Marine Corps Ontos in \

Volume One: 1965

by the

HISTORY SECTION
HISTORICAL FOUNDATION
FEDERAL WAY, WASHINGTON

Marine Tanks and Ontos
Vietnam: 1965 to 1970
by
Those Warriors Who Served during the Vietnam War
Compiled and Edited by
The Marine Corps Vietnam Tankers Historical Foundation Staff

LtCol Ray Stewart, USMC (Ret)

Copyright © 2018 by LtCol Ray Stewart, USMC (Ret).

Library of Congress Control Number: 2018905385
ISBN: Hardcover   978-1-9845-2597-0
              Softcover   978-1-9845-2598-7
              eBook   978-1-9845-2599-4

All rights reserved. No part of this book may be reproduced or transmitted in any form or by any means, electronic or mechanical, including photocopying, recording, or by any information storage and retrieval system, without permission in writing from the copyright owner.

Any people depicted in stock imagery provided by Getty Images are models, and such images are being used for illustrative purposes only.
Certain stock imagery © Getty Images.

Print information available on the last page.

Rev. date: 06/11/2018

To order additional copies of this book, contact:
Xlibris
1-888-795-4274
www.Xlibris.com
Orders@Xlibris.com
742075

CONTENTS

Foreword v
Preface vii
Introduction xi

How It Started 1
What the Hell Happened? We Were Winning the War
　When I left! 24
Shipboard Follies 30
Jesse and Me Take a Ride 39
Third Tanks—D-day RVN 68
California-Based Seventh Marines, 1st Marine Division 103
Attack on Third Tank Battalion Headquarters 106
The Vietnam War and the Special Landing Force 116
Qui Nhon, 1 July 1965 129
Vietnam War 132
Operation STARLITE: The First Big Battle
　(17–24 August 1965) 155
Operation STARLITE, Aug. 18 1965 178
Binh Son 198
Tom Tuck's Vietnam Tour of Duty with Ontos 204
Operation PIRANHA 212
Company C, 3d Tank Battalion, 9/5/64–10/7/65 216
VC Assault on Hill 22 30 October 1965 232
A Rainy Night in Chu Lai 242

Index 641

Foreword

This is the chronological history, prepared by the Marine Corps Vietnam Tanker Historical Foundation, intended to cover the entire span of Marine Corps tanks and Ontos involvement in the Vietnam War between 1965 and 1970, published in six by-year volumes. This series details tank and Ontos activities, from preparation for landing of the 9th Marine Expeditionary Brigade (MEB) across Da Nang's Red Beach 2 in the Republic of Vietnam (South Vietnam) on 9 March 1965 through the war as it escalated from a North Vietnamese–supported mostly guerilla insurgency, to a head-to-head, often hand-to-hand battle between the regular forces of the North Vietnamese Army (NVA) and those of the ARVN (Army of the Republic of Vietnam) supported by the U.S., with major American combat units increasingly committed to the conflict. This narrative traces the landing of the nearly five thousand Marines (the 9th MEB, subsequently renamed the 9th MAB—Marine *Amphibious* Brigade); its transformation into the Marine Amphibious Force (MAF), which, by the end of the year 1965, comprised more than thirty-eight thousand Marines until less than two years later when there were two full Marine divisions, plus the activation of the 5th Marine Division (26th and 27th Marines in-country) by 1966; then the deactivation of the Ontos battalions, the winding down of offensive combat and combatant units, to the final withdrawal of essentially all Marine ground forces in the mid-1970s; and the Marines' establishment of three enclaves in South Vietnam's northernmost corps area, I Corps, as their presence, their tactical areas of responsibility (TAORs), expanded from their initial mission—the raison d'etre being the defense of the Da Nang Airbase—and huge complexes fully able to support both ground and air units, to a balanced strategy involving the bases' defense, offensive operations, and pacification.

The Foundation's editors, who compiled the massive amount of often-confusing and contradictory official documents and the equally difficult personal accounts, rely heavily on such authors as Oscar "Ed" Gilbert (*Marine Corps Tank Battles in Vietnam*), Ed Murphy (*Semper Fi Vietnam: From Da Nang to the DMZ*), Jim Coan (*Con Thien: The Hill of Angels*), and Bob Peavey (*Praying for Slack*). Both Coan and Peavey have authored their own books based on on-the-ground and in-the-fight personal experience. Gilbert has a unique talent for putting personal stories in basic chronological order. Murphy provides a *Reader's Digest* version of the Marine Corps History Division's *U.S. Marines in Vietnam* series but adds so much more. These authors, especially Gilbert, have given a voice, almost literally, to the Tanker combatants. Until now, no author or publication has given a similar voice to the exploits of those Marines who crewed the Ontos.

We hope you will enjoy the series and will feel free to weigh in with your comments.

Lieutenant Colonel Raymond A. Stewart, USMC (Ret)

Preface

The six-volume series of *Marine Corps Tanks and Ontos in the Vietnam War: 1965 to 1970* is written largely by, and mostly about, the Tankers and Ontos crewmen who participated in one of longest and arguably one of the most controversial and nationally divisive wars in the history of the United States. The framework of this series is provided by two primary sources: the previously classified unit command chronologies, which are the by-month, detailed chronicling of every battalion-size Marine unit's activity, and the U.S. Marines in Vietnam series, which we refer to as the Green Books, published by the History and Museums Division, Headquarters, U.S. Marine Corps in the early 1960s and '70s. The value in this approach is that the reader/researcher can read of the exploits of the subject of this series—Tankers and Ontos crewmen—and follow the links back to the expanded coverage in the U.S. Marines in Vietnam series. And the reverse is also true. Within this structure is more than two hundred personal interviews and stories by Marine veterans who served in Vietnam, as well as the oral histories of as many Marines interviewed in-country, who often "lived" on the field of battle itself, literally on the heels of a just-completed operation, or of those Marines who just recently returned to CONUS—many via medical facilities—from the Vietnam War's arena. A plethora of secondary sources, so important in order to present the full story of Tankers and Ontos crewmen, are cited in the "Foundation Library" annex.

The Marine Corps Vietnam Tankers Historical Foundation, established in 1999, concentrated the efforts of its two-to-three-person "staff" on developing a viable history-oriented organization during its first few years. That accomplished, the Foundation commenced planning to write the history of Marine tanks in Vietnam. At some point along the evolution, the Foundation's board of directors agreed to include the antitank community and tell of the exploits of that "thing" called the Ontos. Since the thrust of the book is about—and most importantly largely *by*—the Marines who crewed these tracked vehicles, acquiring the "by" element has proven both challenging and labor-intensive on the one hand while exciting beyond description on the other.

The decision to present the six-book series in its present form and format was arrived at over many months of asking multiple questions and logging even more opinions. Our efforts to write about Tankers—and later to include Ontos crewmen as well—could have been one of merely gathering and editing for publication hundreds of stories based upon written articles, previously recorded interviews, and real-time interviews of Vietnam vets unconnected to the context of the Vietnam War itself. This would be of interest primarily to those who related their own personal experiences. Publishing the personal experience stories in chronological order would also offer little added value for the labor-intensive effort of our Foundation's volunteers. Alternatively, another option was to just stick to the presentation of the impersonal unit command chronology format with little involvement of the personal side of the war. The thinking then—and confirmed time and again subsequently—was that not even the contributors would read the finished process. In short, we decided to go with a hybrid of the noncontextual sea story within the framework provided by the by-month chronologically produced battalion-level and above command chronologies. Now, when reading the personal story of a warrior's fight, the reader will be able to better understand, when provided this context of where, when, and which supported infantry unit(s) actually took place. So these volumes are hundreds of personal sea stories placed in the framework of military history.

In addition, Foundation-conducted interviews of dozens of Marine Veterans, other than members of the tracked vehicle community, provide an even broader picture of the significant role tracks played in the success of hundreds of offensive operations they supported. The Foundation maintains a library of approximately three hundred books from which are drawn quotations and which provide background information about the many-facetted Vietnam War. The citing and attribution of sources convention is provided in the bibliography.

In addition to these primary sources, the Foundation's staff has researched the official records of the U.S. Marine Corps; records of other military and civilian organizations—both U.S. and allied— when appropriate; the Marine Corps' Oral History Collection of the History and Museums Division; Texas Tech archives; Veterans History Project of the Library of Congress; comment files of the Marine's History and Museum Division; and pertinent published primary and secondary works featured, among other publications, in the *Leatherneck*, *Marine Corps Gazette*, and *Vietnam* magazines. Although none of the information in this history is classified, some of the documentation on which it is based still may have a classified designation. Comment drafts of the manuscript were reviewed by several persons, most of whom were directly associated with the events they describe, and many of their remarks have been incorporated into the narrative. Lists of all those interviewed, another providing names of the authors of personal stories, and interviewees are included in the appendices.

I have used the actual names of the Marines who are in this series. Those authors who have had the latitude and propensity to choose disguises for their characters by using fictional names and possibly backgrounds have exercised an option not available to those who write history. In those areas where quotes are used, except for excerpts taken directly from printed documents, there is an attempt at capturing what the character *may* have said or thought under the circumstances detailed. For example, as a lieutenant strained his vision through the rain and blowing salty ocean mist, made more difficult by the pitching ship responding to the lifts and drops of 5-foot waves, to identify the intended landing beach, he reviewed his planned deployment of his Marines and the several possible variables he might have missed. He thought outloud, "Have I covered everything? Have I trained my men well enough? How will I react in the face of possible injury or dying?" While the lieutenant may not have actually said this, those thoughts crossed every small-unit leader's mind in similar situations. It is considered as "creative nonfiction," which adds depth, realism, and humanness to otherwise often rather dry situations without altering the situation.

The production of this volume has been a cooperative effort on the part members of the History Foundation. The manuscript was prepared under the editorial direction of Raymond A. Stewart, Lieutenant Colonel, U.S. Marine Corps (Ret) and president and founder of the Marine Corps Vietnam Tankers Historical Foundation. The authors, of course, assume sole responsibility for the content of the text, including opinions expressed and any errors in fact.

Editorial Staff

Introduction

The idea of a book to chronicle the Vietnam War exploits of Marine Tankers and our Ontos crewmen brothers has been around for a long time—nearly fifty years now. When the Foundation undertook this project. This is how it came together.

Members of the Foundation's board of directors and the book committee agreed to take on specifically identified tasks and projects to address each part of the six-volume series. The series includes major/named operations, timelines, unit designations, and locations for starters. Also provided is the chain of each battalion's command and staff to include company commanders. And, there is the ongoing Foundation's effort to gather personal stories of Tanker and Ontos crewmen. This effort will not stop with the launching of each volume. Rather, we expect, at least initially, that there will be an increase in interest and the submission of personal stories.

Along the chronological format path are many personal stories told by Tankers and Ontos crewmen. Most of the personal recollections agree with the official version, but many do not. Occasionally, participants in the same fight have differing thoughts on many of the details of the who, what, where, when, and often why of an outcome. A "Glossary of Terms, Abbreviations, and Acronyms"; a composite list of "Personal Awards for Valor"; recognition, by name, of author-contributors; a list of financial supporters; a bibliography; a reading list of books and publications of interest; and links to websites are provided.

We began the decades-long journey of compiling material for writing this publication with the Foundation's logo directed to the Tankers and Ontos Crewmen: "You made history. Your Foundation is making it known."

Ray Stewart

Important Note to Readers and Researchers: Because the historical series has been drawn from a multitude of sources, we have used a streamlined citing convention that will both facilitate the reading of the material and lead the reader to the source of the material in the most convenient way. Annex A is the source-citing key, and annex B identifies the source. For example, a quote or a suggested reading may be "SF-EM." Should the reader desire additional details, it's a matter of turning to annex B and locating "SF-EM," which is listed alphabetically. Adjacent to "SF-EM," one will find *Semper Fi: Vietnam: From Da Nang to the DMZ Marine Corps Campaigns, 1965–1975* by **Edward F. Murphy**.

For more detailed information, simply email or call the VTHF, and we will answer your questions or address your comments. You will not have to acquire a copy of *Semper Fi*. We have it in the Foundation Library to assist in your research. Additionally, in some circumstances, we can lend a copy of a publication or you can purchase a copy at a reduced rate.

How It Started

"Know your enemy" is one, and arguably the most important, of the basic precepts of war. "Know your friend" is a given of everyday life. But by order of magnitude, this pair of "knows" is an absolute in winning the fight on the kinetic battlefield. In the case of the American armed forces' involvement in the Vietnam War, its leadership had ". . . no such general guide to North Vietnam's armed forces". (PA-DP). "For reasons not at all clear, neither scholars nor government analysts have ever given the PAVN (People's Army of Vietnam variously NVA or North Vietnamese Army) the attention it deserves." Douglas Pike, in *PAVN: People's Army of Vietnam*, observed, "While the DIA (Defense Intelligence Agency) had volumes on the PAVN armed force's order of battle (OB) which could throw some light on the PAVN capabilities," there was "little on the *intentions* of PAVN generals. The United States never developed a strategy appropriate for the war it was fighting, in part because it assumed that the mere application of it vast military power would be sufficient" (AW-GH). "Through the entire Vietnam War, in and out of the U.S. government, such matters as the composition and mindset of the PAVN High Command, the operational code used in the military decision making, an assessment of Hanoi's strengths and vulnerabilities, even PAVN's grand strategy, went virtually unexamined" (PA-DP). No plausible excuse was provided for this blindness in the face of our enemy, whose martial prowess deserved the widely known assessment as the "Prussians of Asia." Did not the American military and civilian leadership wonder how the Vietnamese earned its widely known reputation?

What is the "fog of war" that one hears bantered about? The "fog" is often cited as the cause for failure of some sort. It is variously defined "as the uncertainty in situational awareness experienced by participants in military operations. The term seeks to capture the uncertainty regarding one's own capability, adversary capability, and adversary intent during an engagement, operation, or campaign" (https://en.wikipedia.org/wiki/Fog_of_war) and a term used to describe the level of ambiguity in situational awareness experienced by participants in military operations. While the term is simply defined, the elements and factors that are present and often not measurable or predictable would include but not be confined to knowledge of the enemy—his military strengths and tactics, his social philosophy, his history, economy, national aspirations, goals, geography. In short, the list of variables, especially in combinations, is endless. It is the level of knowledge of the enemy matched to the knowledge of the "friendlies" that determines the outcome of battles at the tactical end of the spectrum and the war at the strategic end.

Loren Baritz, in his *Backfire: A History of How American Culture Led Us into Vietnam and Made Us Fight the Way We Did* (BF-LB), leaves little doubt the most basic elements that comprise the fog of war were ill-considered by those who sent Marine Corps Tankers and Ontos crewmen to fight and die in what he refers to as the "national calamity"—the Vietnam War. He cites the personal memoirs of Robert McNamara, secretary of defense in both the Kennedy and Johnson administrations, and General Colin Powell that "center on our monumental ignorance of the enemy—the Viet Cong and North Vietnamese—as well as of our presumed friends in South Vietnam." He goes on to opine, "There is no longer any serious debate about the ignorance of the men who made the war." Baritz quotes McNamara as acknowledging that the State Department and the Pentagon "played a lethal game of blind-man's buff [*sic*]: 'Our misjudgments of friend and foe alike reflected our profound ignorance of the history, culture, and politics of the people of the area (both the South and the North Vietnamese), and the personalities and habits of their leaders.'" "We did not understand the Vietnamese—ourselves—or why we felt it necessary to fight in the first place" (BF-LB).

The Players

The Vietnamese for centuries have lived in an armed camp (PA-DP). From 111 BC, for a thousand years, the Vietnamese struggled to expel the Chinese (PV-JT). The hundreds of war heroes in the centuries-long fights are honored to this day: the Trung Sisters in AD 43, Ly Bi in the sixth century, Ngo Quyen in the tenth century, Tran Hung Dao in the thirteenth century, and Le Loi in the fifteenth century. These are but a few of the dozens of heroes whose names are found on street signs and public places throughout Vietnam.

By 1883 the colonial French completely controlled all of Vietnam and formed the French Indochina entity, which incorporated Cambodia and Laos. With the French occupation came a pattern of abuse by the colonizers and constant rebellion by the "conquered." And here was born the first inkling of American military involvement in the region it referred to as Southeast Asia in support of America's European ally amid the purge of anti-French revolutionaries.

Background

By post–World War II treaties and agreements among the victors, Vietnam was divided along the 17th Parallel. A Communist government ruled the north, and in the south, a series of coup-prone anti-Communist regimes attempted to govern. Long before 1965, the United States had been involved in maintaining stability in the government of South Vietnam as a counter to Communist North Vietnam's quest to unite the two under the North's leadership. To assist in keeping South Vietnam free of the dominance of its northern brethren, a U.S. Military Assistance Advisory Group (MAAG) was established in South Vietnam as early as 1950 and continued to function after the formal division of Vietnam into North and South. For example, at the end of 1954, the United States agreed to support the South Vietnamese Armed Forces (ARVN) initially in conjunction with the soon-to-depart French and subsequently assumed the entire advisory effort (YW-DZ).

In 1962, with an increased agitation from the North in the form of both military and economic support of the Viet Cong insurgents south of the DMZ, President Kennedy directed a series of U.S. military and political steps—including the introduction of military equipment, U.S. military and civilian advisors, and other administrative, logistics, and intelligence support units in the South to prevent a Communist takeover under the umbrella of the "domino theory." By the end of the year (1962), more than twelve thousand U.S. technicians, advisors, pilots, supply, and administrative personnel were in Vietnam, including eighteen Marine Advisors to the South Vietnamese Marine Corps and a U.S. Marine helicopter task group (Marine Task Unit 79.3.5) code-named SHUFLY to provide air support during the Vietnam War beginning in 1962. The tasking represented the first large unit commitment of a Marine unit to Vietnam during the anti-Communist struggle in Southeast Asia.

The mission was to provide assault support, offensive air support, and air reconnaissance, with primary objective being troop lift and resupply to United States Military Assistance Command, Vietnam (USMACV) and the Army of the Republic of Vietnam (ARVN) forces engaged in combat operations. The challenges experienced while in Soc Trang established tactics and procedures still used by Marine helicopter units today (http://www.marines.mil/Community-Relations/Commemorations/Operation-Shufly/).

HMM-362 (Marine Medium Helicopter Squadron) and MABS-16 (Marine Air Base Squadron), SubUnit 2 were the first units to deploy in Operation SHUFLY. New squadrons rotated in approximately every four months until 1965 when the United States' involvement in Vietnam drastically increased. Each squadron was deployed on a four-month rotation with four months in Okinawa, Japan, four months aboard ship, and four months in Vietnam.

The government of South Vietnam remained unstable due to turmoil in its leadership and religious fracturing between the Catholic president Diem's faction and the Buddhists bent on burning themselves to ashes.

The results were—among other things—the assassination of the controversial President Ngo Dinh Diem and his brother in the cloak of a military coup. A drastic realignment of the South Vietnamese civil and military apparatus followed. Spiraling downward toward anarchy, dozens of corrupt high-ranking officials, both civilian and military, were replaced by equally corrupt but increasingly less qualified candidates. Between the chaos and confusion, the MAAG advised the U.S. double down on its commitments to a stable South and was sent even more men and equipment of all types—an increase to twenty thousand by the end of 1964—and material to South Vietnam, some of which was used by the new government to crush the remaining opposition. And by now (1964) Marine presence increased to over eight hundred spread thinly, mainly throughout South Vietnam's Tactical Zone One (ICTZ) comprising the five northern provinces, as advisors to the Vietnamese Marine Corps, SHUFLY personnel, Marine security guards at the American Embassy in Saigon, and a few more on the Military Assistance Command, Vietnam (MACV) staff.

During 1964, the U.S. government continued to examine the possibility of sending U.S. combat troops to South Vietnam for the defense of critical U.S. installations in light of the increased offensive activity of the Viet Cong and the dramatic improvement of their lifeline—the Ho Chi Minh Trail that paralleled the South Vietnamese border in Laos and Cambodia. In the meantime, offshore activity involving U.S. and North Vietnamese naval surface forces had become engaged amid conflicting reports of activity resulting in "the determination of the President, as Commander-in-Chief, to take all necessary measures to repel any armed attack against the forces of the United States and to prevent further aggression.'(GB-65) To this day, the degree, intensity, accuracy, political expedience, justification, reaction, and result of the NVN and the U.S. Navy, North Vietnam and U.S. cause, effect, response, result, and final tragic outcome of these several elements comprise volumes of facts, data, opinion, and blame.

The possible involvement of American forces in Southeast Asia was an ongoing concern and of special focus by the Marine Corps. In the summer of 1964, the most combat-ready American troops in the Far East were those of the Third Marine Division (3d MarDiv) located on the Japanese island of Okinawa, and the First Marine Aircraft Wing (1st MAW) at Iwakuni, Japan, with elements on Okinawa. The combination of these two was the III Marine Expeditionary Force (III MEF) with subordinate units combined into a Marine expeditionary brigade (MEB), essentially composed of a regimental landing team (RLT) and a Marine aircraft group (MAG). Following the reports and verification of the attack against the U.S. destroyers in the Gulf of Tonkin, the U.S. Pacific Command activated the Ninth Marine Expeditionary Brigade (9th MEB). On 6 August, the six thousand Marines of the MEB embarked on board Seventh Fleet amphibious shipping. A composite Marine aircraft group (MAG), with headquarters and fixed wing squadrons in Japan and helicopter squadrons on Okinawa, was alerted to support the MEB.

Ho Chi Minh

Into this morass was the spawning of two men whose names and exploits would dominate American, South and North Vietnamese, and much of the world's attention for years to come: Ho Chi Minh, the nom de guerre of Nguyen Sinh Cung or Nguyen, and General Vo Nguyen Giap. In early 1900, Ho and Giap became the closest of friends and allies, opening their military and civilian leadership resumés with the building of a self-defense force in the mountains of northern Vietnam to fight first against the Japanese invaders who had taken over temporarily until its defeat in 1945 from the French with the help of the American OSS. After the Japanese were ejected, the re-occupiers—the French—were next on the Ho/Giap hit list. The pair used the same strategy and tactics to defeat the American-supported French as did Tran Hung Dao to defeat the Mongols centuries earlier.

And after the disastrous 1954 defeat of the French at Dien Bien Phu, the Americans would find themselves next on the roster of those who did not "know the enemy."

Ho Chi Minh (1890–1969). Ho's father lost his job as a history teacher in what became North Vietnam when he refused to learn French. He then spent his time helping the peasants and taught his family to believe in the importance of resisting the French and their colonization of Vietnam. Ho's sister received a sentence of life in prison for stealing weapons from the French while working for them. Ho attended a grammar school and became a schoolteacher himself. He then left Vietnam for England. By 1914, Ho was working in the kitchens of a London hotel, and in 1917, he departed for Paris, where he studied the writings of Karl Marx and became an avowed Communist. He was instrumental in the founding of the French Communist Party in 1920 and then, in 1925, set up the Revolutionary Youth League of Vietnam, followed by the Vietnamese Communist Party in 1930 and the Revolutionary League for the Independence of Vietnam in 1941. He firmly believed that the Communist doctrine was the best—maybe only—governing philosophy that would "save" Vietnam (taken from VW-DW) (Ho Chi Minh—"He who enlightens") (AW-GH).

General Vo Nguyen Giap

General Vo Nguyen Giap (1911–2013). As a student in secondary school, Giap became a Communist and joined Ho Chi Minh's Revolutionary Youth League of Vietnam in 1926. In 1939, Giap fled to China to avoid arrest by the French, but his sister was apprehended, incarcerated, and executed. His wife died while in a French prison. From 1941 to 1945, Giap served as Ho's assistant in the guerilla war against the occupying iImperial Japanese. He commanded the Vietminh against the French between 1946 and 1954. The victory against the French at Dien Bien Phu was his greatest triumph. Giap remained commander in chief of the Viet Minh throughout the Vietnam War against the U.S. until 1975. When the new Vietnamese Republic was set up in 1975, Giap became the vice premier.

His chest festooned with medals for bravery and other personal and unit citations from the top of his left blouse pocket to the shoulder epaulette, it was plain for all to see that Lew Walt was no stranger to war. Reading

the lengthy accounts of his personal bravery, his battle experience, and the Marine Corps organization he commanded leaves little doubt that General Walt was the right man to carry the U.S. land to war with the Communist enemy in the Vietnam War. Of interest is that he did not believe that the use of conventional weapons of war could win the battle against the Vietnamese guerilla forces. He championed the "other war"— the war of hearts and minds. More of that later. Suffice it to say at this point that Marine Tank and Antitank organizations wrote many chapters in the civic action book.

Major General Lewis W. Walt assumed command of III Marine Amphibious Force and 3d Marine Division in Vietnam in June 1965. He was also Chief of Naval Forces, Vietnam; Senior Advisor, I Corps; and I Corps coordinator, Republic of Vietnam. Ten months later, General Walt was nominated for lieutenant general by President Lyndon B. Johnson, and his promotion was approved by the Senate on 7 March 1966. He continued in Vietnam as commanding general of the III Marine Amphibious Force, Senior Advisor of the I Corps, and I Corps coordinator, Republic of Vietnam.

General Walt led Marines in three wars during his more than thirty-four years as a Marine officer. His lengthy list of valor, personal, and unit awards included two Navy Crosses and the Silver Star medal during

World War II; a Legion of Merit and Bronze Star medal in the Korean War; the Distinguished Service medal in Vietnam; and a Gold Star in lieu of a second Distinguished Service medal as Assistant Commandant of the Marine Corps from 1 January 1968 until 1 February 1971. There is only one assistant commandant and his title is capitalized

When the war in Vietnam escalated, Westmoreland, after gaining a third star, became, in January of 1964, deputy to General Paul Harkins, the Commander of U.S. forces in Vietnam (COMUSMACV). In June 1964, Westmoreland replaced Harkins, and he would hold the top post in Vietnam for the next four years. When, in the spring and summer of 1965, President Lyndon B. Johnson began sending U.S. ground forces to Vietnam, Westmoreland's attention turned from advisory matters to the employment of those combat forces. *Time* magazine named General Westmoreland its 1965 "Man of the Year."

General Westmoreland decided on a war of attrition, one in which the enemy body count was the key (but not the only) measure of merit, and "search and destroy" was the dominant tactical approach. In response to repeated requests from Westmoreland for more forces, the American commitment eventually grew to well over a half million troops. Despite inflicting very heavy casualties on Viet Cong (VC)

and their supporting North Vietnamese Army (NVA) Communist forces, that approach faltered as the enemy was able to make up for the losses, though be it with increasing difficulty, as the war dragged on and personnel replacements from the North were both older and younger with much less training than in the early days. Meanwhile, support for the South Vietnamese and attention to pacification (championed by Marine senior leadership) efforts suffered from Westmoreland's focus on and intense interest in combat operations. Domestic support for the war in the United States also declined precipitously as casualties mounted with little apparent payoff. The antiwar movement gained strength, bringing intense political pressure to bear.

During 1967, Westmoreland was active in the Johnson administration's Progress Offensive, a public-relations campaign designed to persuade an increasingly restive public that the United States was winning the war. On three trips to the United States, General Westmoreland made very (unrealistically) optimistic comments about how the war was going before such audiences as the National Press Club and a joint session of the U.S. Congress. In a yearlong controversy over enemy "order of battle" assessments (intelligence estimates of the strength and organization of enemy forces), he put an arbitrary ceiling on the numbers that his intelligence officers could report and omitted certain categories of irregular forces that had long been included. That was done despite evidence obtained by Westmoreland's own headquarters staff that showed significantly higher troop-strength figures.

Note here that not only did COMUSMACV not "know the enemy," he *could* not.

The case in point was Lê Văn Nhuận, known better by **Lê Duẩn** (7 April 1907–10 July 1986), who was a Vietnamese Communist politician. He rose in the party hierarchy in the late 1950s and became General Secretary of the Central Committee of the Communist Party of Vietnam (VCP) at the Third National Congress in 1960. He continued Ho Chi Minh's policy of ruling through collective leadership, from the mid-1960s, when Ho's health was failing, until his own death in 1986. Though little known and studiedly off the skyline, he was the top decision-maker in Vietnam. He made the decisions to mount the major offensives in South Vietnam—including the Easter and Tet Offensives—against the will of either General Giap or Uncle Ho, one might add.

But the Americans were not new at the game of war and struggle for independence—a country born and sustained by revolutions against foreign tyranny and whose unity was sustained and maintained by bloody civil war, steeled by men of great courage and led by men of legendary bravery and ability who not only "read the book" on guerilla warfare and were students of the art but also wrote books and implemented successful additional techniques to that of Mao Tse Tung. Marine Lieutenant General Victor Krulak (during much of the lead-up to and fight in Vietnam was the Commander, Marine Forces, Pacific) did write the book on fighting the guerilla titled *Small Wars*. And our successes were, in days gone by, marked by fierce jungle fighting in the Banana Wars in 1915 and the islands across the South Pacific in World War II. However, the Marine forces that landed across the beach at Da Nang on 8 March 1965 surely did not look like a force configured—or trained—to defeat the Communist insurgency in South Vietnam, or anywhere else for that matter.

The basic, self-sustaining unit of the Marine Corps was the Battalion Landing Team (BLT), which comprised, for starters, such ill-suited and ill-designed tools for guerilla warfare as tanks, Ontos, and amphibious tractors manned by Marines who knew little or nothing of guerilla warfare in general or the culture, language, and structure of the South Vietnamese population in particular. And while the senior Marine leaders attempted to direct its efforts to winning the hearts and minds of the locals, the direction from COMUSMACV, who was running the war from Saigon at one end of the spectrum and the on-the-ground Grunt at the other, dictated the philosophy of killing everyone who was found in areas referred to as "free-fire zones," with success and failure measured by "body count"—and not just the number of enemy killed but the ratio of enemy KIAs to Americans killed was divined out determine by what degree we were winning.

Even as the governments—loosely termed—of South Vietnam rotated through Saigon from the 1950s and through the 1960s, and the hinterland descended into uncontrolled anarchy, the United States *could have* extricated itself from Vietnam until the August 1964 Gulf of Tonkin incident changed the game. Contrary to the good counsel of the CIA, leading political and military minds, the "hawks," sustained the call for engaging North Vietnam with air and naval forces in order to thwart the predicted fall of South Vietnam to the North Vietnamese forces, whose presence south of the demilitarized zone (DMZ) that separated the two Vietnams had increased to General Giap's three full divisions poised a mere 50 miles from Saigon, with logistics support directly overland from Haiphong/Hanoi via the ever-expanding Ho Chi Min Trail along the western border of Vietnam with Laos and Cambodia. That maze of tangled routes threaded westward out of three North Vietnamese passes, through the mountains into Laos, then south and east through that country for 200 to 300 miles. It was actually a series of trails, dirt roads, and river crossings eventually stretching at least 30 miles wide and covering a 6,000-mile network. Much of it was covered by jungle. The Ho Chi Minh Trail was so complex that trucks sometimes seemed to disappear suddenly. One Air Force officer described it as a "spider web and another spider web lying on top of it and another and another." There were between 1,250 and 1,700 truck parks and storage areas on the trail. It was believed the North Vietnamese had a fleet of about 5,000 trucks, most of them Russian-made Zils, similar to American Ford trucks. Rolling stock came from

East Germany, Poland, China, and Czechoslovakia (HO-RS) (BR-JP) (VU-JP) (AV-GL) (IV-ML) (SA-SM) (VW-PD) (VH-SK).

There were estimates that as many as 75,000 people worked to build, support, and maintain the trail network. Destruction of the trail to stem the flow of men and material south to support the Viet Cong (VC) and, increasingly, the North Vietnamese Army (NVA) became one of the most important objectives of the United States in Indochina. For a time, most of the American airpower in Southeast Asia was concentrated on it (TR-CR). See http://www.laosgpsmap.com/ho-chi-minh-trail-laos/ map on page 332 (VH-SK).

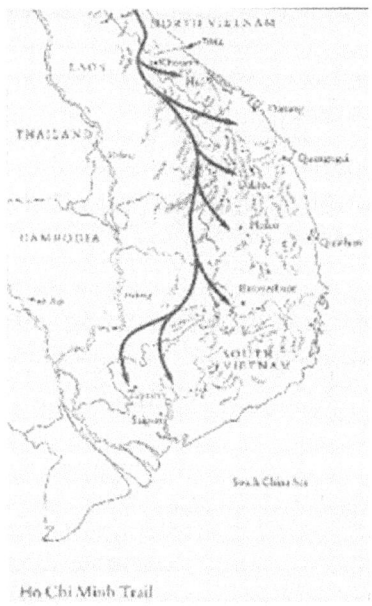

Ho Chi Minh Trail

The North Vietnamese had under early development a sea "Ho Chi Minh Trail" that grew in sophistication, tying its port facilities in Haiphong to Cambodian ports. After the overthrow of Cambodian prince Norodom Sihanouk in March 1970 and the closing to the North Vietnamese of the Cambodian port of Kampong Som on the Gulf of Siam, the Ho Chi Minh Trail became the Communists' only alternative route for moving war material southward.

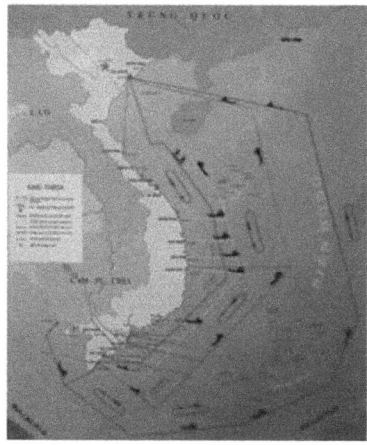

Ho Chi Minh's "Water Trail" (VTHF Archive, 1533)

However, by then, the Ho Chi Minh Trail had grown to such a level of sophistication (e.g., three pipelines that carried POL from Haiphong's storage facilities to support upwards of six hundred Soviet/Chinese-made tanks less than 100 miles from Saigon) that the loss was barely felt by the enemy.

In fact, by early 1965, the local Viet Cong controlled all the major transportation arteries—rail, road, and communications—in South Vietnam itself. "South Vietnam was poised on the brink of collapse" (FB-OL).

And as William Colby stated, "The [American] Embassy used its influence to try to establish some legitimacy in the new Government in Saigon. As a result, a dreary series of antique civilian politicians were named Prime Minister in a revolving-door sequence of so-called 'Governments' resting on little more that the American insistence that they be there" (LV-WC). Only the threat by the Americans to withdraw its support kept any semblance of order or stability.

"[By] 1963 it was becoming increasingly clear to American observers that the Viet Cong was winning the war in South Vietnam" (VW-AW).

Meanwhile, the United States was also in an unsettled state with the assassination of President John Fitzgerald Kennedy on 22 November 1963. Stated the American secretary of defense, Robert Strange McNamara, "Transitions often bring uncertainty, confusion, and error and this was never more the case than in the six months that followed President Kennedy's assassination. President Johnson, who approached Vietnam differently than did his predecessor, inherited a host of unanswered questions and unsolved problems. These became more and more troublesome as we slid toward a deeper involvement in Vietnam" (IR-RM).

In *Mounted Combat in Vietnam*, written by General Donn Starry, USA (MC-DS), he states in chapter 3, "Growth of U.S. Armored Forces in Vietnam":

> The American elections of 1960 brought John F. Kennedy to the White House and Robert S. McNamara to the Pentagon. The change spelled the end of the strategy of massive retaliation and of the pentomic division with its five battle groups designed to fight nuclear wars. The Army reorganization of 1963 restored the infantry battalion and provided a structure for the whole Army that, at battalion and brigade level, was much like the separate battalions within the combat commands of U.S. armored divisions after World War II. It was clear that the new policy of flexible response demanded a force that could fight in any kind of war, including so called wars of national liberation.
>
> In armored units there was little change. The 1963 reorganization reduced each tank and mechanized infantry battalion to three line companies, but each division had more battalions and support echelons. No one in armor seriously believed that armored unit tactics needed to change. In 1957 Field Manual 17-1,

Armor Operations, Small Units, devoted only two and one-half pages to guerrilla warfare. By the early 1960's that coverage had been broadened; Field Manual 17-35, Armored Cavalry Platoon, Troop and Squadron, carried an expanded treatment of guerrilla fighting under the title, Rear Area Security.

Many of the tactics set forth in the manual for employing armored cavalry in rear area security missions proved useful in Vietnam. Road security, base defense, air reconnaissance, reaction forces, and convoy escort were described. Field Manual 17-1 included discussions of base camps, airmobile forces, tailoring of forces for specific missions, encirclements, and ambushes. Both books stressed surveillance, the use of the combined arms team, and the need for mobility. Yet most counterinsurgency training was limited to work on patrols, listening posts, and convoy security; the Army did not foresee a whole theater of operations without a front line or a secure rear area.

By 1965 when the U.S. Army began to send units to Vietnam, divisional armored cavalry squadrons had three ground cavalry troops and an air cavalry troop, tank battalions had three identical tank companies, and mechanized infantry battalions had three mechanized companies mounted in APC's. Armored units were equipped with a mixture of M48 and M60 tanks, M113 armored personnel carriers, and M109 self-propelled 155-mm. howitzers.

On the eve of the Army's major involvement in Vietnam, however, most armor soldiers considered the Vietnam War an infantry and Special Forces fight; they saw no place for armored units. The Armor Officer Advanced

Course of 1964–1965 never formally discussed Vietnam, even when American troops were being sent there. Armor officers were preoccupied with traditional concepts of employment of armor on the fields of Europe; a few attempted to focus attention on the use of armor in Vietnam, but in the main they were ignored. Many senior armor officers who had spent years in Europe dismissed the Vietnam conflict as a short, uninteresting interlude best fought with dismounted infantry.

The Marine Corps' Tracked Vehicle Officers School, Camp Del Mar, Camp Pendleton, taught no courses about Marine tanks in guerilla warfare, though the role tanks played in combined tank/infantry tactics was emphasized. And while the freshly minted second lieutenants were introduced—some rudimentary level—the concept of tank/infantry tactics, the senior-level infantry officers who employed tanks that were attached or in direct support of their units in Vietnam in their tactical offensive planning apparently missed that class.

Meanwhile, the team that would lead the American forces committed to the defense of South Vietnam had evolved. On 20 June 1964, General William Westmoreland, USA, replaced General Harkins as COMUSMACV; and General Maxwell Taylor, USA (Ret.), succeeded Ambassador Henry Cabot Lodge during July 1964. The Tonkin Gulf incident occurred in August of 1964, followed by ARVN-led abortive coup at Phat Duc in September, the attack of Bien Hoa on 1 November '64, and then the Tan Son Nhut attack.

During this period, the government, such as it was, parsed the country into five administrative/tactical zones (CTZs) with the head of each best qualities being well placed politically and usually with a senior military rank. The Marines would be assigned the northernmost CTZ the first zone but referred to as I—as in "eye" Corps. I Corps was further divided into five provinces. The RVN commander of I Corps was Major General Nguyen

Chanh Thi, ARVN, not to be confused with Major General Nguyen Van Thieu, the South Vietnamese IV Corps commander (SV-EM).

General Westmoreland (COMUSMACV) declared Da Nang to be in great danger of falling to the North Vietnamese, an event that could be facilitated by a Soviet-supported air attack from the North in conjunction with an NVA ground attack across the DMZ. Since the president's declaration of Operation ROLLING THUNDER (a result of the Gulf of Tonkin incident) and the Da Nang air facility, a key base to facilitate the conduct of that offensive (and the somewhat covert air support of the ARVN—Operation SHUFLY), Da Nang must not fall. So commenced the step-by-step escalation of the political and military tragedy known simply as Viet Nam.

The five northern provinces that comprise South Vietnam's I Corps. I Corps operations were mainly the responsibility of the Marine Corps. Even though during the last years of the war U.S. Army units were deployed to I Corps, they came under the operational control of the Corps.

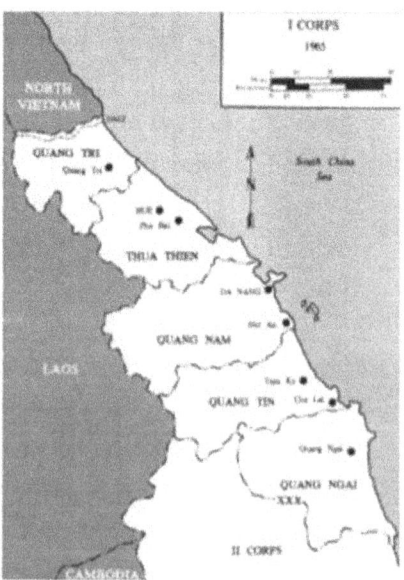

To protect the Da Nang air base against an attack from the air, General Westmoreland requested an antiaircraft missile unit. That request was given to the Marine Corps' 1st Antiaircraft Missile (LAAM) Battalion.* "The nose of the camel is under the tent!" On the night of 8–9 February 1965, Battery A, 1st LAAM flew into Da Nang.

The remainder of the five-hundred-Marine LAAM Battalion arrived by amphibious shipping during the following week. By 16 February 1965, the battalion occupied positions surrounding the Da Nang Air Base. This was the Americans' first step in the attempt to persuade the North Vietnam's government to curtail its terrorist attacks. As with all the other dozens of subsequent attempts to persuade the North Vietnamese to curb its assault of South Vietnam through the gradual escalation of military forces that followed over the next several years, it was paid scant attention.

A Marine Hawk missile launcher is in position at the Da Nang Airfield. The Hawks were designed to defend against low-flying enemy Vietnamese aircraft of the type flown by the North (GB-65).

USMC photo A184433

---

* In an interview of the LAAM battalion's logistics officer (S-4) (CD-22), he was asked, "Major Hessel, when you first arrived in Vietnam did you have any problems with unloading of men and equipment?" His response was, "Yes we did to a certain extent. This was due to the fact that adequate port facilities were not available at that time in the Da Nang area. It was necessary for us to unload in the (Da Nang) Bay and use small craft to bring our supplies up the (Tourane) river and unload in the city along the main streets. The difficulty there, besides moving the distance, was there was little room in which to stage equipment and between unloading and actually moving it out. It was obvious to us at the time, we were practically the first unit to land in Vietnam, it was obvious at that time, that extensive improvements would be needed in that area to support increased operations" (CD-22A).

One can only imagine the administrative and logistics challenges in bringing five hundred Marines and a Hawk battery into a country that had none of the most basic facilities or infrastructure to accommodate the organization. Eventually, there were two LAAM battalions with batteries spread from Chu Lai to the south and Monkey Mountain and beyond to the north.

The base was located south of the peak of Sơn Trà (Monkey) Mountain, overlooking Danang Harbor/China Beach (https://en.wikipedia.org/wiki/Monkey_Mountain_Facility).

In *Where We Were in Vietnam* (WW-MK), Kelley states, "LAAM Sites (AT and BT) Light Anti-Aircraft Missile sites deploying Hawk AA Missile. Each LAAM Battery had 36 missiles mounted on 12 launchers holding 3 Hawks each. 1st and 2d Battalions deployed to South Vietnam beginning in '65, with 1st Battalion protecting Da Nang Air Base and 2d Battalion later at Chu Lai AF as it was developed. 1st LAAM Battalion (479 men): Battery A was set up on Hill 724, north of Hai Van Pass during Aug '66 (according to Ed Escoffier, the USN at Hai Van Pass site offered 'Best chow in Vietnam!'); Battery B was on Hill 327 (Division Hill) just west of Da Nang; Battery C was on north end of Tien Sha Peninsula, east of the USAF CRC; and Assault Fire Unit of 15 Hawks was put on Hill 55, southwest of Da Nang. 2d LAAM Battalion (460 men): Battery A on Ky Hoa Island north of Chu Lai; Battery B at the north end of Chu Lai Air Field; Battery C at the south end of Chu Lai

Air Field (Battery C moved to Hill 141 further south east of Chu Lai Air Field to better cover the Song Tra Bong Valley)." To the author's knowledge, "[N]o HAWK missiles were ever fired in anger, although two were fired accidentally in '66." Some data per USMC in Vietnam, 1966, pp. 271–72 (GB-66).

The new COMUSMACV, General Westmoreland, had reason to believe that the security of the five-hundred-Marine LAAM bBattalion could not be entrusted to the local ARVN, and he asked for two battalions of Marines to guard the LAAM bBattalion that was guarding the Da Nang complex. The newly accredited U.S. ambassador to South Vietnam, a retired army general, Maxwell Taylor, was opposed to the introduction of U.S. ground troops to South Vietnam. On 27 February, a cable to Taylor informed him that ground troops were "on the way." Any who may have entertained thoughts or desires that the landing would be "inconspicuous" was shocked to learn that Marine landing teams—RLTs, BLTs, MEBs—are task-organized and that tanks, Ontos, amtracs, and their supporting logistics equipment and rolling stock are part and parcel of that "package," i.e., formal "Table of Organization and Equipment (TO/E)." Further, rotary-winged and fixed-wing aircraft are included in the TO/E of the MEB. Marines fight as an integrated air/ground force (MAGTF). With the additional air assets came the requirement for more air support facilities. Thus was the thinking behind acquiring the existing airfield at Phu Bai to the north and the planned construction of Chu Lai AirfField to the south of Da Nang, both of which required ground forces to protect them and the aircraft that protected the ground forces.

Both Westmoreland and Maxwell, four-star and former four-star army generals, no doubt agreed with the U.S. Army's opinion as expressed in the Department of the Army's *Mounted Combat in Vietnam* by General Donn A. Starry: "On the eve of the Army's major involvement in Vietnam, however, most armor soldiers considered the Vietnam War an infantry and Special Forces fight; they saw no place for armored units. The Armor Officer Advanced Course of 1964–1965 never formally discussed Vietnam, even when American troops were being sent there. Armor officers were preoccupied with traditional concepts of employment of armor on the fields of Europe; a few attempted to focus attention on the use of armor in Vietnam, but in the main they were ignored. Many senior armor officers who had spent years in Europe dismissed the Vietnam conflict as a short, uninteresting interlude best fought with dismounted infantry" (MC-DS).

Irrespective of the Army armor's views of Vietnam, its opinion of how the tanks might (or probably would not) be employed there, the Marine Corps was structured to remain flexible and nimble faced with any number of contingency operations worldwide. The Army's focus was on a land war on the plains of Europe. With the 1st Marine Division posted at Camp Pendleton—looking west across the Pacific Ocean—and the 3d Marine Division, at home on the Japanese island of Okinawa, in the middle of the Pacific Ocean, the Corps was the obvious choice to be sent to Vietnam. The first ground troops would be from the 3d Marine Division's Marines, and the 1st Marine Division at Camp Pendleton was placed on high alert for possible deployment as well.

Initial Marine reinforcements were to consist of both ground and air units. With growing tension in the Far East, General Krulak had made plans at the beginning of the year for the movement of Marine forces and large-scale preparatory maneuvers. In early February, he alerted two U.S. Marine fixed-wing squadrons in the United States for deployment to Japan in late March. Coincidentally, the FMFPac commander scheduled the largest landing exercise since World War II to take place on the West Coast of the United States in early March. The scenario for the exercise, code-named SILVER LANCE, reflected the situation in Vietnam, featuring guerrillas, hard-core aggressor forces, and political-military problems. In Hawaii, the 1st Marine Brigade, consisting of the 4th Marines and MAG-13, made preparations to reinforce the 1st Marine Division and the 3d Marine Aircraft Wing in SILVER LANCE. With the imminent landing of the 9th MEB in Vietnam, the Pacific Command ordered the curtailment of forces for the exercise at the last minute. At this time, 7 March, the Marines of the 1st Brigade were already embarked in amphibious shipping. Crediting General Krulak for "the amazing coincidence of the readiness of the Brigade" for movement, Lieutenant Colonel Rex C. Denny Jr., then the Brigade G-3, eleven years later recalled, "We were on again/off again for Okinawa. Then on precisely the planned sailing date for SILVER LANCE . . . the shipping sailed from Pearl Harbor and turned right instead of left. Perfect timing for the movement to the Far East to be in position for the April troop deployment to Vietnam. The hastily planned deployments of Marine units from Hawaii and the West Coast to Okinawa and Japan went smoothly. The 4th Marines, reinforced by a reconnaissance company, antitank company, and by an artillery battalion, the 3d Battalion, 12th Marines, arrived and reported to the 3d Marine Division on Okinawa by the end of March. At the same time, MAG-13 became part of the 1st Marine Aircraft Wing in Japan" (GB-65).

The most massive and elaborate war game staged by U.S. Armed Forces since WWII, Exercise SILVER LANCE, ended three days ahead of schedule at Camp Pendleton. Operations began on 12 February and ended 9 March.

> On 8 March 1965 the Marines landed at Danang. Their presence in South Vietnam illustrated the failure of American policy there. Since 1954 the US had been trying to establish a South Vietnam that could stand on its own in defense of containment. The mere presence of US ground forces showed that the efforts of 11 years had been a failure. American involvement in the Vietnam War had begun. (VW-AW)

What the Hell Happened? We Were Winning the War When I left!

by Lieutenant Colonel R. A. Stewart, USMC (Ret)

I, and most of my A Company, 1-65 Class of newly commissioned Marine officers, first heard of "Vietnam" during the summer of 1964. As one of nearly one hundred freshly minted second lieutenants attending the Marine Corps' Officer Basic School (TBS), Marine Corps Base, Quantico, Virginia, I was anticipating, upon our 22 December 1964 graduation, assignment of my military occupational specialty (MOS) that would be a major determinant of my career path in the Marine Corps. We were slouched in various positions at our tables in a classroom at TBS at the end of an unseasonably cold and wet three-day final field exercise, eager to clean our weapons, scrape the Virginia mud from our 782-web gear, shed our foul-smelling utilities, and stand under a hot shower. Thoughts of Thanksgiving dinner outprioritized whoever that young Marine officer was on the stage, behind the podium, droning on about his experience as an advisor to the Vietnamese Marine Corps in "Vietnam." Vietnam?

The first lieutenant wore a Purple Heart ribbon. If my memory serves me correctly, his name was Herb Pierpan. His talk was to brief us on a place few, if any, of us had heard of and—to be candid—it inspired little to no interest among us: the cold, wet, and mud-soaked, blackened-faced second lieutenants. Little were we to know that in less than eight months, many of our graduating TBS class of new officers would represent American "boots on the ground" in the Republic of South Vietnam (RVN). By then, some of these officers had been wounded (WIA), a few killed (KIA), and recognized for their bravery in the face of the Communist enemy, being awarded to individual second lieutenants (Navy Cross, Silver Stars), Vietnamese Crosses of Gallantry, as well as entire Marine infantry and their supporting arms units—tanks, artillery, Ontos, amtracs, trucks, communications, Marine Air—receiving the Presidential, Navy/Marine Corps, and Meritorious Unit Citations (PUC, NUC, and MUC).

At that time, the troubles in Vietnam, in the context of the Southeast Asian domino theory, may have been discussed at various levels by a spectrum of American professionals—military and civilian—and probably found in some newspapers and other publications in early 1964, but for those of us recently graduating from college, attaining a commission in the Marine Corps, preparing ourselves for our future, and several of us recently married consumed most of our attentions. Further, once reporting into Marine Corps Schools' TBS, and for the follow-on six months, we barely had time to meet the rigorous mental and physical requirements designed to fill our average twenty-five-hour days of intense classroom instruction, field exercises, and physical training. Reading a newspaper or watching the evening news with David Brinkley and Chet Huntley was not found in the TBS curriculum.

Upon completion of TBS at Quantico, Virginia, just prior to Christmas 1964, most of the class of second lieutenants departed Quantico to report to our just-assigned units. I, and a few of my classmates with an 1801 MOS, reported to the "Tank and Amtrack Officers Course, Class 2-65" at Camp Del Mar, Camp Pendleton, California, in early 1965. After graduation, some would be assigned to amtrac units leading to an 1803 MOS; others, to first tanks and antitanks to become 1802s.

Del Mar, Camp Pendleton, CA, January 1965 (VTHF Archives)

Then, for me, to Embarkation School at Camp Pendleton, followed by preparing for the MEBLEX "Silver Lance"—attacking across the beach at Camp Pendleton. Then I received orders to "B" Company, 1st Tank Battalion, Camp San Onofri, Camp Pendleton, California. I met briefly with my new company commander, a somewhat aged "mustang" captain, Allan Lamb; my platoon sergeant, a supercool pipe-smoking staff sergeant, Peter Frano; and a few of my reinforced tank platoon NCOs and troopers. I drove back to my apartment in San Diego, packed my sea bag, and was driven down the hill by my new bride to the San Diego port to find the USS *Alamo* (LSD-33).

S.Sgt. Peter J. Frano guiding
tank onto LCU

Debarking LCU into the well deck
of USS *Alamo*, M48A3, 3d Platoon,
B Company, 1st Tanks

(LSD-33) USS *Alamo*
ballasted down

Alamo's interior ramp system from
well deck to flight deck

Members of 3d Platoon,
B Company, 1st Tanks
The original Third Herd

USS *Alamo* ballasting up
Next stop Vietnam via Okinawa

Pictures provided by Lee Tannehill of the Third Herd of B Company,
1st Tanks, June 1965 (VTHF)

I'd never actually been aboard an LSD but was familiar with the layout of this class of amphibious ship from my classes at the just-completed Embarkation School. My tanks were in the "well deck," three of them preloaded in LCU-1454. The other two tanks, along with some rolling stock—including the small but mighty Ontos—were packed and lashed together into the remainder of the well deck. I located the rest of my vehicles tethered together topside on the flight deck. The USS *Alamo* (LSD-33) was preparing to sail east within two days in support of the 3d Battalion, Seventh Marines (3/7), which comprised the ground elements of the Battalion Landing Team (BLT 3/7). Where we were headed was "a secret," and we were told not to tell *anyone* (that we didn't know where we were going, I'd guess). Ahh, the Marine Corps' definition of a "senior cruise." Aside from a very rough sail to and a brief stop to offload and backload in Okinawa onto the USS *Point Defiance* (LSD-31, *Alamo*'s sister LSD), we were on our way south—to Vietnam! Or so the scuttlebutt had it.

Tom Snyder's description of activities and shipboard life for Marines is accurate and typical of that experience to which the Corps rode the Navy to war. His story starts just from his stateside preparations activity, after the landing of Marine tanks and Ontos in Vietnam, so may be a bit out of sequence, and then continues until just after Operation STARLITE—"The First Battle," when his unit came ashore in Chu Lai.

Shipboard Follies

Aboard the (LSD-33) USS *Alamo* and (LSD-31) USS *Point Defiance*

by Tom Snyder

Avast there, mateys, and I will attempt to refresh your memory of what shipboard life was like as seen through the eyes of a nineteen-year-old Marine lance Corporal (E-3) motor transport pogue aboard two different LSDs on my 1965 "Summer Cruise"; although they were the same size/class ship, life was vastly different.

When we heard the scuttlebutt that we were getting orders for Vietnam—possibly—we started making preparations at Marine Corps Base, Camp Pendleton before the actual orders arrived. New 5-ton M-54 6×6s were picked up by a driver detail at Marine Corps Supply Depot, Barstow, CA, and driven back to Camp Pendleton to replace our fleet of aging 2-1/2-ton M-35 6×6 trucks. I'm sure a then Second Lieutenant, Carl Ludecke, remembers this event in his fledging military career due to the behavior of certain Marines in that detail once let out in the public sector! But that's another story.

We did get the new trucks from Barstow to Camp Pendleton in good shape. These trucks were then loaded with various cargo—mount-out boxes filled with supplies and small equipment needed to set up the outfit in the field, tents of various sizes, and ammunition picked up at underground storage magazines within the confines and security of Camp Pendleton. The trucks, with M-105 trailers, and M-38 jeeps were then driven across Marine Corps Base, Camp Pendleton, CA, west to the beach area at San Onofri, CA, which was a section of Camp Pendleton, and loaded via LCM and LCU to the (LSD-33) USS *Alamo*, which was anchored offshore.

After loading all the cargo and vehicles necessary for anticipated combat operations into the hold of the *Alamo* and on the various deck levels—well deck, mezzanine, and flight—and securing the cargo and vehicles to the decks with chains, dunnage, and ratchet binders that were rusted and corroded by salt water, the *Alamo* weighed anchor and sailed to the U.S. Naval Base at San Diego, a few miles to the south, to await all ship's personnel and anticipated Marine "embarked troops," take on stores/supplies, fresh water, etc., and the contingent of deploying Marines that were arriving by cattle car from Camp Pendleton. This included Bravo Company, 1st Tank Battalion (3d Platoon) and supporting/attached B Company's H&S Platoon sections, all commanded by then Captain Allan W. Lamb and Second Lieutenant Ray Stewart. Unknown to most of the troops (all this movement and the destination were "classified"), this was to be our home for the next two weeks. Destination: Nonstop to Okinawa.

(Editor's Note: The forward movement was "nonstop," but the up/down, side-to-side was anything but. We hit a storm that pitched up and down, rolled from side to side, and yawed [a corkscrew motion when the ship pitches and rolls at the same time] the ship to a degree that even the seasoned ship's crew was sent to the rail, shouting for "ORRORK." And unfortunately for the Tankers and Ontosmen who were required to work in the dark and smell of the well deck to reinforce the equipment tie-downs to keep tanks from breaking loose and causing no end to damage to the ship. Tom was sent to the flight deck to reinforce the tie-down of his 5-ton M-54 truck, which was no mean task in itself. In the driving wind and rain, Tom lost his footing and received a concussion when his head lost the battle with a steel gear locker.)

3d Platoon (Rein.), B Company, 1st Tank Battalion, FMF. (LSD-33) USS *Alamo* flight deck O/A, 10 June 1965, in transit from San Diego, CA, to Okinawa, Japan (VTHF Archives)

We got settled into the troop quarters. The canvas-laced bunks were sometimes seven or eight high, and it was quite an ascending climb if your bunk was on the top, near the overhead. The first day at sea, classes were held by 3/B/1st Tank platoon sergeant, the pipe-smoking Staff Sergeant Frano, on the various military subjects. Regulations and rules for aboard-ship living and off-limits areas were explained: the bridge, officer's country, engine room, etc. We did almost daily physical training (PT) and preventive maintenance (PM) on our equipment to keep busy and out of trouble.

The sSkipper (captain) of the *Alamo* and crew were, at most, very troop friendly. There were no fights, arguments, etc. between the crew and Marines. We dovetailed the chow lines. The ship's PX was open daily with no restrictions on purchases. Chatter could be seen between the ship's crew and the Marines. The captain/skipper of the *Alamo* came on the communication squawk box almost daily, updated everyone on stateside news and any advancing weather conditions, and gave us our location in this vast expanse of ocean.

As Marines, this was, for most of us, our first exposure to life aboard ship and the various general orders including lifeboat drills and general quarters, given to all via the squawk box (ship's internal intercom), the bosun's mate piping chow, and other routine ship chores such as, "Sweepers, sweepers, man your brooms. Let's have a clean sweep down, fore and aft," and "Now hear this: Starboard section 3, lay down to the laundry to pick up same." With all my time spent aboard ship in the Marine Corps, I never did find out what that damn "same" was!

One aspect of shipboard life that was announced unexpectedly, but was necessary, was the dreaded "Stand by to take on stores" directive, which amounted to a gigantic work detail that was usually all E-3s and below in rank. Another ship would rendezvous at sea with the *Alamo*, usually a reefer (refrigerated cargo ship); and fresh food supplies, mail, movies, days' old newspapers, etc. would be transferred to the *Alamo* via helicopter with a cargo net. These food staples would be deposited on the flight deck by the chopper, and the work parties would hand-transfer the cases of food and perishables down the narrow walkways and passageways, into the reefers of the *Alamo*. Huge amounts of food were handled case by case in this manner.

When the order was sounded to "secure stores detail" and the total case lots were accounted/unaccounted for, there would be a complete "shakedown" (search) for any missing items throughout the ship, mostly concentrating on troops/crew quarters, where someone would try to "sidetrack" a case or two of canned fruit (usually) for private consumption later. Woe be to the culprit, or culprits, whose lockers contained the missing items, as surely a trip to stand tall before one's officer for reprimands and punishment would be forthcoming!

Another vital commodity for the forward propulsion of the *Alamo* would be fuel. This was also accomplished by rendezvous with another ship, an oiler (tanker), which would pull closely alongside the *Alamo*. Forward speed was reduced, and direction/course was maintained between the two ships. An order was given to "stand by for shot line," and a firearm similar to a shotgun would be fired containing first a weighted object called a monkey fist attached to a string, which would be attached to a small rope, which would then be attached to a larger line, then finally a cable used to support a large-diameter hose. Hose connections were made, pumps were started, and thick bunker grade-oil would flow from the tanker to the *Alamo*. Again, mail and movies would be exchanged between ships as well.

For Marines, replenishments at sea were interesting to watch, especially if a personnel exchange was in order. It had to be a thrill for anyone to ride a bosun's chair, on a cable over water, as a means of transfer from ship to ship. The transfer of goods, small pieces of equipment, and personnel was even more interesting in heavy seas with both ships being battered by wind and wave.

Another encounter the *Alamo* had while steaming to Okinawa was a typhoon, name unknown. It is virtually impossible to tell someone a story about it; you had to witness one firsthand. The size of the *Alamo* and the weight of the cargo she hauled tossed the ship like a cork. Huge waves/swells caused the bow to dip with waves often reaching the bridge, and when she recovered, the stern would lift from the sea, causing the props to spin in the air, creating a shudder-like vibration that was felt throughout the ship, then the bow would smack down upon the water with a bang, and the process would repeat again and again.

This continued for approximately four days straight before calmer seas were attained. The eating trays on the tables in the galley slid back and forth, walking in passageways was very difficult, and needless to say, Mariner's "flu" was abundant among both the Marines aboard and even some of the ship's crew. The very innards of the ship reeked of vomit. It was quite an ordeal!

One of the duties as Marines aboard a ship is brig (ship's jail) watch, or brig chaser. Brig watch was to ensure the health and safety of any prisoner in the ship's brig, and being a chaser meant escorting a prisoner to sick call or wherever he had to report to on the ship. Interesting duty as a Marine, but I don't think I would enjoy being locked in a tiny cell deep within the ship for days at a time. A prisoner remained there until the next port of call, usually, and then he was transferred to a shore detention facility.

Another aspect of ship living for Marine "landlubbers" was the good old-fashioned "Navy shower." A ship's freshwater tanks and freshwater-generating system could hold, or produce, only so many gallons of fresh water per day. With priorities given to drinking, cooking, and laundry, shortcuts must be followed, hence the Navy shower, a.k.a. step in, turn on, wet down, shut off, lather, quick rinse, turn off, step out—you're done! One may use all the salt water for showering that you want or need, but fresh water used for bathing was curtailed and, in restricted times, even forbidden.

Troop quarters aboard ship were much the same as barracks' rules. Living quarters and heads had to be neat, clean, and orderly. Lights out meant lights out, and silence shall prevail. Any reading or studying was allowed in the galley within reason.

There was also a "watch-stander's chow" or "mid-rats" available to anyone who was on duty or going to or from duty. This usually consisted of soup, a sandwich, and coffee. Many hungry Marines used this extra chow even if they had no duty, without repercussion, especially if regular chow was of disliked or reduced portions until the ship's resupply.

Mail call aboard ship was no different from land-based connections, with the exceptions of unpredictability and infrequency, naturally. Many a lovesick "boot Marine" was the subject of a long-standing joke called mail buoy watch, where-in he was sent topside to scan the horizon for a drop-off/pickup point, a mail buoy, which, of course, was nonexistent!

We, 3d Platoon (Rein), B Company (-), 1st Tank Battalion (-), (The Third Herd) arrived at Okinawa and disembarked at White Beach.

With all our gear, tanks, trucks, and other equipment organized on the beach, we traveled up to Camp Hansen.

Liberty call commenced, and after getting into the activities, sights, sounds, and smells of Okinawa, fourteen days later, we reversed direction and hauled everything back down to White Beach and reloaded this time on (LSD-31) USS *Point Defiance* and mounted out attached to BLT 3/7, the ground component of the Special Landing Force (SLF), in support of any combat operations the Navy might undertake throughout the Pacific theater, including Vietnam—a highly mobile floating amphibious strike force that will be off the coast of Vietnam in varous configurations for the duration of the Vietnam War.

One may think that the *Point Defiance* would be similar to the *Alamo* as far as being the same size and class of ship, but it was not. While aboard, there were no dovetailing chow lines and the ship's crew just straggled and cut into the head of the chow line at will, for just one example of dissention. Fights broke out between the ship's crew and the onboard Marines. PX purchases were restricted sales to Marines but were wide-open and unlimited for sailors. The captain/skipper never came on the squawk box to broadcast any news or significant events occurring back in the Continental United States. Nary a word was heard from him; it was like he wasn't even on board. We had not a clue as to our present location either. These may seem petty, but it created a hostile environment between the onboard Marines and the ship's crew, and there was very little civil conversation that took place between the two.

The *Point Defiance* was called upon to support the rescue of a Navy destroyer, the USS *Frank Knox*, that had run aground, midship/high centered, on Pratas Reef (someone was in deep doo-doo for this event), a charted coral reef in the South China Sea. As the Marine 7th Engineers had heavy equipment aboard the *Point Defiance*, including a Bay City, large crane, the powers that be decided they would try to lighten the destroyer by offloading equipment and material from the *Frank Knox* onto the *Point Defiance* in an effort to float her off the reef. But to no avail, not even at high tide. Towing with lines attached to her, was unsuccessful as well.

The *Point Defiance* was on-location twice, and this was a gala event for the Marines. The LSD's tailgate was lowered, opening the well deck at the stern of the ship, ballasting down i.e, partially flooding the well dack, and swim call commenced. I was amazed at the warm temperature of these tropical waters. There was also fishing allowed for those who liked the sport.

After three runs to Subic Bay, Philippines, to drop off or pick up naval supplies and rigging to support the salvage attempt of the *Frank Knox*, someone decided it was a no-win situation, and the civilian contractors—with oceangoing tugboats—arrived and finally towed her off the reef and departed for a ship repair dry dock in Japan.

After the second visit to Pratas Reef, the BLT/SLF was called to begin a critical operation South of Chu Lai that evolved into the first major offensive of the Vietnam War: Operation STARLITE. But that's another story/event.

After Operation STARLITE, we returned to Subic Bay, Philippines, one last time, briefly, and then back to Chu Lai, RVN, for final offloading. Our SLF duties were resumed by a nother BLT. There were quite a few broken hearts in Olongapo, Philippines, from our three visits there. The girls will never be the same! Most of the Marines were elated to be off that ship, the USS *Point Defiance* (LSD-31), where the crew shared the same indifferent attitude of its captain and the often open hostility of his crew.

Semper Fidelis,

Sergeant Tom Snyder, USMC
B Company, 1st Tanks
Motor Transport
Driver and Dispatcher

(*Above*: With Tom's permission, his original article has been lightly edited for printing.)

(*Below*: Editor's Preamble: We are going to build upon John Hunter's [nicknamed Leadfoot by his tank section leader, Sergeant Art Allen] original story. More of that name later. Pictures have also been added and a few editorial embellishments. All this with John's most generous approval.)

Jesse and Me Take a Ride

by John M. Hunter

Private First Class Jesse Salinas and Corporal Tom Snyder (see add-on below) were the two motor transport drivers assigned to 3d Platoon (Rein.), Bravo Company, 1st Tank Battalion attached to the 3d Battalion, 7th Marines, 1st Marine Division, Special Landing Force (SLF 3/7). These two guys were as much into tanks as the rest of us! We went to Okinawa, Japan, by ship—the USS *Alamo* (LSD-33), leaving San Diego in May of 1965. We were supposed to go to Hawaii, but that stop was canceled, so we went directly to Okinawa. Our trip was in an arch, which took us way up into the Northern Pacific. I remember some really cold days en route. And seasick? The entire ship—ship's personnel as well as embarked troops—was calling for "Ralph" over the side. Our B Company cCommander, Captain Allan Lamb, never left his stateroom. Second Lieutenant Ray Stewart, our Platoon Commander, brought him soda crackers and 7-Up for seven to eight days on our way to Okinawa.

After we debarked from the ship, driving the tanks (52-ton M48A3s) across the island to Camp Hansen was a cool experience, especially since it was my first time driving on an asphalt road. But going into the village was a doubly good experience.

Typical main street in "The Ville" (VTHF)

We passed all those bars with the good-looking women and all those stores with everything that you could ever want to buy. I was driving B35, which was the last tank in the seven tank column. As we entered the Camp Hansen back gate, my brakes failed, and I rammed into the back of B-34, Sergeant Allen's tank. I remember the look on his face. I guess that he thought I was messing with him and that he did not realize I had no brakes, hence the nickname Leadfoot. Bad things could have happened crossing Okinawa without brakes on an M48A3. We were lucky that day. As it turned out, this was just one of my "lucky days" that were to follow.

While in Okinawa, I bought my first 35 mm camera, a Petri 7s. I think that it cost me $25. It was a good camera, and it worked well until it fell off the back of a 5-ton truck one day while we were in the field in Chu Lai, RVN. After that, it never worked correctly again . . . but I did not know it. I just kept clicking all those wasted pictures and now those lost memories. That was the day we had to fill in for a Grunt unit that was called out to help another unit that was being pressured by the Viet Cong. I remember occupying sandbagged bunkers as a Tanker without his tank. That was a lonely feeling for sure.

After we were in Okinawa for a couple of weeks, we again loaded everything on a ship. This time it was the USS *Point Defiance* (LSD-31) as part of the Special Landing Force (SLF 3/7) and took off for parts unknown. The date was June 24, 1965. We were headed for a place named Vietnam, where our Tanker brothers from 3d Tanks had already landed and were fighting the enemy—whoever he was. Actually, I don't remember if we were officially told that or not. We cruised around for two months, stopping at Subic Bay in the Philippine Islands. We unloaded the tanks at Subic Bay, did some maintenance work, and drank "some" Miller High Life beer in the clear glass bottles and plenty of the ubiquitous San Magoo (San Miguel) beer. I have since learned that the ship and some of our Marines went on a rescue mission to help get a stranded/grounded USN destroyer (USS *Frank Knox*) off Pratas Reef and left some of us ashore.

We embarked the *Point Defiance* at Subic Bay, Philippines, and got under way in the LSD's well deck. It was August 31, 1965, when I drove B-35 onto an LCU in the well deck of the USS *Point Defiance* and took it to the beach at Chu Lai, RVN. I think that I am pretty typical for a Viet Nam vet where the memory (or the lack thereof) is concerned. According to my service record, I spent over a month at Subic Bay—I wish! Before landing at Chu Lai, we made a short stop at Qui Nhon on July 1, 1965. We took just two tanks ashore (B-34 and B-35). That fact is in my service record (SRB). I remember this well because I have photos to prove it. Sergeant Allen (TC of B-34 and light section leader) was in charge of the three of us: recently promoted Lance Corporals Tookolo and Reed and (not yet promoted) me. We had spent seven days at Qui Nhon acting as a stationary deterrent on the beach until SLF 2/7 (with the 2d Platoon, B Company, 1st Tanks) could relieve us. It was kind of like a vacation! Don't blame me, I was just following orders. I was a PFC, low man on the totem pole.

We offloaded at Chu Lai, RVN, where we had our tank park and living area located in a nice sandy area next to the beach of the South China Sea, where we joined the headquarters of B Company, 1st Tanks.

B-34, Third Herd of Bravo Company, 1st Tanks on the beach at Chu Lai, August 1965. B-34 without track. Thrown track and broken torsion bars were a problem that experienced driving in the bottomless sand minimized. Chu Lai—the world's largest butt kit.

VTR M-51 tank retriever nicknamed Nadine in B Company's tank park 1st Tanks' tank park on the shores of the South China Sea in Chu Lai, September 1965

Setting up the B Company, 1st Tanks' shower on the beach at Chu Lai, September 1965

Our only fresh water was from the "water buffalo" and was for drinking and personal cleaning only. To get "fresh" water in some quantity, Lieutenant Stewart devised a plan to dig a well, which would yield somewhat brackish water but less salty and corrosive than that in which we swam in the South China Sea accompanied by our "rubber laides". I remember some of the guys trying to dig a water well in the sand. It did not work too well, since it kept caving in and filling with sand. Lieutenant Lemon, platoon commander of the 1st Platoon, Company "B", and Sergeant Charley Waggle, section leader of 3d Platoon, Company "B", lent a hand in this picture. So we drove wooden 4×4 posts down at each of the four corners of the well. On the outside of these, as we dug down, they laid 2×6s. As they dug down more, they'd drive the 4×4s on the corners down and add rows of 2×6s along each side. At about 6 feet, the hole started filling up with water. They kept digging until there was about 4 feet of water in the well. We took turns jumping in and rinsing the sand off. After five to six days, the brackish water turned ugly and started to smell. Our Doc came by, took one look at the situation, and declared the well polluted and ordered the hole filled back up. Great while it lasted.

Chu Lai Beach w/chow line galley and emersion heaters used for cleaning eating utensils. On the beach at Chu Lai.

2d Lt. Carl Lemon (in the middle with shovel), platoon commander of 2d Platoon, B Company, 1st Tanks; and Sgt Charlie Waggle (foreground), section leader of 3d Platoon, B Company, 1st Tanks, dig a "well" at the B Company CP, Chu Lai (VTHF Archives).

We had a big sand dune ridge behind the camp with some air defense missiles located up there (LAAMs). Behind that ridge, you could hear artillery firing, Huey helicopters flying around, and Douglas A-4s taking off and landing from the just-built Chu Lai AirfField. Every evening around dusk, two or three Third Herd tanks left the tank park to become a key part of the defensive perimeter around the airfield. We had hardback tents to sleep in when we were back in that area. There were 55-gallon drums elevated for showers and the old pit toilet near the bottom of the ridge. There was also a big tent where the motor transport people hung out. They had weights there to work out with, and sometimes we would spend the evening there, pumping iron. It didn't help me much since I was the skinny one of my tank platoon.

M49C Tank Truck

One morning, I believe in October or November of 1965, I was in my tent when Jesse Salinas came by and asked me to accompany him, or asked if I wanted to go with him, to pick up a load of diesel fuel at the local fuel dump. Since Jessie was a good friend, I said, "Sure." I checked out with my tank commander (TC), Sergeant "Mac" Mackenzie, and we took off. We were not too far down the road when Jessie asked me if I wanted to take the long way and to see some sights. Of course I said, "Yes!" Big mistake! We went north along the beach and then took a dirt road inland toward Highway 1. The road was completely deserted. We were peacefully traversing this road when we came upon what looked like a big puddle. I should mention we were in a 2-1/2-ton (I think), 1,000-gallon tanker truck (M49C). When we came to this "large puddle," we stopped and examined the situation. It looked OK, so we proceeded into the "large puddle," and that was when the truck sank to the bottom of what, to our surprise, turned out to be a river! Where we first entered was the deepest part. The water was up to the top of the seat cushions. Of course, the truck engine stalled, and it would not start. We had to swim out of the thing, and then we decided to walk on west on the dirt road instead of going back the way we came, since we knew there was nothing behind us for several miles.

So we started our walk down the road in the middle of nowhere with one .45-caliber pistol, which was mine. Jessie was unarmed. Talk about two lucky dumb asses. The first thing of note that we saw on the road was a large bamboo snake that was about 3 to 4 feet long. It crossed the road in front of us and entered a stand of . . . what else? Bamboos.

Next to happen on our stroll, we saw some jeeps coming up the road toward us. As they approached, we could see that both jeeps were full of officers. Riding shotgun (front passenger seat) in the first jeep was a full-bird colonel. I have no idea who he was, but I would bet he was the 7th Marines regimental commander (Colonel Oscar Peatross). The first question he asked me was, "Where is your cover, Marine?" not "What the hell are you two doing out here?" But "Where is your cover?" I told him that I left it in the truck when it stalled in the water and we had to swim out. It was a very lame excuse, but he accepted it, and the two jeeps went on their way . . . and so did we. Not long after that, we came upon something that was almost as good as a tank, an amtrac! Really—an amtrac coming down the road many miles from the ocean. Coming to rescue us? He pulled up to us and stopped. We spoke to the crewmen and described our problem. They told us that they were glad to help. We hopped aboard, and back down the road we went to our drowned truck, to the Bean Burner, which was Jesse's name for his truck. The amtrac crew hooked up the tow cable and pulled us out and then dragged us all the way to Highway 1 and onto the asphalt. You might have thought we would have tried to pop the clutch and get it started when the amtrac was pulling us, but we did not try that. They dropped us on the highway, and we flagged down a Marine driving a big dump truck. He pulled us a short distance, and we got the truck jump-started. We drove back to the tank park, arriving four hours and thirty minutes later.

No one said a thing to us. I guess they thought that was how long it took to pick up a load of fuel (which we had failed to do!), but we did not get anything except water in the cab. A few days later, I saw Jesse and he told me the engine in his truck had blown up and it needed a major overhaul. No one ever knew about our wild ride, and we were very fortunate that day. Not only could we have gotten shot or drown, we also could have gotten in even bigger trouble if our wild ride had been discovered.

My advice to people is, if they have a job to do, just do it and leave the side trips alone. A short cut—or a long cut—unless it's your "lucky day," can lead you to a place you don't want to go.

Semper fi.

John M. Hunter, Corporal, USMC
"B" Company, 1st and 3d Tank Battalions
Vietnam 1965–1966

So to this piece of literary magnificence, added are some insights from former sergeant (then corporal) Tom Snyder:

Hi, Ray.

Although I don't remember this incident *when it occurred*, I do have a recollection of the aftermath. Both John Hunter and Jesse Salinas were PFCs at the time, and I was a corporal. My job was as chief dispatcher, and I was responsible for the knowledge of the status of each vehicle assigned to "B" Company, 1st Tank Battalion, and all drivers. As the "senior" motor transport driver, I was delegated to this position by then Staff Sergeant Pete Frano, platoon sergeant, 3d Platoon, shortly after departing San Diego, en route to Okinawa.

By using the word *aftermath*, I am referring to damage to the 6×6 Tanker truck. What they said about the lake/stream depth was true, unfortunately. The deep-water fording kits were removed after our arrival at the Chu Lai beach area. The water was sucked into the intake manifold and crankcase of the engine. When Private First Class Jesse Salinas finally got the engine started and returned to the motor pool, the diluted engine oil had already done its damage to bearings and cylinder walls. As this type of repair was above the echelon of our 3516 MOS mechanics, the Ttanker truck was shipped to Third FSR up the beach for engine replacement. It was a fortunate incident, however, that the truck did not take on a load of diesel fuel at the fuel dump, because without the truck-engine-driven PTO pump, gravity offloading would have taken awhile, and we did not have any on-site storage tanks to hold it.

When "mounting out" with "B" Company, 1st Tank Battalion, each platoon of five tanks "rated" a certain number of motor transport vehicles, i.e., jeeps, 5-ton 6×6 trucks, "water buffalo" water trailers, jeep trailers, cargo trailers, and two 6×6 Tanker trucks, one for diesel fuel and one for 84 octane gasoline. All motor-driven vehicles used in a mount-out situation are labeled Prime Movers, and the motor transport platoon's duties are to keep these vehicles up and running. Needless to say, this Tanker truck was placed in a high-priority repair status at Third FSR's engine-replacement facility, and turnaround time was ASAP!

Private First Class Jesse Salinas's nickname was the Bean Burner, labeled by motor transport drivers before we even departed Camp Pendleton, California, and he painted that name on the engine cowling of his truck.

SF,

Tom

As an addendum, Ray . . .

I have been enlightened that John Hunter's nickname was Leadfoot, given to him by Sergeant Allen for missing a turn driving his tank and also running into the back of Sergeant Allen's.

SF,

Tom

With both of these stories, and many more similar ones, the young trooper went off to war knowing virtually nothing of the physical and mental hardships he would endure. Luck held for these two young Marines just out of high school; they served their thirteen months—hard ones at that—and came home uninured physically, though with some emotional scarring.

So, as we sailed west, even with a nearly total news blackout, we suspected we just might be facing a shooting war against an "enemy" and in places that were unknowns. If asked, we most probably would answer that we understood that the enemy, his tactics, and his weapons were those that we had been trained to fight over the past many months of class and fieldwork. Surprise!

To get a better feel for the environment—terrain and weather, for starters—of the rumored confrontation, I planned to conduct classes for my platoon. I tried to locate some FMFMs (Fleet Marine Force Manuals) and FMs (Army Field Manuals) in the ship's "library" to match the tactics described in them with the environment presented with negatives on both. Among the embarked Marine unit leaders, ship's staff, or members of my reinforced platoon, zero results. Lotsa shrugs. One morning, while steaming east, I gathered my platoon in the officers' wardroom to talk about what might be facing us, but without maps or any material—let alone knowledge—about Vietnam. All the more frustrating was the ringing in my ear of the basic tenet of warfare: "Know your enemy." I had no clue about the enemy or the terrain, the weather, tactics, or what the beef was all about. I knew possibly less about our friendly order of battle: one helluva way to go to war.

I have related my truncated introduction to the Vietnam War as an example of the level of knowledge and preparation that was typical of virtually all the American military personnel arriving in Vietnam, irrespective of service or at any level of leadership and those he led.

Ray Stewart

The 3d Tank Battalion, 3d Marine Division stationed on the Japanese island of Okinawa was the first of the three Marine Corps tank battalions to move its flag to Vietnam, though both the 3d Tanks and a bit later 1st Tanks, stationed at Camp Pendleton, California, had subordinate units already fighting the South Vietnamese Viet Cong (VC), which had major support by the North Vietnamese (NVA). The 3d Tanks, a few thousand miles (and logistically seemingly light-years) from Marine Corps Supply Depot (MCSD), Barstow, California, was at the small end of the logistics/supply pipeline. Additionally, the M48A3 52-ton, 90 mm gun tanks, formerly gas driven, had been refitted with a 650 horse power V-12 *diesel* power pack, which changed the spare parts requirements. The 3d Tanks, farthest from its source of resupply, was also closest to the anticipated fight.

First Lieutenant Kevin Flynn arrived at 3d Tanks on Okinawa in early 1964. He was assigned to the 3d Tanks' maintenance section as the Maintenance Officer to find the battalion's tanks in very poor condition. Many of the tanks were deadlined, and most of the others were less than fully operational. He was directed to get the battalion's tanks ready to rumble. His major—just one of many—challenge was the gas-to-diesel engine swap out.

Lieutenant Flynn's article sheds light on what took place. The last sentence says it all.

> In early 1964, I attended the Track Vehicle Maintenance course at the 1st Marine Division, was shipped to Okinawa, and phased in the new diesel tanks.
>
> The Maintenance Section, at that time, was under the guidance of Gunnery Sergeant Metz and Staff Sergeant Getz, who had been jerry rigging and cannibalizing the battalion to keep the tanks in the field and doing an excellent job of it. The problem arose when we phased in the new M48A3 diesel (engine-powered) tank and had very few spare parts. The maintenance section had parts on back order for well over a year, and the problem continued.

Upon my arrival in (mid) '64, the battalion had failed a CG inspection, and the BN commander was replaced. Lieutenant Colonel Q. V. Earl became the new CO. As I was the only senior fFirst Llieutenant with grease under his nails, I became the Maintenance Officer. My first job was to barter with the Army for a truckload of olive drab (OD) paint. Paint was the most important commodity when preparing for the CG inspection. At the next inspection, all missing parts were on order; the jeeps, trucks, and all tracked vehicles were on line and looking like new money. We passed with flying colors, even though 20 percent of our vehicles were inoperable. (But they "looked good"!)

Months later, Lieutenant Colonel States Rights Jones Jr. took over the battalion, and our parts problem was still a disaster. I went to Colonel Jones and said I thought the only way to solve our parts problem and get USMC's help was to deadline the battalion. The gun companies were more than slightly angry, but we were getting no response from (Marine Corps Supply Depot) Barstow. Colonel Jones deadlined the entire battalion.

One day in the tank shed at Camp Hansen, someone yelled "Ten Hut!" and someone said, "Who's Lieutenant Flynn?" I replied, "Who wants to know?" There was no response, but around the corner came a general with a tank jacket on and a pearl-handled pistol on his hip, and he said, "I do." It was General Masterson (Bat) from Headquarters Marine Corps. After giving me the evil eyeball, he wanted to know what our problems were. After about an hour meeting with all hands and another hour with Colonel Jones, he left saying he would correct this problem PDQ. Two weeks later, all sorts of parts began arriving, including turret motors, which we hadn't seen for several years. After three months, we had all the parts we rated and a few extra. On 8 March '65, it all paid off.

Kevin D. Flynn

Marines splash ashore across Red Beach, Da Nang, RVN, 8 March 1965

Da Nang Area

Of course, the "8 March '65" First Lieutenant Flynn is referring to is the date of the landing of the 9th Marine Expeditionary Brigade across Red Beach, Da Nang, Republic of Vietnam, which included 1st Platoon, A Company (-) (Rein.), 3d Tanks, which actually landed on the adjacent Red Beach 2 on 9 March and fought the insurgent Viet Cong (VC), the North Vietnam–supported Main Force VC, and the professional Army of North Vietnam—Mr. Charles of the NVA.

B-31, the "command tank," aboard an LCU, making it ashore over Red Beach 2, Da Nang, 9 March 1965

B-31, Tanks A-11 and A-13 of the 1st Platoon, A Company, 3d Tank Battalion, which accompanied the 9th MEB landing in March 1965. Note how clean and uncluttered these early-war vehicles are (NARA).

It is a tribute to Marine Tankers (and their Ontos brothers) that the full capabilities of the vehicles they operated were realized in the challenging environment presented to them and for which they, and their supported infantry Marines, received little, if any, prior training.

The exclamation of surprise voiced by the U.S. ambassador to South Vietnam (he a retired four-star Army general officer) echoed the four-star Army general running the Vietnam War when Marine tanks and

Ontos crossed Red Beach 2 in Da Nang City on 8–9 March of 1965 and is a testimonial to the degree of preparation for the war that followed.

Though the basic principle of war ("Know your enemy") was violated and the 7**P**s (**p**rior **p**roper **p**lanning **p**revents **p**iss-**p**oor **p**erformance) ignored by those charged with developing the strategy to fight the Viet Cong (VC) and the North Vietnam Army (NVA) and win, these unforgivables were addressed—and largely corrected—in the prosecution of the war at the tactical end by the dedication, loyalty, and imagination of the Marine trooper and noncommissioned officers (NCOs); with the diligence, dedication, and grit of company grade officer leadership; and the steadying hand and experience of staff noncommissioned officers (SNCOs). They won every battle. However, the war was lost—some say from the start—at levels far above their pay grade.

A major training exercise named SILVER LANCE, conducted across the beach of Pendleton, California, presupposed a situation in which Lancelot,* a small, underdeveloped nation, became enmeshed in political upheaval sponsored by its northern neighbor, Merlin.

*The exercise code name given the friendly (blue) country that nominally represented South Vietnam.

^The exercise code name given the enemy (red) country that nominally represented North Vietnam.

The exercise was the creation of Lieutenant General Victor H. Krulak, commanding general, Fleet Marine Force, Pacific (CGFMFPac), former special assistant for Counterinsurgency and Special Activities, organization of the Joint Chiefs of Staff (JCS). General Krulak, stationed in Hawaii, was to play a major role in the philosophical differences between the Marine Corps (III MAF, General Walt) and the Army (COMUSMACV, General Westmoreland) in fighting the Vietnam War. General Krulak was a recognized expert in the conduct of guerilla warfare.

For Operation SILVER LANCE, the Corps amassed an armada of 60 ships, including three aircraft carriers, to take part in the operation. Over 500 Marine and Navy planes and helicopters, 3,200 motor vehicles, and 66 tanks were used by the force of 20,000 sailors and 25,000 Marines participating in the training exercise. Some 5,000 of the Marines played the part of Lancelotian (a.k.a. South Vietnam).

natives and infiltrators from Merlin (a.k.a. North Vietnam).

Lieutenant General Krulak and his staff began planning the exercise in September (1964). They finished with a script that covered the histories of the make-believe countries, the developing political situation, and the events that led to the Lancelotians' request for U.S. military aid. Also in the script were 2,000 "incidents" or problems, with which the CG wanted his troops encumbered. These were things such as pesky natives on the beach, a Lancelotian request for school textbooks, and scores of requests for medical aid. There was also a village chieftain who refused to deal with anyone less than the U.S. commander.

That Brigade Commander, Brigadier General E. H. Hurst, was given little notion beforehand of the difficulties that had been set up for him. This was to reinforce the realism of the situation. Needless to say, the situation was soon well in hand.

SILVER LANCE started with a Marine Brigade landing (unopposed, which was the only similarity to what actually happened on 8 March 1965 at Da Nang, RVN) to restore law and order in Lancelot (a.k.a. South Vietnam). Its arrival triggered an invasion by a Merlinese division (a.k.a. NVA), which soon drove the brigade into a pocket and threatened its annihilation.

The whole affair came to a climax with an all-out invasion by an expeditionary force of 20,000 Marines under the command of (none other than) General Krulak.

Original estimates were that it would take about one week to drive the aggressors from Lancelot and restore the civilian government to power.

However, in keeping with the realism that prevailed throughout the exercise, Major General W. T. Fairbourn, CG 1st Marine Division, seized an opportunity to accomplish the mission earlier than planned. A pincers movement executed by an armored column combined with a two-battalion helilift squeezed the last remnants of the "enemy" into a complete encirclement. Aggressor opposition ceased, and Exercise SILVER LANCE came to a successful conclusion (MG-4/65).

In an article written by Herb Brewer, First Sergeant, USMC (Ret), in *The 1st Word, 1st Marine Division (REIN) FMF*, vol. 1, no. 1, titled "1st Marine Division in the Field; 5 Feb 1965," he states,

> Operation Silver Lance was conceived by Lieutenant General Victor H. Krulak during the period of 19 February 1965 through 12 March 1965. The objective was to prepare the Marine Corps for its war in Vietnam. Silver Lance consisted of 70,000 Sailors and Marines, and 80 ships.
>
> It was to be the largest operation ever held on the west coast with a contingency of 31,000 Marines. It was to include 6,000 Marines from the 1st Marine Brigade out of Kaneohe, Hawaii, and *would have been* [italics by VTHF] the first time the 4th Marines ever set foot on U. S. soil since the end of World War II. They never made it to the shores of Camp Pendleton: reducing the III Marine Expeditionary Corps to 28,000 Marines from Pendleton. A difference of four ships between the two operations. One might ask "Why would having an actual war to fight limit the participation in an exercise!"
>
> In route to the Operation Silver Lance, the 4th Marines, with its complementary forces, were [*sic*] ordered to Okinawa, and then to Vietnam to continue the buildup

of American Forces in Vietnam. On 14 April 1965, the 3d Battalion, 4th Marines made an amphibious landing at Da Nang on Red Beach 2.

Fifty-five miles to the south, the 1st and 2d Battalion, 4th Marines; supported by 3d Recon Battalion; and 3d Battalion, 12th Marines (Artillery) landed on 7 May 1965, to provide security for the construction of Chu Lai Airfield. On 12 May 1965, the 3d Battalion, 3d Marines landed to reinforce the security of the airfield. As predicted by General Krulak, twenty-five days later, Chu Lai Airfield became operational during the first week of July 1965.

Note: rResearch shows that the 3d Battalion, 9th Marines (3/9) TAOR was in and around the Da Nang area, and never participated in the Chu Lai Enclave region.

By the end of 8 July 1965, there were over thirty thousand Marines deployed to Vietnam. Including supporting arms, air wing groups, service support groups, and heavy equipment support. The war continued for ten years after the first landing in Vietnam.

References used were.

1. Victor H. Krulak, First to Fight, An Inside View of the U. S. Marine Corps.
2. The Marines In Vietnam 1954–1975, An Anthology and Annotated Bibliography.
3. GySgt V. Mroz, Editor: The 1st Word, 1st Marine Division (REIN) FMF; Vol. 1. No 1; 1st Marine Division in the field; 5 Feb 1965.

Semper Fi,
Herb Brewer
1st Sgt USMC (RET) (SG-HB)

"On 8 March 1965 the Marines landed at Danang. Their presence in South Vietnam illustrated the failure of American policy there. Since 1954 the US had been trying to establish a South Vietnam that could stand on its own in defense of containment. The mere presence of US ground forces showed that the efforts of 11 years had been a failure. American involvement in the Vietnam War had begun" (VW-AW).

When the decision was finally made to introduce ground combat forces into Vietnam, it was at the end of a very long, complicated, and in-depth debate with several conditions, concessions, and assumptions made between and among both military and civilian officials at the highest of levels of their respective offices. "By early 1965 the American command in Vietnam had concluded that the South Vietnamese could not hold off the combined Viet Cong and North Vietnamese Army forces without U.S. assistance, and in February American forces began a limited air and sea bombardment of North Vietnam and jet aircraft strikes in South Vietnam. In late February General William C. Westmoreland, Commander, U.S. Military Assistance Command, Vietnam, requested two U.S. Marine battalion landing teams to assist South Vietnamese forces in making the airfield at Da Nang secure" (MC-DS).

The decision (to introduce combat arms) was based on the assumption that U.S. military presence would be of relatively short duration (i.e., undefined. And, by the way, Marines, during Operation SILVER LANCE across the beach and up the road at Camp Pendleton, defeated the "enemy" military, pacified the guerillas, won the hearts and minds of the villagers, and restored the legitimate government in five days on which to base this decision!). "During the first half of 1965 the three principal ground strategies were described as security, enclave, and search and destroy. Under the security strategy American Marines were sent to Vietnam to defend an airfield ——." However, the planners—mostly senior Army types—failed to understand or realize that when called to deploy a Marine Battalion Landing Team (BLT), included in that task organization were tanks and Ontos, among other elements of heavy equipment to support and maintain tanks and Ontos, and that this was the same scenario for artillery, amphibious tractor (amtracs), bridge builders, and bulldozers.

Since the Marines saw no reason to leave their tanks and Ontos behind (they were not dining regularly with General Westmoreland or retired general ambassador Taylor in Saigon's finest facilities), here they came! So on 9 March 1968, the second day of offloading the 9th MAB across Red Beach in Da Nang, Staff Sergeant John Downey, USMC, drove his 52-ton M48A3 tank (loaded with sixty-two rounds of mixed-capability 90 mm main gun ammunition and hundreds of rounds of .50- and .30-caliber machine gun bullets) off a landing craft onto Red Beach 2 and was followed by the other four tanks of 3d Platoon, Company "B", 3d Marine Tank Battalion. Then in March, the 1st Platoon, Company "A", 3d Marine Tank Battalion, followed by the 3d Tank Battalion Command Group commanded by Lieutenant Colonel S. R. Jones Jr., came ashore in Da Nang on 2 April. The first lines of a new chapter, "U.S. Marines in Vietnam," in the 190-year history of the Marine Corps were written. The role of Marine Corps armor—tanks and Ontos—was to play in America's longest war, and while significant, it *was not* well understood. Today, nearly six decades on, the role of tanks and Ontos still *is not* well-known, let alone understood.

And the U.S. aAmbassador's comments were correct: "Tanks" and fighting a "guerilla war" in the same sentence is nearly oxymoronic. In defense of the criticized, and not that it would have changed the composition of the BLT, the mission statement that propelled the Marines into Vietnam and the several changes that followed, no mention is made of fighting guerilas. In fact, it was clear that the mission was purely defensive (of the Da Nang Airfield and the Marine LAAMs in place to defend the airfield against enemy air attack). The Marines were ordered ashore and prepared to fight on the beach if necessary but in any case to proceed to the Da Nang airfield and establish perimeter security and send units west up Hill 327 to provide security for the LAAM site there to protect the airfield. Further, the Marines were able to sustain themselves once ashore until the logistics connection to CONUS would be established. (See an abbreviated description of a self-sustaining Marine MEU in the "Glossary of Terms"). The Army's nominees were not prepared to take on the mission, so the Marines were a stopgap. This situation was repeated down the road at Qui Nhon, when BLT 3/7 of the SLF was landed (2 July 1965), followed by BLT 2/7 (7 July 1965)* and *finally* the Army.

Major General Ray Davis, Assistant Division Commander of the 3d Marine Division on Okinawa, as he related in his autobiography, "also saw the 3dMarDiv as competition to the U.S. Army unit co-located on Okinawa" (SD-RD). He wanted the Marines to be first to land in Vietnam and take on the enemy. (Note: There is no indication that he was prepared to fight a guerilla war and even less that he wanted his Marines employed in a static defensive role.)

He "snuck" into Vietnam during SHUFLY, where Marine helicopters were supporting ARVN Ops. He saw the air base's need for upgrading to accommodate fixed wing (to support his ground Marines in an offensive) and also reconned possible landing sites from which to select amphibious entry into Vietnam, starting 8 March '65. General Davis was called to task by COMUSMACV's Saigon-based headquarters for this breach of military protocol.

"A major effort was concerned with the rapid deployment of units. We (3dMarDiv) were in effect competing with an Army airborne brigade (173d) which was stationed near Kadena Airfield (United States Air Force Base) and which had some priority over Marines in terms of transportation." Davis streamlined the process to beat them to the punch. "This got us into Vietnam quicker that the Army could get

---

* *Located at Qui Nhon 7 Jul–4 Nov. During the period 7 Jul–4 Aug., III MAF had operational control of 2/7. After that period, the U.S. Army's Task Force Alpha, which became I Field Force, Vietnam in November, had the operational control of the unit (GB-65). First Marine Division's 1st Antitank Battalion and 1st Tank Battalion, Company B, 2d Platoons were attached to BLT 2/7 as elements during this period.*

there." And his new, innovative system allowed the Marines to get into Qui Nhon, a few months later, more quickly than the 173d—again.

"On 8 July 1965 the 3d Marine Tank Battalion, commanded by Lieutenant Colonel States Rights Jones, Jr., debarked at Da Nang—the first U.S. tank battalion in Vietnam. Consistent with U.S. Marine Corps concepts of tank employment, the battalion's primary mission was to support Marine infantry. As Marine tactical areas of responsibility (TAOR) expanded throughout 1965, so did the areas in which tank units operated in support of infantry reaction forces, as support for infantry strongpoints, or in sweep and clear operations" (MC-DS).

So, doctrinally, if Marine infantry is employed to prosecute a conventional offensive operation and tanks and Ontos are attached, the tracks will be employed. And, as tribute to the "Tracksters," they would find any and every way possible to make themselves relevant—be it in the triple-canopy jungle crushing foliage for attacking Marine infantry, wallowing through the rice paddies to facilitate search-and-clear infantry operations, or blowing down buildings and smashing walls to defeat the enemy's cover and concealment efforts in urban combat. And though employed as such, too late to support the infantry in a face-to-face fight with the enemy, to transport the Marine dead and wounded to the rear.

The sequence of introduction of Marine combat support units, especially tank and antitank units, into Vietnam may appear somewhat reversed from initial perceptions. And to say that the separation of a tank or antitank platoon from its parent company and its attachment to or in direct support of an infantry battalion (or companies in DS or attached to their respective infantry regiments) did not present a number of challenges would be an understatement. The concept of task organizing these supporting units with additional supplies ("combat loading") and supplementing refuel and communications equipment allowed the tank and antitank units to operate ashore in support of the infantry units for a predetermined time.

Landing and Deployment of Tanks and Ontos

The day of 8 March 1965 slowly broke through a clouded overcast and a drizzle of wind-blown rain and a sea off the coast of South Vietnam in the Da Nang harbor running with four- to six-foot waves. It was difficult to focus on and define the shoreline, but the troops knew it was close, and they had been preparing their departure from the torture that only a ship's embarked troops can adequately explain. Arriving at Red Beach, Da Nang, Republic of South Vietnam, the U.S. Navy's 7th Fleet Task Force 76, comprising the flagship USS *Mount McKinley* (AGC-7) (https://en.wikipedia.org/wiki/ USS Mount McKinley), USS *Henrico* (APA-45), USS *Union* (AKA-106) (https://en. wikipedia. org/wiki/USS Union (AKA-106)), and USS *Vancouver* (LPD-2) (https://en.wikipedia. org/wiki/USS Vancouver (LPD-2)), was preloaded M-48 tanks in LCMs and M-50 Ontos in its well deck. As the time for the command to "land the landing force" came closer to H hour, the seas became increasingly rough and the wind brought the rain to an even more horizontal state paralleling the turbulent sea. The Tankers and Ontos crewmen stood by or in their vehicles, with growing apprehension of the long-anticipated amphibious landing as the movement of the *Vancouver* rose vertically and fell with a severe jar, now encountering 8- to 10-foot swells. The pitch and roll made it difficult to move from place to place without holding on. Then H hour was delayed, first with no predicted time announced and then predicted to be "within the hour" while the sea calmed.

Finally, the long overdue command "Stand by—land the landing force" rang through the ship's 1-MCs of the USS *Vancouver* (LPD-2) and the other ships of TF76. The tanks and Ontos were ready to move. Keeping their vehicles serviced in the cramped, suffocating well deck for the past few months was pure torture. Lighting was poor, and air usually fouled by the exhaust of running vehicles exacerbated by the ship's woefully inadequate ventilation system. Now the exhaust, increased several-fold as nearly all the tracked vehicles were running, though watering their eyes and burning their lungs was a prelude to the much-anticipated thrill of putting their feet on solid ground. If the delay in departing the ship by an hour or so was disappointing, it was trivial compared to the full-day delay finally announced, which meant that Tankers, Ontos crewmen, truck drivers, and equipment operators all attached to the reinforced, task-organized platoons would be spending the night sleeping in, around, or under their vehicles, or at least close by, since the Navy had already secured the crew's berthing areas. The tanks and Ontos were shut down as all hope for debarking on the eighth faded with the sinking sun. The Cs were broken out since the chow deck was also now "secured," i.e., closed to embarked troops. The much maligned "ham and m——r f——s" and the much disdained canned apricots were culled from the menu and tossed overboard with a brief ceremony earlier than anticipated.

And while the movement of heavy equipment and rolling stock stayed put in the bowels of *Vancouver*'s well deck, the troops on the *Henrico* were over the side, down to the waiting Mike boats, which were still pitching dangerously, causing some Marines to lose their footing, as well as breakfast, while descending the side of the ship. Personal equipment was lost, and several minor injuries were sustained. The most serious was when crushed between the pitching Mike boats and the ship's side, requiring treatment in the ship's sickbay. But no event would now slow the movement to contact prepared for on reaching the beachhead that lay in the mist to the west.

In the meantime, in the city of Da Nang, South Vietnam's "Third City" (after Saigon and Hue), the Vietnamese's preparations to meet and greet the American Marines were continuing apace. The city's band had been practicing the American national anthem, and something that sounded vaguely like the Marine Corps Hymn, without stop for

Though "well decorated" by the Da Nang mayor and his staff, Brigadier General Karch remains somber. (GB-65)

nearly a week. Da Nang City's government officials had written and rehearsed their opening remarks with which to welcome the Americans.

The governor of the province of Quang Nam, ARVN General Thi, and his civilian and military entourages were present and arranged in the reception line adjacent to Red Beach by order of seniority in their finest clothes. The several groups of schoolchildren had been excused from class to attend the event—the largest in their recollection—and were excited beyond words, chattering and giggling among themselves.

Brigadier General Frederick J. Karch, the commanding general, 9th MEB, watches the landing bedecked with flowers presented to him by South Vietnamese schoolgirls lining both sides of the road, waving and cheering. This picture received wide distribution in the U.S. press. (GB-65)

(Photo courtesy of Associated Press and Wide World Photos.)

Thuy Dao, a teenager, dressed in her finest clothes, had never seen so much excitement and so many dignitaries gathered in one place. To be excused from the rigors of the classroom was testimonial enough that this was a "very big thing." Thuy said that what she witnessed that day, seen through the eyes of innocence that had known only the quiet life of rural Vietnam, was to leave an indelible imprint. She looked back at the several events of the day and attempted to tell what she thought *at that time* in detail. She had little to compare what she saw with her rather limited experience: the noise of the huge trucks, the men dressed so different than she could have imagined, splashing through the water from the front of boats, to flop down on the beach with guns pointed inland for *no apparent reason*. So much entrenched in her memory was the event of many years ago. Little was she to know then that she would, speaking nearly perfect English, within two years be employed by the U.S. Navy's JAG (judge advocative general) office in Da Nang; or that in a few more years her country would be ripped apart in war. She would become a boat person with her family left on the beach, waving her goodbye; and her father, a colonel in the ARVN, would soon "disappear," never to be seen again, shortly after the NVA stormed the city in defeating the South Vietnamese Army in detail (personal interview with Dao in Turkey 2013).

From the moment the first Marine of Brigadier General F. J. Karch's 9th MEB set foot on the beach, to be followed by another 5,000 of his brothers in the pipeline, the world would be changed forever and not so much as that of the United States of America and the citizens of a united Vietnam. By the end of 1965, there would be more than 38,000 Marines in RVN. This, the first (mis)step of the march into the most divisive conflict in America's history.

Members of the 9th U.S. Marine Expeditionary Force (the name was later changed to Marine Amphibious Force) scramble ashore onto the beach at Da Nang on March 8.

A day later, on 9 March 1965, Marine Staff Sergeant John Downey, 3d Platoon, Company "B", 3d Tank Battalion, drove his 52-ton M48A3 Patton tank off the landing craft onto Red Beach 2 in I Corps, South

Vietnam. Staff Sergeant Downey's tank became the first U.S. tank to enter the Vietnam War, to be followed by two tank battalions—the remainder of 3d Tanks posted on the Japanese island of Okinawa and the 1st Tank Battalion at Camp Pendleton, California—and elements of a third tank battalion, the Fifth, yet to be activated (http://www.marines.mil/).

(VTHF Archives)

Third Tanks—D-day RVN

by Joe Tyson

[Spelling and sentence structure corrected with no change of subject content.]

Sir,

The pictures I sent you a few days ago on the landing at Red Beach, Da Nang, 1965, were correct, but dates need to be corrected. After some memory-jogging thought and some research, I stand to be corrected. For so many years, I tried to put the hellhole of Vietnam and my tour there completely out of my mind.

Third Platoon, Bravo Company, 3d Tank Battalion landed across Red Beach, Da Nang, Republic of (South) Vietnam (RVN) on 9 March 1965. This was the first contingent of an American armored unit to land in Vietnam.

This is a picture of Bravo 31, my tank, with then me (Lance Corporal Joe Tyson) driving it from a navy U-boat onto Red Beach (2) Da Nang, South Vietnam. Later, after a field promotion to sergeant, I became the tank commander of this tank. We lost the tank some months later (Feb. 1966). Marine engineers inspecting the blast site estimated the mine we triggered to be 100 pounds of TNT electrically detonated. B-31 was totaled with minor injuries to some of my crew.

Staff Sergeant Downey's tank was in front of my tank on the U-boat (LCU). As you probably know, a Navy U-boat can transport 3 medium (M48A3) tanks. When the U hit the beach, Sergeant Downey's tank off-loaded to Red Beach first, making his tank the first American tank to land in Vietnam. My tank—B-31—was the second tank to land.

(Note: Marine tanks and Ontos were identified by the alphanumerics painted on each M48A3 tank turret. For example, "B-31" would be a B Company, 3d Platoon Tank, and by convention, it would be the "command tank," i.e., the tank usually occupied by the platoon commander. The antitank battalions followed a similar protocol with their M50A1 Ontos.)

This identifier and the battalion logos were painted out once in-country.

The 3d Platoon remained in the vicinity of Red Beach for at least 24 hours, waiting for our ammunition to off-load. Once loaded with ammunition, the 3d Platoon proceeded to the Da Nang Air Base to bolster security there.

The following is paraphrased from *Lullabies for Lieutenants* by Frank Cox (LL-FC):

Since the tanks, Ontos, and other rolling stock and heavy equipment landed across Red Beach 2, a day after the large celebration experienced by the Grunts with the initial landing over Red Beach 1, ours was a rather tame greeting—a few fishermen and curious onlookers. After recovering from the weeks in the well deck and adjustment to being on solid ground, the tanks turned south into Da Nang.

The streets were teeming with Vietnamese peasants setting up shop on the side of the road, having brought rice and vegetables in from the countryside to sell to the mobs in the city.

Fishmongers placed their products on wide frond baskets in market cubicles. Crabs scuttled in large glass jars, bluefish and catfish slowly flopped, and basa, tra, and sole, all just landed from the nearby shimmering South China Sea, lay in lines of fillets. The smell of nudc [*sic*—nouc] mam, the Vietnamese ubiquitous fish sauce, hung in the air like foul incense and hit me like a sledgehammer, triggering my gag reflex. The treads of several tanks in our convoy pulverized chunks of asphalt that had torn loose from the roadbed. The steel monsters whined terrible mechanical noises and spewed diesel exhaust that hung in the air like black-grey filmy clouds.

The convoy raced along the river and through the city. Young children poked heads out of their makeshift homes crafted from cardboard and smiled and whistled. Older children brazenly and desperately raced up to our vehicles when we slowed, begging for cigarettes and candy. The adults didn't smile. They dispassionately observed us with cold, stoic faces.

We passed peasant women bouncing along the side of the road in knee-flexed jogs that helped them balance their load distributed at both ends of a bamboo pole atop their shoulders. The humid smell of rottenness and new growth filled the air. Brown-eyed eight-year-old boys smiled and waved at us straddling their fathers' water buffalos in the rice fields. The fathers in the nearby villages were absent, doing whatever mischief the Vietcong were into at the time.

Lance Corporal Joe Tyson continues:

> I remember not being at the base location very long. I was assigned as driver on a blade tank. The name of the tank commander (TC) of the blade tank was Sergeant Reed, a big black guy, good man and a great sense of humor. Have some great stories about my stint on blade tank with Reed, but I'll leave them for a later date.
>
> The blade tank was ordered to the intended 3d Tank Battalion Command Post (CP) on Hill 37 to clear fields of fire for the soon-to-arrive Tank Battalion H&S Company and its command group. On 8 July 1965, the rest of 3d Tanks landed at Da Nang. It was commanded by Lieutenant Colonel S. R. Jones.
>
> I remember being on watch the night 3d Tanks was mortared along with small-arms fire. I never will forget the sounds of that attack, the extreme loudness of the 82s (mortars), and the screaming shrapnel along with the zips of the small-arms fire. I could clearly see the flashes of the enemy mortar tubes off to my right and muzzle flashes of the small arms. I was in the tank by myself, and I traversed the turret to the right but could not fire because our blade tank was in hull defilade and a mound of dirt was blocking the 90 mm main gun tube. I stood by for a frontal assault, which I thought was definite. The TC, Reed, and John Saikley were pinned down in a sandbagged hooch behind the tank, so they couldn't get on board. We tied a string to the On switch in the driver's compartment, which made

it easy (and safer) to power up from outside the tank, and a canister round was already up and loaded in the main gun. I flipped the safety and was ready. There was a gun tank off to my right on the corner of the defensive perimeter that had a perfect down to the right and a straight-ahead view of those enemy tube flashes, but they never fired a single round. Could never figure out why.

After the battalion CP stint, the blade tank was sent to Marble Mountain, where I was transferred back to B-31, which was Captain Lee's tank. He was our company commander. Captain Lee was a great CO and leader. I have often wondered whatever happened to him.

I have many stories of my time at Marble Mountain with Bravo Company and the 9th Marines we were attached to, but they too are for a later time. My tour of duty in Vietnam was a long, long 15 months.

Joe Tyson sent the letter below just a few days later:

Sir,

The pictures I sent you a few days ago on the landing at Red Beach, Da Nang, 1965, were correct, but dates need to be corrected. After some memory-jogging thought and some research, I stand to be corrected. For so many years I tried to put the hellhole of Vietnam and my tour there completely out of my mind.

Third Platoon, Bravo Company, 3d Tank Battalion landed across Red Beach, Da Nang, Republic of (South) Vietnam (RVN) on 9 March 1965. This was the first contingent of an American armored unit to land in Vietnam.

Staff Sergeant Downey's tank was in front of my tank on the U-boat (LCU). As you probably know, a Navy U-boat can transport two medium (M48A3) tanks. When the U hit the beach, Sergeant Downey's tank off-loaded to Red Beach first, making his tank the first American tank to land in Vietnam. My tank—B-31—was the second tank to land. The 3d Platoon remained in the vicinity of Red Beach for at least 24 hours, waiting for our ammunition to off-load. Once loaded with ammunition, the 3d Platoon proceeded to the Da Nang Air Base to bolster security there. I remember not being at the base location very long.

Since 1970, when the last of the Marine tank battalions with the antitank battalions, with the Ontos included, left Vietnam, there has been multiple additions, deletions, and mission adjustment of the Marine Corps ground organizations. We will address briefly and only as necessary to clarify tank and Ontos participation, the at-that-time command and control arrangements and organizations.

At that time, and little has changed since, there were three categories and missions or types of ground organizations. They were referred to as combat (infantry), combat support (artillery, tanks, Ontos, etc.), and combat service support (medical, logistics, etc.). The infantry battalion was the basic ground combat element. To fit the anticipated fight, the Marine Corps infantry units were task-organized by adding the combat support and combat service support elements to the infantry battalion that could best accomplish the specific mission based on the likely enemy, situation, and terrain. For example, the scenario might be one where tanks would logically be employed to best support their overland capabilities of massive and unmatched fire and maneuver; Ontos may be employed in anticipation of facing enemy armor and fortified enemy positions. Of interest, in the context of the Vietnam War, there was no suggested task organization or BLT configuration—or philosophy—that addressed Marines in the defense or Marine infantry in guerilla operations.

During the Vietnam War, the resulting organization was referred to as a Battalion Landing Team (BLT) when embarked aboard amphibious shipping, which was built to be adaptable to any contingent the Navy's Seventh Fleet might face in its area of responsibility (AOR), basically the Pacific Ocean and its literals. bordering land masses. The BLT was the ground element of the MAGTF (Marine Air Ground Task Force), which included air assets of rotary- and fixed-wing airplanes that were also task-organized. Further, the combat support units, specifically tanks and Ontos, were "attached" to or in "direct support (DS)" of the infantry battalion in specific configurations: the tank battalion in support of an infantry division, a tank company in support of an infantry regiment, and a tank platoon supported an infantry battalion. Again, in Vietnam and in general, the designation of a unit as a BLT included an artillery battery, a tank platoon, and an Ontos platoon of the combat support units and the appropriate size and type of unit from the combat support organizations. In general, these attached units were the responsibility for reporting and supporting by the BLT, especially in the case of the Special Landing Force (SLF). As the SLFs landed in Vietnam, the BLT designation was usually dropped and the supporting units reverted back to the command and control of their respective parent organizations, to be later parsed back out to the support of an infantry organization usually for specific operations. (Note: Refer to the "Glossary of Terms" for the definition of *attached* and *direct support*.)

As the tank platoon was detached from but remained in support of the 3d Battalion, 9th Marines, 3d Marine Division (BLT 3/9), the defensive positions 3/9 was establishing around the Da Nang Air Facility. The tanks were placed into defensive positions along the west side of the airfield's defensive wire. There were no sanitary facilities of any kind. "Field heads" (toilets) and "piss tubes" (urinals) were dug into the sand. A close-by stream was used for "bathing." C rations were broke out. Cots were scrounged, and the tanks were dug in by hand. The Air Force fed a hot meal in trade for Marine trinkets. The Tankers were kept busy digging zigzag trench line and filling and placing sandbags. Exactly how the mission to defend the Da Nang airfield was to be accomplished was left to the experience and imagination of the new occupiers. The company's fFirst sSergeant, Don Gagnon, put his Tankers to work, setting up aiming stakes with set parameters to avoid hitting friendly troops with outgoing ordnance. The Tankers avoided using or even setting adjacent to the existing abandoned French concrete bunkers, knowing that they would be the first to be hit in the advent of a mortar or sapper attack.

K/3/9 carved out and fortified postions on Hill 327 using sandbags and help from earth-moving equipment from Marine engineers. (Photo by GySgt R. F. Halahan, USMC.)

Marines from the 1st Battalion, 3d Marines disembark from U.S. Air Force C-130 transports at the Da Nang Air Base on 8 March. The airlift of the battalion was held up for twenty-four hours shortly after these Marines arrived. (USMC Photo A184402)

Lieutenant Colonel H. J. Bain's 1/3 had been alerted but a few days earlier and was saddled up and moved to the Kadena Air Base to begin its airlift from Okinawa directly to the Da Nang Air Base, which was complete by 12 March, with the exception of 1/3's attached tanks, Ontos, and low-priority vehicles. These combat support and combat service support assets were moved by surface, shipping from Okinawa's White Beach to Da Nang harbor for general unloading and administrative landing of other 9th MEB units. "Because of a fire fight on the night of 8–9 March between VC elements and Vietnamese Army troops only two miles north of RED Beach, the ships of the amphibious task force had moved to anchorages near the mouth of the Song Han (Da Nang/Tourane River). The next day unloading continued up the river over a ramp into the city" (GB-65).

This is a distillation of Staff Sergeant A. B. Peavey's oral history interview on Marine Corps History Division (CD #159).

Marine Tanker Staff Sergeant Peavey began his eight months, eleven days tour in Vietnam when he landed at Da Nang Airfield with 1/3 on 9 March 1965. He was the liaison NCO representing Alpha Company, 3d Tank Battalion, which came across Red Beach, Da Nang, a few days later. His unit re-embarked amphibious landing craft and proceeded north up the South Vietnam's coast and overland to Phu Bai, where his tanks supported 3/4 in their operations in the expanding Hue/Phu Bai TAOR.

During Staff Sergeant Peavey's interview, he answered the questions of the interviewer:

Q. Would you discuss for me briefly, how your tanks were deployed? What effectiveness you found? With what effectiveness were they used? Perhaps mentioning what problems you ran into and some of the areas where they weren't very effective?

A. The main areas where they [tanks] were not too effective were the areas you could not travel. The roads were very limited, and the tank weighs about 52 tons. We could not travel [across country] in that terrain over there with the exception of staying on the roads. The way they employed us, we would go on patrols, go out 5 or 6 miles and shoot the 90 mm gun into suspected VC areas. One day when we were in the process of doing this, we had a couple of tanks mined. Blew the whole suspension off the right side on two tanks, took us all that day and most of the night to get back in from towing our tanks in. Then the way they employed us again was the show of force. They [the Marine infantry] would go to these little villages, and we'd set up a blocking force. The ARVNs then would flush them [the VC] out into the areas where the tanks were employed along the river . . . set up blocking force.

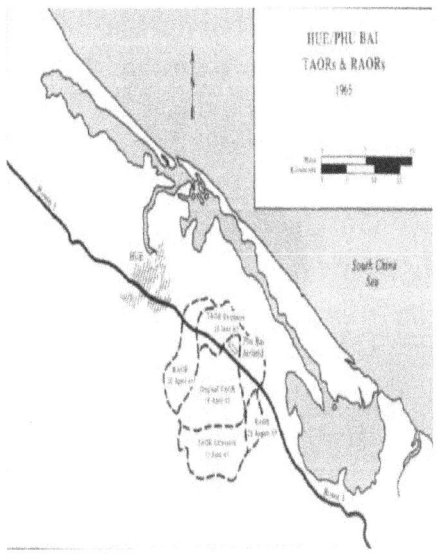

Hue/Phu Bai TAOR's & RAOR's 1965 (GB-65)

We would take maybe a squad of infantry for security purposes, and we'd take one tank platoon, maybe four tanks. Most of the time we took four tanks, Ontos . . . four or five Ontos would maybe go on these patrols. We'd go just as far into these areas as we possibly could to see, if we could spot, any areas where the VC was located and shoot into these areas.

Q. When employing tanks in the artillery role?

A. The way we'd do it, we'd have to work with the artillery, sir. They'd have to build us a ramp to ramp the tanks, about 45-degree ramp. We'd have to ramp these tanks so we could get the angle of the most range so we can shoot like artillery. And the artillery personnel would tell us we got to read the azimuth indicator within our tanks, and he'd tell us what to set this on, and we'd set it there and fire a round [of 90 mm]. Sometimes he'd say, "Willy Peter [white phosphorous] five rounds" and we'd fire Willy Peter five rounds. He'd tell us what to set on the azimuth indicator, and it'd go off just like the artillery . . . he'd give us the read-in of the quadrant. We had the M13 quadrant, that's for elevation, and then the indicator is for deflection. We also used the M1 quadrant, which is more accurate than the M13. We'd set that read-in on, what <u>the</u> Artillery Officer would give us: then we'd shoot.

Thus, with about one-third of the Marine Western Pacific ground forces committed, a new phase of the five years of tanks and Ontos involvement in Vietnam War had started. Though the beginning started rather innocently with the Joint Chiefs of Staff 7 March announcement that "U.S. Marine Force will not, repeat will NOT, engage in day-to-day action against the Viet Cong," and while the ground forces—the infantry battalions and their supporting tanks and Ontos—were assigned initially approximately 8 square miles around the Da Nang facility, that restriction was soon loosened. 1/3 deployed to, further developed, and manned the defenses along the perimeter of the airfield, while 3/9 moved to advance positions on and around the hill mass 268–327 west of the air base from which they ran limited patrols with tank and Ontos support, terrain allowing. On 1 April, the mission of the 9th MEB was expanded, allowing it to use its Marines "in active combat under conditions to be established and approved by the Secretary of Defense." Along with this expansion was the movement of the Regimental Landing Team (RLT) 3 comprising BLTs 2/3 and 3/4, as well as Marine Air and the RLT Headquarters. 3/4 departed Okinawa on five LSTs, having recently completed exercise JUNGLE

DRUM III in Thailand. On 10 April, BLT 2/3 landed over Red Beach and at the Tiensha Peninsula across from the Da Nang River with two companies joining Task Force Alpha to be helilifted to the Phu Bai airstrip 45 miles north of Da Nang near Hue to assume the defense of that area and await the arrival of 3/4.

On 14 April, the 9th MEB assumed control of the three MEB ground units upon coming ashore. On 12 April, the RLT-3 commander, Colonel E. B. Wheeler, and his headquarters arrived to assume command of all BLTs ashore. On 14 April, Lieutenant Colonel D. R. Jones's BLT arrived and moved to Phu Bai, where he relieved Task Force Alpha. On 15 April, elements of 3/4 (First Lieutenant Warner, Platoon Leader, 3d Platoon [-] [Rein], B, 3d Tanks; and First Lieutenant Bates, Platoon Leader, 3d Platoon, A, 3d ATs attached) embarked at Da Nang and proceeded to the mouth of the Hue River to off-load on LCMs and LVTPs and to depart for Hue 11 miles up the river to debark, to be welcomed by a band and five hundred cheering Vietnamese, and then by trucks to Phu Bai to relieve the elements of 2/3, who landed there four days earlier.

2/4 Marines are flown north 40 miles to Phu Bai awaiting orders to occupy the positions vacated by 2/3 (Photo by GySgt R.F. Ayers, USMC)

Coincidentally, "On 14 April, General Westmoreland provided the MEB with a concept of operation which he divided into four phases: establishment of defensive bases; deep reconnaissance patrols of the enemy's avenues of approach; offensive action as a reaction force in coordination with the Vietnamese; and finally, 'undertake in coordination with RVN I Corps, an intensifying program of offensive operations to fix and destroy the VC in the general Da Nang area.'" One might note here that there's no mention of what was a great bone of contention between COMUSMAVC and Marine Corps leadership termed "Hearts and Minds" (GB-65).

On 19 April, RLT-3 was reorganized as 3d Marines (Rein) and the Da Nang TAOR was established, as was a TAOR established at Phu Bai for 3/4. The following day, COMUSMACV headquartered in Saigon authorized a change in Brigadier General Karch's ground force's mission to include the following:

Aggressive combat patrolling within the respective TAORs

Preparation for conducting offensive operations as a mobile reaction force

The landing and deployment of III MEF to Da Nang and the landing of one of its MEBs at Chu Lai to assume control of a newly assigned TAOR

April witnessed the first real Marine ground action with the Viet Cong enemy. A Marine reconnaissance company on patrol spotted what appeared to be an armed group of Vietnamese males carrying a mix of weapons. The Viet Cong, seeing their first American Marines, though surprised but apparently well drilled, deployed and fired on the Marines. The Marines were outmanned by the "10 to 150" enemy soldiers. The box score was representative of what became referred to as "the long war" that was to follow—one Marine WIA (slightly) and one VC KIA and the estimate of the enemy strength questionable.

"In a war without front lines and territorial objectives, where 'attriting the enemy' was the major goal, the 'body count' became the index of progress. Most authorities agree(d) that the figures were notoriously unreliable. The sheer destructiveness of combat (to say nothing of the results of bombing by B-52's from 50,000 feet) made it difficult to produce an accurate count of enemy killed in action" (AW-GH). And where civilians were used by the Viet Cong guerillas for cover, said Caputo, "If it's dead and Vietnamese, its VC, was a rule of thumb in the bush" (RW-PC). Tankers and Ontos crewmen referred to a captured Vietnamese, male or female, as VCS, or Viet Cong *Suspect*. Should the "suspect" expire, for whatever reason, he/she was reported as VCC—Viet Cong *Confirmed*.

In late April, the 3d Tanks' CP was relocated to the vicinity of Hill 327, into the sparse living conditions, which the 3d Tanks Headquarters personnel set about improving. The assigned mission of the tanks was to provide indirect fire in support of the infantry patrols sent to expand the TAOR. This employment of Marine tanks was also a preview of the future of tanks in the war that never saw tanks used in their intended primary role of tank-on-tank. Training to use their tank as an artillery piece was rudimentary for most crewmen and not of high priority in most field exercises. That is not to say the use of tanks in the indirect fire mode was not effective and, in this case, responsive and effective. The range of the 90 mm tanks was greater than that of the 105s. And while the bursting radius of the 90 mm high explosive (HE) and white phosphorous (WP) was less than that of the 105s, the accuracy was arguably greater and time-to-target was considerably shorter. Tankers traded their services for hot chow; services like towing and manual labor were rewarded with ice and accompanying beer.

In the meantime, three reinforced Marine battalions and Marine Air MAG-12 were planned for deployment at Chu Lai, 57 miles to the south of Da Nang and 20 miles north of Quang Ngai City on the coast of the South China Sea adjacent the to-be-constructed SATS (short airfield for tactical support).

USMC Photo A 184206 South Vietnamese troops secure the Chu Lai area. Their U.S. Army advisors have made a sign to greet the Marines.

General Carl's 3d MEB was reconstituted comprising RLT-4 with its headquarters near the beach in Chu Lai with Captain Joe Sanders's C Company's Headquarters Platoon, 3d Tank Battalion in direct support (DS); BLT 1/4 with Second Lieutenant B. R. "Bucky" Massie's 1st Platoon, C Company, 3d Tank Battalion attached; and 2/4 with Second Lieutenant P. J. Harris's 2d Platoon, C Company, 3d Tanks attached, 3d Recon Battalionn, MABS-12, and a CB's Battalion. The landing was both across the beach at Chu Lai and inland by helicopter. Even at this early stage, the Marine Corps' actions and decisions and tactics in fighting the war were at odds with the Army-heavy staff of COMUSMACV in Saigon. However, to meet somewhere in the middle, the two sides agreed to add 3/3 and K/3/9 deployed from the Da Nang TAOR to provide beach security to the 3d MEB mix during that landing and off-loading phase and to remain in that mode until the amphibious forces were properly deployed ashore.

H hour for the amphibious elements of the landing was planned for 0800 on 7 May across Red Beach, Chu Lai, and by helicopter farther east to LZ ROBIN. The amphibious Marines were met with the usual flower maidens, press corps, and hand-painted signs by those friendly units, which preceded the Marines. Captain Joe Sanders, CO C, 3d Tanks, said, "I remember very little about the landing on the beach at Chu Lai. I think we may have used the nets and a regular personnel landing craft. I don't remember getting my feet wet but Chu Lai had a good beach for landing craft so I may not have. We were greeted on the beach by Vietnamese officials and young girls dressed in white. I thought it was kind of strange to see all the heavily armed Marines and these young girls in white greeting them with flowers." Captain Sanders moved his tanks north and set up his company CP on a hill overlooking the South China Sea beach.

It was a routine festive day enjoyed by all, but the Marines were hard at work to grind through the sand of what was called the world's largest butt kit and more precisely described by General Krulak (who picked the place and for whom it was named) "as great a challenge as any foreshore that I have ever seen. The sand is of powdered sugar consistency and no wheeled vehicle can negotiate it with success." And tank drivers learned early on that thrown track resulted unless turns were made with caution. By the end of the day, the 4th Marines Headquarters and all the supporting units were in place with the defensive perimeter established. However, the off-loading of the airfield supplies and equipment was a different matter. Because of the difficulty negotiating the sand, all progress literally ground to a halt. Beach matting was ordered, and by 10 May, it arrived to commence the movement of SATS material and equipment to the landing strip site.

"At noon on 12 May, the [Chu Lai] amphibious operation officially came to an end. On this date, the first elements of BLT 3/3, arriving in amphibious shipping from Okinawa," brought First Lieutenant Ken W. Zitz on the USS *Thomaston*, the Platoon Commander of the 3d Platoon, A Company, 3d Tank Battalion, which was to land across Red Beach, Chu Lai.

Lieutenant Zitz always made a "splash" wherever he entered, and the landing of his tank platoon was in-character. Tanks (and other rolling stock) are routinely prepared to enter the water from landing craft with the installation of fording kits. For tanks, the maximum water depth is 8 feet. As the LCU on which two of Zitz's 52-ton M48A3 tanks were loaded backed out of the well deck of the ballasted-down LSD USS *Thomaston*, it executed a 180-degree turn toward the Chu Lai beach and powered up for the run. Some distance from the actual beach, approximately 50 feet, the LCU allegedly hit a sandbar that ran somewhat parallel to the beach. Thinking that the bottoming signaled a safe and shallow beach to the shore, the Navy controller signaled to Lieutenant Zitz in A-31 to debark. Taking the lead, -Ken keyed his helmet mic and told the driver to "move out." His tank surged forward and down . . . down . . . down! Instead of the zero-entry beach, his tank dropped into 10 feet of water. Following closely and suffering the same submergence and similar results, A-32 also drowned and, it too, died.

Both tanks were ingloriously towed ashore. The salt water destroyed the generators, and with no spare parts any place to be had, the deadlined tanks sat on the beach for several weeks. With 3/3, to which 3/A/3d Tanks was now in support of (rather than attached to), assuming the defense of the southern portion of the TAOR, Lieutenant Zitz's "heavy section," i.e., three tanks (the "light section" sitting deadlined on the beach), proceeded to the "Song Cai Bong" (OB) with a squad of Grunts on board. At the river's edge, Lieutenant Zitz observed nearly a dozen Vietnamese boats. He told his Vietnamese interpreter, armed with a bullhorn, to order the "fishermen" in to the riverbank. One boat took off, and the tank's gunner, Ken Zebal, was given the command by Lieutenant Zitz to fire his 90 mm loaded with a high-explosive (HE) round. With a hit, Zebal then fired a white phosphorous (WP) round, also a dead center hit with a number of secondary explosion following. Since the Rules of Engagement (ROE)—termed as "ridiculous" (phrased more colorfully with a Marine dialect)—specifically proscribed Zitz's decision to use his 90 mm without prior approval, he was called, as anticipated, to the 3/3 Command Post (CP). He expected a chewing, but the prayer meeting was not a reprimand for his decision, but rather it was actually a congratulation by the regimental CO. The positive results of Zitz's decision caused the Rules of Engagement to be modified.

With the completion of the Chu Lai amphibious landing, seven of the nine infantry battalions of the 3d Marine Division with its ground support units—artillery, tanks, and Ontos—as well as most of the 1st MAW were deployed in three areas of South Vietnam. The 9th MEB was deactivated, and the III Marine Amphibious Force (III MAF) was stood up. The Marine Corps Division / Wing Team was in place and ready to expand its operations within their much-expanded TAORs, anticipated with the soon-to-be announced offensive role.

From his Saigon-based headquarters, Commanding General Military Assistance Command, Vietnam (COMUSMACV) "General Westmoreland observed that American operations would take place in three successive stages: base security, deep patrolling, and finally search and destroy missions" (GB-65). And Marine forces were positioned to defend and expand three enclaves' TAORs at Da Nang (172 square miles), Chu Lai (104 square miles), and Phu Bai (61 square miles) by conducting long-range patrolling, setting ambushes, conducting major search and destroy missions, and initiating a comprehensive pacification Civic Action Program.

Evidence attained from communication intercepts, aerial reconnaissance, and active patrolling by Marine recon units of growing threats adjacent to and within each TAOR required additional assets be employed; hence, the call for more Marines came from both MACV and III MAF. Then the VC spring-summer offensive opening on 30 May grabbed the attention of both the Vietnamese government and U.S. military. The 1st VC Regiment Headquarters in place a scant 20 miles south of Chu Lai, reportedly reinforcement from the east with units "on the move," first engaged the ARVN when they surprised and soundly trounced the ARVN forces within mere shouting distance of the Chu Lai TAOR. And to make matters more complicated, the South Vietnamese government was experiencing considerable difficulty resolving systemic and chronic internal conflicts. "During June, the South Vietnamese Army was losing the equivalent of one infantry battalion a week to enemy action" (GB-65). General Westmoreland called for a division of the Republic of Korea Army. More of the ROK Marines later. The call for more troops—up to forty-four battalions to include Korean, New Zealand, and Australians—was accompanied by the request to launch offensive operations across the country to be known as the "search and destroy tactic."

The Republic of (South) Korean soldiers and Marines established their reputation as being a tough, no-holds barred, nearly autonomous force, certainly not the embodiment of the "hearts and minds" philosophy prescribed for the conduct of the "other war" early in the war. Their record working with Marine Tankers (*Praying for Slack: A Marine Corps Tank Commander in Vietnam* by R. E. Peavey [PS-RP]) will be detailed in a follow-on segment, but one example story first.

In Lewis B. Puller Jr.'s *Fortunate Son: The Healing of a Vietnam Vet*, called in the *New York Times* "a dark and corrosive autobiography," Chesty's son, Marine lieutenant and platoon commander of the 3d Platoon, Gulf Company, 1st Marines operating in the Riviera during the summer of 1968, described as "a lethal stretch of beach, hedgerows and unfriendly thatched villages along the South China Sea" south of Marble Mountain, alludes to the South Korean's reputation for brutality.

True to his word, Captain Woods [G Company's CO] devised an ambitious operation as a way to settle the score in the Riviera. He knew that it would be unacceptable from a political standpoint simply to level Viem Dong, the hamlet at the edge of the Riviera, a known Vietcong stronghold, from which we had been taking an increasing amount of hostile fire, but he also knew that the South Korean allies were free to operate without the political constraints that figured so heavily in all our planning. He therefore seized on the idea of a joint operation in which our company would be lifted at first light into the Riviera. We would then form a cordon around Viem Dong, and a South Korean company would sweep through the village and drive the unsuspecting enemy into our field of fire. Whatever else the Koreans did in the village was their own business, *but with their reputation for brutality* [author's italics] we all knew that the village would be loath to support the Vietcong so openly in the future." (FS-LP)

Unfortunately, Lewpy (the Puller family's nickname for Lewis Jr.) was not to witness the completion of the operation. As he was running from the enemy soldiers he was facing with a jammed M-16. He turned away, running back to the company's CP, when he tripped a booby trapped 105 mm artillery round, which exploded, losing both his legs and most of both hands, ending his career though not his life.

The 2/4 Marines are flown north 40 miles to Phu Bai, awaiting orders to occupy the positions vacated by 2/3.
(Photo by GySgt R. F. Ayers, USMC.)

Hue/Phu Bai TAORs and RAORs 1965 (GB-65)

On 10 April, Lieutenant Colonel David A. Clement's BLT 2/3 landed at Da Nang. Task Force Alpha of the BLT was helilifted to the Phu Bai airstrip 45 miles north of Da Nang near Hue to assume the defense of that area.

RLT-3, commanded by Colonel E. B. Wheeler, landed at Da Nang, RVN, at 0800 on 12 April 1965.

with CO Company A (-) (Rein.), 3d Tank Battalion First Lieutenant E. T. Metz and

CO Company A (-) (Rein.), 3d Antitank Battalion First Lieutenant R. J. Donohue attached.

Upon landing, RLT-3 assumed OpCon of 3d Marines (-) (Rein), defended key terrain, and provided security for the airfields at Da Nang/Hue-Phu Bai.

On 19 April, tanks and ATs were detached from the RLT and placed in direct support (DS) under AdCon of parent units.

On 22 April, tanks deployed with one platoon in DS 2/3 and 3/9 and AT's one platoon to each battalion, 1/3, 2/3, 3/9.

And on 14 April, Lieutenant Colonel Donald R. Jones's BLT 3/4 arrived in Vietnam and moved to Phu Bai, where it relieved Task Force Alpha. Coincidentally, "On 14 April, General Westmoreland provided the MEB with a concept of operation which he divided into four phases: establishment of defensive bases; deep reconnaissance patrols of the enemy's avenues of approach; offensive action as a reaction force in coordination with the Vietnamese; and finally, 'undertake in coordination with RVN I Corps, an intensifying program of offensive operations to fix and destroy the VC in the general Da Nang area'" (GB-65).

On 19 April, Regimental Landing Team-3 (RLT-3), cutting its tie to the Navy's 7th Fleet, was reorganized as 3d Marines (Rein.) and was given a larger Tactical Area of Responsibility (TAOR) centered on Da Nang; and the following day, 3/4 at Phu Bai was assigned a TAOR, the size of which allowed for active patrolling, and defensive area large enough to more adequately protect the airfield. Ground forces under General Karch received an expanded mission tasking from COMUSMACV that, among other provisions, included (1) aggressive combat patrolling within the TAORs and (2) preparation for conducting offensive operations with constituted mobile reaction force. At the same time, President Johnson, on the recommendation of the Joint Chiefs of Staff (JCS) and COMUSMACV, ordered the deployment of the III MEF to Da Nang and the landing of a MEB-size force at Chu Lai.

By 20 April 1965, the 9th MEB comprised Headquarters 3d Marines (-) (Rein), 1/3, 2/3, and 3/9—just under four thousand Marines.

By late April, the Company "A", 3d Tanks' CP was relocated to the vicinity of Hill 327 (AT 985742). Living conditions improved. The assigned mission of the tanks was to provide indirect fire in support of the infantry patrols sent to expand the TAOR beyond the constraints previously imposed by the TAOR's as far as six miles.

One might note here that there's no mention of what was to become a great bone of contention between COMUSMAVC and Marine Corps leadership termed "hearts and minds" (GB-65).

In the meantime, three reinforced Marine battalions and Marine Air MAG-12 were planned for deployment at Chu Lai, 57 miles to the south of Da Nang and 20 miles north of Quang Ngai City on the coast of the South China Sea, adjacent to the to-be-constructed SATS Airfield.

South Vietnamese troops secure the Chu Lai area. Their U.S. Army advisors have made a sign to greet the Marines. (USMC photo A184206.)

General Carl's 3d MEB was reconstituted, comprising RLT-4 Headquarters with Captain Joe Sanders's C Company's Headquarters Platoon, 3d Tank Battalion DS; BLT 1/4 with Second Lieutenant B. R. "Bucky" Massie's 1st Platoon, C Company, 3d Tank Battalion attached; and 2/4 with Second Lieutenant P. J. Harris's 2d Platoon, C Company, 3d Tanks attached, 3d Recon Battalion, MABS-12, and a CB's battalion. The landing was both across the beach at Chu Lai and inland by helicopter. Even at this early stage, the Marine Corps' action and decisions in the war were at odds with the Army staff of COMUSMACV in Saigon. However, to meet somewhere in the middle, the two sides agreed to add 3/3 and K/3/9 down from Da Nang to provide beach security to the 3d MEB mix. H hour for the amphibious portion was planned for 0800 on 7 May across Red Beach, Chu Lai, and by helicopter to LZ ROBIN. The amphibious Marines were met with the usual flower maidens, press corps,

With the completion of the Chu Lai amphibious landing, seven of the nine infantry battalions of the 3d Marine Division with its ground support units (artillery and tanks and Ontos) as well as most of the 1st

MAW were deployed in three areas of South Vietnam. The 9th MEB was deactivated, and the III Marine Amphibious Force (III MAF) was stood up. And the Marine Corps Division / Wing Team was in place.

COMUSMACV "General Westmoreland observed that American operations would take place in three successive stages: base security, deep patrolling, and finally search and destroy missions" (GB-65). And Marine forces were positioned to defend and expand three enclaves—tactical areas of responsibility (TAOR)*—conduct long-range patrolling, set ambushes, conduct major search and destroy missions, and initiate a comprehensive pacification Civic Action Program.

But the evidence of growing threats adjacent and within each TAOR required additional assets be employed, hence the call for more Marines. Then the VC spring-summer offensive opening on 30 May really got the attention of both the Vietnamese government and the U.S. military. The 1st VC Regiment, a scant 20 miles south of Chu Lai, was reportedly "on the move." The VC forces surprised and soundly trounced the ARVN forces within shouting distance of the Chu Lai TAOR. And to make matters more complicated, the South Vietnamese government was experiencing considerable difficulty resolving its internal political conflict. "During June, the South Vietnamese Army was losing the equivalent of one infantry battalion a week to enemy action" (GB-65). General Westmoreland called for a division of the Republic of Korea Army. (More of the ROK Marines later.) The call for more troops—up to forty-four battalions, to include Korean, New Zealand, and Australians—was accompanied by the request to launch offensive operations across the country to be known as the "search and destroy tactic."

"On 8 July 1965 Headquarters, Third Tank Battalion debarked at Red Beach Two, Da Nang Port, Republic of Vietnam and established the Command Post adjacent to Company 'A' at (AT 985742). On 10 July,

---

* Da Nang, 172 square miles; Chu Lai, 104 square miles; and Phu Bai, 61 square miles.

the Command Post moved to the southern perimeter of the Division Area of Responsibility at (AT 988711). Extensive defensive positions were established in coordination with the Ninth Marines, Third Anti-Tank Battalion, and the First Amphibious Tractor Battalion" (CC-XX). Within three days—barely time to unpack their kit—a two-tank (light) section was dispatched to Monkey Mountain (BT 0284) to enable direct fire against harbor targets. In another two days (14 July), a light section from Company B was sent to guard the northern approach to the Highway One bridge over the Song Cau Do (AT 998708)" (CC-3Tk, 7/65).

"The 3d Antitank Battalion (-) arrived and disembarked at Da Nang [sic], Republic of South Vietnam 9 July 1965. Moved into bivouac (AT 983744). On 10 July, relocated at (AT 987711). Company 'A' (-)(Rein) arrived via surface transportation at Da Nang on 12 April. Company 'B' (-)(Rein) arrived via surface transportation at Chu Lai on 7 May. Company 'C' (-)(Rein) arrived 8 July via surface transportation and disembarked at Da Nang" (CC-3AT, 7/65).

The 3d Antitank Battalion (-) comprising the Command Element and H&S Company embarked APA 27 at White Beach, Okinawa, on 30 June 1965 and sailed 030300 July 1965. They arrived and disembarked at Da Nang, RVN, on 9 July, bivouacked (AT 983744), and relocated next day to (AT 987711). Company A (-)(Rein) arrived at Da Nang on 12 April. Company B (-)(Rein) arrived at Chu Lai on 7 May. Company C (-)(Rein) arrived on 8 July at Da Nang. The 3d Antitank Battalion was in general support (GS) of the 3d Marine Divisions and the letter companies in direct support (DS) of the infantry regiments. The 3d AT's companies were deployed in all three of the TAORs—Da Nang (H&S and A Company), Hue/Phu Bai (C Company), and Chu Lai (B Company). Platoons were initially assigned either in DS of or attached to infantry companies, but the great swap of companies among regiments commenced, AT platoons among infantry companies, and deploying light (two Ontos) and heavy (three Ontos) sections among infantry platoons would become the norm. The use of the Ontos was immediate, not as a "tank killer," but the Ontos's weapon system was flexible and adaptable. The 106 mm recoilless rifle knocked down bunkers and closed caves, The .30-caliber machine gun was employed against smaller and softer targets—the Viet Cong (GB-65).

True to the Marines' philosophy on how to fight a guerrilla war, the Tankers set up "a Civic Action Program in the adjacent hamlet of Phong Le Bac (AT 983705) where fourteen patients were seen" (CC-3Tk, 7/65) for various health-related conditions. By 19 July, a similar program was started by the Ontos crewmen of Lieutenant Colonel B. A. Heflin's 3d Antitank Battalion in the hamlet of Yen Bac (CC-3AT, 7/65) (from which, by the way, is where the mortar barrage is suspected to have originated).

Staff Sergeant J. M. Dodgens's Interview by Marine Corps History Division (CD-417-A)

Interviewee's Name: SSgt Jimmy M. Dodgens #1433001, USMC Emman: SSgt - no spaces, no periods is correct
Date of Interview: Circa Aug.–Sep. 1966
Conflict: Vietnam War
Military Unit: B Company, 3d Tank Battalion, 3d Marine Division
Duties: Section Leader, B Company, 3d Tanks
Interviewer: SSgt Herbert W. Chenault, USMC
Length: Approx. 25:00
Location of Interview: Headquarters Company, Headquarters and Service Battalion, MCB, Camp Lejeune, North Carolina
Individual Completing Summary: Aryn Willhite
Recording Format and Number of Recording: CD #417-A
Documents Submitted with Interview: None
Related Material: None
Classification: Unclassified
Transcription Priority: Note: The following is a verbatim transcript.

SSgt Jimmy Dodgens, in an interview given in the fall of 1966 at Camp Lejeune, NC, relates in detail his year in tanks operating south of Marble Mountain, RVN.

"I was in Vietnam from July 1965 to July 1966. On the 8th of July we landed in Da Nang area and we moved on into the Tank Battalion (CP) which was (on) Hill 421, I think this is the number, and for the first month or two we sat in a defensive position. They really didn't have no use for the tanks at this time, and I stayed there up until the 9th of September 1965. I moved up to Da Nang, Marble Mount east of Da Nang about 15 miles out (south) of Da Nang, there we started going out on small operations.

"The Viet Cong started mining the roads for these tanks. They started using very small mines which would maybe bend a wheel or break a track, just minor damage that they were doing. But as the weeks went by, they found out the small mines weren't doing much damage to the tanks, so they started making the mines bigger and they kept getting bigger and bigger until they'd finally blow the side of the tank off which would take all day to put it back in action. Then they started mining all the channelized areas; we tried to get into a village, and the only available road into the village would be mined, something like 75–80-pound mines. Most of them would be dud 105s or 155 rounds. Most of the time they were set off by pressure, but some would be electrical and they kept trying to shoot us with small arms. This was earlier in the war; it was the first time they'd seen tanks in the war. They tried carbines and small-caliber weapons, which they found out, it wasn't doing much harm. Then they tried using 57 mm recoilless rifles, which wouldn't do too much damage; it'd knock a small hole in the tank, nothing big enough to hurt the crew but delay the tank. Then they tried mortaring us several times. In one operation, I took on 3 direct hits, 81 mortars; it practically cleaned everything off the vehicle, but inside no one was hurt. I got a bump on the head but nothing big. And they tried to dig tank traps; they dug one and we run into this hole, it must have been about 12 feet wide and 12–13 feet deep; the gun tube went right into the ground. Sand and dirt came inside, right through the gun tube; we got out of that and right back into action. A couple of tanks pulled us out.

"They (the supported infantry) wouldn't use us too much. Every operation they put us in the blocking force until they found out the tanks could do a really good job out there.

"Maybe a company or platoon size sweep and they'd get pinned down, the Viet Cong would have them pinned down, they couldn't move no place. They called in the tanks and we'd go and bail them out. The small arms wouldn't hurt the tank, and the 57s. We'd go on out and move forward and shoot the Viet Cong and give them (the supported infantry) time to move on out and we kept doing this on several operations.

"Like one night, this platoon went out and he got pinned down by the Viet Cong around 360 degrees. I called up the tanks that were attached to me, and I told them to follow behind me. We was going out to bail out the infantry platoon that was pinned down and evidently they didn't receive my message and I got out there, it was raining and dark and come to find out my (other) two tanks weren't with me. I just sat there by myself and I went out to the grid coordinates the (infantry) Platoon Commander told me to report to, and I found the platoon there and the Viet Cong was shooting at the tank. I could hear them hitting the tank; it sounded like little raindrops, small drops hitting the tank, and he (the infantry platoon commander) showed me where all of his men was and I started firing canister and HE and WP in about a 360-degree circle along with small arms and that ran the Viet Cong off. One area called Ha Dong Bridge. It had been an old railroad trestle crossing the river and the Viet Cong mined it and broke it in half and the bridge was down in the river like a V. We used this bridge to cross to the other area Ha Dong and get back and they used this bridge to cross and the Viet Cong started booby trapping it and mining it. We'd lose Engineers about every day, they'd go down and clear the road and they'd get blown up. The Viet Cong started putting these electrical mines and they'd wait until we'd get up there and they'd set them off. We lost about 15–20 men, engineers and infantry. And one morning, the Company Commander gave me a mission just at the break of dawn, which I did. I had 2 tanks, and I ran down the railroad tracks just as fast as my tank could run and ran to the bridge and saw 2 sampans just leaving the bridge, and they were just paddling that thing as fast as they could. It looked like it had a motor on it, going as fast as it was. So I gave a fire command to my gunner and he got the front boat, I think it was 2 or 3 Viet Cong in the front one and he destroyed them with .30 caliber, and I did the same thing to the rear one, killed the VC that was in the boat and sunk it. It was the last time that bridge got booby-trapped. I was there another 2 months and that was the end of it.

"We went back Kilo Company 2/9; they started out company size in an open rice paddy with water about 2-1/2 feet deep. I was in my tank looking through my telescope and I saw a Viet Cong ambush set up over there, something like a horse shoe. So I called ahead and got ahold of the Company Commander of Kilo Company, Captain Brooks, I think was his name. I told him this ambush was set up and requested permission to firing a killing cross. [Note: "Killing Cross" is found under "Area Fire" in FM 17-21 "Tank Gunnery" p. 130, para 145.]

"He called back and gave me permission to fire a killing cross in there and after they moved through, they found a few dead ones there, not too many and some weapons. We found out a week later that those rounds killed about 20 something Viet Cong and wounded a big number of Viet Cong. The Village Chief told us this and the Captain: He was pretty proud of these tanks.

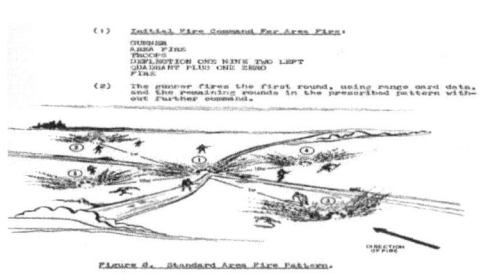

Standard Area Fire Plan

"In one area, I think Lai Song (1), we set up with Kilo Company, and every afternoon about sundown the Viet Cong would start sniping at us, started H&I fire. So one evening we caught a couple of men coming in real close, so we captured them. They were Viet Cong and as soon as we turned them into the CP, the Viet Cong cut loose, firing at the CP, seemed like a company or battalion-size Viet Cong rounds coming from everywhere. So me and my crew, we crawled across the CP, we only had one man on the guns; we crawled over there and got in, and the Company Commander Kilo Company gave the command to fire and destroy this village across in front of us, Lai Song (1), which we did. We opened up over there, and we killed just about everything in the village, chickens, buffalo, cows, and the next morning they brought in 60–70 Vietnamese women and children who were wounded, but we didn't see a man. My crew alone saw 8 to 10 men with weapons; we never did find out how many we got in this operation. We did get quite a few of them.

"In one operation, east of Marble Mountain, called the Leprosy Colony, we got information, intelligence that there was a Viet Cong Battalion operating in there. This Company, I believe, Charlie Company 2/9, we moved out and went on into Marble Mount area and into the Leprosy Colony and I was the lead tank, and all of a sudden everything broke loose. There was rounds coming in from every place, mortars, 60 and 80s, pouring like rain falling, bullets hitting the tank so fast it sounded like popcorn popping. My platoon Staff Sergeant Thibodaux got shot in the head, and we applied first aid to him. We put 2 pressure bandages on his head to stop the bleeding, but we never stopped the bleeding. We got a corpsman but he couldn't do much good. We were down in a channelized area; we was the only tank there. We'd slid down this embankment, and we couldn't get back out. The firing kept getting thicker and thicker and our FO got wounded and our Platoon Commander got wounded; our mortar men were wounded. I think it was 9 men wounded and approximately 2 men killed. We kept shooting small arms out the tank. I think 2,300 rounds of .30 caliber and I fired several canisters and about emptied my tank of .50 caliber. We seen the Viet Cong in the rice paddy; they'd stick their head up and shoot, then down they'd go. We kept pouring it on 'em, everything we had, and at one time I had to command the tank, and gun it, and everything. The Platoon Sergeant was out of commission, and when it (the VC incoming) slowed down, I moved around to all the empty positions and moved the wounded to the rear to the evacuation point and got them out. This is the day I picked up a Bronze Star with a Combat "V" for saving several lives. That's where the tank really helped me, if it had been something smaller than a tank, it might have been destroyed and I believe they could have destroyed this entire company if I hadn't been there. I could put out a large volume of fire with that tank and small arms didn't hurt anything, and that day I got hit with 3 mortars and I was carrying water for the infantry, about 9 water cans, several cans of oil and food, and small arms ammunition on the tank and that didn't get destroyed; it just got swept off like someone took a broom to it and swept it off.

"My loader in this same operation, the Viet Cong was coming real close to the tank and they was trying to get close enough to throw grenades in. He was sticking his head out of the tank and with a grease gun, M381 sub machine gun, he killed 5 with his. So this kept them from coming in real close, and we were traversing the turret all he could and still stay in the safety limits. It was empty on both sides of us, and we could have done a lot better if we could move forward, but there was a big paddy and that was as far as we could go.

"That night we moved on back and we hadn't been in the CP for more than an hour; we'd been fighting all day and had been back long enough to refuel and resupply with ammunition when an ambush come up, and I guess there was about 200 to 300 around the CP. The CP was near Marble Mountain, and we fought about 2-1/2 hours and all of a sudden the firing quit. We had no ways of getting out front; it was pretty swampy to the right and the left, so we stayed in position all night and the next morning we went out and we found about 10 or 15 Viet Cong laying around and found pieces of weapons so we knew that the 90mm had hit some mortar positions and found several pieces of 57 recoilless rifles.

"A week or so later we left the CP and went on another operation up to a place called Miller's Ridge. All the infantry and tankers around there hated this place because every time we went there we got ambushed, most of the time from 3 directions. They have, like, a horseshoe set up there and we can never see anybody; they was dug in so well. I could run over these holes with my tank and they wouldn't even break in. This area I'm talking about, Miller's Ridge, is about 15 miles south of Da Nang, and this one day we had swept all day and destroyed several building and several bunkers and we were moving back out and we had an Army Observer plane up there and we saw tracers going towards it and heard heavy volumes of fire fight just across the ridge. So right away I ordered my section to drive up to the top of the hill as fast as we could get there, so we did, and when we got there we saw approximately 40–50 Viet Cong in the open. So I gave the command to all the tanks to fire killing cross, and I saw anywhere from 10–15 bodies completely leave the ground where we shot 'em up, and the infantry company commander came up and patted me on the back for a good job and again I think we saved this AO because they were sure was putting fire on him. He called down later, we had communication with him, and he said he sure appreciated that, "if you boys wouldn't have pulled in there and destroyed them, I believe they would have got me." They hit his plane 5 or 6 times but they didn't hit where it'd hurt it too much, and he made it back to the airstrip without trouble.

"How they deploy the tanks now in Vietnam is different than how they deployed them before and all the training I ever had done. The rice paddies and the roads, they weren't big and wouldn't hold the tanks up. And most of it was right out of the rice paddies which was anywhere from 2–3 feet of water and a tank would go on through this without any problem, and we didn't have anything big to fire at, which is bad. A tank should be fighting other tanks, but there wasn't anything there like that, and we had to do most of our firing on buildings and bunkers and what have you. We found it very, very hard to get into some of these places due to the rolling hills they had and most of them were sandy and we had problems getting the tanks in, but once we got in, we could do a good job with them. They didn't have anything that could knock them out; we got delayed a few times, but that was about it.

"And as time went by, the Viet Cong, they knew we couldn't operate too good, and areas that we could get through they'd have mines laid everywhere; it restricted us a lot and we'd get across these rivers. The bridge companies would lay bridges for us and we'd get out and cross the rivers and go on into these villages.

"We noticed in most villages, has wells and big ditches dug around them. Every time we'd cross these ditches, the tanks would be buried up to the belly-up and we'd be delayed there for a few minutes. We never had any problems—we come right on out. We never got into anything we couldn't get out of. It's real good on fuel; we could go 2 or 3 weeks without refueling. They were diesel tanks, I believe if they would have been gasoline, we'd have lost more than what we did. Diesel just didn't seem to catch on fire where these big mines would have hit it. They were so big that they'd knock the engine right through the firewall part of the way through the turret, and all that would happen was the engine would die.

"Some mines we'd hit would knock all the controls loose and the tank would just keep right on running. We could move it right on back to the rear with no problems. So overall I think it's a nice vehicle for Vietnam, if it was a little lighter it might help some. When it gets where they want it, it can do the job.

"This area I was in near Da Nang, we had this little boy that kept coming in; he'd sell pencils, paper, and bananas and finally he started running around with the barber they had there. He was really good to that boy; he had a small sister and sometime she'd come with him. The barber even bought the girl some dress and the boy a pair of trousers and some shoes, and everyone took a liking to him. He was about 12 years old. He kept coming in off and on for approximately 2 months. And one night we got overran there, and the Viet Cong came through the wire and started grabbing our own grenades and threw them around the CP. We cut loose fire with the tank; we had 2 tanks in the perimeter. Opened up and fired for about an hour and the next morning we went out to clean up the dead. There was about 40 around the perimeter, and this little boy was out there! Everyone thought he might have led the attack, this young boy 12 years old. There were several young ones, 12–15 years old. These are the same ones we'd been buying things from and being real good to, feeding them; we did a lot of favors for them, then they turned right around and led the attack, is what everyone thinks happened. Other places around here, I heard of some of the Sergeants talking about the same thing but in different areas. But this one I actually seen it; I'd given the kid several items myself. We never gave him any information or that would help the Viet Cong out. He was about there every day. After that we got everything secured and didn't let the Vietnamese near the CP.

"We had a little OP that they'd come to trade with them, and finally they stopped trading with the Vietnamese completely after the PX started keeping supplies. Of course when we first got there, we couldn't get pencil, paper, and anything like that.

"That sure taught me to not to be good to them. Some people you just can't be good to. They knew where the ammo bunker was, the mess hall, the command post and everything there. They knew where it was at just like they'd built the place themselves. They came in and grabbed what they wanted and got out.

"One of the reasons I never mention the units I was operating with because I was a supporting unit tanks. I was just with a unit maybe a week, 10 days some units, I was with them for up to 2 months. We'd just go on these operations through the villages; half the time I didn't even know where I was at. I knew about what grid square I was in, but that was about it. We went through so many villages on sweeps that it's hard to remember those names. And Company Commanders, you'd just about get to know them, they'd be leading you and then another unit would move in. As a tank in a supporting unit, we'd stay there in the outer perimeter the whole year I spent in Vietnam. In infantry, they'd take 2 or 3 months and go back and guard the airstrip and areas in the rear; they always got relief, which we didn't.

"So you can see why it's hard for me to remember these names, companies, and the units that I worked with. We were always on the go, and we never knew who we were working with.

"This just about concludes my tour in Vietnam. I rotated back to the States in July '66."

California-Based Seventh Marines, 1st Marine Division

First Tanks and Antitanks at the Tip of the Spear

3/7—On 24 June 1965, Battalion Landing Team, 3d Battalion, 7th Marines, 1st Marine Division (BLT 3/7) commanded by Lieutenant Colonel C. H. Bodley, commenced embarkation aboard the USS *Iwo Jima* at White Beach, Okinawa, with its attachment and those units in direct support. Second Lieutenant N. M. "Manny" Wood, the Platoon Commander of the 3d Platoon, Company C, 1st Antitank Battalion—3/C/1stAt's (Rein)—and Second Lieutenant R. A. "Ray" Stewart, the Platoon Commander of the 3d Platoon, Company B, 1st Tank Battalion, 3/B/1stTk's (Rein.) were under way on 26 June for the Republic of Vietnam (RVN).

Upon arrival offshore of Qui Nhon, RVN, "personnel from the Tank, Antitank, Motor Transport, and Amphibious Tractor Platoons landed, without heavy weapons and equipment, to man positions on the defensive perimeter *in order to gain experience under such conditions*" (CC-3/7, 9/65) (italics for emphasis by the editor).

On 8 July, the BLT was reembarked and remained offshore until 20 July, when it was diverted to Pratas Islands (actual a reef) to support the salvage of the USS *Frank Knox*, which had ran aground there. The group was then split up with the tanks and antitanks aboard the USS *Point Defiance* (LSD-31) sent to Subic Bay, PI. The *Point Defiance* was ordered back to Pratas Reef and to make room on the LCU and LCMs in the well deck of the *Point Defiance*; the preloaded rolling stock (tanks) and equipment was left behind at Subic Bay. The BLT was subsequently reconstituted at Subic Bay, all set ashore, tanks and other equipment reloaded, and on 17 August, the task group was under way for RVN and participation in Operation STARLITE. On 24 August, the units sent ashore reloaded. Once again, tanks and Ontos did not have to reload.

The BLT returned to Subic Bay and then back to Chu Lai, RVN, on 31 August at which time Manny and Ray checked out of BLT 3/7 and into their respective parent companies already ashore.

2/7—BLT 2/7 relieved BLT 3/7, commanded by Lieutenant Colonel Leon Utter, in Qui Nhon, RVN, on 7 July 1965. Lieutenant John Warner was the Platoon Commander of the 2d Platoon (-)(Rein), B Company, 1st Tank Battalion, 1st Marine Division (2/B/1stTk's); and Lieutenant Harvey Schmitt was the 2d Platoon commander, Company C, 1st Antitank Battalion, 1st Marine Division (2/C/1stAt's).

1/7—BLT 1/7 was commanded by Lieutenant Colonel James P. Kelly. BLT 1/7 "by 8 August 1965 was completely embarked (at Okinawa) and enroute to the RVN" (CC-1/7, 8/65). The BLT included 1/B/1stTk's with First Lieutenant Carl Lemon, the Platoon Commander (6 through 7 September) and 1/C/1stATs Platoon Pommander, First Lieutenant H. Connolly (6 through 10 September)—attached. It commenced landing at Chu Lai, RVN, on 14 August. On 20–24 August, 1/C/1stAT's supported 1/7 in Operation STARLITE against the "Van Tuong Village Complex, South Vietnam (Quang Ngai Province), and Van Tuong Peninsula" (CC-1/7, 8/65).

Both platoons participated in Operation PIRANHA, landing on White Beach and moving to assembly area at (BS 759862). Tanks provided a light section in support of B/1/7 and C/1/7 at (BS 773868), and Ontos provided a light section for support of A and C/1/7 and D/1/7 at (BS 756859). After Operation PIRANHA, each platoon returned to the OpCon of their respective companies.

The 9 August 1965 Attack on 3d Tank Battalion Command Post

"At 092330 August 1965 small arm and automatic weapons fire was received along the southern portion of the Battalion perimeter followed by a mortar barrage of twenty rounds (81 and 60mm) within the Tank Battalion's Command Post (AT 986709 to AT 988712). An additional six to ten rounds (of mortar fire) impacted in the village of Phuong Bac (1) (AT 990712). Casualties, two DOW (died of wounds), eighteen WIA (wounded in action). Two tents destroyed, two trucks damaged" (CC-3Tk, 8/65). The WIAs were medevaced.

Marine Tanker Corporal Joe Tyson detailed his reaction to the attack with the following article (HA-JT):

Attack on Third Tank Battalion Headquarters

Excerpt from *Vietnam Memoirs*

by Joe Tyson, B Co., 3d Tank Bn., 65/66

On August 9th 1965, I had the second watch on the blade tank from 1000 to 0200. I was the gunner during this time on the vehicle. At 2330, I heard a muffled *whoop, whoop, whoop,* and many more of those sounds were coming in secession. I immediately saw mortar tube flashes forward of the far right perimeter position, out across a rice paddy in an elevated wood line, with numerous muzzle flashes from small-arms fire, all from that same location. For an instant, I looked up at the sky to the far right, and I saw scores of small orange sparked contrails arcing up, then down towards to us. I knew immediately the mortars would be on top of us in seconds. I screamed back towards the sleeping bunker where Saikley and Reed were, "Keep your heads down!" Rounds were whizzing and zinging right over my head, and I heard continuous ricochets off the tank turret. Green and red tracers were flying and ricocheting every which way. Then 82 mm mortars started blasting, throwing pieces of screaming shrapnel everywhere.

I had already pulled the string we had run from the driver compartment "On" switch, to the top of the turret, to power up the tank. I quickly flipped the manual 90 mm main gun safety to the "On" position, knowing there was a canister round already up in the chamber. I traversed the turret to the right, knowing the canister round would have no effect at that range, but it was the fastest way to unload it so that I could get an HE (high explosive) round up to blast the enemy positions. Once the turret was traversed, I saw that there was mounded dirt left from putting the tank in hull defilade, which caused the gun tube to be blocked. Well, forget that. I charged the .50 caliber (machine gun) and fired fifty or sixty rounds in the direction of those tube flashes, trying to zero in with my tracers on the targets.

There was a gun tank on that far right corner position. Why wasn't he unloading on those muzzle and tube flashes? I threw two illumination grenades forward past the concertina wire to my front and traversed the turret forward, watching for the frontal attack I felt sure was coming any second. Enemy rounds were still whizzing and zinging all around. The dinks were walking the 82s back into the center of the big tent (living) areas. This was bad. The tank on the far right position and the bunkers near it still had not fired a shot. Maybe the dinks had got the crewman on watch and the rest of the crew was pinned down and couldn't get on the vehicle. I yelled, "Reed, Saikley, where the hell are you?" They were still pinned down in the sleeping bunker at the right rear of the tank. I heard a tank firing to my right rear. Maybe the ground assault was coming at that side? I kept my eyes peeled forward. The 82s started blasting us again all around, and the enemy small-arms fire was as heavy as from the start. I threw another illumination grenade down by the wire, just waiting for the frontal attack. I had made sure the Claymore (mine) trigger was right where I could reach it. Then I recharged the fifty and commenced firing out to the far right again twenty or thirty bursts. All of a sudden, SILENCE! Reed and Saikley quickly jumped up on the tank. I dropped into the turret, ready to load the main gun if need be. It was quiet.

Cpl Tyson: I think it's over.

Sgt. Reed: Good job, Tys. Good job.

Cpl Tyson: I couldn't get a 90 shot off at those tube flashes. Maybe I could have stopped that mortar fire, but the dirt pile from the hull defilade was blocking the gun tube.

Sgt. Reed: Listen to me. You got .50 caliber on them. That gun tank in the far right corner position had perfect targets of opportunity and did not fire anything, neither did the bunkers on that side with the office pogues manning them.

Cpl Tyson: I tried to radio that tank. I don't think they even had their radios on. What the f—— is going on?

Sgt. Reed: Well, number one, this was the first combat for these Marines here—including us. Yes, we have had some experience with some enemy small-arms fire, light mortars, and a few RPGs at the air base, but these Marines have had none until now. That tank that fired on the other side of the perimeter was a B Company tank, the one your buddy Bennett is on. They picked up some experience when they were attached to the 2d Battalion, 9th Marines a few weeks back; when they were out further in "Happy Valley" on those daily sweeps. They knew how to react. It's been too quiet here for too long a time people got complacent. Didn't you think that when the brass started the daily inspections? The goofy rules that were implemented, like, no magazines allowed in your personal weapon; or absolutely no firing of any weapon on the perimeter without first getting permission; or your ass would be in a sling—shine your brass, shine your boots, clean your web gear. Now you feed a Marine. Bullshit like that in a place like this for too long. Instead of teaching him that the enemy is constantly watching them and preparing him for an attack just like the one we just experienced, and then you have a big problem, he will hesitate. Dude, they set it up to fail with poor leadership. Hell, you and I have discussed this many times.

Cpl Tyson: Yes, I know, Tthe Marine Corps is an assault force. What are we doing here pulling security on a perimeter? I think it will change now though.

Sgt. Reed: I hope so.

Cpl Tyson: Sgt Reed, I can't believe no one is up on the radios. I have it on the frequency they gave us.

Sgt. Reed: Dude, I told you inexperience, sort of on-the-job training for combat.

Cpl Tyson: You know, Sgt Reed, the Marine Corps has not been in combat since Korea, what does that tell you?

Sgt. Reed tells me after Korea, twelve years of shining brass and spit shining boots, but no combat experience left in Mother Green's combat machine except a few older gunnery sergeants and master sergeants.

Cpl Tyson: Exactly!

Sgt. Reed: Still no radio contact. Head back into battalion to see what is going on, put a magazine in your forty-five.

Cpl Tyson: Way ahead of you, dude, put it in during the attack.

I grabbed a flashlight and headed back into battalion. There was a heavy odor of nitro and ammonia mixed with the dust in the hot humid, still air. I could taste it in my mouth. Reaching the big sleeping tent, I noticed five Marines still in the long shallow fire trench. I asked them if they knew what was going on.

Marine: No, but a lot of mortars hit the cluster of tents in the center of the camp.

I noticed that none of them had their weapons.

Cpl Tyson: Where are your f——g weapons?

Marine: When the mortars started, we jumped from the cots to the trench.

Cpl Tyson: Go get your f——g rifles and never leave them anywhere, remember hearing that in boot camp? Get them now, put a magazine in them, and keep them locked and loaded. What would you have done if the dinks got past the perimeter? How would you have defended yourselves? While you are at it, put your bayonet on your rifle belt and stay alert and dig this trench out tomorrow, so if you're standing in it, is at least up just past your waist.

Glad none of those Marines were over the rank of Lance Corporal. If any were, I probably would have been told to f——k off. I left and headed for the cluster of tents; great idea to put all your leadership all in one big target area. I saw one of the company gunnery sergeants.

Cpl Tyson: Gunny, what is going on?

Gunny: So far twenty-two wounded, one KIA, First Lieutenant Kraus, Battalion XO.* Two more of the wounded are really bad, probably won't make it.

Cpl Tyson: What about the radios? Nobody is up—our perimeters are cut off from battalion.

Gunny: Don't know what's going on with the radios.

Just then I heard the medevac helicopters coming in to pick up the wounded.

Gunny: Nothing you can do here, Corporal, this is under control, head back to your tank.

Jesus, I said to myself, under control, like those five Marines I ran into unarmed. What the hell were they thinking? I headed back to the tank, stopping by Bennett's tank to get his story.

---

* First Lieutenant Ronald C. Kraus, 32, Grandview, IN (KIA), was the 3d Tank Battalion's adjutant—not executive officer.

L.Cpl Bennett: Yo, Joe, what the f——k. We fired a few canister and thirty cal at those cocksuckers, but what was up with the tank on the corner of the perimeter? Didn't fire a f——g shot?

Cpl Tyson: Believe me, I noticed.

L/Cpl Bennett: What's up with the radios? L/Cpl is correct. No period

Cpl Tyson: Don't know. All I know is one dead and twenty-two wounded so far.

L/Cpl Bennett: Who bought it?

Cpl Tyson: Battalion XO. (Note: He meant the Battalion Adjutant.)

L/Cpl Bennett: Jesus.

Cpl Tyson: Talk later—got to get back to my tank.

I climbed up on the tank and dropped into the loader's hatch and put on my helmet.

Sgt. Reed: What did you find out? Sgt is correct, No period

Cpl Tyson: Twenty-two wounded so far and the battalion XO dead, two more of the wounded probably will not make it, no word on the radios being down.

Sgt Reed: Damn, it's started. Saikley, you sleeping down there?

Pvt Saikley: No.

Sgt Reed: Start the tank to recharge the batteries.

I showed Sgt Reed my hands; they were shaking.

Sgt Reed: Normal reaction, dude, mine are too.

Reed told me to run my hand over the top of the turret. I did, then jumped inside the turret and shined the flashlight on my hand, damn hundreds of small metal fragments were stuck to the sweat on my hand.

Sgt. Reed: Tank took a lot of small-arm ricochets.

Cpl Tyson: No s———t. Remember, I was on top when that shit rained down on us. The tank also took some heavier metal fragments.

Sgt Reed: I know, we'll check it out in the daylight. You did the right thing, Corporal, glad you didn't get hit.

It was quiet the rest of the night.

Daylight came, and I climbed down on the sponson box and checked the tank all around. There were lots of small metal fragments from small-arms fire and many fragments all different sizes from the enemy 82 mortars. There were a few bigger dings in the right side of the turret. There was a hole in the right side sponson box right through, about the size of an orange, and one smaller one in the rear fender toolbox.

There was not one tank or bunker on the front or right side of the perimeter that did not sustain some damage. One bunker got a direct hit with a mortar. It was piss-poor reaction from us. Basically, we got our asses kicked by a well-coordinated enemy attack, and we only put out one sixty-fourth of the firepower we were capable of producing. Their taking out of our command center first was nothing but genius. Having no radio contact with any part of our command center meant no coordination.

Cpl Tyson: We were lucky we did not have many more killed and injured. I don't even want to think about a wire penetration with those five unarmed Marines I ran into last night.

Sgt. Reed: Agreed! I hope we will not be at battalion much longer; would rather be out with the infantry. At least we could move, maneuver, and shoot. We lacked any infantry here and tanks need infantry—they were our eyes and ears. Infantry would have had patrols out and ambushes set up to nip that in the bud.

Cpl Tyson: Dude, I agree, but if those bunkers on that side would have opened up with their M-Sixties and that gun tank on that corner position would have unleashed its firepower, it would have been over quick. Wish we were on that point.

Sgt. Reed: Tyson, belay the wishful thinking. Nobody was injured on our crew, be thankful for that. All things happen for a reason. We will get our chance soon enough. Look at the freaking holes in this tank, for Christ's sake. First thing we do is knock down these mounds of dirt on our sides to open our fields of fire to our extreme right and left in case somebody drops the ball again. This attack was an important learning lesson for us. Let's take what we have learned from this and leave the rest lay.

Cpl Tyson: Got it.

Sgt. Reed: Now, what was this you said about five unarmed Marines you came upon last night?

Cpl Tyson: With all the adrenaline rushing, I forgot to tell you. When you sent me back into battalion to see what I could find out last night, I found five Marines lying in the long fire trench by the sleeping tent, all unarmed.

Sgt. Reed: Damn, piss-poor training, bet their web gear was clean and their brass was shining though.

Cpl Tyson: Maybe so, but I know one thing that was not clean and shining.

Sgt. Reed: What was that?

Cpl Tyson: Their skivvies after that mortar attack.

Sgt. Reed: Tyson, you are something else. Even in the worst circumstances, you always got a one-liner.

In a short time we would be ordered to Marble Mountain, the forward command post for B Company, 3d Tanks; we would be in support of the 9th Marines.

At battalion we had approached the Gates of Hell but now would pass through hell's main gate on operations with the 9th Marines south of Marble Mountain.

Joe Tyson

The following named Marines received a Purple Heart on 10 August: Aguilar, S.; Bocchinfuso, J.; Bradley, M. L.; Clark, Richard P.; Crabtree, Jr. John E.; Cruz, M.; Daniels, E. C.; Hawley, J. G.; Hubbard, L. J.; Jones, D. E.; Laduca, J.; Maur, W. H.; Odette, A. B.; Ryals, J. L.; Smith Jr., W. S.; Sullivan, Daniel H.; Whitworth, J. R.; Wingert, Donald E.

The following is taken from the 3d Tanks' August 1965 Command Chronology (CC-3Tk, 8/65):

> At 2330, the Battalion Command Post received a considerable amount of small arms and automatic weapons fire from positions directly in front of the southern portion of the perimeter. Within a very few seconds a heavy mortar barrage began landing throughout the Command Post. Two living tents, the S-1, and the one defensive bunker received direct hits. The barrage lasted for approximately five minutes and approximately thirty rounds exploded within the perimeter and six in the Hamlet of Phong Bac (1). Muzzle flashes were seen coming from Yen Bac (Third Anti-Tank's CAP) at (AT 984702) and Cam Ne (1) (AT 982694). The 60 mm mortar were probably fired from the latter. An artillery fire mission was called on

the suspect gun positions however due to the distance the results were not immediately known. The Battalion sustained twenty-three WIA, three of whom later died of wounds including the Battalion Adjutant. At 2338 emergency helicopter evacuation was requested.

Reference

United States Marine Corps Chronology Report. August 1965. Declassified.

Marine Corps Vietnam Tankers Historical Foundation.

During the month of August, Ontos companies of the two antitank battalions were landing in Da Nang and Chu Lai and joining the fight.

Additional deployment of (Ontos) units during the month of August (1965).

Company C (-) (Rein.), 1st Antitank Battalion (2d and 3d Platoons) landed at Chu Lai on 14 August 1965. The 1st Platoon, Company C was assigned direct support of the 1st Battalion, 7th Marines.

The 3d Platoon, Company C, 3d Antitank Battalion landed at Da Nang on 16 August 1965 and joined Company C, 3d Antitank Battalion. They were assigned a direct support role for the 3d Battalion, 9th Marines.

The 3d Platoon, Company C, 1st Antitank Battalion landed at Chu Lai on 18 August 1965 and was assigned a direct support role for the 3d Battalion, 7th Marines.

The Vietnam War and the Special Landing Force

by Ray Stewart

The means to setting foot on *terra firma* South Vietnam, if by amphibious ship of the U.S. Navy, was basically one of two ways:

One, across the beach on foot or by vehicle—wheeled or tracked—and/or by rotary-winged aircraft, i.e., helicopter. At the early stages of the war, that would have been the single rotor UH-34.

Or, two, by military or military-contracted commercial passenger aircraft. And entry was prepared for by an anticipation of a hostel greeting or an uncontested administrative landing met by friendlies ranging from young ladies passing out leis in the company of South Vietnamese local officials to Shore Party Marines with red patches on their trousers directing the operation. Of these basics, there were any number of hybrids that affected both the physical and mental conditions and preparations by the participants. Emman: "Shore Party" is the official name given to the organization that runs the beach during an amphibious operation.

The arriving in South Vietnam at the Da Nang Airfield via military or military-contracted civilian aircraft became a rather routine, administrative exercise after 1965. Initially, entire units arrived in the

Navy's amphibious bottoms, i.e., the Gator Navy accompanied by their material, weapons, equipment, and vehicles, trained and equipped to face the enemy on the beach.

It didn't take long for the Corps to realize that the units landing in Vietnam would need replacing by like units at some point and that there were no such units. So the challenge was met by the design and implementation of Operation MIXMASTER, which saw, rather than unit replacements, individual Marine replacements. Except for the military flavor of the greeters and the greetees, not much different than what was customary at a civilian airport (except, almost to-the-man), the heat was described variously as "brutal," "wilting," "soul destroying," "lethal," or worse, as thousands of Marines and soldiers streamed into Vietnam through several airports.

Of more interest is the story told by Marines who anticipated and were prepared to meet the enemy across a hostile beach or in a hot LZ farther inland. Several authors have described in some detail the preparations of the infantry—the Grunts. Fewer have attempted to capture the thoughts and detailed steps taken by preassault Tankers and Ontos crewmen to ready themselves *and their fighting vehicles* to support the Grunts who most often preceded armor to the beach in their mission to move inland and carry the fight against the hostile defenders. In an amphibious operation, Ontos might be in the third or fourth wave and the tanks further back than that—maybe the sixth or seventh wave.

First Lieutenant William Van Zanten, USMC, was the Executive Officer of Company I, 3/7, 1st Marine Division, FMF, and embarked aboard the USS *Iwo Jima* (LPH-2) on 17 August 1965 as "*Iwo Jima* steamed out of Subic Bay for Vung Tau, Republic of Vietnam, to join in Operation Starlight [*sic*], a five-day search-and-destroy operation that eradicated some 600 Viet Cong." In Bill's book *Don't Bunch Up: One Marine's Story* (DB-WV), he details the workup of his company of Marines for what was anticipated to be a helicopter assault into the heart of the 1st Viet Cong Regiment ensconced in well-prepared caves and fighting holes arranged in mutually supporting defensive killing zones into a labyrinth of hot landing zones. His description captures in general terms the Grunts' perspective. Subtract the M-14 semiautomatic, 7.62-caliber rifle operated by a single Marine, and add the 52-ton, 90 mm main gun, M48A3, Patton Tank crewed by four Marines: the common denominator is "Marine," and the emotions are shared understanding that they were facing an unknown future.

As the amphibious ships of the Special Landing Force (SLF) arrived in the *Amphibious Objective Area (AOA) off the coast of South Vietnam, Lieutenant Colonel Charles H. Bodley, Commanding Officer of BLT 3/7, called a final briefing of the officers and senior staff noncommissioned officers (SNCO's) to impart his preassault "pep talk" in the wardroom of the *Iwo Jima*: "'This is war, gentlemen. No time for thinking about liberty or time off. We have a job to do. An important job and one which we will be proud of." It was impossible to sleep after the Old Man (Bodley) had done his John Wayne impression in the wardroom. Humor aside, last-minute checks of last wills and testaments, powers of attorney, and letters home to wives, girlfriends, and moms were double-checked for completion.

From the USS *Point Defiance*, there were no tank or Ontos officers or senior staff noncommissioned officers at Colonel Bodley's pep talk on the *Iwo Jima*. We, embarked on the *Point Defiance*, had little knowledge of what was going on. Wild rumors circulated the LSD-31 USS *Point Defiance* ships' crew and embarked Tankers, Ontosmen, and others. We may just as well have been orbiting Mars as being a few hundred feet from the *Iwo Jima* as we approached and dropped anchor in the waters of the AOA off the coast, but in sight and sound of the shoreline. We'd been left in the well deck of the *Pont Defiance* for the Qui Nhon landing and expected this one would be the same. It was.

I left my Platoon Sergeant—Staff Sergeant Peter J. Frano—in charge and worked my bolt to get ashore with the BLT 3/7's command group. My idea was to be at the BLT 3/7's Operations Officer (S-3) side and proselytizing for getting my tanks into the fight and not bring them to the beach, only to be staged there "out of the way" for a subsequent admin tour. Staff Sergeant Frano, with tanks ready to move ashore, poised in the well deck of the *Point Defiance* to come ashore, never got my call.

At least at Qui Nhon my platoon came ashore—though be it as Grunts—with our .45-caliber pistols and grease guns. And unbeknownst to me—or Staff Sergeant Frano, who was with me—the ship decided that it needed the preloaded (with three of my tanks) LCU for something other than whatever the tanks might be used for to bring them to the beach, off-load them, and there they sat for a few days!

Shortly, the SLF with BLT 2/7 and the 2d Platoon, B Company, 1st Tank Battalion relieved 3/7, and it was off to Subic Bay, Philippines, for the latter.

Years later, the landscape had changed considerably. Virtually all entry into Vietnam was considered administrative. The Viet Cong (VC) and the North Vietnamese Army (NVA) were being killed and were killing Americans in record numbers, but it was happening far from entry points. *Praying for Slack: A Marine Corps Tank Commander in Vietnam*, authored by Robert Peavey (PS-RP), paints a different picture of anxiety facing Marine Tankers landing in Vietnam.

Of course the Tanker and Ontos crewman is not designed to be helilifted into an LZ—"hot" or not. But getting off that amphibious ship into the LCM or LCU to the beach and, when reaching the beach, wading ashore carries the same concerns and requires similar preassault preparations.

The following is taken in part from https://en.wikipedia.org/wiki/USS_Iwo_Jima_(LPH-2)#Vietnam_War and modified to identify the Marine units that the USS *Iwo Jima* (LPH-2) supported. She was the first ship to be designed and built from the keel up as an amphibious assault ship. She carried Marine helicopters and a detachment of embarked Marines for use in the "vertical envelopment" concept of amphibious operations.

During May 1965, the USS *Iwo Jima* remained off the Chu Lai coast of South Vietnam, for a month, protecting Marines and Seabees establishing the new SAT's air field. Besides helicopter support ashore, including defense perimeter patrol, she was a support center for laundry, showers, fresh provisions, store, and mail service. She also supervised the continual off-load of ships over the beach for the entire month, then on 7 June 1965, landed Marine squadron personnel and helicopters ashore up the coast of South Vietnam at Hue-Phu Bai, some 30 miles north of Da Nang. After a few days rest in Subic Bay, she steamed to Buckner Bay, Okinawa, where she embarked the SLF BLT-3/7 Marines and equipment. This was completed on 26 June 1965, when she sailed for Qui Nhon, Republic of Vietnam, in company with the USS *Talladega* (APA-208) and, where tanks and Ontos were located, the USS *Point Defiance* (LSD-31).

This group of ships was designated by the Navy as Task Group 76.5, that part of the 7th Fleet which carries the

Marine Special Landing Force (SLF). On 30 June, she arrived at Qui Nhon, about 100 miles south of Chu Lai. The following day, the Marines of BLT-3/7 landed ashore to take up defensive positions for the protection of US Army engineers and communications units. The operation was a stopgap measure, waiting for the Army's 101st to saddle up and take the assignment. (Note: This is the same outfit that was unable to answer the call to land in Da Nang on 8 March.)

The USS *Iwo Jima* remained off Qui Nhon for defensive support of the Marines until 20 July 1965, then steamed for Pratas Reef, about 240 miles southwest of Taiwan. Arriving the morning of the 22d, her helicopters were immediately pressed into service to aid the salvage of destroyer USS *Frank Knox* (DD-742). Then left the Qui Nhon area with the USS *Point Defiance* (LSD-31) to work the destroyer off the reef. Second Lieutenant Ray Stewart's Third Platoon, "B" Company, First Tank Battalion remained on the *Point Defiance*—in part. Three of his five tanks were left sitting on the docks of Subic Bay. They had been "pre-loaded" on the ship's LCU, resting in the well deck but, since the LCU was required by the USS *Frank Knox's* extraction team's salvage equipment, the Navy made the decision that tanks to fight the war was less important than re-floating the grounded ship.

To say that the Marine Corps was furious over the preempting of its fighting capability for a strictly Navy non-combat salvage activity would be an understatement. In fact, the Navy/Marine Corps chain-of-command philosophy came under scrutiny by the Joint Chiefs. When the *Knox* was cleared, the *Point Defiance* sailed for Subic Bay. On 17 August

1965, *Iwo Jima* and other ships of the SLF steamed out of Subic Bay for Vung Tau, Republic of Vietnam, to join in Operation Starlight [*sic*], a five-day search-and-destroy operation that eradicated some 600 Viet Cong. The successful Navy-Marine Corps amphibious operation, backed by gunfire support from the cruiser USS *Galveston* (CLG-3) and two destroyers, came to a close late on 24 August. She landed her Marine Special Landing Force (SLF) at Chu Lai on 1/2 September, embarked 800 Marines of a rotation draft, and sailed for Buckner Bay, Okinawa, Japan.

By the time of the final landing, across the beach at Chu Lai after Operation STARLITE, of elements of the SLF (BLT 3/7), Stewart had all five of his Third Herd tanks in one place, i.e., in the *Point Defiance*'s well deck, after having them scattered across the Pacific from Pratas Reef through Subic Bay and Qui Nhon with their crews left to fend for themselves. That was the good news. Less "good" was that only two tanks of the five tanks could run (kinda/sorta), but only on one bank each of the V-12 diesel power packs. Captain Allan Lamb, an old Mustang, Commanding Officer of B Company, 1st Tank Battalion, was said to have tears in his eyes as the engineers and Shore Party Marines literally pulled and dragged three deadlined and two seriously impaired M-48 Tanks ashore and into the adjacent tank park. He had not seen or heard from me for months as there was no communication protocol between the Navy's SLF and the Marines ashore under III MAF, except improbably via a few vague references in a BLT's command chronologies. Captain Lamb never seemed quite the same after this less-than-warrior-like entry to the war zone. In fact, he had just been selected for major and said, "There are two idiot ranks in the Marine Corps—and they both wear gold."

The USS *Iwo Jima* landed the rotation troops at Okinawa, then arrived off Qui Nhon, 10 September 1965, to cover the landing of the Army's 1st Air Cavalry Division and extraction of the Lieutenant Colonel Leon

Utter's BLT 2/7 (with the 2d Platoon, Company B, 1st Tank Battalion commanded by First Lieutenant John Warner), which had earlier relieved BLT 3/7.

She had supported three amphibious assault search-and-destroy raids (Operation DAGGER THRUST) along the coast by 1 October. Several months later, she again joined the 7th Fleet Amphibious Ready Group (ARG), a fast-moving assault force that had completed more than twenty search-and-destroy operations along the South Vietnamese coast between March 1965 and September 1966. (Both the Operations DAGGER THRUST and DECK HOUSE series are covered in detail elsewhere.) One of these missions hit only 3 miles south of the demilitarized zone to search out and decimate a regiment of the North Vietnam Army's 342B Division, which had infiltrated South Vietnam through the neutral zone. More on the Iwo Jima in subsequent volumes of *Marine Tanks and Ontos in the Vietnam War*.

As explained earlier, in the context of task organizing, combat support units (tanks, antitank, artillery) and service support (medical, supply) that were either attached to or in direct support of were either OpCon or AdCon by the supported infantry organizations. What that meant in the terms of chronicling the supporting units' activities was often marginal, usually checkered, and occasionally not at all. Thus, tank and antitank units' activities were left undocumented, personnel records left uncomplete (or in error), personal or unit valor either not reported on by the supported infantry unit, or recommendations for medals and awards misplaced in the lengthy administrative chain, exacerbated by prioritizing assets to the fighting of the enemy—and the weather, terrain, resupply of ammo, food, water, insects, leaches, disease, immersion foot, heat/cold, thirst, hunger, personnel shortage, ROE's, etc.

Tank and antitank units arrived by platoon attached to a battalikon landing team (BLT), usually reinforced with additional rolling stock, communications, and mount-out kits, to name a few, specifically configured to operate independent of the parent tank/antitank company but only for a specified and limited duration. The platoon commander had virtually no contact with his company commander once the BLT was underway, often for months. Seldom was the occasion when either knew of the whereabouts of the other, especially when part of the Special Landing Force (SLF) whether afloat or ashore and still in support of an infanfry battalion.

This lack of communications and other support for subordinate platoons and companies at the next echelon up, for that matter, was partially rectified when the tank and antitank battaion's headquarters and service companies came ashore and took Op/AdCon from the supported infantry organizations. The case in point is the production of the battalion's monthy command chronologies. The 3d Tank and Antitank Battalions were the first of the two battaions that were committed to the Vietnam War. The others, the 1sts, intitially stationed at Pendleton, California, finally relocated their flags to Chu Lai, RVN.

Information about the activites of the 3d Tank and 3d Antitank in-country units has been researched from personal interviews of Tankers and Ontos crewmen, infantry battalion command chronologies that *may*—and most *not*—cite the activities of their attached units.

The first reporting on the record from Lieutenant Colonel S. R. Jones Jr.'s 3d Tank Battalion with its command post (CP) located at Da Nang (AT 988711) was published in August 1965. Third Tank's Platoons and Companies had been operating in-country since 9 March. As stated in CCA-3Tk, 5/01, commenting on 3d Tank's publication, the *Command Diary*,

> [It] . . . (pre-dates command chronologies) is mostly illegible and pages missing and out of sequence. There is no S-level staff Officers identified. There are only a few incidents reported of 2–3 shots from a sniper from time-to-time during this reporting period. It may be noted that the Captain Joe Sanders's Company "C" located at Chu Lai is also not reported on. Today, he may take

exception to that "non-reporting" covering the time he was aggressively fighting a war.

Background. During the first week in June 1965 Third Tank Battalion (-) was alerted for deployment to the Republic of Vietnam. Two of its companies were already in-country and a couple of those companies' platoons had preceded them.

Note: The (-) indicates that some organic element(s) of the 3d Tanks is attached to another unit; without exception, that unit would be a Marine infantry organization. The official location of the tank battalion is where its commanding officer and his headquarters group is, no matter where other elements (companies) are located.

At this time, Company "A" was located at Da Nang, Republic of Vietnam (AT 985742), attached to the 3d Marines.

Company "C" was located at Chu Lai, Republic of Vietnam, attached to the 4th Marines.

Third Tank Battalion Headquarters, H&S and Company "B" (-) was located at Camp Hansen, Okinawa.

Note: Company "B"(-) indicates that at least one of its platoons was detached. In this case, a platoon was attached to the Special Landing Force (SLF)

On 25 June 1965 Third Tank Battalion (-) consisting of Headquarters and Service Company and Company "B" (-), attached to Regimental Landing Team – Nine (RLT-9), departed Camp Hansen, Okinawa and embarked aboard amphibious shipping of the Seventh Fleet. Headquarters, Third Tank Battalion (Command Group) was located aboard the USS *Washtenaw*

County—LST 1166. On 3 July 1965, Battalion Headquarters and Headquarters and Service Company, Third Tank Battalion departed Naha Port, Okinawa for Da Nang Port, Red Beach Two, Republic of Vietnam.

Original Message-----
From: Gene Hika
Sent: Thursday, December 4, 2014 10:47 AM
To: USMCVTHF
Subject: Pictures

Col. Ray: The pics that I sent to you were taken of the 3d Tank Battalion in 1965. We boarded LSTs in Naha, Okinawa in late June (1965) and headed for Vietnam. Most of us did not know where Vietnam was, but we were soon to find out.

Gene Hika (VTHF)   Gene Hika (VTHF)

My fondest memory of the trip was the fireworks that the lead ship put on for the convoy on July 4, 1965. It was not the best that I have seen thru the years, but it is one that I'll never forget.

We made an unopposed beach landing at night and went thru a small town called "Dog Patch," I think. The next day found us going to where our base camp was to be, Hill 34, if I remember right. Geeez, it's been a long time. We were to dig two-man foxholes on the perimeter, and the digging was tough, seeing as how the ground was like cement. I never thought we would get thru, but we did.

The second and third day we had GP tents but spent very little time in them cuz they were so very hot in them. The rest of my time in country was spent on patrol with that Bull's Eye they called a PRC-10 on my back. When we went on patrol, we carried only a .45 in a holster. But not me, I also took my M-14 (semiautomatic 7.62 cal. rifle replaced by the M-16) with me which someone said to me, "You can't handle your rifle if you had to." My comment was, "Watch me."

Besides going on patrols, we spent quite a bit of time in the Command Bunker on radio watch. I often wondered why traffic would pick up at times and almost stop at other times. Well, it was because of operations that were taking place, 9 of them in while I was in country.

Eventually we got to go into the city of Da Nang on liberty: That was before they changed from using green backs to MPCs or "funny money." I wonder what happened to the money in the Monopoly games. Every so often we would take a radio jeep to get washed, and that was almost as good as going on liberty.

I have a lot of good memories and some bad ones in country, but one that I won't forget is that smell of Viet Nam. The only place that reproduces that smell is the Marine Museum (NMMC) outside of Quantico. And I will never forget the takeoff in the C-130 from the Da Nang Air Base and going back to Okinawa; then to catch a flight back to stateside—to MCAS, El Toro, CA, Air Base; then off to home for 30 days' leave. This was before they called us "baby killers" and spat all over you and you could travel in uniform and stand up proud.

I had one more year to go, and that was spent at MCAS, Cherry Point, NC, 2d Marine Air Wing where I was discharged from the Corps in '67. Thanks to a lot of Marines who helped me along those 4 years.

Cpl Eugene E. Hika (aka GUNNY)

H&S Company, Communication Platoon, 3d Tank Battalion, RVN—1965

(VTHF Archives: With permission, lightly edited for publication)

Qui Nhon, 1 July 1965

Ray Stewart

South of Chu Lai and I Corps was an Army logistics base in the Central Highlands of II Corps near the city of Qui Nhon. With mounting pressure by the enemy on this strategically important supply center and the scheduled arrival of the Army unit selected to defend unacceptably delayed until mid-July, the decision was made by General Westmoreland to deploy the 7th Fleet's Special Landing Force (SLF) comprising Lieutenant Colonel C. H. Bodley's BLT 3/7, newly arrived from Camp Pendleton, California, with Second Lieutenant R. A. Stewart's 3d Platoon (Rein.), B Company, 1st Tank Battalion attached.

On 1 July, according to plan, elements of BLT 3/7 were brought ashore and took position of the high ground south of the city, Stewart's Marine Tankers, as heavily armed infantry with .45-caliber pistols, "grease guns," and a few M-14 rifles, as Second Lieutenant Manny Wood's 3d Platoon, C Company, 1st Antitank Battalion Ontos crewmen dug in along the assigned defensive perimeter. The 3/7's commanding officer, Lieutenant Colonel Bodley, would not land nor employ his tanks or Ontos.

(Note: When Lieutenant Colonel Bodley made the same decision later—during Operation STARLITE, which followed—it was the consensus of the supporting units' officers, i.e., company-grade embarked on the USS *Point Defiance*, especially the unit commanders of tanks and Ontos, that the battalion commander had "no clue" how to use them.)

In the book by Bill Van Zanten *Don't Bunch Up* (DB-BV), you may read about Lieutenant Colonel Richard Owens, alias C. H. Bodley. With the continued delay of Army forces in sufficient numbers and/or ability, the decision was made to return BLT 3/7 to the SLF and land BLT 2/7 with Lieutenant Colonel L. N. Utter's 2/7 2d Platoon, B Company, 1st Tanks and his Ontos, an operation that was completed by 7 July.

A footnote may be in order here. When Second Lieutenant Stewart landed with his 3d Platoon personnel, including his Platoon Sergeant, Staff Sergeant Peter J. Frano, support truck drivers, and communicators, he left a token contingent back on the *Point Defiance* to maintain three tanks (B-31, B-32, and B-33) of the 3d Platoon. In order to bring personnel, supplies, and equipment to the landed troops, two of the five preloaded tanks were brought to the beach and off-loaded from the ship's LCMs, freeing it up to provide logistic support for the ashore elements of BLT 3/7.

Private First Class John Hunter was the driver of B-34. Sergeant Art Allen was the tank commander of B-35 and the Section Leader of the B-34/B-35 Tank Light Section on the beach during this weeklong operation. Hunter recalls, "According to my personnel record, we were there between July 1, 1965 and July 20, 1965. The unit included the following people: Sergeant Allen, Lance Corporal Reed, Lance Corporal Tookolo, Lance Corporal Kuczek, and Private First Class Hunter. B-34 and B-35 were the two tanks that were on 'Mike' boats (LCM's), and I guess they wanted to use the boats for other purposes, and that is why they moved the tanks ashore. One of the photos shows the equipment being brought onto the beach. All this was being coordinated by the Shore Party guys with the red patches on their trousers, and covers."

Hunter continues, "During the time we were on the beach, we did not do much, swam, and ate: The guns were in the travel lock the entire time. I have no clue why Sergeant Allen did not have us ready to battle, but I guess he did not think there was a need to do so.

"I also think there may be a photo missing as there is not one of Kuczek standing by the tank. I think the boonie hat belonged to Reed, and we all posed with it, trying to look macho. We did have our .45's on, so we were half-assed ready for a fight.

"And Ray, I hope I don't see the picture of me and Kuczek on some porn site, as we are looking good in our skivvies.

SF

John"

John, thanx for the pics. Yours were the first 1st Tanks tanks to land in Vietnam. I don't know if 1st Tanks has written that in their history but they should. We will definitely cite you (with pictures if we can make them work) as well as your Okinawa road march from the beach to Camp Hansen in our history book.

S/Fi,

Ray

BLT 2/7 Tanks (2d Platoon, Company B, 1st Tanks) Platoon Leader First Lieutenant John Warner—tall, thin, swarthy, rather taciturn officer—and a platoon of five Ontos were loaded on the USS *Alamo* (LSD-33) in support of the 2/7 SLF. The *Alamo* was the same ship we (3d Platoon, Company B, 1st Tanks attached to BLT 3/7) left San Diego in. We then off-loaded on Okinawa, road-marched up the island to Camp Hansen, remained at Camp Hansen, tank park of the recently departed 3d Tanks, for 3 weeks, then back onto the USS *Point Defiance* (LSD-31) at White Beach for the BLT 3/7 SLF float. Elements of 3/7 went ashore at Qui Nhon late June and then relieved by 2/7 on 7 July to resume the SLF (RS-Comment).

Vietnam War

Second Platoon, B Company, First Tanks—1965

The following notes are taken from a phonecon interview of Master Sergeant Robert Fierro (USMC, Ret.) on 5 September '16 from the Foundation office to Bob's home in Oceanside, California. The interview was recorded on Tuesday, 6 September, as read from my notes, and covers primarily his participation in the Vietnam War.

Robert joined the Corps in January 1951 and retired April 1971. He trained on the M-4 tank at Camp Pendleton, California. He said in those days the "old Salts"—veterans of both WWII and Korea—were like brothers, fathers, and mentors. I offered that the great training had as much to do with the eagerness and trainability of the students, which we agreed on, is seldom found today or even a few years after his training. While he and his platoon had fairly adequate training in the mechanics and operations of the tank, they received no training (then or after) that would prepare them for the enemy, situation, or terrain they would face when fighting the VC/NVA later in the Vietnam War.

As a run-up to going in-country Vietnam, he—with the XO of B 1st Tanks—flew to Okinawa, in Camp Hansen, during the spring of 1965. It was a convoluted trip via Guam, Japan, etc. That took a number of days. They secured the Quonset hut barracks for billeting and a place in 3d Tanks Tank Park / Motor Pool in preparation for B

Company's arrival from CONUS. No specific dates were given but it was anticipated to be "early June" of '65.

(Note: CO of B Company was Captain Allan Lamb, who boarded the USS *Alamo* in San Diego with 3d Platoon Second Lieutenant R. A. Stewart, Platoon Commander; Staff Sergeant P. J. Frano, Platoon Sergeant, and sailed on 7 June for Okinawa.)

I write and provide the 2/7 Command Chronology of the brouhaha raised by Lieutenant Colonel Leon Utter's CO of 2/7 with the use of CS gas in operations against the VC after landing at Qui Nhon. Robert had heard about the issue sometime after the incident but had no comment on it.

The BLT 2/7, to which 2 Bravo (2d Platoon, Company B) was attached to for the duration of the SLF, did not include tanks in any of its named operations. (Also note that Fierro had no contact or dealings with the Ontos personnel aboard ship, at Camp Hansen or once ashore.) What appears to be about the one (and only) time documented by 2/7 of tank support was when the 2d Platoon went to the field in an unnamed operation NW of Qui Nhon. The tanks (no specific mention of Grunts) were to destroy a village known to harbor VC. The difficulty in crossing the only subpar bridge was significant but successfully accomplished by the two tanks still operable (bad fuel from Camp Pendleton, the same problem encountered by 3d Platoon while on SLF 3/7, which preceded and was relieved by 2/7 at Qui Son). When the tanks arrived at the village, they found it essentially unoccupied. Ample evidence of logistics support for the enemy was uncovered—food, clothing, meds—but no weapons or other ordnance. Once determined to be all clear of civilians, the village was burned down. They made it back across the river via an engineer-provided fording.

End of Phonecon Interview

The following is taken from the 2/7 July Command Chronology. It's a cut/paste from a PDF doucment, which is done in block, so there'll be verbiage before and after the pertinent tank info.

```
At 070800H July 1965 BLT 2/7 landed on Green Beach S. of Qui Nhon City to
execute relief of BLT 3/7. Relief completed without incident at 071800H July
1965. BLT 2/7 CP at CR (073213). Off loading completed at 080450H and ships
working party ashore by 080855H. On 8 July one company BLT 2/7 occupied ridge
dominated by hill 586 CR (043182). To CR(043178). BLT 2/7 CO and staff briefed

on situation in Qui Nhon area. BLT CP displaced to CR (018197) 101330H. Dis-
placement completed at 101800H. Left combat support/combat service supports in
old CP area. CR (073213), forming an LSU. One company designated BLT 2/7 Reserve
and Mobile Reaction Force Unit. Companies relocated their base of operation
during week to avoid static positions where possible. One company requested

CG 3rd MarDiv on situation in Qui Nhon area. On 15 July Co H moved by foot and
helo to encircle and conduct village search in Phu Tai (4). CR (027163) on
16 July. One rifle Plat (Rein) moved by motorized-mechanized column from BLT
2/7 CP to the town of Phu Tai (4) to clear Route 1 from CR (007200)to CR (028160)
stayed one night and returned to CP. CG 22nd ARVN Div rep with American Advisors
Village deserted at ime of entry. Engineer Plat constructed by-pass of stream
at CR (999251) to permit Tank Plat to join CP Forward. 18 July - Co F con-

28 July Engineer Plat cut by-passes along route one CR (014183) and CR (026159)
S. of BLT CP for move of Tank Section to Phu Tai (4). Co E elements provided
```

The BLT 2/7, to which 2 Bravo was in support, did not include tanks (and Fierro had no contact or dealings with the Ontos personnel aboard ship, at Camp Hansen or once ashore) in any named operations. What appears to be about the one and only time the 2d Platoon went to the field was in an unnamed operation NW of Qui Nhon. The tanks (no specific mention of Grunts) were to destroy a village known to harbor VC. The difficulty in crossing the only subpar bridge was significant but successfully accomplished by the two tanks still operable (bad fuel from Camp Pendleton, the same as encountered by 3d Platoon while on SLF 3/7, which preceded and was relieved by 2/7 at Qui Son). When the tanks arrived at the village, they found it essentially unoccupied. Ample evidence of logistics support for the enemy was uncovered—food, clothing, meds—but no weapons or other ordnance. Once determined to be all clear of civilians, the village was burned down. The two tanks made it back across the river via an engineer-provided fording.

Major A. Doublet was the Operations Officer (S-3) of 2/7. He was interviewed by a member of the Marine Corps History Division upon his return from Vietnam. Major Doublet details the use of, and issues surrounding, employing riot control CS gas to clear tunnels occupied by the enemy. The interview, the operation (named STOMP), and the use of CS gas did not directly involve tanks or Ontos but, at the time, was a high-profile news item in U.S. newspaper and TV, which did include interviews by the news media of Tankers and Ontos crewmen. Major Doublet and Lieutenant Colonel Leon Utter, CO, did make use of 2/7's attached tanks and Ontos whenever their employment would provide a force multiplier. However, in the case of Operation STOMP's area of operation, which encompassed terrain that was unfavorable to the use of tracked armor, it was not feasible.

(Note: That which follows is a modified copy of the summary of an interview of Major Alvin Doublet, former Operations Officer (S-3) of BLT 2/7, by Lieutenant Colonel D. J. Hunter. The Foundation was on grant to the Marine Corps Historical Division, Quantico, Virginia, to develop written summaries of one hundred of the interviews conducted by the history division of in-country, or recently returned to CONUS, Vietnam Marines.)

UNITED STATES MARINE CORPS
HISTORY DIVISION
ORAL HISTORY INTERVIEW WRITTEN SUMMARY

Interviewee's Name: Major Alvin Doublet, USMC, Service #060073 USMC
Date of Interview: 3 June 1966
Conflict: Vietnam War
Military Unit: BLT 2/7
Duties: Battalion Operations Officer
Interviewer: Lieutenant Colonel D. J. Hunter, USMC
Location of Interview: MC Base Camp Pendleton
Length of CD:
Summary: Major Doublet's experiences while serving as the Operations Officer, 2d Battalion, 7th Marines in South Vietnam, 7 July 1965 to 19 December 1965
Prepared by: Lieutenant Colonel R. A. Stewart, USMC (Ret)
Unclassified

Abstract: In this interview of Major Doublet, he details the very successful operations of BLT 2/7, in which he served as the Battalion Operations Office, in the Qui Nhon (II Corps) area of South Vietnam in September 1965 during Operation STOMP followed by Operation HARVEST MOON in December 1965. His "Lessons Learned" provided near the conclusion of the interview are worthy of study but only to a point, i.e., they took place in the early days of a very complicated and changing five years that followed. These two battles were fought between rather conventional forces using and validating the then-schoolbook solutions.

Key Words: BLT 2/7, Qui Nhon, COMUSMACV, CS/CN riot control gas, Operation STOMP, man-pack flamethrowers, Operation HARVEST MOON

Hunter: When did 2/7 first go into South Vietnam, and where?

Doublet: BLT 2/7 landed in Qui Nhon, South Vietnam, 7 July 1965. Its mission at that time was to relieve BLT 3/7, which landed earlier in the month (approx. 1 July) then in coordination with 2d Corps of Republic of Vietnam to deploy forces on key terrain in the Qui Nhon area in order to reinforce the Republic of Vietnam's armed forces in defense of the airfield, port, and logistic facilities and U.S. supporting installations in the Qui Nhon area.

Hunter: Who did the 2/7 work for?

Doublet: The operational control (of 2/7) was under initially COMUSMACV (Commander, U.S. Military Assistance Command Vietnam, General Westmoreland) until the Task Force Alpha, later to be called Field Force Vietnam, was established in Na Trang under Major General Stanley Larsen (USA). This occurred on 5 August 1965. In summation, I can say from 7 July to 4 August we worked for COMUSMACV and from 5 August to 7 November, when we left Qui Nhon, we worked under Field Force V(ietnam) under (Army) General Larson.

Hunter: Focus on two actions in which 2/7 took part. Let's turn our attention to 2/7's employment of CS and CN (riot control gas). Can you tell me the background on this particular operation, when it took place, what the mission was, and how you came to employ these agents?

Doublet: Late in August (1965), it was our desire, as was the desire of Field Force Vietnam, to have us coordinate operations north of Qui Nhon where it was known that VC forces were causing considerable harassment to the local populace as well as posing a threat to the security of Qui Nhon. A target was decided on, which contained roughly a company supposedly of regular North Vietnamese Forces (NVA). The target area was described as a considerable number of tunnel complexes and underground storage area where the VC was storing ordnances for possible destruction of facilities in the Qui Nhon area. Prior to this or just a couple of weeks prior to our notification of this target, Operation STARLITE in Chu Lai had taken place. The (2/7) Battalion Commander had directed me to go up to see the 7th Regiment to find out what their experiences had been in this particular locale. While I was there, I noticed or observed a considerable number of caves and tunnels that the 7th Marines had contacted with and the difficult time they had in getting the civilians out of the tunnels in order to get (to) the VC forces. When I came back from Chu Lai, I reported this to the Battalion Commander, Lieutenant Colonel Utter, and in conjunction with our plan at this time north of Qui Nhon, we decided we would use riot-control agents in any of the tunnels that we would experience in our operations, which was titled Operation STOMP. Then (we) cleared (got permission for) the utilization of the riot-control agents with the Field Force Vietnam Headquarters in Na Trang. D-day for this operation was 5 September 1965. It was to be a coordinated operation in that a company of regional force units under the tutelage of (US) Special Forces camp, which was also north of Qui Nhon. We were going to make a combined helicopter and amphibious landing. One of our companies would go in by helicopter to the north side of the target area, while another landed across a riverbed and the 3d Regional Force (Vietnamese) would go into blocking positions to the west.

Hunter: This operation took place 5 September. Can you give us a location for the target area?

Doublet: The location of the VC target was approximately 10 air miles from Qui Nhon due north. The concentration of (enemy) forces was expected to be a company of VC. The operation commenced with the landing of our Company H on the riverbank and followed closely with the landing of the helicopter north. The regional force company (Vietnamese Regional Force) had already moved into position some two hours before, and they were to the west. It soon became quite clear that the earlier information on the existence of tunnel complexes was true and the riot-control agent was employed by company commanders with a great deal of success in that the entire operation, which lasted approximately two and a half days. There were some three hundred to four hundred civilians who were forced out of the caves and tunnels by the riot-control agents and a total of fifty-six VC captives and twenty-eight VC were killed during the course of the operation. We estimated if we had not utilized the riot-control agent, the civilians that had been placed in front of the tunnels (as human shields) would have had a considerable number of casualties inflicted upon them.

Hunter: This situation was that the VC in control of the area had herded the civilians into the tunnels, kept the civilians between the VC in the tunnels and the Marines outside. Is that right?

Doublet: That's correct.

Hunter: Were they bringing fire to bear from the tunnel or tunnel entrances?

Doublet: In a number of instances, there were some small spider holes that were other exits to the caves and tunnels, where the VC could fire upon us. We were unable to detect where these firing holes were at the time of the engagement, but after the tunnels and caves were cleared, we were able to see how they utilized this tactic of using the civilians in the front while they operated from the rear, either as a hiding place or as a location where they could drop out of sight in the spider holes.

Hunter: Al, do you have interpreters or PA systems with you to, more or less, alert civilians in the tunnels to the fact that you were going to use this stuff, or did you just put it in the tunnels?

Doublet: That's correct. We had—from the 22d Airborne Division (USA) whose headquarters were in Qui Nhon—a Psychological Warfare (PsyOps) Team who were equipped with speakers, in addition to some six interpreters that we had with our battalion. At that time, we didn't have all six employed, but all the people were warned and they were encouraged to come out of the caves and tunnels before we engaged the riot-control agent. In no case were we able to convince them to come out, and I'm sure that the fact the VC were behind them threatening them was one of the reasons they didn't come out prior to the use of riot-control agent.

Hunter: At this time, during the operation, did you have these little handy dandy blowers to put the stuff in the tunnel?

Doublet: No, the Mighty Mite blowers only came available to use after Operation STOMP.

Hunter: So you just took the grenades and tossed them into the tunnel entrances or spider holes and it's how it came about?

Doublet: That's correct, sir.

Hunter: Did you recover any weapons from the VCs in these tunnels?

Doublet: Yes, our total kill, body count, as I repeated before, was twenty-eight. We captured some twelve weapons and considerable amount of storage rice and food supplies.

Hunter: Al, what was the reaction at your level and higher levels once the fact that you had used CS and CN became apparent?

Doublet: We had, at the onset of this operation, some five new photographers from various agencies here in the States, and of course, they evidently followed the reports concerning our utilization of riot-control agent(s). Later the next day (after the use of the agents) that we received word from Field Force V, General Larson's headquarters in Na Trang, to be prepared to furnish additional information on the utilization of riot control agents. Contacts from Na Trang indicated that an officer representing General Larson would be up to query members of the battalion on the plan and actual employment of the riot=control agent. COMUSMACV, with a dispatch, said that there had been no approval on the use of the riot-control agent. In immediate response to this, General Larson sent a message back to

COMUSMACV that the utilization of the riot-control agent had been with his approval and had been used in a humanitarian way and some three hundred to four hundred civilian lives had been spared in contact with the VC. It progressed steadily from that particular point. As the time period elapsed, we were visited by numerous personnel, both Marines from III MAF, with correspondence received by the battalion commander from Lieutenant General Krulak (USMC) backing his utilization of riot-control agent, and in general, there was a feeling that our utilization of this agent had been a (in a) humanitarian vain and there would be no complications. It was later that a revision to the policy of riot-control agent came about. I had the good fortune of attending a chemical warfare briefing at Field Force V in Na Trang sometime later on where additional instructions were put out on its use. And it became, as weeks, months passed, a common fact that unit commanders were able to use it, and we felt that our utilization of it successfully during Operation STOMP had a lot to do with this reappraisal of the use of riot-control agent, and finally, when we finished up our operation in Qui Nhon, General Westmoreland came by and visited and talked to the officers and SNCOs available in the CP. I commented to Lieutenant Colonel Utter that our successful utilization of riot-control agent at that time had changed the world's opinion and had a direct bearing on later employment of this previously unheard of riot-control agent—unheard of from the standpoint of bad publicity that had earlier been connected with it.

Hunter: So you had actually a fine hand in changing national policy with your employment of CS and CN in these particular caves and tunnels.

Doublet: We feel that we did, Colonel.

Corporal Mark Suthers was a Tanker with the 2d Platoon, B Company, 1st Tanks. His comments capture the essence of the tank platoon's activity during its deployment with 2/7 in the Qui Nhon AOR.

I have reviewed the command chronologies and have a reasonable picture of the BLT 2/7 ops around Qui Nhon. The operation around An Khe was an Army effort, and General Larson was using a different grid coordinate system from UTM conventions that Lieutenant Colonel Utter (CO of BLT 2/7) used. (I also noted that Colonel Utter was much more organized than was Larson based on these records.)

The references around An Khe all use BR coordinates that do not plot on the UTM metric maps I have downloaded. Some of Larson's references at 1:250,000 and others are 1:50,000, so I can only assume his maps were either using English units? Some reference points are observable from Colonel Utter's order to the Recon element, which was to secure a hamlet and radio comm's site and some mountain peaks are pinpointed. However, where tanks operated with Company "F" (2/7) or 101st Airborne is something I have not been able to figure out. Gunnery Sergeant Fieros as well as Sergeant Gibson's tank + crew, Bol, Shukitas, and I got stuck at some point off of Route 19 (CP for 101st I guess), along with a few paratroopers for this ops. We did some H&I firing at night and killed a pig, which we tried to roast and eat, but that was about it.

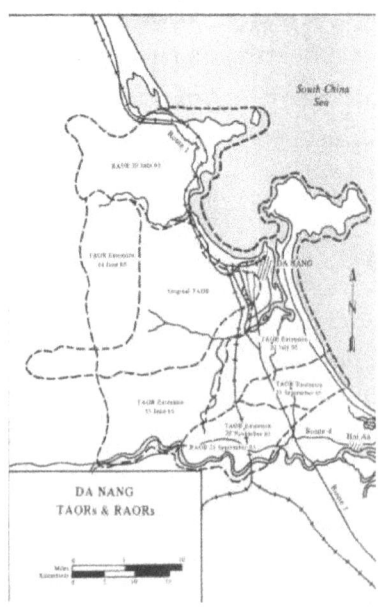

DA NANG
TAORs & RAORs

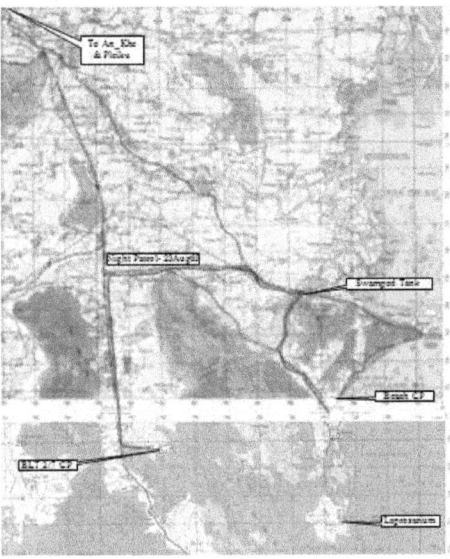
BLT-2/7 Qui Nhon Map 1 positions 1965

Meanwhile, further north, between Qui Nhon and Chu Lai, the 1st Viet Cong Regiment was increasingly posing a threat to the Chu Lai Airfield now heavily populated with lucrative targets of multiple aircraft, a huge fuel farm, and other

highly valuable and vulnerable equipment, supplies, and CC-2/7 ordnance of all types and sizes. Spread over a wide area, the facility was impossible for the thinly manned perimeter to stop either a sapper assault or to protect the valuable assets from long-range mortar or artillery.

In the meantime, the Viet Cong operating in the Da Nang TAOR were eager to mount a coordinated, well-rehearsed sapper attack against the aircraft, equipment, and facilities at the Da Nang Airfield. That this attack could be so well planned and executed was a preview of coming attractions for the defenders of the Chu Lai Airfield just being completed 50 miles to the south.

"On 1 July, a Viet Cong mortar and ground attack on the Da Nang airfield exposed the vulnerability of the base to enemy hit-and-run tactics" (GB-65). Lieutenant Colonel V. E. Ludwig's 1/9 was responsible for the defense of the Da Nang Airfield. The offensive-minded Marines were not content to "sit on their ditty bags," as one Lieutenant General Victor Krulak had said recently. The VC, watching the Da Nang Air Base activity from their homes in the adjacent villes,* observed Lieutenant Colonel Ludwig stripping two companies from his 1/9 Battalion's airfield defensive perimeter and sending them out "looking for the enemy," thus allowing the enemy, who were in fact no farther than across the airfield's perimeter road just outside the perimeter wire, to choose any number of open avenues through the Marines' wire to get into and run rampant through the air base. The offensive-minded Marines never thought for a minute that the solution to thwarting such attacks was to build a better *defensive* mousetrap but, rather, go on the attack and ensure the safety from attack by denying the enemy free movement to its target by clearing him from an extended TAOR. It was stated that sometimes the best defense is a good defense.

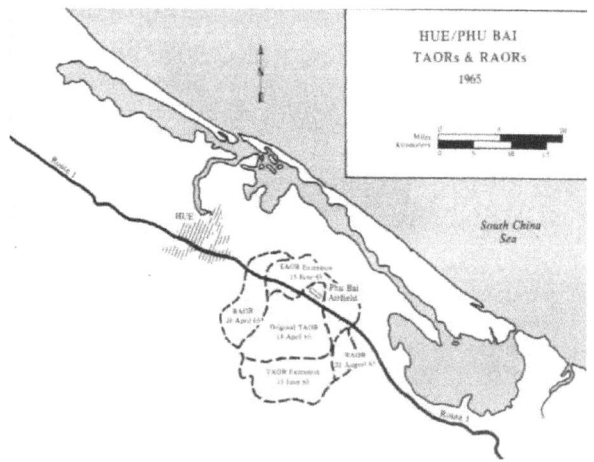

Hue/Phu Bai TAOR 1965

---

* "The term *village* in Vietnam denoted an administrative unit, while the true local community was the hamlet, several clusters making up a village." Often several hamlets would have the same name and were differentiated with a number on Marine maps. None of this hodgepodge made much difference to the Marines, calling them all "villes" (GB-65).

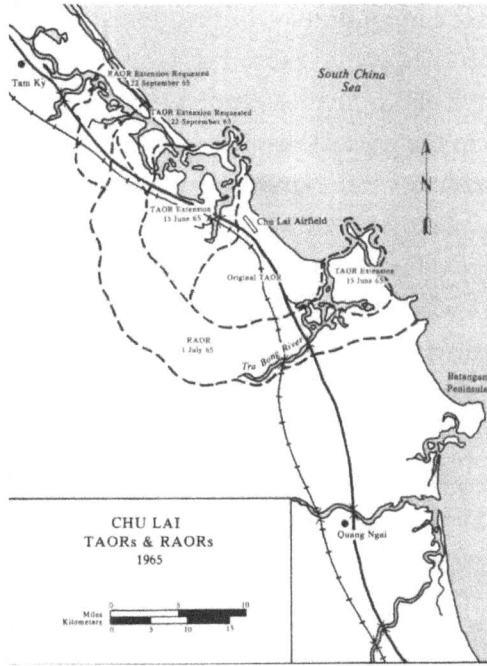

Chu Lai TAORs and RAORs, 1965

In the meantime, at the other two TAORs assigned to the Marine (Chu Lai and Phu Bai), the Marines were shedding the cloud of hunkering down behind the wire, waiting for the enemy, and had moved out in active patrolling in an attempt—more often than not met with frustrating three to four days' "walks in the sun"—to find, fix, and destroy him. And while the three to four days' walks in the sun somewhat satisfied the needs of the offensive warrior to "do something" and provided the opportunity to stretch their legs, the Viet Cong homegrown guerilla was tending his rice paddy that the Marines were wading through, looking for him. As the sun set, the farmer became what the Marines were looking for.

The Marine Tankers and Ontos crewmen were looking for ways to become actively involved in the effort, to become relevant in the kind of war none were trained to fight. On the surface, "guerilla warfare," "counterinsurgency," "hull-down defense," and "armored operations" are not found in the same sentence. But become relevant they did—from the difficulties inherent in amphibious operations, such as the Operations DAGGER THRUST and DECK HOUSE; to jungle-encountered, triple-canopied foliage; to fender-deep rice paddies with ten-foot dkes; to sugar sand up to the tracks' carrier rollers; to city fighting with streets so narrow that tanks took the front from buildings on both sides of the "street" at the same time. And tank and Ontos unit leaders became great salesmen for their "product," selling it to the supported infantry commander, who was drawing up his next scheme of maneuver to show how the use of his supporting tracks could best assure success. Alas, there are more pictures of tanks and Ontos piled with Marines dead and dying *coming back* from the fight that they didn't get to fight than tanks and Ontos leading or supporting the charge that started the fight. Some infantry commanders used their attached tracks as ambulances at best and hearses at worst.

Bridge bypass (MCVTHF photo)

The many streams and rivers encountered were a constant problem for Tankers from several aspects. Most bridges could not support a 52-ton tank, and none of them could be trusted to support the 60-ton VTR tank retriever. The engineers solved part of the river-crossing dilemma by the use of pontoon boats used to ferry the tanks one at a time across the larger rivers, but the seasonally adjusted flows that took the wide, shallow stream easily forded without the use of fording equipment preparation to a raging ten-foot deep river, often with scant warning, posed a challenge. The smaller streams could be equally as challenging in a different way. For example, the steepness of a stream or riverbank could be nonnegotiable, which meant an on-foot reconnaissance to find an egress was required, exposing the ground guide to enemy small-arms fire and the tanks—lined up "bumper-to-bumper waiting to cross"—vulnerable to RPGs and B-40s. The enemy would be able to preplan ambushes at the likely crossing points going into and/or coming out of the river. Major bridges along the main roads also required guarding to stop both ground attack and swimmers placing explosives to destroy them.

So, unfortunately, the tanks were used to guard each end of a major bridge. Of all the ways tanks can be used—and were used in Vietnam to adjust to the situation and terrain—static positioning of tanks was the most onerous.

Expanded TAORs posed challenges for both the infantry units and supporting arms alike. None so significantly than to tanks and Ontos. Within short distances of but a few kilometers—often in any twenty-four-hour period and on a single operation—the terrain to be negotiated could change rapidly from coastal sand dunes to low rolling hills covered by scrub forest, swamps with mazes of waterways navigable by small boats, or steep jungle-clad mountains impassable to vehicle of any sort. One must keep in mind that tanks and Ontos are employed as force multipliers in direct support of and/or attached to infantry units. However, tracks, being as vulnerable as they are to enemy antitank weapons (RPGs and B-40s, mines, and sappers with satchel charges), are most effective when the concept and tactics of tank-infantry teams is adhered to. Operation STARLITE, with the "Lost Column," is case in point and will be discussed in some detail. The point of this reminder is that even when tanks and Ontos might be able to move well, their support from the infantry may be difficult to assure. The tank infantry (TI) phone mounted on the right rear of the tank fender is the direct line between an infantryman outside the tank with the tank crew.

However, after brushes with the heavy foliage often encountered by the tank and the occasional mine, the TI phone is a casualty. The most consistent and reliable method for tank/infantry to communicate is via the compatible radio. When asked how—or even if—the infantry used the TI phone, Dick Carey wrote, "The only time the TI phone was used or I should say not used when a captain with 2/9 ripped my ass when I told him I was already listening to 3 separate nets and the Phone had been disconnected." Pappy Reynolds writes, "On the M48 and M48A1 the TI phone was on the center rear of the tank in an armored box. It had a 50 foot cord. In training at Pendleton, the grunts used it. On the M48A2 and A-3, the phone was in a tin box on the right rear fender. It had a very short cord. The grunts were reluctant to use it as they had to almost stand in the tank's exhaust to use it. Lieutenant Fitzgerald got hit because our TI phone didn't work and he had to lean out of the tank to talk to the grunts." This is a testimonial to the use, or attempted use, of the TI phone and the communications capability of the tank.

In FMFM 9-1 "Tank Employment," section VI, in the paragraph "Special Situations," eight of the eleven "situations" at one time or another were faced by the Marine Tanker. But the training received by both officers and enlisted personnel did not address these in depth. That Marine Tankers and Ontos crewmen being able to get the most from their respective weapons was a testimonial to their initiative, hard work, and innovativeness.

On 8 July 1965, Headquarters, 3d Tank Battalion debarked at Red Beach 2, Da Nang Port, Republic of Vietnam, and established the command post adjacent to Company A at (AT 985742).

On 10 July 1965, the command post moved to the southern perimeter of the Division Area of Responsibility at (AT 988711). Extensive defensive positions were established in coordination with the 9th Marines, 3d Antitank Battalion, and the 1st Amphibian Tractor Battalion.

"The Third Tank Battalion mission is to provide combat support for the Third Marine Division in current operations utilizing mobility, armor-protection, fire power, and shock action to close with and destroy enemy forces, fortifications, and materials. The Third Tank Battalion (-) is in General support of the Third Marine Division with a tank company (-) in direct support and under the operational control of the Ninth Marines, and a tank company attached to the Fourth Marines" (CC-3dTk, 7/65).

On 24 July 1965, 3d Marine Division Operation Order placed the 3d Tank Battalion (-) in general support (GS) of the 3d Marine Division. The 3d Tank Battalion was directed to provide one company (-) in direct support (DS), under the operational control (OpCon) of the 3d Marines, and to provide one company (-) in direct support (D/S), under the operational control (OpCon) of the 9th Marines.

Captain F. W. Jarnot's Company A (-) (Rein) was placed in direct support (DS) (and under the) operational control (OpCon) of the 3d Marines in the Chu Lai TAOR.

Captain A. E. Lee's Company B (-)(Rein.) was placed in direct support and operational control of the 9th Marines in the Da Nang TAOR.

Captain Joe Sanders's Company C (-)(Rein.) remained attached to the 4th Marines in Chu Lai. His 3d Platoon, Company C remained attached to the 3d Battalion, 4th Marines in Phu Bai (CC-3Tk, 6/65).

At Chu Lai was the CO of Company B, 1st Tank Battalion, Captain A. W. Lamb, with his Headquarters Platoon and Lieutenant John Warner's 1st Platoon. His 2d and 3d Platoons were attached to BLT 2/7 and 3/7 Special Landing Forces (SLF), respectively.

(From CC-3Tk, 7/65).

SUMMARY

1. Mission Assigned

The 3d Tank Battalion's mission is to provide combat support for the 3d Marine Division in current operations utilizing mobility, armor protection, firepower, and shock action to close with and destroy enemy forces, fortifications, and materials. The 3d Tank Battalion (-) (Reinforced) is in general support of the 3d Marine Division with a tank company in direct support operational control of the 3d Marines, a tank company in direct support operational control of the 9th Marines, a tank company attached to the 4th Marines, and a tank company (-) attached to the 7th Marines.

2. Chronological Summary of Events

1 August 1965 Company "B" conducted two fire missions in support of 2d Battalion, 9th Marines sweep and clear operations in Cam Ne (1). Targets were defensive bunkers and trenches located at (AT 987683) and (AT 987687). Both targets were damaged and one bunker was destroyed.

2 August 1965: Company A in direct support of 3d Marines' Operation BLAST OUT I in southwest portion of Da Nang TAOR. Company conducted patrol and sweeping operations on the western flank with elements of the 3d Reconnaissance Battalion. No enemy activity encountered. Marines from Company B, 1st Battalion, 3d Marines were seen in Operation BLAST OUT southwest of Da Nang. The 1st Battalion, 9th Marines conducted its search of the Cam Ne village complex, four miles to the north, in conjunction with this operation.

3 August 1965: Company A continued to provide tank support to 3d Marines' Operation BLAST OUT I. Tanks were employed to clear village fortifications of booby traps and antipersonnel mines. No enemy troop units were encountered. Company B conducted fire mission in support of 2d Battalion, 9th Marines' sweep-and-clear operations in

Cam Ne (1). One bunker where automatic weapons fire was coming from was destroyed (AT 979675). During the evening, Company B displaced to the Marble Mountain area in preparation for operations with the 1st Battalion, 9th Marines.

4 August 1965: Company A returned to command post from Operation BLASTOUT I after having provided security for two damaged LVTE-1s during the night of 3–4 August. Company B conducted tank-infantry sweep-and-clear operations south and west of Marble Mountain. Three tanks were temporarily mired in rice fields but were back in action in less than an hour. There was no enemy contact with the tanks, although an LVT was extensively damaged when it struck a mine while operating with the tanks.

5 August 1965: Company B continued the tank-infantry search-and-destroy operations southwest of Marble Mountain. Tank fire was used to destroy enemy bunkers, emplacements, and trench lines. The tank received a considerable amount of small-arms fire from a fortified building at (BT 037656) shortly after noon. The structure was destroyed, and the enemy small-arms fire ceased as a result of the tank fire.

6 August 1965: Company A was assigned a mission to crush and burn a suspected enemy district headquarters at (AT 876692). Upon reaching their destination, they found the area deserted. A flame tank was used to destroy suspected enemy emplacements and meeting places in the immediate vicinity. Company B concluded its support of the 1st Battalion, 9th Marines' sweep southwest of Marble Mountain without further enemy contact.

7 August 1965: Company A continued to support search-and-destroy operations of the 1st Battalion, 3d Marines near Cau Song (1) (AT 875695). Additional enemy emplacements were destroyed, and the operation concluded during the early evening hours without enemy contact.

8 August 1965: In response to a request from the 2d Battalion, 9th Marines, tanks located at the battalion command post conducted a fire mission against a known enemy ammunition storage area at (AT 987688). Eleven rounds were fired, and the target was destroyed, as well as ammunition contained therein. The battalion completed proficiency firing with all command post weapons. Medical personnel continued to provide first-aid and basic treatment to the residents of the hamlet of Phong Bac (1). This activity occurred approximately four times each week and attracted nearly half the village population of eighty.

9 August 1965: Company B responded to a request for assistance from Company B, 1st Battalion, 9th Marines, which was under attack by small arms and automatic weapons. Tank fire was directed at the structure where the fire was coming from. A search of the area failed to reveal any enemy or weapons, although spent cartridge cases from .30-caliber weapons were found. At 2330, the battalion command post received a considerate amount of small-arms and automatic weapons fire from positions directly in front of the southern portion of the perimeter. Within a very few seconds, a heavy mortar barrage began landing throughout the command post area. Two living tents, the S-1 tent, and one defensive bunker received direct hits. The barrage lasted for approximately five minutes, and approximately thirty rounds exploded within the perimeter and six in the hamlet of Phong Bac (1). Muzzle flashes were seen coming from Yen Bac at (AT 984702) and Cam Ne (1) (AT 982694). The 60 mm mortar rounds came from the first firing position, and the 81 mm mortar rounds were probably fired from the latter. An artillery fire mission was called on the suspected gun positions; however, due to the distance, the results were not immediately known. The battalion sustained twenty-three WIA, three of whom later died of wounds, including the Battalion Adjutant. At 2338, emergency helicopter evacuation was requested. Killed in action / died of wounds were First Lieutenant R. C. Kraus, Corporal L. I. Hildenbrand, and Lance Corporal P. A. Devers.

10 August 1965: At 0023, helicopters began arriving, and all persons injured during the mortar attack were evacuated to the 3d Marine Division hospital by 0500. Crater analysis revealed that the mortar rounds had come from the vicinity of the suspected gun position; however, a search by a patrol from the 2d Battalion, 9th Marines failed to discover any evidence of activity in those locations. The battalion command post was reorganized, and deeper and more heavily constructed bunkers were built. Company B, operating with the 1st Battalion, 9th Marines, captured six Viet Cong near (BT 054697) and turned them over to Hoa Vang District Headquarters for interrogation.

11 August 1965: Thirty-five Vietnamese were treated by battalion medical personnel, and thirty pairs of shower shoes were distributed to the residents of Phong Bac (1). Company B captured clothing, ammunition, and other military items during a tank patrol south of Marble Mountain. At 2000, four rounds of sniper fire were received in the battalion command post from positions near (AT 996712).

12 August 1965: The artillery forward observer assigned to the tank battalion observed numerous Vietnamese entering a small shrine 1,000 meters forward of his position carrying long boxes. A patrol was sent to the area in coordination with the 3d Antitank Battalion. No unusual activity was observed, and the boxes could not be found.

13 August 1965: Company B participated in a tank-infantry sweep in coordination with 1st Battalion, 9th Marines southwest of Marble Mountain. At (BT 069689), tank returned fire on a Viet Cong emplacement. One Viet Cong was wounded and was seen being dragged off by another. No further enemy activity occurred as the patrol continued its operations throughout the night.

14 August 1965: Company A conducted a tank-infantry patrol with elements of Company C, 1st Battalion, 3d Marines in the western portion of TAOR. No enemy contact. Company B conducted search-and-destroy operations near Marble Mountain without contact.

Battalion Headquarters command post defense weapons were fired for training and proficiency of crew members.

15 August 1965: Two rounds of small-arms sniper fire were received in the battalion command post area. Location of weapons could not be determined. Company A continued its patrol with the 1st Battalion, 3d Marines. Sniper fire was received from a position near (AT 879689); however, the area could not be searched due to dense underbrush.

16 August 1965: At 2315, several voices shouting "You die" were heard along the southern sector of the battalion command post perimeter. This was followed by small-arms and automatic weapons fire along all sides of the perimeter. Four 81 mm mortar rounds fell along the eastern sector. Contact was broken when defensive automatic weapons returned a heavy volume of fire. The artillery forward observer called a fire mission at the suspected mortar position, which resulted in six Viet Cong confirmed KIA. Reports indicated that approximately thirty Viet Cong were involved in the attack with approximately six automatic weapons being used. A late report from the chief, Hieu Duc District, indicated that twenty-six Viet Cong were killed by artillery fire.

Operation STARLITE: The First Big Battle (17–24 August 1965)

Originally written for the USMCVTA "Sponson Box"

by Lieutenant Colonel Ray Stewart, USMC (Ret)

When the 9th Marine Expeditionary Brigade (MEB) came across Red Beach 1 in Da Nang, Republic of Vietnam, under the command of Brigadier General Frederick J. Karch, USMC, on 8 March 1965, it had orders to "dig in and hold." The Army of the Republic of Vietnam (ARVN) was in command, and according to Brigadier General Karch's statement to the press, "Our job is to secure the area. We'll be operating strictly in a defensive role."

(Note: Marine Corps' 3d Tank Battalion M48A3 tanks landed across Red Beach 2 the following day.)

So while the ARVN troops were free to seek out and engage the enemy, Marines were relatively confined to "behind the wire." The Da Nang enclave was referred to by some Marines as "The Alamo." From the Alamo, Marines could fire only when fired upon. In some instances,

Marines observed "troops in the open," but by the time they could obtain permission to shoot, the opportunity was lost.

A MAG-16 helicopter evacuates STARLITE casualties, while a Marine M-48 from C Company, 3d Tank Battalion in Chu Lai stands guard. The Marine on the lower left caries an M-79 40 mm grenade launcher (GB-65). (USMC photo A184966)

Further to the south in an area called Chu Lai, 55 miles from Da Nang, things were a bit different. In June of 1965, Company L, Marine Support Battalion, intercepted and reported an increase in message traffic between several known Viet Cong units concentrated on and around the Van Tuong Peninsula just 15 miles south of the Chu Lai enclave. The Marine cantonment included a new U.S.-built airfield. These intercepts alerted the aerial intelligence collection assets, which confirmed "unusual activity," including the building of bunkers and other positions to the south increasingly closer to the airfield.

During mid-August 1965, an enemy deserter informed his interrogators that the 60th and the 80th Viet Cong Battalions, with reinforcement from the 52d Weapons Battalion, comprised a unit called the "First Viet Cong Regiment." Further, that this 1,500-man regiment intended to attack the just-being-built Chu Lai enclave and airfield from its staging area on the Van Tuong Peninsula in order to disrupt the systematic buildup of American forces "before they could become organized and interfere with the North's takeover of their southern brethren" (LN-7/15).

(Note: The purported source, a "defector," was a ruse to shield the fact that this information was obtained through highly sensitive electronic intercept of the enemy's radio traffic [SIGINT].)

Army General Westmoreland, the commander in charge of all military operations in Vietnam (COMUSMACV), located in Saigon, and his staff grew increasingly concerned that the Viet Cong were preparing to mount an attack on Chu Lai with "up to 3 regiments of Viet Cong." The concern was shared by Marine Lieutenant General Lewis Walt, commanding general of the III Marine Amphibious Force (MAF). General Westmoreland "encouraged" General Walt to take the offensive. General Walt "reminded" General Westmoreland of the 6 May letter limiting Marines to support of the ARVN. General Westmoreland told Walt that these constraints were "no longer realistic" and ordered General Walt to rewrite the rules of engagement (ROE).

General Walt had already rewritten the onerous, defensive-oriented ROE and was merely waiting for the word to implement it. On 6 August, General Westmoreland gave General Walt "official permission to take offensive action against the enemy." In less than a week, the 7th Marines were landed in Chu Lai. RLT 7 (-) (Rein.), commanded by Colonel Oscar F. Peatross, with Captain Allen W. Lamb's Company B (-), 1st Tank Battalion in direct support. BLT 1/7, reinforced by the Lieutenant John Warner's 1st Platoon, Company B, 1st Tanks, arrived on 14 August.

Lieutenant Colonel S. R. Jones, commanding officer of the 3d Tank Battalion (-), headquartered in Da Nang, had already deployed two of his companies to the Chu Lai Tactical Area of Responsibility (TAOR) in support of the 3d Marines (Company A, commanded by Captain Fidelas W. Jarnot) and the 4th Marines (Company C [-], commanded by Captain Joe P. Sanders).

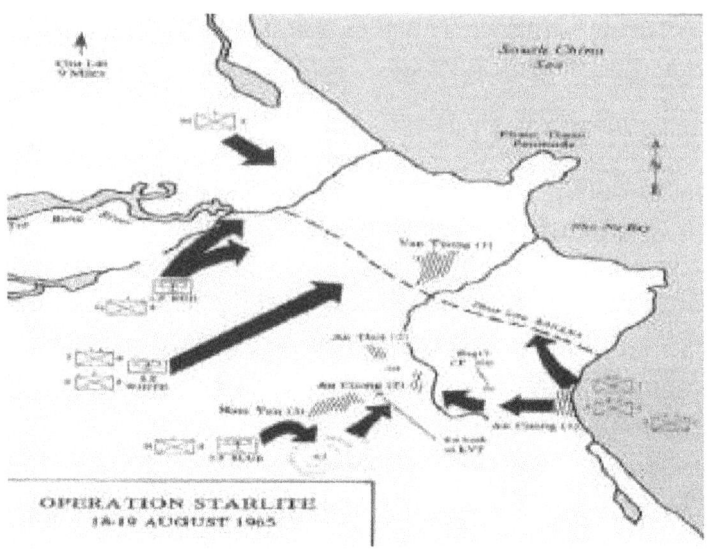

Map of Operation STARLITE (GB-65)

Captain Sanders's 3d Platoon remained attached to the 3d Battalion, 4th Marines (3/4) in Phu Bai.

With increased enemy activity reported around the Van Tuong village complex and the arrival of the 7th Marines—along with permission to engage the enemy—General Walt and his staff flew to Chu Lai from Da Nang. There was but one of two choices: "sit on our ditty bags" and wait for the "battle-hardened 1st Viet Cong Regiment led by Le Huu Tru who had commanded the regiment against the French at the iconic Battle of Dien Bien Phu in 1954 and more recently mauled the ARVN's 51st Regiment, to organize an attack" (LN-J/15) or take the battle to the enemy. Predictably, the Marines chose the latter and Colonel Peatross (CO, 7th Marines [-]) was given command of the attacking force. Colonel Don Wyckoff, 3d Marine Division operations officer, designated the operation "Satellite," but as a young private first class typed out the plan, the generators failed and the clerk—with only a candle for light, altering history—typed "Starlite" instead of "Satellite" throughout the document. Colonel Wyckoff, realizing the difficulty of changing the error and probably smiling at the originality of the PFC's misspelling, allowed the operation order to be disseminated among the participants.

The operation was to be a two-battalion combined air and amphibious assault using the tactical "double hammer and anvil" plan—Lieutenant Colonel Bull Fisher's 2d Battalion, 4th Marines (2/4) and Lieutenant Colonel Joseph E. Muir's 3d Battalion, 3d Marines (3/3). Lieutenant Colonel Muir's 3/3 was to land across the beach, leaving his supporting tanks aboard ship, and Lieutenant Colonel Fisher's 2/4 to vertical assault by helicopter further inland. A third battalion—the 3d Battalion, 7th Marines (BLT 3/7), commanded by Lieutenant Colonel Charles H. Bodley and reinforced by Second Lieutenant Raymond A. Stewart's 3d Platoon (Rein.), Company B (-), 1st Tank Battalion—embarked on the USS *Point Defiance* (LSD-31) and was designated as the floating reserve. Artillery support was to be provided by Marine batteries at Chu Lai. Naval guns were on-call, and MAGs -11 and -12 were to fly close air with Helicopter Squadrons 261 and 361 supporting the vertical envelopment.

If the creation of the attacking regimental-size force under Colonel Peatross—drawing units from both the 1st and 3d Marine Divisions (3d Marines from Okinawa, 4th Marines from Hawaii, and 7th Marines from Camp Pendleton)—was complicated and difficult, Marine Tanker Captain Lamb's supporting job was no less so. He was tasked to provide tank, both gun and flame, support into an area 12–15 miles south of Chu Lai that was only marginally "tank country," making both reinforcement and resupply tricky at best. The infantry-supported units did not use tank fuel (diesel), main gun (90 mm rounds), or small-arms ammunition (.30-caliber machine gun) or have the means to provide it. Captain Lamb made plans for overland resupply of his tanks and men, as well as the means to affect repairs and the retrieval of disabled tanks. This required review of his B Company, 1st Tanks' assets, those of Captain Sanders, commanding officer of A Company, 3d Tanks, who landed earlier and whose command post was located to the north of his (Captain Lamb's) command post, and also the Operation STARLITE's logistics officer located within a stone's throw in Colonel Peatross's 7th Marines compound. Captain Lamb handpicked the Tankers with which he would join the battle "just down the road."

On 17 August, selected 1st and 3d Tank Battalion tanks loaded into amphibious craft at Chu Lai in support of the amphibious assault phase, while the others moved overland from Chu Lai to link up for the follow-on assault on the 1st VC Regiment bunkered on the Van Tuong Peninsula.

On 18 August, Company B (-) (Rein.), 1st Tank Battalion moved out. It comprised the following:

> Company B (-), 1st Tank Battalion with (1) M-48 Gun Tank, (3) M-67A2 Flame Tank, (1) VTR M-51, with RLT-7
>
> Tanks: B-51, F-33, F-53, and F-55. (B-51 was Captain A. W. Lamb's. He was the "Gagle Commander." He received the Silver Star for his action. The *F*s were all flame tanks.)
>
> 3d Platoon, Company A, 3d Tank Battalion with BLT 3/3
>
> Tanks: A-31, A-32, A-33, A-34, and A-35
>
> Section, 2d Platoon, Company C, 3d Tank Battalion with BLT 2/4
>
> Tanks: C-22, C-24
>
> 3 officers, 43 enlisted USMC, 1 USN
>
> Casualties for tank units: 1 KIA, Corporal William C. Laidlaw, C Company, 3d Tanks; 15 WIA

Further, the tank elements were organized into three separate increments:

> The section of 2d Platoon, Company C, 3d Tanks was attached to Lieutenant Colonel Fisher's BLT 2/4.
>
> 3d Platoon, Company A was attached to Lieutenant Colonel Muir's BLT 3/3.
>
> Captain Lamb's Company B (-), 1st Tanks was with Headquarters, RLT-7 in a general support (GS) role.

BLT 3/3, after an amphibious landing with gun tanks and flame tanks, of the 3d Platoon (Rein.), Company A, 3d Tank Battalion, commanded by Second Lieutenant Ky Thompson, and Ontos of the 3d Platoon, Company B, 3d Antitank Battalion, commanded by Lieutenant McCoy, and 2/4, with their supporting tanks attached, joined up outside the hamlet of An Cuong (2). The terrain was "primarily rolling, weeded or brush-covered interspersed with dry crop fields, wet rice paddies, and paddy dikes." Hedgerows of small trees and brush from 6–10 feet divided up the terrain.

Company C reported that two of their tanks were extensively damaged during "Operation Starlight" [sic]. The tanks had been involved in a very close and intense battle with the Viet Cong near Van Tuong. Tanks were damaged by antitank rockets, 81 mm mortars, 57 mm recoilless rifles, and well-aimed small-arms fire. Due to the fluid nature of the situation, the exact disposition of the tanks was unknown at this time. Company C reported one KIA and seven WIA. Company B, 1st Tank Battalion reported one flame tank damaged and four WIA. Killed in action was Corporal William C. Laidlaw (CC-3Tk, 8/65).

On 19 August 1965, Company C sustained extensive damage on two tanks and moderate damage to three others during "Operation Starlight" [sic]. One tank was damaged beyond repair and was destroyed by a demolition team. One other tank required evacuation, and the remainder could be fully restored. Tanks destroyed numerous enemy fortifications, captured twenty-nine weapons, and accounted for sixty-eight confirmed VC KIA (CC-3Tk, 8/65).

Editor Comment: The time and effort by the 3d Tank Battalion Headquarters S-3 Shop to write about Operation STARLITE (note spelling) and enter it into its command chronology is questionable. However, it is crystal clear that either the three tank companies in Chu Lai, from each of the two tank battalions and both reported by the 3d Tanks, that had some considerable skin in Operation STARLITE combat, did not report "up" as they should have and/or the reports were given only cursory interest when reaching 3d Tanks' operations. For example, the following Marines were awarded Purple Hearts on 20 August: Denton, C. L.; Hearn, J. E.; Myers, R. E.; Stanford, V. R.; Thompson, J. B.; Thompson, K. L.; Vickery, W. L.

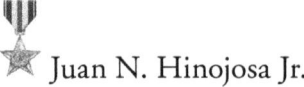

Juan N. Hinojosa Jr.

The President of the United States of America takes pleasure in presenting the Silver Star to Lance Corporal Juan N. Hinojosa, Jr. (MCSN: 2110369), United States Marine Corps, for conspicuous gallantry and intrepidity in action while serving with Company B, Third Tank Battalion, THIRD Marine Division (Rein.), FMF, in connection with combat operations against the enemy near Da Nang, Republic of Vietnam on 26 September 1965. While on an armored patrol in direct support of Company D, First Battalion, Ninth Marines, the tank on which Lance Corporal Hinojosa was riding took a direct hit from an insurgent communist (Viet Cong) guerrilla 57 millimeter anti-tank weapon which seriously wounded the driver and rendered him unconscious in addition to destroying tank inter-communications. Simultaneously, heavy small arms fire was brought to bear on the tank and the accompanying infantry, pinning them down. Realizing the driver's condition and knowing the danger to the immobile tank and the infantry, Lance Corporal Hinojosa unhesitatingly climbed outside of the tank from his loader's position, removed the driver and helped carry him to a safe position among the infantry. Still under heavy small arms fire, he courageously returned to the front of the tank and directed it with hand and arm signals, bringing it to a position where it could effectively fire on the enemy. His fearless aggressiveness and aplomb under fire was instrumental in helping the infantry gain the fire superiority which neutralized the hostile fire. By his daring actions and loyal devotion to duty and fellow man in the face of grave personal risk, Lance Corporal Hinojosa upheld the highest traditions of the Marine Corps and of the United States Naval Service.

Action Date: September 26, 1965
Service: Marine Corps
Rank: Lance Corporal
Company: Company B**Battalion:** 3d Tank Battalion
Division: 3d Marine Division (Rein.), FMF

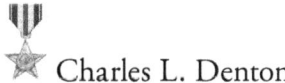

Charles L. Denton

The President of the United States of America takes pleasure in presenting the Silver Star to Corporal Charles L. Denton (MCSN: 2073195), United States Marine Corps, for conspicuous gallantry and intrepidity in action while serving with Company C, 3d Tank Battalion, THIRD Marine Division (Rein.), FMF, during Operation STARLITE in the Republic of Vietnam, on 18 August 1965. While engaged in an attack against determined, well entrenched insurgent communist (Viet Cong) forces, Corporal Denton's tank was hit by an enemy anti-tank rocket. As a result of the hit, Corporal Denton, his platoon commander and the tank's gunner were wounded and the tank was set afire. With complete disregard for his own wound and the intense enemy fire, he climbed out of the turret and assisted his seriously injured Platoon Commander to a position of relative safety. Realizing that the burning tank was a hazard to the wounded Marines in close proximity to it, Corporal Denton returned through the heavy enemy mortar and small arms fire to the tank. Boldly utilizing hand and arm signals while in a completely exposed area, he successfully guided the tank to a protected position where the fire could be extinguished. Once again returning to the open area, Corporal Denton assisted in evacuating the numerous wounded.

Having completed this task, he selflessly refused to be evacuated and returned to his tank. By his heroic actions and inspiring devotion to duty throughout, Corporal Denton was instrumental in saving the lives and reducing the suffering of several wounded Marines, and upheld the highest traditions of the United States Naval Service.

Action Date: 18-Aug-65
Service: Marine Corps
Rank: Corporal
Company: Company C
Battalion: 3d Tank Battalion
Division: 3d Marine Division (Rein.), FMF

Quote from *Medals, Marines and Vietnam* by William Myers (MM-WM)

Cpl Denton: In the sector controlled by Hotel Company 2/4 Jenkins and his men were again moving against the village of Nam Yen 3. They were aided in the assault by two M48A3 tanks from Company C Third Tank Battalion. Tonucci climbed onto the back of one of the vehicles and was trying to direct its fire onto a heavy .51 caliber enemy machine gun by using the tank-infantry phone. The tank was hit by a large antitank rocket and he was thrown into a rice paddy by the explosion.

> The driver of the tank Corporal Charles L Denton of Detroit Michigan, his platoon commander, and the tank's gunner were wounded by the same blast and the tank was set on fire. Denton disregarded his own wound and the intense fire and pulled his platoon commander from the tank and assisted him to a place of relative safety. He then returned to the burning tank and guided it away from the large group of wounded Marines and to a protected position where the fire was then extinguished. The tank could not be repaired so engineers destroyed it in place. Corporal Denton was awarded a silver star medal for his bravery.

DECLASSIFIED

COMFAST B
1st Tank Battalion, FMF
3d Marine Division (Rein), FMF
c/o FPO San Francisco, California 96601

AWG/jmr
3Sep65

From: Commanding Officer
To: Commanding Officer, 3d Tank Battalion, FMF

Subj: After Operation Report, Operation Starlite

Ref: (a) Map, VIETNAM, 1:50,000 AMS L7O1 Sheets 6737 II, 6737 III, and 6736 I

1. **Units.**
   CoB(-), 1stTkBn, FMF
   3dPlat, CoA, 3dTkBn, FMF
   Sec, 2dPlat, CoC, 3dTkBn, FMF

   a. CoB(-) consisted of one (1) Gun Tank, three (3) Flame Tanks, and a VTR, M51.

2. **Total Strength.**
   5 Officers USMC
   43 Enlisted USMC
   1 Enlisted USN

3. **Date.** 18 August 1965.

4. **Time.** Approximately 0900-2400.

5. **Place.** Vicinity of Hamlet Complex An Cuong (1) and (2).

6. **Casualties.** USMC 1 KIA 13 WIA.

7. **Organization.** The Tank elements of RLT-7 were organized into three separate increments. The Section of 2d Platoon, Company C was attached to BLT 3/4. The 3d Platoon of Company A was attached to BLT 3/3. Company B (-) was with Headquarters, RLT-7 in a General Support Role.

8. **Scheme of Maneuver.** Companies of BLT 3/4 and BLT 3/3 advanced abreast on the left of the regimental zone (see overlay). The boundary between Companies was the streamline. Due to trafficability the tanks of both units advanced generally along the same axis.

9. **Terrain.** The area was primarily rolling, wooded or brush covered interspersed with dry crop fields, wet rice paddies, and paddy dikes. The dry crop fields were set apart by hedgerows of small trees and brush ranging from six (6) to ten (10) feet high.

DECLASSIFIED

DECLASSIFIED

UNCLASSIFIED

10. Trafficability. With the exception of the wet rice paddies and the streamline areas, movement was fair to good. The dry crop fields were generally at different levels and movement through the hedgerows was slow until it was determined how much lower the next field was.

11. Observation. Direct line of sight rarely exceeded two (2) to three (3) hundred meters. Most often, either a tree line, a wooded knoll, or hedgerow restricted visibility to fifty (50) or one hundred (100) meters.

12. General. At approximate coordinates 700923 the advancing companies, with supporting tanks, came under enemy small arms, mortar, and anti-tank fire. Enemy positions were well concealed. The action continued between the first point of contact through the streamline and paddy area to approximate coordinates 702930. Near this point A54 was put out of action by Anti-Tank fire at close range. The Section of Company C Tanks assisted in evacuating the crew and returned to the defensive perimeter of Headquarters Company 2/4 at approximate coordinates 703916. Two Tanks of 3d Platoon, Company A, having lost contact with supported infantry, also returned to the area of the perimeter. A55 had previously had track problems and returned to the beach in company with A33.

During this time RLT-7 Headquarters was moving into a CP at approximate coordinates 703927. Situation reports from the companies in contact had not been received and neither their position nor situation was known.

At approximately 1100, India Company 3/5 requested a Flame Section at their position. India Company was in contact with the enemy, but reported the route between them and RLT-7 CP was clear. The Flame Section moved out in company with five (5) LVT's with resupply for India Company. The Flame Tanks had not been assigned as escorts for the resupply column, but since going to the same destination, moved out together.

The column passed the area in which Company E 2/4, with supporting tanks, were engaged by a matter of meters. The column proceeded to approximate coordinates 700931 and was hit by small arms, mortars, and Anti-Tank weapons. B55 was put out of action and the wounded crew evacuated. The LVT's, attempting to get cover, drove into the rice paddies and bogged down. B53 having expended the .30 Cal. ammunition, with the .50 Cal. out of action, and the driver wounded by blown out fragments of the driver's periscope, broke contact and returned to RLT-7 CP.

A company of BLT 3/5 was mounted on LVT's and with B51 moved out to the point of contact.

At approximate coordinates 703926 the gun tank stopped to fire .30 Cal. at enemy running across the front. While firing, B51 was hit by Anti-Tank fire from the direct front. The Anti-Tank fire continued, from a well concealed position, at and even the tank into the LVT column that had closed up behind. When the column dispersed the gun tank again came under fire from the right flank before pulling back into a covered position. 90mm fire returned was limited to canister since friendly positions were not known. When the Anti-Tank positions could not be determined by a foot reconnaissance contact was broken.

2

UNCLASSIFIED

A further attempt was made to relieve the column. At approximately 1600, Company A 3/7 with B51, A33, and the TPR moved north and then west to approximate coordinates 702932. Contact was made with the enemy. By the time the Company could advance it was too dark to determine the exact position of the column.

Radio contact was made between A33 and A32. It was reported that they had not had enemy contact for several hours. With the two elements separated by a rice paddy running five (5) to six (6) hundred meters long, contact was again broken at approximately 2340.

Early on the morning of 19 August 1965 the wounded were evacuated by helicopter. Two Companies of 3/7 with B51, A33, and the TPR moved into the area shortly thereafter. Evacuation of the dead and burial of enemy dead was accomplished. Recovery of vehicles was started. One LVT was recovered from the paddy and all tanks returned to MLT-7 CP. On 20 August 1965, recovery of the remaining vehicles was accomplished except for one LVT and A34. Both the LVT and tank had received multiple Anti-Tank and Mortar hits. Both had burned in excess of thirty-six (36) hours.

Upon personal inspection by the Company B Commander it was determined that A34 was not of sufficient salvage value to risk attempting to evacuate or cannibalize it. Both fuel tanks, when ruptured, had burned. The engine compartment was completely gutted. The right track was burned off. The right air cleaners, stowage boxes, and fenders were fused together from the heat. The left side had been hit, and though not burned, was of little value. In the turret the radio was melted in a mass. The deciding factor was the condition of the 90mm ammo. The bases of the shell cases had swelled and over the deck half dozen of the ready racks. It was assumed that any ammo stowed under the turret deck, nearer to the heat source, would be in even more dangerous condition.

As requested, engineers blew the same in place.

13. Remarks. The account as relates to the initial activities of both Company A and Company C was compiled from reports of participants. The account as relates to Company B results primarily from the participation of the Company B Commander.

LESSONS LEARNED

1. As a result of a very brief planning period and the attachment into three (3) tank elements there was a total lack of coordination except spontaneous assistance as the situation developed.

RECOMMENDATION: That in future operations of this nature Tank units be placed in direct support under central control and coordination of the Regimental Tank Officer.

2. That in the absence of knowledge of friendly troops' disposition the main gun of a tank cannot be fired without danger to friendly troops.

RECOMMENDATION: That subordinate unit situation reports be accurate and

frequent enough to determine their disposition in so far as the situation permits.

3. That in the type of terrain in which this action took place it is not only possible, but probable, that the enemy can position a strong force in between two advancing elements.

RECOMMENDATION: That units requesting support from the rear provide necessary guides and/or security into their position as the situation and terrain dictates.

4. That when an infantry unit with attached tanks continues to advance through terrain impassable to tanks the tank unit loses contact and becomes an easy target for Anti-Tank weapons.

RECOMMENDATION: That if a tank unit cannot continue the advance the supported unit must give specific instructions as to a rally point, another unit location or leave them adequate security to provide close in Anti-Tank defense.

5. That in an area where concealment favors the defender tanks are particularly vulnerable to close in Anti-Tank fire.

RECOMMENDATION: That in terrain encountered in this operation infantry precede tank elements until the absence of Anti-Tank positions is assured.

A. W. LAND

Operation STARLITE after-action report

And here is a verbatim reproduction of the above after-action report:

Company B
1st Tank Battalion, FMF
3d Marine Division (Fwd), FMF
c/o FPO San Francisco, California 96601

AWL/jar
3Sep65

From: Commanding Officer
To: Commanding Officer, 3d Tank Battalion, FMF

Subj: After Operation Report, Operation Starlite

Ref: (a) Map, VIETNAM, 1:50,000 AMS L701 Sheets 6757 II, 6757 III, and 6756 I

1. <u>Units.</u>   Co B (-), 1stTKBn, FMF
   3dPlat, Co A, 3dTkBn, FMF
   Sec. 2dPlat, CoC, 3dTkBn, FMF

   a. CoB (-) consisted of one (1) Gun Tank, three (3) Flame Tanks, and a VTR, M51

2. <u>Total Strength.</u>   3 Officers USMC
   43 Enlisted USMC
   1 Enlisted USN

3. <u>Date.</u> 18 August 1965.
4. <u>Time.</u> Approximately 0900–2400
5. <u>Place.</u> Vicinity of Hamlet Complex An Quang (1) and (2).
6. <u>Casualties.</u> USMC 1 KIA 13 WIA
7. <u>Organization.</u> The Tank elements of RLT-7 were organized into three separate increments. The Section of 2d Platoon, Company C was attached to BLT 2/4. The 3d Platoon of Company A was

attached to BLT 3/3. Company B(-) was with Headquarters. RLT-7 in a General Support Role.

8. <u>Scheme of Maneuver</u>. Companies of BLT 2/4 and BLT 3/3 advanced abreast on the left of the regimental zone (see overlay). The boundary between Companies was the streamline. Due to trafficability the tanks of both units advanced generally along the same axis.

9. <u>Terrain.</u> The area was primarily rolling, weeded or brush covered interspersed with dry crop fields, wet rice paddies, and paddy dikes. The dry crop fields were set apart by hedgerows of small trees and brush ranging from six (6) to ten (10) feet high.

10. <u>Trafficability</u>. With the exception of the wet rice paddies and the streamline areas, movement was fair to good. The dry crop fields were generally at different levels and movement through the hedgerows was slow until it was determined how much lower the next field was.

11. <u>Observations</u>. Direct line of sight rarely exceeded two (2) to three (3) hundred meters. Most often, either a tree line, a weeded knoll, or hedgerow restricted visibility to fifty (50) or one hundred (100) meters.

12. <u>General</u>. At approximate coordinates 700925 the advancing companies, with supporting tanks, came under enemy small arms, mortar, and anti-tank fire. Enemy positions were well concealed. The action continued between the first point of contact through the streamline and paddy area to approximate coordinates 702930. Near this point A34 was put out of action by Anti-Tank fire at close range. The Section of Company C Tanks assisted in evacuating the crew and returned to the defensive perimeter of Headquarters Company 2/4 at approximate coordinates 703926. Two tanks of 3d Platoon, Company A, having lost contact with supported infantry, also returned to the area of the perimeter. A35 had previously had track problems and returned to the beach in company with A33.

During this time RLT-7 Headquarters was moving into a CP at approximate coordinates 709927. Situation reports from the companies in contact had not been received and neither their position nor situation was known.

At approximately 1100, India Company 3/3 requested a Flame Section at their position. India Company was in contact with the enemy, but reported the route between them and RLT-7 CP was clear. The Flame Section moved out in company with five (5) LVT's with resupply for India Company. The Flame Tanks had not been assigned as escorts for the resupply column, but since going in the same destination, moved out together.

The column passed the area in which Company H 2/4, with supporting tanks, were engaged by a matter of meters. The column proceeded to approximate coordinates 700931 and was hit by small arms, mortars, and Anti-Tank weapons. B55 was put out of action and the wounded crew evacuated. Five LVT's, attempting to get cover, drove into the rice paddies and bogged down. B53 having expended the .30 Cal. ammunition, with the .50 Cal. out of action, and the driver wounded by blown out fragments of the driver's periscope, broke contact and returned to RLT-7 CP.

A Company of BLT 3/3 was mounted on LVT's and with B51 moved out to the point of contact.

At approximate coordinates 703928 the gun tank stopped to fire .30 Cal. at enemy running across the front. While firing, B51 was hit by Anti-Tank fire from the direct front. The Anti-Tank fire continued, from a well concealed position, at and over the tank into the LVT column that had closed up behind. When the column dispersed, the gun tank again came under fire from the right flank before pulling back into a covered position. 90mm fire returned was limited to canister since friendly positions were not known. When the Anti-Tank positions could not be determined by a foot reconnaissance, contact was broken.

A further attempt was made to relieve the column. At approximately 1600, Company L 3/7 with B51, A33 and the VTR moved north and then west to approximate coordinates 702932. Contact was made with the enemy. By the time the Company could advance it was too dark to determine the exact position of the column.

Radio contact was made between A33 and A32. It was reported that they had not had enemy contact for several hours. With the two elements separated by a rice paddy running five (5) to six (6) hundred meters long, contact was again broken at approximately 2340.

Early on the morning of 19 August 1965 the wounded were evacuated by helicopter. Two Companies of 3/7 with B51, A33 and the VTR moved into the area shortly thereafter. Evacuation of the dead and burial of enemy dead was accomplished. Recovery of vehicles was started. One LVT was recovered from the paddy and all tanks returned to RLT-7 CP. On 20 August 1965 recovery of the remaining vehicles was accomplished except for one LVT and A34. Both the LVT and tank had received multiple Anti-Tank and mortar bits. Both had burned in excess of thirty-six (36) hours.

Upon personal inspection by the Company B Commander it was determined that A34 was not of sufficient salvage value to risk attempting to evacuate or cannibalize it. Both fuel tanks, when ruptured, had burned. The engine compartment was completely gutted. The right track was burned off. The right air cleaners, storage boxes, and fenders were fused together from the heat. The left side had been hit, and though not burned, was of little value. In the turret the radio was melted in a mass. The deciding factor was the condition of the 90mm ammo. The bases of the shell cases had swollen out over the deck hold down of the ready racks. It was assumed that any ammo stowed under the turret deck, nearer to the heat source, would be in even more dangerous condition.

As requested, engineers blew the ammo in place.

13. <u>Remarks.</u> The account as relates to the initial activities of both Company A and Company C was compiled from reports of

participants. The account as relates to Company B results primarily from the participation of the Company B Commander.

LESSONS LEARNED

1. As a result of a very brief planning period and the attachment into three (3) tank elements there was a total lack of coordination except spontaneous assistance as the situation developed.

RECOMMENDATION: That in future operations of this nature Tank units be placed in direct support under central control and coordination of the Regimental Tank Officer.

2. That in the absence of knowledge of friendly troop's disposition the main gun of a tank cannot be fired without danger to friendly troops.

RECOMMENDATION: That subordinate unit situation reports be accurate and frequent enough to determine their disposition in so far as the situation permits.

3. That in the type of terrain in which this action took place it is not only possible, but probable, that the enemy can position a strong force in between two advancing elements.

RECOMMENDATION: That units requesting support from the rear provide necessary guides and/or security into their position as the situation and terrain dictates.

4. That when an infantry unit with attached tanks continues to advance through terrain impassable to tanks the tank unit loses contact and becomes an easy target for Anti-Tank weapons.

RECOMMENDATION: That if a tank unit cannot continue the advance the supported unit must give specific instructions as to a rally point, another unit location or leave them adequate security to provide close in Anti-Tank defense.

5. That in an area where concealment favors the defender, tanks are particularly vulnerable to close in Anti-Tank fire.

RECOMMENDATION: That in terrain encountered in this operation infantry precede tank elements until the absence of Anti-Tank positions is assured.

A. W. LAMB

Allan W. Lamb
Home of record: Ellensburg, Washington

Silver Star

The President of the United States of America takes pleasure in presenting the Silver Star to Captain Allan W. Lamb (MCSN: 0-65948), United States Marine Corps, for conspicuous gallantry and intrepidity in action while serving as Tank Officer attached to Regimental Landing Team SEVEN during Operation STARLIGHT in Quang Ngai Province, Republic of Vietnam, during the period 18 to 24 August 1965. When an armored column of five amphibious tractors and two tanks were pinned down as a result of heavy enemy fire, Captain Lamb courageously led a relief column of a mounted rifle company on five LVTP5's to aid the stricken column. Disregarding the extremely accurate enemy 57-mm. recoilless anti-tank fire which had already scored a hit on his tank from the direct front, Captain Lamb covered the dispersal of the LVTP5 column and escorted them to a covered position. Undaunted by the strength of the enemy fire power, he resolutely led the relief column back into the hazardous enemy fire. Through his insistent determination, after more than eight hours of continuous engagement with the enemy, the Viet Cong forces broke contact and the trapped Marines and equipment were rescued. By his daring actions and loyal devotion to duty in the face of great personal risk, Captain Lamb upheld the highest traditions of the Marine Corps and of the United States Naval Service.

Action Date: August 18–24, 1965
Service: Marine Corps
Rank: Captain
Regiment: Regimental Landing Team 7

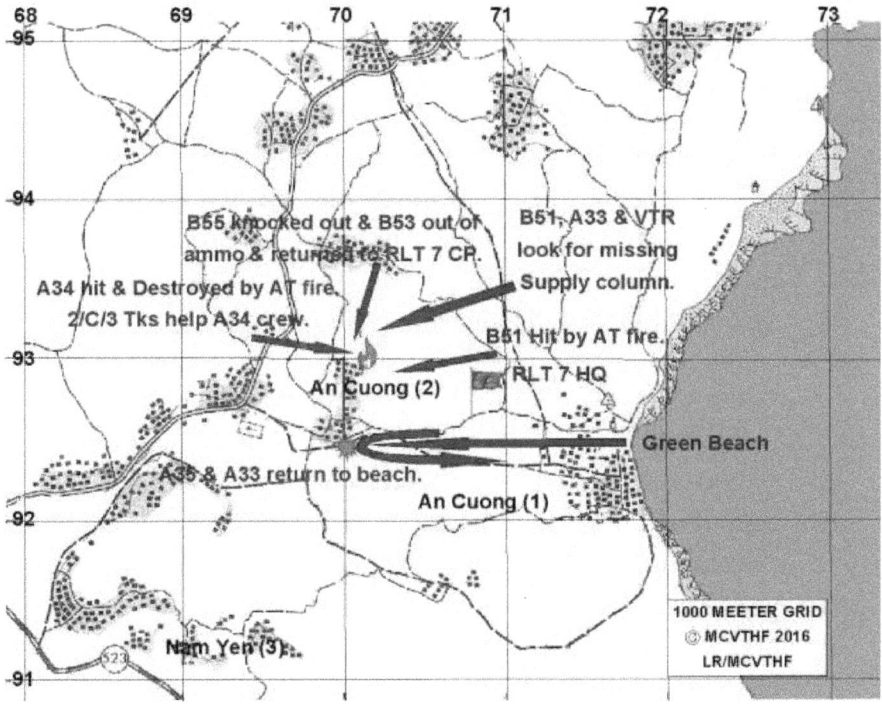

The "Missing Column" Map created by Lloyd Reynolds (VTHF)

For maps, after-action reports, and other statistics, go to the VTHF website at http://mcvthf.org/Maps/Op_Starlight_Aug65.htm and *U.S. Marines in Vietnam: The Landing and the Buildup* (GB-65).

Colonel D. P. Wyckoff, Service #013545, Oral History Interview (transcribed from CD-762)

There were some peculiarities in the STARLITE Operation. First, it was the initial Main Force unit of any substantial size that we had encountered. Second, the operation itself was a unilateral one, cooked up by the 3d Marine Amphibious Force. The only Vietnamese who was in on the details of the operation until the H hour was the (ARVN) commanding general of I Corps, General T. General Tie was alerted to the circumstances and our plans and agreed to keep everything quiet and to himself until the launch of the assault in the STARLITE area.

Another peculiarity we found, or made the assumption, was that this was a relative Viet Cong standard practice to back off into the small peninsulas along the coast as a secure area because the ARVN had not been closing into them in the peninsula. They were using the peninsula as a rest area—a rehabilitation and resupply area.

It was in this circumstance that we found the 1st Viet Cong Regiment. STARLITE was again peculiar because the entire operation from the decision to move in there until the H hour, it lasted less than 72 hours including the planning. The circumstances down in Chu Lai did permit this (longer planning period) because the landing of the 7th Marines into the Chu Lai area a matter of days before the STARLITE Operation commenced. The 4th Marines was the regular unit down there and preceded the 7th Marines in (to Chu Lai).

The 7th Marines (headquarters) had just landed (in Chu Lai) when STARLITE came up, and they were utilized with the ship they arrived on to conduct the amphibious assault with the helicopter assault from the Chu Lai Complex.

This Operation was an outstanding success as I recall 600 Viet Cong killed and 300 weapons Captured. (CD-762)

Capt. Allan W. Lamb, Ellensburg, Washington, a tank officer attached to the Regimental Landing Team 7, (C.O. "B" Company, 1st Tank battalion) led a relief column consisting of a mounted rifle company (India 3/3) on five LVTP5's to aid the stricken column. When his column was hit directly in its front by a well-placed round from enemy 57mm recoilless rifle, Lamb continued on undaunted and after more than eight hours of continuous action, the Viet Cong broke contact and the trapped Marines and their equipment were rescued." (Capt. Lamb was awarded a silver star medal for his bravery.)

Operation STARLITE, Aug. 18 1965

Milo W. Plank Jr.

Lance Corporal Milo Plank taken
by unremembered tank crewman (VTHF)

I was a tank driver on A-32, 3d Tank Battalion, 3d Marine Division and landed on shore near An Cuong (1). Our crew consisted of Corporal Bill Laidlaw as tank commander, Lance Corporal Court as gunner, Lance Corporal Milo Plank as driver, and Sergeant Dan McQueary as loader. Sergeant McQueary was our platoon chief mechanic and was conscripted as a loader because our regular gunner, Ken Zebal, was on R&R.

Left to right: Lance Corporal Milo Plank, Private First Class Cunningham, Lance Corporal Court (VTHF)

My tank platoon of five tanks was attached to I Company and H Company, 3d Battalion, 3d Marines, 3d Marine Division.

We boarded LSD-16 (USS *Cabildo*) on the morning of August 17 and headed east over the horizon. On the morning of August 18, at about 0500, we were offshore near An Cuong (1) and made an uneventful landing.

Operation STARLITE landing of tanks (Picture by Plank to VTHF)

3d Platoon, A Company, 3d Tanks was nominally under the AdCon of Captain Joe Sanders, C Company commander, but OpCon to Captain Lamb's composite company for STARLITE.

Captain Joe Sanders (Picture by Milo Plank to VTHF)

The platoon was split into two sections: a heavy section of three tanks, including A-31, A-32, and A-34. A light section consisting of two tanks, A-33 and A-35, was left at the (7th) Reg. CP and held in reserve.

My section headed inland then turned north on line with I and H Companies and met heavy resistance near An Cuong (2). On our right was a trench line running parallel to our line of advance. To our front was a trench line across our line of advance.

A-31 was in the center with A-32 on the right flank and A-34 on the left flank.

Squad leader Corporal Robert O'Malley (I/3/3) split up his squad and put a four-man fire team on our tank. When we approached the trench on our right flank, automatic weapons opened fire on the fire team, and they all became casualties. We moved to the edge of the trench to engage the enemy with our .30-caliber machine gun. There was thick brush growing up on both sides, and we couldn't see very far. The gunner traversed the gun to right and lowered it to fire. Then there was another burst of (enemy) automatic weapon fire; one round hit the blast deflector and ricocheted up the gun barrel and struck Sergeant Dan McQueary in the arm, and two more hit the searchlight. The corpsman got into the turret and gave him first aid. When he was ready to be removed, I opened the driver's hatch to get out and help get him down. Before I stuck my head out, I looked out of my periscopes to see if it was safe. In my right periscope, there was an opening in the brush, and I could see a VC in the trench about five feet away, pointing a rifle toward the top of the turret. As I raised up to fire my pistol, the VC swung his rifle toward me. In trying to keep my head out of his line of fire, I fired with my face too close to my .45, and the slide came back and hit me on the right eyebrow and I thought I was shot. I put my hand on the wound and didn't find a hole, so I knew it wasn't my time to go.

I could hear some movement in the trench, then more shooting. Several rounds hit my periscope and stopped the rounds from hitting me.

There were M-79 (40 mm grenade launcher) rounds being fired at the trench, but they would explode in the brush without being effective. I had a high angle of fire from my position and could fire down through the brush and might suppress their action. I quickly fired all my pistol ammunition and attempted to get topside, but I noticed a large number of VC coming down the trench, and I knew I couldn't get out. The VC would be on our flank in force and be able to fire into our troops at point-blank range. To my left, about ten feet away, Corporal O'Malley was dressing the wounds of one of his men and saw me shooting. He turned my way, and I shouted at him that the trench was full of Gooks and were coming this way. Without hesitating, he jumped into the trench, firing his weapon, and as he moved out of sight, I could hear the explosion of grenades and rifle fire. I never thought I would see him alive again.

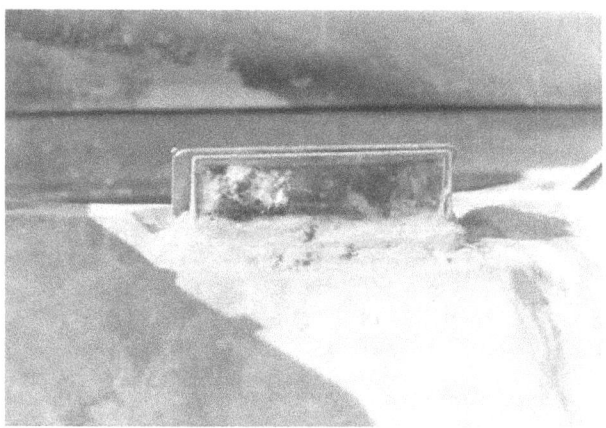

Operation STARLITE: "My periscope likely saved my life."

I wasn't going to get out of the tank without loading my weapon, so I told Lance Corporal Court to throw me some .45-caliber ammo. I got the ammo and reloaded my magazines just in time to see Corporal O'Malley climbing out of the trench, his arms loaded with weapons. We loaded them onto the tank, and we evacuated the casualties. Corporal O'Malley received the Medal of Honor.

Weapons captured by Corporal O'Malley
(Picture provided by Plank to VTHF)

We continued advancing to the front, when A-34 was hit on the left side of the turret by a 75 mm recoilless rifle round. The blast wounded everybody on board. Tank commander Sergeant Ed Sipel was hit in the leg and was evacuated. The rest of the crew suffered minor wounds and the tank was still operational, so A-34 continued with the mission.

A-31 was then hit on the right side of the turret ring. With the gun over the right side at 90 degrees, it could not be traversed. Platoon Commander, Second Lieutenant Ky Thompson, was hit in the heel of the foot and had to be evacuated. The rest of the crew took minor wounds, but the tank was still operational, and A-31 continued with the mission as planned.

A-32 moved into a position to knock out the gun. We fired two rounds of WP from the 90 mm (main gun) and destroyed it.

We shifted west and met heavy resistance near An Cuong (2). Our communications were damaged, and we could not get radio contact with A-34. So we moved in close to them to communicate by voice. A 75 mm hit A-34 on the left rear corner of engine compartment and penetrated the left fuel cell. The tank caught fire and had to be abandoned. My tank commander, Corporal Bill Laidlaw, was hit by shrapnel and was killed. Driver, Private First Class Cunningham, transferred from A-34 to A-32 and gunner, Lance Corporal J. B. Thompson, transferred to A-31. The dead and wounded were loaded onto the tanks, and we returned to the evacuation area.

Later that afternoon, we got orders to proceed to Hill 43 and help secure the hill. A-31 and A-32 moved west, but we were confused and disoriented and became lost. It was getting dark, and we knew we were in big trouble if we didn't make contact at Hill 43 soon. Our radios were damaged and periscopes shot up, and A-31 could not use its main gun or its .30 caliber. It became dark when we came upon some burning vehicles (Supply Column 21, five LVTs and two flame tanks). A-31 managed to make radio contact with Charlie 6 (Captain Joe Sanders, C Company commander, located in his CP at Chu Lai), explain the situation, and ask for further instructions. He told us to stay put and defend our position as best as we could. (Note: It appears that the CO of the Composite Company, Captain Lamb, was not on the same frequency as some of his tanks.)

(Note: The exact location of Captain Sanders was unknown at that time. In an exchange of written correspondence and personal telecons, Captain Sanders cannot recall the details of the operation. If he was at his C Company CP in Chu Lai, he was out of the fight itself. If he was at the 7th Marines CP, neither he nor Captain Lamb recalled him there. In any case, the dilemma in which Plank found himself should have been reported and made known to Captain Lamb, the officer in charge of the tanks. Creating a tank unit for the operation from three different parent units and not having a communications plan and protocol established is a testimonial to the rapidity that Operation STARLITE was implemented. Captain Sanders, though not putting Plank in contact with Captain Lamb nor apparently contacting Captain Lamb himself, nevertheless was correct in his instructions for Plank to stop and prepare for the defense of A-31 and A-32 as night fell.)

Supply Column 21 made the same mistake earlier that afternoon and became lost. They got into an ambush, faced extremely close fighting, suffered heavy casualties, and could not escape. Two LVTs tried to escape by crossing the rice paddy and got stuck. Even though they had radio contact, they could not describe their exact position, and it was unknown to the higher command.

It was dark, and the only light we had were the glowing hulks of the burning vehicles. It was quiet except for an LVT that sounded like a popcorn popper as the .30-caliber ammo, and the occasional "whomp" of a grenade, cooking off. We didn't know if anyone was still alive, but we had no other choice but to stay there and wait for daylight.

A shadow moved in front of my driver's periscope, and I thought we were in for an explosive charge on my driver's hatch. I was about to open the hatch and start shooting when I heard a voice ask if we had any more room in there. I could see that it was a Marine, and I said we would make room. He climbed on top of the tank and dropped down into the loader's hatch. He told us that he was an LVT crewman and had been wounded and playing dead. It was about 110 degrees out there, and he didn't have any water left. We had very little, but we shared what we had.

It was about 0100, and we became extremely dehydrated. If we didn't get some water, we wouldn't last till morning. We had two five-gallon cans of water strapped to the side of the turret next to the loaders hatch, so I decided to go out and get one. The flickering light of the burning vehicles was not enough to illuminate me, so I proceeded to go outside and unstrap them. They were both shot full of holes, but one had about a gallon left in it, so I handed it down the loader's hatch. That small amount didn't last very long, so I decided to find another can. The LVT crewman said that the LVT directly across the clearing from us with the ramp down had a full store of water. If I was going to get some water, I'd better do it before daylight, or I would be an easy shot for a sniper. At about 0400, I quietly got out of my tank and walked the twenty-five yards across the opening, and stepping over some bodies, I made it inside the LVT. I was going to carry two cans, but I decided on only one because I wanted to carry my .45 in my free hand.

As daylight approached, all was quiet, and people began to stir. The remaining Marines came out of their vehicles and set up a defensive perimeter.

On August 19th, at about 1000, the rescue force arrived.

We stayed at the regimental command post till August 25th, then we boarded LCUs and shipped out, back to Chu Lai.

Operation STARLITE: Tanks defending medevac area
(Picture provided by Plank to VTHF)

Operation STARLITE: Reinforcements arrive
(Picture provided by Plank to VTHF)

Lance Corporal Court
(Picture provided by Plank to VTHF)

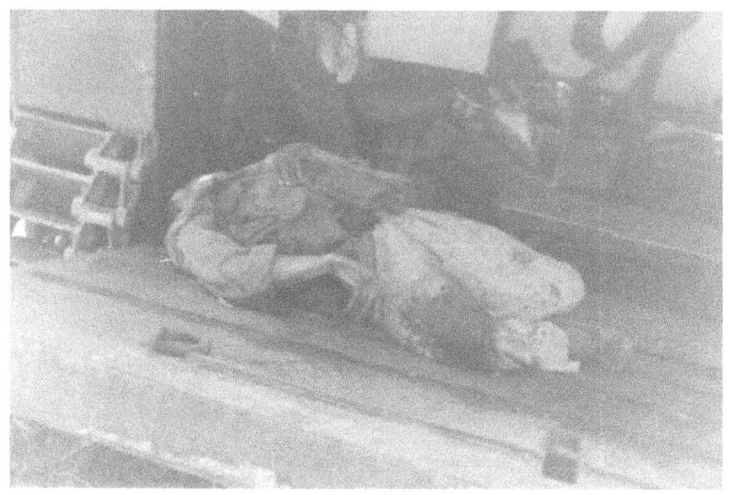

Operation STARLITE: This attacker was shot off the top of this LVT. (Picture provided by Plank to VTHF)

Flame tank with bullet and shrapnel damage to left rear of tank (Picture provided by Plank to VTHF Archives)

Supply Column 21 ambush site
(Picture provided by Plank to VTHF Archives)

Captured weapons. Notice 75 mm recoilless cases.
(Picture provided by Plank to VTHF Archives)

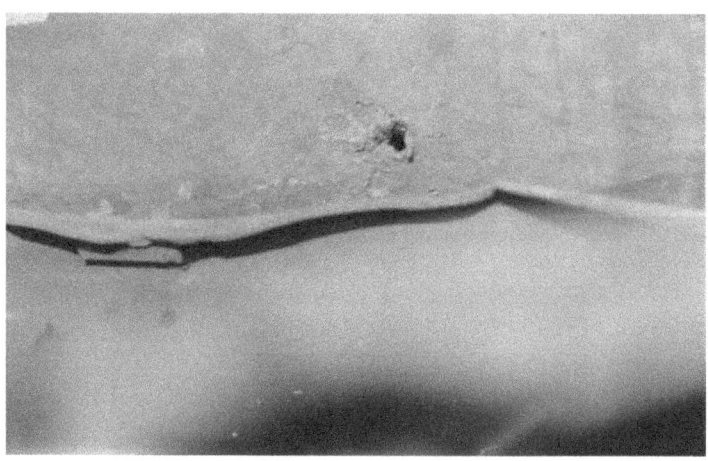

Hit on A-34 went through left side
of turret and blew the fuse out of a WP round.
(Picture provided by Plank to VTHF Archives)

Column Lumbers to Death in Rice Paddy

Attack ... **Viet Nam sweltering** midday sun, U.S. Marine Supply Column 21 lumbered to its death Wednesday in the morass of a Vietnamese rice paddy.

By the end of the day the armored column, 287 tons of steel, was no more. Some of the 30 Leathernecks survived the withering Viet Cong attack but none escaped unmarked.

In the battlefield lay the ruins of the column — five steel-clad amtraks — 35-ton amphibious vehicles — and two M48 tanks. They were part of the tail to the battle of Van Tuong peninsula, where the Marines engaged in the heaviest U.S. fighting of the Vietnamese war.

'EASY RUN'

The "supply pokes" of Column 21 had figured on an easy run. Their mission was to get to the beachhead, resupply a line company, and return to the 7th Fleet mother ship anchored a mile off shore.

Once out of the water, the huge amtraks flopped from one rice paddy to another, unwieldy behemoths unable to find their way. Again and again, the Marines called out to combat men in the field but failed to locate the line company they had been designated to resupply.

At 11 a.m., the column found itself deep in enemy territory.

Black-clad Viet Cong suddenly rose like taunts out of hedge rows and swamps. Explosions erupted all around the column, recalled a survivor, Lance Cpl. Richard Pass of Homewood, Ill. An armor-piercing shell hit the leading tank, wounding two men inside.

THREE BOG DOWN

The amtraks tried to maneuver into good firing positions, but three of the five bogged down in a deep paddy. The supply men had not been trained for the strange, terraced terrain.

A Viet Cong knocked out one of the remaining amtraks by dropping a grenade in the hatch as it edged toward the tanks for protection. The blast killed two Americans and wounded others inside the vehicle.

Communist shells punched three holes in one tank. Bullets riddled the wounded driver after he squeezed himself through the 18-inch escape hatch under the tank.

Mortars bounced off the American vehicles, and Pass watched as Viet Cong with ammunition bandoliers, black pajamas uniforms and camouflaged steel helmets attacked an amtrak 50 yards to his left.

DRIVERS KILLED

One of the two drivers was killed as he leaped out of the beleaguered vehicle. The other was cut down by bullets in the paddy field. He still held his Marine knife when his body was recovered later.

It was a little after noon now. With the sun beating down on the bloodied rice paddy, the Viet Cong fire from positions on top of the vehicles. "I couldn't maneuver up there," explained Pfc. James Roeff of Seattle, Wash., who escaped with a slight wound.

The interior compartments of the metal monsters became cauldrons. Staff Sgt. Jack Merino of Lomita, Calif., said the men splashed water on each other from resupply cans to prevent heat exhaustion.

Suddenly, a young corporal shouted: "Okay, men, we're Marines! Let's do the job!"

CORPORAL SHOT

He started to climb out but a bullet hit him between the eyes before he could raise his rifle.

In midafternoon, Merino heard a frantic whisper from outside, "Amtrak, amtrak." It was a wounded tank crewman. Merino and others pulled him inside.

The Marines held off the enemy into the late afternoon, when air strikes began to ease the pressure on the remnants of Column 21. They stayed at their positions through the night.

A solitary helicopter landed at daybreak, mistaking the body littered field for a landing zone. The Americans rushed from their vehicles to the chopper, carrying the wounded.

The helicopter evacuated the seriously injured in two flights. The dead were left behind.

Ground forces arrived to relieve the other survivors.

The men of Column 21 wanted to cart off their vehicles, but an officer told them:

"Take your personal belongings out of the vehicles. We are going to blow them up."

The relief forces counted 13 Viet Cong bodies.

With the wreckage of the amtraks in the mud, Cpl. Earle Eberly of Sycamore, Ill., summed up the feelings of the survivors:

"We don't like being here and killing people and being killed. But this is a job we've been told to do, we have to do and we're going to do."

Searchlight (Picture provided by Plank to VTHF Archives)

From the perspective of the Grunts' action in Operation STARLITE, see First Lieutenant D. M. Ryan's interview on CD-128.

First Lieutenant Richard "Dick" M. Purnell, #086430, USMC, Company Executive Officer, India Company, 3d Battalion, 3d Marines (I/3/3), tells of his tank and Ontos-supported fight with the 1ˢᵗ Viet Cong Regiment at the height of Operation STARLITE (CD-66).

UNITED STATES MARINE CORPS HISTORY DIVISION
ORAL HISTORY INTERVIEW

Interviewee's Name: 1ˢᵗ Lt. Richard "Dick" M. Purnell #086430, USMC
Date of Interview: 10 February 1966
Conflict: Vietnam War
Military Unit: Company I, 3d Battalion, 3d Marines (I/3/3)
Duties: Company Executive Officer
Interviewer: Lt. Col. D. J. Hunter, USMC
Location of Interview: Marine Corps Base, Camp Pendleton
Length: 35:35
Individual Completing Summary: Raymond A. Stewart, Lieutenant Colonel, USMC (Ret.)
Recording Format and Number of Recordings: Originally audio tape re-recorded on CD #66
Documents Submitted with Interview: N/A
Related Material: N/A
Classification: Unclass./FOUO
Transcription Priority: Unk.

Abstract: Lieutenant Purnell's participation in Operations STARLITE, Republic of South Vietnam, 18 August 1965, while serving as XO I/3/3

Key Words: Operation STARLITE, Chu Lai, amtracs, LSD, blocking force, An Cuong (2), tanks

Interview Log: Note to researchers: Except for words in quotes, this is *not* a verbatim account of the interview. The recording itself should be used to verify this summary.

00:00–11:40: November of 1964, Dick went overseas with 1/1, which became 2/3 upon arriving at Okinawa, Japan. He was a company XO until 18 July 1965, when he left 2/3 for Chu Lai as XO I/3/3 on Chu Lai perimeter, then Operation STARLITE. Returned to CONUS 22 November 65.

Now to Operation STARLITE: From manning Chu Lai Airfield perimeter next to 4th Marines. During AM of 17 August got word to stage and move aboard ship in approximately three hours. Gathered all the units for pickup by amtracs. Within four hours moved to amphibious shipping. Went ashore in amtracs on STARLITE on left flank of battalion CP with two other companies up the beach to the right. Departed amtracs at shoreline. One large explosion. Checked out what was command-detonated mine. One company of 3/3 came overland to set up blocking position on AM of 18 August. I/3/3 was to advance inland 2,000 m and sweep to north and flank 2/4. Got to streambed and started receiving enemy small-arms fire. An Cuong (2) on the left and out of I/3/3's area of responsibility. I Company CO, Captain Bruce D. Webb, got permission to engage village. Friendly WIAs evacuated. *Was joined by a platoon of tanks to which an infantry squad was assigned to protect and pushed on against fairly heavy fire. Tank/infantry assault on An Cuong (2) ringed by an old trench 6 feet wide by 10 feet deep. 2/4 in sight in firefight. Tanks with infantry went down trench line and took casualties.* VC observed running away. After fifteen to twenty minutes, helo landed/took off with wounded company commander, Captain Webb. Dick is now in command. All thought An Cuong (2)—quite heavily fortified—was neutralized but found out later, far from it.

11:41–23:10: Dick returned to company CP. Found also that two FOs, company gunny, et al. killed or wounded and medevaced. K/3/3 and L/3/3 had swung to the right and pushed to the north with minimal enemy contact. Ordered to proceed to north, guiding on the streambed and join battalion CP. Huey helo shot down in area. *Ordered to leave tanks and two squads with downed chopper and move out.* Security detail ordered to follow as soon as helo got out. Then ordered to move entire company back toward beach then head south. *This is due to a supply column of LVTs and tanks in trouble and needing help. Proceeded to beach and 7th Marines supply point to pick up 4-LVTs and 2-tanks and 2-ONTOS comprising a relief column to go find the lost supply train around An Cuong (2).* Major Comer, 3/3 XO, and his group went along. Passing hill on the left while on the trail, tank was hit by an RPG and stopped. Entire relief column stopped and started taking enemy small arms. Infantry dismounted LVTs, and the entire column came under increased small arms and deadly accurate mortar. LVT hit from An Cuong (2). Moderate casualties. Helos called to evac. Major Comer and command group remained with casualties. Other two platoons moved down slope to village. Heavy enemy fire from previously cleared An Cuong (2). An H/2/4 platoon moved through. *From the north two squads with tanks rejoined I Company.* Had sustained heavy casualties. Continued to look for lost supply train. Called in air on An Cuong (2). Two 250-pound bombs quieted enemy fire. Went through village with light contact. Hedgerows were 10 feet and came as a surprise. Another hour-long firefight. After 700–800 meters past village and now pitch black dark; 2,000–2,500 meters from 3/3 Battalion CP—4th Marines also some distance. Told to return to LZ. Without finding lost supply train, commenced return to LZ.

23:11–35:35: Started withdrawal but 4.2 ("four deuce") mortar illumination provided to help the lost supply train hampered the movement, i.e., every time there was a flare, troops had to hit the deck. Coming up on An Cuong (2) from trench at 25–30 meters, incoming small arms and taking casualties. Continued SE direction. Heavy fire taken to rear of column. Point killed one enemy. Three friendly casualties (one KIA, two WIA). Brought in helo for evac using only a shielded flashlight. Helos were outstanding in every respect. First Platoon commander was Staff Sergeant William Wright, 3d Platoon commander was Second Lieutenant Major T. Benton, 2d Platoon commander was Second Lieutenant Jim Kooney—at LZ. Moving along trench line back to rear, killing six to seven VC. Could hear VC shouting all around them. Next day, 7th Marines and ARVN found more than 150 enemy KIA in the area. Took almost all night to get out with all the various activity. No ammo or water resupply—fought on two canteens of water. VC were loaded down with ammo. Packs full of M-79 ammo. Weapons in great shape—BARs, M-79s, M-14s. Well camouflaged. VC were quite aggressive but invariably broke and ran when fired and maneuvered upon. VC comm wire in every trench. Silver Star awarded to Lieutenant Purnell.

END OF INTERVIEW

>Robert Fishel Cochran Jr.
>Date of birth: January 4, 1942
>Date of death: August 18, 1965
>Home of record: Poplarville, Mississippi
>Status: KIA

Navy Cross

The President of the United States of America takes pride in presenting the Navy Cross (Posthumously) to Second Lieutenant Robert Fishel Cochran, Jr. (MCSN: 0-89648), United States Marine Corps Reserve, for extraordinary heroism in Company A, First Amphibian Tractor Battalion, THIRD Marine Division (Reinforced), Fleet Marine Force, during Operation STARLITE near Chu Lai, Vietnam, on the morning of 18 August 1965. While leading an amphibian tractor supply column to the front lines, he had momentarily stopped the column in order to check his positions, when it came under intense enemy mortar, recoilless rifle and small-arms fire. Although he was exposed to enemy fire, he calmly and unhesitatingly directed his vehicles into defensive positions. The amphibian tractor on which Lieutenant Cochran was located was hit by recoilless rifle fire. Disregarding his own safety he ordered his crew to evacuate the vehicle and alertly pointed out a good position for them to occupy. Despite the imminent danger of the amphibian tractor exploding and the attempts of the enemy to enter the vehicle, he, in order to deprive the enemy of this source of supply, removed the machine gun ammunition before he left the tractor. With full knowledge of the situation and complete disregard for his own personal safety, Lieutenant Cochran moved through intense enemy cross fire to his disabled vehicle, directing the wounded and dazed personnel to the safety of two amphibian tractors which had gained hull defilade positions behind a rice paddy bank. When he was assured that all of his men were safe, he determined which vehicle would afford the best observation of the battle area. As he moved toward this tractor he was severely wounded. Knowing that to ask his men to open the main ramp of the tractor would endanger their lives, he unselfishly chose to mount the vehicle through the top hatch. As a result of his heroic action he succumbed on the top of the amphibian tractor. His personal bravery, and fearless devotion to duty reflected great credit upon himself and the United States Marine Corps and were in keeping with the highest traditions of the United States Naval Service. He gallantly gave his life for his country.

General Orders: Authority: Navy Department Board of Decorations and Medals
Action Date: August 18, 1965
Service: Marine Corps

Rank: Second Lieutenant
Company: Company A
Battalion: 1st Amphibian Tractor Battalion
Division: 3d Marine Division (Rein.) FMF

Bobby Cochrane was an "1801"—that is, his military occupational specialty (MOS) was a "Tracked Vehicle Officer, Basic." As with most of the student officers attending the Tracked Vehicle Officers School at Camp Delmar, Camp Pendleton, California, in early 1965, Bobby wanted to become an 1802 tank officer. However, that was not assured, since amtracs drew its officers from this same pool of 1801 students. These officers would work toward and eventually attain an 1803 MOS. Bobby, though somewhat disappointed, was assigned to the 1st Amphibian Tractor Battalion upon his completion of TVOS and eventually deployed to Vietnam with it.

To that time, at track school, Bobby was one of the hardest-working, most dedicated officers I'd known. He excelled at every level of training—classroom, in the field, driving tanks (and amtracs). Besides being fearless, he was a genuine gentleman.

We went our separate ways after graduating track school. I was assigned to 1st Tanks and started on my career as a Tanker 1802. Long story short, as was with many of us from that class, we served in Vietnam. Bobby and I, though I didn't realize it at the time, participated in Operation STARLITE. It was only shortly later that I "heard" that Bobby was killed. And even later—years later, while I was researching for this book—that I discovered that Bobby was the recipient of the Navy Cross medal in recognition of his unbridled bravery during Operation STARLITE.

He died doing what he was destined to be: a brave man who will live in the memory of all those who knew him as a Marine's Marine.

Ray Stewart

Binh Son

by Carl Lemon

I have never been known for my brilliance, but this stunt was probably one of the dumbest decisions I ever made while serving in Vietnam. The SNCOs and junior officers of Bravo Company, 1st Tank Battalion can probably relate to this story.

About two or three weeks after Operation STARLITE, our company commander, Captain Al Lamb, had just returned from his daily staff meeting at the 7th Marine Regimental Headquarters. He called me into his office (tent) to inform me of an armed convoy traveling to Binh Son and that I was to accompany it on this trip. Binh Son was about 10 mile south of Chu Lai and was occupied by a South Vietnamese battalion of Marines with a small cadre of U.S. Marines acting as advisors.

I jumped in my jeep, armed only with my .45-caliber pistol, no driver, and no shotgun rider, and headed for the convoy launch point: a Marine roadblock on Highway 1, about a mile south of Chu Lai.

By the time I got there, the convoy was long gone and nowhere in sight. The Marines at the gate told me they had left about five minutes before and I could probably catch up with them. Now I am in a real quandary. Do I try and catch up with the convoy, or do I dare go back and explain to Captain Lamb why I missed the convoy, in the first place? I had (and have) absolutely the utmost respect for Captain Lamb; he was one of the best officers I ever served under during my time in the Marine Corps, but he was very demanding of his junior officers and had little room for screw-ups. Captain Lamb could dress you down among the best of them, and believe you me, I had been dressed down on more than one occasion and really wasn't looking forward to another one. As you can probably guess, I made one of the dumbest decisions I have ever made in my entire life, because my life was definitely on the line. I proceeded to take off after the convoy as fast as my little jeep would take me, which wasn't very fast at all. If I remember correctly, the jeeps were governed to max out at 40 mph, and this particular time felt more like 5 mph. I swear, I think a horse could have made better time.

On the way south, I drove through several small villages known to harbor the enemy, and little did I know at the time, but this entire territory belonged to several NVA battalions. A few weeks later, we would conduct Operation BLACK FERRET along this same route.

I never did catch up with the convoy or even come close to smelling their dust; in fact, by the time I arrived, they had been there a good 30 minutes or so. When I came driving up, you wouldn't believe the astonished look on everyone's faces. Never having been to the ROK compound before, I wasn't sure what to expect, or if I would even find the place. Trust me when I tell you, I certainly wasn't on a sightseeing excursion or a joy ride.

All I could think of was, "What in the hell am I doing here with nothing but my .45 to defend myself?" After, my right leg was in enormous pain from pressing on the accelerator so hard, and my knuckles were white from gripping the steering wheel. That was without a doubt the longest 10-mile drive I have ever made in my life.

It would be sometime later when I would learn just how dangerous this area really was, and to this very day, I still get cold chills when I think about it. I never did tell Captain Lamb what I had done. It's stunts like the one I pulled that cause MIAs. No excuses, just plain stupidity. All I can say is, Lady Luck must have been with me on that day.

The Marines we served with at that time can probably relate to my story and understand why I chose to do what I did. I truly risked my life foolishly just to avoid an ass eating. An ass chewing for missing the convoy would have been nothing compared to what I faced if Captain Lamb ever found out what I had done.

Carl obviously would match his short judgment with "long" bravery as a recipient of the Navy Commendation Medal with "V" on Operation PIRANHA on the Batangan Peninsula against the vaunted 1st VC Regiment.

20 August 1965: A twenty-six man patrol was conducted from 200001H to 200600H in the area 2,000 meters west of the battalion command post. No enemy encountered.

25 August 1965: The Vietnamese Regional Force Training Center (HOA CAM) immediately adjacent to the tank battalion's western perimeter was attacked by a Viet Cong force of unknown strength. No casualties occurred in the battalion area. The training center sustained two KIA and thirty-seven WIA.

27 August 1965: Company B, while on a search-and-destroy operation south of Marble Mountain, received substantial small-arms and automatic weapons fire. One Marine was WIA. Tank fire was returned on the sources of enemy fire, destroying the emplacement. Due to flooded area between tanks and target, it was not possible to confirm enemy casualties.

29 August 1965: Company B conducted a patrol south of Marble Mountain with A Company, 1st Battalion, 9th Marines. Significant amounts of enemy small-arms and automatic weapons fire were received by the tanks. Fire was returned, resulting in three confirmed Viet Cong KIA. Additional casualties could not be confirmed since it was not possible to maneuver between the tanks and the main target area.

Following closely on the heralded success of the amphibious and subsequent ground operations against the 1st Viet Cong Regiment in Operation STARLITE was the somewhat less so with Operation PIRANHA (7–10 September 65).

Colonel Wykoff CD Interview

This (Operation STARLITE) was followed then by another attempt to do a similar thing south of the STARLITE area. What is now called Operation PIRANHA. Here again, it was a peninsula that jutted out into the sea area. Photographs indicated a very complex system of fortifications and storage caves in the PIRANHA area. However, in the interim between STARLITE and PIRANHA, instructions had been received from MACV to no longer conduct unilateral operations because apparently there had been quite a stir in Saigon from the Vietnamese side that they had not been in on this STARLITE Operation with the exception of General T being informed.

As a result, MACV indicated to us, to the III MAF, that subsequent operations would include planning with the Vietnam forces and participation of the Vietnamese forces wherever possible in operations. We recognize that this is a disadvantage for a number of reasons. I personally was aware of the attitude of several senior commanders, General T and the general whose name I can't remember now who had the first ARVN division in Hue. I talked to this gentleman in Hue, prior to the STARLITE Operation. He had run a very successful show in the Hue area, keeping the VC under control, and the way he was doing it was on the basis that the VC had infiltrated his personnel staff, his general staff, and he made the basic assumption in all his operations that if he told something to his staff, the VC knew about it.

As a result, he would plan an operation and objective that was not the real one, and all the plans would be developed based on a hypothetical objective, and once all the organization had been launched on this operation, he would personally change the direction of the attack and change the objective, utilizing the same forces used in the hypothetical objective; and this, he contended, was the means in which he kept the Viet Cong off-balanced and was successful in the Way area.

07:31–08:25

However, we knew that when PIRANHA kicked off with the 2d ARVN division being involved in the operation, with some Vietnamese Marines, that there was a strong possibility that the operation could be compromised. This proved to be true, and we did go into the PIRANHA area and found all the installations, but the personnel had largely fled and had largely been able to evacuate their supplies.

There was some product of this in the form of a medical cave that was entered. Some of the medical cases had not been evacuated. The PIRANHA area looked like it had been used as a rest and rehabilitation area. It was a rather pleasant little peninsula down there.

However, there was not much pay dirt in connection to this operation.

Let it be known, however, that the Marines suffered but one KIA and a dozen WIAs for an enemy KIA confirmed count of 168 and an innumerable amount, possibly in the hundreds, died in sealed in caves.

Company B, 1st Tank Battalion, attached to the Seventh Marines at Chu Lai participated in Operation Piranha from 5-11 September. Landing over Green Beach on the morning of 7 September the Company moved along the beach to the south to a point along a high escarpment at (BS 774858). Here the steep terrain prevented further inland movement. The Company remained in this location for the remainder of the operation providing direct fire support to the maneuvering infantry elements. Since opposition was scattered and weak the tanks were not required to fire and the company returned to Chu Lai on the morning of 11 September. For the remainder of the month the company provided two tanks at the southern roadblock on highway 1 and retained the other tanks in the company as a reaction force.

This is taken from the September CC of 3d Tanks (CC-1stTk, 6/65).

Loading aboard ship for Operation PIRANHA, Chu Lai 1965

Tom Tuck's Vietnam Tour of Duty with Ontos

by Tom Tuck

When RLT-7 mounted out from Pendleton in the summer of 1965, Charlie Company (1st Antitanks) mounted out with them. First Platoon was attached to 1/7, 2d Platoon was with 2/7, and 3d Platoon was with 3/7. When I staged at Pendleton in the spring of '65, I was in the replacement draft going to 3d Antitank Battalion on Okinawa. By the time we all got together, they carried us down to Broadway Pier, San Diego, and put us aboard the USS *General William Mitchell* on 1 July 65.

We went the "long way": Hawaii, Japan, Taiwan, then to Naha, Okinawa, on the 18th of July. My orders changed from 3d Antitank Battalion, 3d Marine Division to C Company, 1st Antitank Battalion, 1st Marine Division, where they were. It so happened that 1st Platoon and Headquarters Platoon C Company, 1st Antitanks were at Camp Hansen. I joined them there, and on 9 August 65, we boarded (LSD-3) USS *Carter Hall*, and on 15 August 65, we landed at Chu Lai, RVN. Operation STARLITE was about to begin. I was put on a work party and went aboard either (LSD-3) *Carter Hall* or (LSD-31) *Point Defiance*. I can only remember the "3". We went around the peninsula and ballasted down to receive amtracs intended to resupply the operation. (I don't remember if we'd found out the name of the operation yet. I guess it wasn't considered important that we knew that!) We loaded water, ammo, C-rats, and such till it was over. We even had a couple of helos land on the flight deck that we loaded with supplies.

After it (Operation STARLITE) was over, they brought back some of the shot-up stuff on LCUs: tanks, amtracs, and wheeled vehicles. A real eye-opener for what was to come. I happened to be the extra 2143 Ontos mechanic, and I mostly stayed with Headquarters Platoon. Most of my work on the Ontos was in the company area in the Ontos park and motor pool at Chu Lai. I went up to Da Nang a couple of times on parts and resupply runs. We flew up and came back on LSTs usually.

On Operation PIRANHA, I landed with the fourth wave, and we stayed around the 1/7 Headquarters area as part of their security. I woke up at daylight on 8 September '65, having to go pee in the worst way. I crawled out from under the mighty mite (small "jeep") I was sleeping under and saw a palmlike tree to lean on while relieving myself, and when done, I stepped around the tree. The ground gave way, and I almost went into a spider hole. All my buddies had a good laugh, but we sure wanted to know what was down in there. It was very sandy ground around there. It was a small hole probably for only one man. We found nothing down there except a woven mat.

Later on that day and the next, the Grunts brought in the bodies of several VC and lined them up on the ground. A couple of women. They said they were maybe VC nurses that were looking after VC wounded from Operation STARLITE.

We did Operation BLACK FERRET, BLUE MARLIN, and HARVEST MOON and went on convoy escort duty up and down Highway 1 several times.

When all of 1st Antitank Battalion got in-country in March of '66, I was transferred into H&S Company, 1st Antitank Battalion, along with Captain Snyder and a couple of others. The rest of my time there, I worked my ass off for Gunner A-Z and Staff Sergeant Blackwell, trying to get the Ontos back up in some kind of fighting readiness. The 2111 armorers were busy also. I did get out a time or two and took my turn on guard duty, but mostly doing lots of long hours of mechanic work, pack pulling, road wheels, and final drive work.

The last month or so there, someone came up with an old soda pop cooler. The ones that had water in them and the soda pops were cooled by setting them in the cool water. I have to apologize to whoever officer that had put a magnum of champagne in the cooler, 'cause around one o'clock, me and a couple of buddies swiped it and sat around the maintenance area and drank it all up. Later that day, I boarded a C-117 for Da Nang and then a commercial 707 to Kadena, Okinawa. Then, on the 14th of July, I got on a Marine C-130. We stopped at Guam for refuel and then to Wake Island so the pilot could sleep. On to Hickam, AFB at Pearl and we mustered. The pilot said that his aircraft would leave there for the mainland at 0800 the morning of 16 July. If we wanted to go home, be there. We all were.

Tom Tuck

(Tom's original article was edited slightly for publication.)

Sep 7, 1965

Marines Launch Operation PIRANHA

U.S. Marines and South Vietnamese forces launch Operation Pirahna [*sic*] on the Batangan Peninsula, 23 miles south of the Marine base at Chu Lai. This was a follow-up to Operation Starlight [*sic*], which had been conducted in August. During the course of the operation, the Allied forces stormed a stronghold of the Viet Cong 1st Regiment, claiming 200 enemy dead after intense fighting. (Taken from the "History" website)

Since early 1963, the Viet Cong and impressed locals in support of the Communists had labored to convert the Batangan Peninsula into a fortified stronghold with a system of tunnels that connected underground billeting areas, hospitals, and equipment repair capability. Following the conclusion of Operation Starlite, on 24 August 1965, Marine intelligence concluded that what was left of the 1st VC Regiment had withdrawn into the Peninsula. Reconnaissance photos of the Peninsula showed a view of older field fortifications pointing inland with the open end to the sea and a new second view further inland under construction. Existing and under construction defensive works were facing inland.

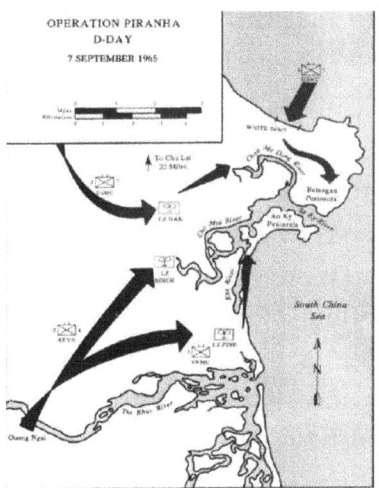

Operation PIRANHA: D-day 7 September (GB-65)

"Having eliminated the threat posed to the Chu Lai base by the 1st VC Regiment, intelligence sources indicated that its remnants had withdrawn to the Batangan Peninsula. Walt considered the time opportune to complete the destruction of the enemy Regiment" (GB-65).

"Col. Peatross once again was to be the commander of the landing force, two Marine Battalions, LtCol. Kelley's 1st Battalion, 7th Marines and Muir's 3d Battalion, 3d Marines would be embarked on ships, Muir's Marines to remain at sea as a floating reserve. LtCol. Bodley's 3d

Battalion, 7th Marines would conduct a heliborne assault of the objective area. Participating Vietnamese battalions, the 2d Battalion, 4th ARVN Regiment, and the 3d Vietnamese Marine Battalion would be moved by helicopter south of Bodley's position" (GB-65).

The Marines, flushed with the earlier victory over the Viet Cong enemy, decided to launch Operation PIRANHA against the Batangan Peninsula, destroying the remnants of the reported 1st VC Regiment. The Marine Corps, being criticized by both the Vietnamese district officials and ARVN senior officers but also by the COMUSMACV and his American, primarily Army, staff located in Saigon, decided to include the ARVN in the initial planning and to use ARVN troops assigned specific objectives.

The plan was for a Marine Battalion Landing Team (BLT), 1st Battalion, 7th Marines (1/7), to make an amphibious landing across White Beach north of the Peninsula and attack to their south, while the 3d Battalion, 7th Marines (3/7) would be helilifted 4 km inland to set up blocking positions. The 3d Battalion, 3d Marines (3/3) would remain available as a floating reserve. The ARVN 2d Battalion, 4th Regiment and the 3d Vietnamese Marine Battalion would be helilifted into the south of 3/7 Marines to conduct search-and-clear operations on the adjacent An Ky Peninsula. The operation was launched on 7 September 1965. The amphibious landing by 1/7 was unopposed, though some unexplained explosions on the beach as the assault began gave the Marines pause.

The ARVN force received some minor ground fire as they came ashore to the south.

On 8 September, B/1/7 discovered a VC field hospital in a large cave near the center of the Peninsula. The Marines captured four of the enemy before coming under fire from the VC that remained in the cave. The Marines briefly returned the fire but decided to attempt to convince the VC to surrender. The Marines and their Vietnamese interpreters were not all that convincing, and the VC would not surrender. Marine engineers then did what Marine engineers do—they placed massive explosives at the entrance to the cave. After the detonation, the Marines counted sixty-six VC dead inside.

As Operation PIRANHA came to a conclusion on 10 September, 178 VC dead were confirmed by body count and 360 enemy and suspected enemy (VCS) had been captured. Allied losses were minimal: two Marines and five ARVN KIA. Once again, the operation failed to wipe out the 1st VC Regiment. They were removed from the active battlefield for a time to refit, but they did so with the assistance of the NVA.

The villagers told the Marines that Viet Cong units had been in the area but had left, some less than twenty-four hours before Operation PIRANHA had commenced. Intelligence reports later indicated that the 1st VC Regiment began leaving the peninsula on 4 September, *coinciding with the increased movement of the amphibious ships at Chu Lai*. Coincidentally, 4 September was also about the time that the Marines were "encouraged" to include the ARVN in planning the operation. Thus the conclusion that the pickings were so slim on the Batangan Peninsula was because the VC occupants had credible prior knowledge of the American intentions. Despite the periodic operations in the area by the U.S. Army and the ROK, the peninsula remained a Viet Cong stronghold throughout the war.

Ontos deployed on Operation PIRANHA,
8 September 1965 (GB-65)

The Enemy: Operation PIRANHA, 8 September 1965

 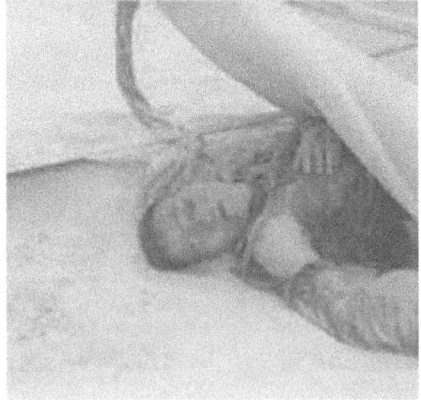

Operation PIRANHA Viet Cong casualties (VTHF Archives)

Operation PIRANHA: Mine clearing LTV-5E (VTHF Archives)

Operation PIRANHA: The run from amphibious assault ship to the beach (VTHF Archives)

Operation PIRANHA

by Carl Lemon

There was virtually no briefing to small unit leaders. The command "Saddle up" was enough to get us formed up, ready to move out to wherever. The Ontos guys were as in the dark as my platoon and me on the pending amphibious operation. I honestly don't recall any specific orders except that we were to make a tactical amphibious landing, expecting heavy, well-fortified resistance. Period.

At 0500, D-1, my 1st Platoon, Company B, 1st Tanks columned out of the tank park 100 yards from the South China Sea, staged north on the Chu Lai Beach. We were attached to the 1st Battalion, 7th Marines as we were earlier on the SLF.

We anticipated the boarding would be quick and orderly, but instead, it was 2200 before we actually were on board in the well deck, preloaded in the LCUs of the amphibious ship. Consequently, we were on the beach, exposed to the heat with no rations for 17 hours. Once aboard, the men were all fed a fine Navy meal, except for myself, as I had to attend a prelanding briefing in the officers' wardroom. The 1/7 Battalion XO informed us that intelligence reports indicated the first three waves could expect up to 80 percent casualties, and it would be a dogfight for several days. That certainly got my attention. The briefing ended around 2300, and then I was interviewed by one of

Walter Cronkite's field correspondents from CBS. As soon as that was over, I headed to the galley to look for something to eat since I hadn't had any food in over thirty hours. In the galley, I found a large platter of chicken fried steak sandwiches, so I proceeded to help myself to one, when this Filipino steward came up from behind me and rudely asked what in the hell did I think I was doing. I told him I was hungry and had had nothing to eat all day. He told me those sandwiches were for the officers standing night watch and that I was not to take any more. At this point, I was not in a very good mood, thinking that tomorrow could be my last day on earth and this guy was telling me to get out of his kitchen. I took another sandwich anyway.

Since we were scheduled for off-loading in less than three hours, I didn't bother going to bed in fear I might sleep through the dismount. I did take a hot shower and spent the rest of the night wondering what the landing was going to bring. At times like this, a person can relive his entire life to this point, thinking about everyone back home and what they are up to.

On D-day, 0300, our LCUs with the tanks loaded, backed out of the flooded well deck, and powered up, moving west with the Batangan Peninsula on the skyline. The Grunts began loading aboard the amtracs and LVT landing craft. Then we sat adrift for what seemed like days, looking at the shoreline. The water was as calm as glass, not a single ripple. I informed the men what I knew and offered everyone the opportunity to write a last letter home to be opened only in the event of death, with the expectation the letters would be returned to each individual in the event they survived the operation. Most all of the men—except for a couple—did write a farewell letter. Fortunately, none of us suffered the anticipated and were able to happily tear up their letters.

Just before H hour, around 0500, the village lights were coming on, and with the sun rising to our rear, we had a good view of the landing area—when all of a sudden, out of nowhere, the preplanned close air support F-4 Phantoms and A-5 Sky Hawks came screaming down the beach, strafing and rocketing the beachhead. They made several passes, and then the naval guns from the accompanying surface combatants opened fire. It was one of the most spectacular exhibitions of Navy-Marine Corps support fire I have ever witnessed. It was definitely something: it gave us a degree of comfort hard to explain. While the bombardment was taking place, the landing craft were formed up in a skirmisher's line and roaring toward the beach. All this was very reminiscent of the movies showing the Marines landing on the islands during World War ll. We had practiced these landing back at stateside, but this was the real thing, and my men and myself were in the middle of it—almost surreal. Our tanks were scheduled in the sixth wave to land on the beach, putting us at the very teeth of the anticipated fight we were expecting. Fortunately for all, the landing was unopposed except for a few snipers left behind by the VC. I think, in all, we suffered only one KIA, a Marine officer, and I don't know the circumstances surrounding his death.

As the day wore on, we continued to move inland and eventually set up in our defensive positions for the night. By this time, I had gone two and a half days without any sleep. The heat was so hot and humidity was so high, and even hotter inside my tank, that I couldn't sleep inside the turret, but I wasn't about to sleep on the ground in fear of snakes, so I lay down on the front fender directly under the main gun and the .30-caliber machine gun and, quite simply, passed out.

Sometime during the night, someone started a firefight, I don't remember if my guys were returning fire or if they started the shooting. I looked up and saw the .30 caliber firing away and, believe it or not, with the noise of the machine gun just a few inches above my head, I actually went right back to sleep. All I remember is everybody was shooting everywhere. To this day, I am haunted with the fact that I couldn't wake up, not only to take control of the situation, but I couldn't wake up to even save my own life if I had to. I still occasionally have dreams that we are being overrun by the NVA and they are inside my tent and I can't wake up to defend myself. I believe that dream is related to this specific incident.

From that point on, I can't remember anything else about the operation. I honestly don't even remember returning to Chu Lai. I assume we backloaded on the ships via the LCUs, but all of this is a blur to me.

I think the Marine Corps learned a valuable lesson form Operation PIRANHA. Operation STARLITE was very successful and the ARVN was *not* included. The South Vietnam politicians and military became extremely upset and insisted that this would not happen again. So Operation PIRANHA was made up of 1/7 making the beach landing, and I believe 3/7 and an RVN battalion made helicopter landings to set up a blocking force. The ARVN *was* included in the planning and operation of PIRANHA, which was considerably less successful— because the enemy had pulled up stakes days before the Marines attacked. Putting the scenarios side by side implied that the ARVN element leaked the dates of the operation, giving the enemy time to clear the area. It was highly likely that someone in the RVN command gave our plans to the NVA. The NVA abandoned their positions on the beach and waited for the RVN troops to land and proceeded to mop them up. The operation did uncover a large underground hospital housing many of the enemy casualties from STARLITE.

Carl Lemon

(Editor's Note: Those, at the time, who stated that PIRANHA was not successful, with "only" 178 enemy KIAs, were a bit spoiled. There was only STARLITE with which to compare it. As the war dragged on and with reality of the situation in which we found ourselves, 178 bad guys moved to the other side of the grass was inviable. Looking back over the duration of the war, through the lens of thousands of Marines' days in the field, ambushes, walks in the sun, innumerable occasions when thirst, hunger, physical impairments caused by vermin and the weather with not one KIA to show for it, 178 enemy KIA in a single operation was to be emulated.)

Company C, 3d Tank Battalion, 9/5/64–10/7/65

by Joe Sanders

On 5 September 1964, after spending thirty-two hours on a flight from Travis Air Force Base in California to Kadena Air Force Base, Okinawa, and half an hour ground transportation to Camp Hansen, I reported to Lieutenant Colonel States Rights Jones, CO, 3d Tank Battalion, and assumed command of C Company. (Please Note: We left Travis on 2 September and arrived on 5 September; at some point we lost 3 September and 24 hours when we crossed the International Date Line.)

From 2 January 1965 to 9 January 1965, I was TAD for 3d Marines Tactical Test of BLT 1/3 at Camp (Mt. Fuji) McNair, in Japan.

From 21 January to 31 March 1965, I was TAD to Jungle Drum III USMC / Thailand MC Exercise as a liaison officer.

Although I had my 1st and 2d Platoons, my 3d platoon was the 3d Platoon from A Company. I never saw them until we landed at Chu Lai. As best I can remember, they were already afloat with 3d Battalion, 3d Marines. My own 3d Platoon stayed behind and was later attached to a battalion that landed in Northern I Corps.

I learned some very tough lessons from this deployment. The amphibian tractor company commander and I were designated to form an alternate regimental headquarters headed by the 4th Marines regimental executive officer. This meant that my executive officer took the company while I was on a different ship. Since they started loading our tanks, almost immediately I lost the assistance of my executive officer and the company gunny in getting personal gear that was not going to accompany us into storage and in preparing the company headquarters for the move. It turned out that once aboard ship, there was no alternate headquarters planning or an office for the use of the other captain or me. We never set eyes on the regimental executive officer on the voyage. All we had was a squad bay with bunks, but no tables or chairs. The recon battalion did not encourage us to hang around their office either. What a waste of precious time that I could have spent with my command. It was a mistake not to have taken this issue to Lieutenant Colonel Jones as soon as I got back from the regimental briefing. I am sure he could have gotten me out of this, but my XO might have had to go in my place. Live and learn.

I remember very little about the landing on the beach at Chu Lai. I think we may have used the nets and a regular personnel landing craft. I don't remember getting my feet wet, but Chu Lai had a good beach for landing craft, so I may not have. We were greeted on the beach by Vietnamese officials and young girls dressed in white. I thought it was kind of strange to see all the heavily armed Marines and these young girls in white greeting them with flowers. I know that it was the next day before I ever got my command back fully under my control. Of course, the platoons were with their battalions, so I did not initially have to worry about them.

The regiment established its headquarters in an open flat sandy area about a mile in from the beach. We stayed in this location for a short time before moving the headquarters to a ridge that overlooked the north end of the beach.

The C Company CP—Chu Lai

Picture taken of Captain Joe Sanders (VTHF Archives)

The mess hall, the cook's tent, and the water point are just over the sand dune in the right of the picture. The picture was taken after we had been there a week or so and only shortly before some Viet Cong slipped in between two outposts and shot up our water point with French .22-caliber submachine guns and threw hand grenades at our cooks' tents. One of my two cooks, a Corporal Joseph Zych, was wounded by a grenade fragment in his elbow. He was the only Marine to return fire at the VCs.

My other cook, Lance Corporal Charles Bumgarner, was very lucky. He had a dud grenade land under the head of his cot. He never woke up during the excitement. The next morning, there was the grenade next to his duffel bag with his name, Bumgarner, clearly stenciled on the bag. That was quite a picture. The only other casualties that occurred from this attack were the totally unnecessary loss of two helicopters and crews that collided on takeoff from the carrier before dawn. They were FRAG to pick up my corporal whose wound was not serious. He could have waited until morning or could have gone out by boat just as my fist sergeant and I did the next morning to see him.

When we left Okinawa, our tanks were in great shape; however, almost immediately we started having track problems. Within the first week, one of the platoon tanks threw a track while driving along a sandy hill. Before the week was out, we had a tank throw another track. These were no real problems, because they were inside battalion perimeters. We tightened tracks, but the next one occurred while out on patrol some distance from a safe area. Because of the slope that the tank was on, we took the retriever out the next day to help get the track back on the tank. The crew and their security team were very lucky as they had not been bothered during the night. Surprisingly, this was the last incident of a tank throwing a track for the remainder of my tour with Charlie Company.

Around this time, the regiment was considering a sweep south along the road to Con (or Son) Tinh and on to Quang Nai. We had a helicopter recon in a Huey of the road, and then someone decided that we should run a jeep recon between the beach and the road on the afternoon before the operation. We had five jeeps counting mine and my 3d Platoon commander's. Mine was the only one that didn't still have a snorkel mounted. We encountered absolutely no one until, as we were approaching a village, we heard a round whine over our heads, followed by the sound of a shot. Everybody bailed out, and the troops spread out and headed for the village. It had sounded like an old M1 carbine. I am not even sure that sniper had intended to hit us as there was no second shot. And while not surprising, it was an eerie experience to drive through a village and not see a soul, not even a dog barking or three to four little guys begging for cigarettes.

After going through the village, we turned west toward the road and immediately saw a problem. The middle of the bridge across a stream had been torn out. This was no challenge for the other jeeps because they could ford the stream, but a really major problem for my jeep. There was no turning back. We found two timbers about 7 inches wide, still intact, and put them back on the still-intact bridge supports. We had nothing to nail the planks to what existed of the bridge, however. My driver, Lance Corporal Allen Odette, pulled up to the two timbers. We'd made the necessary adjustments to the two boards. Then I got on the other side of the stream and ground guided him forward inch by inch across. The jeep was about six feet in the air and between supports. If it had fallen, I don't think we could have gotten it out of the water and the thick mud it was flowing over. Lance Corporal Odette and I made a great team built on skill and trust.

When we got back to our CP, I had quite a surprise waiting for me. Lieutenant Dan Sullivan, my XO, who had been using C-41 to help with an infantry sweep just northeast of our headquarters, had gotten my command tank stuck in a peanut field. This was no ordinary peanut field. The plants were in long, straight, foot-wide rows with about a foot wide and 2-foot-deep gap filled with water between each row. When Dan realized what he had gotten into, he had the driver floorboard the tank, and as they churned through the water and mud, they were just about a hundred yards shy of getting the tank out of the paddy when the tank lost traction. The tracks spun in place with the only discernable movement not forward but, rather, down deeper in the muck.

By now it was fully dark. We used both of the searchlight tanks from one of the platoons, one on each side, to illuminate the area. We had security out, and they did catch a local who had walked up wanting to know what was going on.

We'd called back to the company for our retriever. Using all of the retriever's cable, we still had to attach several tank cables together to reach the C-41. Pulling a tank out of fender-deep mud is a slow, nerve-racking process, since one never knows if the operation will end in success or require the tank to be blown in place by the engineers.

It was very close to daylight before we had the mud-encased tank out, checked out, and ready to be the lead tank in the operation. Although my maintenance chief, Staff Sergeant James Shaffer, the retriever driver, Lance Corporal Leroy Kile, and the tank's crew were instrumental in getting the tank out, the real hero was Sergeant Donald Siron. In addition to all the work he did, he placed himself in a dangerous position where he could see the tank, the cables, *and* the retriever so that he could signal the retriever operator when to take up the slack, the tank TC and driver when to put it in gear, and the retriever when to pull and when to stop. We were very lucky that we did not have any cables break. I wrote Sergeant Siron up for a meritorious commendation, but it was turned down by 4th Marines, and I was told to resubmit it at the end of Siron's tour. It is a shame, as he did an outstanding job and was truly in danger, with two searchlights pointed at him and a taut cable where if something broke, it could have cut him in half. (Someone said we should have fired a couple of shots. I don't think so. It should have been enough without that.)

When I left Chu Lai by air in October of 1965, you could still see the trench we had created getting my command tank out of the peanut paddy.

We were having a continuing problem, sniper fire coming from an area on our west perimeter. I suggested that we put one of our flame tanks out in that area and provide a demonstration of what could happen to him if he continued his harassment. We did that, and after this demonstration, we were not bothered again for the remainder of our stay in that location. We were pretty sure it was someone from the local village, and maybe he could read English well enough to read the logo on the flame tank's tube "Crispy Critter."

Flame Tank puts on a fireworks display adjacent to "C" Company's CP, Chu Lai.

While we were still in the sandpit, we had a visit from a U.S. Naval officer who was an Adviseor to a Vietnamese River Security Group just north of our perimeter. A couple of nights later, their base was overrun and the officer killed. Early the next morning, I visited my 1st Platoon, which was located on high ground overlooking the base and waterways. My platoon leader told me they had watched boats leave the area but had been unable to get clearance to engage the boats. The problem was identifying fishermen as "legitimate," i.e., friendly or going out to fish for the Viet Cong. Of course, they may have been one and the same at any given time of the day. This is the only time I became upset with my driver to the point of it showing. As we left the main road and started into the brush to go to the platoon's position, I looked in the back for the driver's rifle to hold while we were in the brush and discovered that he did not have his M-14. He was wearing a .45 instead. I asked him what would happen if we were ambushed by party not of little boys begging cigarettes but "big" boys with even bigger guns and we with only our .45s. I think I made the point, as thereafter, we always had his rifle with us.

Shortly after the road operation, we relocated to the high ground on the northeast of the beach with a beautiful view of the South China Sea and the white-sand beach. We settled in and remained in this location for the remainder of my tour.

I must mention my first Sergeant. He was a very effective scrounger. He traded two cases of C-rations in at Da Nang for a large tent, which we used for the company offices and sleeping quarters. We had a refrigerator, a washing machine, and an elevated water barrel shower. We kept canteens of cold water in the refrigerator for each of the platoons. They could send a jeep in to pick it up, or we would take it out to them if we had someone going that way. We also had trenches dug beside the tents so that we could take shelter in them if we suffered a mortar attack. This never happened while I was there. We can probably thank Operations STARLITE and PIRANHA for that.

FSR (Force Service Regiment) was located east of my CP and up the road. One of our tanks was deadlined with a transmission problem. We were told that we did not have a high enough priority to get a new one in. However, the Navy Seabees were able to have beer and Coke flown in. I guess building an airstrip had a higher priority than keeping a tank in operation.

One of the many things the Regimental Supply Officer did was to start an Officers' Club (unofficial, of course). Each of us kicked in a few bucks and our ration of beer and the hard stuff. I kept my Coke ration. Not sure about the others. The club was very popular with the aviators and some others operating at the just-built airfield. At some point they decided to start their own—and official—club. The members closed our club's financial books and divided the cash and other assets among those of us who had invested in it. I don't remember how much I received but recall that it had been a very good investment. Probably on a percent basis, the best I ever made.

For some time I stood watch on certain nights each week in the regimental CP. I think they were four-hour watches and only once or twice a week. If a shot was heard anywhere on the regimental perimeter, the battalion involved was supposed to call in to let us know what was happening. If we did not get a call after a few minutes, we were expected to call and see what was going on. The joke was that we had to find out before we had a call from Washington, DC, wanting to know who had fired a shot and why. They finally dropped us out of the rotation. After all, we weren't "infantry" officers.

One afternoon, as a CH-34 helicopter was taking off from the takeoff/landing area next to regimental headquarters, we heard an explosion. Everyone bailed out of the tents in time to see the helicopter make an autorotation landing. The pilot did a good job, but he still hit pretty hard. Not much damage and no one hurt. About a week later, as another helicopter was taking off, we heard another explosion. This time the pilot did not hit quite as hard. I guess he was better prepared for it. Kind of makes you reluctant to fly with them.

Speaking of which, the first Sergeant and I flew to Da Nang to visit the tank company that was there. On the way back, they had loaded the helicopter with fresh-baked bread to bring back for the regiment. We did not lift off; we had to take off like an airplane rather than a helicopter. It was very exciting.

The problem with the CH-34s turned out to be the engines that had been rebuilt in Japan. I am not sure how they got the problem solved, but we didn't have any more incidents like that for the rest of my tour.

Not long after we moved to the location on the higher ground, we received some promotions for members of Charlie Company, so we decided to have a real company formation with our Marines, tanks, and retriever. Not sure why I didn't think to include the truck, the com jeep, and our other four jeeps in the formation. The picture was taken with my little Kodak Pony 828, so the quality was not the best.

C Company, 3d Tank Battalion commanding officer, Capt. Joe, Chu Lai (VTHF Archives)

From 2 January 1965 to 9 January 1965, I was TAD for 3d Marines Tactical Test of BLT 1/3 at Camp (Mt. Fuji) McNair, in Japan.

From 21 January to 31 March 1965, I was TAD to Jungle Drum III USMC / Thailand MC Exercise as a liaison officer.

On 24 April 1965, I received the following PCS orders with the three attachments:

ORIGINAL ORDERS

HEADQUARTERS
3d Marine Division (Rein), FMF
FPO, San Francisco 96601

7B/TEP/cmc
1320/2
24 April 1965

From: Commanding General
To: Captain Joe P. SANDERS, 071521/1802 USMC
Via: Commanding Officer, 3d Tank Battalion

Subj: Permanent Change of Station Orders

Ref: (a) FMFPac msg 312225Z MAR65
(b) III MEF msg 121101Z APR65
(c) Par 4100 JTR (Group Travel)
(d) Par 7005 JTR (Dep)
(e) Par 8008.2 JTR (HHE)
(f) Par 8253.2D JTR (HHE)

Encl: (1) Roster of personnel

1. In accordance with reference (a) and (b), on 24 April 1965, you and the personnel listed on enclosure (1) will stand detached from your present duties and report to the CO RLT-4 for transportation to such place as the 9th MEB is located and on arrival there report to the Commanding General for duty.

2. These orders constitute permanent change of station orders for yourself and the personnel listed on enclosure (1). Copies of these orders, counter-signed by you will constitute permanent change of station orders for all personnel listed on enclosure (1).

3. These orders constitute group travel as defined by reference (c).

4. In accordance with FMFPac Order 8370.1 privately owned weapons are not permitted in the Republic of Vietnam.

5. Effect immunization requirements in accordance with BUMEDINSTs 6230.1D and 6230.13 and have in your possession your immunization card at all times.

6. In accordance with reference (d), travel of dependents is not authorized. Shipment of household effects is authorized in accordance with references (e) and (f). In addition no advance pay is authorized.

7. TravChar appn 1751105.2753;MPMC-65; OC 21 EAN 74152 OffTvl; 74162 EnlTvl; OC 12.

W. R. COLLINS

Copy to:
CG TF-79 (G-1); DivDisbO; DivPostalO; DivRot; F I L E

NAME	RANK	SERNO/MOS	RTD
HARRIS, P. J.	2dLt	088858/1802	Nov65
SUMNER, J.H.	GySgt	669176/1811	Jul65
ASH, F.	Sgt	618257/1811	Jul65
FANNING, J.D.	Cpl	2024653/1811	Jul65
MATTHEWS, G.R.	Cpl	1619316/1811	May66
BALDWIN, F.G.L.	LCpl	2024897/2531	Spe65
CARR, D.B.	LCpl	2059845/1811	May66
COURT, T.	LCpl	2059158/1811	May66
DAGUE, P.J.	PFC	2077397/1811	May66
DEAR, J.	LCpl	2078039/1811	May66
ELMER, R.L.	LCpl	1844733/1811	Jul65
GORDON, E.W.	LCpl	1982860/3531	Dec65
HIPSHER, G.A.	LCpl	2036518/2141	Apr66
KEIR, J.A.	LCpl	2019848/1811	Jun65
LANE, R.W.	LCpl	2041725/1811	Jun65
MAYHUGH, P.P.	LCpl	2052526/1811	Apr66
ONEILL, J.M.	LCpl	2036678/1811	Jun66
WENDT, P.O.	LCpl	2042532/1811	Jun65
TOWNER, J. F.	LCpl	2063626/1811	Mar66
CLAVAN, R.E.	PFC	1991938/1811	Jun65
HOLLAND, R.K.	PFC	2080875/1811	May66
SERVOSS, W.R.	PFC	2068694/1811	Mar66

NAME	RANK	SERNO/MOS	RTD
MASSIE, M. R.	2ndLt	089829/1801	Apr66
BRINGHAM, G. L.	SSgt	1208233/1811	Dec65
HERR, V. F.	Sgt	1193840/1811	Jun65
JOHNSON, F. M.	Sgt	1221018/1811	May66
BOONE, H. G.	Cpl	1666748/1811	May66
HOLLAND, R. E.	Cpl	1863724/1811	May66
SHAW, M. L.	Cpl	2052192/2141	Apr66
EPTING, B. A.	LCpl	1984515/1811	Aug65
FLOER, R. C.	LCpl	2026748/1811	Jul65
LAWROSKY, R. M.	LCpl	2022557/1811	Sep65
MASON, T. S.	LCpl	2061865/1811	Dec65
PIERSON, J. S.	LCpl	2062872/1811	May66
POLICKA, R. A.	LCpl	2017812/2531	Apr66
SERRANO, R.	LCpl	2041510/1811	Jul65
WHITE, C.	LCpl	1918541/1811	May66
ANDERSON, R. R.	PFC	2076722/1811	May66
LESSARD, J. G.	PFC	2061084/1811	Sep65
MCAFEE, A. S.	PFC	2076447/1811	Apr66
OLSEN, C. K.	PFC	2072900/1811	May66
POWERS, D. E.	PFC	2061119/1811	Apr66
REDWINE, M. E.	PFC	2053127/1811	May66
REESE, J. E.	PFC	2053018/1811	Mar66
ROCHE, R. T.	PFC	2075865/3531	Mar66

Headquarters Platoon, "C" Company 3d Tank Bn

NAME	RANK	SERNO/MOS	RTD
SULLIVAN, Daniel H.	1stLt	087663/1802	May66
ARGETSINGER, Donald R.	1stSgt	975156/9999	Apr66
SHEWELL, Jules V.	GySgt	579220/1811	Oct65
SHAFFER, James H.	SSgt	1040370/2149	Dec65
MILLER, Samuel W. Jr	Sgt	1428303/1811	Jul65
SIRON, Donald L.	Sgt	1368593/2141	Aug65
CARRILLO, Luis A.	Cpl	2013063/0141	Sep65
ROCKS, Francis A.	Cpl	1986619/2531	Jul65
WONGAN, Ivan A.	Cpl	1631970/1811	Dec65
ZYCH, Joseph M.	Cpl	1970085/3371	Jul65
BUMGARNER, Charles D.	LCpl	2037740/3371	Aug65
HARRINGTON, Joseph W.	LCpl	2035257/1811	Jun65
KILE, LeRoy D.	LCpl	1983685/2141	Mar66
MOBLEY, Ronnie T.	LCpl	2062269/1811	Mar66
ODETTE, Allen S.	LCpl	1834972/3531	Dec65
OSBORNE, George C.	LCpl	2036554/0141	Nov65
THOMPSON, Robert R.	LCpl	2041808/2841	Jun65
GATES, Harry D.	PFC	2017345/1316	Feb66
JOLLY, Franklin L.	PFC	2051527/3051	Jul65
MAPEL, William D.	PFC	2065197/1811	May66
MEJIA, Johnny	PFC	2082341/1811	May66
PALMIGIANO, Anthony F.	PFC	2098070/0141	Nov65
TRIMBLE, James D.	PFC	2064456/1811	Jun65
KLAAS, Robert A.	Pvt	2088875/1811	May66
ROWLEY, Jack B. (USN)	HN	591 05 98 /8404	Jul65

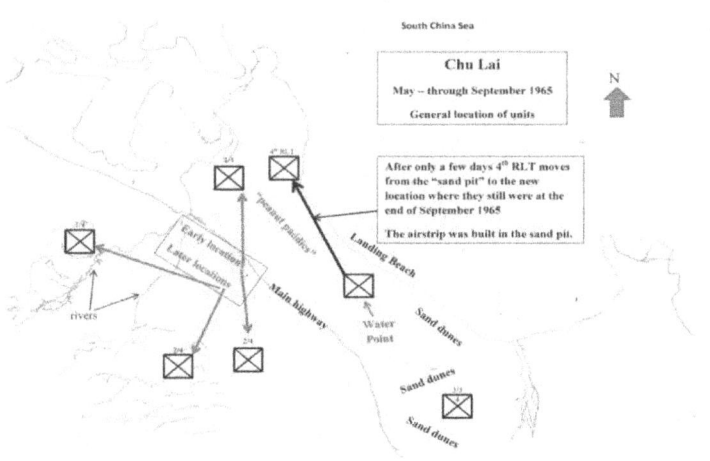

May–September RLT-4's dispostion ashore at Chu Lai

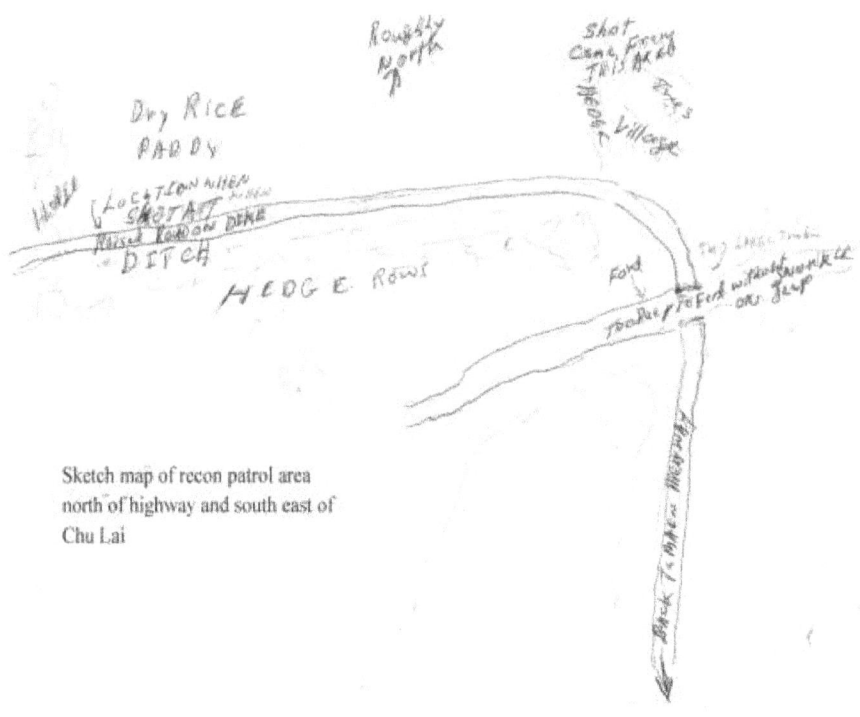

Sketch map of recon patrol area north of highway and south east of Chu Lai

Company C sketch map of recon patrol

Captain Sanders's article

Hill 22 Southwest of Marble Mountain

Edward E. Murphy, in his book *Semper Fi: Vietnam: From Da Nang to the DMZ—Marine Corps Campaigns, 1965–1975*, in concluding his 1965 chapter, states, "Unfortunately, the Marine Corps' policy of rotating its troops out of the war zone after a thirteen-month tour, assuming they had survived death or serious injury, meant that many of the lessons learned in the early days were doomed to be relearned over and over again as the years passed" (SF-EM). In fact, often there were no "lessons learned"; there were barely "lessons observed." Yes, a few facts were recorded, and a paucity of these, but there was no meaningful "cause and effect" sought, documented, and placed in lesson plans to train the Marines at the Marie Corps' Parris Island, South Carolina, or

San Diego, California, boot camps; its Officer Basic School minting second lieutenants, its midlevel officer Amphibious Warfare School (AWS), its senior officer Command and Staff College (C&SC) at Quantico, Virginia, or Tracked Vehicle Officer School (TVOS) at Camp Delmar, Camp Pendleton, California.

The "Battle of Hill 22" provides an example of how much could have been learned but was not.

This is an abstract of CC-3Tk 10/65 taken from the VTHF October 2014 *Breech Block*, quoted from 3d Tank Battalion October Command Chronology (CC-3Tk, 10/65):

> CO Company A: Captain F. W. Jarnot
> Location: Da Nang (AT 946762)

> "A" Company remained in direct support of the Third Marines occupying strong points along the MLR and providing rapid reaction alert forces. Since the situation in the Third Marines TAOR was relatively stable tanks were committed on only three occasions. A two tank patrol was conducted to the most southwesterly sector of the TAOR to the hamlet of An My (3). No enemy activity was noted. <u>On 30 October 1965 at 0200 a large attack against A Company, 1st Battalion, 1st Marines located at Hill 22 (AT 953667) was launched by the Viet Cong. The tank located on this position was slightly damaged by two 57mm recoilless rounds and a direct hit from a mortar shell. The tank remained operational, fired nineteen major caliber rounds, and killed between six and eight Viet Cong.</u> Concurrently the tank in support of M Company, 4d Battalion, 4th Marines on Hill 41 (AT 934663) directed ten rounds of 90mm High Explosive ammunition, at a range of 1200–1500 meters, against two confirmed enemy mortar positions neutralizing their

fire completely. At 2200 on 30 October a tank reaction force at the 2d Battalion, 3d Marines was committed against a substantial probe being launched near the Battalion's Command Post. Three 90mm canister rounds were directed against the enemy and contact was broken.

This is taken from 1/1's October CC. It will be noted that in describing the assault in detail, there is no citing of the key role a single tank played in stopping the attack, actually credited by the infantry company commander in keeping the VC from overrunning the company, and driving the survivors from the A/1/1's defensive perimeter.

> characterized by small arms fire and grenades. Company "A" was attacked on the night of 29-30 October by a Main Force Company and three guerrilla companies, estimated 3-400 men, using "Mass" tactics, 60mm mortars, 57mm RR, Inerga Rifle Grenades, and French Rifle Grenades.

"Company 'A' was attacked on the night of 29–30 October by a Main Force Company and three guerilla companies, estimated 3–400 men, using 'Mass' tactics, 60mm mortars, 57mm RR, Inerga Rifle Grenades, and French Rifle Grenades" (CC-1/1,10/65).

Following is a clip from 3d Antitank Battalion's October Command Chronology (CC-3AT, 10/65). Note the scant reference to the fight that A/1/1's CO describes in detail.

> (b) Company "A" (-) (Rein) supported two infantry Company operations, one infantry platoon operation, one infantry platoon ONTOS/Tank patrol and one infantry squad/ONTOS patrol. On 300210H Oct65, an ONTOS vehicle from the First Platoon was hit by a VC 57mm recoilless rifle when it was supporting Company "A", 1st Battalion, 1st Marines. The VC assault on the infantry company, with the ONTOS vehicle manning their MLR, caused the first seriously damaged ONTOS as a result of enemy gunfire in the Vietnam operation. (Note SITREP number 111). The ONTOS were used extensively as a night perimeter security/mobile reaction force. Two M21 fire missions were conducted during the month, expending 12-106mm HEAT rounds; 181-106mm HEP-T rounds; 338-.50 caliber spotting rounds and 1000-.30 caliber rounds (machine gun). For details see enclosure (1) SITREP DTG 021800H/031800H Oct65 and SITREP numbers 92, 97, 105, and 112 with attached weekly summary.

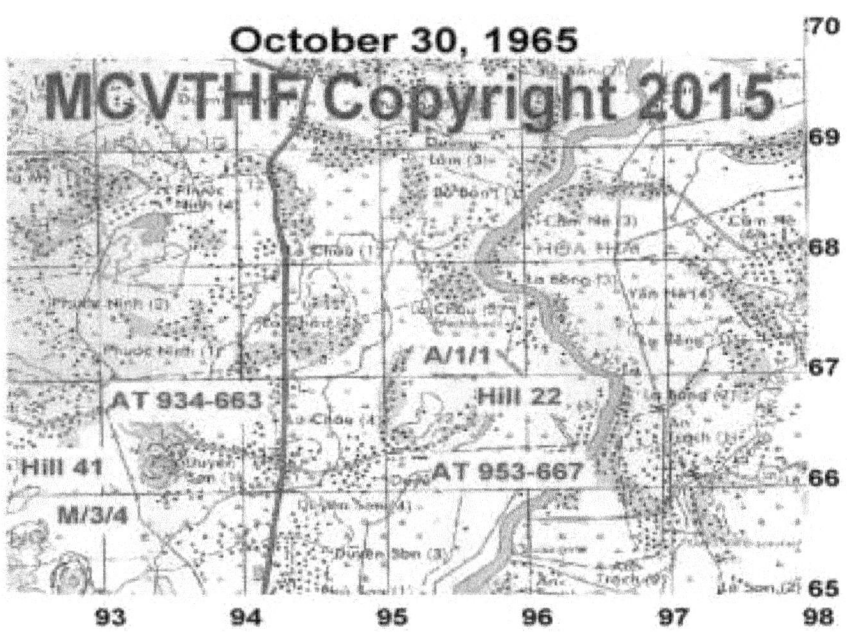

This is taken from the interview of Captain Maxwell,
the company commander of A/1/1

VC Assault on Hill 22 30 October 1965

Captain Maxwell, Company Commander A/1/1 (CD-128)

I'd like now to discuss the artillery as best I can and discuss the 81 mortar section actions the best I can. I want to describe the action of the tank commander. As I stated earlier, the tank commander, I do not know his name, he is a Negro sergeant in the Marine Corps and of course a Tanker. He was not located in his tank when the attack started. He and his crew were in holes right next to the tank, and when the attack started, he and his crew climbed into his tank. I did not see him during the attack; I was unable to contact him during the attack. After a while, he was buttoned up in his tank, and he had received, I know at least, one 57 recoilless rifle hit on the turret of his tank. The round did not penetrate the tank. He also received some direct hit mortar fire, knocking out the searchlight that he had on the tank. So he was obviously under heavy attack. He may have received more than one hit by the 57 recoilless rifle, I'm not certain. He, very fortunately, took it upon himself to start firing his tank. I need to discuss this here a little further. He attempted to get his tank—as I mentioned earlier, his tank was his hull defilade. He attempted to get his tank out of the position it was in so he could move his tank into a more favorable position to deliver fire upon the VC that was attacking the position. He told me later that a couple of Marines who had become seriously wounded had crawled underneath the tank to a hole for protection, and he was unable to get them out. He was unable to move his tank because of Marines were seriously wounded; therefore, he did not move his tank and began firing his 90 mm and I believe the .30-caliber machine guns that he had mounted on his tank as best he could in the general direction of the attack. In my opinion, this tank was the most effective, the single most important weapon, that we had fighting the Viet Cong and blunting its attack. As I recall, he did not start firing his tank until approximately 15–20 minutes after the attack had begun. Once he started to fire his 90 mm gun, this seemed to be the turning point in the attack. The fire was slacking off, and we could no longer see large groups of VC attempting to penetrate our position. He fired initially three rounds of canister at approximately 100–200-meter range directly into the attacking forces of the Viet Cong. If he did this as he told me he did, I am certain that these three rounds caused very heavy casualties among the Viet Cong. I might also point out that by him firing in the position which he was firing from, which was located right in the center of the hill, that he unquestionably inflicted some friendly casualties from firing where he did. Not to be critical of his action, but merely pointing out, in all probability, that some of our wounded were from this tank's firing. In addition to the three rounds of canister that he fired, I believe eighteen rounds of heavy explosives and many, *many* hundreds of rounds of .30-caliber machine gun fired directly into where the Viet Cong had massed into their forward attack. I'm certain inflicted casualties on the enemy forces and in my opinion turned the attack away from us and kept us from being completely overrun that along with the 81 mm mortar fire that we were receiving from our own section.

Note: First Lieutenant F. Stolz, 3d Platoon commander, A/1/1 also details this action

UNITED STATES MARINE CORPS
HISTORY DIVISION
ORAL HISTORY INTERVIEW SUMMARY

Interviewee's Name: 1st Lt. Frank V. Stolz, #088989, USMC
Date of Interview: 2 March 1966
Conflict: Vietnam War
Military Unit: 1st and 3d Marines, 3d Marine Division
Duties: Rifle Company Platoon Commander, F/2/3 and A/1/1
Interviewer: Lt. Col. D. J. Hunter, USMC
Location of Interview: Marine Corps Base, Camp Pendleton, CA
Length: 52:19
Individual Completing Summary: Raymond A. Stewart, Lieutenant Colonel, USMC (Ret)
Recording Format and Number of Recordings: Originally audio tape, re-recorded on CD #88
Documents Submitted with Interview: N/A
Related Material: N/A
Classification: Unclass./FOUO
Transcription priority: 3

Abstract: Experiences of First Lieutenant Frank Stolz while serving in the Republic of South Vietnam as a rifle platoon leader initially with 2/3 and then 1/1 during the period 10 April 1965 to 31 October 1965

Key Words: Okinawa, Transplacement Battalion, Mixmaster, Hill 22

Interview Log: Note to researchers: Except for words in quotes, this is not a verbatim account of the interview. The recording itself should be used to verify this summary.

00:00–16:17: Arrived in Okinawa, Japan, with 1/1 November 1964, became 2/3. Went through* transplacement battalion training. Training was primarily for standard infantry operations but found out that scouting and patrolling was what was required in Vietnam. Great shortage of maps and compasses in all prior training, which impacted negatively in-country. Stolz was a rifle platoon commander in F/2/3 in the Da Nang TAOR from 10 April when landing in Vietnam. Northwestern part of Da Nang TAOR. "Fox Fort" (AT 902775) Company CP. Some company sweeps. Occasionally battalion sweeps but primarily platoon-size operations. Some brushes with the VC guerillas, which were mostly untrained and poorly armed. Some mines and booby traps. Hill 71 ops at AT 89746 on 30 August 65. Thick brush, poor movement, poor visibility. Grenade booby trap with four WIA, one KIA. Lieutenant Stolz describes the composition, deployment of booby traps. VC campsites described—cover, concealment, size, shape, type, location, disposition, food, water, ammo. Besides basic load, his platoon carried extra ropes and described uses of them.

16:18–32:24: Then went to from F/2/3 to A/1/1 with his rifle platoon at SW sector of Da Nang TAOR on 29 October 1965 as part of the Mixmaster Program. Hill 22 AT 954667 near Lac Chau (4). Took basic load without M-79s or ammo. Assumed defensive perimeter as 3d Platoon. Located on hill was one tank and one Ontos and some mortars. Surrounded by three villages with good fields of fire. Cover and concealment with tombstones with sandbags and one strand of wire. On night of 30 October, no moon, dark, ill-prepared positions. Frank detailed the layout of the CP. Two platoons in place. Then described the firefight. At 0230, one incoming mortar that wounded company XO. Then RPGs and 57 mm RRs incoming—two rounds hit the tank. Volume of incoming increased, and men were scattered trying to get dressed and man their positions. Then attack from the north and the west with heavy hand grenade support on line by forty to fifty VC. Called for illum from organic mortars. Friendly fire returned. VC assault generally stopped at wire.

Editor Note: A key to defeating the enemy assault on a well-structured friendly defensive perimeter was the emplacement and activation of the Claymore mine.

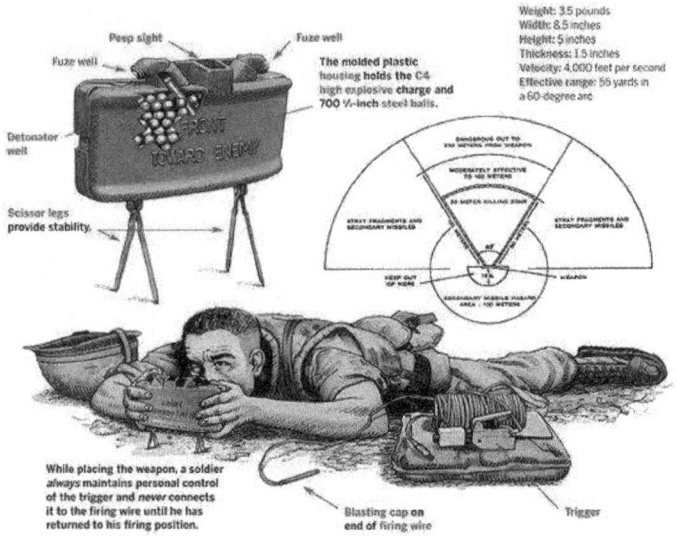

Emplacement and activation of the Claymore mine
(Picture provided by Tom Snyder) (VTHF)

Some few went into perimeter and tents, searching for weapons. VC had no coordination between VC mortars and assaulting enemy. Hand-to-hand combat ensued. Ontos knocked out by 57s right away. Tank could not move due to casualties underneath and could not fire 90 mm because of unknown location of friendlies to the front.

32:25–45:17: Tank then fired into the village to the west and then canister into groups of twenty to thirty. Comms became checkered. First squad in NW sector with two corpsmen was hit. Meat hooks used by VC to drag their WIA/KIAs away. Hill 41 to the west gave some 81 mm and tank support but were also pinned down by mortar fire. VC force of estimated three hundred comprised two hard-core VC companies of 120 and one guerilla company of 60. VC were a number of eleven-to-fifteen-year-olds and a few old men—all with eight to nine grenades hanging from body. VC interrogation resulted finding out what it would take to attack a Marine position. VC had been walking for a week or two. Attack had been planned for a month. Marines had no prior knowledge of pending attack. VC casualties—56, actually dragged into perimeter and buried. Also lots of freshly dug graves around perimeter villages. Marines lost six weapons and captured forty plus.

45:17–52:19: Marines fought in place. Stood and died in place. Great pride. Some VCs were brave, professional, and dedicated. Many were not. Majority of casualties came from guerilla. POWs stated fear of firepower of Marines, i.e., the "test" attack. Arty support came in after ten minutes of the attack. Illum first with few HE into village later. Some air support around 0410–0415—actually after fight was over. Huey's (helicopters) brought ammo and carried out casualties. 31 October—on there was incoming small arms from local villages until 18 October when Stolz left.

END OF INTERVIEW

Captain Pasquale "Pat" Demartino, #062965, USMC, company commander of L Company, 3d Battalion, 3d Marines (L/3/3), occupied Hill 22 just after Captain Maxwell departed. He reported improved relationship with the locals but ended his interview with his medevac to the hospital due to severe—life/limb threatening—wounds due to shrapnel from a local-planted mine (CD-96).

Operations HARVEST MOON and GOLDEN FLEECE were the last-named operations in 1965. And though it appears that neither of these two operations had tanks, antitank, Ontos attached to or in direct support of the infantry units, their presence was nonetheless reported, if not detailed.

"In mid-August, the battalion (1/9) was released from duty as the (Da Nang) airfield defense battalion and was assigned to the area south of Marble Mountain bordering the South China Sea. Operating from a central base area, Lieutenant Colonel Ludwig (C.O.) sent out small patrols to bait the VC. When these units made contact, a mobile reaction force, composed of Marines mounted on tanks (from Captain Arthur E. Lee's Company "B," 3d Tanks [CC-3dTk, 8/65]), Ontos, and amtracs, sped to the point of contact. On 29 August, the battalion defeated a Viet Cong company, killing 12, capturing 12 more and dispersing the remainder" (GB-65) (CC-1/9, 8/65).

Lieutenant Colonel Ludwig's idea was to enlist the help of four of the local villages' chiefs which was a new tactic. With the success of this operation, it became the genesis of the Operation GOLDEN FLEECE, which followed. Ludwig continued to use these tactics into September and depended heavily upon the participation of his attached tanks, Ontos, and amtracs. Rice was successfully harvested, and VC were killed. GOLDEN FLEECE morphed into HARVEST MOON as most of the other Marine units in the area which soon included the entire Chu Lai TAOR.

"During this period, III MAF started what was to become the COUNTY FAIR technique, a cordon and search operation with psychological overtones" (GB-65). Once again, the infantry battalions in each of the three TAORs—Chu Lai, Da Nang, and Hue/Phu Bai—with support from attached and direct support tanks, Ontos, and amtracs weighed in with all the manpower that could be mustered and still not jeopardize either the active offensive operations or base security.

"The best that could be said for the III MAF pacification effort (Golden Fleece, Harvest Moon, and County Fair) by the end of 1965 was that the Marines realized the problems and had started to challenge the VC control of the countryside. There was still much to learn and do" (GB-65). A major challenge was posed by the poor showing of the Popular and Regional Forces. They were the government of Vietnam's (GVN) face to the locals. It was not a pretty face.

The units, once ashore, immediately set up housekeeping. General Purpose (GP) tents and the smaller CP tents were pitched for billeting and offices. Mess tents were erected with adjacent eating utensils' cleaning apparatus—GI cans filled with water and emersion burners (gas-fired heaters) to provide boiling water for mess kit cleaning and sterilization. Most Marines used their "meat can with cover and knife, fork, and spoon" and sequentially submersed them, holding the assembly by the handle, through the 3-GI can sequence. The Marine who brought the standard metal mess tray as a souvenir from his stint aboard ship with an SLF was much envied, and three-tray was a prized possession to be passed down upon its owner's departure from the war. Part of the repertoire the Tanker's black humor was, "If you buy the farm on this next operation, can I have your mess tray?"

Heads (outside "crappers," mostly "two holers") were built over open 55-gallon drums. These were serviced daily. Keeping it short, diesel fuel was poured into the 55-gallon drums to burn, thus reducing the volume of the content. It maintained passable sanitation requirements but upset the flies, which quickly evolved into 2 pounds of ugly black things, so fat they had difficulty in gaining flight, so just crawled around inside the screened-in facility. They reproduced their new strain by the thousands (well, may be hundreds), defying all means of exterminating.

Potable water tanks were set atop wooden towers, as were makeshift showers.

Electricity was provided to the camp with organic gas generators. The motor pool / tank park maintenance areas were among first priority in order that twenty-four-hour repairing and servicing of the tanks, Ontos, trucks, and other rolling stock would be assured. Priority of electricity, after the maintenance capability was provided, was to the chow hall, sick bay, administrative offices, and then billeting—troops, NCOs, SNCOs, officers in that order.

Then there was the constant "upgrading" that continued to provide more comfortable living conditions. Wooden floors (decks) were set inside and to the approaches to and between the tents. Eventually, wooden strong-back framing was built for the tents. The ultimate was the "hootch," which was mostly wooden framed and decks screened with tie-down shutters, and tin roofs. And more reliable electricity generation was brought on-line and access to water assured.

Laying the deck for a strong back hootch
(Photo by Shup [VTHF])

Makeshift bunkered hootch
Photo by Shup (VTHF Archives)

Prepping for hootch "upgrade"
Photo by Shup (VTHF Archives)

When tanks and Ontos were deployed to the field, all sorts of shelters were innovated. Here's a Tankers story.

A Rainy Night in Chu Lai

by John Hunter

I was the driver of B-35, for (3d Platoon) B Company, 1st Tanks at Chu Lai in 1965. Our company tank park and adjoining motor pool was situated near the beach of the South China Sea, just to the north of the Song Tra Bong (River) and co-located near the 7th Marines command post (CP). For a lot of evenings during my time there, every evening after chow, we would make a run north up the beach, then inland, drive out to the Chu Lai Airfield to guard the perimeter.

The crew of B-35 consisted of Sergeant "Mac" Mackenzie, tank commander (TC); Lance Corporal Richard Tilden, gunner; Lance Corporal Eugenio, loader; and me, Private First Class John Hunter, driver. On one such evening, we proceeded to the airfield. Shortly after arriving, it started to rain. I mean to say it RAINED! The first thing we did was get into our tank at our respective assigned positions and close the hatches. I can remember sitting in the driver's seat, as the rain poured in around the leaking rubber gasket, which I first discovered when my tank was briefly submerged during our run to the beach from an LCU when landing in Okinawa and again across the beach at Chu Lai. Of course, there was someone watching the wire from the TC's hatch, most likely Sergeant Mackenzie. After only a few minutes of this, we all decided we needed to vacate the tank and get outside where it was actually a little dryer.

For those who have "been there, done that," there is no disagreement that it does get mighty cold in Vietnam—especially with a wind off the ocean. We did find some relief from the cold (if not the rain), for when we would run the engine to charge the batteries, we would crowd around behind the tank, breathing diesel exhaust fumes in an attempt to get a little heat. I might add that every Grunt within one hundred yards joined the standing room only, shivering, wet, windblown tank crew behind the tank.

After a while, one of the Tankers came up with the idea of taking the tank tarp, tying it to the rear of the tank, and propping up the other end so the crew members not on watch could get under it and keep dry. About this time, the wind started blowing even harder, one would think that the wind could not move wet sand, but by dawn, the tarp was half buried under a foot of wet sand. Now that makes a heavy tarp, wet and cold, and trying to pull a wet tarp out of the sand, scrape off the sand, and fold it up to go back to the tank park—where the "Chu Lai Hilton" was waiting for us—a real pain. The Chu Lai Hilton was the name of our tent. It was not a hard-back tent like the one I was to later sleep in at Marble Mountain with 3d Tanks in Da Nang. That area too was all sand, but dry, not windblown, and a heck of a lot better than that wet, sand-covered tarp.

As a Tanker I know we are not supposed to complain about the fact we lived in tents in the area, rode everywhere on our tanks, always had hot food, and had armor plating to protect our asses. But little hardships like "the rainy night" just make one a better Marine! It is like taking a bath in a rice paddy with the leeches, or drinking a warm beer with the mosquitoes. All part of character building and the Vietnam experience we enjoyed on our "senior trip."

John M. Hunter
RVN 1965–66
1st and 3d Tank Battalions

And the pacification effort "though not wholly supported by MACV, the III MAF pacification efforts seemed to be taking hold. General Walt felt positive that his forces would soon have the upper hand" (GB-65). When III MAF (G-5) staff officers came to visit the tank and antitank battalions south of their CP on Hill 327, they were toured through the villages of Phong Bac and Yen Bach, supported by the Tankers and Ontos crewmen, respectively. They were indeed jewels in the crown of the III MAF Combined Action Program (CAP). And the success of these programs must have given heart—if not confidence—to General Walt. However, "If he had any idea of what the future (in fact) would hold, though, he might not have been so optimistic" (SF-EM).

In the meantime, tank and antitank units were beginning to experience shortages that the Marine Corps Logistic System could not have identified and therefore prepared to meet. One small example (or two): The tank's drive sprockets at the "meeting" of the suspension and drive systems, due to the super abrasive Chu Lai beach sand, were wearing out two to three times faster than the *established* usage data was prepared to support. Means had to be found to reset the system to accommodate this new data, and that would take time. The high heat and humidity took their tolls on every type of rolling stock and piece of equipment in one or more of several adverse results. Cannibalizing deadlined vehicles to keep others operational became an art form.

3d Tank and 3d Antitank Battalions as of 31 December 1965

As 1965 came to an end, most of the 3d Marine Division and its supporting organizations were on the ground in some strength in South Vietnam. And the 1st Marine Division, with some units on the ground in the fight, and others on the Special Landing Force (SLF) in the coastal water of South Vietnam, was on full alert at Camp Pendleton, California, to join them in the fight in early 1966 against the largely unknown and ill-understood Vietnamese enemy (VC) on the bidding of their only slightly better known, but still misunderstood, Vietnamese allies (NVA). The Ho Chi Minh Trail extending for hundreds of miles between Hanoi/Haiphong Harbor in North Vietnam feeding the enemy through an ever-growing logistics supply system that they became impossible to interdict.

The table that follows reflects only the tank and antitank organization attached to their respective infantry battalions and thus on the ground. It does not identify those afloat organizations comprising the Special Landing Force (SLF) or units in the process of transiting to/from Vietnam, usually via Okinawa.

The basic ground Marine organization comprising the Special Landing Force (SLF) is the Battalion Landing Team (BLT), which is task-organized (i.e., armed, equipped, and trained) to fight the anticipated enemy. As an organization, the SLF is not found in the Marine Amphibious Force (MAF). As a result, those units comprising the SLF are not reflected here. SLF operations, other than Operations STARLITE and PIRANHA—for example, DAGGER THRUST and DECKHOUSE—as well as other amphibious operations and organizations are found in the annexes section.

To be clear, the chart is but a snapshot of the organizations taken only on 31 December 1965. A day later, or earlier, the detailed numbers and strength of lll MAF may have looked quite different: a BLT coming ashore with the supported infantry battalion, then the attached units reporting to their parent unit; a supporting unit (e.g., an Ontos platoon) of the BLT may remain attached to that infantry battalion or commence reporting to its parent company or battalion and may, or may not, continue to be in direct support of that infantry battalion. This chart also reflects the location of the infantry regiments and the tank and antitank battalions, subordinate units' positions and locations changed by the minute.

The reporting and supported/supporting units were and are more than a bit convoluted and, in any case, confusing to the historian; and even more so to those warriors who fought the enemy of the day. Every effort to keep things straight has been and is being made. There is mostly truth to the statement "Most of the time I didn't know where I was, who my boss was, or where in the hell we were going." And when todays' reunions find buddies not seen in over fifty years, if one thought he knew any of the above, there is always one or two who will have a completely different and equally plausible recollection—and pictures to "prove" it.

(Note: Tank and Antitank Units in red)

3d Marines (-) (Rein.) (Da Nang-Phu Bai) (4182*)
    HqCo (Rein.) (Da Nang)
        (1) Det., HqBn, 3d MarDiv
    1st Bn, 1st Marines (Da Nang)
    1st Bn, 3d Marines (Da Nang)
    2d Bn, 1st Marines (Rein.) (Phu Bai)
        2d Bn, 1st Marines
        Det., HqBn, 3d MarDiv
        1st Plt (Rein.), Co A, 1st ATBn (20*)
            (5 M5OA1 Ontos)
        1st Plt (Rein.), Co A, 1st EngrBn
        1st Plt (Rein.), Co A, 1st TkBn (28*)
            (5 M48A3 Tanks)

4th Marines (-) (Rein.) (Chu Lai) (2895*)
    HqCo (296*)
    1st Bn, 4th Marines (1063*)
    2d Bn, 4th Marines (1063*)
    Co B (-) (Rein.), 3d ATBn (71*)
        Co B (-) (41*)
        Det., H&S Co, 3d ATBn (30*)
    Co B (-) (Rein.), 3d EngrBn (124*)
    Co A (-) (Rein.), 1st AmtracBn, FMF (177*)
        (34 LVTP-5, 1 LVTC, 1 LVTR-1, 2 LVTE)

Co C (-), 3d TkBn, FMF (101*)
    (12 M48A3 Tanks)
    Co C (-) (89*)
    Det., H&S Co
        (3 M67A2 Flame Tanks) (12*)

7th Marines (Rein.) (Chu Lai) (3917*)
   HqCo (-) (Rein.) (307*)
      HqCo (-) (246*)
      Det., HqBn, 3d MarDiv (61*)
   1st Bn, 7th Marines (1083*)
   2d Bn, 7thMarines (1010*)
   3d Bn, 7th Marines (1039*)
   Co C (Rein.), 1st ATBn (90*)
      (15 M5OA1 Ontos)
      Co C (61*)
      HqCo (-) (29*)
3d ATBn (-) (Rein.) (Da Nang) (330*)
   H&S Co (163*)
   Co A (-) (Rein.) (10 M5OA1 Ontos) (67*)
   Co C (Rein.) (20 M5OA1 Ontos) (100*)
3d TkBn (-) (Rein.) (Da Nang) (524*)
   H&S Co (-) (290*)
      (2 M48A3 Tks)
Co A (-) (Rein.) (94*)
   (12 M48A3 Tks and 3 M67A2 Flame Tks)
   Co B (Rein.) (117*)
      (17 M48A3 Tks and 3 M67A2 Flame Tks)
   Co C, 1st Plt (23*)
      (5 M48A3 Tks)

* Total Personnel: USMC, USN, officer, enlisted, and attached units with primary components (i.e., tanks—gun and flame; Ontos)

Note: Edited statistics (GB-65)

1965: A Recap of Marine Operations
Chronology of Significant (Mostly) Marine Events

1 Jan.—TE 79.3.3.6 at Da Nang was designated Marine Unit, Vietnam (MUV), TU 79.3.5, by direction of CG FMFPac. The organization and its operations remained essentially as before.

7 Feb.—Communist guerrillas attacked a United States compound at Pleiku, and U.S. aircraft retaliated by striking targets in North Vietnam, initiating a new phase of the war. U.S. forces in South Vietnam totaled 23,000. U.S. dependents were ordered evacuated from RVN.

8 Feb.—Battery A, 1st LAAM Battalion arrived at Da Nang via C-130; it was operational the next day.

10 Feb.—The Viet Cong blew up a U.S. military billet at the coastal city of Qui Nhon, killing twenty-three soldiers.

13 Feb.—More elements of the 1st LAAM Battalion (-), commanded by Lieutenant Colonel Bertram E. Cook Jr., arrived at Da Nang by sea and air. Two full batteries and supporting elements were deployed and 100 percent operational five days later.

17 Feb.—Company C, 7th Engineer Battalion began arriving at Da Nang by LST. HMM-163, commanded by Lieutenant Colonel Norman G. Ewers, relieved. Lieutenant Colonel Joseph Koler Jr.'s HMM-365 as the operating squadron of TU 79.3.5. (Note: Helicopter squadrons located on the Da Nang Air facility.)

28 Feb.—USMC tactical unit strength in RVN was 1,248, broken down as follows:

HMM-163: 230
Sub-Unit I: 203
Security Company (D/1/3): 260
Total MUV: 693

1st LAAM Bn (-): 405
CO C, 7th EngrBn: 150
Total, New Elements: 555
Total, USMC (Tactical): 1,248

These figures do not include USMC Advisors, embassy Marines, MACV staff personnel, and various other categories of Marines assigned outside the Da Nang area.

8 Mar.—The 9th Marine Expeditionary Brigade (MEB) commanded by Brigadier General Frederick J. Karch, landed at Da Nang. The MEB included two Marine Battalion Landing Teams (BLTs)— 3/9 (Lieutenant Colonel Charles E. McPartlin Jr.), which landed over Red Beach 2; and 1/3 (Lieutenant Colonel Herbert J. Bain), which arrived by air to the Da Nang Air Facility from Okinawa. The 9th MEB mission was to defend the Da Nang Air Base. This was the first U.S. ground combat unit to land in RVN.

9 Mar.—The MUV (TU 79.3.5) was placed under operational control of the 9th MEB and designated MAG-16, commanded by Colonel John H. King Jr. HMM-163 remained in direct support of ARVN I Corps; other elements of the expanding MAG (Sub-Unit 2, MABS-16) were in direct support of the 9th MEB. The 1st LAAM Battalion was placed under operational control of MAG-16 with a mission to defend Da Nang Air Base from air attack.

23 Mar.—Current composition of 9th MEB is as follows:

9th MEB: 4,612
HqCo: 145
BLT 1/3: 1,124
BLT 3/9: 1,115
Brigade Logistic Support Group: 583
Brigade Engineer Group: 224
Brigade Artillery Group: 235
MAG-16 (-): 1,214

H&MS-16 (-): 88
MABS-16 (-): 208
HMM-162: 233
l-IMM-163: 246
1st LAAM: 411

2 Apr.—The United States announced the intention of sending several thousand more troops to Vietnam.

10 Apr.—Lieutenant Colonel David A. Clement's BLT 2/3 landed at Da Nang. Task Force Alpha of the BLT was helilifted to the Phu Bai airstrip, 45 miles north of Da Nang near and to the south of Hue, to assume the defense of that area.

12 Apr.—The RLT-3 commander, Colonel Edwin B. Wheeler, and his headquarters arrived; he assumed command of all BLTs ashore.

14 Apr.—Lieutenant Colonel Donald R. Jones's BLT 3/4 arrived in Vietnam and moved to Phu Bai, where it relieved Task Force Alpha.

19 Apr.—RLT-3 reorganized as 3d Marines (Rein.); a larger tactical area of responsibility (TAOR) was established at Da Nang, and a TAOR was established at Phu Bai for 3/4.

20 Apr.—COMUSMACV authorized a change in General Karch's mission for ground forces to include (1) aggressive combat patrolling within TAORs and (2) preparation for conducting offensive operations as a mobile reaction force. High-level Honolulu conference recommended to President Johnson the deployment of III MEF to Da Nang and the landing of an MEB at Chu Lai.

20 Apr.—The landing of additional Marine Corps units at Da Nang resulted in the following organization:

9MEB
HqCo 240

3d Marines (-) (Rein): 3,751
HqCo: 286
1st Bn, 3d Marines: 1,099
2d Bn, 3d Marines: 1,267
3d Bn, 9th Marines: 1,099
Brigade Artillery Group: 548
HqBtry (-), 12th Marines: 26
Btry A, 1st Bn, 12th Marines: 120
Btry B, 1st Bn, 12th Marines: 119
Btry F, 2d Bn, 12th Marines: 120
Btry L, 4th Bn, 12th Marines: 112
1st 8" HowBtry: 51
Brigade Engineer Group: 299
Brigade Logistics Support Group: 656
MAG-16: 1,613
H&MS-16 (-): 111
MABS-16 (-): 232
VMFA-531 (-): 300
HMM-162: 126
HMM-163: 233
1st LAAM Bn: 413
MASS-2: 100
VMCJ-1: 98
BLT 3/4 and Det HMM 162: 1,500
Total 9th MEB: 8,607

All units were located at Da Nang, except for BLT 3/4 and a detachment of ten UH-34 helicopters from HMM-162, located at Phu Bai.

22 Apr.—The first real Marine ground action with the Viet Cong occurred—a reconnaissance company on patrol was fired on by an estimated 10 to 150 Viet Cong; VMFA-531 provided air support; one enemy was killed, and one Marine was slightly wounded.

28 Apr.—Companies E and F 2/3 participated in the first coordinated ground operation with ARVN forces in RVN.

3 May—The advance party of the III MEF, including its commander, Major General William R. Collins, arrived at Da Nang.

5 May—COMUSMACV promulgated a Letter of Instruction (LOI) giving the mission of III MEF: "In general render combat support to RVNAF (Republic of Vietnam Armed Forces). In coordination with CG, I Corps, participate in or provide for the defense of Hue/Phu Bai, Da Nang, and Chu Lai airfields and ancillary facilities. Maintain the capability to conduct, on order, deep patrolling and offensive operations and reserve reaction operations in coordination with CG, I Corps. Be prepared to execute U. S. contingency plans as directed by COMUSMACV."

6 May—The III MEF headquarters was established at Da Nang Air Base, commanded by Major General Collins, who was also designated the Naval Component Commander (NCC) for COMUSMACV. The 9th MEB was deactivated as an operating unit, and the 3d Marine Division (Forward), also commanded by Major General Collins, was established and assumed command of its assigned units in RVN. With the Chu Lai landings on 7 May, seven of the 3d Division infantry battalions were committed in RVN, supported by most of the 12th Marines and substantial portions of all other elements of the division.

7 May—Ill MEF was redesignated III MAF. Third MAB, commanded by Brigadier General Marion E. Carl, consisting of RLT-4 (Colonel Edward P. Dupras Jr.), the advance elements of MAG-12 (Colonel John D. Noble), and Naval Mobile Construction Battalion 10 (Commander John M. Bannister, USN), landed at Chu Lai with the mission of occupying the terrain necessary to construct an expeditionary airfield there.

11 May—2/3 cleared the village of Le My, liberating it from over two years of Viet Cong control. The village became a model of the Marine Corps' Civic Action Program (CAP).

12 May—Lieutenant Colonel William D. Hall's BLT 3/3 landed at Chu Lai. Brigadier General Carl was designated III MAF deputy commander. RLT-4 was redesignated 4th Marines as the Chu Lai amphibious operation terminated.

31 May—USMC strengths by area:

Da Nang: 9,224
Chu Lai: 6,599
Hue/Phu Bai: 1,614
TAD in-country: 121
Total: 17,558

4 Jun—Major General Lewis W. Walt assumed command of III MAF and the 3d MarDiv (Fwd) relieving Major General Collins.

13 Jun—COMUSMACV directed III MAF to prepare an emergency contingency plan for the movement of two infantry battalions to Pleiku in II Corps area. The plan was completed and forwarded to COMUSMACV on 14 June.

17 Jun.—Lieutenant Colonel Verle E. Ludwig's 1/9 relieved 3/9 at Da Nang and assumed the responsibility formerly held by 3/9 in the defense of the air base; 3/9 was the first Marine battalion to be rotated from RVN.

18 Jun.—Brigadier General Karch returned to Da Nang and assumed duties as assistant division commander (ADC), 3d MarDiv (Fwd).

30 Jun.—III MAF strength in RVN not including Seabees was as follows:

Da Nang: 9,618
Chu Lai: 6,771
Phu Bai: 1,652
Other: 115
Total: 18,156

Total arrived by area during June:
Da Nang: 1,496
Chu Lai: 2,002
Phu Bai: 204
Total: 3,702

1 Jul.—Viet Cong forces conducted a mortar/infantry attack on the Da Nang Air Base under cover of darkness, providing cover for demolition teams that broached the tactical wire surrounding the field, and severely damaged six USAF aircraft. The one Viet Cong captured in the attack reported that he was from the 3d Battalion, 18th Regiment, 325th People's Army of Vietnam (PAVN) Division and that the attack force trained and rehearsed for thirty days before executing its mission. The SLF, composed of the 3/7 (Lieutenant Colonel Charles H. Bodley) and HMM-163 (Lieutenant Colonel Norman G. Ewers), landed at Qui Nhon to protect an enclave at the seaward end of Route 19, the main highway from Pleiku.

6 Jul.—RLT-9 (Colonel Frank E. Garretson) with BLT 2/9 (Lieutenant Colonel George R. Scharnberg) landed at Da Nang.

8 Jul.—At Qui Nhon, Lieutenant Colonel Leon N. Utter's BLT 2/7 relieved the SLF battalion, Bodley's BLT 3/7, which then reembarked in ARG shipping.

21 Jul.—Written confirmation was received for expansion of the Da Nang TAOR and for the establishment of a reconnaissance zone for the Chu Lai TAOR.

29 Jul.—Official sources announced plans to increase the U.S. active duty military force by about 300,000 men. The 1st Brigade, 101st Airborne Division arrived in RVN on this date.

31 Jul.—Ill MAF strengths in RVN not including Seabees were as follows:

Da Nang: 15,204
Chu Lai: 6,949
Phu Bai: 2,052
Qui Nhon: 1,644
Other: 115
Total: 25,964

Total arrived by area during July:
Da Nang: 5,743 + 395
Phu Bai: 178 + 1,651
Total: 7,967

2 Aug.—Operation BLAST OUT, a coordinated USMC/ARVN operation involving 1/3 and elements of the 4th ARVN Regiment, was conducted 10 miles southwest of Da Nang.

3 Aug.—Company D, 1/9 conducted a one-day operation in the vicinity of Cam Ne, south of Da Nang. A CBS television crew accompanying the company filmed a Marine setting fire to a Vietnamese hut. This film, which was shown on the evening news, led to a heated debate in the press about U.S. tactics in Vietnamese villages.

5 Aug.—The Viet Cong attacked the Esso POL storage terminal at Lien Chieu, destroying two JP-4 storage tanks and inflicting extensive damage on three more. Operational control of 2/7 (at Qui Nhon in the II Corps area) passed to U.S. Army Task Force ALFA, the Army field command in RVN.

7 Aug.—The CG III MAF was designated as the senior adviser (SA) for I Corps and assumed operational control of the I Corps Advisory Group.

14 Aug.—The Navy announced four-month involuntary extensions of duty for Navy and Marine Corps enlisted personnel. Coordinating headquarters were established at Chu Lai under the 3d MarDiv ADC, Brigadier General Karch.

15 Aug.—The headquarters of RLT-7 and 1/7 came ashore at Chu Lai. Colonel Oscar F. Peatross commanded the regiment. At Da Nang, elements of 3/9 came ashore, making it the first battalion to be reintroduced into RVN (see 8 March and 17 June 1965 entries).

16 Aug.—3/9 relieved 1/9 as the base defense battalion at Da Nang.

17 Aug.—2/4 and 3/3 were assigned to the 7th Marines for Operation STARLITE.

18–24 Aug.—Operation STARLITE. Three Marine battalions—1/7, 2/4, and 3/3—attached to the 7th Marines, and supported by air, artillery, and naval gunfire, conducted an amphibious-heliborne search-and-destroy operation in the Van Tuong village complex south of Chu Lai. The purpose of the attack was to eliminate an enemy force—the 1st VC Regiment, reportedly 2,000 strong—which had built up for an attack on Chu Lai. Strong resistance was encountered, requiring the support of BLT 3/7 from the SLF. The USMC units advanced through the objective area in two days and then were joined for mopping-up operations by Vietnamese forces.

Casualties were as follows:

USMC
KIA: 45
DOW: 6
WIA: 203

VC
KIA: 614
DOW: 9

The Viet Cong dead were confirmed by actual body count. It was estimated that the actual enemy KIA total ran much higher because of the large number of caves and tunnels that were sealed or destroyed.

(On 9 September, an agent source reported that the VC had suffered 1,430 KIA in Operation STARLITE.)

26 Aug.—In response to a CG III MAF request made in June, eleven sentry dogs and handlers arrived as the initial element of the 1st Provisional Dog Platoon, which was planned to consist ultimately of two squads, a sentry dog squad and a patrol dog squad.

28 Aug.—1/1 arrived at Da Nang to relieve 1/3.

31 Aug.—President Johnson called for "a new and mighty people-to-people program to bring American aid to victims of the war in RVN." The total III MAF strength in RVN, not including Seabees, was broken down as follows:

Da Nang: 1,806 + 10,277
Phu Bai: 2,114 + 1,616
Other: 92
Total: 32,162

Total arrived by area during August:
Da Nang: 4,725
Chu Lai: 2,684
Total arrived: 7,409

Total departed by area during August:
Da Nang: 1,029 (1/3 departed)
Phu Bai: 68 + 35
Total departed: 1,132
Net Gain, August: 6,277

1 Sep.—1/3 departed RVN for Okinawa, where it was relieved by BLT 3/5, and then returned to CONUS. A total of 10,919 personnel of FMFPac remained in Okinawa and Japan.

7–10 Sep.—Operation PIRANHA. Following the decisive Marine Corps victory over the 1st Viet Cong Regiment in Operation STARLITE (18–24 August), intelligence information disclosed that other VC forces were building up on the Batangan Peninsula, still farther south of Chu Lai. Operation PIRANHA, another regimental-level amphibious-heliborne attack, was executed to clear the area. It exacted at least 163 Viet Cong killed and served notice once again upon the VC of the hazards of concentrating their forces. Subsequently, the VC reverted to small unit operations in I Corps area.

11 Sep.—BLT 2/1, which arrived on Okinawa 27 August from CONUS and subsequently embarked as the SLF, assumed a position within six hours' reaction time of Qui Nhon, prepared to land and provide security, if required, for debarkation of the Army's 1st Cavalry Division (Airmobile).

18 Sep.—The first elements of the Army's 1st Cavalry (Airmobile) Division landed at Qui Nhon.

23 Sep.—The Defense Department said that General Westmoreland had the authority to permit use of tear gas.

25 Sep.—Operation DAGGER THRUST I (II CTZ, Vung Mu), SLF (BLT 2/1 and HMM-261).

27 Sep.—Operation DAGGER THRUST II (II CTZ, Ben Goi), SLF (BLT 2/1 and HMM-261).

28 Sep.—The total III MAF strength in RVN not including Seabees by area was as follows:

Da Nang: 18,641 + 13,601
Phu Bai: 2,172 + 1,773
Total: 36,187

Total arrived by area during September:
Da Nang: 3,222
Chu Lai: 3,384
Phu Bai: 327
Total: 6,933

Total departed by area during September
Phu Bai: 26
Net Change: 6,907

1 Oct.—Operation DAGGER THRUST III (II CTZ, Tam Quan), SLF (BLT 2/1 and HMM-261).

14 Oct.—The CG, I Corps approved extension of the Chu Lai TAOR. A USMC sniper team was formed in the Hue/Phu Bai TAOR.

18 Oct.—Operation TRAIL BLAZER, a six-day deep patrol and series of ambushes by the 3d Reconnaissance Battalion, began from a patrol base about 15 miles southwest of Da Nang. Two companies from 3/3 launched Operation TRIPLE PLAY, a two-day search-and-destroy effort conducted 12 miles north of Chu Lai. The results: 16 VC KIA, 6 VCC, and 18 VCS, with only 2 Marines wounded.

26 Oct.—Operation DRUM HEAD, a coordinated two-day sweep effort involving 3/7 and an ARVN platoon, began southwest of Chu Lai. Results: 1 VC killed and 26 suspects captured; 1 USMC killed and 2 wounded.

27 Oct.—Operation GOLDEN FLEECE (begun 8 September 65) was terminated. This operation by the 9th Marines was an effort to deny as much rice as possible to the VC during the summer/fall 1965 rice harvest. USMC units provided protection for Vietnamese farmers in their fields while the rice crop was harvested. It is estimated that 512,400 pounds of threshed rice were denied the VC as a result.

28 Oct.—On the night of 28 October, Viet Cong suicide squads launched simultaneous and coordinated attacks on Marine installations at Marble Mountain near and south of Da Nang and at Chu Lai. Even though most of the attackers were killed, the few who got through used satchel charges to blow up nineteen helicopters and damage the hospital at Marble Mountain, while at Chu Lai they destroyed two fixed-wing attack aircraft. Ground actions during the night indicated that other planned attacks were thwarted by Marine patrols.

3 Nov.—Operation BLACK FERRET, a three-day combined USMC/ARVN search-and-destroy operation of regimental scope, began in an area 10 miles south of the Chu Lai airstrip, on the north side of the Song Tra Bong. Participating was two companies from 1/7; two companies from 3/7; 3/11; two platoons from the 1st Reconnaissance Battalion; and two battalions from the 4th Regiment of the 2d ARVN Division. A booby-trapped 81 mm mortar round wounded six Marines and killed Ms. Dickie Chapelle, the war correspondent who was accompanying USMC units on the maneuver. Helicopters returned the Marines to Chu Lai upon conclusion of the operation on 5 November.

7 Nov.—BLT 2/7 was withdrawn from Qui Nhon (see 10–12 November entry below); HMM-161 remained at Qui Nhon in support of II Corps forces.

10–12 Nov.—Operation BLUE MARLIN, a combined USMC/VNMC operation between Chu Lai and Tam Ky, 20 miles to the north, took place. On 7 November, BLT 2/7 was lifted in amphibious shipping from its former TAOR at Qui Nhon to Chu Lai, where it was joined by the six-hundred-man 3d Battalion, Vietnamese Marine Corps. The two units conducted a combined amphibious assault on 10 November across beaches just north of Tam Ky. Four companies of BLT 2/7 in one LVT wave and two LCM waves landed unopposed, followed by the remainder of the BLT and the 3d Battalion, VNMC, in on-call boat serials and helicopters. Surf at the beach was very high, and the anchor chains of the APA *Paul Revere* and the LST *Windham County* parted.

After sweeping inland to Route 1, the landing force pivoted southward astride the highway and executed a search-and-destroy operation to the Chu Lai TAOR. Resistance was light, and casualties were few. A Vietnamese civilian reported that the VC had withdrawn from the objective area two days previously. At the conclusion of the operation, the RVN Marines were returned by helicopter to their base area south of Quang Ngai; 2/7 rejoined its parent regiment at Chu Lai, replacing 3/3, which embarked for phase II of BLUE MARLIN (see 16–18 November entry) and subsequent operations at Da Nang.

16–18 Nov.—Operation BLUE MARLIN (phase II), similar in scope and concept to phase I (10–12 November), was conducted. At Chu Lai, 3/3 embarked in the same amphibious shipping used in phase I and landed on 16 November over beaches south of Hoi An, about 22 miles south of Da Nang. The landing was accomplished smoothly, with one wave of LVTs and two of LCMs, followed by artillery, tanks, and Ontos in on-call serials. Ashore, the landing force was joined by two RVN Ranger battalions and two RVN special companies in a coordinated search-and-destroy operation north to the Song Cua Dao; 3/3 was lifted to the Da Nang area by amphibious shipping and helicopter.

17–18 Nov.—Marine air elements from III MAF were instrumental in preventing a Viet Cong victory at Hiep Duc, about 25 miles west of Tam Ky. The helilifted troops were successful in defeating the assault on Hiep Duc but were unable to clear the VC from the critical areas to the northwest. At the request of CG I Corps, 3/7 was alerted to reinforce the ARVN units. Extremely bad weather prevented the heliift of 3/7 into Hiep Duc. While awaiting improved weather, the battalion was diverted to assist an ARVN Ranger battalion under siege at Thach Tru, south of Quang Ngai (see 22–24 November entry).

22–24 Nov.—On the late afternoon of 22 November, at the request of CG I Corps, 3/7 began reinforcing an ARVN Ranger battalion, which had come under attack by an estimated VC regiment about 20 miles south of Quang Ngai. At the same time, the 7th Fleet SLF moved to position off Quang Ngai, ready to land on two hours' notice. On the morning of the twenty-fourth, the situation was stabilized and 3/7 returned to Chu Lai. Losses in the encounter were two Marines killed and one wounded in the downed helicopter.

30 Nov.–1 Dec.—Operation DAGGER THRUST IV (III CTZ, Lan Ke). On 30 November, the SLF (BLT 2/1 and HMM-261) executed an amphibious raid at Lang Ke Ga, on the coast 17 miles southwest of Phan Thiet and about 70 miles east of Saigon. Immediately prior to the landing, leaflets were dropped along the routes of advance, giving brief warning to the villagers. Contact was negligible.

November III MAF Summary
Patrols: 3,488
Ambushes: 2,576
Sniper posts: 175
Total offensive ground operations: 6,242
Enemy contacts: 226
Enemy KIA: 126
Enemy WIA: 33
Enemy captured: 22

Rainfall more than 30 inches. Most rain in one day recorded as 7.8 inches.

30 Nov.— The III MAF strength in RVN not including Seabees and naval support activity was as follows:

Da Nang: 21,948
Chu Lai: 14,452
Phu Bai: 2,328
Qui Nhon: 254
Other: 89
Total: 39,071

Operation MIX MASTER, intended to level-load arrival and departure of troops, resulted in personnel strengths fluctuated by area during November due to reassignment between enclaves, replacement, attrition, and movement of battalions. Net strength change for November: 422

5 Dec.—Operation DAGGER THRUST V (II CTZ, Phu Thu), SLF (BLT 2/1 and HMM-261).

8–20 Dec.—Operation HARVEST MOON was conducted approximately 25 miles northwest of Chu Lai. Units involved were Task Force DELTA, 2/7, 3/3, 2/1 (from SLF), and three ARVN battalions. These units were supported by USMC aircraft and artillery and by B-52 strikes.

USMC
KIA: 51
WIA: 256
MIA: 1

Enemy
KIA: 407
VCC: 33
VCS: 231
Ralliers: 3

22 Dec.—The U.S. Military Command in Vietnam ordered a thirty-hour Christmas ceasefire. A military spokesman said that similar instructions had been issued by South Vietnamese government military leaders. No action would be taken by allied or RVNAF forces except in sell-defense. The Viet Cong paid little heed. For them it was "business as usual."

31 Dec.—USMACV released the following figures to news media in Saigon:

U.S. Military Strength in RVN 1 Jan. '65: 23,000
U.S. Military Strength in RVN 31 Dec. '65: 181,000
RVNAF Total Strength 1 Jan. '65: 559,500

RVNAF Total Strength 31 Dec. '65: 679,000
Enemy Military Strength in RVN 1 Jan. '65: 103,000
Enemy Military Strength in RVN 31 Dec. '65: 230,000
U.S. losses during the year: 1,300
RVNAF losses during the year: 11,000
Enemy losses during the year: KIA 34,000
Enemy losses during the year: Captured 6,000

III MAF total arrived during December:
Da Nang: 188
Chu Lai: 138
Phu Bai: 81
Total: 407

III MAF total departed during December:
Chu Lai: 452
Qui Nhon: 25
Total: 477
Net Change: –70

31 Dec.—Ill MAF strength in RVN not including Seabees and naval support activity was as follows:

Da Nang: 22,464
Chu Lai: 13,995
Phu Bai: 2,354
Qui Nhon: 226
1st Anglico: 73
Total: 39,092

31 Dec.—Ill MAF ground operations for the week ending 31 December were as follows:

Patrols: 1,169
Ambushes: 633
Platoon-size Operations: 40

Company-size Operations: 6
Battalion-size Operations: 3
VCKIA 81
VC Captured: 6

31 Dec.—Results of III MAF Operations since 8 March 1965:

USMC
KIA and DOW: 342
WIA: 2,047
MIA: 18

VC
KIA: 2,627
WIA: 314
POW: 535
VCS: 2,827

31 Dec.—A total of 14,528 FMFPac personnel remained in Okinawa and Japan.

Additionally, either already deployed or soon to be were the American forces allies. "The combination of the combined Australian and New Zealand forces to the conflict are relatively well reported, as are thus of the Republic of Korea (ROK) (better known as South Korea). The contributions of the Kingdom of Thailand and the Republic of the Philippines are less well known. Fear of involvement by the People's Republic of China meant that the contingent from the Republic of China (also known as Taiwan) was purely advisory. FWAF contributions peaked in 1969, with almost seventy-thousand personnel deployed from all six nations" (AV-JT).

Marine Tanks and Ontos in Vietnam

Volume Two: 1966

by the

HISTORY SECTION
HISTORICAL FOUNDATION
FEDERAL WAY, WASHINGTON

**Marine Tanks and Ontos
Vietnam: 1965 to 1970**
by
Those Warriors Who Served during the Vietnam War
Compiled and Edited by
The Marine Corps Vietnam Tankers Historical Foundation Staff

CONTENTS

Foreword 273

Vietnam—a Strange Experience from a Western Perspective 287
January 1966 Operation Mallard 294
POOP 301
Blessings in a Small Bottle 309
Operation EAGLE FLIGHT 49er 315
The Marble Mountain "Mad Dog" Caper 372
50 Years Ago—21 May 1966—My Longest Day 392
I Remember 412
Tanks in Operation LIBERTY, June 1966 420
In Country 464
The Move North 470
We'll Wait on the Other Side 496
Operation HASTINGS 505
The August 26, 1966, Attack on Cam Lo: Golf and Hotel 3/12 ... 515
Night of the Tigers 558
Gibson Recalls a Day in Vietnam 585
The Betrayal—The True Story 635

Index 641

Don't fight a battle if you don't gain anything by winning.

—Erwin Rommel

Foreword

This is the second volume in a planned seven-volume operational and chronological series covering the participation of Marine Corps tank and antitank organizations in the Vietnam War. This volume details the continued buildup during 1966 of tank and Ontos units in South Vietnam's northernmost corps area—I Corps—and the accelerated tempo of fighting during the year in what has become known in official documentation as an "expanding war" (GB-66).

Volume 1 detailed the establishment and expansion of the III Marine Amphibious Force (III MAF) in the three enclaves of Chu Lai, Da Nang, and Hue/Phu Bai, employing a balanced strategy of base defense, offensive operations, and pacification. The year 1966 was intended to be a year of consolidation and expansion of those three Tactical Areas of Responsibility (TAORs).

III MAF had nearly doubled its size during 1965 and closed the year with cautious optimism that 1966 would see measurable success in the prosecution of the war against the North Vietnam–supported Viet Cong. However, the "high hopes held by the Marines in 1966" were somewhat dampened by South Vietnam's internal political crisis in the spring, halting the Marine pacification campaign south of the Da Nang Air Base. In July, the North Vietnamese Army (NVA) removed any doubt of its commitment to bolster the Viet Cong's efforts to defeat the existing government of South Vietnam by attacking across the

Demilitarized Zone (DMZ), which caused the Marines to begin the move of its forces north to counter the enemy thrust. The Marines were stretched the 265-mile length of I Corps—"too much real estate—do not have enough men" (GB-66).

R. A. Stewart
Lieutenant Colonel, U.S. Marine Corps (Ret*)

In *A World Lit Only by Fire*, author William Manchester writes of the medieval era, over which his book spans, "I had no grasp of the way the webs of action were spun out, how each led inexorably to another, then another," and uses the Vietnam War to make his point. "Yet I knew from experience that such chains of circumstances are always there, awaiting discovery. To cite a small, relatively recent example: In the first year of John F. Kennedy's presidential administration, four developments appeared to be unrelated—America's humiliation at the Bay of Pigs in April, Kennedy's confrontation with Nikita Khrushchev in Austria six weeks later, the raising of the Berlin Wall in August, and, in December, the first commitment of ground troops to Indochina. Yet, each event had led to the next. Khrushchev saw the Cuban fiasco as evidence that the young president was weak. Therefor he bullied him in Vienna. In the mistaken belief that he had intimidated him there, he built the (Berlin) Wall. Kennedy answered the challenge by sending four hundred Green Berets to Southeast Asia, explaining to those around him that *'we have a problem making our power credible, and Vietnam looks like the place'*" (italics by VTHF) (WL-WM).

The sun rose on South Vietnam on 1 January 1966 to a Marine in-country force of over forty-one thousand men: an increase of the thirty-six thousand Marines of the 9th MEB that crossed the Da Nang beaches less than a year earlier on 8–9 March. And it was not only the numbers of Marines but the organizations and types of units that comprised the Marine forces: A reinforced 3d Marine Division, the 1st Marine Aircraft Wing, and all their supporting units to sustain the Corps' division/wing team. The Marine forces were parsed to three Tactical Areas of Responsibility (TAORs) in the northernmost of South Vietnam's four military regions—the 10,000 square mile I Corps Tactical Zone (I CTZ) comprising five provinces inhabited by 2.6 million people, the bulk of which lived in the coastal region engaged primarily in fishing and rice farming. The terrain spanned the spectrum from the lofty, nearly impenetrable, sparsely inhabited Annamite Mountains in the west that gave way, moving east, to densely vegetated hill masses, then interlaced with rivers and valleys, to the alluvial coastal plain with its dense population.

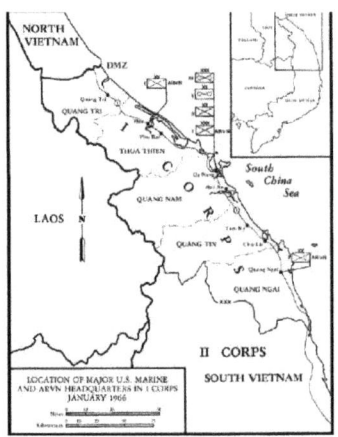

(GB-66)

From north to south: Quang Tri, which bordered on the demilitarized zone (DMZ) with North Vietnam; Thua Thien, with the ancient imperial city of Hue, one of the three largest South Vietnamese cities and its cultural center; Quang Nam, with Da Nang, the second-largest city in South Vietnam and a major port and air facility; Quang Tin, with the just-created U.S. Airfield named by the Americans "Chu Lai"; and the southernmost province of Quang Ngai, with II ITZ on its southern border. Marine TAORs were established in Thua Thien (Hue/Phu Bia), Quang Nam (Da Nang), and Quang Tin (Chu Lai).

The Da Nang TAOR was home to III MAF's, the 3d Marine Division's, and the 1st Marine Aircraft Wing's Headquarters, the 3d and 9th Marines, and the 12th Marines artillery regiment.

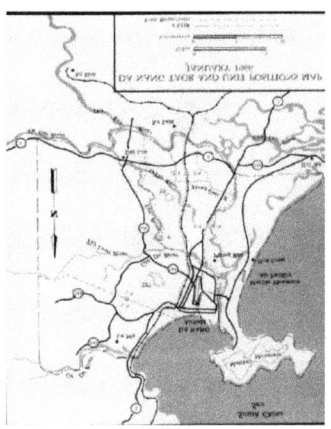

(GB-66)

At Chu Lai was the 4th and 7th Marines with supporting artillery (GB-66 and SF-EM)

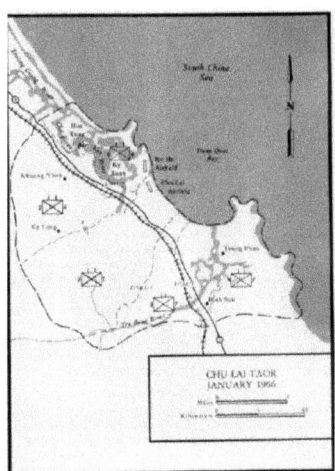

(GB-66)

At Phu Bia was 2/1 and 4/12. Air wing assets were parsed to support operations from these TAORs commensurate with the size of the unit, the area of responsibility, the terrain, and the enemy's disposition.

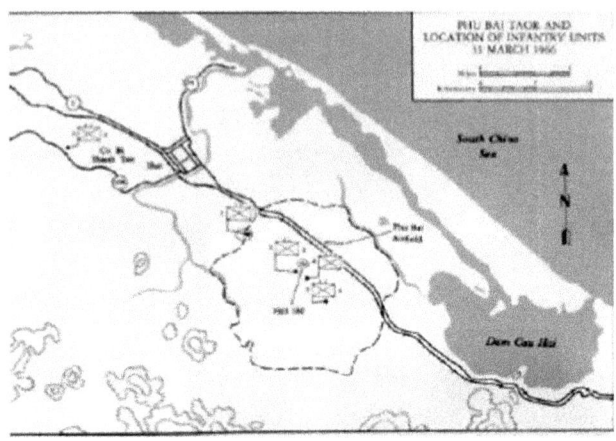

(GB-66)

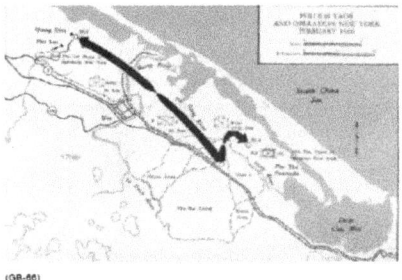

(GB-66)

(Insert Image #6)

III MAF's Commander, General Walt, studying his on-the-ground resources matched to that of the enemy, had reason for optimism even as the Communist-led enemy supported through its pipeline from the north with NVA fighters and supplies fed by the Communist Chinese and Soviet ships through the port of Haiphong, had matched the build-up U.S. Forces with its increase in strength, numbers, training, and equipment of the Viet Cong units in South Vietnam which, by intelligence estimates, with the help of the North Vietnamese Army (NVA), increased from a possible 138,000 in March of 1965 to over 226,000 fighters by the end of the year. Of the mix of South Vietnamese Viet Cong was an estimated seven regiments of the NVA which had already been bloodied by U.S. forces in pitched battles, (Ia Drang and Starlite) acquitting themselves well.

As observed by Edward F. Murphy (SF-EM) "Though the Marines had conducted several large-scale operations against Viet Cong main force units in 1965, the Marine Commander's (General Walt) major concern (though not shared by his boss, Genarl Westmorland, COMUSMACV, headquartered in Saigon) was still "the well-organized Viet Cong political and guerilla substructure" that remained in place and undisturbed. General Walt believed that to win the Vietnam War, the guerilla component of the fight had to be "defeated", which did not mean that he must necessarily be killed but "turned".

General Walt's boss in Saigon, COMUSMACV, Army General Westmoreland had a quite different view of the enemy and the strategy and tactics by which he could be defeated.

(GB-66)

III MAF's commander, General Walt, studying his on-the-ground resources matched to that of the enemy, had reason for optimism even as the Communist-led enemy, supported through its pipeline from the north with NVA fighters and supplies fed by the Communist Chinese and Soviet ships through the port of Haiphong, had matched the buildup U.S. forces with its increase in strength, numbers, training, and equipment of the Viet Cong units in South Vietnam, which, by intelligence estimates, with the help of the North Vietnamese Army (NVA), increased from a possible 138,000 in March of 1965 to over 226,000 fighters by the end of the year. Of the mix of South Vietnamese Viet Cong was an estimated seven regiments of the NVA, which had already been bloodied by U.S. forces in pitched battles (Ia Drang and STARLITE), acquitting themselves well.

As observed by Edward F. Murphy (SF-EM), "Though the Marines had conducted several large-scale operations against Viet Cong Main Force units in 1965, the Marine Commander's [General Walt] major concern [though not shared by his boss, General Westmoreland, COMUSMACV, headquartered in Saigon] was still the well-organized Viet Cong political and guerilla substructure" that remained in place and undisturbed. General Walt believed that to win the Vietnam War, the guerilla component of the fight had to be "defeated," which did not mean that he must necessarily be killed but "turned."

General Walt's boss in Saigon, COMUSMACV, Army General Westmoreland, had a quite different view of the enemy and the strategy and tactics by which he could be defeated and so was spawned and nurtured the strategy that required the enemy to be killed and at a rate that would attrite his military capability by attriting the soldiers directly rather than, as in a guerilla war, by removing his support system (i.e., locals); and thus the VC "stacks their weapons" (i.e., lays down their arms and cease fighting) and becomes a productive contributors to the community welfare. As Murphy opines, "Although General Westmoreland acknowledged the benefits of the Combined Action Program (CAP), he did virtually nothing to encourage their use." He based his opposition on the shortage of personnel to carry out the labor intensiveness of successful guerilla operations.

This then was Westmoreland's, and tacitly the Marines', "tactical plan for victory" in three easy steps: First, "search and destroy" using large units operating in the field to "find, fix, and destroy" enemy forces and base areas. This was to be the responsibility of American troops using the kill ratio*—i.e., "kill more of them than they kill of us" was one of the two ways (the other was to count large units' "days in the field")—to quantify and thus measure success, since territorial gains were not a goal of this war. Second was referred to as "clearing operations," essentially mopping up those enemy escaping the U.S.-led offensive operations. This was to be the responsibility of the ARVN. Third was to be the "securing operation," which was intended to provide a secure defense and a return to normal life without the threat of the VC Guerilla.† The South Vietnamese Regional Forces (RFs) and locally recruited Popular Forces (PFs) would secure the villages once cleared of the enemy.

---

* VTHF comment: The "Westmoreland Plan" was meant to quantify for the chart makers in Saigon the progress of the campaign. "Quantifying" was Secretary of Defense Robert Strange McNamara's mantra. "Cost-effectiveness" was the measure of success. If the enemy killed [supposedly confirmed by actual body count] was some percent greater than the friendly casualties sustained, an operation was termed a success. Putting any sort of value on human life—from either side of the fight—was macabre.

† VTHF comment: This appears as a serious flaw in the understanding of the guerilla. Basically, there were two categories of Viet Cong, with a large gray area between the two. There was Main Force Viet Cong. The best example was the 1st Viet Cong Regiment encountered, met and defeated by the Marines in Operations STARLITE and PIRANHA. They were referred as Main Force because these VC were organized roughly along standard military organizational concepts with a cadre of NVA "advisers" and with a direct tap into the Ho Chi Minh Trail logistics system for arms and supplies. Each village comprised its local Viet Cong organization of various size, level of training, and support for these citizen soldiers by day and combatants at night. The Main Force stood and fought toe-to-toe and then melted away into the safety of the interior or cross-border into Laos. The latter stayed at home, tended his or her rice paddy, and changed his (or her) modis based on the time of day.

If the ARVN was incapable (as was widely held and often confirmed) of completing the second phase (the "Ruff-Puffs" were largely missing roll call altogether) to implement the third phase, even if on the odd chance, the second phase succeeded was doomed to failure as well.

From the earliest days of the landing of tank and antitank units, Civic Action (i.e., working closely and in collaboration with the locals) was a priority for Marines, which became institutionalized at the battalion level; as well as the establishment of a staff position (S-5) on the battalion staff with a line item budget, office, equipment, and regularly assigned officers, SNCOs, and enlisted personnel.

At 3d Tanks' command post in Da Nang, which had adopted Phong Bac, a local village just a few clicks down the road, to build schools, dig wells, farm pigs and chickens, and provide security, Second Lieutenant Bob Mattingly received a Silver Star defending the VC-attacked village.

The 3d Antitanks' command post was also in Da Nang. They adopted the sister village to Phong Bac—Yen Bac—and carried out an equally aggressive and successful support plan.

The tank battalion commander, Lieutenant Colonel William Corson, who championed the concept of winning "hearts and minds," left his position as 3d Tanks CO in Da Nang to head up the CAP on the 3d Marine Division/III MAF staff. He subsequently wrote a book, *The Betrayal* (TB-WC), critical of Westmoreland's conduct of the war that very nearly cost him his Marine Corps career and, though he denied it, led to his early retirement. Even then, his retirement pay and benefits were threatened, but Colonel Corson stayed the course and was proven to be largely correct in his assessment of the conduct of the war and the U.S. prospects of success.

(VTHF comment: As a note, should anyone doubt the commitment tank and antitank battalions and their subordinate units made in the support of the Combined Action Program, access to their units' monthly command chronologies details the daily activities and accomplishments of their respective CAP's effort in taking under their arms the villages of Phong Bac and Yen Bac, respectively.)

General Westmoreland and his, largely U.S. Army, staff in Saigon were also not thrilled with the Marine Corps' stated strategy of the "spreading ink blot," which planned the expansion of their three TAORs outward; securing villages and hamlets; the clearing of the local VC guerillas by denying them local support (that is, those guerillas not killed as the Marines moved into an area); and finally, eventually tying the three TAORs—Chu Lai, Da Nang, and Phu Bai—together along the coast, making 265 miles of the most populated and productive areas of South Vietnam secure and under South Vietnamese government control.

In late 1965, after Brigadier General William E. DePuy's "visit" to I Corps, he reported to General Westmoreland that he (DePuy) was "disturbed . . . that all but a tiny part of the I Corps area is under the control of the VC" and, further and unfairly, that the Marines were "stalled a short distance south of Da Nang." He recommended that the Corps be "ordered" to spend two weeks of every month in the field conducting large-scale, multibattalion offensive operations against the VC. Acting on General DePuy's recommendation, Westmoreland all but actually ordered General Walt to the field. In response to this brewing controversy, prior to the end of 1965, planning for Operation DOUBLE EAGLE, to be conducted in the Chu Lai area, was set in motion as the first operation of the overall 1966 Plan III MAF submitted to COMUSMACV for approval.

Oscar "Ed" Gilbert opens the second chapter, "1966: The NVA Moves South," of his book *Marine Corps Tank Battles in Vietnam* with a quote attributed to General Westmoreland: *"We'll just go on bleeding them until Hanoi wakes up to the fact that they have bled their country to the point of national disaster for generations"* (General William Childs Westmoreland) (TV-OG). The general obviously missed his OCS class on the need to "know your enemy" if one expects any chance in conquering him. Pretty basic stuff.

Following this link "http://www.mcvthf.org" to the annex, a table lists the maneuver battalions of the United States Marine Corps in chronological order of their arrival in-country. These battalions are the line units for all ground combat operations conducted during the Vietnam War that were supported by the 1st and 3d Tank and Antitank (Ontos) Battalions.

In the table, some units show **** instead of a numerical value. This is because the cited unit was broken down into company or smaller-sized units for combat operations. Therefore, these units were not counted for operations purposes in this chat. Only battalion-sized units and operations are included.

Detailed information on the specifics of tank and antitank (Ontos) companies and smaller units, primarily platoons, will be found scattered through the history series. However, as a general rule, tank and Ontos platoons were attached to the BLTs when they left CONUS, Hawaii, or Okinawa in transit to RVN and while they were afloat with the Special Landing Force (SLF). The attached elements were detached upon arrival in RVN, rejoined to their respective companies/battalions, but often continued in the role of direct support of the ground unit to which they were previously attached on the BLT/SLF. Tank and antitank platoons operated in RVN before their parent companies, and finally, their parent battalions came ashore.

As the Marine participation in the war drew down, personnel and equipment departing Vietnam were accomplished on an ad hoc basis, not tied to specifics of their support of infantry, and all but impossible to track and document. In the case of antitank, Ontos crewmen were randomly reassigned to other organizations when their units were deactivated, and the Ontos were assigned to Army and ARVN units to become stationary "pillboxes" in the static defense of base camps. Those that made it back to CONUS found their way to military "bone yards," employed as electric generators, and some found mowing the medians on interstate highways.

Also, please note that the departure dates on the chart are the dates that the battalions' command group—the commanding officer and his principal staff officers—folded their colors, pulled up stakes, and departed Vietnam. Some of their subordinate units may have departed earlier, and some followed at a later date. In the case of antitank (Ontos) companies and platoons, the parent battalion was sunset and its subordinate units were folded into, and came under the command of, the respective tank battalions for a time before they too were deactivated.

(GB-66 revised by VTHF)

"Consistent with his policy of forcing III MAF to go on the offensive, on 7 December (a day that shall live in infamy) 1965, General Westmoreland issued ORDERS" (VTHF emphasis). According to (GB-66), the Marine Corps' version was that "General Walt had 'received approval' for it (III MAF) to conduct an operation in late January 1966 against enemy forces concentrating along the border between the I and II Corps' tactical zones" (SF-EM). Operation DOUBLE EAGLE would be the first major operation of the war that was coordinated across Corps (military) boundaries. The area of operations consigned to the Marines posed particularly challenging terrain. In short, it did not favor tanks and Ontos participation in the planning of the operation. The CG of the just-formed Task Force Delta, Brigadier General Jonas M. Platt, concluded that he would rely on the heavy use of helicopters and that the rough terrain definitely favored the enemy forces of an estimated 6,500 NVA, Main Force VC, and local VC units in the defense.

Intelligence sources identified the enemy forces as the 18th and 95th NVA Regiments and the 2d VC Main Force Regiment. Additionally, the area of operation was home to more than a dozen independent VC companies and smaller units.

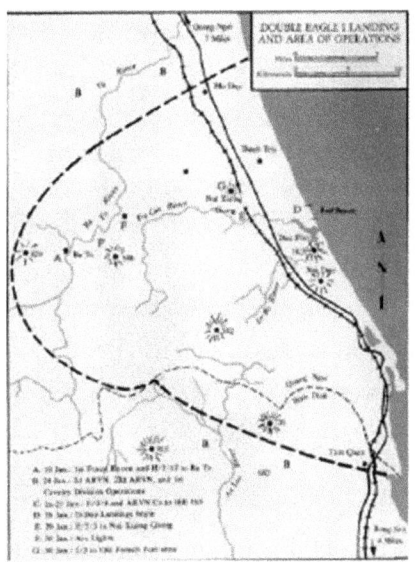

(GB-66)

The U.S. Army's 1st Cavalry Division (with some prodding from COMUSMACV) launched Operation MASHER/WHITE WING, attacking overland for its "half" of the joint operation. January 28 was D-day for the Marines' amphibious landing phase of DOUBLE EAGLE. In short, the bulk of the NVA/VC enemy escaped the traps set for them; and although the participants declared—lukewarmly and with a definite lack of conviction—a "success" for both DOUBLE EAGLES I (declared closed by the task force commander, General Platt on 17 February) and II (following on the heels of I and closed by 1 March) (SF-EM), CGFMFPAC, Lieutenant General Krulak, disagreed at the time and "insisted, several years later, that the lessons of Double Eagle (I and II) operations were largely negative. He pointed out that the operation FAILED [VTHF emphasis] because the VC and NVA had been forewarned." Furthermore, and even more important, Krulak contended that both operations taught the people in the area that the Marines "would come in, comb the area, and disappear; whereupon the VC would resurface and resume control." There were no "lessons learned" (in fact, barely "observed") from the previously conducted

285

Operation PIRANHA, i.e., that the enemy knowledge of our operation was most likely provided them by "friendlies," the forewarning resulting in the largely "failed" operations.

"The body count was the paramount measure of success. Every month, General Westmoreland required a massive collection of statistical data from all units, and no number was more important than the body count. Commanders reporting low body counts were routinely punished with poor fitness reports and passed over for promotion. Careers were on the line. High body counts, on the other hand, led to medals, rapid promotion, and plum assignments" (AReCA).

One has to wonder, though in retrospect, if COMUSMACV knew that of all the patrols conducted during the Vietnam War, less than 1 percent resulted in enemy contact. Further, that, statistically, the battalion-sized operations were the least productive and that the enemy-initiated contacts far outweighed those of friendly forces.

Vietnam—a Strange Experience from a Western Perspective

by Michael Giovinazzo, Ontos Loader

Sergeant, 3d Platoon, A Company, 1st Antitank Battalion

I doubt if anyone who served in Vietnam was not aware of the differences in culture and behavior compared to the American mind-set. The following are some of what I observed that are indelible in my mind:

- A Shell gas station* in the middle of nowhere
- Vietnamese women moving water from a canal to a rice paddy for hours, using what looked like a conical bucket stretched between two ropes
- A rice paddy that serves the dual role of toilet and growing rice
- Reconstructing burned-down huts by slicing bamboo for days
- The sight of a small bus overloaded at least five times what it should be, with people and animals both in, hanging from the sides and out the windows of, and clinging tightly (sometimes tied) together on top
- Bicycles loaded with enough items that would fill a six-by

---

* VTHF comment: Even stranger is finding that in a deserted Shell gas station on the outskirts of Hue were found the only maps the Marine tank-enforced convoy that joined the Battle of Hue City during Tet of '68 had of Hue.)

- Rice in a bowl covered with flies, so it looked black, until they were shooed away
- Small children smoking cigarettes, and the ability of children, in the middle of nowhere, to get you anything you wanted, including ice, liquor, watches, pornography, etc.
- Sweeping for mines on a road as Vietnam civilians are walking past

Picture provided by article's author, Michael Giovinazzo

The funny part is, this all became normal. It was such that if someone said a flying saucer landed in the rice paddy, no one would pay much attention.

The blowing up of my tender nineteen-year-old mind started with my entrance into country by amphibious landing, on Operation DOUBLE EAGLE, in late January 1966. This episode had to take ten years off my life.

The night before the landing, I was told by a lance corporal from the 3d Reconnaissance Battalion, whom I recognized as a guy stationed with me in my previous duty station, that there would be 65 percent casualties on the beach. Of course, not everyone knew this. He was "in the know," and I was nineteen and naive enough to believe him. I kept my thoughts of doom to myself. To think I volunteered to be there, because I broke up with my girlfriend, only to become engaged to her after signing up, prior to leaving.

I was on the USS *Catamount* (LSD-17), one of a five-ship Battalion 3/1 landing team. I had a sleepless night. Reveille was sounded sometime about 0400, and we were told to go to chow for a steak and egg breakfast. Who could eat? Besides, it didn't look much like steak or eggs—wet scrambled eggs and a thin, tough-as-leather form of beef.

As light appeared, I saw what I had seen in the movies, prior to the invasion of a WWII Pacific island: It looked like a hundred ships of all kinds. I could hear what sounded like big guns being fired from some of the ships and the impact explosions inland. After the ships stopped firing, I saw jets flying over, going inland, and could hear more explosions. I carefully observed the Marines I saw, and no one was saying anything. They probably didn't have the "classified information" I had. My platoon commander and platoon sergeant didn't mention any particular doom that would befall us when they explained the particulars of the operation prior to us getting into the boats in the well deck of the LSD. I guess they didn't get the word either.

I had participated in amphibious landings in the Mediterranean and one in the Philippine Islands, just prior to Operation DOUBLE EAGLE. They were practice and this was real. None of the platoon had any combat experience, but I did have some security in the faith I had in our NCOs. All Ontos commanders were sergeants, except for two senior corporals. They were all career Marines and were expert in the Ontos and tactics. I would trust my life to them, even though I didn't have a choice.

We eventually departed the ship with our Ontos loaded on the ship's LCUs and circled in formation with the other landing craft, awaiting our time to reconfigure the formation into an assault line parallel to the beach and power up for the landing. I was buttoned up in my Ontos's loader's compartment. There wasn't a square centimeter of room to move around in the space stuffed with equipment over and under me, and it was totally dark. Though I couldn't see anything, I finally felt the boat slam to a stop, and with the ramp dropped, we proceeded off. Our Ontos went (sank!) underwater, and water was leaking in the rear doors and from above. I thought this was the end of the line for me. I could then feel the Ontos grinding forward and then going up the incline from the water onto the beach. After about a minute, the Ontos commander said I could get out. What I then saw was surreal.

I saw Vietnamese walking around the beach, carrying wood and whatever they carried on those poles with two baskets, one attached at each end. My mind was blown. I went from a WWII war movie, which I felt I was prepared for, to some other dimension. This was only the beginning of the absurdities that I would experience for the next year.

Michael Giovinazzo

Please go to the annexes "http://www.mcvthf.org" to read a letter from Sergeant Giovinazzo.

Gilbert, in *Marine Corps Tank Battles in Vietnam*, in covering Operation DOUBLE EAGLE, stated, "The putative mission was to clear the enemy from the region around the new base at Phu Bai, but the implicit mission was to seek open battle with the NVA. The plan was an enlarged and more elaborate version of [Operation] STARLITE [Note: Actually, the operation took place] . . . in southern Quang Ngai Province near Duc Pho" (GB-66). In any case, as it turned out, the results were more like Operation PIRANHA due to leaks to the enemy forces and their "dee dee" from the AO.

Gilbert interviewed a number of the veteran Tankers involved in Operation DOUBLE EAGLE. They told similar stories to those Tankers involved in Operation STARLITE: "Sam Binion's Platoon from Charlie Company, 3d Tanks was assigned to a force including BLT's 2/4 and 3/1 that would land along the coast on 28 January. 'We left our tanks on ship, and they sent us ashore as Grunts, which was a fiasco. We weren't trained as Grunts. We were Tankers!' The Tankers carried their assigned weapons—(.45 cal) pistols (and grease guns)—and were hastily supplied with M-14 rifles. The Platoon served as the Provisional Rifle Platoon." Unfortunately, the platoon commander, Second Lieutenant Bruce B. Warner was shot and seriously wounded by a sniper while riding in an amtrac, LVTP-1. Lieutenant Warner was medivaced but died of his wounds two months later.

The 3d Tanks January CC states, "The 2d Platoon arrived in Da Nang with the BLT 2/3 SLF. While assigned to BLT 2/3 the Platoon operated ashore during Operation DOUBLE EAGLE as part of a composite infantry unit while their tanks remained aboard ship. This type of employment is not desirable since replacement tank leaders and crewmen are not available nor easily trained. Combat operations of tanks require complete crews and casualties sustained would result in deadlined tanks. The Tank Platoon Leader (Warner) was severely wounded in action and is not expected to return to this organization. Subsequent employment of tanks during [Operation] DOUBLE EAGLE would have necessarily been under the command of the Platoon Sergeant. Since the battalion is short Officers, the Platoon Sergeant (a Staff Sergeant) commands the Platoon" (CC-3Tk, 1/66).

This paragraph should have been a cut/paste to add to the tank battalions' command chronologies whenever float Platoons were detached from their respective BLTs and rejoined to their parent tank company/battalion, since the "standard employment" of tanks—and to some extent Ontos as well—was to leave the tracks in the well decks of their transporting ships.

Note: As with the tanks, Ontos battalion subordinate units had been fighting in Vietnam several months before their parent unit was to join them and provide them the log/admin support needed to sustain operations. Keep in mind that communications at that time—nearly five decades ago—was nowhere near what we have today. Reports and messages were handwritten (and often hand carried) for starters, then converted to documents with many "addees" up and down the chain of command, scattered across the Pacific, which were then to be endorsed and "forwarded" by message or hard copy to the next senior command. Reports and other correspondence were finalized on mechanical typewriters and reproduced on ditto paper mechanically. This was accomplished, often by a Marine not usually skilled much above the "hunt and peck" level, in spite of every challenge. Add to this challenge the constant mobility of all the units, personnel, and the "office"—a field desk sitting on the bare ground, a semifunctioning mechanical Remington, with a tent overhead, seldom shielding (but marginally) from the sand, wind, dust, sounds, rain, and "incoming."

According to Ed Murphy, "Pacification remained the main objective of both the 3d and 9th Marines operating in the Da Nang TAOR" (SF-EM). The Da Nang TAOR was divided in two, with the 3d Marines assigned the area south and west of the city and the 9th Marines given the Civic Action responsibility to the north and west of Da Nang. The emphasis on Civic Action was reflected to, and through, every organization in the 3d Marine Division. The 3d TKs and 3d ATs each adopted an adjacent local village and poured major efforts into showcasing their considerable accomplishments.

January 1966
Third Tanks
Commanding Officer: Lt. Col. M. L. Raphael
Executive Officer: Maj. J. G. Doss Jr.
Operations Officer: Maj. H. L. Maxwell
Logistics Officer: Maj. F. W. Coates
Location and Operations Summary: Da Nang (AT 989708)

While neither tank nor antitank units appear to have been attached to, or in direct support of, the infantry units in Operation MALLARD conducted in the An Hoa area, south of Marble Mountain, the reported details of that operation in early January '66 are predictive of what the future held for all units operating against both the local Viet Cong, the Viet Cong Main Force supported by the NVA, and eventually, the NVA itself.

Antitank and personnel mines salted the area. Seemingly, every village hosted and supported their "home team" of VC that planted every type of IED imaginable. Tunnels and caves of every size, shape, and location were all-pervasive. Marine tanks—and to a somewhat less extent, Ontos—were participants in totally destroying some of the villages that could not be pacified, literally grinding them into dust.

The following is an adaptation from Alan Waugh's treatise on An Hoa.

January 1966 Operation Mallard

by Alan Waugh

Operation LONG LANCE, which took place from 3–8 January 1966, had been a search-and-destroy operation that was conducted from Hill 41 in the north of Dai Loc district. The operation made no significant contact with the enemy, but it did disrupt the Viet Cong logistic bases. Three days later, the Marines began Operation MALLARD, which would be conducted further south in the Dai LocDistrict Annam: Please see several examples of District capped in "U.S. Marines in Vietnam" and would also cover an area west of An Hoa. The Viet Cong had been making frequent raids on the An Hoa industrial complex, and with the success of Operation LONG LANCE, III MAF decided that Operation MALLARD would continue the harassment of the Viet Cong. The area of the operation was southwest of the Song Vu Gia and south to the hamlet of An Bong (2), which was southwest of An Hoa. This region would be later called the Arizona Territory.

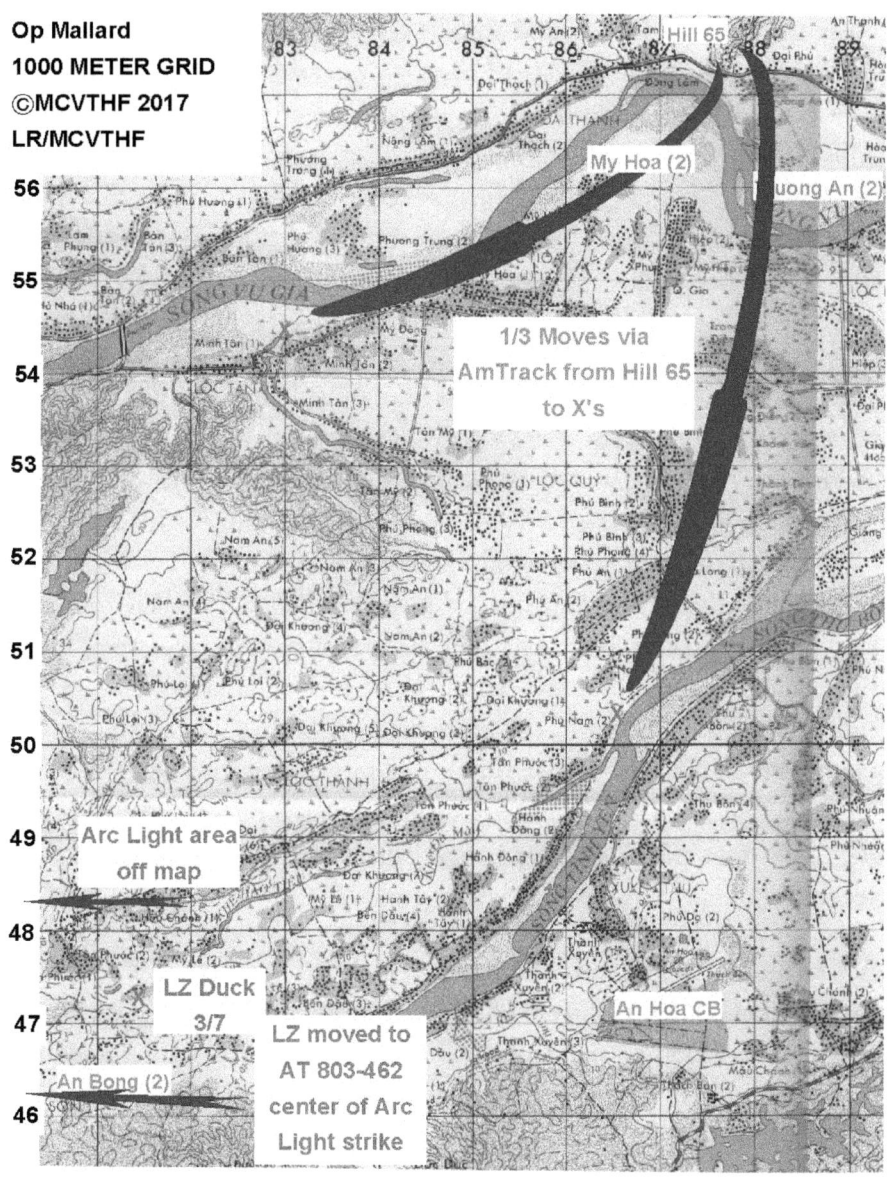

The infantry units taking part in Operation MALLARD were 3/7, 1/3, G/2/9, and ARVN elements. Intel reports had indicated that the following enemy units were in the operational area: R-21, R-24, 5th Battalion HQ, V24, V25, and V26. It was felt that in the objective area, there were an estimated 630 VC and an unestimated number of local Viet Cong. There were also, outside the objective area, an estimated 2,080 NVA who could be called for reinforcement, some just minutes—to a few hours—away. Again, there were other local VC units that could be called upon to move into the objective area. The terrain would be that of flat rice fields, tree lines, and hedges.

Operation MALLARD commenced at 0815 on 10 January, when an advanced motor party from 1/3 in Da Nang left for Hill 65 and the nearby operational area. By 2100, all elements of 1/3 were in position at Hill 65 and the hamlet of Truong An (2), which was on the east bank of the Song Vu Gia. The 3d Marines set H hour for D+1 at 0730. Company B, 1st Amtracs would cross the Song Vu Gia at two points. Fire support would come from LVTP-Hs. The tractors had problems negotiating the river, and the landing party came under small-arms fire from an enemy force located in the hamlet of My Hoa (2). The .30 caliber and the 105mm of the armored LVT soon silenced the enemy! Company B/1/3 had left at 0630 and moved east without incident. They landed at 0730. By 1100, Company C/1/3 had crossed the river. All units were moving toward their objectives, and so far, the enemy seemed to be just few snipers.

As darkness fell, all the companies began to set up Night Defense Perimeters (NDP). LPs were posted and ambushes set up. Throughout the night, all companies reported sporadic contact with small bands of the enemy. At first light, the B-52s began an Arc Light strike. The sound of the carpet-bombing would have put fear into the enemy. The bombing lasted thirty minutes. That night a four-man ambush team from G/2/9 came into contact with a significant enemy force. The Marines killed four VC and captured some weapons.

A/3/1 had found over 5,000 kilos of rice in an enemy cache. Further searches found more rice caches and some tunnels, which they destroyed with C-4. The 3/1 sent a patrol to make contact with an RF company that was reported to be in the neighborhood, but after they searched the area, the *RFs could not be found.* (VTHF comment: Another "preview of coming attractions," i.e., the no-show of the South Vietnamese Regional Forces.)

In Da Nang, the first wave of 3/7 lifted off in thirty-two UH34d helicopters right into the middle of the (B-52) Arc Light strike. The 3/1 received smoke blowers from Division. These would be used to flush any VC from tunnels and caves. Numerous tunnels and caves were found and destroyed. This was to be the blueprint of things for the rest of the operation. On the seventeenth, at 2130, Operation MALLARD was terminated. There were 36 VC KIA and 229 VCS captured with 5 Marines KIA and 66 WIA. There were no Tankers or Ontos crewmen involved in or casualties from this operation. (VTHF comment: However, this area was to become "home" to both Tankers and Ontos crewmen in subsequent operations due to the comments of several Marines expressing their potential support operating in the An Hoa area.)

While Operation MALLARD was not a huge military success in terms of large body counts or VC captured, since the NVA had withdrawn to the mountains and jungle to the east, the favorable reaction of the villagers, who lived near An Hoa, was significant. Many had asked to be evacuated to a more secure area. They had also stated that they wanted the Viet Cong driven out of their hamlets, and they looked to the Marines to do this.

Alan Waugh

The increase in strength of the tank battalion over the last reporting period may be explained partially through the joining of programmed replacements to this organization, but more important to this increase was the joining of A Company, 1st Tank Battalion heretofore attached to RLT-1. The joining of A Company established this organization with five gun companies. The flame section did not arrive with A Company, nor did any of the company's gun platoons. Only the A Company Headquarters element of two officers and thirty-nine enlisted Marines and one Navy corpsman were joined. Since A Company, 1st Tank Battalion was directed to assume the tactical obligations previously assigned to C Company, 3d Tank Battalion, two platoons from C Company, 3d Tank Battalion were transferred to A Company, 1st Tank Battalion.

On 3 January, elements of Company B (Captain W. A. Coomes), Company A (Captain F. W. Jarnot), and Tank Battalion Headquarters (Captain A. E. Lee) participated in Operation WAR BONNET in support of 1/9. (Captain Lee was the composite company commander) (CC-1/9, 1/66). This search-and-destroy operation involved the largest number of tracked vehicles used by the Marine Corps thus far in Vietnam. The commanding officer of 3d Tank Battalion was coordinator and tracked vehicle adviser to the infantry battalion commander. The tanks were used as the point and rear guard for the armor column, reconnaissance, destruction of fortified positions, and perimeter security.

According to 9th Marines January Command Chronology (CC-9, 1/66), "At 030530H a tank attached to B/1/9 struck a mine at (BT 090640) resulting in one Grunt WIA and damage to one track of the tank. One squad and a second tank were left as security for the disabled tank." This happened while crossing the line of departure (LOD). The 1/9 reported nothing on the operation. (VTHF comment: It is not difficult for a battalion commander to disparage tanks when at his LOD—i.e., just prior to stepping off in a combat formation—he loses a squad of his infantry to protecting one tank.)

There are no other specifics recorded for tank action for Operation WAR BONNET the 3d Tank Battalion Reaction Platoon was deployed.

On 28 January, Operation WAR BONNET II was conducted. (Captain Coomes was the composite company commander.) With the exception of there being fewer tracked vehicles, this operation was the same as the operation held earlier on 3 January. The same problems of tracked vehicle control and coordination existed in the conduct of this operation, and again the commanding officer of 3d Tank Battalion was tracked vehicle coordinator and adviser for the infantry battalion commander. The tanks had the same mission as in the first operation.

On 20 January 1966, Company A (-) (Rein.), 1st Tank Battalion came under AdCon of 3d Tank Battalion while remaining attached to the 1st Marines. The 1st and 2d Platoons of Company C (-) (Rein.), 3d Tank Battalion were assigned to Company A (-) (Rein.), 1st Tank Battalion. Company C remained attached to 4th Marines. Company B (Rein.), 1st Tanks remains attached to 7th Marines. All were supporting operations in the Chu Lai enclave. OpCon was exercised by the supported (infantry) units. AdCon and logistical support was exercised and provided by the commanding officer of the 3d Tank Battalion.

Companies A and B, 3d Tank Battalion remained DS 3d Marines and 9th Marines, respectively. Operations were in support of the Da Nang enclave (TAOR) with one platoon supporting operations in the Hue/Phu Bai enclave (TAOR).

Command and control of tank units operating in the three enclaves were exercised through frequent command and staff visits, a monthly command and staff conference, daily communications with each company, and submission of periodic reports of activities by each company.

In addition, Major Franklin W. Coates's S-4 shop had implemented a schedule of contact teams to call on the several units employed away from the CP, operating in the bush.

CO H&S Company: Captain A. E. Lee
Location and Operations Summary: Da Nang (AT 989708)

During the month of January, H&S Company conducted twenty-two daylight (foot) patrols and nine night ambushes in areas adjacent to the battalion CP. The battalion continued to provide one infantry platoon on standby for immediate employment in the 3d Marine Division TAOR. And members of H&S Company, employed as infantry, participated in Operation WAR BONNET. (VTHF comment: Being a member of the reaction platoon and/or other Grunt-type activities was, to many Marines in H&S Companies of both tank and antitank battalions, a welcome assignment and usually implied that being a Grunt for a day meant being excused from the routine housekeeping duties within the CP. For example, this, a composite article from H&S Company troopers.)

POOP

Anonymous

Burning the Sh——ers

Burning our excrement deprived local farmers of valuable fertilizer, used large amounts of gasoline and diesel fuel, served as punishment duty, and fouled the clear blue skies over Vietnam with dark black smoke. Human waste was a staple fertilizer in Vietnam. Ours was much richer than that of locals, and each of us outproduced even the best-fed farmer. We could have auctioned it off to raise some money for the Civic Action Program. Talk about winning hearts and minds! In base camps, it was often a paid job for Vietnamese, but in fire or combat support bases, it was usually assigned to some shitbird (wonder where that term came from) that was out of favor with someone in power.

As all things military, there was a unit SOP. Written or not, these were the steps usually followed.

The size, shape, configuration of the crapper were determined by the command and limited by the building supplies available. At a bare minimum, they were completely open air with a door set atop and supported by dirt-filled ammo boxes on each end. Some were works of a frustrated "civil engineer trooper"—actual "three-holers"! And?

This it was not.　　　　　　　　　　　How about this?

Source of pictures:

https://www.google.com/search?q=vietnam+war+phrases+%22there+it+is%22&rlz=1C1CHBD_enUS688US689&espv=2&tbm=isch&imgil=9V1CYoxDZdVfqM%253A%253BnodJcnP0-v9f_M%253Bhttp%25253A%25252F%25252Fwerejustsayin.blogspot.com%25252F2011%25252F03%25252Fthere-it-is.html&source=iu&pf=m&fir=9V1CYoxDZdVfqM%253A%252CnodJcnP0-v9f_M%252C_&usg=__NaiD6YJ_GqWM9Nj_AFOMDDqSCgA%3D&biw=1018&bih=662&dpr=1.25&ved=0ahUKEwiAnvO_9tbSAhUC-GMKHYFnA9IQyjcIVQ&ei=w17IWMCwJ4LwjwOBz42QDQ#imgrc=9V1CYoxDZdVfqM:

Approach the "facility" and then:

Assemble empty replacement cans, heavy rubber gloves, gasoline and diesel fuel, some long (4–5 feet) stir sticks, and a long stick wrapped with gas-soaked skivvy paper on one end, which will be used to ignite the mix from a safe distance. And be careful: Too much gasoline in the combustion mix could launch ignited turds a good distance.

Pulling the always-too-full cans from under the thinking platform and slopping the contents around and most often on the person pulling the can—one at a time—take a certain touch. The burn location needs to be away from the crapper (20–30 feet) so heat from the fire does not stop our brothers from answering nature's call, many of which were emergency calls. Before a new can is placed under the door, some diesel fuel is added to dampen the odor, repel the huge black stick-to-your-face flies, and allow the new deposits to marinate in a combustible liquid. The diesel, soaked into the solids, makes the next burn more efficient.

Our food, antimalaria pills, and native bacteria conspired, so each man would have diarrhea most days. The cans (the lower one-third of a 55-gallon metal drum) to be burned were half-full of a dense liquid with floating solids and a layer of scum at the bottom. We urinated into fiber shipping tubes (piss tubes) that came with each 105 mm howitzer round, stuck in a dirt pile. We had several located around the FSB. This system was to reduce the volume of water to be burned off shitters and keep men from urinating where they stood.

My first assignment was to cut new cans from 55-gallon drums using a hacksaw. Less than 12 inches into the first cut, my hands were sliced and bleeding from the rough cut edge. My FDC mates were making fun of my struggles, and that was not helping my sense of humor. Fortunately, an engineer walked by, had a good laugh, and then showed me how to wrap detonating cord around the barrel and light one end. It burned fast and hot, yielding a smooth edge. Bless that man! Being an FNG meant being assigned the worst duties and having practical jokes played at every turn.

The two-to-four-hour job of burning was weather dependent. Rain slowed the burn, while wind could whip the smoke up. If it was too calm, the smoke hovered over the base. The smoke's black particles—mimicking the flies—clung to anything they touched, especially the "sanitation engineer." A change of clothes and a shower were a must before being welcomed around others after completing this work. The odor was horrific, and the smoke was black as night. The burning cans needed to be spaced far enough apart to allow a cool space to move around while stirring. Once ignited, the mixture was stirred, and more diesel added as the fire cooled; gasoline was very dangerous to add but was necessary at times. Time passed slowly and it seemed the contents would never burn away, but hours later, a dark dry residue was all that remained. After the can cooled, the contents were dumped into a hole and covered.

Men not on burn detail, including senior enlisted or big-shot officers, seldom came close, so it was an escape in a crazy sort of way. Social stigma was written all over this detail for very sound reasons, but it provided a time to be alone and not be instructed (harassed) by leadership (lifers). Some men turned it into an all-day work detail. Our artillery was on call 24/7, and a fire mission would bring work details to a stop, at which point the two main jobs became shooting the guns and getting fused 105 mm rounds ready and in place at each howitzer. The burning cans were on their own while we were creating more piss tubes!

Many problems happened with this detail, and one of the worst was when the cans were filled too close to the top. This meant part of the contents needed to be poured into an empty can and the only grip was the bottom of the can. There is no way to avoid having your face very close to this smelly treasure, and any rapid movement set off tidal waves of overflow that landed—yes, just where you are thinking. You needed to keep the stir stick in motion to prevent it lighting on fire, or you'd end up with a shortened tool to complete the job. Being assigned this detail was not a good thing; it was a hot job in a very hot country.

Anonymous

(VTHF comment: See volume 4 for a companion story by the then Second Lieutenant Dick Peksen.)

Tanks were particularly valuable for the illumination they could provide the infantry. There were other ways to acquire illumination when needed—artillery, air—but the tank provided instant, directional, and focused light on suspected targets, especially those close in. The M48A3s arrived in-country with the standard round coaxially (with the 90 mm main gun) mounted searchlight that was soon after replaced by the xenon searchlight. The advantage of the xenon light, besides its more powerful standard illumination, was that it could be utilized in the infrared mode. Essentially, what that meant was that we could see the enemy (actually anything that emitted heat—body or other) at night, and he had no idea he was being "painted."

Ray Stewart (then first lieutenant) tells of the time in early 1966 when the first xenon searchlight replacement was made on the tanks on Hill 55 southwest of the 3d Tank Battalion CP.

"I was the assistant logistics officer (S-4), 3d Tanks, Da Nang. I was brand-new on the job and under the wing of Major Franklin W. Coates. He knew my preference for out-of-tent fieldwork and never failed to get me on the road—or in the chopper—at every chance. As luck would have it, an M-54 5-ton truck loaded with the new xenon searchlights (twenty-eight, if my memory serves me) had just come in from Logistics Support Group (LSG) in Da Nang. After figuring out which unit would get however many, the decision was made to get two of them out to Hill 55, where we had five M48A3 tanks. I was to be the convoy commander who would form up a small convoy to get the searchlights, the OJT turret experts, and several tons of ammunition, camp improvement material, food, and beer loaded up and out to Hill 55. Thirteen trucks (a lucky number), comm jeep, and a few other vehicles made up the convoy. PRC-25s were placed in the vehicles, frequencies assigned, radio checks made, and finally the command "Move 'em out" got us underway for the two hours road trip through (and into) Indian country. We arrived to Hill 55 without incident.

The several drivers took their cargo to the appropriate tents—food to the mess tent, etc.—and the much heralded xenon searchlights to the tank park. Ours was by far the more interesting of the cargo (well, second to the beer), and quite a crowd gathered as they were unwrapped and laid out in preparation for the installation. If I recall, there was an FLSG technician to guide the process of removing the old searchlights and mount the new ones. With even the abbreviated break for lunch, it was touch-and-go whether we'd get the job done much before dark. The convoy was on a schedule to depart Hill 55 at first light the next day close on the heels of the engineer road sweep team. Later than that, it would take the chance that Charlie would have mined the road after the team made its run, out of eyesight of the sweep team or the follow-on convoy.

After the searchlight swap-out was made, it was indeed getting dark and deemed too late to backtrack through Indian country to the 3d Tank Battalion CP in an unescorted jeep. So I decided to stay the night on Hill 55 and join the convoy at first light. And besides, there was the prospect of seeing the new night-vision light in action. The two tanks moved up to their positions on the defensive perimeter and prepared for their watch.

As the story went, two Viet Cong suspects (referred to as VCS; all VCSs became VCC—Viet Cong confirmed upon expiration) nearly every night around midnight, visible only by moonlight—these two black-pajamaed agents crossed the field in front of the 3d Tanks LPs, checked into a small grass hootch about 300–400 meters to our front, and then, after a short time, one of the VCS would leave the hootch for a scraggly old tree a few yards from it. The observations from the hill positions were spotty due to limited light and rather limited night-vision capability. These VCS were thought to be the ones—the enemy FOs—who were instrumental in bringing mortar fire on to the hill from time to time with way more accuracy than one would normally expect with known VC locations further out than direct line-of-sight to call in mortar fire.

That night (actually the next morning), about 0100, I was shaken awake to observe the first demo of the new xenon light. Surprised that the installation had been complete so soon, I quickly pulled on my boots and grabbed my .45 from under my rolled-up field jacket and jogged over to the first tank. I climbed up on the tank, joining a dozen other Tankers, was given a pair of binoculars, and without a whisper, motioned the direction of twelve o'clock. There they were! I could barely make them out, even through the IR binoculars, but the xenon searchlight—invisible to the agents—illuminated them like a Christmas tree.

There is no doubt that the next series of steps had been rehearsed down to the last detail to coordinate the planned event between the two xenon-mounted tanks. Between the removal of the old searchlights, mounting of the new xenons, checking everything out, and dry runs, it had to take the full cooperation of all hands—without rest.

Following the two pairs of pajamas with the coaxially (with the 90 mm main gun) mounted xenons, the VCSs appeared to be replicating their routine, entering the hootch for ten to fifteen minutes. As they emerged from the grass hut, one proceeded to the scraggly tree and climbed up. Then he decided to relieve himself. The other stopped, just outside the door of the hootch, to relieve himself at the same time. The "pissing contest" looked like mini flame tanks due to the heat of their streams. The 90 mm WP had been previously loaded in each of the two tanks. At the TC's commands, the tracking infrareds were switched to blinding white, and the WPs were sent to greet their targets with a brilliant phosphorescent burst. When the smoke cleared, the two Viet Cong suspects, the tree, and the adjacent hut—all had just disappeared—evaporated. With the instant disappearing trick, the two agents were called into the tank battalion S-3 Operations as "2 VC KIA (Probable)." Note the *S* was dropped.

At first light, an eight-man reaction squad, far smaller than the fifty-plus volunteers, made it down Hill 55 to where the tree and grass hut once stood to verify the demise of the two enemies. There was nothing to count—nothing but two large converging circles of charred earth. The skipper allowed as how, since there were no body parts, we could reasonably assume that they were literally "blown away" and to add two to the tank battalion's January body count score card, "2 VC KIA (Confirmed)."

This is what was noted in the 3d Tanks' January Command Chronology:

> During the month of January 3d Tank Battalion units received 28 Xenon searchlights. These lights primarily

are deployed on strong points and airfield perimeters for surveillance and target acquisition. The tanks on hill #55 have two confirmed VC KIA as a result of detecting VC snipers with the infra-red capability of the light. (CC-3Tk, 1/66)

There was no reference as to which "VC KIA" won that pissing contest.

Blessings in a Small Bottle

by Major Willard F. Lochridge IV

Sometimes in combat, our Marines are spared their lives in various and strange ways. In this personal account of his first task in combat, the author is saved by a wing and a prayer.

In early 1966, I arrived in South Vietnam as a brand new Marine Second Lieutenant, just out of Officer Basic School (TBS) at Quantico, VA, followed by graduation from the Tracked Vehicle School, Camp Delmar, Camp Pendleton, CA. As a young Marine Officer after my flight into Da Nang, RVN and my dusty ride, I reported in to the Headquarters and Service Company Office, 3d Tank Battalion, 3d Marine Division. At the time, 3d Tanks was located just south of Da Nang on Hill 34. I was not the only Second Lieutenant reporting in, there were five of us.

"Combat action" was what we young lieutenants most desired. We wanted to go where the action was, and where it was then was in a place called "The Horseshoe." Named after a horseshoe shaped lake, it was in an area south of Da Nang, south of China Beach and Marble Mountain, along the coast of the South China Sea.

Before any of the five of us would be given our operational assignments our Battalion Commander (LtCol Raphael) would hold us at battalion headquarters for 3 weeks in order to observe our individual capabilities and receive area orientation briefings. Besides instructing us about Viet Cong (VC) tactics, weapon systems, and particularly their (the local VC) use of booby traps and vehicular landmines, we spent time performing numerous headquarters duties fit for junior officers. We spent several days visiting the battalion's line companies in the field where, again, we were instructed about how they were using their M48A3 tanks against the enemy. We were told over and over again not to follow in old tracks—the VC planted large mines in them when we weren't looking.

Finally, word came down about our assignments. Surprisingly, I was selected to go to the Horseshoe to take over 2d Platoon of Bravo Company. Within 24 hours, I was spirited off in an old UH-34 helicopter that had large, vicious-looking black eyes and a shark-like jaw full of teeth painted on its nose. I supposed this was intended to intimidate the VC. The helicopter, armed with a single M60 machine gun, took off flying south over Highway 1. In about 20 minutes flying time we began a corkscrew descent into Kilo Company, 3d Battalion, 9th Marines' base camp. Scrubby looking pine trees, bamboo stands, and tall grasses surrounded cleared fields of fire that rolled up to strings of barbed wire and bunkers. The helicopter landed just outside the wire. Several Marines ran out to help off load supplies. I asked one of them where I could find their company's commanding officer (CO) and the tank platoon leader. He yelled, "Over there," and motioned toward a sandbagged tent next to a shattered pagoda. Halfway to the pagoda, I met the Officer who I believed was probably the one I was to replace coming toward me with his ditty bag. He vigorously clasped and shook my hand and said I should hook up with the platoon sergeant for a briefing. He shook my hand again: wishing me luck, he ran off to catch the helicopter I had just come in on.

Before meeting my new platoon, I paid my respects to the infantry CO who was busily laying out patrol routes for the coming night. Afterwards, I met my platoon sergeant. We walked to each tank, inspection style, and met the crews. By now it was getting dark, so we settled down in an open fly tent for the night.

As the new platoon commander, I was informed which tank would be assigned to me. I learned a little about each of my Marine Tanker crewmen before we turned in for the night. My tank driver was a young private from Boston. The gunner, a Lance Corporal, was a full-blooded Cherokee from the western branch of the tribe. My loader, a corporal, who had been the tank commander until I showed up, was from Chicago.

Sleep finally came—until the Grunt CO suddenly woke me at 0430. Apparently, one of his patrols was ambushed, pinned down, and surrounded by VC. They had taken several casualties and were running low on ammunition. Worse, medevac and supply helicopters could not get in due to intense ground fire. The CO wanted us to go out and break through to pull them out. We immediately saddled up three tanks—the heavy section. We loaded ammunition, water, C-rations, and other supplies on top of each tank's engine armor plate. A squad of infantry also joined us. It was evenly dispersed to ride on the second and third tanks. My tank was to lead the column.

As the sun was just beginning to rise, we moved out of the infantry company's position at an accelerated rate. Diesel smoke and sand flew as we headed south to rescue our embattled Marines. Spaced about 75 yards apart, we raced forward with my tank in the lead. Remembering not to follow in old tracks, we came to a large field with a bamboo tree line on the far side. Glancing over the area, I noted that the bamboo ended just short of an old pagoda. There was a small break, perhaps 20 feet wide with no old tracks running through it. Leading off, my tank went through without a hitch. As the second tank went through there was a tremendous explosion. A huge cloud of black smoke and flying debris momentarily hid the tank from sight. Then, the vehicle lurched forward out of the smoke and came to a dead stop. The Marine infantrymen riding on the fenders of the tank, having been blown off the tank, lay on the ground among boxes of ammunition and supplies. Smoke surged out of the turret along with the crew. The tank was on fire! My platoon sergeant, who was the tank commander, ran forward to the driver's hatch and pulled the main fire extinguisher handle. All of the extinguishments went off in the driver's compartment but NOT in the turret or engine compartment as they should have. Gathering up fire extinguishers from the other two tanks and aggressively attacking the fires, we finally put them out before the tank's 90 mm, .30 caliber, and .50 caliber ammunition cooked off. Fortunately, none of the infantrymen was seriously injured. However, the smoldering tank appeared inoperable.

Placing the other two tanks into defensive positions, I ran back to the crippled vehicle. It was charred and the under hull was ripped apart bow to stern. The diesel engine had been blown off its mounts and thrust through the firewall into the turret. Both fuel cells were ruptured. It was a "Code X"—a total loss.

While I was sitting on a log next to the rather large crater made by the mine explosion; one of my men came up to me with the detonating device. The device was simply two wooden planks with copper wire zigzagged on opposing surfaces. The planks had been held apart by four wooden pegs. A battery had been attached to the ends of the copper wire. When the tank drove over the planks the pegs were crushed and the wires made contact with each other causing an electrical current to set off the mine. It was a simple instant pressure device. Holding the device in my hands, I looked at the crater. It was several feet in diameter and about four feet deep. I said aloud, "How come we didn't get blown up?" The slot between the bamboo trees and the pagoda was just wide enough for a tank to pass through with no leeway on either side. The answer came from my driver. He said, "Sir, I know why we didn't get blown up." I said, "How's that, Joe?" He then explained how his girlfriend had sent him a bottle of holy water, and during the night before, when we—the crew—were asleep he went around and poured a small amount on each of us. He then put some on himself and emptied the remainder over our tank. I was spell bound. A warm feeling filled my body. I said, "Joe that must be why . . . Heaven certainly knew this tank crew."

Shortly thereafter, we were able to tow the destroyed tank forward a short distance to link up with the ambushed infantry and successfully pull the Marine squad out to safety.

To this day, whenever I think of this story it brings warmth and a respecting belief to me. I thank Joe and his girlfriend always, and most of all, I thank God above for his blessings in a small bottle.

Lieutenant Colonel Lochridge, USMC (Ret.), of the New York Naval Militia (NYNM) and a retired Marine, is the officer in charge of naval forces attached to the New York National Guard's 27th Brigade. He commands small coastal vessels, crewed by Navy personnel, protecting the Indian Point nuclear power plant in Buchanan, New York.

This article first appeared in the Marine Corps Gazette, *Quantico, in the June 2005 issue.*

It is reproduced here with expressed permission of the copyright owner and its author. Further reproduction or distribution is prohibited without permission.

Then Second Lieutenant Willard Lochridge received the Silver Star medal in recognition of his valorous actions subsequent to this event.

And years later, 9/11 found Will Lochridge in the middle of the death and destruction from which he incurred serious, permanent lung damage.

CO Company A: Capt. F. W. Jarnot
Location and Operations Summary: Da Nang (AT 946762)

Company A remains DS 3d Marines, occupying strong points along the MLR and providing a mobile reserve force for the regiment. Tanks in the company were also used for indirect long-range fire (CC-1/3, 1/66). The 3d Platoon, Company A, attached to 2/1, occupies strong points on Highway 1 and provided the battalion with mobile reserve force.

This platoon had three contacts while in support of Marine and ARVN operations. The tanks are credited with an estimated forty-eight VC KIA (forty of these according to ARVN count). Company A participated in Operation WAR BONNET.

CO Company B: Capt. W. A. Coomes
Location and Operations Summary: Da Nang (AT 067719)

Company B remains in direct support (DS) 9th Marines. One platoon is in support of 2 and 3/3, while the remainder support the 1/9. The 1st Platoon, Company C is also in support of 2 and 3/3. As in the past four months, this company continues to have the majority of tank offensive actions.

During January, elements of Company B participated in twenty-eight search-and-clear or search-and-destroy operations, five armored patrols, and were used three times in a mobile reserve capacity. The company had thirty-seven VC contacts and killed an estimated thirty-four VC and wounded an estimated thirteen VC. The company has six tanks on Hill 55 (AT 970620). These tanks are being used extensively to fire deep H&Is south of Hill 55. Company B participated in Operation WAR BONNET.

Operation EAGLE FLIGHT 49er

Submitted by Robbie "Harvey" Robinson
Written by Randy Conrad
Photos by Robert Embesi

[This story, with accompanying pictures, is reprinted from the Sponson Box magazine with the permission of its publisher, the USMC Vietnam Tankers Association.]

Randy Conrad made these notes in his diary on 24 January 1966. Conrad was driver on T. J. Siva's tank.

24 Jan 1966

Went on a raid called Operation EAGLE FLIGHT 49er (same place as 5 Jan., Hill 163, this was the 4th or 5th time to the same place). A-25 was always lead tank, but today A-24 was lead because the lieutenant (the platoon's commander) was on-board A-25.

While going across a very narrow saddle between two hills, A-24 ran over a 100-pound mine (TNT) with the outside edge of the left track. A-25 was about 50 yards behind A-24 when A-24 detonated it. The blast broke A-24's track, ripped off two road wheels, and slammed them up into one of the support rollers, shearing it off. All this debris slammed up into the top portion of the track, forcing it into the fender above. As the fender peeled upwards, three of the Grunts riding on it were flung up into the air. Two were not hurt too badly, but the third came down on his back on top of the 90 mm gun tube and messed up his back. The tank crew was very lucky. Burrell (the driver) banged his mouth on the hatch rim and cut his lip. Robbie, Pop Kelly, and the loader were all OK.

Pictures by Sgt Bob Embesi of Operation EAGLE FLIGHT 49er, 24 January 1966 (from VTHF Archives)

A-25 was sent around A-24 to protect her blind side. This made the grass too slippery for any other tank to pass. A retriever came to pull A-24 back to the battalion CP, but ran out of fuel before reaching us. Battalion sent out a tanker truck and topped off the retriever.

While waiting for help, the tanks and Ontos fired down the hill and across the river into a VC Village. Civilian newspapers claimed 660 VC dead. The Grunts did a body count of 440. During the firing, A-25 had a white phosphorus (Willy Peter) round misfire. Three times we manually cocked the 90 mm; every time it failed to fire. Finally, Sergeant Siva, the tank commander and section leader, said to pull the round out of the breech. Larry Roalson eased the live Willy Peter out and handed it up to me (I was standing on top of the tank turret). I took it from Larry, gently laid it on the fender, jumped down. Again picked it up, carried it about 30 yards away, and laid it very carefully on the ground. I climbed back on the tank and we begin firing again.

When we were ready to return to camp, the process had to be repeated in reverse: pick up the Willy Peter, lay it on the fender, climb on board the tank, pick it up, and hand it to Larry. Then I got busy getting the tank started while the rest of the crew took care of the round.

Since the retriever was busy pulling A-24, we hooked up to A-24's track. For some reason, we were unable to go back down the slope we had come up, so we went straight down the hill. It took both feet on the brakes to maintain any form of control. We got back to Highway 1, and to keep from tearing up the road or the track, I drove on the shoulder of the road.

I saw a Vietnamese in front of me riding a bicycle. As I got close to him, I pulled out to pass. When I *knew* I was past, I pulled back in. Just as I pulled in, I realized (and Sergeant Siva yelled at the same time) that, in fact, I was not completely past the bike rider. I had 15 feet of tow cable and nearly 50 feet of track stretched out behind me, so I flipped the steering wheel to the left. This caused the towed track to whip to the right and toward the Vietnamese. When he saw this 2-1/2-ton chunk of steel and rubber coming towards him and nowhere to go, he just jumped from his bike. Fortunately, the track didn't whip that far, just far enough to trash the riderless bike. THAT WAS ONE PISSED VIETNAMESE, and neither a heart nor a mind was won on this trip.

(With slight editing for clarity. This story is reprinted from the USMC Vietnam Tankers Association's *Sponson Box* magazine.)

CO Company C: Capt. E. L. Erickson
Location and Operations Summary: Chu Lai (BT 531094)

Company C, attached to the 4th Marines, occupied strong points along the MLR and provided a mobile reserve force in the Chu Lai enclave. The headquarters tanks were used to support G/2/4, while the 2d Platoon is DS 2/4 and the 3d Platoon supports the 1/4. On 20 January, the two platoons of Company C were placed under OpCon of Company A, 1st Tank Battalion, just recently arrived in RVN. The Company C Headquarters remains attached to the 4th Marines. Company A, 1st Tank Battalion is attached to the 1st Marines.

CO Company A, 1st Tanks: 1st Lt. J. D. Sparks
Location and Operations Summary: Chu Lai (BT 533080)

Note: Company A comprised only the HQ personnel who came ashore at Chu Lai with no tanks. Rather reminds one of the many times the infantry battalion COs came ashore, leaving their tanks and Ontos sitting in the well decks of their respective amphibious shipping.

Company A (-), 1st Tank Battalion landed in Chu Lai. The 3d Tank Battalion was directed to transfer the 1st and 2d Platoons of C Company, 3d Tanks to A Company. The transfer of supplies and equipment, the sorting of the outstanding requisitions pertaining to the transferred platoons, and the transfer of personnel are a problem, which will require close supervision. Just keeping track of who was coming into RVN was a major administrative issue. The organizations charged with that responsibility were often victims of the "system" over which they had little control.

(VTHF comment: The rotation of personnel, redesignation of units, and constant movement as attachments to supported infantry units meant keeping track of money, men, and materiel—a daunting task.)

CO Company B, 1st Tanks: Capt. H. A. Bertrand Jr.
Location and Operations Summary: Chu Lai (BT 548060)

Company B, 1st Tank Battalion, attached to the 7th Marines, supported operations within the TAOR, participating in search-and-clear and search-and-destroy operations and support of patrols. The company conducted beach patrols in the TAOR and provided one section nightly for the defense of the Chu Lai Airfield.

(VTHF comment: There was little to no difference in the mind-set of the Marine warrior between "search and clear" and "search and destroy" operations. And to the Grunt, saddling up to "destroy" had a certain ring to it that "clear" missed.)

January 1966
Third Antitanks
Commanding Officer: Lt. Col. B. A. Heflin
Executive Officer: Maj. O. R. Edmondson
Operations Officer: Capt. R. F. Lanphier
Logistics Officer: Capt. S. R Stewart
Location and Operations Summary: Da Nang TAOR

3d Antitank Battalion (-) (Rein.) is in general support of the 3d Marine Division.

H&S (-) (Battalion CP) located Da Nang TAOR (AT 987711)

Company A (-) (Rein.) DS 3d Marines
   1st Platoon, Company A DS 1/1
   1st Platoon, Company A 1st ATBn DS 1/3
   2d Platoon, Company A 1st ATBn attached to the 2/1

Company B (-) (Rein.) attached to the 4th Marines
   1st Platoon, Company B DS 1/4
   2d Platoon, Company B DS 2/4
   3d Platoon, Company B DS 3/3

Company C (Rein.) DS 9th Marines
   1st Platoon, Company C DS 2/9
   2d Platoon, Company C DS 1/9
   3d Platoon, Company C DS 9th Marines

Company C (Rein.), 1st ATBn attached to the 7th Marines
   1st Platoon, Company C DS 1/7
   2d Platoon, Company C DS 2/7
   3d Platoon, Company C DS 3/7

CO H&S Company: 1st Lt. J. T. Mathews
Location and Operations Summary: Da Nang TAOR

H&S Company (-) A vigorous program of patrolling our assigned patrol area was conducted. In the month of January, two reinforced squad, ten squad, and twelve fire team-sized patrols worked the area. Three fire team-sized night ambushes were conducted in selected sites within our patrol area of responsibility. All patrols resulted in negative reports. On 21 January '66, a special security patrol was employed when the Battalion Civic Action Team visited all homes within the battalion area to give individual gifts for TET.

Carlos Figueredo, Lance Corporal, age 22, New York, New York, died on Friday, 28 January 1966, while serving in H&S Company, 3d Tank Battalion of hostile gun fire.

On 29 January, the battalion's reaction platoon was committed in defense of the Marble Mountain Complex.

The H&S Company's Reaction Platoon (the same will be said for 3d Tanks Reaction Platoon), while called a reaction platoon, was in fact not that. It was very *pro*active. Many of the H&S Company personnel—"cooks and clerks"—sought inclusion in this platoon. Patrolling out in front of the wire broke the boredom of many of the duties provided by these young Marines who were eager to get into the fight and found this the only way. With luck, they could see combat 1:1. And the platoons that rotated through the Marble Mountain posting came with a promotion, though temporary.

This is how that promotion came about. Understand that this was unconventional, if not illegal. When the thirteen or so H&S Company Marines fell into formation at the battalion CP staging area, preparing to board the six-by (truck) to Marble Mountain, the senior enlisted—and sometimes by drawing straws—was frocked as a "second lieutenant" and had a rotating set of gold bars affixed to his collar. It was found that the ARVN soldiers, with whom the platoon deployed, respected rank. The cooperation of the ARVN was obtain best by an officer. Little cooperation was obtained from nonofficers, so we "created" officers and were, by that innovation, assured much better relations.

UNITED STATES MARINE CORPS HISTORY DIVISION
ORAL HISTORY INTERVIEW WRITTEN TRANSCRIPTION

Interviewee's Name: 1st Lt. Dale K. Caswell, #090813
Date of Interview: 26 Jan 1967
Conflict: Vietnam War
Military Unit: While not cited specifically, it's assumed he served in the 3d ATs
Duties: Platoon Commander, Company Commander, 3d AT Battalion Operations Officer (S-3)

Interviewer: Capt. Carl D. Lemon, #088906, USMC
Length: Approx. 12:00
Location of Interview: Headquarters Marine Corps, Henderson Hall, Arlington, VA
Individual Completing Summary: Lt. Col. R. A. Stewart, USMC (Ret.) (AW)
Recording Format and Number of Recording: CD#329-A
Documents Submitted with Interview: None
Related Material: None
Classification: Unclassified
Transcription Priority: Note: The following is a verbatim transcript.

Abstract: Lieutenant Caswell provides an entire range of topics about the Ontos—tactics, "Rough Rider" convoys, logistics, and maintenance.

Key Words: Ontos, maintenance, track, logistics, supply, training, tactics, operations

00:00–06:20 Caswell: I was in Republic of South Vietnam from 2 January 1966 to 18 December 1966, during that time I served as a Platoon Commander for 8 months, 2 Jan 66 to 25 Aug 66. From 26 Aug 66 to 18 Nov, I was Company Commander of H&S Company, and from 19 Nov to 18 Dec, before I returned home, I was S-3. I was stationed all that time in Da Nang.

I'd like to talk about Ontos tactics. The second day I was there, I was on a Rough Rider (truck convoy) down Highway One from Da Nang to Chu Lai. I had 2 Ontos in the lead of the convoy and 2 in the rear. This was a mistake, as I found out later. We got hit (ambushed), first from the one side and then the other, then both sides at the same time. The mine that stopped the convoy was detonated right in the center. This leaves me to believe that all Ontos, with the exception of perhaps one or two to be used as a maneuver element, should be stationed in the center of the convoy; this way, when either end is hit (ambushed), the Ontos in the middle can move to either end without running into traffic.

Another hint I found while I was stationed in Da Nang was to stay well behind the advancing infantry on a search-and-destroy mission. The reason for this was because the Viet Cong, upon sighting the Ontos, would immediately disperse and perhaps not even open fire at all. I usually kept my Ontos at least 50 meters behind, or out of sight, or out of hearing of the advancing friendly units. When the Viet Cong fired on the infantry, I then moved my Ontos up on line with them, taking the target under fire.

There were certain times when I'd have the Ontos go right through the infantry formation, stop about halfway to the target, and fire on it from there. This way it provided a good protective cover for the infantry on their advance on their particular maneuvers toward the enemy.

Other times, we'd roll right through the infantry with .30 cal. Five Ontos with .30 cal. chattering away had good psychological and casualty effect upon the enemy, and in that particular instance, we'd go right through the enemy positions and break right and left to cover the flanks of the infantry's advance.

Other times tanks and Ontos should be employed to cover the flanks of the enemy position. Most often, if the enemy doesn't withdraw right away to the rear, they will try to escape to the flanks and the Ontos and tanks with their long-range capability can effectively cover both flanks.

The Ontos was used at certain times very effectively as an artillery piece. It has good direct fire capability—unobserved and observed. This is an infantry commander's personal artillery. The Ontos can be used in lieu of mortar or with mortar, with very good effect on night patrol coverage or search-and-clear missions.

Ontos could go places where tanks could not, as far as trafficability is concerned, in Vietnam, especially in Vietnam. They have a better track, not the parade track of the M48A3, but good rubber with metal cleat track. There is one drawback as far as using the Ontos as a tank. They should not be used to break down a tree line or run through a village, across houses or revetment or ditches. The one drawback this stems from is that the Ontos is more or less a tin box. It's an expendable antitank weapon, and one mine, even one under 30 lb., will render the Ontos completely ineffective. Many times the tanks, when the infantry was approaching a village, would roll down the tree line so that any antipersonnel mines that might be there would be detonated and cleared for the advancing infantry. We tried to use the Ontos doing this job, and it was quite ineffective.

The loader, driver, and Ontos commander (OC) previously had all been routinely riding on the vehicle. Because of heavy mining incidents in and around the Da Nang TAOR, I insisted that the loader, the radioman, mechanic, and the OC follow the advancing vehicles by at a least 50 meters to be out of the casualty radius of any antitank mines that might be detonated by the advancing Ontos. In this way I also had more effective control of my PIGS and could use my radioman right next to me and spot targets for the Ontos from a position of better visibility.

06:20–12:00 One thing I found a need for was a target-marking weapon. The Ontos itself had a spotting rifle with a phosphorus element, but the OC, if there was a breakdown in radio communications, should have some kind of weapon to mark a target. I had my radioman carry, in addition to the radio and LAWs, a rifle grenade, a Willy Peter type, to mark targets that I wanted to select firing on.

Another disadvantage in this situation was that the Ontos needs more small-arms firepower for sustained infantry support. Since the Ontos's primary role is antitank destruction, and we are fulfilling a secondary mission, that of support of the infantry and destruction of revetments and so forth, the Ontos does need more small-arms firepower. I have recommended in the command chronologies and other records that the Ontos carry either Quad .50s or 20 mm's, and a GE Gatling gun would also be an outstanding weapon for this particular vehicle. I recommend taking off the #3 and #4 guns, that is the two guns—one on the left of center and one right of center of the Commander's cockpit—and mounting a heavy-firepower weapon in this position.

(VTHF Comment: Lieutenant Caswell's suggestion/recommendation, whether as a result of his earlier reports or more widely recognized deficiencies, appears to have had some resonance at the antitank battalion level while its headquarters were still in Okinawa, as witnessed with this 1966 3d ATs Command Chronology.)

> a. Testing of .50 Caliber Machine Gun Mounted on Ontos.
>
> Operational reports from Marine forces in the Republic of Vietnam have indicated the desirability of a light tracked vehicle for use in direct fire support of infantry. The Ontos has proven its ability to negotiate terrain which is not accessible to tanks or wheeled vehicles, however its main armament is designed for antitank use. The backblast, relatively low ammunition capacity, and burst characteristics of the 106mm recoilless rifles have inhibited its effectiveness as a counterguerrilla weapon.
>
> It was theorized that the replacement of two of the six 106mm rifles on the Ontos with .50 Caliber coaxially mounted machine guns would increase its flexibility as a fire support weapon, and permit more rapid ambush and counter ambush fire in situations where the smaller caliber round would be more appropriate, or where the firing of the 106mm weapon would be precluded due to friendly troops or equipment in the backblast area.
>
> The theory was tested on 15 March 1966 at the Camp Hansen, Okinawa firing range. Using a locally fabricated mount, one caliber .50 caliber machine gun was fired in place of the number 4 rifle on the Ontos. (See pictures 1, 2 and 3) As with the 106mm recoilless rifle, the weapon was charged manually from outside the vehicle. It was fed from a 200 round ready box. Target acquisition, aiming and firing were accomplished from within the vehicle, using the Ontos fire control system.
>
> The test showed that the emplacement of .50 caliber machine guns can be done without modification to the Ontos, that room is available for belts of up to 600 rounds per machine gun, and that well aimed .50 caliber fire can be delivered in this manner.
>
> On 28 March 1966, this battalion requested sufficient M85 machine guns to arm thirty (30) Ontos as described above.
>
> The theory was tested on 15 March 1966 at the Camp Hansen, Okinawa firing range. Using a locally fabricated mount, one caliber .50 caliber machine gun was fired in place of the number 4 rifle on the Ontos. (See pictures 1, 2 and 3) As with the 106mm recoilless rifle, the weapon was charged manually from outside the vehicle. It was fed from a 200 round ready box. Target acquisition, aiming and firing were accomplished from within the vehicle, using the Ontos fire control system.
>
> The test showed that the emplacement of .50 caliber machine guns can be done without modification to the Ontos, that room is available for belts of up to 600 rounds per machine gun, and that well aimed .50 caliber fire can be delivered in this manner.
>
> On 28 March 1966, this battalion requested sufficient M85 machine guns to arm thirty (30) Ontos as described above.

There appears to have been no follow-on reports.

The other disadvantage as far as the 106 mm recoilless rifle is concerned is that they are basically a guide tube for the round. They are not a gun tube. There is no metal protection for the round itself. It's quite exposed. This was shown to us when a Viet Cong fired a small rifle grenade at the Ontos which, of course, if he had been properly trained, he would have never tried, but he did. The grenade itself detonated one of the rounds in the tube in turn because of the very thin shell on the guide tube of the 106 itself detonated all 6 rounds. This completely destroyed the vehicle.

In the area of logistics, concerning tactical maneuvers, fuel delivery was a major problem. It was delivered in 55-gallon drums. There was the problem of pumping it into the vehicles by hand pump and the delivery and return of the barrels for refill, the rusting of the barrels resulting in contaminated gasoline, and many other problems. I would recommend, as I did over there, that the LVTP5s, which continually accompany movements to resupply and bring the mail and other stuff, should or could have in it either one or two rubber bladder-type fuel cells. Half of the cell could contain diesel fuel for the tanks and half gas for the Ontos. In this way, it'd be much easier to pump the gas into the vehicles and also return to the base with any gear that must go to the rear with an empty tank.

Maintenance was not a major problem in the field. Parts, originally in the first of it, were hard to get, but after a while, there was no problem with parts. The vehicle itself, in what little experience I have with tracked vehicles at maintenance school and other places, I've decided that the Ontos has probably the best track support system of any of our armored vehicles. Track again was a problem in so far as a logistical situation was concerned; we couldn't get it. They either were not manufacturing it or someone forgot where it was. After much pain, and turning the Ontos into permanent pillboxes until something was done, we found track in Okinawa. But this is a logistical bookkeeping problem that should never have happened.

In maneuvering and following in-trace of infantry on an operation, we always tracked larger vehicles. That is, we drove usually in the right-hand track of a larger vehicle like a tank or LVT. Since our treads weren't as wide as a tank, we drove in the right track to protect the driver, who drives from the left, from the blast from any command or pressure-activated antitank mines.

As far as special training goes for individual personnel, reloading and driving were two big problem areas. We constantly conducted drills in reloading the Ontos—everyone working as a specialty routine and constantly timed. Driving over the rice paddy dikes was another problem. Many times Tankers, not wishing to slam the front road wheels into the side of a dike, often resulting in broken torsion bars, would slow down when they came to a paddy dike, which was raised portion in the paddy about 12–24 inches in height. Once the tank slowed down, it lost all momentum carrying it forward and then had only traction, which was also lost in the mud. This situation was made even worse when the driver would allow the tracks to spin in the mud and dig the tank in even deeper. Ontos upon command would drive at the paddy as hard as they could and drive either over it or through it. This took training of the individual personnel in the vehicle.

END OF INTERVIEW

CO Company A (-) (Rein): Capt K. E. Sharff
Location and Operations Summary: Phu Bai TAOR

Company A (-) (Rein.) continued DS 3d Marines. The 1st Platoon DS 1/1 maintained their defensive posture, providing one Ontos to Company B CP (AT 921692) and one Ontos to the battalion CP for security. The 1st Platoon, Company A, 1st AT Battalion DS 1/3, with a light section positioned at Company D CP and the heavy section at 1/3's CP. On the 29th and 30th of January, a reconnaissance was conducted in the western areas of responsibility to determine suitable firing positions for long-range direct fire support.

On 22 January, Ralph Beck received a Purple Heart.

CO Company B (-) (Rein.): 1st Lt. M. H. Chang
Location and Operations Summary: Phu Bai TAOR

Company B (-) (Rein.) attached to the 4th Marines until 20 January, when the 1st Marines assumed control. With the 2/4 participating in Operation DOUBLE EAGLE, the company realigned the platoons' defensive positions to insure maximum coverage, by fire, of probable avenues of approach and key terrain features. The 1st Platoon DS 1/4 maintained defensive positions along the MLR. On 18 January '66, the platoon conducted a direct fire H&I mission on an island at (BT 5214), expending ninety rounds of 106 mm. The 2d Platoon DS 2/4 maintained defensive positions along the MLR. On 2 January '66, the platoon provided escort for G and E/2/4, and a light section provided escort for G/2/4 on 11 January '66. The platoon participated in direct fire H&I mission on 11 January '66, expending eighty-three rounds of 106 mm. On 16 January, a heavy section supported G/2/4 at (BT 513059) in an attack of VC. On 26 January, the platoon came under the control of 1/4.

CO Company C (Rein.): 1st Lt. A. J. Anderson and Capt. F. Firing
Location and Operations Summary: Phu Bai TAOR

Company C (Rein.) continued in direct support (DS) of the 9th Marines. The 1st Platoon remained DS 2/9. On 4 January '66, one section was dispatched to reinforce a patrol receiving heavy small-arms fire. A total of

250 .30-caliber machine gun rounds were fired resulting in one VC KIA (possible). The platoon moved to Hill 55 (AT 971620) on 15 January '66, where they emplaced and fired for registration. Escort was provided on 17 January '66 for a sweep of Chau Son (3) (AT 950606) and Chau Son (2) (AT 945605). The platoon supported a sweep of Bo Mung (BT 027649), directing 250 rounds of .30-caliber machine gun fire at suspected VC positions with unconfirmed results. On 29 January '66, the platoon reinforced by the 3d Platoon supported operation WAR BONNET II.

CO Company C (Rein.): 1st ATBn: Capt. C. F. Snyder
Location and Operations Summary: Phu Bai TAOR

Company C (Rein.), 1st ATBn remained attached to the 7th Marines. The 1st Platoon DS 1/7 continued to man defensive positions along the MLR. Ontos/infantry patrols were conducted almost daily behind the MLR. The 2d Platoon DS 2/7 continued to man defensive positions along the MLR. On 15 January '66, the heavy section escorted a convoy to (BS 562894) southwest of Binh Son, where they assumed a defensive posture until 18 January '66, when they escorted the convoy's return to Chu Lai. The 3d Platoon DS 3/7 continued to man defensive positions along the MLR. On 24 January '66, a light section escorted a convoy from Chu Lai to the military compound AT Quang Ngai.

J. R. Gipe, lance corporal, age 21, Harrisburg, Pennsylvania, a radio operator serving with Company C, 3d Antitank Battalion, died on Thursday, 6 January 1966, due to injuries sustained from the explosion of an enemy mine.

Note: 1ˢᵗ Tank and 1ˢᵗ Antitank (Ontos) Battalions Headquarters came into Vietnam during March. The tank and antitank companies that preceded their parent battalions were reported on respectively by the 3d Tank and 3d Antitank Battalions.

Note: In the context of "unintended consequences" were the refugee surges resulting from the disruption caused by major-sized operations. Gilbert, in *Marine Tank Battles in Vietnam*, wrote, "The big battles that MACV sought, created a flood of refugees that overwhelmed both the civil authorities and the Marines. The Marines, for their part, resented the refugees for the disease, sanitation, and administrative (to say nothing of the security) problems they caused, as well as for the inevitability of VC included in the mass of people" (TV-OG).

February 1966
Third Tanks
Commanding Officer: Lt. Col. M. L. Raphael
Executive Officer: Maj. J. G. Doss Jr.
Operations Officer: Maj. A. W. Lamb
Logistics Officer: Maj. F. W. Coates
Location and Operations Summary: Da Nang (AT 989708)

It should be noted that the battalion will, within the next six months, face a tremendous rate of personnel attrition due to rotation to CONUS. There are, at the present time, several large blocks of personnel having a like RTD, particularly in June and September. The two attached companies from the 1ˢᵗ Tank Battalion are primarily responsible for these blocks of RTDs, since they were deployed to WestPac from CONUS as units. In order to alleviate the problem of these two companies rotating back to CONUS as units, and thus losing the effectiveness of two tank companies at once, the battalion has sought to distribute personnel with like RTDs equitably throughout each of its six companies. While personnel reassignments within the battalion will partially alleviate the problem of losing, en masse, an entire company in a given month, it will not alleviate the prospect of losing vast blocks of personnel who have the same RTD. Such losses will certainly result in a critical personnel shortage unless a like number of personnel are programmed into the battalion on a timely basis. A tank and Ontos are crew-served weapons—four crewmen to operate a tank and three crewmen to operate an Ontos. Any fewer Marines results in a severe degradation of the armored firepower capability of that tracked vehicle.

Command and Control

As in the past, command and control of tank elements in the III MAF area remained decentralized. Tank units (and often a single tank) were employed (scattered) throughout the three enclaves, as well as deployed afloat in support of the SLF.

The 3d Tank Battalion exercised complete control of the Battalion Headquarters tanks and the 1st and 2d Platoons of Company C. The headquarters tanks were employed on the battalion command post perimeter. The 1st Platoon supported 3/3 under the supervision of Tank Battalion Headquarters. The 2d Platoon was in reserve.

Companies A and B, 3d Tank Battalion were DS infantry regiments in the Da Nang enclave, while Company C was attached to 4th Marines in the Chu Lai enclave. Companies A and B, 1st Tank Battalion were attached to the 1st and 7th Marines, respectively, in Chu Lai.

OpCon of tank elements was primarily exercised by supported infantry regiments. Ad/LogCon of all five gun companies remained with the 3d Tank Battalion.

When OpCon is exercised by the infantry, the requirement for close and frequent liaison with the supported unit is paramount. Command and representative liaison is constantly maintained to ensure mutual understanding and to promote coordination and cooperation.

Supervision of tank support continues to be exercised through frequent command and staff visits and conferences, daily communication, and submission of periodic reports.

CO H&S Company CO: Capt. A. E. Lee
Location and Operations Summary: Da Nang (AT 989708)

During the month of February, H&S Company conducted twenty-three security patrols and five night ambushes in the vicinity of the battalion CP. Two platoon-size search-and-clear operations were conducted in the Phong Bac Hamlet Complex adjacent to the CP. The battalion continued to provide one infantry (reaction) platoon on standby for immediate employment in the Da Nang TAOR. This platoon was employed on two occasions during the month to reinforce infantry battalions.

CO Company A: Capt. F. W. Jarnot
Location and Operations Summary: Da Nang (AT 946762)

Company A continued to support 3d Marines. Primary employment consisted of occupying strong points on the MLR, maintaining blocking positions on the MSR and Route 1 and participating in planning and employment of a mobile reserve force. Forward positions have been selected and occupied to provide H&I fires as required.

CO Company B: Capt. W. A. Coomes
Location and Operations Summary: Da Nang (AT 067719)

Company B, supporting 9th Marines, had the majority of tank offensive action and enemy contact. The area in which they operated is primarily flat, open terrain with few water obstacles. The company participated in thirty-one search-and-clear and search-and-destroy missions, eighteen armored patrols, and once as a mobile reserve. These actions resulted in thirty enemy contacts for a total of forty-seven VC KIA and two WIA.

CO Company C: Capt. E. L. Erickson
Location and Operations Summary: Chu Lai (BT 531094)

Company C remained in support of 4th Marines in the Chu Lai TAOR but had no operational tank platoons in that area. Their 1st Platoon supported 3/3 in the Da Nang TAOR, and their 3d Platoon operated with the BLT 3/4 SLF. The 2d Platoon arrived in Da Nang with the BLT 2/3 SLF. While assigned to BLT 2/3, the platoon operated ashore during Operation DOUBLE EAGLE as part of a composite infantry unit while their tanks remained aboard ship. This type of employment is not desirable, since replacement tank leaders and crewmen are not available or easily trained. Combat operations of tanks require complete crews, and casualties sustained would result in deadlined tanks. The tank platoon leader was severely wounded in action and is not expected to return to this organization. Subsequently, employment of tanks during Operation DOUBLE EAGLE would have necessarily been under the command of the platoon sergeant. Since the battalion is short of officers, the platoon sergeant commands the platoon.

CO Company A, 1st Tanks: 1st Lt. J. D. Sparks
Location and Operations Summary: Chu Lai (BT 533080)

Company A and Company B of the 1st Tank Battalion continued to provide tank support to the 1st Marines and 7th Marines, respectively, in Chu Lai. The terrain between the Song Am Tan to the north and the Song Tra Bong to the south poses formidable obstacles to tank operations in that TAOR. Again, a bridging capability or sufficient lighterage must be made available to fully exploit the offensive capability of this weapon.

CO Company B 1st Tanks: Capt. H. A. Bertrand Jr.
Location: Chu Lai (BT 548060) (No report)

February 1966
Third Antitanks
Commanding Officer: Lt. Col. B. A. Heflin
Executive Officers: Majs. O. R. Edmondson and E. H. Graham

Operations Officers: Capt. R. F. Lanphier and Maj. O. R. Edmondson
Logistics Officers: Capts. S. R Stewart and K. E. Sharff
Location and Operations Summary: Da Nang TAOR

On 1 February 1966, the battalion was deployed as follows:

3d Antitank Bn. (-) (Rein.) is in general support of the 3d Marine Division.
    H&S Co. (-) (Bn. CP) located at Da Nang TAOR (AT 987711)
    Company A (-) (Rein.) DS 3d Marines

Company A DS 1/1
    1st Platoon, Company A, 1st ATBn DS 1/3
    2d Platoon, Company A, 1st ATBn attached to 2/1
Company B (-) (Rein.) attached to the 1st Marines
    1st Platoon, Company B DS 1/4
    2d Platoon, Company B DS 1/4
Company C (Rein.) DS 9th Marines
Company C DS 2/9
    2d Platoon, Company C DS 1/9
    3d Platoon, Company C DS 9th Marines
Company B DS 3/3
Company C (Rein.) 1st Antitank Battalion attached to the 7th Marines
    1st Platoon, Company C DS 1/7
    2d Platoon, Company C DS 2/7
    3d Platoon, Company C DS 3/7

CO H&S Company: 1st Lt. J. T Mathews
Location and Operations Summary: Da Nang TAOR

H&S Co (-), during the reporting period S-2/S-3, was relocated in the command bunker. The company continued its vigorous patrol activity within the assigned patrol area. Emphasis was placed on night ambushes during the period. On 6 February, the Battalion Reaction Platoon, all from H&S Company, was committed in defense of an area within the 9th Marine's TAOR.

COs Company A (-) (Rein.): Capts. K. E. Sharff and S. R. Stewart
Location and Operations Summary: Da Nang and Phu Bai TAORs

Company A (-) (Rein.) continued DS 3d Marines.

The 1st Platoon was DS 1/1.

One section was with A/1/1 (AT 921692); the other section was with the 1/1 CP (AT 954719).

On 3 February, the section with A/1/1/ conducted H&I fire into Hills 122 (AT 889668) and 36 (AT 895695).

On 6 February, the platoon continued H&I fire from the vicinity of Hill 41 (AT 935663) into GS (AT 9365).

On 16 February, the section with the 1/1 CP displaced with C/1/1.

On 18 February, while attempting to break trail in some dense underbrush, this section became disabled in a ravine. The Ontos remained immobile at the site (AT 894718) until recovery and repair could be effected on 24 February with the assistance of the 3d Engineer Battalion, which built a road to the scene.

On 26 February, one Ontos from this section fired two 106 mm rounds from (AT 889727) at a suspected VC location at (AT 885707), no confirmed results.

The 1st Platoon, Company A, 1st ATBn was DS 1/3. One section in support of D/1/3 at Le My (AT 899820) and one section at the 1/3 CP.

On 5 February, the section at Le My conducted H&I indirect fire from (AT 900821) into an area bounded by (AT 896835) to (AT 905857).

On 10 February, the same section supported an S&D mission with an infantry platoon and two amtracs.

On 11 February, the section at Le My supported an S&D mission with D/1/3. While on the mission, they sealed two caves located at (AT 869837) and (AT 872836), utilizing fourteen rounds of 106 mm HEP-T.

On 16–20 February, night H&I missions were fired into an area north of Son Ca De.

On 19 February, the section at Le My augmented a fire mission laid on the artillery and 81 mm mortar units adjacent to the D/1/3 positions. Targets were located at (AT 870844), (AT 887844), (AT 870855), and (AT 885856).

COs Company B (-) (Rein.): 1st Lt. M. H. Chang and Capt. R. F. Lanphier
Location and Operations Summary: Chu Lai TAOR

Chu Lai Enclave

Company B (-) (Rein.) attached to the 1st Marines.

The 1st Platoon was DS 1/4. They maintained defensive positions at the 1/4 CP (rear).

On 4 February, they displaced to the 1/4 CP (forward) on Hill 69 (BT 464073).

On 5 February, the platoon reinforced by the 2d Platoon participated in convoy escort duty for D/1/4 and the Battalion HQ group in support of Operation DEAD END. The convoy proceeded along Highway 1, and when the troops dismounted for the operation, they assumed blocking positions. After the operation that evening, the 1st Platoon escorted M/3/7 (OpCon 1/4) and the 1/4 HQ group back to their area.

On 18 February, the platoon provided escort duty for M/3/7 S&D mission in the vicinity of Hill 54 (BT 396145). One Ontos destroyed a trench line at GS (BT 4313) on 19 February. The platoon concluded the month located on the 1/4 MLR, located at GS (BT 5209) and (BT 5210).

The 2d Platoon was DS 1/4. They started the month with one section on Hill 69 (BT 464073) with the 1/4 CP (forward). One section was located at (BT 465070).

On 2 February, one Ontos fired an indirect H&I mission from a defilade position at (BT 461073). The target was at (BT 424049). With the platoon commander acting as FO, excellent target coverage was obtained.

On 5 February, the platoon reinforced the 1st Platoon on Operation DEAD END. Upon completion of the operation, they escorted D/1/4 back to their positions.

On 14 February, one section accompanied D/1/4 to (BT 441099), a site where an ARVN platoon was surrounded by VC. Upon arrival at the scene, one Ontos was brought under small-arms fire by the VC. Fifty rounds of .30-caliber machine gun fire was returned, with no confirmed results.

On 18 February, one section provided convoy escort duty for an infantry platoon and an engineer unit to (BT 411128) and (BT 396145). Later that same day, this section, now with D/1/4, linked with the 1st Platoon escorting M/3/7 and supported them in a joint S&D mission of the area surrounding Hill 54 (BT 396145).

On 19 February, four VC crossing a ridgeline were fired on by one Ontos. Later on the VC were observed emerging from behind the hill; they were taken under fire by artillery. The results were two VC KIA (possible).

On 20 February, the section withdrew with D/1/4 back to Hill 69.

On 23 February, one section escorted D/1/4 to (BT 419123).

On 28 February, the section again escorted D/1/4, this time to Hill 43 (BT 396145).

CO Company C (Rein.): Capt. F. Firing

Location and Operations Summary: Da Nang TAOR

Company C (Rein.) continued DS 9th Marines.

The 1st Platoon was in support of 2/9. The month commenced with one section with F/2/9 at Yen Ne (AT 988665) and one section at the Platoon CP (AT 990678).

Richard H. Main, PFC, age 21, Palmyra, New York, died in a vehicle crash on Friday, 4 February, of nonhostile injuries sustained in the accident.

On 8 February, one Ontos from the Platoon CP location was dispatched to evacuate a wounded Marine. The Ontos, then working with E/2/3, was taken under VC small-arms fire. The crew returned fire with no confirmed results; the VC broke contact. The Ontos remained with E/2/9 after this mission.

On 14 February, the section with F/2/9, while supporting an infantry platoon, made contact with the VC at Ha Dong (AT 999643) and fired fifty .50-caliber spotting rounds with no confirmed results. While on the mission, three AP mines were detonated and one tank trap was encountered, with no friendly losses or damage.

On 18 February, the Ontos with E/2/9, reinforced by one Ontos from the 3d Platoon, were given the mission of aiding a patrol pinned down by the enemy at (BT 009632). Five 106 mm, five .50-caliber spotting rounds, and one hundred rounds of .30-caliber machine gun were directed at the VC, who withdrew.

On 28 February, one Ontos with M/3/3 destroyed VC prepared positions at (AT 963649). The same day, the section with G/2/9 and a section from the 3d Platoon test-fired their weapons in the vicinity of Ha Dong Bridge.

The month ended with one section (made up of one Ontos from 1st Platoon and one Ontos from 3d Platoon, Company B with M/3/3, at An Trach [1]), one section 1st Platoon with G/2/9, and one section (made up of one Ontos from 1st Platoon and one Ontos from the 3d Platoon with H/2/9 and one Ontos 1st Platoon at the 2/9 CP).

The 2d Platoon started the month DS 1/9.

One section was at Tra Khe (3) (BT 073669) and one section at Man Quan (2) (BT 044688).

On 6 February, the section at Tra Khe (3) supported an infantry sweep of Tra Khe (2), with no VC contact.

On 8 and 9 February, the sections changed locations, one to Ngan Trung (3) (BT 065643) with D/1/9 and the other section to Viem Dong (BT 065683) with A/1/9.

On 11 and 13 February, the section with A/1/9 participated in a sweep and an ambush with no VC contact.

On 17 February, the section at Viem Dong participated in a night patrolling the vicinity of (BT 092653) and (BT 094643), no VC contact.

Between 15 and 17 February, 3/9 replaced the 1/9 in the left sector of the 9th Marines TAOR. The 2d Platoon switched support to 3/9 for the remainder of the month.

On 18 February, the section at Ngan Trung (3) conducted a FIREX.

On 20 February, the same section, now with M/3/9, engaged in a firefight with VC at (BT 052654), destroying several houses at that location, no confirmed VC casualties.

On 26 February, the section at Viem Dong, now with L/3/9, participated in a sweep at (BT 108637), no contact. On 27 February, the entire platoon participated in Operation HUNTER in the vicinity of Phong Ho village. No contact.

CO Company C (Rein.), 1st ATBn: Capt. C. F. Snyder

Location and Operations Summary: Chu Lai TAOR

Company C (Rein.), 1st ATBn was attached to the 7th Marines. This is in support of the 7th Marines' beach security plan.

The 1st Platoon was DS 1/7.

One section manning MLR positions at (BS 605995) with B/1/7; the other section was at (BS 568997) with D/1/7. The Platoon Headquarters was displaced from (BT 560048) to (BT 584016), the 1/7 CP location.

The 2d Platoon was DS 2/7.

One section was manning the MLR at (BT 495036) and the other section on the MLR AT (BT 504030).

The Platoon Headquarters was displaced from (BT 560048) to (BT 509028), the 2/7 CP location.

On 26 February, a FIREX (indirect fire) was conducted. An artillery officer acted as FO; the results were considered excellent.

The 3d Platoon was DS 3/7. One section was manning the MLR at (BS 549996) and the other section on the MLR at (BT 528002).

On 3 February, the section located at (BS 549996) fired seventy-five rounds of caliber .50 from (BS 547995), into suspected VC positions at (BS 552989), (BS 553991), and (BS 549989), no confirmed results.

On 3 February, the other section conducted an H&I fire mission into GS (BS 5198) and (BS 5298). Twenty-three 106 mm and sixty .50-caliber spotting rounds were expended. No confirmed VC casualties.

Hue/Phu Bai Enclave

2d Platoon, Company A, 1st ATBn attached to the 2/1. One Ontos was deployed nightly for the 2/1 security element.

On 10 February, the platoon conducted H&I fire from (YD 900072) into an impact area 4–6,000 meters southwest, no confirmed VC casualties. A total of 184 106 mm rounds were expended.

On 26 February, the platoon was totally committed to an operation within the 2/1 TAOR. As the operation was still in effect as the month ended, no detailed information is available at this time. Spot information from the 3d Marines indicates that no casualties have been reported as of the end of February.

Note: First Tanks and 1st ATs (Ontos) Battalions came into Vietnam during March. The tank and antitank companies that preceded their parent battalions were reported on respectively by the 3d Tank and 3d Antitank Battalions.

All the Chu Lai tank and antitank units were getting the word that "moving north" was in the stars as reported NVA activity was sighted with disturbing frequency and intensity.

Between 23 February and 3 March at Phu Bai, 2/1 under Lieutenant Colonel R. T. Hanifin Jr. conducted Operation NEW YORK, a joint operation with the ARVN against the village of Pho Lai, seven klicks northwest of Hue. The operation netted zero enemy KIA, but 2/1 reversed its direction and went after a VC force located on the Phu Lai Peninsula counting more than 120 VC KIA as they chased the scattered enemy for several days (GB-66 and SF-EM).

From 3–6 March in the Chu Lai TAOR, Colonel Peatross's 7th Marines conducted Operation UTAH against the 21st NVA Regiment northwest of Quang Ngai City with the 2d ARVN Division using Lieutenant Colonel Utter's 2/7. As it turned out, when confronted with face-to-face combat, the ARVN faltered, and 2/7 came to their rescue; and then the ARVN, after being rescued by 2/7, failed to rejoin the fight. The 3/1 did join the fight. "In all, the Marines claimed to have killed nearly 600 NVA. Beside the casualties that Young's battalion (3/1) suffered on 5 March (50 KIA), another 66 Marines were killed and 188 wounded."

On 29 March, Major General L. W. Fields arrived in Chu Lai to officially plant the flag of the 1st Marine Division. He took command of all the ground forces in the Chu Lai TAOR and became the deputy commander of III MAF. General Fields went right to work. Between April and June, wasting no time, he presided over ten battalion-sized operations *outside* the Chu Lai TAOR. Though in total they resulted in only minimal contact with enemy, the totals of "Battalion Days in the Field" kept on the COMUSMACV charts generated smiles among the air-conditioned staff officers in Saigon.

"Despite these search and destroy operations, the major efforts of the 1st Marine Division continued to focus on pacification. Besides the combined-action platoons that the division fielded, the two other main pacification programs were County Fair and Golden Fleece" (SF-EM). (Covered in detail in GB-65 and GB-66.) (VTHF will publish a separate document focusing on the Civic Action Programs and Projects of the tank and antitank battalions)

March 1966
First Antitanks
Commanding Officer: Lt. Col. W. Moore
Executive Officer: Maj. R. E. Harris
Operations Officer: Maj. A. J. Eagan
Logistics Officer: Maj. J. J. Keefe
Location and Operations Summary: Camp Hansen, Okinawa, to Chu Lai, RVN

The 1st Antitank Battalion moved from a training status at Camp Hansen, Okinawa, to counterinsurgency operations in the Chu Lai Combat Base, Republic of Vietnam, during the period covered by this report.

On 1 March 1966, the following task organizations were reactivated, and elements of the 1st Antitank Battalion were attached to them as listed below:

RLT-5: Company B (-), 1st Antitank Battalion (Company Headquarters only)

BLT 2/5: 2d Platoon (Rein.), Company B, 1st Antitank Battalion

The 3d Platoon (Rein.), Company B, 3d Antitank Battalion, which had been refurbished and trained by this battalion on Okinawa for a two month period

H&S Company CO: Capt. J. W. Schroeder
Location and Operations: Camp Hansen, Okinawa, to Chu Lai, RVN

CO Company A, 1st ATBn: Capt. G. R. Van Horn
Location: Camp Hansen, Okinawa

CO Company B, 1st ATBn: Capt. J. E. Felker
Location and Operations: Camp Pendleton, CA

Joined RLT-5 on Okinawa on 8 March upon arrival from Camp Pendleton

CO Company C, 1st ATBn (-): 1st Lt./Capt. W. F. Snyder
Location and Operations: Chu Lai, RVN

March 1966
First Tanks
Commanding Officer: Lt. Col. A. W. Snell
Operations Officer: Maj. J. G. Collier
Logistics Officer: Maj. R. E. B. Palmer
Locations and Operations Summary:

The battalion was prepping, staging, and loading on to USS *Winston* (AKA-94), USS *Vernon County* (LST-1161), USS *Whetstone* (LSD-27), and USS *Cavalier* (APA-37) at White Beach, Okinawa, for transport to Chu Lai, South Vietnam.

12 to 18 March: The battalion staged supplies at Camp Hansen, Okinawa.

18 to 20 March: Staging was at White Beach on an around-the-clock operation.

21 to 23 March: Found the battalion loading aboard two ships, USS *Cavalier* (APA-37) and USS *Whetstone* (LSD-27).

25 March: The rear echelon loaded aboard the USS *Winston* (AKA-94) and USS *Vernon County* (LST-1161).

27 March: Departed Okinawa.

28 March: To rejoin the battalion underway.

During the latter part of the reporting period, the battalion landed and established the Battalion CP on Hill 43 vicinity (BT 571041) within the Chu Lai enclave. While H&S Company established the new CP, unloading of the USS *Cavalier* continued. Cargo and equipment sustained minimum damage and loss, estimated to be less than 1 percent.

Immediately upon arriving ashore, liaison was made with Companies A and B, and action was taken to prepare to support these units and assume OpCon as of 29 March and AdCon as of 1 April 66.

2 March: End of Battalion Command Post and Logistical Exercise.

11 March: BLT 3/4 was activated for operation, detaching 3d Platoon (Rein.), Company A, 3d Tank Battalion.

19 March: Advance party departed from Okinawa aboard USS *Colonial* (LSD-18).

23 March: Advance party arrived at Chu Lai enclave.

23 March: First Tank Battalion (-) departed from Okinawa.

27 March: First Tank Battalion (-) arrived in RVN.

28 March: First Tank Battalion (-) CP was established in the vicinity of (BT 571041).

29 March: As of 1500, 1st Tank Battalion regained OpCon of Companies A and B.

Comments from the Tankers: From our knothole, it was about time the 1st Tank Battalion finally got off their ditty bags, got it together, and came to the war. Actually, at first we thought it (the war) would be over by the time we saw the REMFs from Camp Pendleton. B Company's Captain, Allan Lamb, CO, had his company on the ground in Chu Lai since August of 1965 (i.e., six to seven months) providing airfield security, supporting the 7th Marines, and had been involved in the largest amphibious assault since Korea—Operation STARLITE. He put together a composite company made up of tanks from three platoons from two different tank battalions with no support from either one and was awarded the Silver Star for his bravery under intense enemy fire and credited with a basket full of enemy KIAs. Refer to the August '65 Third Tanks CCs (CC-3Tk, 8/65) to get an abbreviated report of, and volume 1 of this series on B 1st Tanks, his leadership in Chu Lai, RVN.

H&S CO: Capt. H. J. L. Reid
Location and Operations Summary: Same as BL&OS above

CO Company A: Capt. J. D. Sparks
Location and Operations Summary:

D/S 1st Marines, Chu Lai. Tanks were credited with preventing the VC from overrunning the airfield and causing inestimable damage to the aircraft

1–28 March: Attached to 3d Tank Battalion, 3d MarDiv, in D/S, 1st Marines.

29–31March: Reverted to OpCon of 1st Tank Battalion, 1st MarDiv, and placed in D/S of 1st Marines.

CO Company B: Capt. E. E. Stith
Location and Operations Summary:

D/S 7th Marines, Chu Lai. Tanks supported infantry routine patrols and provided defensive positions security.

1–28 March: Attached to 3d Tank Battalion, 3d MarDiv, in D/S, 7th Marines.

29–31March: Reverted to OpCon of 1st Tank Battalion, 1st MarDiv and placed in D/S of 7th Marines.

CO Company C (-) (Rein.): Capt. F. U. Salas
Location and Operations Summary:

On 8 March arrived Okinawa from Camp Pendleton, California, and off-loaded over Kin Blue Beach and was attached to the just-activated RLT-5, which was deactivated on 27 May upon arrival at Chu Lai, RVN. Tanks supported routine infantry patrolling, road security, and bolstered defensive positions.

March 1966
Third Antitanks
Commanding Officer: Lt.Col. B. A. Heflin
Executive Officer: Maj. E. H. Graham
Operations Officers: Majs. O. R. Edmondson and E. R. Larson
Logistics Officer: Capt. K. E. Sharff
Location and Operations Summary: Da Nang TAOR

CO H&S Company: 1st Lt. J. T Mathews
Location and Operations Summary: Da Nang TAOR

COs Company A (Rein.): Capts. K. E. Sharff and S. R. Stewart
Location and Operations Summary: Da Nang TAOR

The company remains DS 1st Marines. The 3d Platoon, Company A, 1st ATBn was joined by this company as of 1 March.

Headquarters Platoon continues in support of the gun platoons, providing maintenance, logistical, and administrative support.

The 1st Platoon continues DS 1/4, manning defensive positions along the MLR at (BT 5209) and (BT 5210). During this reporting period, the platoon did not participate in any operations.

The 2d Platoon on 1 March reverted to the direct support of 2/4 Marines with defensive positions on Hill 69 complex. At 010715H, the light section escorted one platoon from G/2/4 to (BT 431109) and then to (BT 431108). At 1100H, the light section escorted the platoon back to their positions and returned to Hill 69 complex. At 071830, the light section escorted E/2/4 to (BT 398149). At 2000, B-25 received three rounds of small-arms fire. Due to mechanical difficulty, the Ontos was unable to return fire.

The 3d Platoon, Company A, 1st ATBn was joined on the rolls on 1 March. They remained DS 3/1. No operations were conducted.

CO Company B (-) (Rein.): Capt. R. F. Lanphier
Location and Operations Summary: Hue/Phu Bai TAOR

The company remains DS 4th Marines.

Headquarters Platoon embarked aboard the (AKA-105) USS *Skagit* on 24 March and departed the Chu Lai enclave 25 March and arrived Phu Bai the evening of 25 March. Initial off-loading began 1730, and Headquarters arrived at the company CP at 0930 on 26 March. The company with two gun platoons is billeted in nine tents.

The 2d Platoon is located in the company area and supports the 2/1. The heavy and light sections alternate on nightly basis defensive positions along the MLR. The positions are (YD 878154), (YD 883153), (YD 889153), (YD 878113), (YD 878117), (YD 880120).

Third Platoon is located in the company area and supports the 3/4.

CO Company C (Rein.): Capt. F. Firing
Location and Operations Summary: Da Nang TAOR

The general disposition of the company remains unchanged: 1st Platoon with 2/9, 2d Platoon with 3/9, 4th Platoon with 3/3, and the 3d Platoon augmenting the 1st and 4th Platoons. There was very little action for this reporting period.

CO Company C (Rein.), 1st ATBn: Capt. C. F. Snyder
Location and Operations Summary: Chu Lai TAOR

"The 3d Marine Division had a hard time pacifying the Da Nang TAOR in the spring of 1966 because of the major South Vietnamese political crisis." III MAF units were threatened with the serious lack of supplies due to the general strikes that paralyzed Da Nang and Hue and stymied traffic between them. The protests were quelled only by late May / early June.

March 1966
Third Tanks
Commanding Officer: Lt. Col. M. L. Raphael
Executive Officer: Maj. J. G. Doss Jr.
Operations Officer: Maj. A. W. Lamb
Logistics Officer: Maj. F. W. Coates
Location and Operations Summary: Da Nang (AT 989708)

The Viet Cong, during March 1966, continued to employ large mines (50–75 lb.) to combat the proven effectiveness of tanks in the Da Nang enclave. As in previous months, their efforts to destroy the M48A3 proved unsuccessful. However, in four instances, tanks were damaged to varying degrees. The incidents in which tanks hit mines were as follows:

11 March 1130H: A tank detonated a mine at coordinates (BT 067633), which resulted in moderate damage to the tank. The mine was rigged with a pressure-type detonating device. The mine probably contained between 40 and 50 pounds of TNT. It left a crater 4 feet in diameter and 3 feet deep.

13 March 1966: At 0700H, a tank detonated a mine at coordinates (BT 100620). The mine was rigged with a pressure-detonating device, which was destroyed by the explosion. The tank sustained only moderate damage from the blast, which yielded a hole 5 feet in diameter and 3 feet deep. This mine contained probably about 50 pounds of TNT.

28 March 1966: At 2045H, a tank hit a mine at coordinates (AT 950600). The mine consisted of 50 pounds of black powder and created a crater 8 feet in diameter and 4 feet deep. The tank sustained moderate damage to the suspension system.

29 March 1966: At 0950H, a tank detonated a mine at coordinates (BT 087619). The mine consisted of approximately 40–50 pounds of TNT. A crater 8 feet in diameter and 5 feet deep resulted from the explosion. The tank sustained moderate damage.

The Viet Cong continued to place mines at points of channelization and in roads and tracks either frequently or recently used by tracked vehicles.

Note: Early in the deployment, it was considered safest from mine damage when a tracked vehicle followed another—wheeled vehicles as well, probably—in its tracks. However, the VC observed the same thing. Result? If tracks were out of sight—for only a moment—the VC would place mines in them that were sure to be detonated when the tank returned.

Although numerous reports have credited the Viet Cong with an increased antitank capability in the form of RPG-2 (B-40) rocket launchers, no tanks from the 3d Tank Battalion have encountered these weapons during the reporting period.

30 March 1966: Corporal H. L. Whaley (#1907395) and Lance Corporal M. Coleman (#2103372) drowned in the field south of Da Nang when the tank they were in submerged while crossing a stream. Not a result of hostile action.

McArthur Coleman, lance corporal, age 22, Masury, Ohio, died 30 March 1966 in a vehicle crash.

Henry L. Whaley, corporal, age 23, New Haven, Connecticut died 30 March 1966 in a vehicle crash.

The 3d Tank Battalion continued to provide tank combat support for the 3d Marine Division.

Company A (-) (Rein.), remained in support of 3d Marines. The tanks were employed at strong points on the MLR, roadblocks on the MSR and Route 1, and provided the 3d Marines with a mobile reserve force. The tanks employed on the forward strong points are also used for long-range H&I fires. As the dry weather continues to improve trafficability in the 3d Marines TAOR, Company A increased its patrol action.

Company B (Rein.) remained DS 9th Marines and continued to have the majority of tank offensive action and enemy contact. Elements of the company participated in eleven armored patrols, seventeen search-and-clear and search-and-destroy operations, and operated twice as a mobile reserve. These actions resulted in forty-six enemy contacts for a total of fifteen VC KIA and one VC WIA.

Both Companies A and B employed flame tanks. They were utilized to clear fields of fire and destroy sources of cover and concealment. Some flame tank missions were fired at night as a show of force and to exploit the inherent psychological effect of flame.

Company C (-) (Rein.) remained in support of the 4th Marines and displaced to the Phu Bai enclave with the regiment. The Company Headquarters joined the 3d Platoon, Company A, which was attached to 2/1 in Phu Bai. This platoon was redesignated as the 1st Platoon, Company C. The former 3d Platoon, Company A returned to Phu Bai with BLT 3/4 upon completion of their deployment as SLF. This platoon was redesignated the 3d Platoon, Company C. The 2d Platoon, Company C displaced from Da Nang to Phu Bai to join the company.

At the close of this reporting period, command and control requirements were reduced by the detachment of Companies A and B, 1st Tank Battalion. The 3d Tank Battalion no longer exercises any control over these companies.

Companies A and B, 3d Tank Battalion continued DS 3d and 9th Marines in the Da Nang enclave. Company C, attached to 4th Marines, displaced from the Chu Lai enclave to Hue/Phu Bai with that regiment.

Operational control of the majority of available tanks continued to be exercised by supported infantry units.

The 3d Tank Battalion retained control of the Headquarters Tank Section and the 3d Platoon, Company A (formerly the 1st Platoon, Company C). This platoon, presently supporting 3/3, is retained under tank battalion control to provide flexibility in filling requests for tank logistic and administrative support.

With the battalion reduced to three gun companies, control has become more centralized. Supervision and direction of the detached company employed in the Hue/Phu Bai enclave are exercised through daily communication, periodic reports, and frequent staff visits.

H&S Company CO: Capt. A. E. Lee
Location and Operations Summary: Da Nang (AT 989708)

During the month of March, H&S Company conducted thirteen security patrols and two ambushes in the vicinity of the 3d Tank Battalion Command Post. The battalion participated in providing night security for an engineer well-drilling team south of the CP on the Song Cau Do.

The Provisional Infantry Platoon maintained on standby was employed for a seven-day period in the 3/9 area of Marble Mountain to augment their defensive effort.

Initial action was taken in the organization of a Combined Action Platoon to increase security of the Hoa Tho Village Headquarters and Phong Bac School. A squad (-) of H&S Company, 3d Tank Battalion was committed to reinforce the undermanned Popular Force unit assigned that security mission.

Plans are being finalized to implement the formal organization of the Combined Action Platoon in accordance with the provisions of Division Order 04900.1.

CO Company A: Capt. J. J. Sucha
Location and Operations Summary: Da Nang (AT 946762)

Company A continued to support 3d Marines. Primary employment consisted of occupying strong points on the MLR, maintaining blocking positions on the MSR and Route 1 and participating in planning and employment of a mobile reserve force. Forward positions have been selected and occupied to provide H&I fires as required.

CO Company B: Capt. W. A. Coomes
Location: Da Nang (AT 067719)

CO Company C: Capt. E. L. Erickson
Location: Phu Bai (YD 879152)

CO Company A, 1st Tanks: 1st Lt. J. D. Sparks
Location: Chu Lai (BT 533080)

CO Company B, 1st Tanks: Capt. H. A. Bertrand Jr.
Location: Chu Lai (BT 548060)

April 1966
First Antitanks
Commanding Officer: Lt. Col. W. Moore
Executive Officer: Maj. R. E. Harris
Operations Officer: Maj. A. J. Eagan
Logistics Officer: Maj. J. J. Keefe
Location and Operations Summary: Chu Lai (BT 512040)

Mission: To provide general support to the 1st Marine Division in the defense of the Chu Lai Combat Base and in unilateral and combined offensive operations as directed, anywhere in RVN.

Note: On 14 April, 2d Platoon, Company B arrived at Chu Lai from float (SLF) and was assigned Company A and redesignated 4th Platoon, Company A.

H&S CO: Capt. W. F. Snyder
Location and Operations Summary: Chu Lai (BT 512040)

CO Company A (-) (Rein.): Capt. G. R. Van Horn
Location and Operations Summary: Chu Lai (BT 531089)

8–9 April: Supported 1st Marines during Operation IOWA

Company was in D/S of the 1st Marines. At 080580, Company A escorted the 1st Marines' motor convoy to Hill 54 at (BT 397145). The 2d Platoon of Company A and 2d Platoon of Company C were placed in D/S of F/2/4 with the 3d Platoon, Company A in D/S of

E/2/4. At 081500, E Company pulled back to Hill 54, and 3/1 took up their position. At 081830, 3/1 was pulled out of the operation, and the 3d Platoon was placed in general support of the regiment and was integrated into the defense of the CP. During the night the situation remained static, and at 090700, 2/4 jumped off from their position on Hill 55 to sweep in a southeasterly direction parallel to Highway 1. The 2d Platoon was DS F Company, the leading element, with the 3d Platoon and a heavy section from 2d Platoon, Company C in D/S of E Company in trace. The light section of 2d Platoon, Company C was part of Company A motorized convoy escort. The operation secured at 091000 at the Ong Co Bridge. This was the first time in the history of the ATBn that an Ontos company was utilized *as* a company in a combat situation.

(Note: A 3d AT Company in the Da Nang TAOR also became the first of 3d ATs—read on.)

26–30 April: Supported 1st Marines during Operation WYOMING

Concept of Operation: The commanding o(s) of the 1st Marines directed Company A to provide direct support to the 1st Marines. At approximately 250800H, Company A was alerted and preparations were made for Operation WYOMING. Initial assignments detailed two platoons of Ontos to escort 1/11 to (BT 395151). After the initial destination was reached, further assignments of Ontos units would be directed from the 1st Marines Headquarters.

CO Company C: Capt. J. W. Schroeder
Location and Operations Summary: Chu Lai (BT 547016)

12–15 April: Supported 7th Marines during Operation NEVADA

Concept of Operations: The commanding officer of the 1st Antitank Battalion directed Company C to provide direct support to the 7th Marines. Company C received verbal orders at 110900H. At approximately 111100H, Company C received its alert, and preparations for Operation NEVADA began. Initial assignments detailed one platoon of Ontos to escort 3/11 to Nui Vo and one platoon of Ontos to escort the regimental headquarters and landing support convoy to Quang Ngai. After the initial destination was reached, further assignments of Ontos units would be directed from the 7th Marines HQ.

The Ontos platoon set up security positions around the artillery positions. At 121030H, a light section of the second platoon with a security element of company headquarters conducted an overland reconnaissance at (BS 635837) for possible link-up with the helo-lifted elements. It was noted that ARVN personnel carriers had been through the area some months earlier, that the road going to the units was wide enough, and that the surrounding rice paddies were basically dry, making bypasses readily available if needed.

At 120700, the 1st Platoon with five Ontos departed the Chu Lai Combat Base, escorting the 7th Marines Headquarters and the landing support area vehicles. The convoy arrived at the Quang Ngai area approximately 120830 without incident.

A helicopter reconnaissance of a route to 2/7 positions was conducted at 121700H. It was noted that many deep, wide ditches, walls, and other tracked-vehicle obstacles had been constructed along the proposed route from (BS 650841) to (BS 687845). It was also noted that the ARVN personnel carriers had stopped their advance at (BS 664842); however, it was felt that with some bridging material and engineer support, the route could be traversed by bypassing and bridging.

D plus 1: Company C (two platoons) with 3d Platoon E/2/7, a detachment of C Company engineers and a forward observer (FO) from 2/7 departed 131030H. The link-up force departed the MSR at (BS 628837) and proceeded east. At 131410H, the 1st Platoon was detached to escort approximately thirty refugees to the MSR and return to the 7th Marines CP for further assignment. At 1610, the link-up was effected with 2/7, and resupply and refueling were conducted with helicopters.

At 132000H, the 2d Platoon was attached to 2/7 for operations, and the 1st Platoon was placed DS 3/11 for security of that unit's firing positions.

D plus 2: The 2d Platoon moved out with one section in support of H Company and one heavy section in support of G Company. At 140915H, after the Ontos had passed the checkpoint of the blown bridges at (BS 695845), the Ontos were detached from 2/7 and directed to return to the 7th Marines CP because of anticipated helo lift of 2/7.

D plus 3: To the completion of the operation, one platoon of Ontos remained DS 3/11, and one platoon provided additional security for the 7th Marines CP. The Company Headquarters and the 1st Platoon secured from Operation NEVADA on order at 181215H. The Ontos escorted convoys back to the Chu Lai Combat Base as they were secured from Operation NEVADA.

20–22 April: Supported 7th Marines during Operation HOT SPRINGS

Concept of Operation: The commanding officer of the 1st Antitank Battalion directed Company C to provide direct support to the 7th Marines. Verbal instructions were received at 202100H April '66. At approximately 202140H April '66, Company C was alerted and preparations for Operation HOT SPRINGS began. Initial assignments detailed one light section to escort the convoy of regimental headquarters and landing support detachment to Quang Ngai and elements of 3/11 to Nui Co and one light section to escort 3/7 from the enclave to the logistical support area to Quang Ngai. After initial destinations were reached, further assignments of the Ontos elements would be directed by the 7th Marines Headquarters.

At 0630, the Company Headquarters, 2d Platoon and one light section of Ontos departed the Chu Lai enclave, escorting elements of the 7th Marines Headquarters, 3/11, and the landing support convoy.

At 0730, one light Ontos section of the 2d Platoon departed the Chu Lai enclave and escorted the truck convoy carrying 3/7 to the Quang Ngai logistical support area.

At 0800, the first convoy reached Quang Ngai without incident. The Ontos elements were emplaced at Nui Thien An with the regimental headquarters to await further deployment.

At 0900, the 3/7 convoy arrived at the logistical support area at Quang Ngai without incident. The light section of Ontos was released and returned to Nui Vo DS 3/11 units deployed in that area. The Ontos were used as security elements for the Nui Vo area.

D plus 1: No Change.

D plus 2: Operation HOT SPRINGS was terminated. The Company Headquarters returned to the Chu Lai enclave with the 7th Marine Headquarters.

The 2d Platoon remained in Quang Ngai to participate in the parade and public ceremonies to be held in honor of the "very successful" joint HOT SPRINGS operation with the Army of the Republic of Vietnam.

April 1966
First Tanks
Commanding Officer: Lt. Col. Albert W. Snell
Executive Officer: Maj. L. R. Burnette Jr.
Operations Officers: Capt. E. E. Stith and Maj. J. G. Collier
Logistics Officer: Maj. R. E. B. Palmer
Battalion Locations and Operations Summary: Hill 43 (BT 571041), Chu Lai Combat Base

27 March '66: Arrived in RVN.
28 March '66: CP established (BT 571041).
29 March '66: Regained OpCon of Companies A and B.

On 1 April 1966, this battalion assumed AdCon of Companies A and B. These companies remain DS 1st and 7th Marines, respectively. On 14 April 1966, 1st Platoon, Company C arrived at Chu Lai. OpCon/

AdCon of this unit was assigned to Company A as directed by the commanding officer, 1st Tank Battalion.

Operations

IOWA, 1st Marines
NEVEDA, 2/7
HOT SPRINGS, H/2/7
WYOMIMG, 2/5

H&S COs: Maj. J. G. Collier and Capt. H. J. L. Reid
Location and Operations Summary: Same as battalion above

Reaction units (squads+) conducted a number of foot patrols throughout the area of the battalion's responsibility. No enemy contact reported.

During two periods this month, 1st Tank Battalion simultaneously provided an infantry company headquarters and a reinforced rifle platoon committed as infantry in defensive positions in the 2/7 TAOR, two tank platoons functioning as four-gun artillery batteries firing indirect fire under fire direction of 11th Marines, while carrying out all normal battalion missions and functions.

CO Company A: Capt. J. D. Sparks
Location and Operations Summary:

Operation IOWA: Two tanks from 3d Platoon, Company A, supported by three tanks, one dozer tank, one recovery vehicle, and two provisional infantry squads from 1st Tank Battalion, moved across the Song Tran, via (BT 531099), and the Song Khou Yen, via (BT 423102). The initial ford of the Song Khou Yen via (BT 423102) proved impassable, and the tanks then crossed via (BT 531099) with assistance from a dozer tank. At 080910H, three rounds of automatic weapons fire were received from via (BT 423109). At 080930H, ten rounds of automatic weapon were received from via (BT 419103). Fire was not returned in either case due to a lack of defined targets and presence of women and children in the area. Numerous punji pits and several new fighting holes were encountered via (BT 419103). Sporadic long-range sniper fire was received via (BT 431099) from via (BT 428092). No casualties. After the fording operation, the supporting vehicles returned via (BT 431099).

COs Company B: Capts. H. A. Bertrand and E. E. Stith
Location and Operations Summary: D/S 7th Marines, Chu Lai

Tanks supported infantry routine patrols and provided defensive positions security including tank gunnery registration of both direct and indirect firing.

CO Company C: UNK
Location and Operations Summary: Attached to 5th Marines

This abstract is taken from the battalion's command chronology. There is no mention in this document of Company C (?).

April 1966
Third Antitanks
Commanding Officer: Lt. Col. B. A. Heflin
Executive Officer: Maj. E. H. Graham
Operations Officer: Maj. E. R. Larson
Logistics Officer: Capt. K. E. Sharff
Location and Operations Summary: Da Nang TAOR

On 1 April 1966, the battalion was deployed as follows:

3d Antitank Battalion in general support of the 3d Marine Division.

    H&S Co (-) (BN CP) located Da Nang Enclave

    Company A (-) (Rein.) DS 3d Marines (Da Nang)
        1st Platoon, Company A DS 3d Marines (Da Nang)
        2d Platoon, Company A DS 2/3 (Da Nang)
        1st Platoon, Company A, 1st ATBn DS 1/3 (Da Nang)

Company B (-) (Rein.) DS 4th Marines (Hue/Phu Bai)
    2d Platoon, Company A, 1st ATBn DS 2/1 (Hue/Phu Bai)
    3d Platoon, Company A, 3d ATBn DS 4th Marines (Hue/Phu Bai)

Company C (Rein.) DS 9th Marines (Da Nang)
    1st Platoon, Company C DS 2/9 (Da Nang)
    2d Platoon, Company C DS 3/9 (Da Nang)
    3d Platoon, Company C DS 9th Marines (Da Nang)
    3d Platoon, Company B DS 3/3 (Da Nang)

CO H&S Company (-): 1st Lt. J. T. Mathews
Location and Operations Summary: Da Nang TAOR

Da Nang Enclave

H&S Company (-): The battalion area of responsibility was covered by twenty-four daylight patrols during the month. In addition, five night ambushes were established in the area. The company furnished a reinforced fire team for security of an engineer well-digging site on six occasions.

A provisional rifle squad was designated for employment as needed by Headquarters, 9th Marines for a rear area defense counterattack strike force composed of units within the 9th Marines TAOR. The company provided a squad-size blocking force to support an ARVN sweep of Cam Ne (3) subhamlet (AT 978697).

On 20 April, a Vietnamese Popular Forces Platoon with U.S. Army advisers passed through battalion lines for employment as a blocking force for a sweep of Yen Bac (AT 985701) and Cam Hoa (1) (AT 965703) and Cam Hoa (2) (AT 976701) hamlets by a company of 51st ARVN Regiment.

CO Company A (-) (Rein.): Capt. S. R. Stewart
Location and Operations Summary: (Da Nang TAOR)

Da Nang Enclave

Company A (-) (Rein.) continued DS 3d Marines.

The 1st Platoon remained in reserve at the company CP with the mission of direct support of the 3d Marines.

During the period of 1–10 April, this platoon conducted practice firing at Le My (AT 699820), firing 106 mm HEP-T and .50-caliber spotting rifles on all Ontos.

On 5 April, the platoon was placed on standby for possible commitment to aid in the evacuation of U.S. citizens from the city of Da Nang, but they were not called out. During the period of 11–20 April, the platoon conducted familiarization firings with all T/O weapons, including the .30-caliber machine gun.

The month closed out with the platoon conducting a 40-mile road march for driver and crew training.

The 2d Platoon continued DS 2/3.

During the period of 1–10 April, the platoon conducted practice firing on the 106 mm recoilless rifles and .50-caliber spotting rifles at True Bao (AT 9071).

From 8–10 April, one Ontos was placed on standby at the 3d ATBn CP for possible employment in an armored column.

During the remainder of the month, the platoon developed defiladed firing positions in support of G-H2/3.

The 1st Platoon, Company A, 1st ATBn continued DS 1/3.

From 1–10 April, H&I missions were fired from a firing point located on Hill 358 (AT 931885) into GS (AT 8988, AT 9087, AT 9088, and AT 9089).

On 8 April, one section was placed on standby at the 3d ATBn CP for possible employment in an armored column. They were released on 10 April, without having been committed. During this same period, one Ontos assumed a defensive role at NAM-O bridge (AT 935867) in place of an M48A3 tank that was on standby for the armored column mentioned above.

For the remainder of the month, the platoon conducted nightly H&I fire missions from positions on Hill 358.

On 28 April, the platoon conducted a direct fire mission in support of D/1/3, achieving good results in target area.

CO Company B (-) (Rein.): Capt. R. F. Lanphier
Location and Operations Summary: Hue/Phu Bai TAOR

Hue/Phu Bai Enclave

Company B (-) (Rein.) continued DS 4th Marines.

The 2d Platoon, Company A, 1st ATBn was DS 2/1.

On 5 April, one section had the mission of reinforcing a roadblock at (YD 875148). They returned the following day, with no enemy contact.

On 10 April, the platoon participated in a company firing exercise at Dong Da Training Center.

The platoon's primary mission during the remainder of the month was that of manning three defensive positions within the 2/1 TAOR. The only other special mission during the month was the support of a reconnaissance patrol to (YD 825245).

The 3d Platoon, Company A, 3d ATBn commenced the month DS 3/4.

On 15 April, the platoon was placed DS 1/4.

On 16 and 17 April, the platoon was given the mission of providing convoy escort for the battalion during the displacement of the CP to (YD 522300).

During the early morning hours of 18–20 April, the battalion received enemy 60 mm, 81 mm, and 82 mm mortar fire within the perimeter.

During the 20 April mortar attack, the Ontos commanders of one section observed muzzle flashes emanating from suspected VC mortar positions (YD 524290). The Ontos section directed nineteen rounds of 106 mm recoilless rifle fire at the position. A morning patrol reported negative results.

On 20 April, one section supported an infantry patrol on an unnamed village at (YD 474276) with no contact.

On 21 April, one Ontos provided security for engineers on a mine sweep.

On 22 April, one section provided direct support for A/1/4, setting up a blocking position at (YD 4827).

On 30 April, one section was placed DS A/1/4, with the mission of reinforcing a blocking force at (YD 521288). Enemy troops were sighted at Don O (YD 5226). Eight rounds of 106 mm recoilless rifle and twenty .50-caliber spotting rounds were directed at the Viet Cong, with unknown results.

The 3d Platoon, Company B, 3d ATBn departed from the Da Nang enclave with a mission of security for a "Rough Rider" convoy. The platoon arrived at the Company B, 3d ATBn CP (YD 894143) with no contact. The platoon was placed DS 4th Marines and assumed defensive positions within the 4th Marines TAOR.

CO Company C (Rein.): Capt. F. Firing
Location and Operations Summary: Da Nang TAOR

Michael R. Cuneen, lance corporal, age 20, Bradford, Pennsylavania, died on Tuesday, 5 April 1966, of nonhostile causes.

Da Nang Enclave

Company C (Rein.) continued DS 9th Marines.

The 1st Platoon was in support of 2/9. The platoon commenced the reporting period with one section in support of F/2/9 and the other section with G/2/9.

On 1 April, the section with F/2/9 supported a sweep of (BT 0161). On returning from that location, they were taken under VC small-arms fire. The Ontos returned .30-caliber machine gun fire with no confirmed results.

On 2–3 April, the section with G/2/9 supported a platoon-size patrol.

One 3 April, the section received small-arms sniper fire from a railroad car (AT 995616). The sniper fire ceased after the section returned fire with eight .50-caliber spotting rounds and three rounds of 106 mm HEP-T.

On 8 April, the section with F/2/9 supported a platoon patrol with no VC contact.

On 9 April, the section reinforced a platoon from F/2/9 in establishing a roadblock at Thanh Quit bridge (BT 042621).

On 10 April, the section with G/2/9 supported a platoon sweep. That evening the section assumed defensive positions at Quang Dong (3) (AT 993617).

On 11 April, at 0100, the defensive perimeter was hit with heavy VC small-arms and automatic weapons fire. One Ontos received a direct hit (weapon or caliber unknown), causing a secondary explosion by detonating the 106 mm HEP-T ammunition in one of the recoilless rifles. The section sustained two WIAs during this action.

On 14 April, the section supporting F/2/9 came under sniper fire from a house at Phong Luc (3) (BT 018624). The Ontos used .30-caliber machine guns in support of the advancing infantry, and then fired three 106 mm HEP-T rounds at the house. Sniper fire ceased.

On 15 April, one Ontos section supported two squads from F/2/9 at a blocking position at Thanh Quit (BT 028625). No contact was reported.

On 17 April, the section with F/2/9 supported a patrol and came under fire from approximately thirty to forty VC who were spotted along the Song Thanh Quit (BT 025612). The section returned .30-caliber machine gun, .50-caliber spotting rounds, and twenty-one 106 mm HEP-T rounds with an estimated fifteen VC KIA (unconfirmed).

On 20 April, E/2/9 relieved G/2/9 and an Ontos section now supported E/2/9.

On 21 April, H/2/9 relieved F/2/9 and an Ontos section now supported H/2/9. On 25 April, this section supported an S&D patrol and was taken under fire by an estimated squad of Viet Cong. The Ontos returned fire with .30-caliber machine gun fire and five rounds of 106 mm HEP-T. A search of the area disclosed expended .30-caliber M-1 cartridge casings and trails of blood, indicating possible VC KIA/WIAs, but no confirmed count.

On 27, 28, and 30 April, the same section supported H/2/9 S&D missions.

The 2d Platoon was in support of the 3/9. The platoon started the reporting period with one section at battalion maintenance and the other section at the platoon CP (BT 074657).

On 2 April, one section supported K/3/9 in Operation GOLDEN FLEECE at Khai Tay (2) (BT 045677).

On 4 April, a section again supported K/3/9 on the same mission.

On 6 April, one section supported M/3/9 on a blocking position between (BT 068677) and (BT 071698).

On 13 April, the 3/9 CP received VC small-arms fire, and one Ontos section was immediately committed on the line and returned fire with .30-caliber machine guns. Proximity of friendly troops precluded the use of 106 mm recoilless rifles.

On 14 April, a section supported an M/3/9 sweep, with no determined results.

On 19 April, while supporting M/3/9 between (BT 063642) and (BT 092588), one VCS was captured. The patrol turned the suspect over to M/3/9 and continued on their mission. At (BT 056654) the patrol received small-arms fire. Return fire resulted in the capture of two VCS and one VC KIA. After the patrol returned to the M/3/9 CP, the Company M commander dispatched two fire teams with the prisoners to the 3/9 CP, the Ontos section acting as escort.

On 21 April, as troops were embarking on helicopters at the 3/9 LZ, .50-caliber machine gun fire from the northeast and southwest of the perimeter was received. An Ontos was sent to the scene, and .30-caliber machine guns neutralized the enemy fire. There was one friendly WIA during this exchange of fire; enemy casualties were undetermined.

On 27 April, M/3/9 received enemy small-arms fire from (BT 062648). An Ontos section returned .30-caliber machine gun and 106 HEP-T fire. The VC withdrew under fire, with no determined results.

On 30 April, the section with M/3/9 supported an S&D operation in GS (BT 0662) and (BT 0661). No contact was reported.

The 3d Platoon continued DS 9th Marines being used to reinforce the 1st and 2d Platoons, Company C, and the 3d Platoon, Company B. One section was in support of 3/3 and Hill 55 (AT 971620).

INTERVIEW

On 14 April 1966, First Lieutenant R. J. Donahue (#084510, MOS 0302) was interviewed for thirty-three minutes at the Marine Corps Recruit Depot, Parris Island, South Carolina, by the Marine Corps History Division personnel about his just-completed tour in Vietnam. Here is an edited version of the summary write-up by R. A. Stewart, lieutenant colonel, USMC (Ret.).

First Lieutenant Donahue was the A Company, 3d Antitank Battalion commanding officer, and the interview covered a spectrum of Ontos employment.

He arrived in the Republic of South Vietnam with RLT-3 on 12 April 1966 via the LST ramp in Da Nang Harbor. Prior to arriving in Vietnam, he had been attached to RLT-3. Upon landing, he proceeded to Hill 327 and Hill 268, about 1/2 mile NW of the Vietnamese village called Dog Patch, west of the Da Nang Air Base. Upon arrival at the cantonment, he took command of Company A, 3d Antitank Battalion (3d ATs) and specifically of the 3d Platoon, Company C, 3d ATs, as well as the other AT platoons attached to various battalions located throughout the country.

Control was admin/logistics, but platoons remained DS (OpCon) their respective infantry battalions. Employment was primarily perimeter security. But they also supported infantry companies on sweep operations, providing fire support.

The Ontos was able to navigate up to 5 feet of water with fording equipment installed. This ability to cross small streams and rice paddies enhanced the ability to accompany the infantry units' operations. The Ontos, with its 6–106 recoilless rifles, fired at caves at a range of up to 2,000 meters with 90 percent degree of accuracy using ATP and HE ammo. (Note: Neither WP or canister rounds were available at that time.)

A reaction platoon of Ontos was kept in reserve for quick response to the supported infantry units' needs. It could move at 33 mph on hard-surface roads and over most flat terrain. They actually fired 8,000 meters when deployed to Lai Me one round at a time (Note: Range is assumed to be 1,100 meters) into the mountains to the west with a high degree of accuracy. The requirement to fire indirect fire missions did not present itself during my tour, though prior training prepared the Ontos crewman for that. A crew mounted two headlights on its Ontos, making "spotlights" with which the crew could see 300 meters at night. They test-fired this arrangement but did not actually employ it. Ontos crewmen could, and almost always did, remind Tankers that they could take their "pig" where tanks could not go.

(Note: Lieutenant Donahue was the company commander of the first Ontos company ever committed to combat—as a company.)

Lieutenant Donahue explained the concept of administrative and logistics support (admin/log). He was the supply officer and the admin officer more than the tactical employment officer. (Note: This was the case in general for both Ontos and tank organizations.) He described in some detail what these duties entailed—working through both the in-country supported units and with his battalion supply located back at Okinawa. A 1,200-gal M-49C gas tanker truck was organic to the company, and so fuel was not a great issue. Maintenance men (2143 MOS) deployed from Company Headquarters to smaller units—one vehicle per day. Again, not a large issue. Radios worked well. The extreme heat, weather, and tracks posed the M-50A1 no great problems. Only one vehicle hit a mine with no major (hull) damage and no casualties. We had no on-hand parts to fix things immediately; anything broken or worn out had to be replaced on a 1:1 basis from Okinawa. Besides the innovation of extremely long-range firing and the headlights add-ons, no other new techniques were invented. All CONUS and Okinawa training was adequate to the employment requirements.

The battalion arrived in May/June. Even with the battalion in-country, all admin/log and OpCon arrangements remained the same. The Ontos is well suited to this type of employment and the terrain encountered. Armor is adequate. The Ontos presence has a great psychological effect on both enemy and friendly. It is quiet and therefore stealthy. (We are more stealthy than tanks.)

Recording format and number of recordings: Originally audio tape re-recorded on CD #105.

"In early April, MACV intelligence sources confirmed Westmoreland's suspicions with information that the 324B NVA Division had taken up positions just north of the DMZ" and "learned that the enemy had created the Tri-Thien-Hue Military Region, with a headquarters location about twenty-five kilometers west of Hue" (SF-EM).

Though General Walt had "misgivings," "under heavy pressure from MACV, General Kyle final ordered Colonel Sherman's 4th Marines to send one battalion to Khe Sanh," and Operation VIRGINIA was launched on 18 April with 1/1 OpCon'd to the 4th Marines. The Marines walked and helicoptered around Khe Sanh for a few days. "They found absolutely no sign of the enemy." The rest of Operation VIRGINIA was canceled. It was not until 23 June when he was found in the form of two battalions of the 6th NVA Regiment (SF-EM).

April 1966
Third Tanks
Commanding Officer: Lt. Col. M. L. Raphael
Executive Officer: Maj. J. G. Doss
Operations Officer: Maj. A. W. Lamb
Logistics Officer: Maj. F. W. Coates
Battalion Location and Operations Summary: Da Nang (AT 989708)

During the month of April 1966, the 3d Tank Battalion had experienced the same basic enemy employment of antitank mines which has prevailed for the past (10) ten months. There was an increase of mining incidents in the Phu Bai area, which is related to the increase in (U.S.) operations. No injuries reported, and damage reported minimal to extensive. The battalion remains in G/S of 3d MarDiv.

H&S CO: Capt. A. E. Lee
Location and Operations Summary: Da Nang (AT 989708)

CO Company A (Rein.): Capt. J. J. Sucha
Location and Operations Summary: Da Nang (AT 946762)

Company A (Rein.) remained in support of 3d Marines. The favorable weather continued to improve trafficability in the 3d Marine TAOR, which resulted in increased tank activity (and enemy mining operations!).

The 2d Platoon, Company A had a tank section at Le My, which fired frequent direct and indirect fire missions in support of infantry operations north of the Song Ca De. This tank section also participated in two search-and clear-operations north on Route 14 to the entrance to Elephant Valley (AT 840855). On these operations, the tanks destroyed a total of seventeen VC huts. (Note: The Ontos unit also reports their activity here as well.)

On 21 April, four tanks from Company A provided an escort for the mechanized force moving elements of 3/9 to the Operation GEORGIA area. The tanks provided security from the vicinity of Hill 41 (AT 933663) to Hill 65 on Route 14 (AT 878576). The 1st Platoon, Company C was redesignated as the 3d Platoon of Company A. This platoon remained DS 3/3 and continued to fire long-range indirect fires from Hill 55 (AT 970621).

CO Company B (Rein.): Capt. E. L. Tunget
Location and Operations Summary: Da Nang (AT 067719)

The Marble Mountain "Mad Dog" Caper

by Lieutenant Colonel Ev Tunget, USMC (Ret.)

When I assumed command of B Company, 3d Tank Battalion in the spring of 1966, the company CP was located just north of Marble Mountain. Two of my platoons were supporting 9th Marine battalions in the general area of Hill 55. My 2d Platoon, under the leadership of Second Lieutenant Bill "Lurch" Lochridge, was supporting 1/1 in the area south of Marble Mountain; 1/1 had built a large "fort-like" command post from which it conducted company operations in the coastal area.

Following a one-company search-and-clear operation, the Grunts found a young calf wandering loose and brought it back to the 1/1 CP area. Since it was so young, it required hand feeding with milk and other "nutrients," a job which the Grunts willingly shared. While trying to come up with a mascot name, someone suggested the name Shits, since that was what the calf mostly did.

In the same company area, some other Grunts had "adopted" a dog, which became very territorial and unfriendly to anyone or anything that invaded *his* "TAOR." Because of his nasty nature, he was named Asshole. One day, Asshole took exception to Shits being in his TAOR and bit him. Several days later, it became obvious that Asshole was rabid, and he was put down. Seems like that should have been the end of a sad story, but it gets much better, i.e., worse!

The several Marines who could be identified as having had contact with Shits following the biting by Asshole were immediately evacuated to the hospital in Da Nang and given a series of rabies shots. Because it was uncertain how many more could be infected, *the entire battalion (1/1) was taken off the line and quarantined in a division rear area* to see if other cases would emerge. I'm sure this did not result in a favorable fitness report for the battalion CO!

Soon after the Marble Mountain "mad dog" caper, division published an order that all dogs within unit perimeters be vaccinated against rabies if they were to be retained as "mascots." There was to be a $3.00 fee per shot to be paid by anyone assuming ownership of the dog. If no one assumed this obligation, the dogs were to be humanely destroyed or otherwise removed from unit perimeters.

Within my tank company CP area, we had a number of dogs, which, after I announced the $3.00 fee per shot per dog for keeping the dog around, all of a sudden, for some strange reason, didn't belong to anyone in particular.

Now I was faced with the decision on how to humanely dispose of the dogs. My company gunny said he had a .22-caliber pistol and could take the dogs to the rear wire of the compound and solve the problem. Somehow, that didn't seem to fit the definition of "humane disposition" to me.

Our company corpsman said he could go up the road to the Seabee's compound and get sodium pentothal from the medical section and put the dogs to sleep with a simple injection. That sounded to me like a more humane way to solve the problem. It turned out that while my corpsman knew how to give shots to people, he didn't have the foggiest notion how to properly put an animal to sleep. He didn't get the injection directly into the bloodstream, and that poor animal screamed, frothed, and writhed for several minutes before succumbing. I said that was the end of *that* "solution."

Lieutenant Bill Lochridge's 2d Platoon was due to head back down south to coordinate operations with 3/9, which had replaced 1/1. I told Bill to load up all the dogs on his tanks and to drop them off in the "villes" as they passed through. I knew that the dogs would be welcomed by the villagers, one way or another! (Vietnamese were known to wok their dogs.) This put a humane end to the Marble Mountain mad dog caper, as far as I was concerned. I also made it clear that any other dogs showing up in my areas of responsibility had better bring their "papers," i.e., shot record, with them!

Ed Tunget

Company B (Rein.) remained DS 9th Marines and, as in previous months, had most of the tank offensive action and enemy contact. Elements of the company participated in nine armored patrols and ten "search and clear" and "search and destroy" operations and were used twice as a mobile reserve. These actions resulted in twelve enemy contacts for a total of eight VC KIA (BC).

 On 26 April, Robert Haller received his first (of two) Purple Heart.

CO Company C (Rein.): Capt. E. L. Erickson
Location and Operations Summary: Phu Bai (AT 946762)

Company C (Rein.) remained DS 4th Marines and provided the battalions with CP defense and a mobile reserve force.

During April and May, 1/5 and 2/5 arrived in Chu Lai, releasing 2/4 and 3/1 to move north to Da Nang. On 27 May, Colonel C. F. Widdecke brought his 5th Marines' flag to Chu Lai.

May 1966
First Antitanks
Commanding Officer: Maj. R. E. Harris
Executive Officer: Maj. A. J. Eagan

Operations Officer: Maj. A. J. Eagan
Logistics Officer: 1st Lt. T. F. Dempsey
Location and Operations Summary: RVN (BT 512040)

Commander's Narrative Summary of Significant Events

At the beginning of the reporting period, Lieutenant Colonel W. Moore was commanding the 1st Antitank Battalion. Company A, reinforced with two platoons from Company B, 1st Antitank Battalion, was DS Chu Lai Defense Command and the 1st Marines. Company B (-) was attached to RLT-5. Company C was DS 7th Marines.

On 1 May, this battalion commenced operational planning to support the 7th Marines in Operation MONTGOMERY. An operational brief, a "Concept of Antitank Support," was prepared and submitted to the CO of 7th Marines to assist him in planning and coordinating Ontos support.

Liaison with the CO of 7th Marines and his staff indicated that (the number of) Ontos support for Operation MONTGOMERY would exceed the number organic to Company C Ontos, their direct support AT company. To fill this requirement, two platoons from Company A were placed OpCon to Company C for the duration of the operation. The 7th Marines Frag Order initially task-organized the 1st AT battalion (-) as a subordinate command for this operation.

Company C, reinforced with two platoons from Company A, participated in Operation MONTGOMERY DS 7th Marines.

On 7 May, the 1st Platoon, Company B, which had been attached to BLT 1/5 since July 1965, CHOP to this battalion. The platoon was attached to Company A (Rein.) pending the arrival of Headquarters, Company B from Okinawa.

On 27 May, Headquarters, Company B, which had been attached to RLT-5 since 1 March 1966, CHOP to this battalion. For the first time since May 1965, this battalion had Ad&OpCon of its three organic antitank companies. Company B rejoined its two organic platoons from Company A. The 3d Platoon, Company B is presently attached to BLT 3/5 on SLF duty.

During the reporting period, units of this battalion participated in three major operations and escorted in excess of thirty convoys outside the 1st Marine Division TAOR.

H&S Company CO: Capt. W. F. Snyder
Location and Operations: Chu Lai, RVN (BT 512040)

CO Company A (-) (Rein.): Capt. G. R. Van Horn
Location and Operations Summary: Okinawa and Chu Lai, RVN (BT 531089)

On 29 May, Company A was placed DS 5th Marines. Company B was placed DS Chu Lai Defense Command by the commanding officer's verbal order.

6–12 May: The 2d, 3d, and 4th Platoons participated in Operation MONTGOMERY.

The Company Headquarters with the 2d and 3d Platoons were DS Chu Lai Defense Command during the reporting period.

CO Company B: Capt. J. E. Felker
Location and Operations Summary: SLF and Chu Lai

Narrative of Significant Events

27 May: Returned to operational control of 1st ATBn, joined 1st and 2d Platoons; 3d Platoon on SLF with BLT 3/5.

29 May: Assigned to Chu Lai Defense Command.

CO Company C: Capt. J. W. Schroeder

Location and Operations: Chu Lai, RVN (BT 547016)

During the period 20–22 May, Company C participated in Operation MORGAN DS 7th Marines.

During the period 24–29 May, Company C participated in Operation MOBILE DS 7th Marines. A 1st Antitank Battalion reconnaissance team was attached to the 1/7 Command Group during this operation.

Narrative of Significant Events

2 May through 24 May: Company C (-) with two Ontos platoons from Company A became OpCon to the 7th Marines for Operation MONTGOMERY.

During the month, Company C escorted twenty-seven convoys outside the Chu Lai enclave and participated in three major operations with the 7th Marines, which placed Company C, 1st Antitank Battalion under OpCon of the 7th Marines twenty-two days of the thirty-one days.

May 1966
First Tanks
Commanding Officer: Lt. Col. Albert W. Snell
Executive Officer: Maj. L. R. Burnette Jr.
Operations Officer: Maj. J. G. Collier
Logistics Officer: Maj. R. E. B. Palmer
Location and Operations Summary: Chu Lai

On 1 May, Companies A and B remained DS 1st and 7th Marines, respectively. The 1st Platoon, Company C remained OpCon/AdCon of Company A until 2 May, at which time it was transferred to Company B.

On 6 May, BLT 1/5 arrived at Chu Lai. At 060800H, OpCon/AdCon of 3d Platoon, Company C was chopped to 1st Tank Battalion, which in turn assigned the platoon to Company A.

On 22 May, Company C (-), attached to RLT-5, arrived at Chu Lai. The company remained under OpCon/AdCon of RLT-5 until 270530H at which time 1st Tank Battalion assumed OpCon/AdCon. Company C established its CP on Hill 43 in conjunction with the battalion CP.

On 30 May, Company C regained OpCon/AdCon of its two platoons previously attached to Companies A and B.

On 30 May, Company C relieved Company A of its mission to support the Chu Lai Defense Command; Company C tank platoons are presently occupying positions within the Defense Command's AO.

At the close of the reporting period, the 1st Tank Battalion has OpCon/AdCon of all its organic units with the exception of the 2d Platoon, Company C, which is presently with the SLF.

Due to the unusual amount of rain experienced during May (highest recorded for month of May in thirty-four years), tank operations, as such, were greatly hindered. However, the planning and coordination training that went into the preparation for subsequent operations will be of great value for future operations.

The 1st Tank Battalion once again proved its flexibility in supporting the 1st Marine Division during the reporting period by continuing to occupy indirect firing positions on OP39 (BS 574965), by providing provisional infantry units when required, and by continuing to maintain and fulfill its primary mission.

H&S CO: Capt. H. J. L. Reid
Location and Operations Summary: Same as battalion above

Reaction units (squads+) conducted a number of foot patrols throughout the area of the battalion's responsibility. No enemy contact reported.

CO Company A: Capt. J. D. Sparks
Location and Operations Summary: Chu Lai

Routine day-to-day activities due to weather making the terrain largely inoperable.

CO Company B: Capt. E. E. Stith
Location and Operations Summary: Chu Lai

Routine day-to-day activities due to weather making the terrain largely inoperable.

CO Company C: Capt. F. U. Salas
Location and Operations Summary: Chu Lai

Routine day-to-day activities due to weather making the terrain largely inoperable.

Foundation Comment: The month of May 1966 experienced the heaviest rainfall in thirty-four years. Rice paddies became several inches to a few feet deep, rivers flooded, raged, and were unfordable, roads became quagmires, bridges were washed out or became impassable, and several planned operations were canceled or delayed indefinitely. Even in the CPs, wooden pallets used as walkways floated away.

May 1966
Third Antitanks
Commanding Officer: Lt. Col. B. A. Heflin
Executive Officer: Maj. E. H. Graham
Operations Officer: Maj. E. R. Larson
Logistics Officer: Capt. K. E. Sharff
Location and Operations Summary: Da Nang TAOR

The 3d Antitank Battalion in general support of the 3d Marine Division.

 H&S Co (-) (Battalion CP) located at Da Nang TAOR

 Company A (-) (Rein.) DS 3d Marines (Da Nang)
  1st Platoon, Company A DS 3d Marines
  2d Platoon, Company A DS 2/3.

1st Platoon, Company A, 1st ATBn DS 1/3 Marines

Company B (-) (Rein.) DS 4th Marines (Phu Bai)
2d Platoon, Company A, 1st ATBn DS 2/1
3d Platoon, Company A, 3d ATBn DS 1/4
3d Platoon, Company B, 3d ATBn DS 1/1

Company C (Rein.) DS 9th Marines (Da Nang)
1st Platoon, Company C DS 2/9
2d Platoon, Company C DS 3/9
3d Platoon, Company C DS 1/9

CO H&S Company (-): 1st Lt. J. T Mathews
Location and Operations Summary: Da Nang TAOR

H&S Company (-): Normal administrative and logistical support of the Ontos companies was provided during the month. In addition, the battalion sector of the 9th Marines rear security area was covered by a vigorous program of nighttime patrols. Members of the H&S Company Reaction Platoon conducted thirty-eight night patrols, eleven night ambushes, and five daylight patrols, all working out of the battalion's patrol base in Yen Bac hamlet (AT 986705).

On 12 May, four Vietnamese Popular Forces (PF) soldiers were assigned to the battalion under permissive orders. These PFs were utilized for reinforcement of the patrol base in Yen Bac hamlet and assisted in the Civic Action Program.

One fire team (Rein.) of the reaction platoon furnished security for an engineer well-digging site at (AT 990699) on seven occasions during the month.

One rifle squad of the reaction platoon was placed under OpCon of 2/9 for CP defense from 7 to 11 May.

On 15 May, the entire reaction platoon was placed on standby alert for possible employment during the political crisis and resultant civil unrest in the city of Da Nang. This standby status was secured on 25 May, without the reaction platoon having been called out.

CO Company A (-) (Rein.): Capt. S. R. Stewart
Location and Operations Summary: Da Nang TAOR

Da Nang Enclave

Company A (-) (Rein.) continued DS 3d Marines.

The 1st Platoon started the month in reserve with one Ontos section at the company CP, their mission being direct support of the 3d Marines. The other Ontos section was in support of D/1/3 at Le My (AT 699820).

On 6 May, the Ontos section at Le My was assigned the mission of locating a patrol from D/1/3 that had lost radio communications with their company CP. It was located approximately six miles up Route 14, and the Ontos escorted the patrol back to their CP.

On 15 May, the reserve Ontos section was placed on standby at the 3d AT Battalion CP for possible deployment as a part of Task Group ROMEO.

On 19 May, the Ontos section located with D/1/3 at Le My (AT 699820) received incoming small-arms fire from an estimated squad of infantry up Route 14. The Ontos fired 1,500 rounds of .30-caliber machine gun ammunition at the fleeing VC. Results were four VC KIA (BC), one of which was directly credited to the Ontos section. The section returned to D/1/3 CP with the enemy dead and some Marine infantry WIAs.

The remainder of the month was devoted to defense of the D/1/3 CP area at Le My.

The Ontos section at the 3d AT Battalion CP was relieved of standby on 25 May and returned to the company CP.

The 2d Platoon continued DS 3/3, with one Ontos section in support of G/2/3, the other Ontos section in support of H/2/3.

On 3 May, the section with G/2/3 supported them in a sweep within the 2/3 TAOR. Sixteen 106 mm recoilless rifle HEP-T rounds were fired at suspected VC positions with unknown results.

On 7 May, one section supported H/2/3 on a sweep of Khuong My (1) (AT 926684), with the Ontos section acting as a blocking force. Although there were no major rounds expended, one VC and seven VCS were captured. The remaining portion of the reporting period was devoted mainly to maintaining defensive positions within the TAOR.

The 1st Platoon, Company A, 1st ATBn started the reporting period DS 1/3, with one Ontos section located on Hill 358 (AT 931885) with a platoon from C/1/3 and one section at the platoon CP, which later provided CP security for K/4/12. Nightly H&I fire missions were fired by the Ontos section on Hill 358.

On 17 May, during a VC probe, one Ontos crewman sustained minor wounds from a hand grenade.

On 21 May, during the civil unrest in Da Nang, one Ontos was utilized on an armored roadblock at the junction of Highways 1 and 1a (AT 974769). The company commander was on the scene throughout most of the period, which terminated on 25 May.

On 28 May, the company commander of C/1/3 called on the Ontos section for a direct fire mission, as small-arms fire was being received from (AT 899875). The location was pinpointed by infantry tracer fire for the section leader. The Ontos section at the target point, and the VC fire ceased.

On 29 May, an infantry patrol from C/1/3 went to the target area. They found substantial evidence of direct hits with the 106 mm rounds. Many pieces of bloody clothing, blood trails, pools of blood, and pieces of human flesh were noted. A weapon believed to be a 57 mm recoilless rifle or large automatic weapon was found. The weapon was destroyed to the extent positive identification was not possible. The platoon continued nightly H&I fire missions during the remainder of the month.

CO Company B (-) (Rein.): Capt. D. C. Satcher
Location and Operations Summary: Hue/Phu Bai TAOR

Phu Bai TAOR

Company B (-) (Rein.) continued DS 4th Marines.

The 3d Platoon, Company B, 3d ATBn commenced the month DS 1/1.

During Operation CHEROKEE (5–7 May), the platoon of Ontos was used to reinforce the assault companies.

On 5 May, one Ontos detonated a large mine at (YD 515263). The vehicle was destroyed and one Ontos crewman was KIA, and infantry USMC WIA were sustained from the resulting explosion. That afternoon the platoon was placed under OpCon of the 4th Marines and assigned to the regimental rear area security. After the operation, they were again placed DS 1/1. During Operation WAYNE, the platoon remained in defensive positions within the 1/1 defensive area.

Wilbert I. Andrews, private, age 19, Providence, Rhode Island, died on 5 May from multiple fragmentation wounds. He was an Ontos crewman serving in Company B, 3d Antitank Battalion.

On 11–20 May, the platoon supported one sweep with elements of 1/1, with no contact reported. The platoon maintained defensive positions nightly on the 1/1 MLR.

On 24 May, 1/1 displaced to the Da Nang TAOR, the platoon displaced to the Company B CP and reverted to direct support of the 4th Marines. The 3d Platoon, Company A, 3d ATBn continued DS 1st Battalion, 4th Marines.

On 25 May, the platoon was used to support the assault companies on Operation CHEROKEE. When 1/4 continued to move northeast during the operation, the platoon remained in direct support.

At the completion of Operation CHEROKEE, the platoon remained at the 1/4 CP, located at (YD 569245), where it manned defensive positions.

On 27 May, 1/4 displaced from the forward area (YD 569245) to (YD 894143). The platoon displaced also and remained DS 1/4. The 2d Platoon, Company A, 1st ATBn was DS 2/1 with the mission of manning defensive positions on the 2/1 perimeter. The Ontos were used extensively for nighttime protection along the MLR.

On 27 May, 2/1 displaced to relieve 1/4, and at this time, the platoon reverted to direct support of the 4th Marines.

CO Company C (Rein.): Capt. F. Firing
Location and Operations Summary: Da Nang TAOR

Da Nang Enclave

Company C (Rein.) continued DS 9th Marines.

The 1st Platoon was DS 2/9. The platoon commenced the reporting period with one Ontos section in support of H/2/9 (BT 015633) and the other Ontos section in support of E/2/9 (AT 992644). One Ontos remained at the company CP.

On 5 May, the section with H/2/9 supported an overnight operation in the vicinity of (BT 033635). No contact was reported.

On 9 May, the same section supported an H/2/9 patrol to (BT 011631), where it set up in defensive positions for the night. No contact was reported, and it returned to the H/2/9 CP the following day.

Bernard A. Teske III, lance corporal, age 21, Excelsior, Minnesota, a repair technician, died on 11 May 1966 while serving with Ontos. He was a member of Company C, 3d Antitank Battalion.

On 15 May, the platoon, reinforced by one Ontos from the 3d Platoon, displaced to the Phong Le Bac Bridge (AT 998707–AT 999705) to act as elements of a blocking force, with A1/1.

On 16 May, one section was displaced from the bridge site to (BT 017658), where it set up another roadblock. The section remained until the seventeenth, at which time it returned to the Phong Le Bac Bridge location. One Ontos section established a roadblock at (BT 042621).

On 18 May, one section from the Phong Le Bac Bridge location displaced to a position south of the Cam Le Bac Bridge at (BT 017705).

On 19 May, the roadblock at (BT 042621) was secure, and the section of Ontos displaced to (BT 017626) to provide security for an infantry platoon at that location.

On 20 May, this section displaced to a location with Company H/2/9 at (BT 015633). The section at the Phong Le Bac Bridge was used to physically delay a "Struggle Force* convoy headed for Da Nang, until

---

* "Premier Ky was convinced that the Buddhist leaders were traitors who wanted to overthrow his government." "For siding with the Buddhists, Ky relieved Thi [Commander of ARVN forces in the northern I Corps TZ and a devout Buddhist] of command on March 10, 1966, precipitating a major political crisis." Gen Thi's backers were referred to as the Struggle Force. III MAF commander, General

permission was received from higher authority to let them pass. No rounds were fired by the Ontos.

On 21 May, the section with H/2/9 displaced to the Anderson Trail located at (BT 027639).

On 21 May, this Ontos section moved from the Anderson Trail to the Than Quit Bridge (BY 042621) where it reinforced an infantry platoon and tank. AT 1700 that afternoon, an estimated twelve VC delivered small-arms and 57 mm recoilless rifle fire at the position, and the Ontos fired two rounds of 106 mm HEP-T recoilless rifle fire in return. There were no determined results, and the VC broke contact.

On 22 May, the section displaced from the bridge to the junction of Anderson Trail and Highway 1 (BT 033644).

On 24 May, the remaining section at the Phong Le Bac Bridge displaced and reverted to a direct support role of E/2/9 (AT 992644). The section at (BT 033644) displaced and reverted to a direct support role of H/2/9 (BT 015633). The platoon CP moved to the new 2/9 CP (BT 015627).

Greg Weaver, private first class, age 19, Abilene, Texas, died on 26 May 1966. He died outright from enemy fire. Corporal Weaver served in the 2d Platoon, Company C, 3d Antitank Battalion as an Ontos crewman.

On 27 May, the Ontos section with H/2/9 supported a patrol from G/2/9 in the vicinity of (AT 9963) and (BT 0063). No contact was reported.

Walt, considered Thi "an exceptional military leader who commanded the 'deep-rooted' loyalty of his soldiers. This potent combination—political support from the Buddhists and military support from the ARVN—allowed Thi to resist American pressure to just fade away. According to the official history of U.S. Marine Corps Vietnam operations in 1966, 'The removal of General Thi caused an immediate shock wave throughout I Corps'" (http://www.historynet.com/the-1966-buddhist-crisis-in-south-vietnam.htm).

The 2d Platoon was in support of 3/9. The month started with one Ontos section in support of K/3/9 (BT 098657) and the other Ontos section at the 3/9 CP (BT 074657).

On 5 May, the latter section supported elements of 2/4 (OpCon 3/9) on a sweep from Ngan Trung (3) (BT 038663) to Quang Loc Dong (BT 067616). No contact was reported.

On 12 and 13 May, one Ontos section provided escort security for a civil affairs detail to Tu Cau (1) (BT 038663). No contact was reported.

On 23 May, the Ontos section AT the 3/9 CP supported H/2/4 (OpCon 3/9) in a search-and-destroy mission in the vicinity of (BT 0669). No contact was reported.

On 24 May, the platoon provided a security patrol on the road from a bridge at (BT 072707) to the 3/9 CP.

On 26 May, one Ontos section supported a K/3/9 sweep of (BT 113625), (BT 120634), and (BT 097634). At (BT 101640), one Ontos fired a single 106 mm HEP-T round at a house in which an armed VC was observed entering. At the termination of the sweep (approximately 1345), as the units were returning to the K/3/9 CP, one Ontos detonated an unknown-type mine at (BT 096658). The explosion resulted in one KIA and five WIA, and the Ontos was destroyed. Shortly after the mining incident, the area received small-arms fire. An Ontos returned .30-caliber machine gun fire, and the VC broke contact.

On 29–31 May, the platoon provided security for engineer road-clearing operations.

The 3d Platoon was in support of 1/9. The platoon commenced the month with one Ontos on Hill 55 (AT 971620), one Ontos section at An Trach (1) (AT 969664), and one Ontos section on Hill 22 (AT 954667).

On 6 May, the section located at An Trach (1) was assigned a mission with C/1/9 Reaction Company, in support of the company at (AT 969647). The section fired fourteen 106 mm HEP-T rounds, twenty-six .50-caliber spotting rounds, and 700 rounds of .30-caliber machine gun ammunition at a group of VC. No confirmed results were obtained.

On 16 May, one Ontos was displaced from Hill 55 and was assigned as part of the roadblock at (BT 017685) (OpCon of the 1st Platoon of this company).

On 17 May, the Ontos remaining on Hill 22 fired five .50-caliber spotting rounds and two 106 mm HEP-T rounds in support of a C/1/9 Platoon that was under VC long-range small-arms fire. No determined results were noted.

On 20 May, the Ontos section located at Na Trach (1) displaced to Hill 55. On this same date, the platoon CP displaced from (AT 967665) to Hill 55.

On 25 May, the Ontos section on Hill 55 supported a C1/9 sweep. The Ontos crewmen killed one VC (BC) with small-arms fire at (AT 956664).

On 31 May, the Ontos section on Hill 22 supported a sweep of Bo Ban (1) (AT 957686), with no results observed.

May 1966
Third Tanks
Commanding Officer: Lt. Col. M. L. Raphael
Executive Officer: Maj. J. G. Doss Jr.
Operations Officer: Maj. A. W. Lamb
Logistics Officer: Maj. F. W. Coates
Location and Operations Summary: Da Nang (AT 989708)

During the month of May 1966, with the diminished rainfall, significant tank activity took place in both the Da Nang and Phu Bai TAORs.

Tank action accounted for seventy-nine VC KIAs (BC), thirty-six KIAs (prob.), seven VC WIA, thirty-three WIA (prob.), nine VCS captured, and two VC captured. Forty-five buildings were destroyed, along with seventeen dikes, 300 meters of trench line, ten-man traps, and two 57 mm recoilless rifles. Tanks supported infantry on twenty-three search-and-destroy/search-and-clear missions and fifteen patrols in the Da Nang and Phu Bai TAORs.

During the month, 352 rounds of 90 mm, 1,470 rounds of .50 caliber, and 12,850 rounds of .30 caliber were expended on combat operations by the three tank companies of the battalion. All 90 mm ammunition was fired on direct fire missions with the exception of forty-two rounds. On four occasions, the M-67 flame tank was employed in support of combat operations. The indirect fire missions from Hill 55 in the Da Nang TAOR was discontinued due to the artillery displacement forward to cover the area previously covered only by tank fire and air.

On 14 May, due to the worsening political situation in the city of Da Nang, the 3d Tank Battalion was directed to form a mechanized task group and be prepared to enter the city of Da Nang to protect U.S. personnel and property.

On receipt of CG, 3d MarDiv Task Group Romeo was formed, which consisted of the following major elements: twelve tanks, five Ontos, twenty LVTs, two provisional companies of infantry. The tank battalion commander was named task group commander. This task group was organized into three mechanized teams for the deployment into the city of Da Nang. One mechanized team was deployed to the 3d Shore Party Battalion CP, where it awaited orders for further deployment. Task group elements were also employed to strategic blocking locations external to the city of Da Nang. These positions were the bridge linking Da Nang and Da Nang East at (BT 048763), the Nam O Bridge area at (AT 930840), and the road junction at (AT 978769).

On 25 May 1966, Task Group Romeo was ordered to stand down from alert status.

The tank companies of the 3d Tank Battalion remain DS three infantry regiments of the 3d Marine Division.

Company A (-) (Rein.) is DS 3d Marines with the 2d Platoon supporting 1/3 and the 1st Platoon supporting 2/3. One platoon of Company A has been assigned DS 1/9, reinforcing Company B in support of that regiment.

Company B (Rein.) is DS 9th Marines. The 1st and 2d Platoons are supporting 1/1, and the 3d Platoon is supporting 2/9.

Company C (Rein.), operating in the Hue/Phu Bai area, is DS 4th Marines. From 5 May until 31 May, Company C (-) (Rein.) supported 1/1, 1/4, and 2/1 in that order during operations in the Co Bi Thanh Tan area, north of Hue, while the 1st Platoon supported either 2/1 or 1/4 in the Phu Bai TAOR.

H&S Company CO: Capt. A. E. Lee
Location and Operations: Da Nang (AT 989708)

During this reporting period, 3d Tank Battalion continued to commit headquarters personnel organized into provisional infantry units to provide maximum support to elements of the 3d Marine Division.

A reinforced squad continued to be provided as part of a composite platoon, which participated in the Da Nang Air Base defense. The platoon's position is adjacent to the MCB-6 compound in Da Nang East.

In the conduct of defense of the 9th Marines rear area defense zone, 3d Tank Battalion continued aggressive local patrolling and establishing frequent night ambushes.

The provisional infantry squad that previously was assigned to support the PFs in the defense of the Phong Bac School and the Hoa Tho village office continued to be provided during the month of May.

CO Company A (Rein.): Capt. J. J. Sucha
Location and Operations Summary: Da Nang (AT 946762)

Company A (Rein.) continued to occupy key strong point positions in the 3d Marines TAOR and in the 1/9 TAOR.

On 21 May, 1st Platoon tanks from Company A, while in position on Hill 22 (AT 954665) with elements of C/1/9, were called to reinforce/extract a patrol that had become engaged with an estimated VC platoon at (AT 954655). The tanks and an infantry squad departed Hill 22 in a southeasterly direction to the position of the engaged squad. A helo-lifted squad reaction force (Sparrow Hawk) was ordered, and it landed at (AT 947637) and advanced in a northerly direction. Two 57 mm recoilless rifles, located in the vicinity of (AT 957650), engaged the tanks and were subsequently destroyed by tank fire. Fire from the 57 mm recoilless rifles caused minor damage to the tanks and wounded the platoon leader and one crewman. Two tanks from the 3d Platoon, Company A moved overland in a northwesterly direction with elements of A/1/9 Marines, who were mounted in LVTs. This force moved from a position on Hill 55 in the vicinity of (AT 970620) to engage the same VC force in the vicinity of (AT 953645). As a result of this action, fifty-two VC KIA (BC) were credited to tank action.

The use of a two-pronged tank-infantry attack to encircle and destroy an enemy is not new, by any means, but this case is one of the few reported where it has been employed in RVN. Its usefulness and effectiveness is borne out by the toll of casualties inflicted on the VC.

50 Years Ago—21 May 1966—My Longest Day

Rod Henderson

I joined the Marine Corps' PLC (Platoon Leaders' Class) Program the summer of 1960, following high school graduation. Boot camp was at Quantico, Virginia, during the summers of '62 and '64. I graduated from college in '65 and off to Officers Basic School (TBS) the rest of '65; then Tracked Vehicle Officer School at Camp Del Mar, Camp Pendleton, California, in January and February '66. I arrived in RVN 22 March '66 and was assigned to Company A, 3d Tank Battalion. A number of new second lieutenants arrived during March, and the battalion commander, Lieutenant Colonel Raphael, had more lieutenants than he knew what to do with! As such, he decided to spread us around to tank sections and let attrition determine who would be platoon leaders. Being that platoon-size action of tanks in Vietnam was not frequent, this worked quite well.

My station turned out to be Hill 22, southwest of Da Nang. The first section of tanks I had, from 1st Platoon, was TC'd by Staff Sergeant Coco and Corporal Williams. Staff Sergeant Coco was the type who always addressed me as sir, but I knew his inner thoughts were, "Oh boy, we've got a training process to go through here!" I learned a lot from him and caught on quickly. My first "baptism under fire" came while he was the section leader.

Toward the end of April '66, the infantry company, H/2/4, was redeployed along with the tank section and replaced by C/1/9 and another section of tanks from 1st Platoon. Staff Sergeant Cosmo and Sergeant Banner were the TCs.

Hill 22 was an active area, with seemingly daily enemy contact. The rice paddies were drying out, but tank movement was still very limited. One of the infantry platoon leaders was Second Lieutenant Dan Brittain, whom I knew from the Basic School. I went out on a foot patrol with him—**one time**! He had the idea that in a firefight, line your troops up like British redcoats and advance! He must have missed our classes on fire and maneuver. This did not go over well with his troops! Lieutenant Brittain was KIA on May 30, 1966.

In early May, the word came down that I had been "chosen" to go to Japan the end of May for a six-week course to learn the Vietnamese language. I don't recall that I prayed about this, but I certainly asked, "Why me, Lord?" There are two things I have never been able to do in life—dance and learn a foreign language. I took French in high school, and after six weeks, the only French I knew was 'Parlez vous francais?' and 'Chevrolet coupe.' The teacher told me she'd give me a passing grade if I agreed to drop the course. I went for it! One of the reasons I majored in engineering in college was a foreign language was *not* required for graduation! I did not want to go to language school but didn't know how to talk my way out of it, nor did I have the cojones to argue with the colonel!

Then, on May 21st, I learned a very valuable lesson—even Marine second lieutenants were not immune to enemy fire! A squad-size patrol from A/1/9 made contact with a large VC unit in the area of Dong Phu (3). We were about 2 miles north and got the word to proceed with infantry to relieve the patrol. The paddies were dry, and we made good time getting to the area. I'll never forget the sight as we came around a tree line and there was the battle right in front of us. Opening fire with everything we had, the VC were emerging from spider holes and tree lines and heading south!

Both tanks had full crews, so I rode on the back of Sergeant Banner's tank, with helmet plugged in and able to see everything going on. The firing continued for fifteen to twenty minutes, moving through tree lines, pushing south.

From across the river, the VC fired a 57 mm, hitting Staff Sergeant Cosmo's tank. Corporal Payne, the loader, was wounded from this blast. He was a tall kid and had to have the loader's hatch open in order to stand up in the turret! We shared a common bond, as we were both country bumpkins, raised on hog farms. Sergeant Banner and I saw the back blast area, and he sent several 90 mm HEs after it. I thought we hit the gun and crew. In the course of a few more minutes, we continued around and through hootches and tree lines. Numerous VC bodies were observed, and a neutral steer was performed over a spider hole, complete with occupant, the gun tube swinging through a grass hootch before we backed off the spider hole. I thought the battle had ended and started filling up the emptied .50-caliber trays. All tankers hated the side mount .50s with only fifty rounds per tray. As I was doing this, the next thing I realized was my left arm was numb. My first thought was, "Oh shit, I lost my arm." Looking at it, I saw that, yes, I had been hit, but no horrible exit wound, and well, that's not too bad! Sergeant Banner yelled at me, "Stay down, we just got hit!" I don't remember the explosion; a 57 mm hit the front of the turret, causing minor damage, but no penetration. Staff Sergeant Cosmo's tank returned fire and knocked out that 57 mm.

A lull in the battle did occur, and the infantry lieutenant and I made the decision that I would stay with the wounded and fallen Marines and get them evacuated—Corporal Payne had already been medivaced—while the rest would push on. Word was received that a Sparrow Hawk was on its way and all would link up. I was left with five wounded and three fallen Marines. All of us wounded were able to move (hobble) and looked like a band of rag-wrapped warriors. We started gathering the fallen, preparing for that medivac, when we came under fire from a few VC still in spider holes, one of which was entirely too close to me! For some reason, he was firing at the Marine the farthest distance from him. I dropped behind a rice paddy dike, pulled out my .45 ACP, and realized I had left Hill 22 with full magazines but had forgotten to lock and load! I went to pull the slide back with my left hand and discovered I had no use of my hand—I couldn't grasp anything! It was at that moment that I experienced sheer panic! Luckily for me, I was next to a fallen Marine. I grabbed his M-14, threw it on the dike, and fired three times before the bolt stayed open—empty! That fallen Marine probably saved my life, and I don't even know his name. That thought has been with me ever since. I yelled to the closest Grunt if he had more ammo. He answered, "Lieutenant, we thought we were getting medivaced, so we gave our full magazines to the Marines moving on. We've got just a magazine apiece." Time for strict fire discipline—control and ammo conservation. As the afternoon wore on, we let our adversaries know we were still there and thinking of them. There was a ditch about 50 yards to the west of us, and we decided that was our best place to make a stand—crawling along paddy dikes wasn't going to work for long.

One by one, we started running for the ditch, zigzagging as we went. I saw several rounds hit the dirt, but all made it to the ditch. When it was my turn to take off, I realized I had been hit in the leg as well. The wound was not major—just lost some meat—but the leg ached. I have never been known to be a fast runner. In high school, there were guys who could run 100 yards faster than I could cover 50 yards! It is said that during times when the adrenaline is flowing, things appear to be in slow motion. So, take a slow runner, in slow motion, and we are talking creeping! I remember getting close to the ditch and jumping for it. I swear, I was still 10 feet from it when I landed! We took count of what we had—ammo, guns, no grenades, a .45 ACP with round chambered, safety on, and fixed bayonets for those that had them. We continued firing a round or two, ever so often. This seemed to work, although by this time, I think the only thing both sides wanted was distance! I remember looking at the sun and wondering if I would see it set that evening.

About 6:00 PM, my two tanks and the infantry returned to our position. We learned that medivacs had been called for us, but the inserted Sparrow Hawk had met with heavy fire. Many casualties and the choppers were rerouted to the south. We heard all the sounds of war—air support, jets and choppers, rockets, napalm, you name it; it was there. A couple more choppers were called for us. I rode out with two other wounded Marines and two fallen Marines lying in front of us. We were taken to Charlie Med Battalion in Da Nang. Landing, the living got off the right side and the fallen Marines were taken off the left side. I can still see that row of covered Marines on the edge of the landing pad. Inside the triage tent, it was like a scene in *Gone with the Wind*—saw horses set up, with stretchers, and doctors and nurses working double time to attend to us. Several years later, I saw the movie *MASH*. I did not like it. In my mind they were making fun of the doctors and nurses who ran these units—nothing could be farther from the truth. My wounds were not serious, so I got to watch the operation of a *MASH*-type unit—wonderful people, lifesavers. By the time they got to me and removed the shrapnel, it was close to dark. I got to a cot in a tent with about ten of us. One Marine had severe head wounds and wasn't expected to make it through the night. On the cot next to me was a Vietnamese who had gotten shot in the ass. When they removed the bullet, they discovered it was a .45 ACP round. They weren't sure if he was friend or foe, so they put him in a plaster body cast, a stick across at his knees, and holes between his legs for obvious reasons. No chance of him running away in the night! I fell asleep that night, totally exhausted—I had never felt that way before or since. This truly was my *longest day*.

Aftermath

Over forty Marines were wounded during that encounter, including several from the Marine Air Wings. The 9th Marines lost about fifteen KIA—thirteen were listed, but a couple more died of wounds. The VC lost over one hundred—I don't think anyone knows for sure. It was a very bloody day! The kid that wasn't expected to make it through the night awoke the next morning, sat up, and told the doctor he felt OK but had a headache. The doctor looked at him, smiled, and said, "I'll be damned; we didn't think you'd make it!" Don't know what happened to the Vietnamese guy—only that he was really pissed, both figuratively and literally! General English came through and presented us with our Purple Hearts that morning.

Second Lieutenant Don Rohleder "inherited" my tank section. Don and I had been in Officers Basic School and Tracked Vehicle School together. We called him the Rommel of our tank class. He was quiet, superattentive, never joking around. Whereas a lot of us were thinking about what "young lovely" we were going to meet at the Sandpiper in Laguna Beach for the $2.95 prime rib and baked potato night special, Don was probably studying tank tactics. Unfortunately, Lieutenant Rohleder was KIA on October 12, 1966. I can't look at the Wall, see his name, and wonder, if I hadn't been wounded, would that be my name? But then I realize, no, if I hadn't gotten wounded, I'd probably still be in Japan, trying to pass Vietnamese 101.

I spent a couple of weeks at the Da Nang NSA Hospital before it was decided to send me to the naval hospital on Guam. The doctor checked my arm, asked where I was from, and called someone saying he had another patient to send to Great Lakes Naval Hospital. He explained the nerve damage may or may not be repaired, but this "tour of duty" was over. I spent another week in Guam, enjoying the island, the WWII history, and I was there when the last Japanese soldier from WWII came out of the hills and surrendered! He was so ashamed of himself, but his relatives were elated!

Several months at the Great Lakes hospital, then a few months at the Marine barracks and the arm and hand were back in working shape. It's still numb from the elbow down, but I have 90 percent use of it. I was slated to return to RVN and went back in November '66. I met Corporal Payne in Okinawa; he was recovering from a gunshot wound to his left hand—accidental discharge of his .45 ACP. He was on Lieutenant Rohleder's tank when Don was KIA. I got assigned to Company B, 1st Tank Battalion and the Third Herd—but that's another story! Staff Sergeant Cosmo got promoted to second lieutenant, and I met him in December '67 at 5th Tank Battalion in California. I ended up a company commander in 2d Tank Battalion and had, recently promoted, Staff Sergeant Banner in my company. I served with some mighty fine Marines and have always been proud of that!

Semper fi,

Rod Henderson (Lt. Fuzz)

CO Company B (Rein.): Capt. E. L. Tunget
Location and Operations Summary: Da Nang (AT 067719)

On 13 May, 3d Platoon Tanks of Company B were employed with elements of 2/9 as a reaction force to assist an infantry platoon that was engaged with an estimated force of 250 VC. The tanks mounted a platoon of infantry in the vicinity of (BT 015635) and moved south to engage the VC force located in grid square (BT 0161). When the tanks and infantry appeared, the VC attempted to break contact and fled across the Song La Tho in the vicinity of (BT 003609). The VC were pursued by fire from the tanks to the limit of observation. Tanks provided supporting fire as the infantry pursued the VC across the river. Initial reports credited tanks with five VC KIA (BC); subsequent reports credited tanks with an additional four VC KIA (BC), for a total of nine during the encounter.

At night on 16 May, 1st Platoon Tanks of Company B, while in night defensive positions, observed five VC in a boat at (BT 100644). VC were detected with the aid of the tank-mounted infrared (xenon) searchlight and were taken under fire. As a result of this action, four VC KIA (BC) were credited to tank fire.

 On 15 May, Francis E. Vining received a Purple Heart.

COs Company C (Rein.): Maj. E. L. Erickson and Capt. J. H. Gary III
Location and Operations Summary: Phu Bai (YD 879152)

1 May: Conducted extensive route and bridge reconnaissance of Route 1 north of Phu Bai to a point 8 miles north of the city of Hue. A request for an LCU ferry to cross the Song Huang was submitted to the commanding general, 3d Marine Division. A request for a Class 60 Raft (ferry) to cross the Song Cua Hua was submitted to the commanding general, 1st Infantry Division, ARVN. Received a warning order to provide a company (-) (Rein.) DS 1/1 during Operation CHEROKEE in Co Bi Thanh Tan area, northwest of Hue.

5 May: Provided direct support to 1/1 on Operation CHEROKEE. No enemy contact, all civilians were evacuated from the zone of action.

6 May: Continued support of 1/1 in deliberate search and destroy with A&C/1/1. No enemy contact. Collected and evacuated approximately 30 tons of rice.

7 May: Operation CHEROKEE terminated. Mission changed to direct support of 1/4 for further operation in the Co Bi Thanh Tan area. At this time, trafficability throughout the Co Bi Thanh Tan area was excellent.

8 May: A heavy section of the 3d Platoon conducted a search-and-destroy operation with an element of 1/4. A section of the 2d Platoon conducted a reconnaissance in force with elements of C/1/4 to an area 2,000 meters

south of the LSA. No contact. Heavy rain for three days did not reduce trafficability, but fording operations became more difficult.

9 May: The 3d Platoon conducted a search-and-clear mission from vicinity of 1/4 CP to Song Bo. One VC KIA, two VC captured.

10–12 May: Company supported elements of 1/4 in conduct of six platoon-size search-and-destroy missions, three squad-size reconnaissance patrols, and one engineer squad demolition mission to destroy remains of Ontos, which hit an antitank mine on 5 May. Captured seven VCS.

13–14 May: Company C (-) with A/1/4 attached, conducted search-and-destroy operations south of Song Ho, westerly from Song Bo. Collected approximately 40 tons of rice. Headquarters and flame section conducted a patrol with elements of D/1/4, no contact.

15 May: Company C (-) (Rein.) with a platoon of Ontos and A and C 1/4 attached, with the tank CO in command, occupied blocking positions in the Co Bi Thanh Tan area and conducted a screening operation to protect civilians allowed to return to the valley for collection of personal effects. Approximately 20 tons of rice collected, no enemy contact. Flame section conducted a patrol with elements of D/1/4. No contact.

16 May: 2d Platoon conducted a search-and-destroy mission with A/1/4. Apprehended one VCS.

17 May: Elements of headquarters section with flame section and 3/D/1/4 deployed against approximately eighty VC in vicinity of (YD 520300). VC attempted to flee and were pursued by tank fire with estimated three VC KIA (POSS), three VC WIA (POSS). Expended three rounds of 90 mm, 1,500 rounds of .30 caliber.

18 May: At approximately 0230, headquarters and flame section operating with D/1/4 received fifty rounds of 81 mm mortar fire during which time an unknown number of VC attempted to infiltrate their

positions. VC casualties unknown, no casualties to tank personnel. One tank slightly damaged by shrapnel, repaired immediately. Unseasonably heavy rains inundated the valley, which reduced trafficability except in the rice paddies. No major problems in trafficability but selected routes had to be utilized.

20 May: At 0450, VC initiated mortar attacks on both defensive positions located at (YD 525264) and (YD 545266). The mortar attack lasted about twenty minutes with no casualties at Company C position. The VC followed the mortar attack at platoon position (YD 525264) with an infantry assault by an estimated VC company supported by 81 mm and 60 mm mortars, 57 mm recoilless rifles, and numerous RPG-2 antitank assault weapons. Intense fire was delivered on the attacking VC by the section of tanks, infantry platoon, and artillery, which was called on the VC assault position and avenues of escape, resulting in eleven VC KIA (BC), estimated thirty VC KIA (POSS), and an estimated thirty VC WIA (POSS). The tank section sustained seven penetrations from RPG-2 rockets but continued in action.

In early June, III MAF intelligence officers learned that the 2d NVA Division had entered the Que Son Valley and, on 13 June, ordered an extensive recon effort to be made between Tam Ky and Hiep Duc.

13 June: Phase 1 of Operation KANSAS kicked off with a half dozen thirteen-man recon teams helilifted into Que Sanh Valley. Every team had enemy contact that ranged from "slight" to the all-out attack sustained by Staff Sergeant Jimmie L. Howard's team that barely escaped with their lives while garnering the dubious honor of becoming the most decorated unit in Vietnam, with his Team 2 receiving two Navy Crosses, fifteen Silver Stars, and Staff Sergeant Howard, the Medal of Honor.

Operation KANSAS ended on 22 June with no further significant contact. Three more named operations followed, and then, with increased fighting elsewhere, operations came to an end until April 1967. Of course, the NVA quickly reoccupied any ground taken from them by the Marines, and by the time the Marines came back, they found the entire valley infested with wall-to-wall enemy occupying caves, dug into supporting fire bunkers, and connecting trenches and tunnels.

June 1966
First Antitanks
Commanding Officer: Maj. R. E. Harris
Executive Officer: Maj. A. J. Eagan
Operations Officer: Maj. A. J. Eagan
Logistics Officer: 1st Lt. T. F. Dempsey
Location and Operations Summary:

Company A: DS 5th Marines
Company B (-): DS Chu Lai Defense Command
Company C: DS 7th Marines

20 June: The commanding officer issued 1st ATBn Frag Order 301/1-66 assigning the following missions to subordinate units of this command:

Company A
   Shift OpCon to CG, 3d MarDiv upon completion of Operation KANSAS.

Company B
   Assume OpCon of one AT platoon from Company C.
   Provide DS 5th Marines with one AT platoon.
   Provide DS Chu Lai Defense Command with two AT platoons.

Company C
   Shift OpCon of one AT platoon to Company B.
   Provide DS to the 7th Marines.

25 June: In modification of his earlier order directing one AT company to shift OpCon to CG, 3d MarDiv, the CG, 1st MarDiv directed one AT company (minus one platoon) to shift OpCon. The commanding

officer of 1st Antitank Battalion directed Company B to join one platoon from Company A pending the arrival in-country of BLT 3/5.

CO H&S Company: 1st Lt. W. D. Webster
Location and Operations Summary:

CO Company A: Capt. G. R. Van Horn
Location and Operations Summary: DS 5th Marines

A heavy section from the 3d Platoon, Company A supported G/2/5 in a company-size search-and-destroy operation.

14 June: A light section from the 1st Platoon, Company A supported G/2/5 in a company-size search-and-destroy operation.

15 June: A light section from the 1st Platoon, Company A operated as a blocking force in support of a G/2/5 heliborne assault on a suspected VC stronghold.

20–26 June: Company A (-) (Company Headquarters and two AT platoons) participated in Operation KANSAS. Company A (-) was OpCon to 3/1 for the duration of the operation.

Company A (-) returned from Operation KANSAS and shifted OpCon to the command pending embarkation to Da Nang Combat Base.

29 June: Company A (-) embarked aboard the USS *Summit County* (LST-1146) for displacement to Da Nang Combat Base and shifted OpCon to CG, 3d Marine Division (Rein.).

The 2d Platoon, Company B supported E and H/2/5

Commander's Narrative Summary of Significant Events:

At the beginning of the reporting period, Company A was DS 5th Marines.

The 1st Platoon was DS 1/5 located on Hill 69 coordinates (BT 468068). The 2d Platoon was DS 1/5 located on Hill 54 coordinates (BT 397145). The 3d Platoon was located at coordinates (BT 434081) DS 5th Marines CP.

On 1 June, a heavy section of Ontos from the 3d Platoon was DS G/2/5. A clearing operation was made from Hill 22 coordinates (BT 423091), north to the Song Trau (BT 422093). The Ontos fired twenty-four 106 mm rounds at trenches and suspected enemy positions. Several trenches were damaged; no enemy casualties noted.

On 14 June, G/2/5 conducted a company-size sweep along the Song Trau (BT 422093). A light section of Ontos from the 1st Platoon supported this operation from blocking positions at (BT 422092). No enemy contact made.

On 15 June, at 1430H, a light section of the 1st Platoon was employed in blocking positions at (BT 434057) overlooking Ky Long (1) in support of G/2/5. No enemy contact was made

On 20 June, A Company Headquarters plus the 1st and 3d Platoons shifted OpCon to 3/1 for Operation KANSAS. The platoon assumed defensive positions DS I, K, and M/3/1. Company A's participation in this operation resulted in two VC KIA (prob.) and one VC WIA (prob.).

On 24 June, 2d Platoon Alpha Company was put under OpCon of B Company, 1st Antitank Battalion, which is DS 5th Marines.

On 26 June, Company A (-) returned to the 1st Antitank Battalion CP and made preparations to board ship for Da Nang. The rear echelon of the Company Headquarters, which remained in Chu Lai during Operation KANSAS, boarded ship on 25 June and sailed for Da Nang on 26 June.

On 29 June, the 1st and 3d Platoons, plus the remaining Company Headquarters, boarded ship. Upon reaching Da Nang, A Company will be DS 1st Marines, shifting OpCon to CG, 3d MarDiv.

During the reporting period, units of this company participated in four operations and escorted one convoy outside the 1st Division TAOR.

CO Company B (-): Capt. J. E. Felker
Location and Operations Summary: Chu Lai Defense Command

Commanding Officer's Narrative of Significant Events:

13 June: First Sergeant Reid assumed duties as first sergeant, Company B.

23 June: Company assigned twofold mission of direct support to the 5th Marines and direct support of the Chu Lai Defense Command. The 1st Platoon, Company C, 1st Antitank Battalion placed under the OpCon of Company B.

24 June: Company CP relocated to the vicinity of Hill 35.

25 June: The 2d Platoon, Company A attached to 2d Platoon, Company B relocated to company CP, and 1st Platoon, Company C assumed 2d Platoon's mission at the Chu Lai airstrip.

27 June: The 2d Platoon, Company B placed DS 2/5 and relocated its CP to Hill 69.

28 June: Company CP fired upon (five rounds SA) by an estimated two (2) VC snipers. Fire returned. No enemy or friendly casualties.

The 2d Platoon, Company A departed Company B CP for Company C CP in preparation for Operation OAKLAND DS 2/7.

June 29: The 2d Platoon, Company B participated in operational sweep in support of 2/5 through the hamlets of Ky Long (1) (BT 4305) and "No Name" (BT 4403). Fifteen (15) major rounds fired in direct support from Ontos ridge (BT 4305). No enemy or friendly casualties.

Late Entry

4 June: An accidental discharge of a 106 mm recoilless rifle mounted on a Company B Ontos resulted in the death of three Marines and the wounding of four others. The commanding officer immediately ordered an investigation to inquire into the circumstances of the accident. Major A. J. Eagan was appointed investigating officer.

The Marines Killed

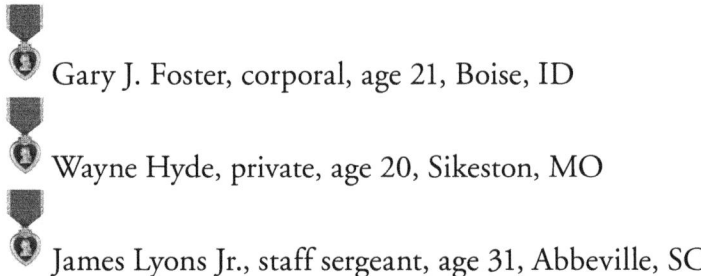

Gary J. Foster, corporal, age 21, Boise, ID

Wayne Hyde, private, age 20, Sikeston, MO

James Lyons Jr., staff sergeant, age 31, Abbeville, SC

CO Company C: 1st Lt. D. R. West
Location and Operations Summary: DS 7th Marines

18 June: A light section from the 2d Platoon, Company C provided direct fire support to D/1/7 in a company-size search-and-destroy operation.

11 June: The heavy section of the 2d Platoon, Company C was placed DS D/1/7 combat base. Operating out of this position, the Ontos were able to provide direct fire support in small unit actions throughout the reporting period.

13 June: The light section (subsequently increased to a heavy section) of the 3d Platoon, Company C was placed DS I/3/7's combat base.

26 June: One Ontos from the 3d Platoon, Company C detonated a mine, which totally disabled the vehicle. One crewman was killed and a second seriously wounded by the blast. Ontos had been operating out of I/3/7's combat base.

The Ontos crewman killed was Alberto A. Avalos, lance corporal, age 21, Brownsville, TX.

June 1966
First Tanks
Commanding Officers: Lt. Col. A. W. Snell and Maj. L. R. Burnette Jr.
Executive Officers: Majs. L. R. Burnette Jr. and R. E. B. Palmer
Operations Officer: Maj. J. G. Collier
Logistics Officers: Majs. R. E. B. Palmer and H. J. L. Reid
Location and Operations Summary: Chu Lai Combat Base, Hill 43 (BT 571041)

(VTHF comment: By now, 1st Tanks had taken over command and control of all its subordinate units and was well settled in the Chu Lai Combat Base (landing on 28 March 1967), conducting around-the-clock operations. Companies A and B were in direct support (DS) of 1st, 5th, and 7th Marines. Company C was in DS of the Chu Lai Defense Command (CLDC), provided one platoon to the Special Landing Force (SLF). First Tanks then moved its headquarters to Da Nang with OpCon to the 3d MarDiv as 3d Tanks moved north. The Ontos battalion followed in trace.)

H&S COs: Capts. J. D. Sparks and J. C. Greene Jr.
Location and Operations Summary: Chu Lai Combat Base, Hill 43 (BT 571041)

CO Company A: Capt. W. J. Britton
Location and Operations Summary: Chu Lai Combat Base

DS 5th Marines

1–30 June: Chu Lai Combat Base.

01–031200H June: DS 1st Marines.

031201H–30 June: DS 5th Marines.

18–30 June: 2d Platoon DS Chu Lai Defense Command.

CO Company B: Capt. E. E. Stith
Location and Operations Summary: Chu Lai Combat Base

DS 7th Marines

1–30 June: Chu Lai Combat Base, DS 7th Marines.

18–30 June: 1st Platoon DS Chu Lai Defense Command.

CO Company C: Capt. F. U. Salas
Location and Operations Summary: Chu Lai Combat Base and Da Nang TAOR

1–18 June: DS Chu Lai Defense Command, with two (2) tank platoons.

19 June: Embarked for Da Nang aboard (LST-1096) USS *St. Clair County*. Arrived Da Nang.

19 June: AdCon 1st Tank's OpCon 3d Marine Division.

19–30 June: DS 1st Marines, Da Nang TAOR.

1–30 June: 2d Platoon, Company C remains on SLF.

June 1966
Third Antitanks
Commanding Officer: Lt. Col. B. A. Heflin
Executive Officer: Maj. E. H. Graham
Operations Officer: Maj. E. R. Larson
Logistics Officer: Capt. K. E. Sharff

Location and Operations Summary:

The 3d Antitank Battalion continued to provide general support to the 3d Marine Division in the Da Nang and Phu Bai TAORS.

On 1 June, the disposition and support roles of units of the battalion were as follows:

H&S Company: 1st Lt. B. M. Mathews
Location and Operations Summary:

CO Company A: Capt. S. R. Stewart
Location and Operations Summary:

Company A DS 3d Marines (Da Nang)
    1st Platoon, Company A DS D/1/3
    2d Platoon, Company A DS C/1/3, H/2/3, and K/4/12
    3d Platoon, Company A DS G and H/2/3

CO Company B: Capt. D. C. Satcher
Location and Operations Summary:

Company B DS 4th Marines (Phu Bai TAOR)
    1st Platoon, Company B DS 4th Marines
    2d Platoon, Company B DS 4th Marines
    3d Platoon, Company B DS 1/4

CO Company C, 1st ATBn: Capt. F. Firing
Location and Operations Summary:

Company C DS 9th Marines (Da Nang TAOR)
    1st Platoon, Company C DS 2/9
    2d Platoon, Company C DS 1/1
    3d Platoon, Company C DS 1/9

CO Company A (-): Capt. G. R. Van Horn
Location and Operations Summary:

Company A (-), 1st ATBn. Moving from Chu Lai to Da Nang, the advanced party arrived via (LST-1096) USS *St. Clair County* at 280730H June. The remainder of the company arrived at 301730H June via (LST-1146) USS *Summit County*. The company was placed under OpCon of the 3d ATBn effective 281400H June. It was placed DS 1st Marines. The company arrived with the 1st and 3d Platoons, both of which were assigned DS 1/1.

VTHF comment: The command chronologies (CC) for each of the AT companies are so detailed, lengthy, and the battalion did not summarize them (by date or by unit) that they do not appear here. Keeping track of forty-five-plus Ontos, deployed across three infantry battalions of four companies with three platoons each spread all over northern I Corps would be akin to herding pigs! You are encouraged to visit the Foundation website, call up the original, complete CC for more detailed analysis of each platoon's action for the month. And for even more detail of the operations of the Ontos, acquiring the CCs of the supported infantry unit is encouraged. For example, 1st Platoon, Company A was DS D/1/3 and participated in Operation LIBERTY. To see what D/1/3 did during the month of June 1966 and particularly in Operation LIBERTY, pull up 1/3's CC, find D/1/3, and see what the Ontos did to support that Grunt company.

June 1966
Third Tanks
Commanding Officer: Lt. Col. M. L. Raphael
Executive Officer: Maj. J. G. Doss
Operations Officer: Maj. E. L. Erickson
Logistics Officer: Maj. F. W. Coates
Location and Operations Summary:

During this period, the command is on record of being unable to continue to support with its tanks all those missions for which the battalion is requested and expected. This is due to the many calls for "warm bodies" to provide *infantry* security throughout the TAOR by

Marines who are in fact trained tank and tank support technicians, and the fill rate for these MOSs is falling far short of the departure of personnel. In addition, there has been a dramatic increase in antitank assaults and mining incidents, which has increased WIAs and required increased repair and maintenance requirements.

During June 1966, the 3d Tank Battalion continued to support the division in the Da Nang and Phu Bai TAORs. On 20 June 1966, the 3d Tank Battalion was once again reinforced when it assumed operational control of Company A (-), 1st Tank Battalion.

Tank action during June has been decidedly more intense than any previous month. The tanks were involved in significantly more combat operations, engaged more enemy targets, and made their presence felt by the enemy more often than in past months. Tank support this month has been a major factor in the division successfully achieving domination of the greater portion of the Song Thu Ban / Song Ky Lam south of the Da Nang TAOR, an area long dominated by the Viet Cong.

The primary effort of the tank battalion this month was devoted to support of Operation LIBERTY in the Da Nang TAOR.

Operation LIBERTY

The mission of Operation LIBERTY was to clear the southern portion of the Da Nang TAOR of VC forces. Assignments of tank battalion units on this operation were as follows:

Company B commenced the operation with the 1st and 2d Platoons in support of 1/1, the 3d Platoon in support of 2/9 and assumed OpCon of the 3d Platoon of Company A, which was in support of 1/9. On 20 June, Company B assumed OpCon of one section of 1st Platoon, Company C, 1st Tank Battalion (OpCon of 3d Tank Battalion). This section was put in support of 2/9. Also on this date, 1st Platoon, Company B that had been in support of 1/1 was replaced by the 3d Platoon of Company C (-), 1st Tank Battalion. This Company B platoon then was committed in support of 1/9.

I Remember

by Pat Rogers, CWO 4, USMC (Ret.)

[This story is reprinted from the USMC Vietnam Tankers Association's *Sponson Box* magazine, volume 4, number 3, June 2001. Edited for form, not content.]

I was in my prep time for the 200 yards rapid-fire stage of the National Match Course "leg match" at the Virginia State Championships at Quantico. The scorer on an adjacent target had been occasionally looking at me since we arrived. Not mean looks but inquisitive, as if he were trying to dig into the recesses of his mind. He was a guy my age, wearing a Marine Corps Shooting Team sweatshirt but obviously not on active duty. He looked vaguely familiar, but after twenty plus years as a cop, most everyone looks familiar to me.

My curiosity overcame common sense. I should have been preparing to shoot, but suddenly I had an overwhelming desire to identify this guy. On a hunch, I asked when he was in-country. "66–67" he said. "You?" "65–66," I replied. "Who were you with?" "3d Tanks," he replied. *Gee, I thought, what a coincidence.* "So was I. I was an 1811." Then his eyes got real wide. The earlier confusion was gone, and a grand smile spread across his face. "You're Mouse, I'm Whitehead! You were Alpha 34!"

I remember . . .

I remember a gangly kid from Georgia coming out to Hill 55 as a replacement on my tank. I don't even believe that Gene Whitehead was a PFC yet. He was brand-new, unblooded and untested. His sincerity was overpowering. He was trying hard to do everything right that he wound up doing most everything wrong or maybe not. I had ten or eleven months in-country and almost three years in the Marine Corps. I had seen the elephant. I had seen Marines killed and wounded, and it was not something I wanted to see again. Not if I could help it. I expected competence in a very imperfect environment. A tank is a very intimate place. You may sink or you may swim, but rest assured you will all get wet together. I was so far intact and wanted all in my sphere of influence to remain so. Circumstance might preclude survival, and I could accept that, but I could not accept a Marine dying because of a lack of training.

I remember . . .

I remember that we pushed Gene Whitehead hard. He probably believed that I considered him somehow unworthy. He once stated that I did not like him, but that was not the case. For all of his inexperience, he had that spark that differentiates the warrior from the rest. He had the makings of a good Marine; he just needed to survive long enough to be one.

I remember . . .

I remember that Hill 55 was not the best place to bring someone up to speed. The OJT was however great.

During the first Indochinese War, two French battalions were wiped out on, or near, this hill. The CO of 3/3, Lieutenant Colonel Muir, was killed there in September 1965. When we occupied the hill in January 1966, we had but two platoons of India Company 3/3, a light section of tanks and an Ontos section. We were not on Hill 55 for more than five minutes before one of our crewmen tripped a mine.

In the book *Small Unit Action in Vietnam, Summer 1966*, the author stated, "In the spring and early summer of 1966 the most notorious area in I Corps was the flat rice paddy and hedgerow complex around Hill 55." I concur. The hill was probed, assaulted, and mortared constantly. Weather and terrain made movement difficult. The enemy apparently had an inexhaustible selection of mines, and he employed them effectively. More importantly, the Viet Cong R-20 (Doc Lap) Battalion had been actively engaging ARVN and U.S. Marine units in the area. Well trained, well equipped, and extremely well led, this unit would continue to be a thorn in the side of Marines operating south of Da Nang.

I remember . . .

I remember that during the late morning of 21 May 1966, a squad from Charlie Company 1/9 made contact with the R-20 Battalion on the west side of the Yen River opposite the village of An Trach (1). Hard-hit, they received support from two tanks and additional Charlie Company Grunts, but they too were stopped.

Observing that enemy troops were also on the east side of the Yen River, 1/9 ordered my section and Alpha Company 1/9 up to engage. A Sparrow Hawk rocket was deployed but landed in the middle of the A/1/9's position. They suffered heavy casualties in a very few minutes.

I remember . . .

I remember listening to the radio on the ride out, hearing the frantic radio calls from the pinned-down Marines, the requests for air and artillery support, and more ominously, the requests for multiple medevacs. "Mr. Charles" was not backing down. He was standing and fighting with all he possessed. It was apparent that this fight would be different.

I remember . . .

I remember that when we made contact, it was sudden and furious. The enemy was close. Engagement was rarely out to 100 meters and usually significantly closer. We were advancing north on the east side of the Yen River. The terrain was flat, with paddies separated by thick hedgerows. We assaulted these positions supported by air, but it was the man with the rifle who had to ultimately remove the other man with a rifle from his position.

I remember that at some point I felt as if I was in a kaleidoscope: the noise of in- and outgoing rounds; UH-1 gunships flying at treetop height, hitting positions merely 25 meters in front of us; friendly ordnance impacting at what could only be described as dangerously close; the constant radio noise squawking over three channels simultaneously; and the distinct whine of an OV-10 (aircraft) directing fast movers (fighter/attack aircraft) or occasionally coming down low and fast to strafe enemy positions when nothing else was available.

Gene expertly maneuvered "O. G. Clank" through the battlefield, punching holes in the hedgerows, making it some small degree easier for Grunts to pass through.

I remember moving through one hedgerow and seeing the tree line on the other side erupt in a wall of recoilless rifle, RPG, and small-arms fire. I had a canister round in the chamber of the main gun. I pressed the trigger, and for a very few seconds, there was relative quiet.

I remember the Grunt company commander issuing orders, calming an excited radio operator, moving his Marines, and overpowering a powerful foe. Many years later, he received a Silver Star for his actions that day. The Marine Corps got away cheap on that one. He deserved more.

I remember . . .

I remember that after several hours of heavy fighting, we were making progress overrunning enemy positions. Moving through one trench line, we momentarily stopped to allow the Grunts to catch up. I looked out to either side of the TC's cupola and saw those wonderful, dirty, and tired warriors get on line and start shooting. I looked to the front and realized that no more than 30 meters away, an enemy platoon was also on line, giving back everything they got. The image of two groups of hard men standing and firing almost shoulder to shoulder, neither giving nor seeking quarter, is one that I will take to my grave.

By now the enemy was attempting to withdraw, and we were not about to let him go. We pushed through another position and stopped. Murphy, who thrives on close combat, came to pay us a visit. A canister round broke open in the chamber, spilling out its deadly load of 1,160 pellets locking up the breach. The coaxial .30-caliber machine gun had finally overheated, quitting in fiery protest. Staff Sergeant Turby Thomas (our tank commander) had run the TC's cupola-mounted .50-caliber machine gun dry. Earlier, I had shot an enemy soldier carrying a pistol and a map case with his weapon at about 10 meters. The effect was devastating. The mount, designed by Boeing, was difficult to reload under normal, peacetime conditions and impossible to load now. "O. G. Clank" was effectively disarmed.

I remember . . .

I remember peering out of the TC's hatch and seeing a large number of enemy soldiers alongside my tank. We had outrun our support. The Grunts had not yet caught up with us, and we were alone. We were in the unique position of having advanced past a retreating, disorganized enemy company. I grabbed my M-14, and as I climbed out of the tank, one of the enemy raised his AK-50 submachine gun and, at a range of 10 feet, emptied the magazine at me. Above the noise of the rest of the battle, the sound of those bullets passing by my head was easily the most distinctive. I put the front sight on his chest, squeezed the trigger, and shot him. He went down, but there were many of his comrades close by. Some were retreating to their perceived survival. I will never again hear the term "target-rich environment" without thinking about this incident. I started engaging as many as I could one at a time with my semiautomatic rifle. While changing magazines, I caught sight of movement below me and saw Gene standing in the driver's hatch, shooting enemy soldiers off of the tank with his .45, buying me time.

I remember thinking for a brief moment that this kid was going to be all right. We continued to shoot as many as we could, but it became rapidly apparent that there were more of them than we had bullets to stop them. I called Gene on the tank's intercom and ordered him to drive forward. About then, I ran the M-14 dry. I called in to the tank for another magazine. The pistol magazine (!) I was handed did not even disturb the soldier I threw it at, but then I was handed a frag grenade. I pulled the pin and threw it at a soldier in front of the tank. I called Gene over the intercom to get him to stop the tank, but my dancing on top of the turret dislodged the yo-yo cord severing communication, so he couldn't hear my command. We rolled forward, and the grenade detonated under the tank with no damage—other than to my ego should I have to explain to the CO why I tried to blow up my own tank.

I remember Gene driving down the trench line, doing neutral steers on top of enemy soldiers, crushing them before they could hurt any more Marines.

Off to the west, I watched a Grunt jump into the trench with the enemy who were firing a machine gun. His rifle apparently had malfunctioned, because he picked up an e-tool and killed them both with it.

I remember a Huey flying low up the river, shooting enemy soldiers who were swimming to the west bank in a vain attempt to escape the carnage in the hedgerows.

I remember . . .

I remember consolidating on the other side of the river. Communications was reestablished, weapons' malfunctions reduced and reloaded. A Grunt platoon commander came alongside the tank with a map in his hand and asked if I knew exactly where we were. I didn't have a clue at that point. He said, "To hell with it. Let's go north and kill some more of these sons a bitches."

And I remember looking at Gene Whitehead and giving him a thumbs-up.

As battles go, this was not one of the big ones. It only lasted seven hours, although it seemed like seven eternities at the time. We destroyed two companies of the R-20 Battalion, killing somewhere between 50 and 130 of them. But we lost twelve Marines KIA and thirty-one WIA. Things happened that day. Things I have never seen or experienced before or since. After this fight, I have seen life with a greater clarity and have a much better understanding of certain emotions.

And I understand completely what courage is; I saw it occur many times on that overcast spring day along the banks of the Song Yen.

I took the rifle sling off of my arm and stood up to hug Gene. Thirty-two years of emotions came out, and we made lots of loud noises reminiscing about days gone by, much to the amusement of all the young Marines, sailors, airmen, soldiers, and civilians on the firing line. Gene got down to the serious business of shooting. Already a distinguished pistol shot, he needed four points to be among the very few who are Double-D. He held hard and shot a 477-9X, enough to earn six points and his Distinguished Rifleman's Badge.

We went to dinner that night and talked about what has transpired since that spring day thirty-two years ago. Married and with three children, he retired as a master sergeant with twenty-three years' service to his country. He became the good Marine I had hoped.

A member of the USMC Rifle Team told me that Gene just received a Bronze Star for an action that occurred after my departure. He had picked up and returned to its original owners a frag that had been tossed into his tent, saving several Marines. The Marine Corps got away cheap on that one too. He deserved at least one more for helping to keep his crew alive so many years ago.

This meeting of two broken-down warriors was too providential to be mere chance. It may not have been divine intervention, but then again, maybe it was. It was extremely emotional for both of us and brought back a lot of memories.

I remember . . .

I remember a time when we answered the clarion's call and strong men, armed, fought a war in a country that no longer exists. I remember a time when the elected and appointed officials of a political party micromanaged its professional military and sacrificed the lives of its best and brightest on the altar of political expediency. I remember working with the finest men I have ever known.

And I will never forget.

Pat Rogers

Operation LIBERTY does not appear in the U.S. Marines in Vietnam series and receives scant coverage elsewhere in the records. However, Sergeant Kenneth Whitehead with his story captures the history of the operation, which included virtually every element of the Vietnam War as fought by the Marines—infantry, supporting arms, close air support, logistics air support, and the support of the Navy's offshore gun support.

Tanks in Operation LIBERTY, June 1966

by Kenneth Whitehead

[This story, with accompanying pictures, is reprinted from the USMC Vietnam Tankers Association's *Sponson Box* magazine, volume 12, number 111, September–December 2010. Edited for form and not content.]

Operation LIBERTY (7–15 June 1966) found my light section of tanks from 3d Platoon, A Company, 3d Tank Battalion (A-34 and A-35) attached to the 9th Marines. But the day in question is 18 June 1966. (See "After Action Report," which follows below.) We were involved in a search-and-destroy operation several klicks west of Hill 55 in 9th Marines' area of operation. We had been experiencing intermittent VC contact and taking a lot of sniper fire since crossing Liberty Bridge many days before, but this day was a smorgasbord of action and incident. I was, by this time, the gunner on A-34 (in my opinion), the most sought-after position on a tank crew (if there is one). Our tank crew consisted of Staff Sergeant Turby Thomas (TC), Lance Corporal Gene Whitehead (gunner), PFC Holmes (driver), and Sergeant Kulick (maintenance man/loader). The Grunts were taking some casualties from mines and a well-trained group of VC snipers. We had two corpsmen and a few Grunts who were the object and result of their (the VC's) keen marksmanship skills, which was not a coincidence. These guys were deliberately targeting our onsite medical life-support system. Nothing hits home and pisses off a Marine more than to know that the enemy is targeting his corpsman.

After we medevaced the wounded as a result of these VC snipers, we got the word to move out. It was not long when we found ourselves directly on top of a large VC unit. I was searching and traversing the turret in order to find a clear target to unload a canister round, when Staff Sergeant Thomas (Turby) yelled, "Gooks 1200!" I swung the turret around, and all I could see were VC running frantically around, firing weapons. Without an order to fire, the main gun recoiled and approximately 1,300 .30-caliber pellets were on their way to the VC's location. Without waiting, and while Turby (Staff Sergeant Thomas) was firing the cupola-mounted .50-caliber machine gun, at the same time giving his fire commands to me, he was telling the loader to insert another canister. By this time, I began to distinguish more clear VC targets. These guys were well prepared, well armed, and it was obvious that we had driven only a short distance directly into their preplanned ambush.

There were so many close-in VC that their movement was not hard to detect. I felt that I couldn't fire fast enough to cover the threat. I heard Staff Sergeant McCormick (Jerry) over the radio, yelling several times, "Scratch my back—there are gooks all over me!" As I swung the turret in his direction, which was to our right front, I could clearly see a few gooks take a burst from Jerry's copula-mounted .50-caliber machine gun. It downed one VC and took off the left arm of another gook, turning him around and putting him to the ground. But to my amazement and disbelief, this guy gets up and starts running down a trench, with my tracers pouring into his knapsack. As A-35 came into my view, I could see why Jerry's calls were filled with total anxiety—there were several VC attempting to lay charges on top of his tank. Without a command, I sprayed A-35 with four to five healthy bursts of my coaxially mounted .30-caliber machine gun. About this time, I was thinking, "This is why I came to Vietnam. This is what it is all about." I felt we had the upper hand in this firefight that was supposed to be an ambush and the source of our enemy-planned demise. Being young and dumb, I was thinking one dimensionally and blindly. We were barely staying afloat in holding our own, and Jerry and Turby knew it.

As I was directing my attention back to my sector of responsibility, I saw some VC attempting to fire an RPG at us, and Turby must have seen the same picture, because by the time he said "RPG," I had let the canister round go and, when the smoke cleared, I was already focusing back on the same area with the infinity sight pressing the red triggers and the gunner's controls sweeping the VC trench line with my .30 caliber. At some point in time, I began to think, "There are more of these gooks than we can kill. Where the hell are the Grunts?"

I was hearing explosions near—and on!—our tank. Then Jerry (TC of A-35) came over the radio and said, "Hey, let's get the hell out of here. There are too many gooks here!" I began to wonder if there was something going on that I didn't comprehend. I said to Turby, "We got them where we want them [that was a very stupid observation on my part]. We can't leave now!" Jerry was adamant about leaving, and about this time, Turby calls back to the 9th Marines Company CO, asking where they were and that we needed their support. It turns out that the Grunts had stopped again due to more Marines getting wounded and, in the confusion, had forgotten to inform their tank section to stop. We were two tanks several hundred meters ahead of the Grunts and being surrounded by at least a company-size VC unit.

Sergeant Kulick, not being an experienced loader, was doing a great job keeping the .30 caliber firing and the main gun fed with rounds. I can remember asking for another canister and he threw in a WP, but anything down range at this point served the purpose. About this time, I heard what could only be described as someone hitting the side of the turret with a sledgehammer. There was no explosion, however. I thought that was awful strange at that time. I continued to put canister and .30 caliber along the tree line and trenches, seeing many VC taking hits but continuing to fire back at us until they received additional bursts of .50 and .30 caliber.

Jerry called again, overly excited, to Turby and insisted that we pull back and call in for supporting fire, and shortly thereafter, the Grunt actual called and said he had fast movers coming in with Nape and 500-pounders, so we need to exit the area. As we backed out, I continued to lay down covering fire for Jerry because his tank was well forward of ours, and the gooks were trying to outflank him on his left.

We moved no more than 50 yards back, when the entire front of our vision was engulfed in flames of red and black smoke. The shock of 500-pound bombs that close shook the vehicle. After several passes by our air support dropping napalm and bombs, we stopped receiving fire, and the only sound that was heard was that of things burning. You could smell the horrible stench of burning flesh saturating the air. By this time, the Grunts had made it forward to our position.

A short while later, the order to "move out!" was given, and we moved through the area that had previously been occupied by the VC company. We drove over the trenches and set up a 360 on the other side. After assessment of what had just happened, the gravity of the event started to set in, and I became suddenly physically and mentally exhausted. There were many VC dead spread out in every direction in grotesque positions. Only two wounded VC were found, one being a young woman. She was brought to my tank, along with another VC man, and they both had their arms tied behind their backs. I was asked to watch them until a chopper that was incoming could pick them up. The Grunts picked them up and sat them on the back of my tank. Turby was checking out A-34 for hits and discovered an unexploded antitank round sitting on our left front fender. That was the sledgehammer sound I had heard during the ambush.

My attention focused back on the two VC that were occupying the back of my tank. I noticed the woman staring at me with hatred in her eyes like I have never seen before—or since. The man was lying down by this time and crying from the pain of his wounds, but as I looked back at the VC female, I noticed that she was wounded worse than he was, but she was not making a sound. She had bad burns and deep shrapnel holes in several places. I asked her with a gesture of my canteen if she wanted some water, but she just continued to stare defiantly at me, and I knew, if she had the opportunity and the resources, she would cut my throat—or worse.

The chopper came in, and the POWs were taken off my hands. We all decided to quickly put down some C-rats. As we were sitting together (very stupid thing to do) on a rice paddy dike, eating chow and talking about the morning contact, snipers opened up on us, along with bursts from automatic weapons fire. Another corpsman was hit. Where they came from was a mystery. Sergeant Kulick and I both just made a mad dash for A-34 as rounds kicked up around us. I still remember to this day that I leaped from the ground, on a dead run, to the fender and into the turret without using the tank to pull myself up. We were both in the tank, and Sergeant Kulick said, "I'm hit!" His eyes were as big as oranges, and he was holding his left arm. I quickly investigated his wound, but what I found was a hole in his left shirtsleeve and a red streak mark on his arm. After he realized this, we both laughed with a bit of anxiety.

A few months later, I was told that Sergeant Kulick experienced a mental breakdown and started shooting at our own Grunts with a .50-caliber machine gun, thinking they were NVA. He was sent back to the States for treatment. I sure hope he has found the help he needed. He was a friend and a good man. It's a wonder that more of us haven't lost our grip! I know I have more than my share of anxiety and other facets of related physiological problems related to my time spent in RVN.

Turby and Holmes finally made it to the tank, and we tried to find the source of the incoming fire. A few rounds of strategically placed 90 mm HET-91 in a few bunkers silenced most of the automatic weapons fire, but the sniper fire continued. A while later, we made a push to renew contact with the remaining VC, but all we got in the next couple of hours was incoming mortars and more sniper fire. A few more Marines were wounded, and we all were scared, mixed with getting more pissed off.

By late afternoon, and after precisely laid arty fire and air strikes called in by the Grunt CO, we managed to finally sweep through this village, which lay in our path and to the banks of a river next to it. The only thing left alive in that village was a couple of pigs and a wounded old woman. I heard Turby say over the intercom, "Where the hell did the gooks go? They have just disappeared!" We set up a 360, and A-34's sector of responsibility was overlooking the river.

As I got out of my tank, a Grunt sergeant came over and asked if he could borrow my .45-caliber pistol. I thought he was going to check out a hole. Without hesitating, I gave it to him already loaded. He just seemed very happy. Then he turned and walked down a trail a short distance. I heard one shot, and within a minute, he came back with my pistol and said, "That old bitch won't feed any more gooks!" I am still dumbfounded, shocked, and stunned to this day. Not only that he shot that old woman, but that he used my pistol! Strangely enough, at that time, I knew why he did it: anger had controlled his actions, and he wasn't thinking clearly at the time. The Marines even shot the pigs. Over the next few days, we were ordered to blow any boats to hell coming down the river. Our tank accounted for destroying nine and no telling how many VC were killed by our fire or drowned when their boats sank.

We lost three corpsmen that day and several Marines either killed or wounded. The enemy took us on and lost a lot of their fighters in the process. How they could just disappear, melt away, is a credit to them. If we could have cornered them that day, more death would have been evident on both sides.

I was told after returning from Operation LIBERTY that when we pulled back from the ambush site and after the air strikes ended, an entire squad of VC with RPGs was found dead from napalm trying to outflank A-34, my tank. So in hindsight, Staff Sergeant Jerry McCormick's concerns and anxiety were warranted, and he deserves full credit for not only saving his tank crew that day, but mine too!

Searching for the VC

After beating the bush for about a month

Just find them and destroy them

A break with a dud antitank grenade on the fender

From the USMC "After Action Report Operation LIBERTY," June 1966:

> With the surrender of the "Struggle Forces" at Da Nang and the restoration of some stability there, the 9th Marines once more renewed its offensive, coordinated with the South Vietnamese. On 2 June, ARVN Colonel Lap, who had replaced ARVN Colonel Yeu as the Quang Da Special Sector Commander, visited Colonel Simmons at his CP. The South Vietnamese commander wanted the 9th Marines to resume COUNTY FAIR operations in the five-village pacification area. He assured Simmons that at least one battalion from the 51st ARVN Regiment would be committed to the pacification campaign. Following Lap's visit, Colonel Simmons revised portions of his previous orders. On 5 June, he ordered his battalions to renew COUNTY FAIR operations with the Vietnamese and extended the deadline for the attainment of Phase Line Brown from 31 May to 20 June.

At this juncture, General Kyle decided to transform the 9th Marines' Ky Lam Campaign into a division-size offensive, involving "a conventional linear type attack of all forward units to push the front lines forward in a deliberate search of every hamlet in the zone." He divided the Da Nang TAOR into three sectors: the cleared, the semicleared, and the uncleared. "The cleared area formed an irregular arc around Da Nang Air Base, delineated by the South China Sea to the east, the Song Cau Do to the south, the foothills to the west, and the Song Cu De to the north. Extending the arc outward from the cleared area boundary, the semicleared sector reached the Thanh Quit River to the south, three to five kilometers into the high ground to the west and the Hai Van Pass to the north. The uncleared region consisted of the area between the Song La Tho and Song Thanh Quit and the banks of the Song Ky Lam and Song Thu Bon. Phase Line Green, the final phase line, paralleled the latter two rivers. The 3d Marine Division commander ordered that only minimum forces be held in the rear and set 30 June as the target date for reaching Phase Line Green."

Continuing arrival of Marine reinforcements allowed General Kyle to make this all-out effort. On 28 May, the 1st MP Battalion arrived at Da Nang from the United States and relieved the 3/3 of its airfield security mission. The 3d Battalion then returned to the operational control of its parent regiment, taking over the 3d Marines western TAOR. Colonel Harold A. Hayes Jr., who had relieved Colonel Fisher on 16 April as 3d Marines commander, at last had command of all three of his battalions. Other reinforcements were scheduled to arrive at Da Nang or were already in place. Colonel Bryan B. Mitchell was slated to transfer his 1st Marines Headquarters from Chu Lai to Da Nang in June. In fact, two of his battalions had already moved by the end of May. The? 3/1 arrived at Da Nang on 22 May, while the 1st Battalion arrived on 31 May. Both battalions were temporarily placed under OpCon of the 9th Marines. The 3d Battalion became the regimental reserve; the 1st Battalion relieved the regiment's eastern flank battalion, 2/4, which rejoined its parent regiment at Phu Bai.

By mid-June, General Kyle could expect to have three Marine infantry regiments consisting of eight battalions at Da Nang. He planned to reduce the extensive 9th Marines TAOR by assigning the 1st Marines to the eastern flank, while the 3d Marines took over that part of the 9th Marines TAOR west of the Song Yen. In effect, Kyle visualized a shoulder-to-shoulder advance to the Song Ky Lam. The operation, codenamed LIBERTY, was scheduled to begin on 7 June, with the 9th Marines bearing the brunt of the campaign in its initial stages. Colonel Simmons divided his TAOR into company-sized objective areas. His reserve battalion, 3/1, was to concentrate on combined operations with ARVN and Vietnamese local forces in the five-village pacification region in the semicleared area. The 3/9 was to continue its two-company holding action in the An Hoa region. All the remaining infantry companies were assigned to the three forward battalions, 1/1 on the eastern flank, the 2/9 in the center, and 1/9 on the western flank.

Thus, each forward battalion was to consist of five infantry companies instead of the usual four, with three companies deployed to the front and two to the rear. The advancing battalions were to secure Route 4 by 20 June and reach the Song Ky Lam by the end of the month.

Lieutenant Colonel Van "Ding Dong" Bell Jr.'s 1/1, on the division's left, had its heaviest engagement just before Operation LIBERTY started. During the evening of 5 June, the battalion commander and his small mobile command group embarked in three Ontos and found themselves stalled on the northern fringes of Phong Ho, a hamlet 10,000 meters south of the Marble Mountain Air Facility and in an area "noted for their hostility toward ARVN soldiers and their allies." Bell's vehicle had run out of gas, and the group had just been resupplied by helicopter. As the aircraft took off for the return trip to Marble Mountain, VC weapons from positions approximately 1,000 meters to the southwest opened fire. Using his command group with its Ontos as a blocking unit, Lieutenant Colonel Bell ordered reinforcements from his Company B, supported by LVTs and tanks, brought up from the south of Phong Ho. According to the battalion commander, "the result was a sound thrashing of the VC" with eleven dead enemy left on the battlefield and a number of captured weapons. Bell remembered several years afterward, "This area was never pacified and later was leveled, and the villagers (who had requested to) removed and relocated."

On 7 June, Operation LIBERTY began with heavy preparatory artillery fires. Marine artillery neutralized thirty-five objective areas in front of the advancing infantry. Initially, the enemy countered the Marine offensive with only small-arms fire and mines. The mines were the more deadly of the two. The most significant mine incident occurred on 11 June in the 9th Marines central sector. Captain Carl A. Reckewell's F/2/9 walked into a large minefield in a grassy plot just south of the Song La Tho. Two detonations killed three Marines and wounded twenty-one. While the wounded were being evacuated, four to five additional explosions occurred and the grass caught fire, but fortunately, there were no further Marine casualties. The following day, the artillery fired a destruction mission, which caused seven secondary explosions in that same field.

On 15 June, the division completed its planned realignment of regiments in the TAOR. Colonel Mitchell assumed OpCon of his two 1st Marines Battalions and took over responsibility for the division's eastern flank from the 9th Marines. With a corresponding reduction in the western sector, the 9th Marines' TAOR now consisted of only 134 square miles, the regiment having given away nearly 100 square miles in the exchange.

With the adjustment of forces and sectors, the 3d Marine Division continued its "scrubbing" actions in Operation LIBERTY. The only serious enemy opposition occurred in the 9th Marines zone of action. On 18 June, Company C, 9th Marines, operating 2,000 meters south of Dai Loc, came under heavy mortar and small-arms fire, suffering eight wounded. The company asked for supporting air and artillery, which ended the enemy resistance. (See Kenneth Whitehead's article above.) Lieutenant Colonel Donahue's 2/9 underwent a similar attack on 22 June in the hamlet of La Hoa, immediately east of the railroad and 4,000 meters north of the Song Ky Lam. Marines once more called upon supporting arms, including naval gunfire from the destroyer USS *Marton* (DD-948), to silence the enemy.

According to U.S. Navy historians, "Between four and nine ships including destroyers, cruisers, and rocket ships were available for gunfire support in Vietnam at any one time and more than half the missions supported Marines in I Corps" (NHD, comments on draft MS, dated 19 June '78 [Vietnam comment file]).

By the end of the month, all three Marine regiments reached Phase Line Green and the operation ended. VC resistance to the Marines' advance had been scattered and ineffective. The 9th Marines observed that the lack of major enemy resistance gave plausibility to the thesis that the momentum of Operation LIBERTY prevented them from gaining any degree of initiative and uprooted them "from what had been a relatively secure operating area." That regiment alone claimed to have recovered 40 square miles from the VC. The Marines were once more optimistic about pacifying the extensive Da Nang enclave.

H&S COs: Capts. A. E. Lee and J. B. Terpak
Location: (AT 989708) Same as battalion CP

COs Company A: Capt. J. J. Sucha and 1st Lt. H. L. Stiegelman
Location and Operations Summary: (AT 946762)

The tank battalion operations of the month of June, exclusive of Operation LIBERTY, were as follows:

Company A (-) (Rein.) continued to occupy key positions in the 3d Marines TAOR.

6 June: Two 1st Platoon tanks supported K/3/9 in a sweep of the area in grid squares (AT 9966 and 9562). There was no enemy contact.

8 June: While in a night position with A/1/9, a third platoon tank using its infrared tank-mounted searchlight observed a VC in the road at (AT 979623). The VC appeared to be preparing to set a mine. Tank .30-caliber machine gun fire was directed on him, and he fled into nearby tree line.

While in support of A/1/9, Company A headquarters' dozer tank destroyed and filled approximately 9,000 meters of trench line in grid squares (AT 9562, 9563, 9564, 9664, 9764).

15 June: Two Company Headquarters tanks operating with elements of 2/9 discovered two camouflaged tank traps each 10' × 10' × 15' at (AT 948268) and (AT 949632). The bulldozer tank covered both traps.

19 June: A 2d Platoon tank, while in support of elements of 1/3 located at Nam O Bridge (AT 928828), received twelve to fifteen rounds of mortar fire. The tanks returned .30- and .50-caliber machine gun fire upon the suspected mortar positions. The tanks then supported an

infantry search of the area. Search resulted in two VC KIA (prob.) and two VC WIA. Three 60 mm mortar rounds and one 60 mm mortar sight were recovered.

29 June: Two 1st Platoon tanks, while in support of elements of 2/3 located at (AT 899579), sank a boat at (AT 878565). Tank 90 mm fire was delivered on target with good effect. Estimate one VC KIA (prob.) and one VC WIA (prob.) as a result of this action.

There were two additional incidents of Company A tanks receiving small-arms fire during the month. In both instances, tanks returned fire with unknown results.

The 1st Platoon of Company A was in support of 2/3 for the duration of Operation LIBERTY.

Tank operations during Operation LIBERTY were conducted in support of infantry units sweeping southward through their TAORs to assigned objectives bordering the north banks of the Song Thu Ban / Son Ky Lam waterway. Tanks provided combat support for their respective infantry units for the entirety of the operation. In the 2/9 TAOR, the infantry and tank advance was blocked by the Song Ai Ngai at (AT 990642). At this point, the tanks supporting 2/9 were transferred to support operations in the 1/9 TAOR. These tanks advanced southward with elements of 1/1, crossed the river at (AT 968607), and then moved back into the 2/9 TAOR to resume operations with 2/9 in the movement to their objective.

CO Company B: Capt. E. L. Tunget
Location and Operations Summary: (AT 989708)

The tank battalion operations of the month of June, exclusive of Operation LIBERTY, were as follows:

2 June: A 2d Platoon tank observed and took fire, three VC located at (AT 055629). Tank 90 mm fire resulted in three VC KIA (conf.).

Flame tanks from headquarters platoon were utilized by 2/9 in two fire missions to destroy enemy fortifications and possible ambush sites.

A Company Headquarters tank acting as security for flame tanks working with F/2/9 observed four VC running into a house at (BT 078619). The 90 mm and .50-caliber fire demolished the house with resulting four VC KIA (prob.).

The following is a chronological sequence of events occurring on Operation LIBERTY:

COMPANY B (Rein.)

11 June: The 1st Platoon supported D/1/1 in a sweep of the area at (BT 096635). Tanks destroyed one booby trap with 90 mm fire. Two hundred feet of trench line and three circular automatic weapons pits were also destroyed by the tanks.

14 June: A 3d Platoon, Company A OpCon to Company B observed six VC in tree line at (AT 947569) and fired 90 mm at the enemy. A search of the area resulted in three VC KIA (conf.).

15 June: The 3d Platoon, Company A OpCon to Company B and supporting B/1/9 fired a 90 mm at suspected VC positions in the village at (AT 927564) and destroyed the same.

16 June: A 3d Platoon tank, while supporting elements of 2/9, observed nine VC in the river at (BT 974565) and two VC with weapons on the north bank of the river. Tanks fired a 90 mm and observed bodies falling, but the probable casualties could not be confirmed as no search was conducted due to in accessibility of the area.

Two 2d Platoon tanks supporting G/2/9 destroyed seven houses and eight fighting holes and detonated one AP mine at (AT 005621). Three 2d Platoon tanks supporting B/1/1 located at (BT 078608) received four hundred rounds of small-arms fire and approximately eight grenades from an estimated VC platoon. The tanks returned 90 mm and .30-caliber fire. The results of this action were unknown as darkness precluded a search.

In this same vicinity, a tank detonated an M-26 booby trapped grenade with no resulting casualties.

17 June: A 3d Platoon tank in support of 1/9 at (AT 9715567) observed nine VC carrying weapons and entering the river. The tank fired 90 mm into the enemy, and the three VC appeared to be hit. Area was not searched as VC were south of the Song Thu Ban River. Three VC KIA (prob.).

18 June: A headquarters flame tank in support of B/1/1 at (BT 080608) burned VC tunnels located in that area.

Two Company A tanks OpCon to Company B, while in support of 1/9 at (AT 925550), received small-arms fire and two rifle grenades. One rifle grenade hit one of the tanks but did not detonate. Tanks returned 90 mm canister fire and .30-caliber fire. The results of this action were one VC KIA (conf.) and one VC WIA (conf.).

Two Company A tanks OpCon to Company B and in support of 1/9 at (AT 915557) received fifteen rounds of mortar fire. Tanks returned 90 mm fire at the suspected mortar sites. The mortar fire ceased. Five infantrymen were wounded by the mortar fire.

A 3d Platoon tank in support of 1/9 at (AT 959555) observed with the tank-mounted infrared searchlight three VC in a boat and four VC on the bank of the river. The tank switched to white light and fired 90 mm, .50 and .30 caliber, upon the enemy. The boat was sunk, and a search of the area resulted in four VC KIA (conf.). In a personal search of the sunken boat conducted by the tank platoon commander on the following morning, the following items were found: thirty-five 100-pound bags of rice, forty-five gallons of kerosene, personal letters, assorted documents, Russian bandages and medical supplies, and a wallet with 200 piasters.

19 June: Two 1st Platoon tanks while in support of 1/1 at (BT 131625) engaged in a firefight with VC at (BT 1346). Tanks fired .30 caliber, and a later search of the area disclosed VC WIA.

Two 1st Platoon tanks in support of D/1/1 at (BT 116629) engaged an undetermined number of VC at (BT 1216). The tanks fired 90 mm upon the enemy. Results of this action were one VC WIA.

21 June: A tank from the 1st Platoon, while in support of elements of 1/1 at (BT 126332), received thirty rounds of mortar fire from (BT 130628). The tank fired 90 mm. Results were unknown as darkness precluded search.

Two 1st Platoon tanks, while in support of B/1/9 at (BT 925535), received small-arms fire from (AT 925528). Tanks returned fire with 90 mm. The tank fire destroyed six boats and four houses. The results were unknown as an intervening river precluded search.

Two 1st Platoon tanks, while in support of B/1/9 at (AT 925534), received small-arms fire from (AT 923526). The tanks returned 90 mm fire, and results were one VC KIA (conf.).

22 June: The 1st Platoon tanks, while in support of D/1/9, observed VC at (AT 947543). The tanks fired 90 mm and .30 caliber and observed direct hit on three VC. Three VC KIA (conf.) were the results of this action.

23 June: Two 1st Platoon tanks, while in support of D/1/9, observed and fired 90 mm and caliber .30 at (AT 947543). Direct hits on the enemy were observed by the infantry commander; however, the area was not searched as the Song Thu Ban River intervened.

On 23 June, Ken Zebal received a Purple Heart.

24 June: The 2d Platoon tanks at (AT 947562) fired 90 mm on four VC located at (BT 947536). Results of this action were two VC KIA (prob.).

25 June: Two 2d Platoon tanks, while in support of D/1/9, fired 90 mm into six sampans located at (AT 947544). VC casualties were unknown as the river made a search impossible. Six boats were sunk by the tank fire.

A Company Headquarters tank in support of B/1/9 at (AT 925529) received small-arms fire from a house at (AT 925529). The tank returned fire with 90 mm and destroyed the house. A search of the area disclosed one VC KIA (conf.).

25–28 June: During this period, Company B and Company C, 1st Tank Battalion tanks (OpCon to 3d Tank Battalion) conducted a small operation in support of 1/1. Fifteen gun tanks, two flame tanks, and one retriever were placed DS 1/1, which was advancing from Phase Line Amber to Phase Line Green. Personnel from Company B were placed in an advisory capacity to the operating sections of Company C, 1st Tank Battalion, as the former had been operating in the area for eleven months and knew it well, while Company C was relatively new to the area.

The vehicles were staged according to plan on the afternoon of 22 June at the LOD (Phase Line Amber). Assignments of tanks were made, placing 3d Platoon, Company C, 1st Tank Battalion and platoon Company B, 3d Tank Battalion DS 1/1. Four tanks were committed on Axis Yellow, and the remaining three tanks were committed to Axis Blue. The tanks from the 2d Platoon, Company C, 1st Tank Battalion were assigned to Axis Red. Three tanks from the 1st Platoon were placed DS Company C, 1/1, on Axis Brown. The headquarters tanks and the retriever and two flame tanks from Company B, 3d Tank Battalion were held in reserve and provided security for the command group of 1/1, which was mounted in two LVTs. Although originally scheduled to begin on the twenty-third of June, the operation was postponed for a period of forty-eight hours.

Tanks expended 90 mm, .50 and .30 caliber on the VC. Results of this action were five VC KIA (conf.) and seven VC KIA (prob.). A total of twelve boats were also destroyed.

29 June: Two 3d Platoon tanks in support of C/1/9 at (AT 902547) fired 90 mm into a VC village. Village was searched by infantry with negative results.

30 June: A 2d Platoon tank, while in support of B/1/9, fired at a sniper at (AT 925529). The tank was then fired on by 57 mm recoilless rifle but not hit. The tank returned fire with 90 mm and .30 caliber. An air observer in the vicinity credited the tank with four VC KIA (conf.). This same tank observed boats landing VC at (AT 912556 and 911531). The tank fired 90 mm and sank two boats and damaged ten more. A search of the area revealed fifteen VC KIA (conf.).

During the month of June, Company B tanks received small-arms fire in an additional thirty-one incidents. In all these VC incidents, the tanks returned fire with unknown results as a search was not made due to inaccessibility of the terrain, pressing operational commitments, or darkness.

CO Company C: Capt. J. H. Garry III
Location and Operations Summary: Phu Bai (YD 879152)

Company C continued to provide tank combat support for infantry units operating in the Phu Bai TAOR.

4 June: Two 2d Platoon tanks supported G/2/1 in a sweep of the area in the vicinity of (YD 526287). An estimated 2,600 pounds of rice was

discovered and turned over to the logistics support unit. Forty civilians were escorted out of the village of Ap Co Xuan.

6 June: Seven gun tanks and one flame tank supported E/2/1 on a search-and-destroy mission along the Song Bo River at (YD 574276).

7 June: Seven gun tanks and one flame tank supported H/2/1 by delivering 90 mm gunfire into probable VC locations on the ridge line in grid squares (YD 4825 and 4925). The tanks fired into suspected VC fortifications in the village of Lou Hoa Hein (YD 4727). The flame tank fired upon the same village. En route back to Company H CP (YD 520300), the tanks, with infantry mounted, received three rounds of 81 mm mortar fire. The tanks returned 90 mm and .30-caliber fire into the suspected mortar site. No casualties were received by the Marines.

9–11 June: The 2d and 3d Platoons supported 2/4 and 2/1, respectively, for the first two days of Operation FLORIDA.

12 June: Five tanks supporting the 5th and 7th Vietnamese Airborne Battalions fired 90 mm into the village of Thanh Thanh at (YD 560240) and (YD 570240). These missions were called by a tank liaison team working directly with the Vietnamese units.

12 June: Three tanks supported 2/1 and fired 90 mm at VC command posts and observation posts in grid squares (YD 4625, 4725, 4824, 4825).

14 June: Company C moved back to the 4th Marines TAOR. En route, tanks encountered many altars placed in the middle of the roads by demonstrating Buddhists. The altars caused some delay in the progress of the tanks. Approximately 375 altars were removed by the Vietnamese special police in order that the tanks could get through.

In Hue, at 0500 on the fifteenth of June, Buddhists demonstrated around tank positions. The demonstration was short-lived, and tanks departed Hue and arrived without incident at destination at 0720.

UNITED STATES MARINE CORPS
HISTORY DIVISION
ORAL HISTORY INTERVIEW WRITTEN TRANSCRIPT

Interviewee's Name: Major John H. Gary, USMC #068303
Date of Interview: 28 December 1966
Conflict: Vietnam War
Military Unit: 3d Tank Battalion
Duties: Commanding Officer C Company, 3d Tank Battalion, 3d Marine Division
Interviewers: SSgt. James B. Schneider and Sgt Gilbert Olds
Length: 0:11:00
Location of Interview: 3d Marine Division Command Post, Phu Bai, Vietnam
Individual Completing Summary: Lt. Col. R. A. Stewart, USMC (Ret.)
Recording Format and Number: CD#306-A
Documents Submitted with Interview: None
Related Material: None
Classification: Secret/Unclass.
Transcription Priority: Note: The following is a verbatim transcript.

Abstract: Relocation of C Company, 3d Tank Battalion, 3d Marine Division from Cobi Than Tan, Quang Tin Province, South Vietnam, to Phu Bai, Thua Thin Province, 17–18 June 1966

Key Words: Tank company CP relocation, Phu Bai, Hue, Buddhist altars, mines, National Police, Gao Lai

00:00–02:28: Gary: After operating approximately forty-two days in the Cobi Than Tan, I received word early morning of 17 June (1966) to move my company at Cobi Than Tan back to Hue/Phu Bai. Initially the move started 0945. I sent one light section of (two) tanks, a mine sweep team, and a platoon of infantry to precede the main column by approximately forty-five minutes. I was in radio communications at all times with my forward elements and did not plan to move the main column until the first two bypasses had been swept. We experienced no difficulty in sweeping the first two bypasses but did find mines in the bypass at the Song Bao.

02:28–03:30: We had commenced the move down Highway 1 and were approaching the bypass, when word was received that a mine was implanted in the bypass. It took approximately thirty minutes to clear the mine, and we proceeded on. Approximately 3 kilometers from the bypass, we experienced difficulty and delays with Buddhist altars along the route. These altars were 15 meters apart and in the center of the road. In some cases, they allowed us only 3–4 inches clearance to get the tanks around them. We had with us at the time one company of National Police, who were instructed to move the altars in the event that we could not pass them without causing damage. We were not allowed to touch the altars ourselves.

03:30–07:14: We proceeded at approximately 2 miles an hour until we reached the Song Kahar, just north of Hue. At this point, the altars were placed almost side by side and in some cases only 2 to 3 meters apart. We were planning on making a river crossing at this point and had to turn off the main road down a side road to make the crossing where we had planned. It was totally impossible for us to pass at this time. I was approached by a Buddhist priest who told me he was the leader of the Buddhists in Hue and asked which direction I was traveling. I told him only that I was heading south. I asked if it would be possible for me to get the tanks through the narrow pass down to the river. He explained to me, at that time, that the demonstration was not against the Americans but the Vietnamese government, and if I would tell him where I was going, he would ensure me that all the altars would be moved out of my path. I did not tell him at that time where I was going, nor at any time did I mention my destination was Phu Bai.

The altars were moved, and I proceeded to move the column down the narrow road to make the river crossing and did not complete the crossing until approximately 1600.

On the other side of the river, we experienced the same difficulty. As we approached the congested area of Hue, the altars became more and more frequent and closer and closer together. We were able to move the column of tanks only inside the perimeter that had been established inside the city by the U.S. troops.

Once inside the perimeter, I requested that Navy shipping move me across the Perfume River. LCUs were not available at this time, and only one LCM could be used for the movement of tanks across the river. At approximately 1800, we started moving the tanks from the north side of the Perfume River to the Hue ramp on the south side. Not until 0200 the next morning did we complete the move of all the tanks across the river.

As I arrived on the south side of the river with the last tank, I was informed that a demonstration had been planned along the route of the tanks from Hue to Phu Bai. While we were waiting for the National Police to return and escort us through the city, a demonstration took place about 0400. I would estimate the number of people that were participating was about 1,000. The demonstration took place at the Hue ramp on our route outside the city.

Upon the arrival of the National Police, the persons participating in the demonstration dispersed. However, the altars remained in our path.

07:14–11:00: We proceeded south out of the city, trying to safely bypass the altars at the same time slowing the column down long enough for the National Police to catch up and move the altars in our path. In certain cases, we had to travel with part of the tank on sidewalks and the rest in the street to make it by the altars that could not be moved—or even touched. As we proceeded south, I was told by the liaison officer, 1st ARVN Division, that information had been received that a demonstration had been planned in Gao Lai for 0600 in the morning. It was very doubtful at the pace we were making that we could reach Gao Lai prior to 0600.

Altars were becoming more frequent. Crowds were gathering, even though it was quite early in the morning, and I was quite concerned about the possibility of one of the tanks striking a civilian or an altar. I insisted that all the altars be moved if there was any doubt in my mind that they'd be hit. This slowed us down. I estimate approximately 375 altars were moved from the time we left the Hue ramp until we reached the city limits of Hue.

At this point, one of the tanks developed engine trouble. In order not to delay the column, I instructed the tank to be towed to Phu Bai. Although this enabled us to move rapidly, it did slow us down in trying to pass areas where altars had been placed in our way.

As 0600 approached, it was very doubtful that we could reach Gao Lai by 0600. My plan was to cut across country and go around Gao Lai, where I had been told the Vietnamese planned to throw civilians in our path to slow us down or stop us and to make an example of us during the demonstration. We did reach Gao Lai at 0555 and were able to pass through the city. There was no demonstration there, other than the normal altars in the road and those that were attending to the altars. We proceeded on and reached Phu Bai at approximately 0730.

This trip normally takes four to five hours; this day it took twenty-two hours. The National Police moved approximately 675 altars during the move. No altars were struck, no civilians hit, no property damaged, and I felt the credit goes to the drivers of the tanks and the patience they had moving this distance.

END OF INTERVIEW

22 June: The 1st Platoon supported 1/4 on a search-and-destroy mission in the vicinity of (YD 860350). The tanks fired preparatory fires of 90 mm into the area prior to the infantry search.

Company C 1st Tank Battalion

Company C, 1st Tank Battalion arrived in Da Nang on 19 June aboard amphibious shipping. This company was put under OpCon of 3d Tank Battalion and committed DS 1/1 on 20 June. All tank operations were conducted in support of Operation LIBERTY.

22 June: Two 1st Platoon tanks participated in sweep in the vicinity (BT 000630 to 013635) with elements of 2/9. The tanks destroyed fifteen houses and three bunkers.

24 June: The 3d Platoon tanks, while in support of 1/1 at (BT 105647), engaged enemy of unknown force. Four tanks fired 90 mm and .30 caliber with unknown results as darkness precluded search.

26 June: Two 1st Platoon tanks, while in support of elements of 2/9, located a minefield at (BT 007610). Tanks fired 90 mm into mines and noted eighteen secondary explosions.

27 June: Two 1st platoon tanks supported elements of 2/9 on a sweep in the vicinity of (BT 009613). Tanks destroyed 2 buildings and one bunker with 90 mm fire.

28 June: Four tanks supported B/1/1 in a sweep conducted in the vicinity of (BT 079613). Two VCS were captured during this search.

July 1966
First Antitanks
Commanding Officer: Maj. R. E. Harris
Executive Officer: Maj. A. J. Eagan
Operations Officer: Maj. A. J. Eagan
Logistics Officer: 1st Lt. T. F. Dempsey
Location and Operations Summary:

Throughout the reporting period, subordinate units of this command were assigned missions as follows:

> Company A (-) OpCon 3d Marine Division, DS 1st Marines
> Company B (-) (Rein.) DS 5th Marines, DS Chu Lai Defense Command
> Company C (-) DS 7th Marines

H&S Company CO: 1st Lt. W. D. Webster

CO Company A: Capt. G. R. Van Horn
Location and Operations Summary:

Robert H. Gage, staff sergeant, age 29, Columbus, Ohio, was a career Marine serving as an Ontos leader with Company A, 1st Antitank Battalion, who went missing from his unit located near Da Nang, in Quang Nam Province, South Vietnam on 3 July 1966. He was declared dead on Tuesday, 30 July 1974.

Ben (Weaver). This is from Dick Carey—our VTA President. Hope it is of some value to you. May be stuff you already know.

Semper Fi,

Ray

In a message dated 02/24/2001 07:51:10, WarVeteran writes:

Ray:

Here is a story of Robert Hugh Gage, 1st Antitank—MIA. Bob and I went to school together from the first grade to high school.

Back in 1998, I made contact via the Internet with the team who was in Laos looking for MIA bodies. They sent me the following information:

On 3 July 1966, at approximately 1500 hours, Lance Corporal Robert H. Gage and another Marine assigned to Company "A," 1st Antitank Regiment [sic], Battalion 1st Marine Division, left their platoon position to go to Hamlet II, Dien Ngoc (formerly Thanh Thuy) Village, in the vicinity of grid coordinates (BT059649), Quang Nam, Danang Province, Vietnam, to find someone to do their laundry.

While the other Marine was bargaining, he noticed Corporal Gage talking to a Vietnamese girl outside a house in the hamlet. That was the last time he saw Corporal Gage. After completing his business, he started back to the platoon position without Corporal Gage. Approximately two hours later, he returned to the hamlet with two other Marines to look for Corporal Gage, but could not locate him. Upon returning to his platoon, he reported that Corporal Gage was missing. During the next several days, members of the platoon conducted a thorough search of the hamlet for Corporal Gage, but failed to locate any sign of the missing Marine. Lance Corporal Gage is unaccounted for.

On 4 July 1966, a Marine counterintelligence agent interrogated Miss Nguyen Thi Luong, a farmer and a small store owner, in Hamlet II, Than Thuy (now Dien Ngoc) Village. Miss Luong said that, at approximately 1430 hours (3 July 1966), two Americans approached her home for the purpose of having her do their laundry. As she conducted business with one of them, the other left her home and was seen talking with three Vietnamese girls, one of whom was Miss Hunh Thi Duoc. She said she did not know the identity of the other two Vietnamese girls. Miss Luong said she did not see the men again. Miss Luong added that the hamlet chief was a Viet Cong and that Viet Cong main force troops occupied the hamlet in the evening. She claimed the Viet Cong had killed her husband, a former government youth cadre, in 1964.

A joint team interviewed Mrs. Nguyen Thi Luong, a farmer and a former store owner in May 1992. She recalled that two American soldiers came to her store. One soldier remained in the store. The other American, a skinny Caucasian about 1.8 meters tall, left the store with a Mrs. Hoan and Mrs. Huynh Thi Dan, both of whom were members of the Viet Cong militia. She said that 30 minutes later, she heard a gunshot and the soldier who had stayed in the store abruptly left. A couple of hours later, this soldier returned with others in his unit and searched the area for the missing soldier. Later that evening, the American unit returned and arrested her and her mother, Mrs. Huynh Thi Trung, and another woman, Mrs. Nguyen Thi Nghiep, and took them by helicopter to Danang for questioning. When she returned a couple of weeks later, Mrs. Hoan had already left the area. Mrs. Hoan was reportedly killed in District III, Danang City. According to Mrs. Luong, Mrs. Hyunh Thi Dan (possibly should be Hyunh Thi Hong), currently the Chief of the People Control Section, An Khe District, Gia Lai Province, may have information pertaining to the incident. Mrs. Luong reportedly heard from Mrs. Phuong Thi Tai, currently living in Dien Ngoc Village, that the body of the American soldier was buried near an irrigation canal near Mrs. Tai's house. According to Mrs. Luong, Mrs. Le Thi Lan, presently living in Hamlet II, Dien Ngoc Village, witnessed the burial. Mrs. Luong stated that Mrs. Huynh Thi Duoc (previously identified as one the girls Gage was last seen talking with) was helping her with the laundry at the time of the incident.

Mrs. Le Thi Lan indicated she was part of a plan to capture an American soldier. She reported that she and Miss Huynh Thi Duoc talked with one of the soldiers and he followed them to Mrs. Diem's house. When the soldier saw the guerrillas waiting for him within the house, he pulled a pistol and attempted to escape. One of the guerrillas, Mr. Nguyen Huu Duoc, shot and killed the soldier. Mrs. Lan said that several local people temporarily hid the soldier's body in the banks Muong Song ditch. According to Mrs. Lan, Mr. Huynh Hao allegedly buried the body in the "Dinh Ba" area. She said the three guerrillas who killed the soldier, Mr. Nguyen Huu Duoc, Mr. Nguyen Huu Hi and Mr. Huynh Vinh, were all subsequently killed in the war. The joint team interviewed Mr. Huynh Hao, a farmer during the war. Mr. Hao denied he buried the body of the American soldier. He said that one evening, he met four guerrillas who had just buried the soldier in the middle of a path through a local cemetery on a sand dune.

He identified the guerrillas who allegedly participated in the burial as Mr. Tran Nguu, Mr. Nguyen Bai, Mr. Nguyen Tan, and Mr. Huynh No, all of whom were subsequently killed during the war. Mr. Hoa indicated the area where the four guerrillas allegedly buried the soldier's body was located on a sand dune in an area 10 meters wide by 20 meters long in the vicinity of grid coordinates (BT 05866531). According to Mr. Hao, remains buried in the cemetery are constantly working their way to the surface and are then reburied. According to Mr. Phan Kiet, the remains of the soldier came to the surface in 1987 and were reburied. Local villagers are allegedly unable to find the remains.

In 1993 a joint team interviewed Mrs. Phong Thi Tai, longtime resident of Thanh Thuy (Dien Ngoc) village, stated she witnessed a U.S. service member being led by three women to Mr. Hai's house in Thanh Thuy in July, 1966 or 67. Around 1500 hrs that same day, she heard a gunshot coming from Mr. Hai's house. She heard that the American had been shot by Mr. Nguyen Huu Duoc, Village Militia Commander. Mrs. Tai identified Mrs. Hong, Mrs. Lan and Mrs. Hoan as the three women who escorted the American. Tai explained that the body was temporarily buried in a ditch and later moved to avoid detection by U.S. forces searching the area. Mrs. Tai did not observe the dead body or the burials. She also heard that Mrs. Phung Thi Long knows the burial location. The team also interviewed Mr. Huynh Duc Kha, a local villager, stated that an American was shot to death in Dien Ngoc and transported to Dien Van for burial. He claimed that he was a participant in transporting the American. Kha also stated that U.S. forces came on the scene and cleared the area encompassing the burial site using a bulldozer. Conclusions: Cpl Gage was shot and killed by local Militia.

Joint Teams have interviewed a total of nine witnesses, two of whom have provided firsthand eyewitness testimony concerning the shooting death of Cpl Gage. The remaining witnesses provided strong hearsay information concerning Cpl Gage's incident as well as firsthand observations of circumstances leading up to the time of his death. The testimony from the several witness interviewed during the field investigations is consistent and indicates that Cpl Gage was killed and his body buried in the local cemetery. However, the exact location of Cpl Gage's grave site is still not known. Therefore, further field activity is required to resolve this case.

END OF OFFICIAL REPORT

CO Company B: Capt. J. E. Feeler
Location and Operations Summary:

2 July: The 2d Platoon, Company B participated in a search-and-destroy mission with companies G and H/2/5.

26 July: Light section 2d Platoon, Company B participated in a search-and-destroy mission in support of a platoon from H/2/5.

CO Company C: 1st Lt. D. R. West
Location and Operations Summary:

7 July: Light section 2d Platoon, Company C participated in a sweep with M/3/7.

12 July: Light section 3d Platoon, D/3/7 at Tien Dao Hill.

15 July: Company M/3/7 attacked by reinforced Viet Cong Company at Tien Dao Hill. A light section provided support throughout attack. Four Marines from Company C, 1st Antitank Battalion were WIA during this action.

26–29 July: Company C (-) supported the 7th Marines during Operation FRANKLIN.

(VYHF comment: The Ontos were phased out halfway through the war and strained through the sieve of the supporting respective tank battalions. From that point on, tanks' reporting and command chronologies mostly mention the now-organic Ontos in passing and very little of what the Ontos did was reported in any great detail. By July 1967, there are thirteen second lieutenants on the battalion staff and companies! This is an indicator that "someone" had placed antitanks as a low priority for manning to T/O.)

July 1966
First Tanks

Commanding Officers: Majs. L. R. Burnette Jr. and R. E. B. Palmer
Executive Officers: Majs. R. E. B. Palmer and J. W. Clayborne
Operations Officers: Majs. J. C. Collier and R. D. McKee
Logistics Officer: Maj. H. D. L. Reid
Location and Operations Summary: CP on Hill 43 (BT 571041) within the Chu Lai Combat Base

Companies A and B remained DS 5th and 7th Marines, respectively; 2d Platoon, Company A supported the Chu Lai Defense Command during 1–14 July; 3d Platoon, Company B supported the Chu Lai Defense Command during the entire period. Company C with two gun platoons, remains with 3d Marine Division, Da Nang TAOR, and the 2d Platoon with the SLF.

H&S COs: Capt. E. J. Hoynes and Maj. J. P. McGill
Location: Same as battalion CP

A Provisional Rifle Platoon, which had reported to the Chu Lai Defense Command on 26 June, was returned to OpCon of the 1st Tank Battalion on 041600H July. On 24 July, H&S Company provided the Chu Lai Defense Company with a Provisional Rifle Platoon and Company Headquarters. As of 31 July, the Provisional Rifle Platoon and Company Headquarters remain with the Chu Lai Defense Command.

CO Company A: Capt. J. C. Greene Jr.
Location and Operations Summary:

Companies A and B conducted operations with the 5th and 7th Marines, respectively. The primary effort of Company A was reconnaissance from (BT 425090) to (BT 375060) in an attempt to open a tank route to the Phuoc Khach area (BT 375055). On 25 July a tank-Ontos-infantry patrol proceeded along the road from Tien Xuan (1) (BT 408090) to Phuoc Khach. Tanks were able to proceed as far as (BT 3878) but were halted due to the narrow road. Ontos and infantry proceeded to the high ground overlooking Phuoc Khach (BT 37662). With minimal engineer effort (blade tank), it should be possible to move tanks to Phuoc Khach.

CO Company B: Capt. E. E. Stith
Location and Operations Summary:

Company B operations consisted primarily of tank infantry sweeps by the 2d Platoon in support of D/1/7 on the peninsula area south of the Song Tra Bong. The 2d Platoon, with elements of Company Headquarters and Battalion Headquarters tanks, participated in Operation FRANKLIN from 26 through 28 July. The tanks supported D/1/7 in blocking positions to the north while the 2/7 swept from Route 1 south of Binh Son to the sea at the Batangan Peninsula (BS 7686).

During the month of July, two tanks were damaged by mines. Both incidents occurred while supporting D/1/7 sweeps. On 18 July, a flame tank with 2d Platoon, Company B in support of D/1/7 struck a mine near (BS 673939), incurring extensive damage to the left front suspension. On 26 July, a tank of 2d Platoon, Company B participating in Operation FRANKLIN detonated a mine near (BS 674960), incurring extensive damage to the left track and suspension system. No Marines were either killed or injured.

CO Company C: Capt. F. U. Salas
Location and Operations Summary:

Company C with two gun platoons remains with 3d Marine Division, Da Nang TAOR, and the 2d Platoon with the SLF.

On Friday, 8 July 1966, Charles C. Roberts, lance corporal, age 18, Newport, Tennessee, a metalworker by MOS, was serving in Company C, 1st Tank Battalion, died in an enemy-caused vehicle crash.

July 1966
Third Antitanks
Commanding Officers: Lt. Col. B. A. Heflin and Maj. E. R. Larson
Executive Officer: Maj. E. E. Brooks
Operations Officers: Maj. E. R. Larson and WO C. C. Harris
Logistics Officer: Maj. K. E. Sharff
Location and Operations Summary: Da Nang

H&S Company CO: Capt. B. M. Mathews
Location and Operations Summary: Da Nang

The company continued its role of providing administrative and logistical support of the Ontos companies during the month. The battalion portion of Subsector I, Southern Sector, Division Rear Area, was effectively covered by night patrols as well as ambushes. The Battalion Reaction Platoon dispatched a squad on three occasions to the village of Yen Bac (AT 985708) to investigate disturbances; no contact was reported. The commitment for H&S Company to provide one squad OpCon of the 3d Tank Battalion to assist in defense of the LAAM battery on Hill 327 continued throughout the month.

COs Company A: Capts. S. R. Stewart and A. A. Compton
Location and Operations Summary:

Company A DS 3d Marines (Da Nang TAOR)
    1st Platoon, Company A DS I/1/3 and G and H/2/3
    2d Platoon, Company A DS C/1/3 and D/1/3
    3d Platoon, Company A DS E/2/3 and G/2/4

The month commenced with one Ontos section in support of F/2/3 on Hill 65 (AT 878577) and the other Ontos section in support of F/2/3 at (AT 913598). One platoon was in support of I/3/3 at (AT 929691).

On 1 July, the section with F/2/3 supported a two-platoon sweep adjacent to Hill 65. No contact was reported.

On 9 July, the Ontos supporting I/3/3 displaced to (AT 944782) where it became OpCon of the 2d Platoon, A Company.

From 1 to 15 July, the platoon expended seventy-two major (106 mm recoilless rifle HEP-T) rounds on (H&I) fire missions.

On 10 July, the section in support of F/2/3 supported a platoon-sized patrol. Negative results were reported.

On 11 July, the same section, supporting a platoon from F/2/3, fired 106 rounds and 2,000 .30-caliber machine gun rounds at VC located by and in houses and haystacks. Results were four secondary explosions sighted.

From 11 to 20 July, the platoon expended 162 106 mm rounds in H&I fire missions from Hill 65.

On 27 July, the section with G/2/3 displaced to (AT 916592), where it had the mission of providing counterfires for 2/3. The Ontos section on Hill 65 expended 163 106 mm rounds on H&I missions from 21 to 31 July.

The 3d Platoon continued DS C and D/1/3, one Ontos section with D/1/3 at Le My (AT 899820), one section with C/1/3 on Hill 358 (AT 931885), and one at AI Van Pass in support of a platoon from C/1/3.

On 1 July, one Ontos provided cover for an infantry sweep of (AT 922792), with negative results.

On 7 July, the Ontos at Hai Van Pass was used to set up a roadblock.

On 9 July, one Ontos was placed OpCon of 2d Platoon from the 1st Platoon and was positioned as part of the company reaction force at the CP (AT 944782).

From 7 to 10 July, the platoon expended 467 106 mm rounds on H&I missions.

On 16 July, the Ontos at the platoon CP was used as a "show of force" at Kim Liem (AT 924857) during the night. The platoon provided a roadblock at Hai Van Pass on 16 and 17 July for a Rough Rider convoy.

From 11 to 20 July, the platoon expended 750 106 mm rounds on H&I missions.

On 24 July, one Ontos supported the infantry security element during a rice harvest in GS (AT 8485), remaining on that mission until 26 July.

From 21 to 31 July, 619 106 mm rounds were expended on H&I fire missions.

CO Company B: Capt. D. C. Satcher
Location and Operations Summary: Hue/Phu Bai TAOR

Company B in direct support or the 4th Marines (Phu Bai TAOR)
    1st Platoon, Company B DS 4th Marines
    2d Platoon, Company B DS 4th Marines
    3d Platoon, Company B DS 1/4

From 1 to 11 July, the 1st Platoon commenced the month DS 4th Marines, maintaining defensive positions.

On 12 July, Company B received a frag order from the commanding officer of 4th Marines to deploy one platoon and the company command group to Dong Ha (YD 244599), in support of Operation HASTINGS. At this time, the 1st Platoon was assigned the mission of providing security in the 1/4 vital area, relieving the 3d Platoon, Company B. The platoon remained in defensive positions for the remainder of the month with the exception of one section, which provided a convoy escort mission.

On 15–16 July, the Ontos section departed Phu Bai, escorting a convoy to/from Dong Ha.

The 2d Platoon commenced the reporting period DS 4th Marines. On 8 July, the company received a frag order to send one platoon to Dong Ha airstrip (YD 244599). The platoon departed Phu Bai at 100640H July, providing convoy escort to Dong Ha. Upon arrival, it was placed DS 2/1.

On 14 July, when Company B (-) arrived at Dong Ha, the platoon rejoined the company for the deployment to Cam Lo (YD 132594) for Operation HASTINGS. Upon arriving at Cam Lo, the platoon was placed in defensive positions guarding the Task Force Delta CP and helicopter LZ.

On 30 July, the platoon was chopped from DS 4th Marines and placed under OpCon of 3/4.

The platoon remained at Cam Lo with 3/4 while the remainder of the company displaced to Don Ha, en route to the Phu Bai TAOR.

The 3d Platoon started the month DS 1/4. Three positions were manned within the 1/4 TAOR from dusk to dawn nightly.

On 12 July, the platoon was relieved by the 1st Platoon for deployment on Operation HASTINGS. The platoon departed Phu Bai for Cam Lo, with the Company B Command Group at 130555H July. It was assigned convoy escort duties for the movement. When the convoy reached Thon My Chanh (YD 404475), it was held up because of a blown bridge. The Ontos, as well as all wheeled vehicles in the convoy, were ferried across the Song Co Lau River by an ARVN bridge platoon. During the crossing, one ARVN truck sank in the river and was retrieved by the

Company B wrecker and crew. A defensive perimeter was established for the night at (YD 412475), the Ontos providing security for the night.

On 14 July, the convoy arrived in Dong Ha (YD 244599). At this time, the 2d Platoon joined the company and continued to the Task Force Delta CP at Cam Lo (YD 132591). The platoon was assigned defensive positions within the TFD CP perimeter. One section practiced indirect fire procedures, firing 36 106 mm recoilless rifle rounds under control of the 3/12 FSCC. The evaluation was excellent.

On 30 July, the company departed for Phu Bai. The platoon was chopped to OpCon of 3/4 and remained at Cam Lo as perimeter security.

Jimmy D. Baccus, private first class, age 20, Lawndale, California, an Ontos crewman, died of illness on 28 July. He served in Company B, 3d Antitank Battalion.

COs Company C: Capt. F. Firing and 1st Lt. S. T. Flynn
Location: Da Nang TAOR

Company C DS 9th Marines
    1st Platoon, Company C DS 2/9
    2d Platoon, Company C DS 9th Marines
    3d Platoon, Company C DS 1/9

Company C continued DS 9th Marines.
The 1st Platoon continued DS 1/9.

On 1 July, one section was DS G/2/9 at (BN 024577). One section was at the 2/9 CP (BT 015627).

On 3 July, one Ontos in support of G/2/9 fired three major rounds at a building (BT 025577), destroying it, with no report of enemy casualties.

On 4 July, the Ontos section with G/2/9 supported them on a search-and-destroy mission, with no contact reported.

On 5 July, the Ontos switched locations; the section with 2/9 CP exchanged mission with the section with G/2/9. During the relief, one Ontos section received twenty-five VC SA rounds at (BT 048607). No casualties were reported.

On 7 July, the Ontos section with G/2/9 provided convoy escort to (AT 992577) and return (BT 024577). No contact was reported.

From 11 to 18 July, the Ontos sections remained in support of G/2/9 and the 2/9 CP.

On 19 July, one Ontos in support of G/2/9 located three minefields in vicinity of a bridge at (BT 012568).

On 20 July, F/2/9 switched positions at (BT 024577) with G/2/9; the Ontos section at that position remained, now in support of F/2/9.

On 20 July, this Ontos section supported an F/2/9 convoy to (AT 964606). On the return, one amtrac detonated a mine at (AT 989580), at which time the VC fired fifteen rounds of SA at the convoy. The Ontos returned fire with 1,500 .30-caliber machine gun rounds. The VC broke contact. No damage to Ontos or crew casualties was reported.

On 22 July, the Ontos section at 2/9 CP escorted two Otters to (AT 996618) and return, with no contact reported.

The remainder of the month was without incident.

The month ended with one Ontos section at the 2/9 CP (BT 015627) and the other section at the F/2/9 CP (BT 024577).

The 2d Platoon started the month at the Company C CP (Rear) (AT 998723).

On 5 July, the rear CP was closed, and all activities moved to Hill 55 (AT 960620). The 2d Platoon moved to Hill 55 at that time.

On 8 July, one Ontos section was placed DS D/1/9 (AT 947547).

On 10 July, this Ontos section fired five major rounds and six hundred .30-caliber machine gun rounds in support of D/1/9 (AT 953544). Three houses were destroyed, with three VC KIA (prob.) credited to the fire mission.

On 11 July, this same section supported D/1/9 on a search-and-clear operation from (AT 941546) to (AT 937554). Two 106 rounds were fired, destroying two houses. A group of VC (AT 937552) were fired at, resulting in four VC KIA (prob.). Fire was later received from (AT 937554). Return fire with two hundred .30-caliber machine gun rounds and four .50-caliber spotter rounds was directed at the VC with no determined results.

On 16 July, this Ontos section supported D/1/9 in a search-and-clear operation from (AT 947547) to (AT 949583). The Ontos fired three 106 rounds and 350 .30-caliber machine gun rounds at the VC located at (AT 946574), resulting in four VC KIA (prob.).

On 18 July, the Ontos section at the platoon CP displaced to support B/1/9 (AT 923543). This Ontos section, while with B/1/9 at (AT 929533), observed VC boats along the riverbank (AT 904526). Twenty .30-caliber machine gun rounds were fired at the boats; however, the range was too great for accurate damage assessment.

On 20 July, the same section sighted twenty-five to thirty VC unloading sampans at (AT 904526). Six major rounds were fired into a tree line located at the junction of the Song Tu Bong and Song Vu Gia Rivers at (AT 914534) to (AT 917535). Two rounds fell short and landed in the Song Thu Bong without detonating. The other four rounds resulted in the destruction of two houses, one secondary explosion, one secondary fire, and three VC KIA (prob.). Later that day, the Ontos section sighted twenty-five VC in khaki uniforms in boats at (AT 904526). Five 106 rounds were fired, resulting in the destruction of one boat and five VC KIA (prob.). Six additional major rounds were fired, resulting in the destruction of four more boats and the collapsing of two caves. A total of seventeen 106 mm recoilless rifle rounds HEP-T, twenty .30-caliber machine gun, and ten .50-caliber spotter rounds were fired during this action.

On 27 July, the Ontos section with D/1/9 fired three hundred .30-caliber machine gun rounds at two VC with no confirmed results.

On 28 July, this same section sank two VC sampans with five hundred .30-caliber machine gun rounds. No VC KIA or WIA were confirmed.

On 30 July, one Ontos from the section supporting B/1/9 fired ten .30-caliber machine gun rounds at a VC boat at (AT 914532), with no confirmed results. Later that day, the Ontos fired twelve .30-caliber machine gun rounds at a VC boat at (AT 912535), and an additional twenty machine gun rounds at a VC boat with five VC observed at (AT 914535), with results unknown. All of the action noted above was on the Song Thu Bong.

The 3d Platoon started the month DS 1/9. One Ontos section was on Hill 55 (AT 960620) at the 1/9 CP, the other Ontos section at (AT 911939) with B/1/9.

On 2 July, the Ontos section with B/1/9 fired twelve 106 rounds, resulting in the destruction of nine boats and three houses at (AT 904538).

On 4 July, the same section supported a sweep of Company B to (AT 920540). No contact was reported. That evening, the Ontos fired seven 106 rounds from the Company B night defensive position at (AT 912539) to (AT 902531) (AT 914534) with undetermined results.

On 5 July, this same Ontos section was positioned at a river block (Song Vu Gia) with D/1/9.

On 6 July, VC sniper fire was received. Nine 106 rounds were fired at the source (AT 927530)–(AT 925534), and sniper fire ceased.

On 7 July, the Ontos section fired fourteen 106, five hundred .30-caliber machine gun, and one hundred .50-caliber spotting rifle rounds into (AT 906539)–(AT 905538), when a USMC helicopter was hit by an estimated twenty VC. Results were undetermined.

On 9 July, the same Ontos section with B/1/9 fired ten 106 and twenty-five .50-caliber spotting rifle rounds from (AT 903542) to (AT 900539), resulting in the destruction of two houses and one newly constructed VC bunker.

On 10 July, the same Ontos section received VC sniper fire from (AT 895544), apparently from a high-powered rifle with a scope. One Ontos returned fire with fifteen 106 rounds, 250 .30-caliber machine gun, and twenty-five .50-caliber spotting rifle rounds. The VC sniper fire ceased.

On 12 July, the Ontos section with B/1/9 fired five 106 rounds from (AT 903543) to (AT 904548). In addition, eight .50-caliber spotting rounds and 250 .30-caliber machine gun rounds were fired at VC sniper. Results were one VC KIA (conf.).

From 14 to 20 July, the platoon displaced to the company CP located on Hill 55 (AT 963612). On arriving at the company CP, one Ontos was sent to reinforce the 2d Platoon, and shared in action noted in connection with support of D/1/9 above. One Ontos was positioned as part of the company CP defensive. The remainder of the platoon was located at the 3d ATBn CP for maintenance.

CO Company A (-), 1st ATBn: Capt. G. R. Van Horn
Location and Operations Summary: Da Nang TAOR

Company A (-), 1st ATBn (OpCon 3d ATBn) DS 1st Marines
   1st Platoon, Company A DS 1/1
   3d Platoon, Company A DS 1/1

Company A (-), 1st ATBn remained DS 1st Marines.

The 1st Platoon started the month at 1/1 CP (BT 073659).

On 2 July, the platoon was placed DS D/1/1 at (BT 083644).

On 5 July, the D/1/1 CP displaced to (BT 080641). The platoon supported a K/3/1 sweep from (BT 073708) to (BT 065705). No contact was reported.

The 3d Platoon started the month at 1/1's CP (BT 073659).

On 2 July, the platoon was placed DS D/1/1. One Ontos remained at the 1/1 CP (BT 073659). One Ontos section was located at (BT 059647) in support of the 1st Platoon D/1/1 and the other section at (BT 104655) in support of 3/D/1/1.

On 4 July, one Ontos was hit by VC small-arms fire on the number 2 and 3 recoilless rifles. Both rifles were taken to FLSG for a service ability check.

On 5 July, the 1/D/1/1 displaced to (BT 069639) and the Ontos displaced with it. The same day the Ontos section with the 3/D/1/1 displaced to (BT 109642).

On 6 July, the Ontos section with the 1/D/1/1 fired three major rounds (106 mm recoilless rifle HEP-T) and eight hundred rounds of .30-caliber machine gun ammunition at VC snipers, with negative results.

On 9 July, the Ontos section with 1/D/1/1 fired six major rounds at snipers at (BT 054650) with negative results. The same day, the other Ontos section at (BT 070650) fired one hundred rounds of .30-caliber machine gun ammunition at VC snipers at (BT 070648) and (BT 067649) with negative results.

On 13 July, one Ontos supporting 2/D/1/1 and one Ontos from the 1/1 CP were dispatched to (BT 050645) where a D/1/1 patrol was under fire from VC snipers. The Ontos fired ten major rounds at the hedgerows (BT 048645) with negative results.

On 15 July, the entire platoon moved to (BT 081642) in support of D/1/1.

On 17 July, one Ontos returning from the 3d ATBn maintenance area to D/1/1 was being led by an M-422 Mighty Mite. The M-422 was ambushed by an unknown number of VC at (BT 069690). The VC fired thirty rounds of small arms at the Marines in the M-422. The Marines returned fire with thirty-five rounds of 7.62 mm and .45-caliber ammunition. When the Ontos arrived on the scene, the VC broke contact. Negative results were reported.

On 17 July, one Ontos section was assigned a direct support mission for M/3/1 (BT 049692) on a COUNTY FAIR mission.

July 1966
Third Tanks
Commanding Officer: Lt. Col. M. L. Raphael
Executive Officer: Maj. J. G. Doss
Operations Officer: Capt. A. W. Facklam Jr.
Logistics Officer: Maj. W. J. Decota
Location and Operations Summary: Da Nang (AT 989708)

Within the Da Nang TAOR, the majority of the operations were centered around the movement south of the Song Ky Lam and Song Thu Bon waterway and into the MACON area. This operation involved the fording of a major river by eleven gun tanks, three flame tanks, and a tank retriever to support the multibattalion search-and-clear operation. The problem of finding a ford with a solid-enough bottom that would support 52 tons at a point where the depth would not rise more than 4 feet was solved expediently by Company B personnel. This effort was not in vain, as tanks demonstrated their inherent mobility and armor-protected firepower with a telling effort on the enemy.

During Operation MACON, tanks expended 212 rounds of 90 mm, 150 rounds of .50-, and 8,330 rounds of .30-caliber ammunition. A total of fifty-three VC (KBGF) confirmed were credited to tank action. Tank units were credited with an additional thirty-seven VC (KBGF) probable, twelve VC (WBGF) probable, and fifteen VC apprehended. Tank action accounted for forty-five buildings destroyed and destruction of two fighting holes and bunkers. An ammunition cache containing 241 hand grenades and 18 claymore mines was discovered by tank personnel.

At the completion of the third phase of Operation MACON, the 2d Platoon of Company B was left in the MACON area and accompanied 3/9 to the An Hoa industrial area. All other tanks were extracted from the MACON area and continued operations north of the Song Thu Bon and Son Ky Lam.

Companies A, B, and C, 3d Tank Battalion and Company C, 1st Tank Battalion (OpCon 3d Tank Battalion) continued DS four infantry regiments within the Da Nang and Phu Bai TAOR during the month of July 1966.

Company A (-) (Rein.) was DS 3d Marines.
Company B (Rein.) was DS 9th Marines.
The 3d Platoon of Company A was OpCon to Company B.

Richard Bright, private, age 20, Chula Vista, California, died of an illness on 21 July 1966 while serving as a tank crewman with Company B, 3d Tank Battalion in Quang Nam Province, South Vietnam.

Lee G. Johnson, lance corporal, age 19, Tulsa, Oklahoma, died while serving with Company B, 3d Tank Battalion as a Marine Tanker in Quang Nam Province, South Vietnam. He was killed by an enemy-planted explosive device on 30 July 1966.

BROWN, JOSEPH C. (KIA)

Synopsis:
The President of the United States takes pride in presenting the Silver Star Medal (Posthumously) to Joseph C. Brown (2047608), Corporal, U.S. Marine Corps, for conspicuous gallantry and intrepidity in action while serving with Company B, 3d Tank Battalion, 3d Marine Division (Rein.), FMF, in connection with combat operations against the enemy in the Republic of Vietnam on July 30, 1966. By his courage, aggressive fighting spirit and steadfast devotion to duty in the face of extreme personal danger, Corporal Brown upheld the highest traditions of the Marine Corps and the United States Naval Service. He gallantly gave his life for his country.

Home Town: Pasadena, Maryland

Joseph C. Brown, corporal, age 20, Pasadena, Maryland, was killed on 31 July by enemy ground fire.

Company C (Rein.) operating in the Hue/Phu Bai area is DS 4th Marines.

The following two articles, written by Ric Langley, present the essence of what a young enlisted Marine routinely experienced transitioning from a civilian to a Tanker; from a local kid, through the Marine Corps' training for combat; from the U.S. to the RVN, and the first steps to confronting the Viet Cong and North Vietnamese enemy bent on killing him and his Tanker family.

In Country

by Ric Langley

Bootcamp graduation, 1966
Left to right: Ina Langley, Ric Langley, and Jake Langley.

In January 1966, the draft had finally caught up with me. I could not avoid it any longer. I made the bus trip to Los Angeles, CA, thinking I would spend the next two years somewhere in the U.S. Army. I left Los Angeles on a bus, to my surprise, headed for San Diego, CA, and Marine Corps Bootcamp. By July, I had finished basic training, ITR (Infantry Training Regiment) Camp Pendleton, Tank School, and Staging Battalion. About the only place you could go now in the Marine Corps was to that great vacation spot on the South China Sea, VIETNAM.

On July 5, 1966, I loaded on a Northwest Orient Airlines plane, with 180 of my new best friends and headed for Nam. It was a long flight with several stops that ended in Okinawa, Japan. After a couple of days of processing and a couple of nights drinking way too much with a friend that I had gone through Bootcamp with, we were back on a plane for Da Nang. I was a clueless twenty-year-old about to embark on thirteen months that would change my life forever.

After a relatively short flight, we arrived at Da Nang, South Vietnam. At that time, Da Nang was where all Marines entered or left the country by air. Upon landing, the airfield looked much like any other airfield. The plane taxied to a stop, and as soon as they opened the door, I, along with everyone else on that plane, knew we were no longer in the good old U.S. of A. The heat, humidity, dust, and smell grabbed me by the throat and would not let go until the day, at that same airfield, I would get back on another plane and head back to the world.

We off-loaded the plane and formed up into a loose formation, waiting for transportation to the processing area. The transportation of course would be the good old cattle cars so loved by every Marine. As the cattle car pulled up, I noticed that all the windows were covered with chain link fencing. I asked one of the guys who had taken charge of this group of FNGs (fucking new guys), "What's up with the fencing?" He said, "That's to keep the grenades that the gooks throw out of the cars." First clue this is very serious business. On the short ride, everyone was laughing and talking until we passed an aircraft being loaded with those soon-to-be all too familiar silver coffins, my next clue.

We arrived at the processing center and of course got into one of the never-ending lines that the Marine Corps has to offer. Things moved fairly quickly, and before I knew it, I was being picked up by a 6×6 truck from 3d Tank Battalion. Being the only guy going to 3d Tanks, I jumped up into the cab with the driver and we headed off for the drive to their headquarters. I asked the driver a few questions to try to get some idea what I had gotten myself into. He had been in-country for only a few months with no problems to speak of. They had tents, cots, hot meals, showers, movies, a club, a PX where you could buy just about anything you wanted: so he thought it was pretty good duty. He then added that the companies in the field were not so blessed; they had things a little rougher. Sometimes they didn't get their movies on time and they had to stand guard duty and things like that. This didn't sound so bad; I can do the next thirteen months standing on my head. Think again, new guy.

As we pulled into the battalion area, the driver pointed out the office where I was to report and wished me luck. I grabbed my seabag and ditty bag and headed to the office where I reported in to the clerk. He told me to have a seat and the battalion XO (executive officer) would see me in a minute. After just a short time, the clerk, pointing to the back of the tent, said the XO would see me now. I made my way to where the clerk had pointed and reported as ordered in my best bootcamp style. I didn't want to get off on the wrong foot this early in my stay in Vietnam. The XO didn't say at ease or anything; he just told me to have a seat and they would figure out where they were going to send me. I didn't have to go anywhere; I thought I could be perfectly happy right there for the next thirteen months. Like that was going to happen. The XO called the clerk in and asked him about the personnel levels in the various companies. He said that most of the companies were in good shape except for C Company, which would be losing a lot of people to rotation within the next two months. He said, "OK, let's send him up there, make sure he gets his weapon and all his gear." He said "That will be all," wished me good luck, and told me the clerk would get me squared away. What's with all this good luck stuff? I followed the clerk back to his desk where he started the process to get me on my way. Without saying a word, he started shuffling a bunch of paperwork and making notes. He typed up a form, ripped it out of the machine, and handed it to me, saying it was my boarding pass for a flight to Phu Bai. I asked where the hell was Phu Bai, acting a little irritated. He must have noticed the irritation in my voice; he loosened up and told me it was up north and that C Company was a good outfit; in fact, if he had to go to a company in the field, he would want to go there. He said it was too late in the day to get a flight, so I would have to spend the night there. He said to follow him and he would show me where I could bunk for the night. I followed him up the dirt street to what he said was their transit tent. On the way, he pointed out the chow hall, showers, and latrine. The tent was completely empty except for a few dust-covered cots. I tossed my gear on one of the empty cots and asked what's next. He pointed across the road and said to go to the armory to pick up my pistol and 782 gears. Hmmm, a pistol, maybe another clue? The clerk bid me farewell with the usual good luck. This is starting to creep me out. At the armory, I was issued my pistol, holster, and a ton of 782 gear. The 782 gear consisted of a pack, cartridge belt, two canteens, helmet, and a bunch of other stuff. With another good luck from the armory, I gathered up my gear and headed back to the tent. I didn't realize until I sat down on the cot that I was exhausted. The heat, the tension, and humping all that stuff around had kicked my ass.

Being well over one hundred degrees, with 90 percent humidity, there was no way that I, not being used to the weather, was going to be able to take a little nap, so I decided I would write some letters to let the folks back home know I had made it this far OK. I reached for my ditty bag, unzipped it, and upon looking inside to retrieve my writing gear, I realized I had by mistake picked up my friend Jim Fite's ditty bag. I headed down to the office to ask the clerk where the amtrac battalion headquarters might be. I lucked out; their headquarters was about a quarter mile down the road. I strapped on my newly acquired pistol, what a strange feeling, and headed in the direction the clerk had pointed me to. I found Jim about the same time he figured out we had switched bags. Being late in the afternoon, we decided to go have a few beers at the Amtrac Club. Another long night and another bad morning.

The next morning, as soon as I heard people stirring around, I got up, got my gear, and headed for the motor pool to hitch a ride to the airfield. Once there, I presented my papers to the guy at the desk marked Departures and was informed they would have a C-47 plane leaving for Phu Bai in a couple of hours. One thing I had learned already was that if you have a chance to get some Zs, you had better take it. I headed for a quiet corner, dumped my gear, lay down, and went right to sleep. Before I knew it, the loud speaker was blurting out my flight number. I found the line to board what I thought was the right plane and fell in behind other Marines, Vietnamese women, children, chickens, and even a goat. Welcome to travel Vietnam-style. Up and away on this vintage aircraft, chickens goats, and all. The flight was short, noisy, smelly, and bumpy. Phu Bai airfield was a little smaller than Da Nang but with what seemed like a lot more military activity. I found the office and was able to get in touch with C Company, Tanks. They told me to hang loose; they would send transportation for me as soon as they could. They also told me that there was another guy there that had flown in from Da Nang that morning. I checked the area and spotted a guy that looked like he may be a Tanker. I approached the guy and asked if he was on his way to C Company as well, and he replied, "Yes," so we sat down and started to chew the fat. He had been to Tank Battalion HQ for Office Hours (UCMJ's NJP) and had been busted from private first class (E-2) to private (E-1). There just seemed to be shit birds no matter where you went in the Corps. He asked why I was hauling around all that 782 gear around. I told him that they had issued it to me and I thought I would need it. He said, "Lose it." I would never in a hundred years use it. I said, "But I'm signed out for it." "Tell them, 'It got destroyed in the field.' They can't verify it wasn't." So I dumped the gear in a corner and forgot it. He was right. I never missed it or needed it the entire time I was in Vietnam.

A jeep pulled up by the side door of the building we were sitting in, and a guy came in, checking the area like he was looking for someone, so we flagged him over and asked if he was from C Company Tanks. Bingo, we had our ride, and in no time, I was standing in front of the company

CO (commanding officer). He asked me a number of questions, like how long I had been in the Corps, what kind of experience I had in tanks, where I was from, and that kind of stuff. I answered all his questions and told him I had been drafted in the Marines but that I would give him 100 percent. He said he didn't care how I got there, that I was now one of the Marines under his command and he expected no less than 100 percent all the time. The commander assigned me to C-12, a brand-new tank just in from the States with Sergeant Jones as tank commander (TC). Because of excess personnel, we had five crew members with me as low man. The company was living in hardback tents with hot showers, a chow hall and movies—almost as nice as Battalion HQ, without all the spit and polish.

I found my platoon's tent and an empty cot and started to settle in. Crewmen started to filter into the tent after completing their day's duties and introduced themselves. You could tell I was straight from the States with my polished boots and dark green utilities. I met the other guys on our crew, and they took me to meet Sergeant Jones. They all seemed to like and respect him and said he was a great tank commander. The crew left me with Jones and went off to shower and get ready for chow. We chatted a little bit about home and how long he had been in Nam and how short he was and how long it would be before I was on my way home. He told me what he expected from me as a tank crewman on his tank. All in all, I felt good, I was finally in my new home with my new family and knew what was expected of me. All too soon, I was to learn that home is where you park your tank and that your family can be torn apart in a heartbeat. In the next few months, Vietnam would teach me many hard-learned lessons, and I would collect many more of those valuable clues, but for now, I was as happy as a guy could be that far from home and loved ones.

The Move North

by Ric Langley

By the middle of July 1966, I had been with 1st Platoon, C Company, 3d Tank Battalion for a couple of weeks, and things were pretty good.

I had a roof over my head, good food, a hot shower, and the maintenance guys had just finished brewing a new batch of applejack. What more could a Marine ask for? Being the fifth crewman on C-12 until someone rotated back to the world, I was odd man out. We were not doing much anyway. I had spent most of my time helping my crew mates getting the new tank checked out and squared away. Like myself, the tank had just arrived from the States. It still had that new tank smell. We cleaned guns, checked suspension, tested radios, and all the other things that had to be done to make sure we were ready when and if we were called on. We did spend a few days out on small patrols but nothing serious. I traded off with the other loader on these patrols; he went one day, and I went the next. I wasn't too fond of the loader job and knew for sure that I did not want to be a gunner. What I really wanted to do was to drive. The guy with that job at the time was the next crewman in line to be sent home. I thought I might have a shot at the position when he left. I asked Sergeant Jones what I had to do to get put in the driver's seat. He told me to be patient, that when the driver was gone, he was going to move Rodriguez, the present loader, up to driver. I was disappointed, but that was the way things worked. I knew the gunner was also close to rotating, so maybe I would get another chance then. In the meantime, I just wanted to do the best job I could do as loader. Later on I would learn how important every crewman on that tank was and how much we depended on each other.

As we mounted up one morning to go out and fam fire our weapons, Sergeant Jones told Rodriguez to take the driver's position for the day so he could get some practice. We moved out through the wire and across the sandy terrain to the area, a short distance away, which we used as a firing range. The tank jerked, bounced, and bucked all the way to the range. I could tell Sergeant Jones was not a bit happy with Rodriguez's debut as driver, and I must agree he was pretty bad. We fired all our weapons, including our .45s, and headed back to the company area. Rodriguez's driving did not improve any on the way back—in fact, it got worse. He just did not seem to have the knack for driving. Maybe there was still hope for me being behind that funny-shaped steering wheel.

Three weeks into my tour in Nam and I was right at home. I was with a good unit with good people and good equipment and hadn't been exposed to anything even close to what you would call combat. During morning formation, sometime in late July, our platoon leader passed the word that he wanted to meet with the whole platoon in the mess tent after we were dismissed. We headed for the mess tent, clueless as to what this meeting was all about. There had been scuttlebutt about a move but nothing concrete. There were all kinds of speculation: we were going back to Da Nang, we were going to Hue, we were going on a float—but none of this speculation even came close to the true story.

Our platoon leader came into the tent and took his place in front of a large map of Vietnam. He began to lay out the plan that was to become our future. In a few days, 1st Platoon would load their five tanks on an LST to be transported north to a place with the name "Dong Ha." We would set up a platoon area and do whatever the powers that be called upon us to do. Like that tells you a lot. All extra personnel—that being me—would travel by convoy up the main highway, past Hue and

Quang Tri, and into the Dong Ha area. At the time, the Air Force, Seabees, and some Marines had established a small compound, so we were told that life would be on the primitive side.

The next few days were spent installing fording gear on all the platoon's vehicles, double-checking everything, and packing and loading the entire platoon's equipment into trucks. Departure day came, and 1st Platoon was up early, making final preparations to head north. The tanks and the truck convoy were staged, and the personnel not manning the tanks were given their assignments. I was assigned to ride "shotgun" with the company first sergeant in the lead jeep. As the first sunlight of the day flooded the countryside, the word was passed to "mount up." I checked my .45, grabbed the M14 I had been issued, checked the safety, slapped in a twenty-round clip, chambered a round, placed the rifle in the rack between the seats in the jeep, and took my place in the passenger seat. The first sergeant climbed into the driver's seat, asking if I was ready for a little drive in the countryside. I replied I was as ready as I would ever be.

The tanks fired up their engines, and after a few minutes, they moved onto the road and headed south to meet up with the LST. The first sergeant pulled the jeep onto the road, made a hard right, and pointed the nose north. At that moment, I got that funny feeling where the hairs on the back of your neck stand up and you get that gnawing sensation in the pit of your stomach. I would know this feeling many more times before I would make my way home. This was the first time I had been in contact with the Vietnamese people. I knew for sure that every time we passed a bus or a group of people that their pockets were full of hand grenades and they were going to whip out their AK-47s and blast us. The first sergeant must have noticed my tension; he told me to relax and enjoy the ride. I took his advice and was able to somewhat enjoy the next few hours of the trip to Dong Ha.

We arrived at Dong Ha, without being gunned down, and late in the afternoon drove through the gate and passed the airfield to what would be 1st Platoon's new CP at the end of the landing strip. Dong Ha looked really sparse at this time. We made our way to the location where we were to set up shop; it sure was not Da Nang or Phu Bai. Being late in the day, the first sergeant said we would start setting up tents and unloading the trucks in the morning and, for now, to break open the C-rations and find a place to bed down for the night. This was my first opportunity to enjoy the gourmet delights found inside those little cardboard boxes. I would eventually learn to almost like these canned wonders. We sat around and talked about home, our families, and told war stories for those guys who had them and just generally relaxed.

The first sergeant set up a watch schedule where each man had an hour watch, so we drew straws to see who got what watch. I drew the time from 0200 to 0300. Sitting there on that warm summer night, I was able to reflect on my time thus far in Vietnam. I realized that the longer I was in-country and the farther north I moved, the more primitive and dangerous my life had become. Was this to be where I would spend the rest of my stay in-country? The members of 1st Platoon did not realize that when they rolled out of C Company compound that day in July that it would be the last time they would have a Company Headquarters to call "home." The 1st Platoon would become the "Gypsy Tank Platoon of Northern I Corps." In some ways, this was a good thing, and in other ways, it was bad. I still had a lot of unanswered questions, but I was learning fast; you had to know that you had no other choice.

Ric Langley served with C Company, 1st Platoon and A Company, 4th Platoon from July 1966 to August 1967, and with D Company from August 1967 until he left the Marine Corps in January 1968.

Company C (-) (Rein.), 1st Tank Battalion is DS 1st Marines.

Note: In addition to the increased kinetic action, the tank battalion was heavily involved with civic action. The records show the width and breadth of its program

H&S Company COs: Capts. J. B. Terpak and P. F. Lessard
Location: Da Nang (AT 989708)

COs Company A: 1ˢᵗ Lt. H. L. Stiegelman and Capt. L. A. Brandt
Location and Operations Summary: Da Nang (AT 946762)

The command chronology and other situation reporting for Company A—as well as the other two letter companies—details the day-to-day activities, which, generally speaking, were quite similar in general terms. They include, for example, fragmentation of the company into platoon-size units and further deployment by sections in support of infantry companies; encountering both antitank and antipersonnel mines; detonating personnel mines—most often on purpose to save the supporting infantry units—was pursued by design. The antitank mining most often only temporarily disabled the tank and damaged the suspension systems. Every type of 90 mm round was used, and .30-caliber, .50-caliber coax- and turret-mounted, respectively, machine gun fire was delivered generously. Most often, body count could not be confirmed due to distance to the target and/or reduced light. And, as often as not, secondary explosions were observed from 90 mm firers. Results of H&I fires were particularly difficult to assess. The use of the tanks' searchlights provided good results. The infantry praised the support of tanks for the timeliness and accuracy of their delivery of ordnance as well as the effective range and diversity of their weapons. The extra elevation of the tank commander provided a wider range of target acquisition than the ground-level infantry. And especially entertaining was the ability to vaporize a sampan and its passengers with a single 90 mm round and turn to dust a bunker that housed the enemy delivering automatic weapons fire on the Marines. Both of these events were enhanced by secondary explosions signaling the probability of destroying arms caches.

The following is taken from *Westmoreland: The General Who Lost Vietnam* by Lewis Sorley (WM-LS). (With minor changes, this adaptation conveys the same information and premise.)

> Not later than the autumn of 1966 the leaders of both services involved in fighting the ground war in Vietnam—Army Chief of Staff General Harold K.

Johnson and Marine Commandant General Wallace Greene—saw Westmoreland's approach as fatally flawed and agreed on a viable alternative.

If Westmoreland had problems with fellow Army officers over the viability of his Big War approach, those problems were compounded when it came to dealing with Marines. The Senior Marine leadership saw the war much differently than did Westmoreland, taking a view entirely compatible with the findings of the PROVN Study (discussed below). In addition—to Westmoreland's disgust—such senior Marines outside Vietnam as Commandant of the Marine Corps General Wallace Greene and Lieutenant General Victor Krulak, Commanding General of Fleet Marine Force, Pacific, maintained close contact with Lieutenant General Lewis Walt, commanding III Marine Amphibious Force on the ground in Vietnam, giving him plenty of their opinion and advice, much of it contrary to what Westmoreland was advocating. Wrote Allan Millett, a Reserve Marine Colonel and distinguished historian, "Marine Generals, like Victor H. Krulak, made life miserable for General William C. Westmoreland because of their obsession with pacification and working with the Vietnamese military and paramilitary forces." Just as the major ground force involvement of U.S. troops was in full swing in October 1965, for example, Krulak followed up a recent visit to Vietnam with a cable to Walt. "I am glad you were able to impress Westy with the magnitude of your activity," he said. "At the same time, I am sure that he has not altered his view that 'find, fix and destroy the big Main Force units' is really the answer, and that patrols, ambushes and civic action are all second class endeavors, more suitable for the ARVN and the paramilitary. I disagree with this, and I know you do, too." Westmoreland was actually quite unimpressed with what the Marines were doing. "I believed the Marines should have been trying to find the enemy's main forces and bring them to battle," he noted, "thereby putting them on the run and reducing the threat they posed to the population." Later, as input for his memoirs, Westmoreland said he "just did not find the same initiative in I Corps as elsewhere. Marines seem complacent about enemy possibilities." Walt [was] said he, "dedicated and sincere but found it hard to grasp the big picture and project into the future." Taking just the opposite tack, Krulak argued that "our effort belonged where the people were, not where they weren't. I shared these thoughts with Westmoreland frequently, but made no progress in persuading him."

The costs in human terms were great, as established by studies conducted by Thomas Thayer. He found that both the one-year tour and the six-month command tour "apparently had the effect of raising the toll of U.S. combat deaths. Twice as many troops died during the first six months of their tour as in the second half. After the first month, the number of deaths decline as the tour progresses, without exception. Thus, the longer one stayed alive after arriving in Vietnam, the better one's chances for survival, presumably as the result of a learning curve, which then had to be repeated for each new arrival." Russell Glenn reported confirmatory findings, including longer-term effects. "The 12-month rotation policy," he stated, "touted for its benefits provided to the individual soldier, seems in fact to have been a significant element in causing greater numbers of men to lose their lives and may have increased neuropsychiatric casualties.

At a commanders' conference in April 1966 Westmoreland told his subordinates that "I continue to be a proponent of the one-year tour, but the price we pay is in the teamwork, proficiency, and competence of tactical units."

While he never said as much, and would no doubt have vigorously denied such a suggestion from others, the conclusion is inescapable: that Westmoreland decided early-on that he could simply take over the war effort, get the job done promptly, then hand it back to the South Vietnamese and depart in glory.

(VTHF comment: NOT!)

August 1966
First Antitanks
Commanding Officer: Maj. A. J. Eagan
Executive Officer: Maj. A. J. Harris
Operations Officer: Maj. A. J. Eagan
Logistics Officer: Maj. J. J. Keefe
Location: Camp Pendleton, CA

H&S Company CO: Capt. J. W. Schroeder
Location: Camp Pendleton, CA

CO Company A, 1st ATBn: 1st Lt. B. J. Bethel
Location and Operations Summary: Tam Ky, RVN

 On 17 August, Michael Giovinazzo received a Purple Heart.

At 052400H, 2d Platoon departed the company CP as security forces for the Regimental Command Group convoy. This convoy arrived at Tam Ky at 060430H. One Ontos remained in a defensive position covering the Song Tam Ky Bridge, providing security for six JP-4 Refuelers, which required a pontoon bridge to cross the river. This Ontos arrived at Tam Ky at 060700H.

CO Company B (-) (Rein.): Capt. J. E. Felker
Location and Operations Summary:

Operation COLORADO

Concept of Operations: Company B was to move to the operating area in three increments. One platoon, on D-day, was to move into a blocking position athwart the Hiep Duc Road in the vicinity of (BT 130360), with 3/5 providing convoy security en route. The other two platoons were to act as security forces for the Regimental Command Group as LSA convoys to Tam Ky. Upon arrival in the operating area and for the duration of the operation, Company B was to be prepared for employment in a direct fire support role or in any other capacity as directed by the commanding officer, 5th Marines.

CO Company C: Capt. R. J. Esposito. No report available.

August 1966
First Tanks
Commanding Officer: Maj. R. E. B. Palmer
Executive Officer: Maj. J. W. Clayborne
Operations Officer: Maj. R. D. McKee
Logistics Officer: Maj. H. J. L. Reid
Location and Operations Summary: Hill 43 (BT 571041), Chu Lai Combat Base

Locations:
    H&S Company
        1–31 August, Chu Lai Combat Base

    Company A
        1–31 August, Chu Lai Combat Base DS 5th Marines
        1–2 August, 3d Platoon DS Chu Lai Defense Command

Company B
    1–31 August, Chu Lai Combat Base DS 7th Marines
    1–31 August, 2d Platoon DS Chu Lai Defense Command

Company C
    1–31 August, Da Nang TAOR DS 1st Marines. AdCon 1st Tank Battalion, OpCon 3d Marine Division; 2d Platoon returned from the SLF and replaced 3d Platoon, Company A at the Chu Lai Defense Command on 3 August 1966.
    3–31 August, 2d Platoon DS Chu Lai Defense Command

During the reporting period, Companies A and B remained DS 5th and 7th Marines, respectively.

On 1 August, 2d Platoon, Company B, and 3d Platoon, Company A continued to support the Chu Lai Defense Command.

On 3 August, 2d Platoon, Company C returned from SLF, replaced 3d Platoon, Company A at the Chu Lai Defense Command. Company C, with two gun platoons, remains with 3d Marine Division, Da Nang TAOR. A Provisional Rifle Platoon and Company Headquarters, provided to the Chu Lai Defense Command on 24 July 1966, remain with the Chu Lai Defense Command as of 31 August 1966.

Company A supported the 5th Marines during the reporting period and reinforced by the Battalion Flame Platoon and other headquarters elements, participated in Operation COLORADO from 7 August to 21 August 1966. On that operation, tanks were used for CP security.

Company B supported the 7th Marines with two gun platoons.

The 1st Platoon supported 1st Battalion operations on the peninsula area south of the Song Tra Bong; 3d Platoon supported 3d Battalion positions west of Route 1. Company B Headquarters and 3d Platoon, with 3d Platoon, Company A, Battalion Flame Platoon, and the

Battalion Headquarters Tank Section attached, participated in Operation JACKSON from 27 to 29 August 1966.

H&S CO: Maj. J. P. McGill
Location: Same as battalion CP

 On 26 August, John Perillo received a Purple Heart.

CO Company A: Capt. J. C. Greene Jr.
Location and Operations Summary: (See above.)

CO Company B: Capt. E. E. Stith
Location and Operations Summary: (See above.)

Bobby G. Corsi, sergeant, age 24, Columbus, Ohio, died on Monday, 22 August 1966, by an enemy-planted explosive device. He was a tank crewman serving in Company B, 1st Tank Battalion.

CO Company C: Capt. F. U. Salas
Location and Operations Summary: (See above.)

August 1966
Third Antitanks
Commanding Officers: Majs. E. R. Larson, K. E. Sharff, and D. E. Newton
Executive Officers: Maj. K. E. Sharff and Capt. D. C. Satcher
Operations Officer: WO C. C. Harris
Logistics Officers: Maj. K. E. Sharff, 2d Lt. C. P. Wager, and Capt. D. C. Satcher
Location and Operations Summary: Da Nang TAOR

H&S Company COs: Capt. B. M. Mathews and 1st Lt. D. K. Caswell
Location and Operations Summary: Da Nang

CO Company A: Capt. A. A. Compton

Location and Operations Summary: Da Nang TAOR

Company A DS 3d Marines
    1st Platoon, Company A DS 2/3
    2d Platoon, Company A DS 1/3
    3d Platoon, Company A DS 3/3

COs Company B: Capt. D. C. Satcher and 1st Lt. S. L. Camby
Location and Operations: Hue/Phu Bai TAOR

CO Company C: 1st Lt. S. T. Flynn
Location and Operations:

CO Company A (-), 1st ATBn: Capt. G. R. Van Horn
Location and Operations:

On 3 August, Operation HASTINGS ended, and Operation PRAIRIE commenced. The Marines believed that the 324B NVA Division had either moved north of the DMZ or moved west under the cover of triple-canopy forest. COMUSMACV believed the 324B Division was still south of the DMZ: further, that it was soon to be joined by two more NVA divisions—the 304th and the 341st—preparing to cross the DMZ.

A Marine tank column is shown advancing along Route 9. M-48 tanks, like those pictured here, provided much needed support to the infantry road reconnaissance during Operation PRAIRIE (GB-66).

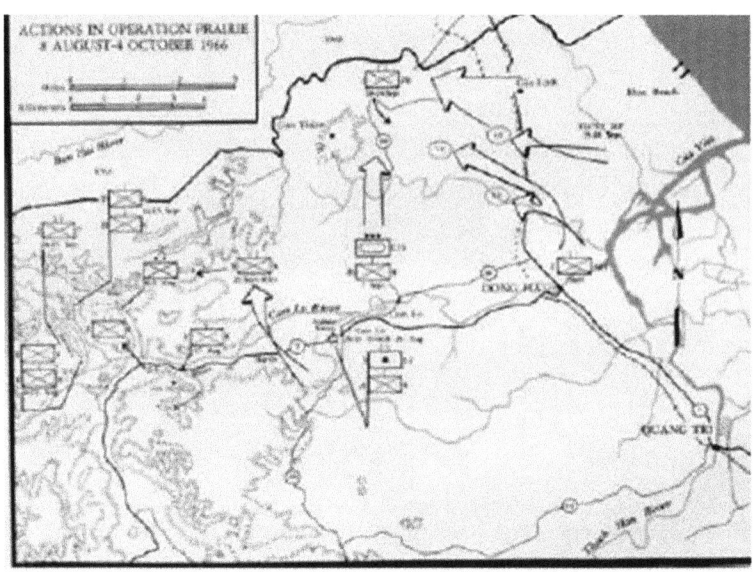

(GB-66) Actions in Operation PRAIRIE

August 1966
Third Tanks
Commanding Officer: Maj. J. G. Doss
Executive Officers: Majs. P. L. Westenberger, E. R. Larson, and J. G. Doss
Operations Officer: Capt. A. W. Facklam Jr.
Logistics Officers: Maj. W. J. Decota and Capt. R. E. Downard
Location and Operations Summary: Da Nang (AT 989708)

During the month of August 1966, the 3d Tank Battalion experienced relatively the same degree and type of VC antitank activity as last month.

Seven (7) antitank mines were detonated by tanks during August as compared to ten (10) during July. In addition, tanks were engaged in VC-initiated exchanges of fire on thirty-one (31) occasions this month, while July's total was thirty-three (33).

To counterbalance these slight decreases in antitank actions, the VC staged mortar attack against the 3d Tank Battalion CP on 17 August and attacked in force a Marine position in the Cam Lo area where elements of Company

C, 3d Tank Battalion were located; according to the infantry commander present, the attack was directed mainly against the Company C tanks.

During the month of August 1966, Companies A, B, and C, 3d Tank Battalion, and Company C (-), 1st Tank Battalion (OpCon 3d Tank Battalion) continued DS four infantry regiments within the Da Nang and Phu Bai TAORs.

Company A (-) (Rein.) was DS 3d Marines.

Company B (Rein.) was DS 9th Marines and 2/1.

The 2d Platoon of Company A was OpCon to Company B until 20 August 1966. At that time, BLT 3/3 assumed OpCon of the 2d Platoon, Company A.

Company C (Rein.) operating in the Phu Bai and Dong Ha area is DS 4th Marines.

Company C (-) (Rein.), 1st Tank Battalion is DS 1st Marines.

On 28 August 1966, 3d Tank Battalion joined the 2d Platoon of Company A, 5th Tank Battalion. This platoon will be redesignated as 2d Platoon, Company A, 3d Tank Battalion. The 2d Platoon of Company A, 3d Tank Battalion was attached to BLT 3/3 on 20 August 1966 for deployment to Okinawa.

H&S Company COs: Capts. J. B. Terpak and P. F. Lessard
Location and Operations Summary: Da Nang (AT 989708)

At 1500H, a 3d Tank Battalion patrol visited the home of a known VC in the village of Phong Bac at (AT 999712) to question the VC's wife. While conducting the interrogation, an M-26 hand grenade was thrown into the house by an unknown party approximately 25 meters from the house. The tank battalion civil affairs officer threw himself on the grenade and shouted for the other members of the patrol to evacuate the area. After several seconds, it was determined the grenade was not going to explode, and the grenade was examined and found to still contain the safety pin. A search of the area failed to reveal the person who threw the grenade.

 MATTINGLY, ROBERT E.

Synopsis:

The President of the United States takes pleasure in presenting the Silver Star Medal to Robert E. Mattingly (0-91273), Second Lieutenant, U.S. Marine Corps, for conspicuous gallantry and intrepidity in action while serving with Headquarters and Service Company, 3d Tank Battalion, 3d Marine Division (Rein.), FMF, in connection with combat operations against the enemy in the Republic of Vietnam on August 5, 1966. By his courage, aggressive fighting spirit and steadfast devotion to duty in the face of extreme personal danger, Second Lieutenant Mattingly upheld the highest traditions of the Marine Corps and the United States Naval Service.

Home Town: Preston, Maryland

Mattingly being presented the Silver Star medal

Lt. Col. Raphael, CO 3d Tanks, presenting award to Phong Bac student (GB-66)

11 August: At 2205H, 3d Tank Battalion received a report from 1st 8" Howitzer Battery, located at (AT 975716), that they were under mortar attack. As southern sector coordinator of the 3d Marine Division Rear Area, all units in the southern sector were alerted, and reserve reaction forces were placed in a standby status. At 120030H, when the threat had diminished, forces returned to a normal state of readiness.

17 August: At 0145H, the 3d Tank Battalion, 3d Antitank Battalion, 1st Amtrac Battalion, and 3d Motor Transport Battalion were attacked by an estimated reinforced VC platoon. The attack began with a mortar barrage of approximately sixty to seventy rounds of both 60 mm and 81 mm. During the initial mortar barrage, the commanding officer and executive officer of 3d Tank Battalion were wounded and the S-4 officer killed. Simultaneously, an estimated VC squad armed with AK-47 assault rifles, RPG-2 antitank rockets, satchel charges, and grenades attacked the 3d Motor Transport Battalion. The VC mortar position located at (AT 983711) were immediately taken under fire by tank 90 mm and small-arms fire. After approximately five to ten minutes, the mortar firing ceased. VC casualties resulting from these fires were four VC (KBGF) probable; 3d Tank Battalion casualties were one KIA, six WIA, and five medevaced.

DOSS, JAMES G., JR.

Synopsis:
The President of the United States takes pleasure in presenting the Silver Star Medal to James G. Doss, Jr. (0-51888), Major, U.S. Marine Corps, for conspicuous gallantry and intrepidity in action while serving with Commanding Officer, 3d Tank Battalion, 3d Marine Division (Rein.), FMF, in connection with combat operations against the enemy in the Republic of Vietnam on August 17, 1966. By his courage, aggressive fighting spirit and steadfast devotion to duty in the face

of extreme personal danger, Major Doss upheld the highest traditions of the Marine Corps and the United States Naval Service.

Home Town: Phoenix, Arizona

WILLIAMSON, ROBERT M., JR.

Synopsis:
The President of the United States takes pleasure in presenting the Silver Star Medal to Robert M. Williamson, Jr., Lance Corporal, U.S. Marine Corps, for conspicuous gallantry and intrepidity in action while serving with Company B, 3d Tank Battalion, 3d Marine Division (Rein.), FMF, in connection with combat operations against the enemy in the Republic of Vietnam on August 17, 1966. By his courage, aggressive fighting spirit and steadfast devotion to duty in the face of extreme personal danger, Lance Corporal Williamson upheld the highest traditions of the Marine Corps and the United States Naval Service.

Walter J. Decota, major, age 33, Pascoag, Rhode Island, a Marine tank officer, was killed on 17 August during an enemy mortar attack on the 3d Tank Battalion Command Post on Hill 32 in Quang Nam Province, South Vietnam.

20 August: From 2158H to 2320H, the 3d Tank Battalion, 3d Antitank Battalion, and 1st Amtrac Battalion CPs located at (AT 989711) received from three hundred to five hundred rounds of small-arms fire from positions in the vicinity of (AT 987711). The three battalions that were receiving fire returned heavy volume of small-arms and M-79 fire. Three VC were observed in position at (AT 994712) and (AT 985715). An LVTH-6 of the 1st Amtrac fired five rounds of HE and three rounds of 105 mm WP at suspected positions. One USMC 1st Amtrac Battalion WIA nonmedevac and one USN (NSA, POL fuel farm) WIA medevac.

A search of the enemy positions was made at 210630H. The search in grid squares (AT 9971) revealed six buildings destroyed, one Vietnamese national wounded in the leg, and one Vietnamese national child that had been killed by small-arms fire. According to villagers, the casualties may have been the result of VC fire.

 JONES, CLARENCE W.

Synopsis:
The President of the United States takes pleasure in presenting the Silver Star Medal to Clarence W. Jones (1460601), Staff Sergeant, U.S. Marine Corps, for conspicuous gallantry and intrepidity in action while serving with 3d Tank Battalion, 3d Marine Division (Rein.), FMF, in connection with combat operations

against the enemy in the Republic of Vietnam on August 26, 1966. By his courage, aggressive fighting spirit and steadfast devotion to duty in the face of extreme personal danger, Staff Sergeant Jones upheld the highest traditions of the Marine Corps and the United States Naval Service.

Home Town: Richmond, Virginia

CO Company A: Capt. L. A. Brandt
Location and Operations Summary: Da Nang (AT 946762)

3 August: At 1925H, a Company A tank at (AT 903546) in support of elements of 1/9 received an estimated ten rounds of small-arms fire. Enemy positions could not be located, and fire was not returned.

7 August: At 1830H, while in support of elements of 2/3 at (AT 878575), fourteen VC were observed at (AT 859568). A heavy volume of 90 mm cannon fire was expended with good target coverage. Due to the range to the target, it was impossible to determine enemy casualties.

10 August: At 1545H, while in support of F/2/3 at (AT 878574), three VC were observed in three boats crossing the Song Vu Gia at (AT 849552). Tanks fired 90 mm cannon and sank all three boats. Area could not be searched, three VC (KBGF) probable.

11 August: At 1301H, while in support of F/2/3 at (AT 878574), three VC were observed in three boats on the Song Vu Gia at (AT 8555), moving in an easterly direction. Tanks fired the 90 mm cannon, sinking one boat and damaging the other two. Three VC (KBGF) confirmed. Again at 1530H, another VC was observed in a boat crossing the river. Tanks fired the 90 mm cannon, sinking the boat with its occupant. One VC (KBGF) confirmed. At 1922H, while in support of F/2/3 at (AT 878574), thirty to thirty-five VC were observed at (AT 821571) moving south. Tanks fired a heavy volume of 90 mm HE and observed direct hits resulting in fifteen VC (KBGF) confirmed.

12 August: At 1220H, while in support of elements of 2/3 at (AT 878574), five VC were observed in two boats crossing the Song Vu Gia. Tank fired the 90 mm cannon and sank both boats. Two VC (KBGF) confirmed.

13 August: From 0100H to 0400H, while in support of elements of 2/3 at (AT 877574), tanks fired an H&I mission into coordinates (AT 895611). All fires were unobserved. Results undetermined.

At 1715H, while in support of elements of 2/3 at (AT 878574), three VC were observed crossing the Song Vu Gia in three boats at (AT 855558). Tanks fired a heavy volume of 90 mm HE and observed direct hits. One boat was sunk, and two were damaged. Two VC (KBGF) confirmed.

15 August: At 0530, while in support of elements of 2/3 at (AT 914598), tanks fired an H&I mission into coordinates (AT 895611). All fires were unobserved. Results undetermined. At 1800, while in support of elements of 2/3 at (AT 877575), tank crewmen observed a number of VC in a boat crossing the Song Vu Gia at (AT 85355). Tanks fired six rounds of 90 mm HE; the boat was not sunk. Two rounds were premature air bursts. Ammunition lot suspended locally pending further investigation.

16 August: From 162000H to 170230H, while in support of elements of 2/3 at (AT 877574), tanks fired H&I fires into suspected enemy positions at (AT 849548). All fires were unobserved, results undetermined.

17 August: From 172000H to 180330H, while in support of elements of 2/3 at (AT 877575), tanks fired H&I fires into suspected enemy positions at (AT 849548). All fires were unobserved, results undetermined. At 1530H, while in support of elements of 2/3 at (AT 877574), tank crewmen observed four VC unloading a boat at (AT 848549). Tanks fired 90 mm HE, destroying the boat and a house nearby. Four VC (KBGF) confirmed.

18 August: From 182200H to 190430H, while in support of elements of 1/3 at (AT 877575), tanks fired three H&I missions into suspected enemy positions at (AT 849548). Results of firing unknown; all fires were unobserved.

19 August: At 1600, while in support of elements of 2/3 at (AT 877575), four VC were observed in a boat at (AT 858562). Tanks fired the 90 mm cannon, scoring a direct hit. The boat was destroyed, and four VC (KBGF) confirmed. At 1445H, while in support of elements of 3/3 at (AT 877575), tanks fired an H&I mission into (AT 855554). All fires were unobserved, results unknown.

20 August: At 2030, while in support of G/2/3 at (AT 915992), tanks fired an H&I mission into (AT 885602). All fires were unobserved, results unknown.

21 August: At 1830H, while in support of elements of 2/3 at (AT 877575), tanks fired an H&I mission into (AT 874577). All fires were unobserved, results unknown. From 212200H to 220200H, tanks in support of elements of 2/3 fired H&I fires from their position at (AT 874577) into (AT 805557). All fires were unobserved, results unknown.

25 August: At 1005H, while in support of elements of 2/3 at (AT 914598), tanks fired an H&I mission into (AT 893613) and (AT 889615). Results unknown, all fires unobserved.

28 August: At 1400H, while in support of elements of the 3d Marines at (AT 877574), tank crewmen observed five VC in a boat on the Song Vu Gia at (AT 854555). Tanks fired 90 mm HE and observed a direct hit. One VC ran from the shore. Results: Four VC (KBGF) confirmed.

CO Company B: Capt. E. L. Tunget
Location and Operations Summary: Da Nang (AT 946762)

2 August: At 0045H, tanks in support of elements of 1/9 at (AT 954544) received approximately fifteen rounds of small arms for the vicinity of

(AT 953533). Tanks returned .30-caliber machine gun fire, and the enemy firing ceased. The area was not searched because of darkness.

3 August: At 1630H, while in support of H/2/9 at (BT 005583) on an antipersonnel mine sweep, an estimated twenty VC were observed in the vicinity of (BT 001582). Tanks fired the 90 mm cannon and .30-caliber machine gun, and the VC broke contact. A search of the area failed to reveal any VC casualties.

At 1720H, while in support of C/1/9 at (AT 953562), ten persons in civilian dress were observed in a tree line nearby. As they were approached by infantry and tanks, they fled. Tanks fired the .30-caliber and .50-caliber machine gun. During the area search, one civilian was found to be wounded and was later medevacuated.

At 2235H, while in support of elements of 1/9 at (AT 905548), tank crewmen observed two VC wading in opposite directions across the river in the vicinity of (AT 901548) and (AT 899542). These sightings were verified by xenon infrared and white light. Tanks fired 90 mm HE and .30-caliber machine gun with a direct hit being observed on one of the VC. One VC (KBGF) confirmed.

4 August: At 1035H, while in support of elements of 2/9 at (BT 008580), tanks received sniper fire from a house at (BT 008584). The house was destroyed by 90 mm cannon fire. Enemy casualties were not determined, as no search of the area was conducted.

5 August: At 1445H and again at 1700H, while in support of D/1/9 at (AT 903545), tanks received enemy fire from the vicinity of (AT 898542) and (AT 902538). Tanks returned 90 mm cannon and .30-caliber machine gun fire, resulting in two VC (KBGF) confirmed and two VC (KBGF) probable.

At 1734H, while in support of A/1/9, tanks fired at an unknown number of VC approaching A/1/9 positions. A heavy volume of caliber

.30-caliber machine gun fire was directed into the VC before they broke contact, resulting in five VC (KBGF) confirmed.

7 August: At 1945, while at (AT 982624) in support of elements of 1/9, four VC ran from a tree line into a house at (AT 984623). The house was immediately destroyed by 90 mm HE fire. Results unknown as the area was not searched.

8 August: At 1615H, while in support of F/2/9 at (BT 019558), twenty to thirty VC were observed wearing pith helmets and khaki uniforms with blanket rolls proceeding in a column in an easterly direction from (BT 022550). Tanks immediately fired a heavy volume of 90 mm HE and observed direct hits and good area coverage. Results: twelve VC (KBGF) confirmed.

9 August: At 1345H, two M67A2 flame tanks in support of 1/9 burned fields of fire at (AT 900545).

10 August: At 1000H, while in support of C/1/9 at (AT 985606), six VC were observed with weapons at (AT 987607). Tanks fired 90 mm HE, WP, canister, and .50-caliber and .30-caliber machine guns with good target coverage resulting in two VC (KBGF) confirmed and four VC (KBGF) probable.

At 1940H, while in support of C/1/9 at (AT 954553), infantry began receiving sniper fire from an estimated three VC at (AT 958558). Tanks returned 90 mm HE and WP, and enemy firing ceased. Area could not be searched because of intervening river.

11 August: At 1306H, a Company B tank detonated an antivehicular mine estimated to contain 50 to 75 pounds of TNT at (AT 986583). The tank was moderately damaged; there were no casualties. Repairs were made on the spot, and at 1700H, the tank proceeded under its own power to Company B CP.

At 1701H, on Liberty Road at (AT 968596), it detonated another antivehicular mine estimated to be approximately the same size as the previous mine. Since this mine was detonated on the same side as the first mine, damage was not extensive to the suspension system. Repairs were started immediately.

At 1720H, heavy small-arms fire was received from a tree line at (AT 967596). In addition to the disabled tank, there were at this time two M67A2 flame tanks, an M-51 VTR, and one M48A3 gun tank on Liberty Road. All tanks returned a heavy volume of 90 mm HE, canister, and .30-caliber machine gun fire before contact was broken. A search of the enemy position failed to reveal any enemy casualties. The disabled tank was then towed to B Company CP without further incident.

12 August: At 1120H, while in support of C/1/9 at (AT 977597), three VC were observed running into a tree line at (AT 977597). The VC were immediately taken under fire with .50-caliber and .30-caliber machine gun, resulting in two VC (KBGF) probable and one VC (WBGF) probable.

13 August: At 0800H, elements of D/1/9 acting as road security at (AT 988635) received sniper fire and observed two VC at (AT 989635). A tank arrived on the scene and expended three hundred rounds of .30 caliber into the VC position. Results unknown as area was not searched.

14 August: At 0955H, while in support of elements of 1/9 at (AT 904549), two VC were observed with weapons at (AT 899549). Tanks fired the .30-caliber machine gun, resulting in two VC (KBGF) confirmed.

At 2045H, while in support of elements of 1/9 at (AT 978606), tanks received approximately fifty rounds of automatic small-arms fire from an enemy position at (AT 980601). Tanks returned 90 mm HE, WP, and .30-caliber machine gun fire. Infantry searched the area with negative results.

16 August: At 1910, while in support of H/2/1 at (BT 024558), fifty to sixty VC were observed at (BT 023535) moving in a column from east to west. Tanks fired 90 mm HE and WP with excellent target coverage. Area not searched because of intervening river. No casualty assessment made.

17 August: At 1645H, while in support of elements of 2/1 at (AT 992578), a section of tanks went to the assistance of an LVT that had been disabled by a mine and was receiving heavy small-arms fire. Tanks expended a heavy volume of 90 mm HE, WP, and .50- and .30-caliber machine gun fire into the enemy position. Results undetermined as area was not searched.

At 1705H, while in support of C/1/9 at (AT 976543), infantry and tanks received a heavy volume of small-arms fire from an enemy position at (AT 977537) and (AT 972535). Tanks returned a heavy volume of 90 mm HE, canister, and .30-caliber machine gun fire, resulting in fifteen VC (KBGF) confirmed. Tanks assisted in the capture of ten VCC and three VCS. Among the documents taken from the prisoners were maps, which outlined forward Marine command post position.

19 August: At 2045, while in support of elements of 1/9 at (AT 904678), tanks received approximately eight to ten rounds of 60 mm mortar fire from enemy positions at (AT 891548); tanks returned 90 mm cannon fire, and the mortaring ceased.

20 August: At 1641, while in support of G/1/9 at (AT 992576), tank crewmen discovered parts of Vietnamese bodies, i.e., foot and intestines, at the above coordinates. Nearby was a crater in an old tank track that apparently was caused by an explosive device. The man appeared to have been blown up by planting a mine. Found near the body were one carbine clip, three Chicom grenades, one document, and pieces of web gear and a pack. One VC (KBGF) confirmed.

On August 20, Robert Adcock received a Purple Heart.

21 August: At 1100, while in support of A/1/9 at (AT 960552), tanks fired 90 mm HE into a bunker complex at (AT 966522), where movement had been observed by an aerial observer. The aerial observer adjusted the tank's fire and reported direct hits but gave no casualty estimate.

22 August: At 1240H, two rounds of sniper fire were received in the B Company CP at (AT 962611). Tanks in the CP fired .30-caliber machine gun fire into the enemy position at (AT 958606). At 221445H, another round was received from the same location. Tanks returned 90 mm cannon fire with good target coverage. The firing ceased; no assessment of casualties was made.

23 August: At 2120H, while in support of G/2/1 at (AT 978563), tank crewmen observed two VC dragging a boat from a tree line at (AT 977567). Tanks expended a heavy volume of .50-caliber and .30-caliber machine gun fire. A secondary explosion was observed. The boat was destroyed, and two VC (KBGF) were confirmed.

24 August: At 0950H, while in support of elements of 1/9 and 3/9 located at (AT 933527), infantry observed enemy movement at (AT 907527), (AT 911532), and (AT 910531). Infantry marked target with 81 mm WP. Tanks fired 90 mm HE. Results unknown as area was not searched due to intervening river.

At 1030H, while in support of G/2/1 at (AT 983546), tanks received automatic small-arms fire from an enemy position at (AT 976545). Seven fully dressed and equipped VC were observed and taken under fire. Tanks fired the 90 mm cannon and both the .50-caliber and .30-caliber machine guns with good target coverage, resulting in five VC (KBGF) confirmed, two VC (KBGF) probable, and one house destroyed.

We'll Wait on the Other Side

by Jerry White

["This story is reprinted from the USMC Vietnam Tankers Association's *Sponson Box* magazine, volume 12, no. III, July–September 2009. Edited for form, not content.]

It was August of 1966, and I was with Bravo Company, 3d Tanks, on Hill 55 (Da Nang).

It sure is a funny thing about memories. Some things are as clear as yesterday, and others have faded. I say that because I remember the action but not my tank crewmates. That is except for tank commander Second Lieutenant Alvarado. He had just been promoted from Gunny.

We were out on a search-and-destroy mission with a platoon of Grunts. There were three tanks including ours, and we had just come out of the jungle to a huge rice paddy. I would say the flooded paddy was at least a 1/2 mile wide. On the other side was a wooded area. Lieutenant Alvarado told the ground-pounder sergeant that we would have to take our tanks across the paddy at a high rate of speed so we wouldn't get bogged down. He said, "Once we get there, we will wait for you and your men to catch up."

Off we went with our engines roaring. Since I was the loader, I got to sit on top of the turret with the TC. What happened next is burned in my memory: When we arrived on the other side of the rice paddy and moved into the wooded area, to my amazement, I saw men in uniforms running every which way. We had driven into a North Vietnamese campsite!

Well of course, all hell broke loose. Three tanks have a lot of firepower as we know. All of our guns were blazing, the .30 caliber, the .50 caliber, and our 90 mm main gun.

As loader, my training really kicked in as I kept loading and our gunner and TC kept firing.

After what seemed hours . . . but was only a few minutes . . . the gunfire ceased as quickly as it had begun. I went up topside and saw our Marine infantry had caught up with us and they were busy securing the area. There were several dead NVA torn apart throughout the campsite.

Looking back on it over forty-two years later, it seems like a dream. I know it really happened. I find myself wondering if there is anybody else out there who was also a part of that mission. None of our guys were hurt that day. One thing happened as a result of that battle: our tank became known as "Ho Chi Minh's Nightmare."

The next month I was sent back to the world, as it was the end of my enlistment.

(Former) PFC Jerry White, USMC

Lake Havasua City, AZ
Retiredqman@yahoo.com

At 241100H, while in support of elements of 1/9 at (AT 973566), tank crewmen observed two boats on the south bank of the Song Thu Bon. Tanks destroyed the boats with 90 mm fire.

26 August: At 0945H, while in support of D/1/9 at (AT 962577), tank crewmen found a 105 mm round rigged as a booby trap. The round was destroyed in place by engineers.

At 2145H, while in support of G/2/1, a tank detonated an antivehicular mine at (AT 996569), causing moderate damage to the tank's suspension system. Three infantrymen were WIA and medevacuated because of the mine.

29 August: At 1130H, while in support of B/1/9 located at (AT 902544), tank 90 mm cannon fire destroyed four boats and two buildings at (AT 899539). Fire mission was requested by infantry.

At 1150H, while in support of elements of the 1st Marines (AT 980609), tanks fired 90 mm canister in support of a passing helicopter that was receiving small-arms fire from an enemy position at (AT 983607). Results unknown, area not searched.

At 2245H, while in support of elements of 1/9 at (AT 902543), tank crewmen heard movement just outside their wire and fired one round 90 mm canister. Results undetermined, area not searched.

Operation MACON

The 2d Platoon of Company B remained DS 3/9 throughout the month of August on Operation MACON. Tank action in this area accounted for eighty-eight VC (KBGF) confirmed, twelve (KBGF) probable, and three VC (WBGF) confirmed.

3 August 1966: At 1815H, while in support of elements of 3/9 at (AT 926526), tanks received three rounds of sniper fire from a position at (AT 934525). Tanks fired into the position with both 90 mm cannon and of .50-caliber machine gun fire. A direct hit was observed on one VC. Tank crewmen continued to observe the enemy position for another ten minutes, when three more VC ran from the area. They were

taken under fire, and again a direct hit was observed. Two VC (KBGF) confirmed and two VC (KBGF) probable.

5 August 1966: At 0845H, while in support of elements of 3/9 at (AT 903546), Company B tanks received sniper fire from the vicinity of (AT 898542). Tanks returned 90 mm cannon fire with good target coverage. Tank crewmen were unable to determine VC casualties as the area was not searched because of an intervening river.

7 August 1966: At 1040H, while in support of elements of 3/9 at (AT 948488), nine VC were observed in the vicinity of (AT 945501) carrying rifles. Tanks fired 90 mm HE and WP with good target coverage. Observed three direct hits resulting in three VC (KBGF) confirmed.

At 1135H, while at (AT 954494), three VC were observed at (AT 954505). Tank crewmen fired two rounds of 90 mm HE but were unable to determine results.

At 1140H, while at (AT 948948), four VC were observed at (AT 946502) wearing green uniforms. Tanks fired 90 mm HE and observed four direct hits resulting in four VC (KBGF) confirmed.

At 1250H, while at (AT 954495), two VC were observed in a tree line at (AT 946502); tanks fired 90 mm HE into the area. Unable to determine enemy casualties as area was not searched.

8 August 1966: At 0905H, a tank detonated an M-26 grenade rigged as a mine at (AT 967493). There was no damage to the vehicle and no friendly casualties.

At 0915H, while in support of K/3/9 at (AT 868498), two VC were observed with rifles in a tree line on the riverbank at (AT 865508). Tanks fired 90 mm HE cannon and .50-caliber machine gun. Observed direct hits with bodies being blown into the air. Two VC (KBGF) confirmed.

At 0930H, while in support of K/3/9 at (AT 868498), a VC dressed in a light-green uniform at (AT 863499) was observed carrying a rifle. Tanks fired 90 mm HE and observed a direct hit. One VC (KBGF) confirmed.

At 1000H, while in support of K/3/9 at (AT 868498), six to eight VC were observed, two of whom were wearing green uniforms. The VC were moving along a trench line to a bunker at (AT 863499). Tanks fired 90 mm HE and observed direct hits with one large secondary explosion being noted. Six VC (KBGF) confirmed.

At 1015H, while in support of K/3/9 at (AT 868498), two VC were observed wearing green uniforms standing in a trench line at (AT 862498). Tank crewmen fired 90 mm HE and observed bodies blown into the air. Two VC (KBGF) confirmed.

At 1017H, while in support of K/3/9 at (AT 868498), one VC was observed crawling along the riverbank at (AT 864497). Tanks fired 90 mm HE, resulting in one VC (KBGF) probable.

At 1030H, while in support of K/3/9 at (AT 868498), eight to ten VC were observed in green uniforms moving through a tree line at (AT 864499). Tanks fired 90 mm HE but were unable to determine results because of intervening river.

At 1615H, while in support of K/3/9 at (AT 868499), two VC were observed with rifles running into a tree line at (AT 862499). Tanks fired 90 mm HE and observed direct hits resulting in two VC (KBGF) confirmed.

9 August 1966: At 1105H, while in support of elements of 3/9 at (AT 936504), two VC were observed wearing green uniforms and carrying weapons at (AT 936504). Tanks fired 90 mm HE and observed a direct hit on one VC; the other VC ran into a tree line. One VC (KBGF) confirmed.

At 1225H, while in support of elements of 3/9 at (AT 936506), six to eight VC were observed in a tree line at (AT 934514). Tank crewmen kept the area under surveillance for approximately ten minutes, when two more VC wearing black clothing and carrying weapons appeared. Tanks immediately fired 90 mm HE into the tree line but were unable to determine results as the area was not searched.

At 1830H, while in support of M/3/9 at (AT 925526), tanks received approximately ten rounds of small-arms fire from an enemy position at (AT 936524). Tanks returned 90 mm WP, .50- and .30-caliber machine gun fire, resulting in one VC (KBGF) probable.

16 August 1966: At 1600H, while in support of I/3/9, tanks received five rounds of sniper fire from (AT 909529). Tanks returned 90 mm HE, .50- and .30-caliber machine gun fire, resulting in six VC (KBGF) confirmed.

18 August 1966: At 1030H, while in support of elements of 3/9 at (AT 993538), tank crewmen observed eight VC in green uniforms with packs moving along a tree line at (AT 993533). Tanks fired 90 mm HE with good target coverage resulting in five VC (KBGF) confirmed and three VC (KBGF) probable.

19 August 1966: At 0915H, while in support of elements of 3/9 at (AT 904543), tank crewmen observed four VC with weapons and packs at (AT 891548). Tanks expended one round of 90 mm WP and fifty rounds of .50-caliber machine gun fire. A direct hit was observed, which resulted in four VC (KBGF) confirmed.

At 0930H, while in support of elements of 3/9 at (AT 904543), tank crewmen observed two VC with weapons and packs at (AT 891548). Tanks fired 90 mm WP resulting in two VC (KBGF) confirmed.

20 August 1966: At 1315H and again at 1330H, while in support of L/3/9 at (AT 881514), infantry units received one rifle grenade and automatic small-arms fire from an enemy position in the vicinity of (AT

881514). Tanks with infantry assaulted the enemy position, delivering a heavy volume of 90 mm cannon and .50- and .30-caliber machine gun fire. The position was overrun; no assessment of casualties.

At 1300H, while in support of M/3/9 at (AT 873524), infantry and tank units received rifle grenade and small-arms fire from an enemy position in the vicinity of (AT 872534). Tanks returned a heavy volume of 90 mm cannon, .50- and .30-caliber machine gun fire resulting in fifteen VC (KBGF) confirmed and the capture of one Russian rifle, assorted small-arms ammunition, grenades, packs, and documents.

At 1830H, while in support of elements of 3/9, tanks received twenty rounds of small arms from (AT 876512). Tanks returned 90 mm HE, and the firing ceased. Results could not be determined because of intervening river.

At 1930H, while in support of elements of 3/9 at (AT 903548), tanks and infantry began receiving a heavy volume of small arms and mortar fire from enemy positions at (AT 905549) and (AT 895548). Tanks returned a heavy volume of 90 mm canister, HE, and WP. Numerous secondary explosions were observed. A search of the area was not made as the tanks were in the process of returning to the north across the Song Vu Gia. Results undetermined.

At 1940H, while in support of elements of 3/9 (AT 925526), tanks received small-arms fire, rifle grenades, and two rounds of 60 mm mortar from enemy position in the vicinity of (AT 925518). Tanks returned 90 mm cannon, .50- and .30-caliber machine gun fire, resulting in six VC (KBGF) confirmed. One secondary explosion was observed 60 meters in front of the tank position.

22 August 1966: At 1815H, while in support of elements of 3/9 at (AT 929517), tanks received small-arms fire from a position at (AT 920514), (AT 924512), and (AT 920512). Tanks returned 90 mm HE, and the firing ceased. A search of the area failed to reveal any enemy casualties.

24 August 1966: At 1405H, while in support of elements of 3/9 at (AT 931492), tanks received four rounds of sniper fire from an enemy position in the vicinity of (AT 936493). Tanks returned a heavy volume of and .30-caliber machine gun fire, and the sniping squad ceased. Results could not be determined.

26 August 1966: At 2145H, while in support of elements of 3/9 at (AT 908507), tank crewmen observed ten armed VC at (AT 908505). The VC were observed by using the xenon infrared light initially, then the white light was used. Tanks fired a heavy volume of .30-caliber machine gun fire into the VC, resulting in three VC (KBGF) probable and three VC (WBGF) confirmed.

27 August 1966: At 1110H, while in support of elements of 3/9 at (AT 905520) as a blocking force, tanks fired 90 mm HE at an unknown number of uniformed VC at (AT 905528). Infantry verified eight VC (KBGF) confirmed.

At 2115H, while in support of elements of 3/9 at (AT 908500), a column of approximately twenty VC were observed carrying packs at (AT 908502). A heavy volume of .30-caliber machine gun fire was fired into the column with good target coverage. Two VC (KBGF) confirmed.

28 August 1966: At 1540H, while in support of elements of 3/9 at (AT 910528), tank crewmen observed six VC at (AT 910531). Tanks fired the .30-caliber machine gun as the VC moved into a tree line. One VC was (WBGF) confirmed.

Again at 1700H, while in the same position, a boat was sighted crossing the river at (AT 906525). Tanks fired 90 mm HE but were unable to determine results.

29 August 1966: At 1315H, while in support of elements of 3/9 at (AT 957494), tank crewmen observed six VC, three of whom were wearing black uniforms and carrying a stretcher; two were wearing

khaki uniforms and carrying rifles. The other was wearing a green uniform. Tanks fired 90 mm HE and observed a direct hit resulting in one VC (KBGF) confirmed and two VC (KBGF) probable.

At 2215H, while in support of elements of 3/9 at (AT 903502), tank crewmen observed fifteen to twenty VC crossing a road at (AT 905495). Tanks fired 90 mm HE, canister, and .30-caliber machine gun fire resulting in one VC (KBGF) confirmed. Found in the immediate area were a pack, camouflage parachute, netting, Ho Chi Minh shoes, 10 pounds of rice, and tobacco.

30 August 1966: At 0150, while in support of elements of 3/9 at (AT 908495), tank crewmen observed eight to ten VC in a rice paddy at (AT 906496). Tanks fired 90 mm HE and .30-caliber machine gun with good target coverage. Area partially searched, four VC (KBGF) confirmed and one female VCC apprehended.

CO Company C: Capt. J. H. Gary III
Location and Operations Summary: Da Nang (AT 946762)

2 August 1966: At 1705H, the 3d Platoon arrived at Dong Ha to support the 4th Marines on Operation HASTINGS.

Operation HASTINGS

by Ric Langley

In August 1966, Dong Ha, Vietnam, was changing from a small outpost a few miles south of the DMZ to a major combat base in Northern I Corps. In the days after the 1st Platoon arrived, the base began to grow by leaps and bounds. Large transport aircraft were coming and going, nonstop, dropping off either troops or combat supplies. Trucks ran continually from the Cua Viet River port in Dong Ha. Landing craft were used to transport cargo from the ships offshore and up the Cua Viet River to Dong Ha. Everybody recognized that something big was in the wind.

The 1st Platoon set up its command post and went about doing its part. Things were extremely different than they had been in Phu Bai. No more hot chow or hot showers and no tents to sleep in. We had a single tent for our CP, and that was it. We lived on our tanks, kind of like an ugly motor home. At night we were assigned a spot on the base perimeter. Each guy on the crew stood a two-hour watch starting at 10:00 at night and ending at about 6:00 in the morning. Each night your watch would move up one spot. Only occasionally was there any activity, and this amounted to minor probing, which was probably just curious kids.

There seemed to be no end to the number of Tanker lessons that came my way almost every day. A few of these include never sleep under a tank hatch when it rains; it will leak. If you hang your pistol on an end connector and forget it, the tank will drive away, grinding up your pistol between the track and the sprocket and you will owe the Marine Corps $61.00 for a new pistol. You can drink hot beer and actually enjoy it and wish you had more. This list grows with every passing day, and as time goes by, the lessons become more and more serious.

(Picture of LCU in Cua Viet river port by author)

As expected, our driver rotated shortly after we moved north, making me the permanent loader, and Rodriguez the driver. Driving just was not Rodriguez's bag. He had improved, but he was by no stretch of the imagination proficient.

Early one morning after a night of heavy rain and cold, we had just made our way back to the CP when we were told that C-12 and another tank would be moving to Cam Lo to train the Grunts (infantry) on what to do and what not to do when operating with tanks in the field. After loading our gear on the tank, we pulled in behind the jeep that was to lead the small convoy west along Highway 9 to the base at Cam Lo. The jeep, C-12, two trucks, and the other tank made our way down the road, and in what seemed like a very short time, we were pulling through the barbed wire gate at Cam Lo. I jumped down to ground-guide Rodriguez, making sure not to walk directly in front of him. I guided Rodriguez to the other side of the outpost where we were to take up our position on the perimeter while Sergeant Jones headed for the Grunt CP to find out exactly what they had in mind for us. We parked the tank, and the gunner and I started making up a range card with all the pertinent information. Rodriguez made himself busy checking track, suspension, and engine and transmission fluid levels. Sergeant Jones returned after a short time with the scoop. Every day we were to take a group of Grunts and pass along information that would help to keep them safe when working with tanks in the field. They were taught how to use the intercom (tank/infantry or "TI" phone) mounted on the rear fender (if it hadn't been torn off), to stay back behind the center of the turret when the tank is firing, to make sure the TC can see you before you try to climb up on the tank, and a lot more. The last thing we wanted was to be running over or blowing away our own troops, so we took this training very seriously.

At the end of the training session, we would ask for questions, and there was always a ton of them. The number one most asked question was how they could get transferred into tanks; they were tired of all the ground pounding. The Grunts were allowed to climb on and into the tanks and were very impressed by the iron monsters. All in all, it was good for both the tank crews and the Grunts, and it did help later on when we began operations.

While in Cam Lo we got word that more tanks had moved into the Dong Ha area; the more the merrier. Cam Lo was quiet with very little activity, just short patrols and listening posts at night. We stood our two-hour watch at night, did our training during the day, and played cards, read, or napped the rest of the time—really boring. It was so quiet it was spooky. Everybody was just waiting for the other shoe to drop. Rumors ran like wildfire through the ranks of the troops at the small outpost. On any given day, you could hear anything from the war was over and we were going home to we would be charging across the

DMZ and invading North Vietnam. At last the word came down; the Marines in and around Dong Ha would move north into the area just south of the DMZ, later to be called "Leatherneck Square," to conduct Operation HASTINGS. Selected units would be inserted by helicopter into the area where the operation would kick off, while others, us included, would move north by ground, hopefully pushing the NVA into the waiting forces.

Recon teams had been working the area for several months prior to the Marine buildup. The reconnaissance had shown extensive NVA activity in and around the DMZ. The troops were not Viet Cong but well trained and equipped uniformed North Vietnamese Army personnel. There was no doubt they were not there on a Sunday picnic.

Sergeant Jones briefed us the day before we were to jump off on what our role in the operation would be. The tone in his voice indicated that this was serious business. At the end of his briefing, Sergeant Jones turned to me and said that I would be doing the driving and Rodriguez would be loading. This came as a total surprise; we had no clue that he was going to make this change. Now I had to step up to do a job even I wasn't sure that I could handle, along with facing my first combat action. No pressure here!

On that sunny morning, we mounted up as many Grunts as we could safely carry on the tanks and headed north; we dismounted the Grunts and began sweeping the villages just north of the river.

Recon had reported enemy bunker and tunnel construction going on in the area during the last week. Several hours later, with all the villages cleared and no contact except for being cussed at by a couple of old ladies and being told we were "number fucking 10" by some kids, we stopped long enough to check fluid levels and grab some C-rats. We had destroyed the bunkers and tunnels that we came across by simply driving over them with the tanks.

With the Grunts mounted up again, we turned north and headed down a narrow road that dwindled into a trail and then to a footpath with jungle close in on both sides and large tree branches overhead. There were signs of enemy presence everywhere we looked. Being the lead tank, Sergeant Jones was starting to become concerned about our inability to maneuver on the narrow path and passed his concern along to the Grunt commander. Just as the decision was being made to turn back and find a more desirable route, there was a large explosion directly over the third tank in the column. The tank's radio antenna had tripped a 105 mm artillery round hung in a tree over the path. Immediately, the jungle to our front and right flank erupted in small-arms and machine gun fire. The Grunts were off and behind the tanks in a heartbeat, with their rifles answering the enemy barrage. Hand grenades were flying back and forth like the Grunts and Charlie were playing catch with each other.

The tanks were able to swing their guns toward the incoming fire and commenced to pound the jungle with canister rounds. Our tank was firing at the muzzle flashes directly to our front. I could not believe the amount of destruction those canister rounds could inflict. Small trees, branches, leaves, dirt and—I am sure—body parts flew everywhere. This intense fighting went on for what seemed like hours, but in reality, it lasted only a few minutes before the enemy fire slacked off and the NVA slipped away, knowing they could not defeat the tanks head-on.

Charlie had made a critical mistake. If the ambush had been placed just a few hundred yards down the path, the tanks would not have been able to traverse their 90 mm guns and therefore would not have been able to bring their massive firepower to bear on the enemy. Lessons were taught to both sides by this small skirmish.

Four Grunts had been killed and several more were wounded by the booby trap in the tree, so we had to find a suitable LZ to bring in medevac choppers. We backtracked to an area on top of a small rise that had a large open clearing for an LZ and called in the medevacs.

Mortar rounds started falling almost as soon as we pulled up on the rise, followed shortly by sniper fire. Charlie was not going to let us get away that easily; he just changed his tactics.

Our machine guns were barking at everything that even looked like it might be a bad guy. We fired several HE rounds just to let them know we had the ability to "reach out and touch" them if they screwed up and showed their position. The sniper fire stopped, and the mortars slacked enough that the choppers were able to get in and get the dead and wounded loaded on board. They lifted off and were out of there without a problem. As the choppers lifted off, we were already getting ready to move out. We had stumbled into a much larger force than we would be able to handle on our own and were ordered to move south back along the route we had taken north that morning.

We would soon learn later this was a huge mistake. Following our tracks, we moved south at a very fast pace, with the Grunts holding on for dear life. After not more than forty-five minutes' travel time, there were again more explosions at the front of the column; this time, the lead tank and the second tank in line had both run over and detonated mines. Charlie had come in after we had passed this way earlier and planted the mines in our original tracks. Luckily for us, he didn't set another ambush along with the mines. Those lessons kept popping up.

One tank was not damaged too badly and could be repaired in the field. The second did not fare so well and would need assistance from a retriever to make it back to Dong Ha. With the sun sinking low in the sky, there was no time for the retriever to make it to our position before nightfall. Our only alternative was to set up a perimeter around the damaged tanks, get them repaired as much as possible, and hold out until morning. We used our tanks to knock down the grass and brush so we would have better fields of fire while the Grunts dug in. It was a tight perimeter with the tanks close together in the hopes that Charlie would think twice before trying to overrun our position.

Throughout the night we could hear movement just outside our lines, but aside from some mortars and some probing, it was a quiet night in the small encampment with very little sleep. First thing in the morning, 1st Platoon was ordered to load two squads of Grunts on board our tanks and head for Cam Lo. Bravo Company tanks would wait with the remaining Grunts for the retriever to arrive and then tow the disabled tank back to Dong Ha. We were more than ready at first light to move out and made it back to Cam Lo without further contact with the enemy before noon. I didn't even get another bath while fording the river. Learned that lesson!

Without much said, we set about doing the things that Tankers do after an excursion into the field. Guns were cleaned, suspension was lubed, fluids were checked, spent ammo was replaced, and all the things it takes to make the tank ready to move out when called. By late afternoon we were all squared away and sat down to have some chow. It seemed funny to me at the time, but our talk did not turn to the day before. The only talk about the operation was what we should do differently in the future. I would notice this behavior the rest of the time I was in Vietnam. There was never a lot of conversation about what happened during times of combat. "How can we make it safer for the tank crews when faced with going into combat?" was the only question asked.

After chow, Sergeant Jones was called to the CP, who returned a short time later with a huge smile on his face. He had, along with our gunner and several other members of the 1st Platoon, received their flight dates. The next morning they would catch the first convoy back to Dong Ha. One thing for sure, I would no longer be the newest guy in the platoon, which felt great. I was finally feeling at home. I was doing the job that I wanted to do and was confident I could do it well. I would, at last, be with crewmates that were going to be around for some time. I had faced combat for the first time and the fear that went with it. I was probably more afraid of what I would do when put in a combat situation than I was of the actual combat. Would I freeze or panic and not perform the way I should? There is no arguing the fact that I was scared to death, but I was able to overcome that fear and focus on what I had to do. I knew that people's lives depended on me to control my fear and drive that tank. I would carry that fear with me, not only for myself, but for every member of our platoon, every time we would go into harm's way. It's true: if someone tells you that they were in combat and they were not afraid, it's a lie. I had found my "home away from home" in Vietnam. It was on the back of C-12, wherever she might be parked, and that would be in a lot of places.

7 August 1966: At 0715, a tank detonated an M16A1 antipersonnel mine in the vicinity of (YD 77161). There was no damage to the vehicle or casualties.

12 August 1966: From 121730H to 131730H, while in support of elements of 2/4, tanks fired five H&I missions into coordinates (YD 030695), (YD 001567), (YD 993569), and (YD 116730) with good area coverage. Tanks were credited with fifty VC (KBGF) probable. This estimate was made by an air observer on station.

13 August 1966: From 131730H, while in support of elements of 2/4, tanks fired three H&I missions into coordinates (YD 9859), (YD 9956), and (YD 1070). H&I missions fired into coordinates (YD 1070) were fired to assist an ARVN outpost that was under siege. Results of these missions accounted for seven VC (KBGF) confirmed, thirty-five VC (KBGF) probable, and the destruction of three recoilless rifles.

On 13 August, 4th Marines Forward CP was established at Dong Ha. The C., Colonel Cereghino, ordered his 1/4 up from Phu Bai, and 2/4 headed west along Route 9 toward the Rockpile. On 17 August, 2/4 was about halfway before taking heavy fire from Hill 252 from the south. The 2/4's CO, Lieutenant Colonel Bench called in artillery and air, but the stubborn enemy could not be budged. He called on tank support from Cam Lo. "When they arrived, the two M-48 behemoths fired point-blank at the enemy positions. This support finally allowed the infantry to capture the hill the next day. The Marines then continued on and established a night defensives perimeter north of the Rockpile" (SF-EM).

14 August 1966: From 141520H to 151530H, while in support of elements of 2/4, tanks fired four H&I missions from the Cam Lo area. Enemy casualties were not assessed.

21 August 1966: From 210001H to 212400H, tanks in support of elements of the 4th Marines fired ten H&I missions into grid squares (YD 2062) and (YD 0869). A total of 325 rounds of 90 mm HE were fired on these missions. Numerous secondary explosions were observed.

ALVARADO, JOSE J.

Synopsis:
The President of the United States takes pleasure in presenting the Silver Star Medal to Jose J. Alvarado (1259372), Staff Sergeant, U.S. Marine Corps, for conspicuous gallantry and intrepidity in action while serving with Company C, 3d Tank Battalion, 3d Marine Division (Rein.), FMF, in connection with combat operations against the enemy in the Republic of Vietnam on August 20, 1966. By his courage, aggressive fighting spirit and steadfast devotion to duty in the face of extreme personal danger, Staff Sergeant Alvarado upheld the highest traditions of the Marine Corps and the United States Naval Service.

Home Town: San Juan, Puerto Rico

23 August 1966: At 0620H, while DS elements of 1/4 in the Cam Lo area, C Company commander departed his CP with fifteen M48A3 gun tanks, one M-51 VTR, four Ontos, and a reinforced company of infantry (A/1/4). The plan called for this completely mechanized unit to conduct a sweep to the north along Route B. During this operation, they received 57 mm recoilless fire from an enemy position at (YD 143729). Tanks destroyed the 57 mm recoilless rifle plus a Russian

machine gun with 90 mm cannon fire. Seven VC (KBGF) as a result of this action. Two tank crewmen were WIA during this engagement. On returning, a tank detonated an antivehicular mine consisting of approximately 60 pounds of TNT encased in a wooden container. There was moderate damage to the tank's suspension system. While halted for repairs, tanks received ten to twenty rounds of mortar fire. One tank crewman was WIA during this action, nonmedevac.

24 August 1966: From 24001H to 251800H, while DS 1/4 at (YD 969577), tanks and infantry received a heavy volume of caliber .50 machine gun fire from an enemy position in the vicinity of (YD 969563). Tanks fired a heavy volume of 90 mm cannon fire into the enemy position, silencing the machine gun. Exact enemy casualties were not assessed. In addition, two H&I missions were fired into (YD 953607) and grid squares (YD 9854), (YD 9954), and (YD 9953). At 1600H, a tank detonated an antivehicular mine at (YD 136616), causing moderate damage to the tank's suspension system. There were no casualties.

26 August 1966: At 0345H, while in defensive positions with H/3/12 and A/1/4 at (YD 110570), an attack by an estimated two hundred to three hundred North Vietnamese commenced. These NVA troops were armed with RPG-2 rocket launchers and satchel charges; the NVA troops infiltrated within 20 meters of the CP. The M-51 VTR was hit with what was believed to have been an RPG-2 rocket fired from close range. Another tank received a satchel charge in the turret, causing extensive damage. This action resulted in twenty-five NVA (KBGF) confirmed, twenty-five NVA (KBGF) probable, twenty WIA probable. In addition, numerous weapons, hand grenades, and demolitions were captured and turned into the S-2 of 1/4 for evaluation.

The following story is reprinted by permission from the USMC Vietnam Tankers Association publication the *Sponson Box* and edited by the Marine Corps Vietnam Tankers Historical Foundation for the series *Marine Corps Tanks and Ontos in the Vietnam War.*

The August 26, 1966, Attack on Cam Lo: Golf and Hotel 3/12

by Dan "Stumpy" Post and Jim Pickett

The attack on Cam Lo and its artillery batteries started about a week before the reported engagement. Hotel and Golf Batteries, 3d Battalion, 12th Marines had positions on the south side of Route 9 at Cam Lo village. Looking back, it wasn't a great location because the village provided cover and concealment to any attacking NVA forces from the north and northwest. Additionally, as 2/4 moved northwesterly, the guns were not always able to provide coverage due to the infantry unit moving beyond their maximum ranges.

To compensate, Hotel and Golf were each given a 155 towed howitzer, helping to achieve better artillery coverage for 2/4. A platoon of tanks with their 90 mm rounds was also used as artillery to supplement the 155s.

Approximately the seventeenth of August, Golf and Hotel batteries moved forward, heading west along Route 9. We set up on a small ridgeline that ran from the northeast to southwest; Route 9 was carved through the position. Golf was the easterly battery; its 155 howitzer parapet dug into the ridge. Sergeant Troester, who was section chief of gun 4, was also the 155 crew chief. Guns 3 through 6 also had parapets carved into the ridge; we started building the ammo bunkers to our rear.

We had "tangle foot" and a triple row of concertina wire in front of our guns; a company of Grunts supplemented our lines from Golf's 155 howitzer, running to the southwest connecting into the lines at Hotel Battery's location. There were two tanks (C-14) and a tank retriever (C-43) inside the lines to our left rear.

Headquarters Battery joined us on August 25, bringing mess and living quarter tents; the site became congested with tents. Our Motor T Section was used on the lines to help coverage; Marines on watch for Golf and, I think, Hotel, were manning lines to their battery fronts as well as the rear lines. I'm sure we had LPs out front, but we didn't know where. We had long days of shooting, building ammo bunkers, and night shooting H&Is along with the normal fire missions. As usual, it was exhausting work for the gun crews.

The batteries transferred one Marine from each 105 to the 155 howitzers to create another two crews. I don't know if this is the right place for this, but in August of 1966, Marines along Route 9 and north of it were pretty gung-ho. There were no antiwar sentiments that I recall. Gun 4 had Corporal Lonergan, Lance Corporal Jones, our driver, JJ Casadena, Private Botts, myself, "Stump," and I think Buder. J" and Botts were new to Nam; Jonesy was a good guy from Alabama. Lonergan was from southern Illinois and was going home in another month. I had a small reel-to-reel tape player that I would use to make tapes, sending them home and to friends "from the world." In turn, they would send me tapes of songs. It was at this location I got a tape with two very weird songs that made everyone think the world was going nuts. Those 2 songs were "They're Coming to Take Me Away Ha Ha" and "Yellow Submarine" by the Beatles. So during work parties, I always had one of those two songs playing.

We had a couple of gooks from the village that would come into our position and give haircuts. This would prove fatal to them on the twenty-sixth. On the twenty-fifth, both 155s moved forward approximately two clicks west to provide better coverage on the reverse slopes of the Razorback. The day of the twenty-fifth was like most, building ammo bunkers, shooting, and filling sandbags. The mess tents were set up; Alpha 1/4 came into our position to take over perimeter security. This evening brought mail call and hot chow, about as good as it gets in the field with the exception of "beer call." As I stood in line for chow with Rhorbach, I looked back; there was Lynwood Inman. Lyn had dated a girl that was friends with a girl I had dated in high school. I think I screamed out his name; we immediately got together and talked about "the world." I had received six newspapers from home that day, and I gave him three of them, keeping three so we could switch the next day.

That night gun 4 shot H&I fires. I took gun watch from 1:00 AM until 3:00 AM; after finishing my watch, I got my replacement up, making sure he was awake. I had been thinking a long time had passed since I "aired" out my feet. Arriving at my tent, I went to my rack, took off my pants and boots; this was something I would never do again at night in the Nam. It seemed like I had just lain down when all of a sudden, explosions went off behind our tent. I could see a red star cluster, and then a large explosion sent the tank retriever into a ball of flames. It seemed all hell had broken loose in a matter of seconds.

The crews for guns 3 and 4 were sharing a tent; after the explosions, it was chaotic getting out. Everyone was trying to get through the entrance at once; as both crews ran for the guns, we realized nobody had grabbed their M-14s; I turned around and ran toward our tent. As I made my way back, there now seemed to be rifle fire everywhere. I knew they (the enemy) were inside the wire; arriving at our tent, I grabbed all the rifles, all the web gear I could find, and ran out of the tent toward gun 4. I wasn't five feet out the door when an automatic weapon started firing at me; I hit the deck and tried to cover my head with rifles. No shit, I was scared.

It seemed like five minutes passed, but I know it was more like thirty seconds, when suddenly, there was an explosion where the rifle fire was coming from. I jumped up and ran to the gun; Jonesy was A-gunning, Lonergan was gunning, J" and Botts were loading. I moved to the parapet wall, covering our front.

Rifles were given out to everyone; as I remember, Jonesy's and Lonergan's were hanging on the shields of the 105. I started seeing green tracers coming from below our gun being fired toward our front. I started firing back, trying to stop anything from coming our way. As the battle progressed, the CO stopped at our gun, asking what I was shooting at. Almost immediately a green tracer passed through our position. I think he said to continue and cover our front.

We had Puff come on station; he started firing at the gook positions. All those red lines from the air to ground, then the buzz of bullets impacting. Everything seemed like slow motion, but it wasn't. We kept firing our 105 until we were out of ammo; as daylight arrived, the jets came in and started bombing runs to our rear. They continued all the way up, into the hills to the southwest where the gooks were trying to escape.

The enemy small-arms fire started dying out; we began carrying ammunition for the gun from the ammo dump. I know I had a rifle over one shoulder and a 105 round over the other. H-34s (helicopters) started bringing in ammo for the Grunts and taking our wounded out; the sun had risen when the last jet dumped his load on the gooks, made a pass over us, wagging his wings. Everyone started policing ammo tubes, getting ready for another attack, trying to make sense of the mess around us.

The mess tents were also "home" to the cooks; they were blown and burned. I think three cooks or mess duty Marines died there. Corporal Clark from Golf Battery had been on mess duty and was never the same again. He was a good Marine, but the war that night had taken a heavy toll on him. I can't recall how many wounded came from those tents, but I believe Clark was the only one not wounded or killed.

The gooks lay dead in weird positions; I recall one NVA soldier was running, then suddenly his midsection was missing and his chest and head lay about 10 feet away from his legs; bullets had hit the explosives on his hips, literally blowing him in two. Everyone started dragging dead NVA to an area where a bulldozer was digging a mass grave; we started throwing them in. The final count was eighty inside our lines; Lord knows how many were outside.

Picture submitted by authors. Note the C-41 Blade Tank at the upper right of the picture.

All the North Vietnamese had tied strings to their pressure points; if they were shot and still capable, the gooks would stop, tighten the string to control bleeding, and continue on. Were they taking opium? Who knows; but usually a rifle wound would take anyone to the ground. Maybe the weirdest I saw was an NVA soldier who had been shot through the head; he had stopped to bandage his wound when someone had finalized his days on earth with a few more rounds to his body.

The Golf Battery Marines on watch that night had more than eleven dead North Vietnamese in front of their fighting hole and more behind and in the hole with them. I know PFC Blain was with Lance Corporal Kowalyk; it may have been Bell or McRae, but all three were wounded, Kowalyk the worst, but he had stopped the NVA from entering the back of their hole, killing one as he tried to get to the other Marines. It was interesting because over the last few nights, Blain, and others in that position, had seen and heard movement to their front. They had tossed grenades but found nothing in the morning. That night the new lieutenant had told the holes, "If you throw a grenade, you'd better have a body out there in the morning." I recall Blain yelling, "There's a gook, there's a gook! You want a body, I've got bodies."

An eight-year-old boy had been induced to attack with these NVA soldiers; they gave him a wooden rifle with a selector. He died charging across our compound, as did the "barbers."

Golf Battery had seven wounded: Blain, Kowalyk, Hite, McCrae, Bell, Schlacter, and Lieutenant Westfall. I believe Kowalyk was awarded the Navy Cross. It was a long time before he recovered from his wounds; I also believe Lieutenant Westfall received the Bronze Star for his actions.

My buddy Inman from A-14 received the Silver Star or Navy Cross, a Purple Heart, and a trip home. I wouldn't see him again until November 10, 1985, when we went to a Marine Corps birthday party; he and I spent the whole night trying to recall August 26, 1966, and the horror of that night. Hotel Battery had three killed in action, as did Headquarters Battery. Wounded from Hotel was six, and four from Headquarters. S-2 was reduced to one person because of the losses.

The next night, at about 2300, we started receiving small-arms fire again but nothing more happened. During the morning hours of the twenty-eighth, the hole manned by the Grunts right beside Golf's gun 4 had an incoming grenade and one additional WIA. I was on gun watch at the time and immediately went forward to the parapet wall, but nothing more happened that night.

I've often wondered about the twenty-sixth, after reading the after-action reports and journal entries, why no one gave us notice; the LPs heard movement, and contact was assured. Then on the twenty-eighth, why that grenade wasn't thrown ten feet to the left of that hole? It would have been me in a big gun pit trying to escape the outcome.

Semper Fi,

Dan "Stumpy" Post (email: postdj@yahoo.com)

Jim Pickett (mail: jpickett4309@yahoo.com)

Sponson Box *Editor's Note: Stumpy was kind enough to send me a news article from* Stars and Stripes *as well as a 3d Tanks sitrep for that night. One retriever, C-43, was hit with an RPG and burned most of the night; a (gun) tank, C-14, was destroyed by a satchel charge dropped inside the turret. The tanks involved were from* C Company, 3d Tanks Battalion. *No Tankers were killed that night. A quote from Major Lavern Larson, XO, 3/12, printed in S&S said, "They have every reason to hate our artillery and tanks. All these weapons are DS Operation Prairie."*

(Excerpt from CC-3TK's, 8/66)

> 26 August 1966: At 0345H while in defensive positions with H 3/12 and A 1/4 at (YD 110570) an attack by an estimated 200 - 300 North Vietnamese commenced. These NVA troops were armed with RPG-2 rocket launchers, satchel charges, the NVA troops infiltrated to within 20 meters of the CP. The M-51 VTR was hit with what was believed to have been an RPG -2 rocket fired from close range. Another tank received a satchel charge in the turret causing extensive damage. This action resulted in 25 NVA KBGF confirmed, 25 NVA KBGF probable, 20 NVA WIA probable. In addition, numerous weapons, hand grenades and demolitions were captured and turned into the S-2 of 1/4 for evaluation.

(Excerpt from CC-3/12, 8/66)

> 26 August
>
> At approximately 0330H the Battalion (fwd) position was attacked by an enemy force of at least company strength. The attack came from the east and southeast and was obviously aimed at the FDC and the howitzers. The fact that the FDC had been moved on the previous day was probably one of the factors most favorable to our side.
>
> Initially, small arms and automatic weapons fire and numerous grenades were received by the security rifle company defending the position. A heavy volume of fire was delivered on the attacking force, while the 105mm howitzers provided self-illumination by expending 412 rounds of Illumination during the attack.
>
> In spite of the heavy fire and the commitment of a reaction squad composed of members of Headquarters Battery in order to reinforce the line, several of the attackers managed to penetrate the position, placing explosive charges in trailers and tents. Six KIA were sustained by the artillery battalion, while the infantry suffered one KIA. A total of seventy-eight bodies of members of the attacking force were counted in and around the position.

26 August 1966: From 262130H to 271800H, while DS elements of 2/4, tanks fired six H&I missions into coordinates (YD 976487), (YD 105702), (YD 120715), (YD 961500), (YD 002535), and (YD 056684). All fires were unobserved, results unknown.

30 August 1966: From 291730H to 301730H, while in support of elements of the 4th Marines on Operation PRAIRIE, tanks fired four H&I missions into (YD 056683), (YD 126743), (YD 096740), and (YD 093688). Tanks expended seventy-seven rounds 90 mm HE and one round 90 mm WP. All fires were observed; twenty VC (KBGF) probable credited by observer.

31 August 1966: From 302150H to 310500H, while in support of elements of the 4th Marines on Operation PRAIRIE, tanks fired two H&I missions into (YD 091691) and (YD 070695), expending 104 rounds of 90 mm HE and two rounds of 90 mm WP. No assessment of damage or casualties was made.

CO Company C, 1st Tanks: Capt. P. E. Byrne
Location and Operations Summary: Dong Ha

3 August 1966: At 2200H, while in support of elements of 1/1 at (BT 059640), tanks received sniper fire from a position in the vicinity of (BT 059644). Tanks returned fire with 90 mm HE, and enemy firing ceased. Results unknown as area was not searched.

5 August 1966: At 1945H, while in support of elements of 1/1 at (BT 053654), tanks fired 90 mm canister at an enemy position at (BT 052653) from which they were receiving small-arms fire. Enemy broke contact, results unknown.

7 August 1966: At 0955H at (BT 089546), a boat was found on the river's edge. The boat contained Vietnamese books, a green utility jacket, fishing nets, and other assorted items. The boat was later sunk and the items confiscated.

13 August 1966: At 1930H, while in support of elements of 1/1 at (BT 057638), approximately thirty rounds of small-arms fire were received from a VC position at (BT 057636). Tanks fired one round of 90 mm canister, and sniping ceased. Results unknown as area was not searched.

14 August 1966: At 1010H, while in support of elements of 1/1 at (BT 128633), infantry observed a man in a boat at (BT 132635). The boat was hailed to come ashore; however, the occupant maneuvered to escape. Tank 90 mm cannon fired and sank the boat. One VC (KBGF) confirmed.

At 1315H, while in support of D/1/1 at (BT 056636), tanks fired 90 mm canister into a position at (BT 053637) from which an LVT had received approximately three hundred rounds of automatic small-arms fire. Enemy fire ceased. Results unknown as area could not be searched because of intervening river.

At 1400H, while in support of elements of 1/1, a tank detonated an antitank mine at (BT 107617). There were no casualties and only moderate damage to tank,

16 August 1966: At 2215H in support of elements of 1/1 at (BT 059652), a tank received automatic small-arms fire from the northwest and east. Tanks fired 90 mm cannon into the enemy positions resulting in two VC KIA probable.

17 August 1966: At 1545H, while in support of elements of 1/1 at (BT 110657), tanks fired on a fishing boat when the boat failed to return to shore as ordered. The boat was sunk by 90 mm HE and .30-caliber machine gun fire. One VC (KBGF) confirmed, one VCC, and twelve VCS apprehended.

19 August 1966: At 1030H, while in support of elements of 1/1 at (BT 105646), a tank fired on a road suspected to have been mined; two secondary explosions were observed.

20 August 1966: At 2255H, the company CP at (BT 069713) received one hand grenade into the company CP. There were no casualties. Returned automatic small-arms fire, and the VC withdrew.

22 August 1966: At 1810H, at (BT 071698), a Company C MRC-36 radio jeep received five rounds of small-arms fire from a position at (BT 069698). Personnel in the vehicle returned twenty rounds of small-arms fire. Two USMC WIA, nonmedevac.

25 August 1966: At 2055H, while in support of elements of 1/1 at (BT 072624), tanks received approximately twenty rounds of small-arms fire from an enemy position at (BT 072625) from which they had been receiving small-arms fire. Area not searched due to darkness, results unknown.

25 August 1966: At 2010H, while in support of elements of 1/1 at (BT 072624), tanks received approximately twenty rounds of small-arms fire from an enemy position in the vicinity of (BT 092628). Tanks returned 90 mm canister fire, and the enemy fire ceased.

26 August 1966: At 1445H, while in support of D/1/1 at (BT 078663), went to the assistance of a USMC truck that was receiving small-arms fire from three houses in the vicinity of (BT 075663). Tanks crushed one house and assisted in the capture of seven VCS.

UNITED STATES MARINE CORPS HISTORY DIVISION
ORAL HISTORY INTERVIEW WRITTEN TRANSCRIPT

Interviewee's Name: S.Sgt. John J. Flynn, #1204677
Date of Interview: 13 June 1967
Conflict: Vietnam
Military Unit: 3d Tank Battalion
Duties: Tank Section Leader
Interviewer: Ma. E. J. Guthrie, 065071
Length: 00:27:00
Location of Interview: Marine Corps Recruit Depot, Parris Island, South Carolina

CD#: 1028B
Individual Completing Summary: R. A. Stewart, Lieutenant Colonel, USMC (Ret.) (AW)
Recording Format and Number of Recording: 1028B
Documents Submitted with Interview: None
Related Material: None
Classification: Unclassified
Transcription Priority: Note: The following is a verbatim transcript.

Abstract: Tank employment in both the southern and northern sectors of I Corps, RVN

Key Words: Tank, infrared, obstacles, antitank mines, RPG-2, antitank weapon

Note: This interview is a Q/A session with short questions and answers. There are no timed segments in order to maintain the flow of the discussion.

Guthrie: Sergeant Flynn, when did you first get to Vietnam?

Flynn: I arrived in Vietnam February 1966 and departed March 1967. I was attached as a tank section leader, 3d Tank Battalion both B and A Companies.

Guthrie: As a tank section leader, you have control of what?

Flynn: Depending on heavy or light section, two tanks in the light section and three tanks in the heavy section.

Guthrie: So you had two or three tanks the entire time, is that affirmative?

Flynn: Yes.

Guthrie: Where were you operating most of the time and what type of terrain?

Flynn: Personally, I operated initially in the Da Nang area, which was the first seven or eight months. Secondly, I worked with tanks in the demilitarized zone (DMZ). In the Da Nang area, the terrain was sandy on the coastal area. The wet season, we were generally road-bound, and we were placed in a better position to function in the south sectors of the Da Nang TAOR as far south as Hoi An and easy access to An Hoa. Again, the various rivers presented a problem in our initial move south. We ran into three different rivers we had to ford; our tanks couldn't go into over 4–5 feet of water. After that, various structures were put up by our engineer element, whether a pontoon or something more permanent with reinforced beams. Initially we did function as a tank platoon in this area because of the sandy type plain of the coast.

Guthrie: Did you run into rice paddies?

Flynn: Yes, I believe we passed through a number of rice paddies.

Guthrie: I would think the tank would be mired down.

Flynn: This is true, in many instances they did get mired down. Initially, through proper reconnaissance, and actual physical one if at all possible, we could then determine what paddies we could negotiate and which we couldn't. The driver would get a sense of the supportability of the ground. Dropping the tank into second (low) gear and floor boarding it was the one technique we found that worked to keep us from getting stuck.

Guthrie: When you are reconning, I know when you were in Korea you had tank reconnaissance experience, what did you look for when you'd actually go up to a rice paddy to decide if you can traverse it?

Flynn: Initial concern is the height and incline of the dike bordering a particular rice paddy. That would be an indication that would show how deep the muck and mire would go. By this I mean some rice paddies in approaching just by visually looking, you may think you can move through it simply because it was bordered with some vegetation growing in it or if you could walk through it, you could then practically determine if there is any traction available for a 52-ton tracked vehicle. Many times there'd be a semihard bottom where if you approached this and accelerated utilizing low gear, I believe it would be more beneficial, you'd find you can pass right through it without getting hung up. Again, proper retrieving and utilization of retrieving equipment such as cables and towing shackles and there was always a great need to ensure prior to moving out on any particular engagement that you had the facilities to extract yourself within your own component. If not, then the call to the rear this would involve a great many people and put them in a position to be ambushed.

Guthrie: How about up by the DMZ, what was the terrain like?

Flynn: Well, if I could use the term, as far as reconnaissance, sort of virgin territory. There was a desire by virtue of the fire team to use the tank to the fullest of its ability in this area. Generally, I found that we were road-bound again; we had to pass streams, and there were bridges that had been blown and I believe all the elements that weren't directly involved in helo operations such as antitank or any other had to depend on the engineers' capability to devise structures for passage.

Guthrie: So was it rocky, hilly, flat, sandy . . .?

Flynn: Yes, it was quite mountainous; there were paddies in the area. We were able to pass through these paddies. There were rivers and streams and forges. A tank can negotiate an incline up to 60 degrees.

Guthrie: How were your tanks employed?

Flynn: First, we were employed as we were taught, tactically with an infantry fire team most, if not all, operations.

Guthrie: Where were you attached?

Flynn: Initially a platoon with a regiment or battalion depending on the infantry commander's discretion, how he wanted to deploy the tanks.

At times, I was with a battalion or directed to operate with a company-type movement perhaps on a sweep or a block in a defensive position.

Guthrie: Offensively, how were you deployed?

Flynn: Again, depending on the operation, we might lay a base of fire for friendly forces to move on through. We were used as a blocking force for sweeping elements. We'd be used as sweeping elements at times.

Guthrie: You have shock action and firepower, do you feel this came into play? Were they (VC/NVA) shocked, or were you just another big gun to them?

Flynn: We never came up against a battalion-size enemy force. In this element, they were hesitant, I believe, to set up an ambush upon a tank with our firepower. They aren't as vulnerable as perhaps an infantry squad.

Guthrie: Were your tanks used in an artillery roll?

Flynn: Yes, that was our secondary role, as armor. We can provide a battery-type fire utilizing five tanks. During the rainy monsoon season, when we weren't able to generally move as we'd like, we were positioned at various locations using roads to gain access to these positions. We did fire in the direct and indirect capacity.

Guthrie: Who provided the fire info?

Flynn: The spotting and fire control did direct our indirect fire.

Guthrie: What fire control?

Flynn: Artillery, in conjunction with the AO and fire direction center.

Guthrie: Where you employed in any firefight to any great extent?

Flynn: Not in a massive firefight, just a defensive or harassing, just wanted to let the enemy know that we did have that capability.

Guthrie: How about your light?

Flynn: Yes, we had a white light.

Guthrie: Were you able to employ your light?

Flynn: Yes, we were able to employ both on the PPB's platoon, Platoon Patrol Base. Sometimes we were out on patrol, and a decision was made to stay overnight rather than return. The tanks played a vast role in this capacity; with this firepower and xenon infrared light, we could reach out to 1,200 meters. It would allow the infantry men to feel a little more secure. I went out in the dense brush, what they call elephant grass, moving our tanks we could push down all the high grass that runs 4–10 feet high and open fields of fire for our tanks and the infantry. The infantry men would disburse around the tank and, with the automatic capacity of our .50s and .30s, 90 mm canister rounds, and infrared and white xenon light, it provided a good amount of security.

Guthrie: How about your regular lights?

Flynn: In the northern sector in the Razorback area, there were dense caves and tunnels. We did have a discussion with the infantry commander throughout the night, flashing a white beam in various locations where suspected fire might be received. Now this wasn't large volumes fire but accurate, devastating sniper fire we were concerned with.

Guthrie: I seem to recall hearing of the deployment of lights where you actually would move around from one area to another, cut your lights, move to another area, and light up the area and move on. Were you employed in this manner?

Flynn: Actually, no, but I can understand where maximum effectiveness or desire for illumination where a tank searchlights could be employed. They teach that the searchlight was generally used in a defensive position even when varied from a light tank section operating with an infantry squad finding themselves in a defensive location overnight and again working all the way up from a platoon, company to a battalion command post whether it would be a rear command post or a forward command post. A tank works in conjunction with adjacent units at predetermined times throughout the night. On avenues of approach, though, if the communication system alerted us that there is movement, we could use a spotlight or the infrared light to search to see if there was any enemy.

Guthrie: I'd imagine it would discourage movement in an area where you had these lights.

Flynn: Yes, in my opinion it would; however, I was not actually there during times where small defensive positions were attacked by the VC. I think in the early stages, I don't think they realized we had a white searchlight. As far as the infrared light, I don't think they knew we had infrared light either.

Guthrie: What kind of countermeasures did you find the VC took? Did you find different type of antitank capability?

Flynn: I believe the countermeasures varied from what we used down south where we were confronted more with antitank mines: 50–75-pound explosives, either pressure detonated or command detonated. In my opinion, they had more materials. In the Da Nang area, they had more opportunities to procure these materials and to improvise the mines. We ran into more antitank mines and vehicular mines in the southern section.

However, in the DMZ area, we ran into less mine incidents, but the enemy had antitank weapon capability, insofar as they used the antitank weapon more profusely and more brazenly, again in my opinion. In the north they basically used RPG-2s, which is an antitank weapon; it penetrates the tank turret and hull with this weapon. They had this weapon in the north because it was the closest point of infiltration and they had difficulty bringing it to the south; or it was the North Vietnamese Army that was more equipped and better trained and they had this weapon in their immediate supply.

Guthrie: What countermeasures were more successful, the mines you would run into in the south sector or the antitank weapons?

Flynn: Oddly, the antitank weapon; the mines' damage was repairable damage. At times to the extent where the vehicle had to be sent to a facility. But the RPG-2, again, could destroy the tank because it could be penetrated. Of course, the occupants would get severely injured or killed. So I think the rocket itself is much worse than any mine incident.

Guthrie: Is this a crew-type weapon? Single-man or two-man?

Flynn: Well, it was loaded by one man and fired by (another) one man.

Guthrie: Is it similar to 3.5 rocket?

Flynn: That is correct.

Guthrie: Did you run into any large weapons like 57 mm or 106s?

Flynn: I guess on a couple of occasions tanks were fired on by a weapon larger than a 57. I don't know the caliber though.

Guthrie: But these were primarily the weapons you ran into.

Flynn: Primarily, although I do have to say on a few occasions we were mortared.

Guthrie: Were the mortars effective?

Flynn: Not as far as demolition of tanks; however, in a defensive position, in the middle of a mortar attack, crewmen tend to get into their vehicles for protection and to be able to operate it when called upon and the infantry under us.

Guthrie: Did you run into any tank obstacles?

Flynn: Yes, in the southern sector, we found many trenches that were deep and wide enough where we couldn't pass over/through them. It did appear at the time that they were intentionally put in as some of them were freshly dug. It was our belief that they were intended to tank traps and were treated as such.

Guthrie: Were they effective?

Flynn: Generally not. We had engineers with us often, and we had a dozer tank we could call on as well.

Guthrie: Did you run into them up north?

Flynn: No, personally I didn't, other than natural obstacles of which there were more than enough.

Guthrie: What about maintenance problems? Did you run into any particular problem? I realize you're not a maintenance man, on a section level you're going to feel it.

Flynn: Well, nothing major, parts were more accessible.

Guthrie: How about the terrain itself, did it call for anything special or extra?

Flynn: Generally preventative maintenance. There was nothing particular, in my opinion, that had greater maintenance problems. Generally, if there was an issue, more attention would be placed on it by the company or the higher echelon of the tank battalion.

Guthrie: Now you were in Korea, correct?

Flynn: Yes, I was.

Guthrie: What field were you in?

Flynn: I was a tank driver.

Guthrie: I would imagine you were not there long enough to be a section leader.

Flynn: No, it was my induction phase. I was a tank gunner too.

Guthrie: Do you recall how much usage is different from Korea to Vietnam?

Flynn: We . . . I didn't make the initial part of Korea; however, I've read and been told of tanks . . .

Guthrie: How about *your* experience?

Flynn: My experience was in the KoKo Ree area and later in the Mon Song Ye area, on the west coast. I was generally moving around the MLR from one site to another. At times, we didn't employ the tanks, infantry moving out and tanks later joining and giving base of fire, obtaining future sites of an MLR, or something like that.

Guthrie: Did you find tanks and infantry working together like they are now?

Flynn: No, actually not, I think tanks' role now is much more profound than it was in Korea. So far, as many times we'd pull into the MLR and expend a load of ammo at known enemy positions and consequently get return fire and we'd back off and the infantry surrounding our tank position would suffer a great many casualties. However, we're exploited more in Vietnam. We got the opportunity to pursue the enemy. I think there is much more movement, more need, and better understanding between the tank and infantry and coordination and a need for both to work much more closely together.

Guthrie: Do you find from your experience in Vietnam and earlier that you have any thoughts or recommendations?

Flynn: Well, while I was in Vietnam, a couple of us thought that a lighter-type vehicle might do a better job over there.

Guthrie: Did you have a chance to see the lighter vehicle operation in the army in Korea or Vietnam?

Flynn: Actually not, I generally worked with Marine elements.

END OF INTERVIEW

September 1966
First Antitanks
Commanding Officer: Maj. R. E. Harris
Executive Officer: Maj. M. F Manning
Operations Officer: Maj. A. J. Eagan
Logistics Officer: Capt. C. R. Vanhorn
Location and Operations Summary: Chu Lai

Company A (-) OpCon 3d Marine Division, DS 1st Marines
Company B (Rein.) DS 5th Marines; DS Chu Lai Defense Command
Company C DS 7th Marines

H&S Company CO: 1st Lt. M. H. Collier
Location and Operations Summary: Camp Pendleton, CA

CO Company A (-): Capt. D. M. Hutson
Location and Operations Summary:

On 20 September, Michael D. Roseman, corporal, age 21, Indianapolis, Indiana, while serving as an Ontos crewman with the 3d Platoon, Company A, 1st Antitank Battalion in Quang Nam Province, South Vietnam, died outright as the result of an explosion of an enemy-planted explosive device.

29–30 September: 2d Platoon, Company A (OpCon Company B) supported 1/5 during Operation MONTEREY.

CO Company B (Rein.): Capt. T. F. Dempsey
Location and Operations Summary:

4–15 September: Company B supported the 5th Marines during Operation NAPA.

CO Company C: Capt. R. J. Esposito
Location and Operations Summary:

8–16 September: Company C supported 1/7 during Operation FRESNO.

17–27 September: Company C supported 1/7 during Operation GOLDEN FLEECE.

September 1966
First Tanks
Commanding Officers: Majs. R. E. B. Palmer and J. W. Clayborne
Executive Officers: Majs. J. W. Clayborne and R. D. McKee
Operations Officers: Maj. R. D. McKee and Capt. R. G. McPherson
Logistics Officers: Maj. T. M. Bryant and Capt. G. E. Hooker
Location and Operations Summary: Hill 43 (BT 515042), Chu Lai Combat Base

During the reporting period, Companies A and B remained DS 5th and 7th Marines, respectively.

On 1 September, 2d Platoon, Company B and 2d Platoon, Company C continued to support the Chu Lai Defense Command.

On 5 September, 3d Platoon, Company B replaced 2d Platoon, Company B DS Chu Lai Defense Command.

On 7 September, Provisional Company headquarters was returned to 1st Tank Battalion.

On 16 September, Provisional Rifle Platoon and Company Headquarters provided to the Chu Lai Defense Command on 29 July 1966 remained with the Chu Lai Defense Command.

On 18 September, 1st Platoon, Company A replaced 2d Platoon, Company C DS Chu Lai Defense Command.

Company C, with two gun platoons, remains with 3d Marine Division, Da Nang TAOR.

On 29 September, the Provisional Rifle Platoon was returned to 1st Tank Battalion from the Chu Lai Defense Command.

H&S Company
1–30 September, Chu Lai Combat Base

Company A
    1–30 September: Chu Lai Combat Base DS 5th Marines.
    19–30 September: 1st Platoon DS Chu Lai Defense Command.

Alan Dance, lance corporal, age 18, New York, New York, died in a nonhostile-caused vehicle homicide accident on Friday, 16 September 1966. He was a mechanic with H&S Company, 1st Tank Battalion.

Company B
    1–30 September: Chu Lai Combat Base DS 7th Marines.
    1–5 September: 2d Platoon DS Chu Lai Defense Command.
    6–30 September: 3d Platoon DS Chu Lai Defense Command.

Company C
    1–30 September: Da Nang TAOR DS 1st Marines. AdCon 1st Tank Battalion, OpCon 3d Marine Division.
    1–18 September: 2d Platoon DS Chu Lai Defense Command.

During the reporting period, Companies A and B remained DS 5th and 7th Marines, respectively.

On 1 August 1966, 2d Platoon, Company B and 3d Platoon, Company A continued to support the Chu Lai Defense Command.

On 3 August 1966, 2d Platoon, Company C returned from the SLF, replaced 3d Platoon, Company A at the Chu Lai Defense Command. Company C, with two gun platoons, remains with the 3d Marine Division, Da Nang TAOR. A Provisional Rifle Platoon and Company Headquarters provided to the Chu Lai Defense Command

Company A supported the 5th Marines during the reporting period and reinforced by the Battalion Flame Platoon and other headquarters elements, participated in Operation COLORADO from 7 August to 21 August 1966. On that operation, tanks were used for CP security. On that operation, the 7th Marines with two gun platoons; 1st Platoon supported 1st Battalion operations on the peninsula area south of the Song Tra Bong; 3d Platoon supported 3d Battalion positions west of Route 1. Company B Headquarters and 3d Platoon, with 3d Platoon, Company A, Battalion Flame Platoon, and the Battalion Headquarters Tank Section attached participated in Operation JACKSON from 27 to 29 August 1966.

H&S CO: Maj. J. P. McGill
Location: Same as Battalion CP

COs Company A: Capts. J. C. Greene Jr. and C. R. Brabec

COs Company B: Capts. E. E. Stith and L. E. Cherico

CO Company C: Capt. F. U. Salas

September 1966
Third Antitanks
Commanding Officer: Maj. D. E. Newton
Executive Officer: Capt. D. C. Satcher
Operations Officers: WO C. C. Harris
Logistics Officer: Capt. D. C. Satcher
Location and Operations Summary: Da Nang (AT 987711)

H&S Company CO: 1st Lt. D. K. Caswell
Location and Operations Summary: Da Nang (AT 987711)

H&S Company: During the month of September, the company continued the normal functions of providing administrative and logistical support for the Ontos companies. The reaction force continued to conduct ambushes and patrols within the battalion's patrol area of responsibility. Two sweeps of the Yen Bac Village Complex were made during the month, acting on information received from the villagers of possible VC activity, with negative results.

James T. Bayne, lance corporal, age 19, El Reno, Oklahoma, died on Sunday, 18 September due to a nonhostile action, accidental homicide.

CO Company A (-) (Rein.): Capt. A. A. Compton
Location and Operations Summary: Da Nang TAOR

Company A (-) (Rein.), 1st ATBn (OpCon 3d ATBn) DS 1st Marines (Da Nang TAOR)
    1st Platoon, Company A DS 3/1
    3d Platoon, Company A DS 1/1
    1st Platoon, Company C, 3d ATBn in direct support 2/1

Company A continued DS 3d Marine Division.

The 1st Platoon remained DS 2/3. The heavy section was located on Hill 65 in support of F/2/3. The light section was located in support of G/2/3. There was no enemy contact or direct fire missions for this period; however, this platoon expended 1,416 major rounds (106 mm recoilless rifle HEP-T) on H&I fire missions with unknown results.

The 2d Platoon remained in support of 1/3 for the entire period with the heavy section supporting A/1/3 at Hai Van Pass and Hill 58 and the light section in support of D/1/3 at positions near Le My. On 17 September, seven major rounds were fired at suspected enemy movement from Le My with undetermined results. This platoon expended a total of 260 major rounds on H&I fire missions with unknown results.

The 3d Platoon continued in support of 2/26 with a light section on Hill 20 in support of G/2/26. A total of 816 .30-caliber MG rounds were fired at suspected VC positions from Hill 20 on 8 September with undetermined results. This section supported a two-day platoon patrol with a G/2/26 platoon on 26 and 27 September. Ontos on this patrol fired fifty .30-caliber MG rounds at VC snipers on 26 September with undetermined results. The 3d Platoon heavy section continued to support F/2/26 on Hills 22 and 41 with a single Ontos on each hill. The third Ontos from the heavy section remained at the platoon CP in support of H/2/26. This platoon fired a total of 731 major rounds on H&I fire missions during the month.

CO Company B: 1st Lt. S. L. Camby
Location and Operations Summary: Phu Bai TAOR

Company B DS 4th Marines (Phu Bai TAOR)
    1st Platoon, Company B DS 2/9
    2d Platoon, Company B DS 4th Marines (Fwd.)
    3d Platoon, Company B DS 3/4

Company B continued to support the 4th Marines.

The 1st Platoon operated in two sections—the heavy section in support of G/2/9 and the light section in support of H/2/9. Both sections accompanied patrols and mine sweep teams and maintained security/reaction forces for their combat bases, as well as providing blocking forces for infantry sweeps.

On 11 September, the heavy section was dispatched to assist G/2/9; however, the VC broke contact when the Ontos arrived on the scene.

From 12 September through 20 September, the platoon remained in defensive positions with 2/9. On 20 September, the 1st Platoon returned to the company CP where they were positioned in defense until 29 September, when they moved into security positions for artillery. There was no further contact during this period.

The 2d Platoon continued DS 4th Marines (Fwd.) with defensive positions at Dong Ha. A light section provided security for Montagnard tribesmen clearing likely ambush sites along Route 9 until 15 September. The heavy section maintained defensive positions for artillery positions near Cam Lo until 29 September when it conducted a patrol in support of 2/9.

On 30 September, the light section displaced to the Rockpile (YD 979568) in support of 2/9.

The 3d Platoon continued in support of 3/4 on Operation PAWNEE through 6 September and returned to the B Company CP at the end of the operation.

On 8 September, Operation PAWNEE II continued. On this operation, the platoon occupied CP security positions at night and conducted patrols during the daylight. Operation PAWNEE II ended on 14 September, and the 3d Platoon returned to the company CP where it was put in support of 2/9 defensive perimeter, with additional task of accompanying infantry sweeps.

On 23 September, the light section on a patrol with F/2/9 sank one VC sampan.

On 25 September, while on a sweep near Hill 163 (YD 799109), Ontos received sniper fire and returned five major rounds, which silenced the VC sniper fire.

The month ended with the 3d Platoon Ontos at the company CP defensive positions.

CO Company C (-): Capt. S. T. Flynn
Location and Operations Summary: Phu Bai TAOR

Company C (-) DS 9th Marines (Da Nang TAOR)
    2d Platoon, Company C (-) DS 3/9
    3d Platoon, Company C (-) DS 1/9

Company C (-) continued DS 9th Marines.

The 1st OpCon of Company A (-) (Rein.), 1st ATBn (OpCon 3d ATBn).

The 2d Platoon continued in support of 3/9, providing security for engineers working on Highway 14.

On the 2 September, while supporting I/3/9 on a sweep, Ontos received VC sniper fire and returned thirteen major rounds (106 mm recoilless rifle HEP-T) and four .50-caliber spotter rounds, which resulted in three VC KIA (prob.) and two VC WIA (prob.).

On 3 September, Ontos were used to resupply I/3/9 and continued on sweep. Sweep was ambushed by estimated VC company, which resulted in one USMC WIA (medevac) and one .30-caliber MG damaged. Ontos returned fifteen major rounds and twelve caliber .50 spotter rounds with eight VC KIA (prob.) and six VC WIA (prob.).

On 5 September, in support of I/3/9 and L/3/9, Ontos were ambushed by VC. One Ontos damaged extensively and three USMC WIA (two medevac). Ontos returned sixteen major rounds and 1,100 .30-caliber MG rounds with undetermined results.

For the remainder of this period, the 2d Platoon continued in support of 3/9 by providing security in defensive positions.

The 3d Platoon commenced this period in support of 1/9 with the light section supporting C/1/9.

On 3 September, Ontos in support of B/1/9 observed three VC and fired one major round plus four .50-caliber spotter rounds at them with undetermined results. This section received two hundred rounds automatic weapons fire from VC positions. Ontos returned fire with five major rounds and nine .50-caliber spotter rounds with undetermined results.

The light section in support of B/1/9 on 8 September expended fifteen .50-caliber MG rounds at suspected VC positions with undetermined results.

The 3d Platoon continued in positions supporting 1/9 until 18 September when they were chopped to BLT 1/9.

On 27 September, the 1st Platoon, Company A, 5th ATBn was chopped from BLT 1/26 into defensive positions in support of 1/26 where they remained throughout the reporting period.

COs Company A (-) (Rein.), 1st ATBn (OpCon 3d ATBn): Capts. G. R. Van Horn and D. M. Hutson
Location and Operations Summary: Da Nang TAOR

Company A (-) (Rein.), 1st ATBn (OpCon 3d ATBn) continued DS 1st Marines.

The 1st Platoon commenced this period with only a heavy section in the Da Nang TAOR in support of K/3/1; however, the light section arrived from Chu Lai on 5 September and assumed position in the support of K/3/1.

There was no enemy contact until 18 September when eleven 106 rounds were fired at VC sniper positions with one VC KIA (conf.).

This platoon occupied defensive positions with K/3/1 until 18 September when two Ontos were dispatched to secure a medevac site for a squad from K/3/1. Ontos fired eleven major rounds at VC positions, VC fire ceased, and the medevac was accomplished. On 22 September, two Ontos were dispatched to support an ambush patrol from K/3/1. These Ontos fired thirty-two major rounds, which silenced VC fire, though enemy casualties were not determined.

On 23 September, Ontos fire eight major rounds at suspected VC ambush positions with unknown results.

On 24 September, Ontos fired seventeen major rounds at VC positions in support of a platoon from K/3/1. VC fire ceased.

On 27 September, Ontos expended one major round at a VC sniper. Sniper fire ceased.

On 28 September, Ontos fired four major rounds at VC ambush with a resultant cessation of enemy fire.

On 29 September, Ontos were dispatched to secure a medevac site for K/3/1. Twelve major rounds were expended at VC positions, which caused VC to terminate their attack. Also on 29 September, two Ontos were sent to a VC ambush site and fired twelve major rounds, destroying three houses from which VC were firing. No confirmed VC casualties. During this period, the 1st Platoon fired ninety-seven major rounds on H&I fire missions with undetermined results.

The 2d Platoon remained at Chu Lai under OpCon 1st ATBn during this entire period.

The 3d Platoon commenced this period in the support of 1/1 with the mission of patrolling a beach with C/1/1.

On 3 September, Ontos fired twelve .50-caliber spotter rounds and one major round at six fishing boats, which fled at approach of Ontos. Also on 3 September, one major round was fired at VC sniper positions with undetermined results.

On 9 September, while in support of a squad-sized patrol, Ontos A-35 hit a mine, believed to be a 155 mm shell. The Ontos was badly damaged, and three crewmen received slight wounds. They were treated and returned to duty. Still escorting C/1/1, Ontos A-34 struck a VC mine estimated at over 100 pounds of explosive. The Ontos was destroyed and one crewmen KIA plus the other two WIA (medevac).

From 22 to 28 September, this platoon assumed blocking positions in support of C/1/1 with no enemy contact. There was no enemy contact for the remainder of this period.

The 1st Platoon, Company C, 3d ATBn OpCon Company A (-) (Rein.), 1st ATBn (OpCon 3d ATBn) began this period in support of 2/1.

On 1 September, Ontos C-14 was submerged while trying to cross a stream. The vehicle was retrieved and coded R-4.

On 4, 5, and 7 September, while in support of H/2/1, Ontos fired 1,700 .30-caliber MG rounds at sniper positions with undetermined results. Ontos fired six major rounds at VC snipers located in a house on 12 September. The house was destroyed, but no confirmation of VC casualties was made.

On 13 September, Ontos received several rounds of VC sniper fire. Seven hundred .30-caliber MG rounds were returned with negative results. Continuing in support of H/2/1, an Ontos commander was WIA (medevac) by VC sniper fire. Fire was returned with six major rounds and seven hundred .30-caliber MG rounds with unknown results.

On 22–26 September, Ontos fired six major rounds and 1,680 .30-caliber MG rounds at VC sniper positions, destroying two houses. VC casualties undetermined. There was no further contact during this period.

September 1966
Third Tanks
Commanding Officers: Maj. J. G. Doss and Lt. Col. W. R. Corson
Executive Officers: Majs. E. R. Larson and J. G. Doss
Operations Officers: Capt. A. W. Facklam Jr. and Maj. E. R. Larson
Logistics Officer: N/A
Location and Operations Summary: Da Nang (AT 989708)

During the month of September 1966, 3d Tank Battalion units operating in the Da Nang TAOR experienced very much the same degree of antitank activity that prevailed over the past two months, i.e., mines, RPGs. However, in the Dong Ha/Cam Lo zone of action on Operation PRAIRIE, Company C, 3d Tank Battalion and the 1st Platoon, Company A, 5th Tank Battalion were subjected to heavy mortar, recoilless rifle, and RPG-2 rocket attacks. On three separate occasions, tank armor was penetrated by what was believed to be RPG-2 rockets. This marked a new phase in Marine tank combat operations in

Vietnam in that the North Vietnamese Army enemy encountered was well equipped, well trained, and was determined to do head-to-head battle with tanks and Ontos.

The following was a chronological listing of antitank mines detonated by tanks during the month of September 1966.

At 031420H, a 3d Tank Battalion tank (B-24) detonated what was estimated to have been a 155 mm round with booster charge at (AT 977543). The resulting crater was 6 feet in diameter and 4 feet deep. The tank was moderately damaged. The tank was second in the column and was tracking the lead tank through open terrain with many tracked vehicle trails. There were no casualties.

At 041650H, a 3d Tank Battalion tank (B-12) detonated an unknown-type mine at (AT 923559). The mine left a crater 5 feet in diameter and 4 feet deep. There was moderate damage to the tank's suspension system. The tank was crossing a rice paddy dike and was second in column. The tank was not tracking the lead tank. There were no casualties.

At 080945H, a 3d Tank Battalion flame tank (F-11) detonated an estimated 70–100-pound mine at (XD 116683). There was moderate damage to the tank's suspension system. The tank was traveling in a channelized area recently swept by Marine engineers. The mine was estimated to have been buried 3 feet deep to avoid detention. There were no casualties.

At 081200H, a 1st Tank Battalion tank (C-15) detonated an unknown-type mine at (BT 085615). The explosion left a crater 4 feet deep and 8 feet in diameter. The tank suffered moderate damage to the suspension system. The mine was placed in an open area and was covered by fire. There were no casualties.

At 090825H, a 1st Tank Battalion tank (C-13) detonated an unknown-type mine at (BT 083629). The explosion left a crater 4 feet deep and 6 feet in diameter. The tank received moderate damage to its suspension system. The mine was placed on a tank trail in open terrain. There were no casualties.

At 091645H, a 3d Tank Battalion tank (B-32) detonated an unknown-type mine at (AT 968597). The explosion left a crater 3-1/2 feet deep and 5 feet in diameter. The tank received moderate damage to its suspension system. The mine was emplaced approximately 100 meters east of Liberty Road in a rice paddy. There were no casualties.

At 131130H, a 4th Tank Battalion tank (B-31) detonated an unknown-type mine at (AT 957583). It was estimated it contained approximately 50 pounds of explosives. The explosion caused a crater 3 feet deep and 7 feet in diameter. The tank received light damage to its suspension system. The mine was emplaced near Route 14. There were no casualties.

At 201530H, a 5th Tank Battalion tank (A-15) detonated what was estimated to have been a 155 mm round rigged as a mine, with light damage to the tank's suspension system. Engineer personnel found and destroyed in place (4) four additional 155 mm rounds in the immediate area. There were no casualties.

At 221355H, a 3d Tank Battalion (C-23) detonated an unknown-type mine at (YD 136667), incurring moderate damage to its suspension system. There were no casualties.

At 231555H, a 3d Tank Battalion (B-32) detonated an unknown-type mine at (AT 953569). The explosion left a crater 3 feet deep and 4 feet in diameter. The tank received moderate damage to its suspension system. The tank was traveling on an old tank trail. There were no casualties.

It should be noted that with but three exceptions, all mines were detonated after 1,200 each day. The three other detonations occurred at 0825, 0925, and 1130. In some instances, it is possible the mines were emplaced by the VC after engineer elements had swept the area. A total of ten antitank mines were detonated during September as compared to seven during August.

During September, a total of forty-five (45) intelligence reports were prepared and forwarded by this command. Within the Southern Sector Rear Area Defense, there were fifteen (15) VC contacts involving exchanges of small-arms fire. This is the highest VC incidence rate for a one-month period since 3d Tank Battalion established its CP on Hill 34.

Intelligence reports received during the month of September from Hoa Vang District Headquarters, Hoa Cam Training Center, and local village officials—plus the marked increase in VC contacts by patrols and ambushes of Southern Sector Rear Area Tenant Units—indicate an increased VC effort to infiltrate and possibly damage the logistics center of the 3d Marine Division Rear Area.

Tank combat operations during the month of September were in support of two major operations, MACON and PRAIRIE, and other operations in the TAORs. These operations accounted for 153 VC (KBGF) confirmed, 95 VC (KBGF) probable, 6 VC (WBGF) confirmed, 46 VC (WBGF) probable, 4 VCC, and 23 VCS apprehended. Additionally, tank action was responsible for the sinking of twelve boats.

Operation MACON

The 2d Platoon, Company B remained DS 3/9 throughout the month of September on Operation MACON. Tank action in this area accounted for forty-seven VC (KBGF) confirmed, nineteen VC (KBGF) probable, two VC (WBGF) confirmed.

Operation PRAIRIE

Company C, 3d Tank Battalion remained DS 4th Marines on Operation PRAIRIE. Tank action in this area resulted in fifty-two NVA (KBGF) confirmed, forty-eight NVA (KBGF) probable, twenty NVA (WBGF) probable.

Note: The wrap-up and main (maybe only) measure of "success" is the body count.

Says Christian G. Appy in *American Reckoning: The Vietnam War and Our National Identity*, "The body count was the paramount measure of success. Every month, General Westmoreland required a massive collection of statistical data from all units, and no number was more important than the body count. Commanders reporting low body counts were routinely punished with poor fitness reports and passed over for promotion. Careers were on the line. High body counts, on the other hand, led to medals, rapid promotion, and plum assignments" (AReCA).

H&S Company COs: Capt. P. F. Lessard and 1st Lt. M. F. Beirne IV
Location and Operations Summary: Da Nang (AT 989708)

10 September: At 1500H, a composite platoon consisting of elements from 3d Tank Battalion, 3d Antitank Battalion, and 1st 8th Howitzer Battery, supported by two LVTP-5s and one LVT H-6, conducted a sweep of the Cam Hoa (2) area at (AT 975702). This sweep was hastily organized when intelligence information received from the Hoa Cam Training Center indicated an estimated VC platoon was in the area. The sweep was completed without incident.

At 2100H, an H&S Company tank received an unknown number of small-arms rounds while in a defensive position within the 3d Tank Battalion CP. The tank identified targets and returned 90 mm HE, WP .30-caliber machine gun fire resulting in one VC (KBGF) confirmed and two VC (KBGF) probable.

20 September: At 2030H, a 3d Tank Battalion ambush patrol observed approximately ten to fifteen VC carrying weapons moving in a northerly direction at (AT 996714). The ambush was not in position to take effective action, so the information was relayed to battalion. Tank battalion coordinated patrols from neighboring units and supporting fires, which were designed to force the VC into another tank battalion ambush established as a result of the original sighting.

At 210100H, the planning paid off as the enemy was engaged by the tank battalion ambush elements at (AT 994714). An exchange of fifty to seventy-five rounds of small arms and approximately three rounds of 40 mm M-79 was made. Several moans and cries of pain were heard during this encounter, indicating VC casualties. A search of the area at daylight resulted in the recovery of one VC (KBGF) confirmed and indications of an additional three VC (KBGF) probable.

22 September: At 220010H, 1st Amtrac Battalion reported receiving approximately fifty rounds of small-arms fire and three to five rounds of 40 mm M-79. They returned small-arms fire and requested illumination. At 230025H, 3d Tank Battalion requested HE concentrations fired. At 230600H, a patrol searched the area with negative results.

23 September: At 232110H, a 3d Tank Battalion squad-size patrol was ambushed by an estimated ten to fifteen VC at (AT 986702). An exchange of small arms and grenades ensued, resulting in one USMC WIA medevac and one female VCS WIA apprehended. A daylight search of the area revealed dried pools of blood and drag marks indicating seven VC (KBGF) probable.

24 September: At 0130H, the NSA POL dump at (AT 989721) reported sighting figures moving among the POL drums. A 3d Tank Battalion tank with searchlight was dispatched to the scene. At the same time, reaction forces of 9th Motor Transport Battalion and 4/12 were alerted for movement. A search of the area produced negative results.

COs Company A: Capts. L. A. Brandt and A. W. Facklam Jr.
Location and Operations Summary: Da Nang (AT 945763)

3 September: At 1930H, while in support of G/2/3 at (AT 877574), tank crewmen observed one VC in a boat in the Song Vu Gia. Tanks fired 90 mm HE and WP with undetermined results because of darkness.

At 1700H, while in support of G/2/3 at (AT 877574), tanks fired an H&I mission into coordinates (AT 855653). All fires were unobserved, results unknown.

4 September: At 1900H, while in support of elements of 2/3 at (AT 877575), tank crewmen observed three VC crossing the Song Vu Gia in a boat from north to south at (AT 841549). Tanks fired 90 mm HE but could not determine the results because of darkness.

At 2013H, while in support of elements of 2/3 at (AT 877574), tank crewmen observed five VC in a boat crossing the Song Vu Gia. Tanks fired 90 mm HE with good target coverage resulting in five VC (KBGF) probable and one boat destroyed.

At 2017H, while in support of elements of 2/3 at (AT 877575), tank crewmen observed six VC with packs crossing the Song Vu Gia from south to north at (AT 853552). Tanks fired 90 mm HE and WP resulting in eight VC (KBGF) confirmed.

5 September: At 2200H, while in support of G/2/3 at (AT 914599), tanks fired H&I missions into (AT 899608). All fires were unobserved. Tanks expended thirteen rounds of 90 mm HE and eleven rounds of 90 mm WP.

6 September: At 2030H, while in support of G/2/3 at (AT 914599), tanks fired H&I missions into suspected enemy positions at (AT 903623) and (AT 891613). All fires were unobserved. Four rounds of 90 mm WP were expended.

7 September: At 2330H, while in support of G/2/3 at (AT 914599), tanks fired H&I missions into (AT 899608). All rounds were unobserved. Tanks expended thirteen rounds of 90 mm HE and eleven rounds of 90 mm WP.

8 September: At 1600H, while in support of elements of 2/26 at (AT 889720), tanks fired H&I missions into (AT 860718) and (AT 862964). All fires were unobserved. Tanks expended thirteen rounds of 90 mm HE and eleven rounds of 90 mm WP.

At 2100H, while in support of elements of 2/26, tanks received small-arms fire from an enemy position at (AT 925668) and returned fire with seven hundred rounds of .30-caliber machine gun fire. Darkness precluded a search, results unknown.

9 September: At 0200H, while in support of 2/26 at (AT 936665), tanks fired 90 mm cannon fire at a suspected VC ambush site at (AT 937666). The area was not searched, results undetermined.

10 September: At 1320H, while in support of elements of 2/3 at (AT 874577), tank crewmen observed two VC proceeding downriver in a boat at (AT 845445). Tanks fired 90 mm HE with good target coverage resulting in two VC (WBGF) probable.

At 1915H, while in support of elements of 2/3 at (AT 875574), tank crewmen observed five to ten VC in two boats and one raft crossing the Song Vu Gia at (AT 843558). The boats and raft were taken under fire by 90 mm HE and .50-caliber machine gun fire. This action resulted in five VC (WBGF) probable.

At 2255H, while in support of elements of 2/26 at (AT 933664), fired 90 mm HE into a mortar position from which they were being mortared. The mortar fire ceased; however, enemy casualties could not be determined.

14 September: From 142200H to 150530H, tanks in support of elements of 2/26 at (AT 933662) and (AT 906718) fired H&I missions into coordinates (AT 864618), (AT 848727), (AT 822704), and (AT 832640). All fires were unobserved. Eight rounds of 90 mm HE and eight rounds 90 mm WP were expended.

15 September: From 142200H to 150400H, tanks in support of 2/26 at (AT 933664) fired H&I missions into (AT 881665) and (AT 865681). All fires were unobserved; four rounds of 90 mm HE were expended.

16 September: From 162000H to 162400H, while in support of elements of 2/26 at (AT 933664), tanks fired H&I missions into coordinates (AT

881654) and (AT 922648). All fires were unobserved. Four rounds of 90 mm HE were expended.

From 162000H to 162400H, while in support of elements of 2/26 at (AT 903719), tanks fired H&I missions into coordinates (AT 835712) and (AT 832742). All fires were unobserved. Eight rounds of 90 mm HE were expended.

At 2100H, while in support of elements of 2/26 at (AT 933664), tank crewmen observed six VC moving in a rice paddy at (AT 923666). Fired .50- and .30-caliber machine gun; enemy casualties undetermined.

17 September: At 0900H, while in support of elements of 2/26 at (AT 933664), tanks fired H&I mission in coordinates (AT 865681). All fires were unobserved. Two rounds of 90 mm HE were expended.

At 2050H, while in support of elements of 2/26 at (AT 933664), tank crewmen observed two squads of VC at (AT 928658). Tank 90 mm HE and WP fire was directed into the enemy position. Results were undetermined since no search was made.

18 September: At 0030H, while in support of elements of 2/26 at (AT 933664), tank crewmen observed two to three VC go into a house at (AT 934661). Fired .50- and .30-caliber machine gun fire, setting the house on fire. A search of the house revealed a body that had been dead at least forty-eight hours. Fresh blood trails indicated one VC (WBGF) probable.

At 0045H, while in support of elements of 1/3 at (AT 885772), tanks fired H&I missions into coordinates (AT 863773) and (AT 861777). All fires were unobserved. Tanks expended nine rounds of 90 mm HE.

From 180001H to 180200H, while in support of elements of 1/3 at (AT 898901), tanks fired H&I mission into coordinates (AT 899935) and (AT 887841). All fires were unobserved. Fifteen rounds of 90 mm HE were expended.

From 181830H to 182130H, while in support of elements of the 3d Marines, tanks fired H&I missions into coordinates (AT 888615), (AT 892613), (AT 901623), (AT 865681), (AT 898663), (AT 888688), (AT 879679), (AT 871691), (AT 839733), (AT 853705), (AT 889726), and (AT 819735). Forty-six rounds of 90 mm HE were expended.

At 02246H, while in support of elements of 3/26 at (AT 933664), tank crewmen observed an undetermined number of VC moving from a tree line at (AT 930660). Tanks fired .50- and .30-caliber machine gun fire. Results could not be determined because of darkness.

19 September: At 190100H, while in support of elements of 2/3 at (AT 877575), tank crewmen observed VC carrying packs and rifles downriver in a boat at (AT 845530). Nearby, they observed three additional boats beached ashore at (AT 845551). Before the tanks could fire, the VC beached their boat and ran into the brush. Tanks saturated with heavy volume of 90 mm HE and WP. No assessment of the area could be made; however, the four boats were destroyed.

From 182000H to 190600H, while in support of elements of the 3d Marines, tanks fired H&I missions into coordinates (AT 862772), (AT 861778), (AT 899836), and (AT 901623). All fires were unobserved. Twenty-four rounds of 90 mm HE were expended.

From 192100H to 200500H, while in support of elements of 2/3, tanks fired H&I missions into coordinates (AT 860775), (AT 861761), (AT 862780), (AT 885834), (AT 899836), and (AT 901623). All fires were unobserved. Twenty-four rounds of 90 mm HE were expended.

20 September: From 202230H to 210430H, tanks in support of elements of 1/3 at (AT 885773) fired H&I missions into coordinates (AT 659769), (AT 862772), and (AT 861781). All fires were unobserved. Nine rounds of 90 mm HE were fired.

At 201545H and 201710H, while in support of elements of 2/3, tank crewmen observed two VC in boats coming upriver at (AT 862859) and three boats beached at (AT 850557) with an estimated five VC in one of the beached boats. Tanks fired 90 mm cannon with excellent target coverage resulting in three VC (KBGF) confirmed and one VC (WBGF) confirmed; in addition, two boats were destroyed.

21 September: At 0030H, while in support of elements of 1/3 at (AT 884773), a tank received six rounds of small-arms fire and one grenade from an enemy position at (AT 884773). The tank could not return fire because of the 90 mm gun would not depress low enough. No casualties nor damage to the tank resulted.

22 September: From 221230H to 221430H, while in support of elements of 2/3 at (AT 914597), tanks fired H&I missions into coordinates (AT 901623). All fires were unobserved. Six rounds of 90 mm HE were fired.

From 222000H to 222300H, while in support of elements of 2/26 at (AT 953667), tanks fired H&I missions into coordinate (AT 881615). All fires were unobserved, results unknown. Ten rounds of 90 mm HE were expended.

23 September: From 231230H to 231530H, while in support of elements of 2/3 at (AT 914597), tanks fired H&I missions into coordinate (AT 897617). All fires were unobserved. Ten rounds of 90 mm HE were expended.

From 232100H to 240100H, while in support of elements of 1/3 at (AT 8982), tanks fired H&I missions into grid squares (AT 8786), (AT 8787), (AT 8886), and (AT 8887). All fires unobserved. Eighteen rounds of 90 mm HE were fired.

24 September: From 242230H to 250100H, while in support of elements of 2/26 at (AT 921674), tanks fired H&I missions into coordinates (AT 899671), (AT 898657), (AT 908654), (AT 912661), (AT 915648), (AT 910639), and (AT 913638). All fires were unobserved. Thirty-five rounds of 90 mm HE were expended.

26 September: At 252354H, 260700H, and 260300H, while in support of 3d Marines at (AT 953667), tanks fired H&I missions into possible enemy positions at (AT 865681), (At 888705), and (AT 878695), expending twelve rounds of 90 mm HE and three rounds of 90 mm WP. All fires were unobserved.

From 260640H to 260815H, while in support of elements of the 3d Marines, tanks provided security for engineers conducting a road sweep from (AT 919599) to (AT 877575). The sweep was conducted without incident.

From 261830H to 262000H, while in support of the 3d Marines at (AT 914597), tanks fired H&I missions into suspected enemy positions at (AT 891613) and (AT 895618), expending three rounds of 90 mm HE and two rounds of 90 mm WP. Results unknown as all fires were unobserved.

From 262005 to 270100H, while in support of the 3d Marines at (AT 880820), tanks fired H&I missions on possible enemy routes of approach at (AT 863810), (AT 850820), and (AT 860830). The tanks expended eleven rounds of 90 mm HE and five rounds of 90 mm WP. All fires were unobserved.

27 September: At 270645H, while in support of the 3d Marines, tanks provided security for engineers conducting a road sweep from (AT 919599) to (AT 877575). The sweep was completed without incident.

From 272000H to 280200H, while in support of elements of the 3d Marines at (AT 898821), tanks fired H&I missions into (AT 801861), (AT 840860), (AT 810880), and (AT 840880), expending eight rounds of 90 mm HE and two rounds of 90 mm WP. All fires were unobserved.

28 September: From 280714 to 280830H, while in support of elements of the 3d Marines, tanks provided security for engineers conducting a mine sweep from (AT 866588) to AT 877575). The sweep was completed without incident.

From 281200H to 281600H, while in support of elements of the 3d Marines located at (AT 914597), tanks fired H&I missions into (AT 902622) and (AT 888615), expending three rounds of 90 mm HE and two rounds of 90 mm WP. All fires were unobserved.

At 281830H, while in support of 2/26, tanks received a report that a vehicle had been ambushed at (AT 938136). A section of tanks and a platoon of infantry investigated and found that a vehicle was damaged by small-arms fire but none of the personnel had been injured. The area was illuminated by the tanks, but no enemy was observed.

From 281900H to 282040H, while in support of elements of the 3d Marines, tanks at (AT 914597) fired H&I missions into (AT 888615), (AT 890612), (AT 895617), and (AT 903621), expending four rounds of 90 mm HE. All fires were unobserved.

29 September: From 290645H to 290825H, while in support of elements of the 3d Marines, tanks provided security for engineers conducting a road sweep from (AT 877575) to (AT 919599). The sweep was completed without incident.

From 291907H to 292245H, while in support of elements of the 3d Marines at (AT 914597), tanks fired H&I missions into (AT 840880), (AT 840860), (AT 810880), and (AT 810860), expending seven rounds of 90 mm HE and nine rounds of 90 mm WP. All fires were unobserved.

30 September: From 300645H to 300825H, while in support of elements of the 3d Marines, tanks provided security for engineers conducting a road sweep from (AT 877575) to (AT 919599). There were no incidents.

At 301620H, while in support of 2/3, tanks located at (AT 882556) observed a boat filled with supplies, with no people around at (AT 882556). Tanks fired six rounds of 90 mm HE, destroying the boat and supplies.

CO Company B: Capt. E. L. Tunget

Location and Operations Summary: Da Nang (AT 965613)

LOCHRIDGE, WILLARD F.

Synopsis:
The President of the United States takes pleasure in presenting the Silver Star Medal to Willard F. Lochridge (0-92140), Second Lieutenant, U.S. Marine Corps, for conspicuous gallantry and intrepidity in action while serving with Company B, 3d Tank Battalion, 3d Marine Division (Rein.), FMF, in connection with combat operations against the enemy in the Republic of Vietnam on September 5, 1966. By his courage, aggressive fighting spirit and steadfast devotion to duty in the face of extreme personal danger, Second Lieutenant Lochridge upheld the highest traditions of the Marine Corps and the United States Naval Service.

Home Town: Scarsdale, New York

Night of the Tigers

by Willard F. Lochridge IV

[This story is reprinted from the USMC Vietnam Tankers Association's *Sponson Box* magazine, volume 14, number I, January–March 2011. Edited and modified for from but not content.]

27th BDE, New York Army National Guard

"Tiger" was the code name for a Marine M48A3 Patton tank that was used in transmissions over radio nets during the early years of the Vietnam War by 3d Tank Battalion (3dTkBn), Third Marine Division (3dMarDiv). Categorized as a medium tank, the M48A3 was a diesel-powered version of the earlier M48A2C tank, which used gasoline for fuel, an explosive component when hitting vehicle land mines or being struck by antitank weapons.

From a historical perspective, the M48A3's origins dated back to the M47 "General Patton" tank, which replaced the Army's M26/46 Pershing series. The first production of the M48 rolled off the Chrysler line in 1952. This version of the M48 was produced primarily for combat in Europe against Soviet tanks. Through many design changes, the M48A3 became the mainstay of armored tanks for the Marines and U.S. Army in Vietnam. Later, after a bewildering number of versions, the M48 would eventually lead the way to the successful M60 Patton tank.

The Marines were the first American forces to bring tanks to Vietnam. On 9 March 1965, Marine Corps Staff Sergeant John Downey drove his M48A3 tank off of a landing craft on to Red Beach 2 at Da Nang, and was shortly followed by the rest of the 3d Platoon, Company B, 3d TkBn. The tanks off the beach and drove south on Highway 1 and were immediately deployed to bolster the defenses around the perimeters of the Da Nang airfield.

Upon learning that "USMC tanks were in country," our government and central command—the U.S. Military Assistance Command, Vietnam (MACV)—in Saigon thought such heavy armor was an overkill and "not appropriate for counterinsurgency operations." Certainly, they would not be able to negotiate the combination of soggy terrain and poor weather conditions, particularly during the monsoon season of South Vietnam. Nonetheless, we had them—as part of our initial landing force—and they were there. Over the coming years, MACV's reasoning would fade as the M48A3 gained a solid reputation as a worthy weapon to be used against the enemy, Viet Cong (VC), and especially—later in the war— the North Vietnamese Army (NVA) troops.

As in wars before, the Marines in Vietnam also developed fighting tactics and techniques to overcome constraints and conditions found on the battlefield. Such creativity was about to be employed in "The Night of the Tigers" during the summer of 1966.

By 1966, both the 3dTkBn and 1stTkBn were in-country. The 3d Tanks was headquartered near Da Nang on Hill 34 (Da Nang TAOR), and 1st Tanks was supporting defensive and offensive operations around the Chu Lai Air Base (Chu Lai TAOR). Both of these battalions were experiencing ever-increasing confrontations with the Viet Cong (VC) within their respective TAORs as their platoons were assigned to support various infantry components that were out in the field.

In the late spring of 1966, 3d Battalion, 9th Marines (3/9) was collectively operating out of An Hoa, about 25 miles southwest from

Da Nang. Their responsibility was to defend the small airfield and village, which supported the only active coal mining operation in South Vietnam. An Hoa also had a hydroelectric power plant and a fertilizer plant operating there. In addition to protecting An Hoa, 3/9's mission included interdicting and stopping Viet Cong Main Force elements—particularly the notorious R-20th VC (Doc Lap) Main Force Battalion—from advancing northward to attack the Da Nang Air Base. Prior to 3/9's arrival, many of these enemy forces (including the R-20th Battalion) freely moved within the region with the support of both the local villages' VC and the NVA. The area also embraced the well-known "Arizona Territory," an area given the name for its Wild West–like characteristics and danger.

At that time, the only way into An Hoa was by air or by driving through the Song Thu Bon, fordable during the dry season. Later the following year, a bridge—Liberty Bridge—would be constructed to allow convoy-type resupply from Hill 55, which lay several miles to the north of An Hoa. During the French Indochina War in the 1950s, it was said that the French lost an entire battalion in a battle on Hill 55. During my time in-country, the area surrounding Hill 55 was still a hotly contested neighborhood.

The? 3/9 requested tanks from 3dMarDiv primarily to support and augment the defenses of the small airfield and, also, to conduct offensive operations with their infantry line companies. The 3dTkBn got the mission and redirected my platoon, 2d Platoon, Company B, which was just completing Operation LIBERTY while attached to 1/1, which was operating in and around the vicinity of Hoi An on the coast of the South China Sea.

Our tanks, especially the tracks and drive sprockets, were literally worn out from continuous use in the sandy terrain, which ran from Marble Mountain south through the "Horse Shoe" to Hoi An. So before deployment to An Hoa, we were directed to return to TkBnHq to refit out with five brand-new M48A3 tanks, each equipped with a new and improved infrared (IR) xenon searchlight, bore-sighted with the main 90 mm gun. The xenon searchlight, producing over one million candlepower, could "reach out" to over 2,000 yards. Close in, should someone look directly into the light, particularly when it was in "spotlight" position, it could cause severe eye injury or the individual would suffer temporary flash blindness.

Weighing in at 52 tons, not including a full load of sixty-two rounds of 90 mm ammunition (the turret alone weighed 18 tons), the M48 could reach top road speed of 40 mph. Performance-wise, it burned one gallon per road mile and two gallons per mile off-road. Total fuel capacity was a little over 300 gallons, which gave it a range of approximately 258 miles; that varied, of course, by terrain characteristics. The transmission had three gear positions: forward high, low, and reverse. Low gear was used primarily when crossing wet rice paddies, streams, and rivers or negotiating steep grades. It also had, at that time, a state-of-the-art fire control system that utilized a stereoscopic range finder, a mechanical ballistic computer (not like today's electronic computerized/laser firing systems that allow you to fire onthe-go and are much more accurate), and an M20 periscope sight that the gunner used to set on his target before firing a main gun 90 mm round. This system would take range data, merge it with the muzzle velocity characteristic of the type round being fired, and elevate the 90 mm main gun sufficiently for the round to overcome the downward pull of gravity while on its way to the target. Typically, we carried sixty-two 90 mm rounds that consisted of HE (high explosive), WP (white phosphorus), canister that contained 1,200 pellets (and later flechettes) to be used against enemy troops in the open and vegetation, and a few HEAT (high explosive antitank). It was said a good crew could put the first round on target 90 percent of the time. In Vietnam, we were probably closer to 98 percent, because the distance to targets was typically less than 500 yards. In addition, we had a coaxially mounted with the main gun .30-caliber machine gun and a cupola-mounted Browning .50-caliber machine gun. Secured around the floor of the turret, we carried ten thousand rounds of .30-caliber and three thousand rounds of .50-caliber ammunition. Each crewman carried a

.45-caliber pistol, and for close-in protection, we had an old .45-caliber "grease gun" in each tank. We also had an assortment of "unassigned" weapons such as M2 carbines, Thompson submachine guns, captured AK47s, and an M79 grenade launcher that allowed us to inexpensively "dust the bushes" when moving into unknown territory or while setting up for night bivouacs. Clearly, we were ready for bear and could light up the night or go IR with our new xenon searchlights.

Departing TkBnHq, we drove south to Hill 55 to spend the night at our Company HQ. While there, we discussed the river crossing with our tank company commander that would have to be made the following day. Small fording stacks were strapped to the engine armor plate of each vehicle in case we needed them to negotiate the water crossing. Aerial maps were studied, and several crossing/fording points were noted. Our first choice was at the end of a bend in the river that flattened out with sandy beaches on either side. It was about 200 yards across but would require a diagonal upstream approach in order to successfully reach the opposite beach.

The M48A3 had a crew of four: the driver, who sat in the front of the tank, not in the turret but with access to it, under the main gun; the gunner, who was situated to the front of and below the tank commander (TC) to the right of the main gun breech; the loader, who stood to the left of the breech, but most often rode outside on top of the loader's hatch; and the TC, who held position in the cupola, a small turret that housed a .50-caliber machine gun that, out of frustration of not working well in such tight quarters, was eventually sky-mounted to the top of the cupola with a semicircle of sandbags for added protection of the TC.

Arriving at the Song Thu Bong in the early morning hours, myself and my company commander, Captain Ev Tunget, scouted out our primary crossing by actually wading across the river at the earlier map-identified fording location. We checked the consistency of the bottom and water depth. Signal flags were posted on the opposite shore as guides. On our way back and still waist-deep in the river, the VC opened fire on us.

With rounds zinging all around us, we made like turtles with just our helmets showing above the water.

We determined that the fording stacks would not have to be used. The hull, and possibly part of the turret, would be submersed, so the drivers would have to "button-up" their hatches and be directed by the TCs, who stood waist-high out of the cupola, via the tanks intercom system by which all the tank crewmen could communicate—transmit and receive. The TCs would eyeball the signal flags, monitor the water flowing over the front slope plates and down along the tank sides to make certain they were on course and remained in reasonable safe freeboard condition from water depth. The gunners and loaders were assigned to topside positions in the event the TCs had to announce "abandon ship." Should that condition happen, the TC and his topside crew would quickly move to aid the driver, who would be underwater, in escaping.

Before going across, we called in 105 mm artillery from An Hoa to prep the other/enemy side of the river to stop them from shooting at us. After several salvos of 105s, the VC left the area. As lead vehicle, we splashed into the river and, running under low gear, began crossing. Our driver, underwater and seeing bubbles wash past his periscope, complained about leaking seals around his battened-down hatch and also claimed he could see fish through his periscopes. Within an hour, all tanks were across, and we began our drive to An Hoa to celebrate a happy reunion with 3/9, with whom we had served earlier in the year in and around the Horse Shoe before 1/1 took over.

The first couple of weeks at An Hoa were spent getting the lay of the land. It was still the dry season, so we could maneuver just about anywhere. We spent many a day and night operating in the field with Kilo, Lima, or Mike Companies throughout our TAOR.

One morning, a jeep coming back from Phu Loc Hill, which overlooked the confluences of Song Tim Bon and Song Vu Gia, hit a land mine;

all occupants were seriously wounded and one was killed. Supposedly, the road had been swept that morning, but somehow, the engineers had missed that mine. The area where the incident occurred was particularly subject to mining. The dirt road traversed a series of stepped rice paddies that were about a mile wide and extended two to three miles on both sides in either direction.

For some unknown reason, the next day, I decided to join the engineers who were assigned to sweep the road. Beginning in the earlier hours, i.e., first light, they began their work with me following a good fifty yards or more behind. As they passed the crater from the mine explosion the day before, we came to a culvert which ran under the road. I noticed dozens of footprints coming out of the paddy, crossing the road and down into the other side. I asked the engineers about these tracks, but no one had an answer, except to say that they had not noticed them the day before.

Returning to TkBnHq, I asked the S-3 (operations officer) if we had had any patrols out in that area the night before. He said, "No." I said, "Then some large body of troops must have crossed that road last night and marched right down the center of those rice paddies."

An idea was forming in my mind about using our tanks to night-ambush the area, but a few technical and tactical issues had to be worked out before presenting the plan to the battalion commander and his staff. Those issues were:

(1) How do we deploy tanks into a night-ambush site without the enemy discovering us? Tanks make a lot of noise when operating in the field, especially when starting.
(2) How many tanks should be deployed?
(3) What primary sites should be selected with appropriate alternate locations, if needed?
(4) How long could we operate our new xenon searchlights on battery power before having to start our engines?

(5) How could we minimize tank-to-tank radio communications, which would also cause battery drain?
(6) How many infantrymen would we need for security?
(7) Size-wise, what would we require for a reaction force to come to our assistance if we made contact? The "Night of the Tigers" was about to unfold.

First, we determined that three tanks or our heavy section, when spread out in a forward-facing fan of fire over the targeted zone, would be sufficient. The tanks would be spaced approximately 25 yards apart with my tank in the center. To protect our rear, two four-man fire teams would go out with us. To reduce battery draw from our radios, we simply would tie pieces of string attached to the wrists of each tank commander. Since I was in the center, I had one string on each wrist. The string had enough play in it to allow us to move our arms while using nightvision binoculars. The idea was, if anyone saw something in their respective area of observation, the strings would be pulled to signal radios up. Our rear tank phone lines tied in the infantry.

Next, and perhaps most critical, came testing our xenon searchlights without engines running. How long could we operate them from battery power only? From the tests, we calculated that each tank could operate for a little over three hours without having to power up engines. So, once in position, a selected flanking tank would use its IR light, while the other two tanks simply observed their areas with night vision binoculars.

We had an amtrac platoon attached to 3/9, so it was easy to visit them and ask for their support. We needed them to cover the noise of moving our tanks at night. The idea was not only to use them for that purpose, but also to have them carry a reaction force out if needed. The plan called for four amtracs and a platoon of infantry (the reaction force) to deploy with us—three amtracs up front followed by three tanks and the fourth amtrac taking up the rear. Once underway as the sun was setting, at a designated time when darkness was complete, this convoy of vehicles would drive past by our primary turn-off point to the ambush site. The tanks would quickly peel off the road, take positions, and cut their engines off.

Without raising suspicion, several of us went out on foot patrols over the course of two to three days to select potential ambush positions. Having completed our homework, we presented our plan to the battalion CO, Lieutenant Colonel Raphael, and his staff. He eagerly approved it. Next morning preparations were made. All was ready for the coming night events. At approximately 2030, the amtracs, tanks, and infantry left An Hoa and headed north toward Phu Loc Hill. By 2130, the tanks were off the road and set in at the primary ambush site. Strings were attached to the tank commander's wrists. The left flank vehicle powered up its xenon searchlight under IR, and nightvision binoculars were put into use by all three tanks. The infantry took up a protective position behind us. Now the wait came as we began scanning the rice paddies to our front.

Time passed when, suddenly, my left wrist felt a solid tug. It was a little past 2300. Radios came up. The left flanking tank commander reported a large enemy force of troops moving in our direction at ten o'clock out about 500 yards. Quickly turning my night-vision binoculars in that direction, I could clearly make out a mass of troops coming our way. Since they were moving toward our front, I ordered all tanks to wait until they were closer, and when told, they were to switch to the xenon white floodlight and begin taking them under fire with coax .30-caliber machine gun fire. Within several minutes, the enemy formation was directly to our front about 100 to 150 yards out. It was time to spring the ambush. The order went out: white searchlight penetrated the night, and three .30-caliber machine guns opened up with devastating interlocking fire. The infantry behind us opened up too. It was a turkey shoot. When we switched from floodlight position on the searchlights to spotlight position, the enemy dropped to the ground. Curiously, when moving back to floodlight, they would stand up and get shot.

Since they were so close, I ordered 90 mm canister rounds to be fired; it only took a few. The field was littered with enemy bodies and supplies.

As the ambush was kicked off, the reaction force was alerted; they came up to help us police the site. By 0100, the ambush position was cleared, and we started our return to An Hoa. As we gained the road, I informed the reaction force commander that we wanted to move to our alternate site. Somewhat surprised, he agreed; we pulled off and set up again.

Within an hour, we had contact. We watched as six enemy troops advanced toward our position. They were probing the rice paddies for either survivors or lost supplies. When they were out about 50 to 75 yards, we switched on our white searchlights, and to our surprise, they simply put their hands up in surrender. We brought them in, tied them up, and gave them some water. One of them was a female, who we were to later learn was a VC cadre officer. At dawn the next morning, we mounted up and returned to An Hoa with our prisoners. However, that was not the last "Night of the Tigers." We went out three more times and had two more nights of solid contact.

Later on, not to be outdone, our light section, consisting of two tanks, used similar tactics at night on the Song Thu Bon and knocked out sixteen enemy troop- and supply-laden sampans.

By the middle of September 1966, our platoon of twenty-two Marines had recorded 244 confirmed enemy KIAs, 58 possible KIAs, 19 WIAs, 5 possible WIAs, and captured 56 enemy troops. Additionally, we destroyed four ammunition bunkers, captured one bunker that contained 271 Chicom (Chinese Communist) hand grenades and 19 Russian claymore-type mines, and destroyed two enemy 57 mm recoilless rifles. We also disposed of a two-man sniper team with three quick rounds of 90 mm WP, who unfortunately had attempted to disrupt our beer party (a party that was held on Phu Loc Hill) after we had completed an operation and our two beer per day per person ration had been airlifted in to us by helicopter. Also, early one morning, we knocked out an entire sniper platoon that was caught on a small island hamlet as they prepared their breakfast meals. One of the enemy who was killed was a Caucasian, later believed to be an East German adviser attached to the unit.

Fortunately, the platoon suffered no personnel lost, and no one had been seriously wounded during our entire time while on operations. However, earlier in our beginning days, we did lose one tank by land mine detonation. Individually, our platoon members received three Silver Star medals, one Bronze Star medal, and three Purple Heart medals.

Will Lochridge

UNITED STATES MARINE CORPS HISTORY DIVISION
ORAL HISTORY INTERVIEW WRITTEN TRANSCRIPT

Interviewee's Name: Capt. W. F. Lochridge IV, #092140, USMCR
Date of Interview: Unk. circa early 1968
Conflict: Vietnam
Military Unit: 3d Tank Battalion
Duties: Tank Platoon Commander
Interviewer: 2d Lt. K. S. Comer, #0100952
Length: 50:00
Location of Interview: Unk.
Individual Completing Summary: Lt. Col. R. A. Stewart, USMC (Ret.) (AW)
Recording Format and Number of Recording: CD#2609A, 2609B
Documents Submitted with Interview: None
Related Material: None
Classification: Confidential/Unclass.
Transcription Priority: Note: The following is a verbatim transcript.

Abstract: Captain. Lochridge's extended tour in Vietnam was from March 1966 to November 1967. He discusses, in the first half of his extended tour as a tank platoon commander (a Silver Star recipient), experiencing intense kinetic action and the last half of his extended tour in RVN as the head of the Civic Action Program at the IIIMAF/3dMarDiv level.

Key Words: Night ambushes, sweep teams, bracket method, rice paddies, Civil Action, Phong Bac, CAP, CAT, PF food supplements, Chu Hoi Ralliers, LAW.

00:00–04:33: Lochridge: On this taped section, I'll start off with one of the first areas I worked in as a tank platoon commander with the 3d Tank Battalion. There are many conventional tactical uses of the armored vehicles in Vietnam, and I'm sure we have multiple references to these types and uses of armored vehicles. However, I have a few things here that might add on to them for perhaps historical and tactical information that could be used presently in Vietnam.

One thing my platoon tried in Vietnam, that was quite successful, was the use of tanks in night ambushes. A lot of people thought, because of the cumbersome size and the noise that the armored vehicle makes, that successful night ambushes would be out of the question. However, we found this to be quite different. We conducted this particular type of tactic down in An Hoa, southwest of Da Nang, during the month of August and September 1966. In the morning, I'd go out with the mine sweep teams covering Liberty Road and look for footprint trails coming from the road. What I found were areas that had been traveled on, and I'd mark these down on my map, and at the same time, I would look over the area for perspective sites for ambushes. The following evening, I'd go back and I'd get my tank crewmen briefed on the area we were going, and I'd get with the S-3, the battalion we were supporting, and we'd be assigned normally anywhere from eight to twelve men depending on the strength of the battalion at the time and what they could let go. After sundown—and this is important—after sundown, we'd take two to three tanks and move down the road to the site for that night's ambush. Moving into the ambush site, we would have the tanks coving a 180-degree area overlooking the supposed or suspect trail that the enemy were going to use, and behind us the other 180-degree area would be our security. Our first night out we had contact around 8:00 that night, and that resolved in twelve KIAs and a couple of prisoners, including the capture of an 82 mm mortar as well as $4,400 worth of equipment. The second night we went out again, and it resulted in a double-type ambush, actually made our first contact 2300, then shortly thereafter, under the cover of engines of amtracs, we moved into our alternate position and caught a body-snatching group that came back into the area and resulted in six KIA and a capture of a cadre female. To make the story short, this does work; this worked four out of six nights and one night twice in a row. Afterward I didn't hear much more that this had been tried again. I do know that it works.

04:33–05:52: Another area to talk about is when out in support of a line company, platoon, whatever it may be and they are pinned down heavily with enemy fire; the forward air controller might be along with this particular unit, may have trouble seeing enemy positions from his area that he's trying to observe. The tank platoon commander has an ideal situation where he can see the enemy a lot better and, consequently, through the use of white phosphorus, Willy Peter rounds, can mark the targets better for air strikes. This was used several times in operation with great success. The tank commander coordinated with the FAC with his radio, and the FAC relayed this to the air support covering the particular operation at the time. The marking rounds are the point target, the smoke comes off pretty well, and it is very clearly observed from the air.

05:52–07:54: Another area we fooled around with was with the 90 mm gun and the .50-cal. machine gun. Since we had problems with parts and keeping the electrical system working with the .50 cal., it was more or less inoperable at various times we needed it, so instead of using it as one of our main weapons in a heavy fire fight, because of its condition due to the electrical solenoid, we decided to use it more or less as sniper rifle. What we would do during the day is line it up—parallel it—with the 90 mm gun so that the only thing that needed to be done or corrected would be elevation. At night, our watch would be on in the tank, and when we got sniper fire, the watch would line the .50 cal. up and start pumping incendiary rounds into the target area. It takes less than a minute and a half to two minutes for the gunner to get the first 90 mm on the way. This resulted in a number of enemy KIA confirmed.

In conjunction with paralleling the two weapons systems, we also found that the bracket method of the target was the best method to use. When shooting at snipers, our first round would be right on target, right where the sniper was shooting from, then bracket about 20 meters to the left with a round and 20 meters to the right with a round. We found that the enemy was running around trenches; they'd fire a couple of rounds quickly from one point then run 20 or 30 yards down a trench or tree line and fire again, so we found that, with bracketing the target the with three rounds from the .50, we got good results.

07:54–08:52: Talking now about the weapons for the tank, the individual weapons—the .45-cal. pistol and the grease gun; my recommendation here would be that the loader of the tank should be armed with an M79 (40 mm grenade launcher). There were several times when I was acting platoon commander where we ran into situations during daylight hours where had we M79s, we would have been better off. Close-in firepower at night, this would also be an ideal weapon for the man standing guard watch on the tank, in that the VC have a tendency to come in close at night. This has happened to me several times—to throw hand grenades—and it would be to our advantage, and add firepower, to the line companies or whoever we are supporting at the time.

08:52–12:10: Now, I'd like to go into the challenges we faced and met with crossing rice paddies. We had a big problem with tank commanders coming into Vietnam faced with having to cross these paddies every day. There are certain measures that one can take going into these areas.

The first thing, before you start crossing, simply halt, get out of your vehicle, and take your tank bar out and, if time and the enemy situation allows, probe the bottoms of the paddy. If the bar slides in real easily, I would hesitate to cross in that area. However, if you find it has a solid bottom with the tank bar, the chances are very good that you would be able to make it across. In crossing the paddy, as soon as you get in to it, make sure the driver has got his in-low gear and it is floored all the way. This pressure on the accelerator should *never* be let up while in the paddy. Be on the lookout, and this is for the tank commander and loader who are looking outside, for small blue flowers. It's a water-type hyacinth that form along the sides of the rice paddies. They are actually small pools or ponds of water. Sometimes they'll be so overgrown that the presence of this water hyacinth the tank crew can't really tell the difference between that and the rice areas. This indicates deep water—stay away from it. It's easy to pick out most of the time. These flowers are growing all season long. They are small blue or purplish flowers. Be on the lookout for those.

The lead vehicle doesn't have much trouble tracking or following a ground guide; however, the vehicles following should make damn sure they don't follow in his tracks. He's already loosened up the bottom, so it's best that they straddle the tracks or take another route altogether. When approaching rice paddy dikes, depending on the side of course, in most areas, the sides of the dike are a foot to two feet high. Be sure that the driver does *not* let up his acceleration. Slam into them; if you slow down to try to cross them "properly," if you are concerned about your breaking torsion bars, you are liable to get stuck. Best thing to do is hit them head-on and take the jar.

Also, concerning rice paddies or any area you might get stuck, it's a good idea to have a 100-foot 1-1/2" steel cable per section, both heavy and light (sections). We found many a times that this cable got us out of trouble. In fact, I would even recommend that at least three vehicles be equipped with these 100-foot steel cables.

12:10–13:15: Going back now about firepower: We found, when entering new areas—areas that are unlikely to have large populations or an area where the population has been evacuated—the best way to go in is reconnaissance by fire. There are no buts about it. We found the use of the .30-caliber coaxis machine gun is our best means. We carried well over the basic load, carrying almost ten thousand rounds per vehicle, simply because we reconned by fire everywhere we went and, we found several times, where reconning by fire paid off and it prematurely sprung ambushes. I can recall a couple of times where we had some VC that we had captured several weeks, after a particular incident had occurred; we found they had been out in that area and had been hit by such things as canister rounds and .30-caliber ammo that we had poured into them in our recon-by-fire.

13:15–14:40: Another means of giving an infantry platoon or line company support, and in particular the small squad or patrol that is going on a short recon or patrol of the area, if tanks can't accompany the infantry, they should find a vantage point from which to support them with direct fire. If the patrol coordinates with the tank commander involved prior to moving out and also if they are carrying something like a 3.5 rocket launchers, or some sort of means to mark their target with smoke, and we found that this was effective. Down in An Hoa, sitting in high vantage points, a couple of times we saw ambushes being set up by the VC far in advance before the friendly patrol got involved or got concerned with the ambush. In cases where a patrol did get ambushed, it could easily mark its target from their flanks and we, in turn, could respond with point target fire. I would not recommend this technique if covering a patrol involved shooting over the friendly patrol. There are cases with short rounds; this should be only used on the flanks of such patrols.

14:40–18:46: My next area I'm going to speak about is civic action.

Note to reader: At this point in the interview session, Captain Lochridge provided details of his extended tour as III MAF's Civic Action Program (for which he was the recipient of the Legion of Merit medal with combat V), which will be covered in a separate annex to this series.

Operation MACON participated in by 2d Platoon, Company B reposted separately.

6 September: At 1205H, while in support of elements of 1/9 at (AT 903541), tanks and infantry received sniper fire from a position at (AT 902539). One round struck one of the driver's vision blocks. Tanks returned 90 mm canister fire, and the sniping ceased. The area was not searched because of intervening river, and results could not be confirmed.

At 1745H, while in support of elements of 1/9 at (AT 904541), tanks and infantry received two rounds of sniper fire from a VC position at (AT 902539). Tanks returned 90 mm WP into the positions. The area was no searched because of intervening river, and results could not be confirmed.

8 September: At 1715H, while in support of D/1/9 at (AT 903543), tanks were requested by the infantry company commander to recon by fire an area in the vicinity of (AT 905537) from which small-arms fire had been received. Tanks fired 90 mm HE, WP, canister, and .50-caliber machine gun fire. Enemy fire ceased. Results undetermined as area was not searched.

At 1730H, while in support of 1/9 at (AT 979606), tanks received sniper fire from (AT 982602). Tanks fired 90 mm canister, .50- and .30-caliber machine gun fire. Enemy fire ceased. Results undetermined as area was not searched.

9 September: At 1645H, while in support of elements of 1/9, a tank detonated an antivehicular mine at (AT 968597). There were no casualties, but moderate damage to the tank's suspension system resulted.

At 1830H, while in support of elements of B/1/9 at (AT 903543), tanks and infantry received light automatic weapons fire from (AT 905537).

A tank returned .50-caliber machine gun fire, and the enemy broke contact.

10 September: At 1810H, while in support of elements of 1/9 at (AT 903543), tank crewmen observed a VC in a tree line at (AT 902538). A tank fired 90 mm WP into the area. The area was not searched because of the intervening river, and results could not be confirmed.

11 September: At 0850H, while in support of an engineer road sweep team on Liberty Road at (AT 969588), tanks received fire from an unknown number of VC at (AT 974589). Tanks fired 90 mm canister, .50- and .30-caliber machine gun fire, and the enemy broke contact.

At 1630H, while in support of elements of 1/9, tanks fired 90 mm cannon fire into suspected mined areas in grid square (AT 9861). Infantry patrols had earlier detonated two M16A1 mines in this area. There were no secondary explosions.

At 1633, while in support of elements of D/1/9 at (AT 903543), tanks and infantry received a number of rounds of sniper fire from an enemy position at (AT 902538). A tank returned 90 mm WP with undetermined results.

Again at 1715H, three more sniper rounds were received from the vicinity of (AT 903539). Tanks returned .50-caliber machine gun fire. Undetermined results as the area was not searched.

12 September: At 1600H, while in support of elements of 1/9 at (AT 909545), tanks were returning from a resupply run, when they received small-arms fire from (AT 902538). Tanks returned fire, and the enemy broke contact.

13 September: At 1130H, while in support of elements of 1/9, a tank detonated an antivehicular mine at (AT 957583). There were no casualties, but moderate damage to the tank suspension system was received.

14 September: At 1855H, while in support of B/1/9 at (AT 903543), tank crewmen observed two VC in uniform at (AT 902538). A tank fired one round of 90 mm HE. Results of firing undetermined as an intervening river prevented a search.

15 September: At 1700H, a Company B tank proceeding to the Ha Dong bridge received a request from G/2/1 to support infantry units pinned down at (AT 995632). Enemy small-arms fire was being received from a pagoda at (AT 994624). The tank fired 90 mm HE and destroyed the pagoda. One secondary explosion was observed. VC casualties were not determined as the pagoda was not searched.

16 September: At 1630H, while in support of elements of 1/9 at (AT 903543), tanks received three rounds of small-arms fire from (AT 902538). Three tank crewmen WIA (medevac). Tanks returned a heavy of 90 mm cannon fire, and the firing ceased. The area could not be searched because of an intervening river.

On 16 September, Robert Haller received his Second Purple Heart.

17 September: At 1630H, while in support of elements of 1/9 at (AT 903563), tanks and infantry received eight rounds of automatic weapons fire from an enemy position at (AT 902538). Tanks fired 90 mm WP and .50- and .30-caliber machine gun fire. Enemy firing ceased. Intervening river prevented search.

ANDERSON, DONALD F.

Synopsis:
The President of the United States takes pleasure in presenting the Silver Star Medal to Donald F. Anderson (2183557), Private First Class, U.S. Marine Corps, for conspicuous gallantry and intrepidity in action while serving with Company B, 3d Tank Battalion,

3d Marine Division (Rein.), FMF, in connection with combat operations against the enemy in the Republic of Vietnam on September 19, 1966. By his courage, aggressive fighting spirit and steadfast devotion to duty in the face of extreme personal danger, Private First Class Anderson upheld the highest traditions of the Marine Corps and the United States Naval Service.

18 September: From 181315H to 181445H, while in support of elements of 1/9 at (AT 903543), tanks reinforced by flame tanks fired a heavy volume of 90 mm cannon fire into suspected sniper positions. The flame tanks burned the area immediately outside the friendly tactical wire. Results of 90 mm cannon fire were undetermined as the areas were not searched.

22 September: At 1345H, while in support of elements of B/1/9 at (AT 903543), tank crewmen observed a boat drifting down the river with no personnel visibly aboard. A tank fired 90 mm HE, sinking the boat.

23 September: At 1555H, while in support of elements of 1/9, a tank detonated an antivehicular mine at (AT 953569); there were no casualties and only slight damage to the vehicle.

24 September: At 1430H, the company CP located on Hill 55 at (AT 956516) received forty to fifty rounds of small-arms fire from an enemy position at (AT 961606). Returned .50- and .30-caliber machine gun fire with undetermined results as the area was not searched.

From 241445H to 241715H, while in support of A/1/9 at (AT 958598), tanks with infantry mounted went to the aid of an infantry platoon which was encircled by an estimated thirty to fifty VC. Tanks fired a heavy volume of 90 mm cannon and tank-mounted machine gun fire, resulting in eight VC (KBGF) confirmed. The remainder of the enemy disengaged.

25 September: At 1245H, while in support of elements of 1/9 at (AT 904543), infantry observed a number of VC at (AT 897538) and requested tank fire. Tanks saturated the area with 90 mm HE and WP plus tank-mounted .50- and .30-caliber machine gun fire. Intervening river prevented a search of the area, results undetermined.

27 September: At 270645H, while in support of the 3d Marines, tanks provided security for engineers conducting a road sweep from (AT 919599) to (AT 877575). The sweep was completed without incident.

From 272000H to 280200H, while in support of elements of the 3d Marines at (AT 898821), tanks fired H&I missions into (AT 801861), (AT 840860), (AT 810880), and (AT 840880), expending eight rounds of 90 mm HE and two rounds of 90 mm WP. All fires were unobserved.

28 September: From 280715 to 280830H, while in support of elements of the 3d Marines, tanks provided security for engineers conducting a mine sweep from (AT ?876553) to (AT 877575). The sweep was completed without incident.

From 281200H to 281600H, while in support of elements of the 3d Marines located at (AT 914597), tanks fired H&I missions into (AT 902622) and (AT 888615), expending three rounds of 90 mm HE and two rounds of 90 mm WP. All fires were unobserved.

At 281830H, while in support of 2/26, tanks received a report that a vehicle had been ambushed at (AT 938136). A section of tanks and a platoon of infantry investigated and found that a vehicle was damaged by small-arms fire but none of the personnel had been injured. The area was illuminated by the tanks, but no enemy were observed.

From 281900H to 282040H, while in support of elements of the 3d Marines, tanks at (AT 914597) fired H&I missions into (AT 888615), (AT 890612), (AT 895617), and (AT 903621), expending four rounds of 90 mm HE. All fires were unobserved.

29 September: From 290645Ht to 290825H, while in support of elements of the 3d Marines, tanks provided security for engineers conducting a road sweep from (AT 877575) to (AT 919599). The sweep was completed without incident.

From 291907H to 292245H, while in support of elements of the 3d Marines, at (AT 914597), tanks fired H&I missions into (AT 840880), (AT 840860), (AT 810880), and (AT 810860), expending seven rounds of 90 mm HE and nine rounds of 90 mm WP. All fires were unobserved.

30 September: From 300645H to 300825H, while in support of elements of the 3d Marines, tanks provided security for engineers conducting a road sweep from (AT 877575) to (AT 919599). There were no incidents.

At 301620H, while in support of the 2/3, tanks located at (AT 882556) observed a boat filled with supplies, with no people around at (AT 882556). Tanks fired six rounds of 90 mm HE, destroying the boat and supplies.

COs Company C: Capts. J. H. Gary and P. F. Lessard
Location and Operations Summary: Da Nang (YD 246599)

Operation PRAIRIE

In early September, "Col Cereghino decided to expand his AO to include the Con Thien region, which lay due north of Cam Lo and just three kilometers south of the DMZ" (SF-EM). He ordered Lieutenant Colonel Bench to make a recon in force sweep of the area with his 2/4 Magnificent Bastards. H/2/4 and a platoon of tanks from C/3dTks headed north from Cam Lo early on 7 September. On 8 September, G/2/4 came face-to-face with an enemy force about one kilometer northeast of Con Thien. The three-hour firefight cost G/2/4 five KIAs.

"On 9 September, Bench's Companies 'E' and 'F,' supported by tanks found a dug-in NVA company just south of the DMZ. From trenches extending deep into the DMZ, the enemy raked the Marines with heavy machine-gun fire. Only the direct fire of the tanks finally broke the enemy resistance" (SF-EM).

From 1 to 8 September, Company C support of Lieutenant Colonel Bench's 2/4 comprised firing H&I missions tank / infantry sweeps.

8 September: A tank detonated an antitank mine, suffering only minor damage but unearthed a large cache of antitank mines, which were destroyed in place. Then a heavy volume of 120 mm mortar and 57 mm recoilless rifle fire from (YD 130717). One tank was hit with the 57 mm, suffering minor damage, and another was hit by a 120 mm mortar round on the cupola, causing severe damage to the cupola, killing one crew member. Tanks returned fire with all their weapons and were credited with twelve VC KBGF confirmed and eight VC (KBGF) probable.

Earl Matthews Jr., staff sergeant, age 28, Florence, South Carolina, a Marine Tanker, was killed on 9 September 1966 while serving as a tank section leader with Company C, 3d Tank Battalion in Quang Tri Province, South Vietnam.

9–22 September: Activity centered on firing hundreds of rounds of 90 mm with results mostly unobserved. However, enemy activity was picking up with tanks receiving 57 mm and small arms incoming. Also the number of enemy KIAs credited was building.

23 September: Reinforced with 1st Platoon, Company A, 5th Tanks, encountered a strong force of NVA when the armored column consisting of nine tanks and two LVTs was ambushed, receiving a heavy volume of 57 mm and small arms. The embarked infantry hit the dirt, and the tanks responded with a large volume of fire from all their weapons and were credited with thirteen NVA KIAs confirmed and many more KIAs and WIAs probable. A large amount of equipment and supplies

were captured. Tanks suffered one tank hit by an RPG-2, which caused severe damage to the power pack.

23–28 September: Tanks provided H&I fires, accompanied engineer road sweeps and patrols, provided perimeter security, returned hundreds of rounds at suspected positions of enemy incoming, and provided covering fire for withdrawal of 2/4 forces.

Note: Company C, 1st Tanks' action is reported on the command chronology from which the above is extracted, but this company is not reflected as part of 3d Tanks in the T/O.

9 September: At 0825H, while in support of elements of 1/1, a tank detonated an antivehicular mine at (BT 083629). There were no casualties, but moderate damage was done to the tank's suspension system.

At 1330H, while in support of D/1/1 at (BT 057640), tanks and infantry received small-arms fire from (BT 055640). Tanks returned fire with 90 mm HE, WP, and canister. A search was not conducted because of trafficable terrain.

At 1330H, while in support of 3/1 anks and infantry received small-arms fire from (BT 041658). Tanks returned 90 mm fire resulting in one VC (KBGF) confirmed, three VC (KBGF) probable, and three VC (WBGF) probable.

Again at 1500H, while in the same position, an unknown number of VC were observed crossing a rice paddy at (BT 055655). Tanks fired 90 mm HE resulting in one VC (KBGF) confirmed.

At 1530H, while in support of elements of L/3/1, tank crewmen discovered five booby-trapped Chicom grenades on a tank trail at (BT 045658). Infantry destroyed the grenades in place.

10 September: At 1400H, while in support of elements of 1/1 at (BT 065619), tanks went to the aid of infantry who were pinned down by fire from two directions, (BT 075614) and (BT 059617). Tanks fired a heavy volume of 90 mm cannon fire, causing enemy to disengage and resulting in five VC (KBGF) confirmed and seven VC (KBGF) probable.

12 September: At 1030H, while in support of elements of 1/1 at (BT 095613), tanks received fire from approximately fifteen VC at (BT 095609). Tanks returned fire resulting in one VC (KBGF) probable.

At 1025H, while in support of elements of 1/1 at (BT 071612), tanks received sniper fire from (BT 075614). Tanks returned a heavy volume of fire, causing enemy to break contact. Search of the area resulted in the apprehension of seven VCS. No other casualties were found.

15 September: At 1200H, while in support of elements of 1/1 at (BT 098621), an aerial observer noted a number of VC at (BT 099624) and marked the target with smoke. Tanks fired 90 mm canister resulting in three VC (KBGF) confirmed.

16 September: At 1030H, while in support of elements of 1/1 at (BT 109629), tank crewmen observed two VC crossing a rice paddy ahead of friendly infantry at (BT 101628). Tanks fired 90 mm HE resulting in two VC (KBGF) confirmed.

At 1030H, while in support of elements of 1/1 at (BT 119630), tanks fired at two VC running at (BT 102626). Area could not be searched because of untrafficable terrain.

At 1300H, while in support of elements of 1/1 at (BT 094637), tanks observed an undetermined number of VC at (BT 099629). A 90 mm HE was fired resulting in two VC (KBGF) confirmed.

At 1700H, while in support of elements of 1/1, tanks destroyed a VC platoon patrol base at (BT 094637) with 90 mm HE and WP fire, resulting in two VC (KBGF) confirmed.

At 1845H, while in support of elements of 1/1 at (BT 082623), tank crewmen observed two VC running across a rice paddy at (BT 085621). Tanks fired 90 mm HE and .30-caliber machine gun fire. A search of the area was conducted; however, no VC casualties were found.

17 September: At 1155H, while in support of elements of 1/1 at (BT 127634), tank crewmen observed four fishing boats at (BT 143634). The boat crews ignored signals to beach and turned away. Tanks fired 90 mm HE and .30-caliber machine gun fire, resulting in three VC (KBGF) confirmed and one VC (KBGF) probable.

From 171945H to 172005H, while in support of elements of 1/1 at (BT 087629) and (BT 082636), tanks fired H&I missions into (BT 080639) and (BT 080628). All fires were unobserved. Six rounds of 90 mm HE, two rounds of 90 mm canister, and three rounds of 90 mm WP were expended.

19 September: At 1500H, while in support of elements of 1/1 at (BT 097643), tank crewmen observed an undetermined number of VC at (BT 097639). A 90 mm HE was fired, resulting in one VC (KBGF) confirmed.

At 1530H, while in support of elements of 1/1 at (BT 097639), two VC were observed in a rowboat on a lake at (BT 098638). Tanks fired 90 mm HE resulting in two VC (KBGF) confirmed. During a search of the area nearby, three VC were apprehended.

At 1545H, while in support of elements of 1/1 at (BT 093658), tanks received sniper fire from their rear at (BT 097658). Returned 90 mm HE, and the sniping ceased. Area not searched, results undetermined.

20 September: At 1930H, while in support of elements of 1/1 at (BT 083603), tanks supported infantry with 90 mm HE fire when they became pinned down by enemy fire coming from a small village at (BT 093609). Area was not searched, results undetermined.

22 September: At 1430H, while in support of elements of 1/1 at (BT 137608), tanks and infantry received sniper fire from an enemy position across a river at (BT 136591). Tanks returned 90 mm HE and canister. Results of firing undetermined because of intervening river.

At 1800H, while in support of elements of 1/1 at (BT 063655), tanks assisted a friendly patrol that had been ambushed by VC at (BT 063660). Tanks fired 90 mm HE, resulting in three VC (KBGF) confirmed.

24 September: At 0800H, while in support of elements of 1/1 at (BT 114650), tanks effected a blocking position and fired a heavy volume of 90 mm HE at VC being flushed from a village and attempting to flee in boats at (BT 120650). This action resulted in ten VC (KBGF) confirmed and four VC (KBGF) probable.

At 1450H, while in support of elements of 1/1 at (BT 098656), tanks received sniper fire from an enemy position at (BT 099653). Tanks immediately returned 90 mm HE fire, and the enemy firing ceased. Enemy casualties undetermined.

At 1615H, a tank detonated an antitank mine at (BT 085615), resulting in moderate damage to the tank suspension system. Immediately after the mine was detonated, hostile arms fire was received from nearby positions. Tanks returned fire, and the enemy broke contact. There were no friendly casualties.

Gibson Recalls a Day in Vietnam

by Garry Gibson

[This story is reprinted from the USMC Vietnam Tankers Association's *Sponson Box* magazine, volume 7, number IV," September 2004. Edited for form but not for content.]

It was either September or October 1966; I was serving with Charlie Company, 3d Tank Battalion. The operation might have been HASTINGS or PRAIRIE; time has taken its toll on those kind of details.

Sergeant Timothy Tews was the tank commander (TC), and I was his driver. We had just received two new Marines who were serving as gunner and loader. They had very little experience. Apparently, they had both been drafted; and as a result, for a while there was some grumbling. Sergeant Tews was experienced enough to handle the loader and the gunner. I was a lance corporal and had begun my first six-month extension in-country.

Captain Paul F. Lessard was the senior tank officer. We were working with the Grunts doing a sweep and broke trail to our operational area. Nothing happened during the sweep until we turned to go back to the rear area. It was getting late, so we gathered all the Grunts on the tanks and began retracing our tracks. I had to keep our tracks just to the right of our old tracks. We were the lead tank; I was worried about mines. Suddenly, the ground gave way, and the nose of the tank dropped into a tank trap that was approximately 15 feet wide, 8 feet deep, and 20 feet long. It is amazing what fast reflexes one gets when he knows he's in the shit.

I slammed the tank into reverse and stomped on the accelerator. As the tank hit bottom, it roared straight back up and out of the tank trap and bounced to a stop about 6 feet from the tank trap. Rifles, helmets, and Marines went flying from the tank as we hit bottom. I stood up in the driver's seat to look into the hole. There was a pile of Marines in the hole, including Sergeant Tews and our new loader. By this time, the entire column had stopped. The word came down that the Marine Grunts would not ride on the tanks on the return to the rear area.

While command was reorganizing the column, I noticed piles of dirt about 20 yards on our right. I asked Sergeant Tews if he could see any movement from his vantage point. Sergeant Tews looked and immediately yelled, "Ambush right!" Sergeant Tews said to haul ass and get out of there. Just then, the NVA (North Vietnamese Army) volleyed RPGs (rocket-propelled grenades) at the column. One RPG hit the front of the company gunny's tank, killing the driver. The dead driver's foot froze on the accelerator, causing their tank's gun tube to ram into the gypsy rack of the tank directly in front. This collision blocked the entire column.

Sergeant Tews directed me out of the "kill zone" then gave me two hard right turns, which put us in line with the NVA assault force that was pouring out of the ravine directly in front of us. Sergeant Tews fired off a canister round into the NVA flank. As a result of our main gun tube hitting bottom in the tank trap, the gun would not return to battery. Then, the coaxial .30-caliber machine gun jammed. Tews told me to keep the gooks off the tank, and he went down into the turret to attempt to get both weapons working.

I had an M1 Garand loaded with 7.62 mm. I had purchased the weapon recently from a Seabee. I kept the M-1 behind the right headlight along with a handful of eight-round clips. From my position, I was able to take out four or five NVA before they noticed me. Once spotted, two NVA began firing at me. I used my last clip on those two and then jumped out of the tank to retrieve two empty clips that had ejected and hit the ground. I reloaded the clips and resumed firing from my driver's seat. Believe me, I was attempting to make every shot count. Through my comm helmet, I heard tactical net say that two phantoms were rolling in to drop napalm on the NVA. This was my cue to haul ass.

The entire column was behind us, so we were in the open and all alone. As a result, we were being hit by a lot of small-arms friendly fire. I dropped the gear shift into low and tried to do a hard right; that's when the left track broke. It had probably been damaged in the plunge into the tank trap earlier. I yelled, "Air strike, abandon tank!" I grabbed my rifle and headed for the rear of the tank. The loader was almost out when his holster hung up upon something. As he was struggling to get loose, I yanked him so hard his holster tore off his pistol belt as I threw him from the tank.

After the action was over, our track was repaired. For the remainder of the road march back to the rear area, we remained tactical with Grunts in a column of files on the left and tanks in column on the right, guns facing outboard.

Garry Gibson

29 September: From 291500H to 291530H, while conducting a search-and-clear operation with elements of the 1st Marines, tanks located at (BT 044659) fired across a stream into (BT 032659), expending twenty-five rounds of 90 mm HE, two rounds of 90 mm canister, and seven hundred rounds of .30-caliber machine gun. Results of fire unknown as the area could not be searched because of intervening body of water.

At 290800H, while in support of elements of the 1st Marines located at (BT 110625), tank crewmen observed four VC running from a village at (BT 110626). The tanks fired one round of 90 mm canister, resulting in two VC (KBGF) confirmed.

In Northern I Corps, the persistent enemy attacks during September appeared to be a desperate bid for a military victory, with its attendant propaganda value, before the fall monsoon hit. Failing in attacks from three different directions, the NVA resorted to a massive attack by fire against a specific target—Con Thien.

During the period 19–27 September, more than three thousand mortar, artillery, and rocket rounds blasted the position. The Americans retaliated by massing one of the greatest concentrations of firepower in support of a single division in the history of the Vietnam War. III MAF artillery units fired 12,577 rounds at known and suspected enemy positions in the region, while ships of the 7th Fleet fired 6,148 rounds at the same area. Marine and Air Force fighter pilots flew more than 5,200 close air support sorties and B-52 bombers of the Strategic Air Command dropped tons of ordnance on the enemy in and *north* of the DMZ. The Con Thien garrison applauded the results; North Vietnamese pressure on the outpost subsided as September drew to a close (GB-66).

In early October, Major General Herman Nickerson took command of the 1st Marine Division and moved his headquarters from Chu Lai to Da Nang. And "during the remaining months of 1966, the 1st Marine Division focused its main effort on pacification programs. A number of GOLDEN FLEECE and COUNTY FAIR operations were conducted throughout the fall months, helping the peasants to feel more secure in their villages" (GB-66).

October 1966
First Antitanks
Commanding Officer: Maj. R. E. Harris
Executive Officer: Maj. M. F. Manning
Operations Officer: Maj. J. J. Burke Jr.
Logistics Officer: Capt. C. R. Vanhorn
Location and Operations Summary:

Throughout the reporting period, 1st Antitank units displaced north DS respective infantry units as III MAF organizations moved closer to the face-to-face confrontation with the large and growing threat of the North Vietnamese Army.

First Antitank Battalion moved from the Chu Lai TAOR to the Da Nang TAOR, RVN.

H&S Company CO: 1st Lt. M. H. Collier
Location and Operations Summary: Camp Pendleton, CA

CO Company A (-): Capt. D. M. Hutson
Location and Operations Summary:

Company A (-)
1–10 October: OpCon 3d Marine Division, DS 1st Marines
11–31 October: OpCon 1st Marine Division, DS 1st Marines

CO Company B (Rein.): Capt. T. F. Dempsey
Location and Operations Summary:

Company B (Rein.)
1–5 October: OpCon 1st Marine Division, DS Chu Lai
6–17 October: OpCon 1st Marine Division, DS 5th Marines
18–24 October: OpCon 1st Marine Division, general support 1st MarDiv
25–31 October: Company B (-) OpCon 1st Marine Division, DS 4th Battalion 503 Infantry 173 Brigade USA

CO Company C: Capt. R. J. Esposito
Location and Operations Summary:

Company C
1–17 October 1966: OpCon 1st Marine Division, DS 7th Marines
18–31 October 1966: Company C (Rein.) OpCon 1st Marine Division, DS 5th Marines and 7th Marines

October 1966
First Tanks
Commanding Officer: Lt. Col. J. W. Clayborne
Executive Officer: Maj. R. D. McKee
Operations Officers: Capts. R. G. McPherson and F. U. Salas
Logistics Officers: Maj. T. M. Bryant and Capt. G. E. Hooker
Location and Operations Summary: Battalion CP, Da Nang (AT 998722)

In addition to support of the Chu Lai Defense Command during the month of October, a unit of this command participated in one major operation.

Operation LEE

On 030710, 2d Platoon (Rein.), Company C, supported by 1-M51 VTR from Company B, departed the Battalion CP for participation in Operation LEE in support of the 2d ROKMC Brigade.

H&S Company provided one rifle squad for participation in Operation LEE, and the assistant S-3 officer was assigned to Headquarters, 2d ROKMC Brigade as tank liaison officer.

On 041500, while moving south to join the 2d ROKMC Brigade, 2d Platoon, Company C received sniper fire from (BS 728894). Thirty rounds .50 caliber were returned, resulting in one VC KIA confirmed.

On 101600, 2d Platoon, Company C secured from Operation LEE and returned to the Battalion CP at 121330.

LESSONS LEARNED

During normal platoon-size operations, the M-51 VTR is not routinely employed. Based on previous experience and information obtained via an aerial reconnaissance on 030915, which disclosed the remoteness of the area to be encountered, the decision was made to employ the VTR.

During Operation LEE, the VTR employed proved to be a tremendous asset to all tracked vehicles operation in the area. Of particular significance was its continued assistance to the 1st Antitank Battalion.

(VTHF comment: Unfortunately, one of the lessons *not* learned was to write up the operation in a way that others can study it. Since Operation LEE was with the ROKMC, no organization above the company logged an after-action report. The Korean units operated with secrecy. It appears that the senior-level leadership studiedly ignored the lack of reporting. In the case of Operation LEE, even lower-level units allowed it.)

H&S CO: Maj. J. P. McGill
Location and Operations Summary: Same as Battalion CP

H&S Company provided logistical and maintenance support for two gun companies until 220800 when it became Battalion Rear Echelon at (BT 515040).

At 271130, additional elements of H&S Company arrived at Da Nang. H&S Company provided one rifle squad for security purposes to accompany 2d Platoon, Company C during Operation LEE.

At 220800, the Battalion Headquarters Section, H&S Company (-), and Company B departed from the CP at (BT 515040) for the Sand Ramp at Chu Lai and embarked aboard the USS *Litchfield* (LST-901) at 231530. These units sailed from Chu Lai at 240510 and arrived at Da Nang 241500. They proceeded to the Bridge Ramp in Da Nang and commenced unloading at 251110.

These units arrived at the present site of the 1st Tank Battalion at 251330.

CO Company A (Rein.): Capt. C. R. Brabec
Location and Operations Summary: Chu Lai (BT 515040)

Company A (Rein.), 1st Tank Battalion, is within the Chu Lai TAOR. The 1st Tank Battalion retains AdCon of Company A.

During the month of October 1966, Company A (-) remained DS 5th Marines until 220800, at which time it moved to (BT 515040), former site of the 1st Tank Battalion Headquarters to provide support for the Chu Lai Defense Command and the Chu Lai TAOR.

One section of three flame tanks is attached to Company A. The 1st Platoon, Company A rejoined its parent company on 220800 and continues to support the Chu Lai Defense Command.

Company A (Rein.) remains under the operational control of Task Force X-ray.

On 4 October, Staff Sergeant Roy T. Sabo of Flint, Michigan, was awarded the Silver Star medal for heroism. His citation read as follows:

 **SABO, ROY T.**

Synopsis

The President of the United States takes pleasure in presenting the Silver Star Medal to Roy T. Sabo (1653906), Staff Sergeant, U.S. Marine Corps, for conspicuous gallantry and intrepidity in action while serving with Company "A," 1st Tank Battalion, 1st Marine Division (Rein.), FMF, in connection with combat operations against the enemy in the Republic of Vietnam on October 4, 1966. By his courage, aggressive fighting spirit and steadfast devotion to duty in the face of extreme personal danger, Staff Sergeant Sabo upheld the highest traditions of the Marine Corps and the United States Naval Service.

Home Town: Flint, Michigan

CO Company B: Capt. L. E. Cherico
Location and Operations Summary: Da Nang (AT 945763)

Company B (-) remained DS 7th Marines until 220800 when it joined the Battalion Headquarters Section for embarkation and movement to the 1st Tank Battalion's present location.

The 3d Platoon, Company B supported the Chu Lai Defense Command until 220800 when it rejoined its parent company for the move north.

At 230559, 1st Platoon, Company B was placed DS 4th Battalion, 503d Airborne Infantry, 173d Brigade.

Company B Headquarters and one platoon provide security for the area now occupied by Company B.

The transportation unit for the 173d ABN BDE and the Army S/5 Civil Affairs Team for segments of the Da Nang area occupy the same area.

COs Company C: Capt. F. U. Salas and 1st Lt. C. E. Barnett
Location and Operations Summary: Da Nang (BT 066715)

Company C was under the OpCon of the 3d Tank Battalion until 260800.

October 1966
Third Antitanks
Commanding Officers: Lt. Col. D. E. Newton and Maj. C. R. Stiffler
Executive Officer: Capt. D. C. Satcher
Operations Officers: WO C. C. Harris and 1st Lt. J. C. Debilio
Logistics Officer: Capt. D. C. Satcher
Location and Operations Summary: Da Nang TAOR

H&S Company CO: 1st Lt. D. K. Caswell
Location and Operations Summary: Da Nang TAOR

H&S Company. During the month of October, the company continued the normal functions of providing administrative and logistical support for the Ontos companies.

The reaction force continued to conduct ambushes and patrols within the battalion's patrol area of responsibility.

CO Company A (-) (Rein.): Capt. A. A. Compton
Location and Operations Summary: Phu Bai TAOR

Company A (-) (Rein.) continued DS 3d Marine Division.

On 100800H, this company started displacement from Da Nang to Dong Ha.

The 1st Platoon continued to support 2/3. The heavy section was located on Hill 65 in support of F/2/3. The light section was located in support of G/2/3.

8 October: The light section accompanied a company-size sweep west of Hill 65 with no enemy contact. The platoon expended thirteen major rounds (106 mm recoilless rifle HEP-T) on H&I fire missions with unknown results.

On 111300H, the 1st Platoon embarked aboard an LCU at Da Nang and arrived at Dong Ha at 121300H.

16 October: They were assigned the mission of supporting K, L, and M/3/4 in defense of Camp J. J. Carroll. The 2d Platoon continued DS D/1/3 at positions near Le My. On 4 October, this platoon fired twelve major rounds at twelve VCS with unknown results. On 6 October, the 173d Airborne assumed responsibility for the 1/3 TAOR. This platoon fired a total of 579 major rounds on H&I fire missions in support of 1/3.

On 111300H, the 2d Platoon embarked aboard an LCU at Da Nang arrived at Dong Ha on 121300H.

17 October: The light section moved to (YD 026561) in support of I/3/4. The heavy section remained at Camp Carroll in support of H&S 3/4. This platoon fired a total of 187 major rounds on H&I fire missions in support of 3/4.

The 3d Platoon continued in support of 2/26. The light section was located on Hill 20 (AT 925691) in support of G/2/26 on Hills 22 and 41 with a single Ontos on each hill. The 3d Ontos from the heavy section remained at the platoon CP in support of H/2/26. On 7 October, the light section accompanied a company-size sweep with no enemy contact. This platoon fired a total of 106 major rounds on H&I fire missions in support of 2/26.

On 101300H, the 3d Platoon embarked aboard an LCU at Da Nang and arrived at Dong Ha on 111300H. From 12 to 15 October, this platoon supported 3/4 in defense of Camp J. J. Carroll.

16 October: The 3d Platoon moved to the Rockpile (XD 977567) in support of 2/9.

22 October: The 3d Platoon fired twelve major rounds at a squad of NVA with unknown results. This platoon fired 1,137 major rounds on H&I fire missions in support 2/9 and 3/4.

24 October: The 3/4 relieved 2/9, and the 3d Platoon continued in support of K/3/4 and M/3/4.

CO Company B: 1st Lt. S. L. Camby
Location and Operations Summary: Phu Bai TAOR

Company B continued DS 3d Marine Division with the company CP at Hue/Phu Bai.

1 October: Began DS 2/4. It was employed as security for mine sweeps and security for a medical infirmary at Goa Lai. One section remained in defensive positions along Route 14.

7 October: One VC grenade was thrown into this position. There were no USMC casualties. One major round was fired at VC with undetermined results.

8 October: This platoon returned to Hue/Phu Bai and occupied defensive positions in support of 2/4. The 2d Platoon continued DS 4th Marines. The light section remained DS 2/9 at the Rockpile (XD 979568).

13 October: The light section participated in a company-size sweep with no enemy contact.

20 October: The light section was relieved by the 3d Platoon, Company A, 2d ATBn.

21 October: The light section joined the heavy section in defense of Dong Ha airstrip in support of 2/4, with no further enemy contact.

The 3d Platoon continued to support the company CP at Phu Bai.

8 October: The platoon relieved the 1st Platoon and assumed support of 2/4. The heavy section provided security for the Gao Lai Medical Facilities in the morning and occupied defensive positions at the company CP at night. This section fired thirty-five .30-caliber MG rounds at VC snipers with negative results. On 8 October, the light section maintained defensive positions at the artillery position on Route 14 and remained there through the reporting period.

CO Company C (-): Capt. S. T. Flynn
Location and Operations Summary: Phu Bai TAOR

Company C continued DS 9th Marines.

The 1st Platoon continued OpCon of the 1st Antitank Battalion until 24 October when the platoon returned to parent organizational control.

28 October: The 1st Platoon moved one section to (AT 914597) in support of G/2/3 and one section to (AT 878576) in support of F/2/3. This platoon expended ten major rounds on H&I fire missions with unknown results.

The 2d Platoon continued in support of the 3/9. The light section in support of L/3/9 provided security for mine sweeps of Highway 14 for the entire period with no enemy contact. The heavy section in support of H&S/3/9 was deployed in defensive positions along the An Hoa airstrip for the entire reporting period with no enemy contact.

The 3d Platoon continued in support of 1/26. The light section was located at (AT 968575) in support of A/1/26. The heavy section (-)

was located at the ferry crossing at (AT 925535) in support of B/1/26. One Ontos remained at the company CP (AT 967617) as an element of a reaction force.

4 October: The heavy section observed twelve VC crossing the river in boats. Ten major rounds were expended, resulting in two VC KIA confirmed.

14 October: The light section received sniper fire and returned two major rounds with undetermined results.

17 October: The light section in support of A/1/26 expended six major rounds at a VC tunnel complex with undetermined results.

24 October: The heavy section (-) moved to Hill 37 to support F/2/3 (AT 878576), and the light section moved to (AT 914597) to support G/2/3. The light section in support of G/2/3 fired twenty-nine major rounds on H&I fire missions.

28 October: The 3d Platoon returned to the company CP.

CO Company A (-) (Rein.), 1st ATBn (OpCon 3d ATBn): Capt. D. M. Hutson
Location and Operations Summary: Da Nang TAOR

Company A (-) (Rein.), 1st ATBn (OpCon 3d ATBn) did not participate in any major operations but continued to support the 1st Marines on squad- and platoon-size patrols and provided a mechanized reaction force for units of the 1st Marines.

7 October: The 1st Platoon DS K/3/1 expended five major rounds at VC positions with undetermined results.

13, 14, and 16 October: The platoon expended eight major rounds, 780 .30-caliber machine gun and fifty spotting rifle rounds at VC snipers with unknown results.

17 October: Two major rounds were fired at VC snipers with results of three VN civilians wounded. During this period, the platoon fired thirty-four major rounds on H&I fire missions.

The 3d Platoon in support of 1/1 took part in blocking force and a sweeping operation with no VC contact.

The 1st Platoon, Company C, 3d ATBn (OpCon Company A [-], 1st ATBn) DS 2/1 expended 10 major, 110 spotter, and 800 .30-caliber machine gun rounds with unknown results. There was no further contact.

24 October: OpCon was dropped to Company C, 3d ATBn. Company A, 1st ATBn OpCon was dropped on 232400H October '66.

The intense fighting around Con Thien, the newly named Razorback Ridge, Rockpile, Mutter's Ridge, and the multiple reporting of NVA activity above, in, and below the DMZ, raised COMUSMACV's concerns that the enemy would push more forces across the DMZ and possibly skirt the Marine forces and take Quang Tri Province with the resulting loss of Dong Ha. The result of these concerns of General Westmoreland and his staff in Saigon "to blunt these movements," Westmoreland "suggested" General Walt put Marines at Khe Sanh" (GB-66). General Walt, with strong approval of his staff, resisted, believing that Khe Sanh had no military significance. General English stated, "It's far away from anything. You could lose it and you really haven't lost a damn thing."

With evidence of a large NVA force just to the northeast of Khe Sanh— and fear of losing face if *ordered* by Westmoreland to occupy Khe Sanh—Walt directed 1/3 to be helilifted into Khe Sanh. Intensive patrolling uncovered no enemy activity.

On 1 October, General Walt reactivated Task Force Delta to set up in Dong Ha and to take control of Operation PRAIRIE from Colonel Cereghino. Even though reports that three NVA divisions were poised to charge across the DMZ and take South Vietnam's northern province of Quang Tri, it did not happen.

October 1966
Third Tanks
Commanding Officer: Lt. Col. W. R. Corson
Executive Officers: Majs. J. G. Doss Jr. and E. R. Larson
Operations Officers: Majs. E. R. Larson and E. L. Tunget
Logistics Officers: Capt. R. E. Downard and 2d Lt. R. J. Bright
Location and Operations Summary: Da Nang (AT 989708) (Hill 34)

Tank combat operations during the month of October were in support of two major operations, MACON and PRAIRIE, and other operations in the TAORs. These operations accounted for sixty VC (KBGF) confirmed, forty VC (KBGF) probable, one VC (WBGF) confirmed, two VC (WBGF) probable, nine VCC, and twelve VCS apprehended. Additionally, tank action was responsible for the sinking of four boats.

Tank mobility was greatly reduced during October because of heavy rains. Certain areas in both the Da Nang and PRAIRIE TAORs became completely impassable for tanks for several days due to flooding, deep mud, and washed-out river and stream fords.

H&S Company COs: 1st Lts. M. F. Beirne IV and R. D. McDaniel
Location and Operations Summary: Da Nang (AT 989708)

CO Company A: Capt. A. W. Facklam Jr.
Location and Operations Summary: Prairie (YD 063544)

1 October: At 012005H, while in support of elements of 2/26 located at (AT 950727), tanks and infantry received sniper from (AT 950724). The tanks returned fire with 90 mm canister, resulting in one VC (KBGF) probable.

4 October: From 041945H to 042325H, while in support of elements of the 3d Marines located at (AT 914597), tanks fired 90 mm H&I

fires. Results unknown as all fires were unobserved. At 042130H, 042230H, and 042330H, while in support of elements of 2/3 located at (AT 877575), tanks fired 90 mm H&I fire into enemy positions at (AT 819565) with undetermined results.

6 to 31 October: Company A was deployed in the PRAIRIE TAOR, conducting operations in support of 3d Marine elements in that area. Significant operational events are recorded under Operation PRAIRIE.

12 October: At 120730H, Company A tanks, while in support of elements of 2/5, departed Cam Lo Area (YD 146603) for 2/5 CP vicinity of grid square (YD 1269). While en route, the tanks and supporting infantry were ambushed at (YD 126666). A heavy volume of small-arms and antitank fire was received. The tanks and infantry deployed, and the tanks returned a heavy volume of 90 mm fire (canister and HE) and .30- and .50-caliber machine gun fire into the enemy positions. Artillery fire was called by an AO on station. The attack came from the left rear as the tanks were leaving a fording site. Three tanks were penetrated by AT weapons, probably RPG rounds.

At 121345H, a platoon of tanks from Company C was dispatched from Cam Lo (YD 146603) to support the ambushed tanks and infantry. The link-up was made at 121415H, and all units proceeded to 2/5 CP located at (YD 115701). One tank platoon leader was KIA, and four tank crewmen were WIA (nonmedevac). Results of the tank fire were eight VC (KBGF) confirmed and fifteen VC (KBGF) probable.

Donald W. Rohleder, first lieutenant, age 23, Baltimore, Maryland, a Marine tank platoon commander, was killed during an ambush of his unit on 12 October 1966.

16 October: At 161930H, Company A tanks, in support of elements of 2/5 at (XD 978585), fired 90 mm rounds in H&I missions into (XD 965614). Results unknown as fires were unobserved.

At 211800H, Company A tanks, while in support of elements of 3/4 (XD 987548), fired H&I missions at close range with the 90 mm gun. Results of fire unknown as the area was not searched.

25 October: From 252000H to 260500H, Company A tanks, in support of elements of the 3d Marines at (XD 981543), fired 90mm H&I missions into (XD 987538) and (XD 975539). Results of fire unknown as the areas were not searched.

26 October: From 261800H to 261855H, Company A tanks, while in support of elements of the 3d Marines located at (XD 983583) and (C+XD 979568), fired 90 mm rounds in H&I missions into (XD 988583) and (XD 973584). Results of fire unknown as the area was not searched.

27 October: From 270800H to 271700H, Company A tanks, while in support of elements of the 3d Marines located at (XD 983545), (XD 983543), and (XD 984543), fired H&I missions with 90 mm rounds into (XD 978538), (XD 988542), (XD 975537), (XD 985541), and (XD 975537). Results of the firing unknown as the areas were not searched.

From 271900H to 280600H, Company A tanks, while in support of elements of 2/9 and 3/4 at (XD 977565) and (XD 976569), fired H&I missions with the 90 mm gun into GS (XD 9855), (XD 9856), (XD 9857), and (XD 9860). Results of fires undetermined as the areas were not searched.

28 October: From 280340H to 280800H, Company A tank, while in support of elements of 2/9 and 3/4 at (XD 983544) and (XD 984574), fired H&I missions with the 90 mm gun into (XD 989538), (XD 987547), (XD 988542), (XD 989543), and (XD 970540). Results of fires undetermined as the areas were not searched.

From 281930H to 290600H, Company A tanks, while in support of elements of 3/4 at (XD 984543) and (XD 984544), fired H&I missions with the 90 mm gun at (XD 978538), (XD 988539), (XD 985541), and (XD 989540). Results of fires undetermined as the areas were not searched.

COs Company B: Capt. E. L. Tunget and 1st Lt. D. B. Garner
Location and Operations Summary: Da Nang (AT 9262611)

6 October: From 061600H to 061930H, while in support of 1/26 located at (AT 975595), tanks went to the assistance of infantry who had entered an enemy minefield and were receiving heavy automatic weapons fire from enemy positions at (AT 976591). The tanks fired 90 mm and .50-caliber machine gun fire, resulting in two VC (KBGF) probable.

8 October: At 080932H, while in support of 1/26 located at (AT 967582), a tank received ten rounds of automatic fire and fifty rounds of small-arms fire from (AT 974582), (AT 980587), and (AT 974589). The tank returned fire with 90 mm rounds. The area was searched with negative results.

10 October: At 101500H, while in support of 1/26 located at (AT 947565), a tank responded to a fire mission request from the infantry who had been receiving sniper fire from (AT 944568). The tank fired 90 mm HE at the area from which the sniper fire had been received. The area was searched with negative results.

12 October: At 120900H, while in support of elements of 1/26, a tank detonated an AT mine at (AT 904545), resulting in moderate damage to the suspension system. Two tank crewmen were WIA, nonmedevac.

14 October: At 141350H, while in support of elements of 2/3 at (AT 877574), tanks fired 90 mm rounds at a boat crossing in the Song Vu Gia at (AT 850552). The boat was destroyed, and there were three VC (KBGF) confirmed. At 141715H, while in support of elements of 2/26 at (AT 970595), tanks returned .30- and .50-caliber machine gun fire

at a sniper who was firing at a road construction crew. Results of the fire were undetermined as the area was not searched.

15 October: At 151215H, while in support of elements of 1/26, tanks and infantry received a heavy volume of sniper fire from (AT 977585). The tanks fired 90 mm rounds into the area with both the infantry and tanks observing direct hits on target. A search of the area revealed evidence of eight VC (KBGF) probable.

16 October: At 161300H, while in support of elements of 1/26 at (AT 963612) and (AT

959602), tanks and infantry received fire from (AT 959604) and (AT 960605). The tanks fired 90 mm rounds into the areas. Infantry searched the areas with negative results.

17 October: At 170720H, while in support of elements of 1/26 at (AT 965612), tanks and infantry received sniper from (AT 971598). The tanks returned fire with 90 mm rounds. Results of the fire unknown as the area was not searched.

At 171905H, while in support of elements of 1/26 at (AT 877574), tanks spotted two boats with VC and equipment on the Song Vu Gia at (AT 855555) and (AT 855553). The tanks fired 90 mm rounds. Results of fire: two boats destroyed, three VC (KBGF) confirmed.

18 October: At 180720H, while in support of elements of 2/3 at (AT 965612), tanks fired 90 mm rounds in support of infantry who were receiving small-arms fire from (AT 971598). The area was searched with negative results.

At 180945H, while in support of 2/3, tanks went to the assistance of one squad from F/2/3 at (AT 877574), which was receiving heavy enemy fire from (AT 873566). The tanks fired 90 mm rounds into the enemy position. Results of the tank fire were not determined due to an intervening river.

19 October: At 191215H, while in support of elements of 2/3 at (AT 876573), tanks fired 90 mm rounds at an enemy supply train at (AT 848557). Results of the fire were undetermined as the area was not searched.

At 191500H, while in support of elements of 2/3 at (AT 876573), tanks fried 90 mm rounds at an enemy supply train at (AT 848555). Results of the fire undetermined as the area was not searched.

At 192210H, while in support of elements of 1/26 at (AT 919546), tanks delivered 90 mm and .30-caliber machine gun fire at a light 100 meters south of the friendly position. Results of the fire were undetermined as the area was not searched, but the light was extinguished.

20 October: At 201700H, while in support of elements of 1/26 at (AT 901549), tanks received automatic weapons fire from (AT 902548). The tanks delivered 90 mm and .30- and .50-caliber machine gun fire into the area. Results of the fire were undetermined. The area was not searched.

21 October: At 211500H, while in support of elements of 1/26 at (AT 968583), tanks and infantry received sniper fire from an enemy position at (AT 965587). The tanks delivered 90 mm and .30- and .50-caliber machine gun fire into the area. Results unknown as the area was not searched.

22 October: At 221415H, while in support of elements of 1/26 and while on a sweep at (AT 968594), tanks and infantry received sniper fire from (AT 968604). The tanks returned fire with 90 mm and .30- and .50-caliber machine gun fire. Results of fire: one VC (KBGF) confirmed.

23 October: At 231615H, while in support of elements of 1/26 at (AT 965612) and (AT 967605), tanks and infantry received a heavy volume of small-arms fire from (AT 973613) and (AT 961602). The tanks

returned fire with 90 mm and .30-caliber machine gun fire. Results of fire unknown as the area was not searched.

30 October: At 302000H, while in support of elements of 1/26 at (AT 967605), tanks received sixty rounds small-arms fire from an estimated two automatic weapons at (AT 969605). The tanks returned fire with .30-caliber machine guns. Results of firing were undetermined as the area was not searched.

31 October: At 311800H, while in support of elements of 2/3 at (AT 878576), tanks fired 90 mm rounds at two VC with rifles by infantry with a 20-power telescope. These VC were believed to be part of a sniper squad operating in the area. Direct hits were observed on the target. The area was not searched due to the intervening river. The tanks were credited with two VC (KBGF) probable.

Operation MACON

The 2d Platoon of Company B remained DS 3/9 throughout the month of October on Operation MACON. Although the tanks were actively engaged, enemy contacts were negligible with no known enemy casualties inflicted through tank action.

Op file, Operation MACON, 4 July–29 October 1966—dated 7/8/1966, document no. 1201063074

3 October: At 031030H, while in support of elements of the 3d Battalion, tanks located at (AT 875507) fired at two VC moving through brush along the riverbank at (AT 874510). Results of fires unknown as the area was not searched.

At 031210H, while in support of elements of the 9th Marines, infantry and tanks located at (AT 866496) received fifteen to twenty rounds of small-arms fire from enemy located at (AT 864499). The tanks returned fire into the enemy location. Results of the fire were unknown as the area was not searched.

At 031830H, while in support of elements of 3/9, tanks and infantry located at (AT 926527) received one round sniper fire from enemy located at (AT 927525). The tanks returned fire into the enemy location. The area was searched by infantry with negative results.

CO Company C: Capt. P. F. Lessard
Location and Operations Summary: Prairie (YD 246599)

All activities are recorded under Operation PRAIRIE.

Op file, Operation BUILD-UP in prairie area, 22 July–16 October 1966—dated 7/26/1966, document no. 1201064003

Op File, Operation PRAIRIE Command Chronology, 1 August '66—dated 8/3/1966, document no. 1201064006

Op file, Operation PRAIRIE, 3 August–1 December 1966—dated 8/4/1966, document no. 1201064007

Company C, 3d Tank Battalion remained DS 4th Marines on Operation PRAIRIE.

6 October 1966: Company A commenced deployment from the Da Nang TAOR to the PRAIRIE TAOR. Deployment was completed on 9 October, and operations were conducted during the remainder of the month in support of elements of the 3d Marine Division on Operation PRAIRIE.

Operation PRAIRIE

1 October: At 011910H, Company C tanks, while in support of elements of 4th Marines at (XD 962619), fired a heavy volume of 90 mm fire in H&I missions into suspected VC positions at (XD 973616). Results of fire were undetermined as the area was not searched.

2 October: From 020800H to 021600H, Company C tanks, while in support of elements of the 4th Marines located at (XD 974565), fired a

heavy volume of indirect fire with the 90 mm gun. Fire was delivered into grid squares (XD 9656), (XD 9661), (XD 9455). Results unknown as fires were not observed.

At 021855H, while in support of elements of the 4th Marines and while providing security for engineers on a road sweep at (YD 025562), tanks fired H&I missions into grid squares (YD 0552) and (YD 0652). Results unknown as fires were not observed. The road sweep was completed without incident.

3 October: From 030630H to 030900H, Company C tanks, while in support of elements of the 4th Marines, provided security for engineers on a road sweep from (YD 061550) to (YD 033561). The sweep was completed without incident.

4 October: From 040900H to 041900H, Company C tanks, while in support of 3/4, fired a heavy volume of 90 mm HE and WP rounds from (XD 975569) to (XD 968617) at a bunker. Two probable secondary explosions were observed. Other results were unknown as area was not searched.

From 040630H to 040900H, Company C tanks, while in support of elements of the 4th Marines, conducted a road sweep from (YD 061543) to (YD 055562) without incident.

From 042000H to 050602H, Company C tanks, while in support of 3/4, fired 90 mm H&I missions into enemy positions on Hill 484 at (XD 967617). Results were unknown as the fires were unobserved.

5 October: From 050900H to 051700H, Company C tanks, while in support of the 3/4, provided direct fire from (XD 974569) to (XD 5617) with 90 mm fire. Hill 484 at (XD 965617) was secured by 3/4 with the assistance of covering tank fire.

6 October: At 061830H, Company C tanks, while in support of elements of the 4th Marines, conducted a road sweep from (YD 061543) to (YD

055562) without incident. At 061830H, while in support of elements of the 4th Marines, tanks and infantry received one mortar round, the type believed to be 120 mm. Also, the round appeared to be a registration round as it landed in the center of the CP.

13 October: At 131100H, Company C tanks were in support of elements of 2/5 on a sweep operation when a tank detonated an AT mine at (YD 134719). The tank received moderate damage to the suspension system.

At 131645H, Company C tanks, while in support of elements of 2/5 at (YD 118718), received mortar and small-arms fire from VC encircling their perimeter. The tanks fired a heavy volume of 90 mm and .30-caliber machine gun fire into the enemy positions. The infantry searched the area and discovered fifteen VC (KBGF) confirmed.

At 131930H, while in support of elements of 2/5, Company C tanks and infantry were ambushed by a VC platoon dug in at (YD 188718). The tanks returned 90 mm fire and a large volume of machine gun fire. Results of the fire were four VC (KBGF) confirmed and four individual weapons captured. One tank crewman was WIA (nonmedevac).

14 October: At 141400H, Company C tanks, while in support of elements of the 4th

Marines at (YD 133959), observed NVAs setting up gun positions at (YD 220717) and (YD 177724). The tanks fired into both positions with 90 mm rounds. Results of the fire were unknown as the area was not searched.

21 October: At 211500H, Company C tanks, while in support of elements of the 4th Marines at (YD 148604), received approximately four rounds of mortars of undetermined size from an unknown enemy position. The tanks attempted to observe further mortar tube flashes with negative results.

November 1966

First Antitanks: From CC-1AT, 10/66, "The Battalion Commander, LtCol R.E. Harris, was killed instantly by sniper fire at 1145 in the Hai Van Pass area (Quang Nam Province, South Vietnam) while visiting units of Company 'B.' The Battalion Sergeant Major and the Battalion Commander's driver were wounded in the action."

🎖 Robert E. Harris, lieutenant colonel, age 37, Sioux City, IA

🎖 Charles L. Isley III, corporal, age 20, Philadelphia, Pennsylvania, an Ontos crewman, was killed on 20 November 1966 while serving with Company C, 1st Antitank Battalion as a result of a mining incident. He died instantly.

November 1966
First Tanks
Commanding Officer: Lt. Col. J. W. Clayborne
Executive Officer: Maj. R. D. McKee
Operations Officer: Capt. F. U. Salas
Logistics Officer: Capt. G. E. Hooker
Location and Operations Summary: Da Nang (AT 998722) (Hill 34)

In addition to supporting the Chu Lai Defense Command during the month of October, a unit of this command participated in one major operation.

Operation LEE (030710–121330)
2d Platoon, Company C, 1st Tank Battalion

On 030710, the 2d Platoon, Company C (Rein.), supported by 1-M51 VTR from Company B, departed the battalion CP for participation in Operation LEE in support of the 2d ROKMC Brigade.

H&S Company provided one rifle squad for participation in Operation LEE, and the assistant S-3 officer was assigned to Headquarters, 2d ROKMC Brigade as tank liaison officer.

On 041500, while moving south to join the 2d ROKMC Brigade, 2d Platoon, Company C received sniper fire from (BS 728894). Thirty rounds of .50 caliber were returned, resulting in one VC KIA confirmed.

On 101600, 2d Platoon, Company C secured from Operation LEE and returned to the battalion CP at 121330.

H&S CO: Maj. J. P. McGill
Location and Operations Summary: Same as battalion CP

H&S Company provided logistical and maintenance support for two gun companies. H&S Company provided one rifle squad nightly as additional security for the Naval Supply Activity Petroleum, Oil, and Lubricants Dump at (AT 987732). In addition, a ten-man security detail was assigned on a temporary additional duty basis to Ammunition Supply Point. This commitment was changed to one officer and four enlisted on 29 November 1966.

At 200330H, the 1st Tank Battalion provided a rifle platoon to the Southern Sector Area Defense coordinator for participation in Operation BALTIMORE. The rifle platoon assumed blocking positions at the north (AT 994728) and south (AT 993715) entrances to Phong Bac hamlet. The operation concluded at 201545H, and the results were four Viet Cong captured.

CO Company A: Capt. C. R. Brabec
Location and Operations Summary: Chu Lai (BT 515040)

During the month of November, Company A (Rein.) remained under the operational control of Task Force X-ray and supported the Chu Lai Defense Command.

CO Company B: Capt. L. E. Cherico
Location and Operations Summary: Da Nang (AT 945763)

Company B remained DS 4th Battalion, 303d Airborne Infantry, 173d Brigade. On 8 November 1966, Company B provided two tanks DS Company E/2/3 at (AT 935664) and (AT 954666), relieving two tanks from Company C, 1st Tank Battalion.

On 1 November, the 2d Platoon, Company B fired forty-six rounds of harassing and interdiction fire in support of the 4th Battalion, 503d Airborne Infantry. The rounds were fired from platoon positions at (AT 895821) and (AT 892771).

On 18 November, a dozer tank from Company B conducted minesweeping operations near the Da Nang Airfield. The dozer tank utilized a locally constructed mine-exploding device. Eleven M-16 and eighty-nine M-14 antipersonnel mines were destroyed.

At 241810H, a fire team-sized outpost manned by 7th Engineers personnel was attacked by an estimated squad of Viet Cong. The outpost, located in the vicinity of (BT 936767), placed a call for assistance over the Zone B Defensive Net. Company B, 1st Tank Battalion monitors this net, and immediately upon hearing the call for assistance, Company B activated its reaction squad and two tanks. As soon as the 11th Marines granted permission, the reaction squad and tanks were dispatched to assist the outmanned fire team. The reaction squad was successful in driving off the Viet Cong, and as they did so, another relief unit managed to contact the outpost. The Company B reaction squad received no casualties and was commended for its prompt and efficient response.

COs Company C: 1st Lt. C. E. Barnett and Capt. P. S. Weigand
Location and Operations Summary: Da Nang (BT 066715)

Company C remained DS 1st Marines. The 3d Platoon furnished two tanks DS E/2/3, from 1 to 8 November.

🎖 On 1 November, Gerald W. Maddox received his first of two Purple Hearts—this month!

At 051400H, a section of two tanks from Company C participated in a search-and-destroy operation with elements of the 3/1. The tank section was credited with two Viet Cong killed at (BT 038664) confirmed by the infantry unit.

🎖 On 30 November, Gerald W. Maddox received his second Purple Heart—this month!

At 251215H, a section of three tanks from the 3d Platoon, Company C established a blocking position at (BT 094613). This section, in support of D/1/1, fired upon four Viet Cong as they fled from the sweeping force. A search of the area resulted in one Viet Cong killed in action confirmed.

At 261100H, a section of three tanks from the 1st Platoon, Company C participated in a sweep operation with elements of Company K/3/1. One Viet Cong was observed running toward a bridge at (BT 106638). The Viet Cong was fired upon, and a search revealed one Viet Cong killed in action confirmed.

November 1966
Third Antitanks
Commanding Officer: Maj. C. R. Stiffler
Executive Officer: Capt. D. C. Satcher
Operations Officer: 1st Lt. J. C. Debilio
Logistics Officer: Capt. D. C. Satcher
Location and Operations Summary: Da Nang TAOR

COs H&S Company: 1st Lt. D. K. Caswell and 2d Lt. C. P. Wager
Location and Operations Summary: Da Nang TAOR

H&S Company. During the month of November, the company continued the normal functions of providing administrative and logistical support for the Ontos companies. The reaction force continued to conduct ambushes and patrols within the battalion's patrol area of responsibility. Work on the improvement of the CP defensive perimeter continued.

CO Company A (-) (Rein.): Capt. A. A. Compton
Location and Operations Summary: Phu Bai TAOR

Company A continued in support of the 3d Marine Division.

The 1st Platoon started the reporting period in support of 3/3 on the Rockpile. The light section was located at (YD 978587) in support of I, K, M, and H&S/3/3; and the heavy section was located at (YD 978587) in support of L/3/3. Heavy rains curtailed any mechanized patrols, and the platoons' positions remained static throughout the reporting period. This platoon expended 657 major rounds (106 mm HEP-T) on H&I fire missions with no known results.

The 2d Platoon continued in support of 2/9. The light section in support of F/2/9 was located at (YD 026561). During the reporting period, the light section participated in three platoon-size patrols with no enemy contact. The heavy section was located at Camp J. J. Carroll in support of H&S, E, H/2/9. This platoon expended 711 major rounds on H&I fires with unknown results. Positions remained fairly static throughout the reporting period with no significant enemy contact.

The 3d Platoon started the reporting period located at (YD 605141) in support of 4/12. On 2 November, this platoon received eight 60 mm mortar rounds and SA fire at (YD 227605). The platoon returned 150 rounds of .30-caliber machine gun fire with unknown results. On 10 November, the "old" 3d Platoon was designated 1st Platoon, Company B and moved to Dong Ha. On 10 November, the new 3d Platoon started Operation LAM SON 328 in support of 4/12 and the 1st ARVN Division. On 17 November, the platoon returned to the company CP (YD 065541) and remained as a reaction force in the defense of Camp

J. J. Carroll. This platoon had no significant enemy contact throughout the reporting period.

On Saturday, 12 November 1966, Juan Torres, lance corporal, age 20, El Paso, Texas, an Ontos crewman serving in Company A, 3d Antitank Battalion, was involved in a vehicle accident and died a day later on 13 November.

CO Company B: Capt. S. L. Camby
Location and Operations Summary: Phu Bai TAOR

Company B continued in support of the 3d Marine Division.

The 1st Platoon continued in support of 2/4 manning defensive positions on the Phu Bai perimeter. On 10 November, the 3d Platoon, B Company was designated 1st Platoon, B Company. The old 1st Platoon rotated with BLT 2/4, and the new 1st Platoon relieved the 2d Platoon of its duties at Dong Ha. The 1st Platoon remained in defensive positions at Dong Ha for the rest of the reporting period with no enemy contact.

The 2d Platoon continued in support of the 4th Marines at Dong Ha until November 10 when they moved by LCU to Phu Bai and relieved the 3d Platoon in place. The heavy section provided security for the medical facility at Ja Lay (YD 819178). On 17 November, a 20-pound mine was discovered at the medical facility and blown in place. The heavy section continued supporting the patrol base and medical facilities until 25 November, when they were relieved by the heavy section of the 3d Platoon. The heavy section returned to the company CP (YD 894143) on 25 November and assumed the defensive missions of the vital area around the airstrip. The light section provided security for the artillery positions at (YD 980050) until 12 November when they moved to support the patrol base along Route 14 (YD 931060). The light section expended fifty-eight major rounds (106 mm HEP-T) on H&I fire missions with unknown results. The light section was relieved in place on 25 November by the 3d Platoon and returned to the company CP for defense of the airstrip.

The 3d Platoon continued in support of 1/4. The heavy section provided security for the medical facility at Ja Lay (YD 819177). On 7 November B-35 hit a mine at (YD 819178), resulting in two WIAs and heavy damage to the vehicle. The heavy section was relieved in place by the 2d Platoon and returned to the company CP to assume defensive positions along the Phu Bai airstrip. The heavy section was relieved in place by the 2d Platoon and returned to the company CP until 25 November when they relieved the 2d Platoon at Ja Lay. They remained at Ja Lay for the rest of the reporting period with no further contact. The light section started the reporting period providing security for the patrol base at (YD 931060). On 10 November, the light section was relieved in place by the 2d Platoon, B Company and returned to the company CP to assume defensive positions along the Phu Bai airstrip. On 25 November, the light section relieved the 2d Platoon at (YD 931060) and continued to provide security for the patrol base with no further contact.

CO Company C (-): Capt. S. T. Flynn
Location and Operations Summary: Phu Bai TAOR

Company C, OpCon 1st Marine Division, continued DS 9th Marines.

The 1st Platoon continued in support of 2/3. The light section remained at (AT 914597) in support of the G/2/3. The heavy section remained at (AT 878576) in support of F/2/3. On 18 November, K/3/7 relieved G/2/3, and I/3/7 relieved F/2/3. This platoon fired one hundred major rounds on H&I fire missions with unknown results.

The 2d Platoon continued in support of 3/9. The heavy section in support of I/3/9 provided security for road sweeps of Highway 14 for the entire period. On 6 November, the sweep team was attacked by a company-size VC force (AT 905505); thirty major rounds were expended with unknown results. Two WIAs (nonmedevac) were sustained. The light section continued in support of K/3/9 with no enemy contact for the entire period.

The 3d Platoon continued in support of 1/26. The light section in support of C/1/26 provided security for daily sweeps of Liberty Road south of Hill 55. On 3 November, this section expended eighteen major rounds at enemy snipers with unknown results. On 5 November, this section, in support of Operation SHASTA, expended five major rounds at snipers with unknown results. On 13 November, the light section expended six major rounds at sniper positions with unknown results. The heavy section began this reporting period in support of B/1/26, providing security for road sweeps and bridge security at night. On 4, 5, and 7 November, this section expended twelve major rounds at snipers with unknown results. On 26 November, this section expended three major rounds at sniper positions with unknown results. The platoons remained in support of 1/26 for the rest of the reporting period with no further contact.

November 1966
Third Tanks
Commanding Officer: Lt. Col. W. R. Corson
Executive Officer: Maj. E. R. Larson
Operations Officer: Maj. E. L. Tunget
Logistics Officer: 2d Lt. R. J. Bright
Location and Operations Summary: Da Nang (AT 989708)

Tank combat operations during the month of November were in support of two major operation, MACON and PRAIRIE, and other operations in the TAORs. These operations accounted for twenty-six VC/NVA (KBGF) confirmed, thirteen VC (KBGF) probable, one VC (WBGF) confirmed, four VCC, and eighteen VCS apprehended. Additionally, tank action was responsible for the sinking of seven boats, the destruction of twenty-four caves/tunnels, and the capture of three individual weapons, two Chinese hand grenades, and numerous medical supplies.

During the month of November, the battalion remained in support of both the 1st and 3d Marine Divisions with elements located in both the Da Nang and Dong Ha TAORs.

The following is a recapitulation of the operational control status of 3d Tank Battalion as of 30 November:

1st Marine Division:
3d Tank Battalion (-) (Da Nang)
H&S Company (-) (Da Nang)
   Company B (Rein.) (Da Nang)

3d Marine Division:
   Det. H&S Company (Liaison Team) (Phu Bai)
   Company A (Rein.) (Dong Ha TAOR)
   Company "C" (Rein.) (Dong Ha TAOR)

Administrative control of 3d Tank Battalion remained with the 3d Marine Division.

H&S Company CO: 1st Lt. R. D. McDaniel
Location and Operations Summary: Da Nang (AT 989708)

CO Company A: Capt. A. W. Facklam Jr.
Location and Operations Summary: Dong Ha (YD 061545)

Company A, 3d Tank Battalion remained DS 3d Marines. Company C, 3d Tank Battalion remained DS 4th Marines.

The tanks of both companies were actively engaged against VC/NVA forces, primarily conducting H&I-type fire missions against known or suspected enemy positions.

CO Company B: 1st Lt. D. B. Garner
Location and Operations Summary: Da Nang (AT 962611)

OPERATION MACON

The 2d Platoon, Company B remained DS 3/9 throughout the month of November on Operation MACON. Although the tanks were actively engaged, enemy contacts were negligible, with no known casualties inflicted through tank action.

Company C: Capt. P. F. Lessard
Location and Operations Summary: Dong Ha (YD 234582)

Company C participated in Operation PRAIRIE.

December 1966
First Antitanks
Commanding Officer: Maj. J. J. Keefe
Executive Officers: Majs. M. F. Manning and J. L. Saul
Operations Officer: Maj. J. J. Burke Jr.
Logistics Officer: Capt. C. R. Van Horn
Location and Operations Summary:

Throughout the reporting period, subordinate units of this command were assigned missions as follows:

Company A, DS B (-)/1/1, 1–2 December
DS 4th Battalion, 503d Infantry, 173 Brigade U.S. Army
   3–31 December 1966 DS 3/9
Company C (Rein.), DS of 7th Marines

1–31 December: Throughout the reporting period, active security patrolling and the establishment of a listening post were executed by this command within Zone B Northern Sector Defense Area under the coordination of the 11th Marines.

1–31 December: During the month of December, the Ontos of this battalion were used extensively for mechanized convoy escort, security for engineer mine-sweep units, and harassing and interdiction fires. The Ontos of this command were not prevented from executing their assigned missions, despite monsoon conditions and marginal trafficability throughout the TAOR.

Note: To attempt to summarize the command chronology of 1st ATs is an injustice. The Ontos were everywhere! There was no job too large or too small for the Ontos to be involved. The command chronologies are detailed down to names of crews. This level of detail is found nowhere else in the archives of command chronologies.

SEQUENTIAL LISTING OF SIGNIFICANT EVENTS

1 December: Company A, DS 1st Marines
Company B (-), DS 4th Battalion, 503d Infantry, 173d Brigade, U.S. Army
Company C, DS of 7th Marines

3 December: Company B (-), direct support of 3/9.

5 December: 2d Platoon, Company A credited with five VC KIA probable.

7–11 December: 3d Platoon, Company A participated in Operation TRINIDAD.

10–12 December: Company B provided a heavy section of Ontos for security of Rough Rider between Da Nang and Chu Lai.

11–15 December: 3d Platoon, Company B supported 3/9 on Operation STERLING.

12–25 December: 3d Platoon and a light section, 2d Platoon, Company C supported 7th Marines on Operation SIERRA.

17–21 December: 1st Platoon, Company A participated in Operation GLENN.

20–21 December: Company B provided a heavy section of Ontos for security of Rough Rider between Da Nang and Chu Lai.

22 December: Ontos A-34 of Company A hit an unknown-type mine, resulting in one KIA, three WIA, one DOW. Vehicle sustained total damage. Ontos C-35 of Company C number 1 gun prematurely fired into lead M-35 truck while moving into position to assist the convoy, which had stopped due to enemy light automatic weapons fire, resulting in one KIA and one WIA.

Michael G. Romanchuk, lance corporal, age 20, Hellertown, Pennsylvania, a field radio operator with Ontos, died of wounds on 26 December 1966 sustained as a result of a mining incident on 22 December.

Victor Tarasuk, lance corporal, age 20, Rachel, West Virginia, an Ontos crewman, died instantly as a result of a mining incident on 22 December. The vehicle he was in was totally dammed by the explosion.

The wounded were

Pandavela, J. S., staff sergeant 1660221

Bedford, C. E., PFC 2276889

Palmer, G. J., lance corporall 2201719

25 December: 2d Platoon, Company B moved from 3d Battalion, 9th Marines TAOR to 2/5's TAOR.

26 December: 2d Platoon, Company B CHOP to 2/5.

H&S Company CO: Capt. M. H. Collier
Location and Operations Summary: Da Nang (AT 991675)

COs Company A (-): Capts. D. M. Hutson and G. J. Forbes

Location and Operations Summary: Da Nang (AT 991675)

CO Company B (Rein.): Capt. T. F. Dempsey
Location and Operations Summary: Da Nang

CO Company C: Capt. R. J. Esposito
Location and Operations Summary: Chu Lai

December 1966
First Tanks
Commanding Officer: Lt. Col. J. W. Clayborne
Executive Officer: Maj. R. D. McKee
Operations Officer: Capt. F. U. Salas
Logistics Officer: Capt. G. E. Hooker
Location and Operations Summary: Da Nang (AT 998722) (Hill 34)

The month of December found the 1st Tank Battalion in basically the same positions as the preceding month. H&S Company, in addition to providing the logistical and maintenance support for two gun companies, spent a considerable time and effort improving the battalion cantonment area and defensive posture.

Company A remained in Chu Lai under the operational control of Task Force X-Ray and supported the Chu Lai Defense Command.

Company B remained DS 4th Battalion, 503d Airborne Infantry, 173d Brigade until 060249H. On that date, Company B was placed DS 9th Marines.

Company C remained DS 1st Marines.

The battalion's defensive perimeter received only four incidents of harassing small-arms fire during December. This was a considerable decrease from the amount received during November and may be attributed to the improved defensive positions and the employment of an infrared weapon sight for night firing.

During the month of December, elements of Company C participated in Operation GLENN. Elements of Company B participated in Operation STERLING, and H&S Company provided personnel support to the 3d Tank Battalion for COUNTY FAIR operations.

H&S COs: Maj. J. P. McGill and Capt. J. C. Winther
Location: Same as battalion CP

The 1st Tank Battalion's area of responsibility was well covered with a total of fifteen night ambushes, six daylight security patrols, and seven night security patrols. On 27 December, this battalion's area of responsibility was altered, and a comparatively new region was available. This new area will also demand constant, aggressive patrolling.

CO Company A: Capt. C. R. Brabec
Location: Chu Lai (BT 515040)

CO Company B: Capt. L. E. Cherico
Location and Operations Summary: Da Nang (AT 945763)

On 5 December, a section of two tanks of the 2d Platoon, Company B, in position at (AT 893772), fired seventeen rounds HE harassing and interdiction fire in support of the 3/9. At 041735H, one tank of the 1st Platoon, Company B, in position at (AT 933632), in support of L/3/7, received three rounds of small-arms fire from vicinity of (AT 934634). Tank B-14 fired three rounds HE. The area was not searched due to darkness.

On 6 December, Company B was placed DS 9th Marines.

On 11 December, at 2130H, a section of two tanks of the 1st Platoon, Company B, in support of Company L/3/7, in position on Hill 41 at (AT 934663), received twenty rounds small-arms fire from the vicinity of (AT 935668). Tanks fired six rounds of HE. No search was conducted due to darkness. At 121100H, a section of tanks of the 1st Platoon, Company B at (AT 956664) fired three rounds HE in support of elements of L/3/7, which were receiving heavy fire from vicinity (AT 959663). Results are unknown. Infantry did not search.

On 12 December, two flame tanks from Company B were assigned the mission of burning and clearing avenues of approach and fields of fire on the ridge line behind the 1st Marine Division Command Post. The flame tanks expended approximately 9,000 gallons of fuel, accomplishing this task. At 191830H, a section of two tanks of the 1st Platoon, Company B, in position of Hill 22, observed two Viet Cong with weapons running west across a rice paddy in the vicinity of (AT 952659). Tanks fired fifty rounds .30-caliber MG with inconclusive results. No search was conducted due to darkness.

CO Company C: Capt. P. S. Weigand
Location and Operations Summary: Da Nang (BT 066715)

At 012000H, a section of two tanks of the 2d Platoon, Company C, in position at (AT 998708), fired at a light on the south bank of the Song Cau Do River in the vicinity of (BT 000705). The tanks expended fifty rounds of .30-caliber MG and one round HE. A search conducted at first light revealed two Viet Cong killed.

At 021020H, a section of three tanks from the 1st Platoon, Company C, in position at (BT 065630), in support of K/3/1, observed several Viet

Cong running toward a tree line in the vicinity of (BT 078625). The tanks fired seven rounds HE. The results were unknown as no search was conducted.

At 041230H, a section of three tanks of the 1st Platoon, Company C, supporting K/3/1, in position at (BT 055644), observed one Viet Cong run into a house in the vicinity of (BT 053649). Tank C-11 fired one round WP. One body was observed being carried away. Infantry conducted a search of the area with negative results.

At 041235H, a section of three tanks of the 1st Platoon, Company C, supporting K/3/1, in position at (BT 058661), observed ten Viet Cong running through a village into a hedgerow in the vicinity of (BT 064665). Tank C-11 fired five rounds HE. Infantry searched the area with negative results.

At 041235H, a section of three tanks of the 1st Platoon, Company C, supporting K/3/1, in position at (BT 058662), observed several VC running into the tree line at (BT 065665). Tank C-13 fired four rounds HE and one round WP. Infantry searched the area and found one Viet Cong killed in action confirmed.

During the hours of 1200H to 1500H on 4 December 1966, the 3d Platoon, Company C, in position at (BT 203570), fired ninety-nine rounds HE and twenty-six rounds WP at targets of opportunity in the vicinity of (BT 199563). Fire was directed by units of the Junk Fleet operating in the area. The results of the firing are unknown. No search was conducted due to a river barrier.

At 041815H, a section of three tanks of the 1st Platoon, Company C moved from the command post of M/3/1 to position at (BT 045533) to support infantry receiving heavy small-arms fire. Tanks fired one round canister, seven rounds HE, 300 rounds .50-caliber MG, and 250 rounds .30-cal. MG at Viet Cong position in the vicinity (BT 036658). Infantry was extracted from the area, and no search was conducted.

At 051430H, a section of two tanks of the 1st Platoon, Company C moved to positions at (BT 057637) to support M/3/1. Tanks fired 12 rounds HE, 2 rounds canister, 250 rounds .50-caliber MG. A search by infantry revealed three VC KIA.

At 051540H, one tank of the 3d Platoon, Company C, supporting 1/1, in blocking position at (BT 077624), observed six VC attempting to flee from the infantry in the vicinity (BT 074630). Tank C-32 fired six rounds HE. Tank crewmen observed three VC drop. Infantry continued sweep and did not search the area. Three VC KIA probable.

On 9 December, tanks of the 3d Platoon, Company C fired 125 rounds 90 mm at targets of opportunity in the vicinity of (BT 199563), resulting in two VC killed and five bunkers destroyed.

On 9 December, at 1810H, the 1st Platoon, Company C, in support of 1/1, in position at (BT 119628), observed three small boats moving downstream in the Song Ha Xan River in the vicinity of (BT 117031). Upon spotting the tanks, the boats hastily retreated toward the north bank. Tank C-11 fired four rounds HE. The results were unknown. No search was conducted due to darkness and a water barrier.

At 092005H, a section of two tanks of the 2d Platoon, Company C, in position at the Highway Bridge at (AT 998708), sighted a small boat moving downstream in the Song Cau Do toward the bridge. Two Viet Cong in the boat fired several rounds of small arms at the tanks. The tanks returned one round HE and sank the boat. One VC was observed swept under by the current. The other VC was observed attempting to swim to the south bank of the river. The tanks swept the area with .30-caliber MG fire and observed rounds striking the VC. One VC KIA confirmed.

On 10 December at 1400H, the 1st Platoon, Company C, in support of K/3/1, in blocking positions at (BT 098659), observed several VC running across a rice paddy in the vicinity of (BT 094663). The tanks fired four rounds HE and two hundred rounds of .50-caliber MG.

The infantry searched the area and confirmed one VC KIA and one captured.

At 111030H, the 1st Platoon, Company C, in support of K/3/1, in position at (BT 102638), observed two VC running across a rice paddy in the vicinity of (BT 106637). Tanks fired three rounds of canister, two rounds of HE, and one hundred rounds of .30-caliber MG. Infantry continued sweep and did not search the area.

At 111100H, the 1st Platoon, Company C, in position at (BT 118638), observed three VC running across an open area in the vicinity of (BT 115634). Tank C-24 fired two rounds of HE. Infantry searched the area, resulting in one VC KIA confirmed.

On the morning of 16 December, the 2d and 3d Platoons, Company C, in support of 1/1, in position at (BT 188589) and (BT 203569), fired fifty-six rounds of HE preparatory fires at V positions prior to landing of 1/1 units.

On 17 December, at 1930H, a section of two tanks of the 1st Platoon, Company C, in support of 3/1, in positions at (BT 053665), received small-arms and automatic weapons fire from a house in the vicinity of (BT 050667). A round ricocheted off the tank and injured a crewman. Tanks returned fire, resulting in one VC KIA. One Marine WIA and was evacuated to the 3d Medical Battalion.

On the afternoon of 18 December, a section of two tanks of the 3d Platoon, Company C, in firing positions at (BT 209577), fired seventy-nine rounds of HE at VC bunkers and fortifications located on the south bank of the Song Cau Bai in the vicinity of (BT 213566) to (BT 216569). The Junk Fleet patrolling the river received fire from these positions and requested tank support to reduce VC positions. No search was conducted due to a water barrier.

At 182115H, a section of two tanks of the 1st Platoon of Company C, in position at the Song Cau Bo Highway Bridge, observed two objects floating downstream toward the bridge. Both objects appeared to have VC flags mounted. Tanks fired at the objects, sinking them both. Secondary explosions were observed from both floats.

At 181605H, the 1st Platoon, Company C, in support of 3/1, in blocking position at (BT 060628), observed two VC attempting to flee from blocking forces in the vicinity of (BT 058621). Tanks fired four rounds HE with inconclusive results. No search was conducted due to river barrier.

On 23 December at 2115H, a section of two tanks of the 1st Platoon, Company C, in response to request of 3/1, moved to position (BT 071708) to support infantry receiving fire from the French Fort at (BT 071708). Tanks fired three rounds HEAT, nine rounds HE, and five rounds WP. No search was conducted due to darkness.

December 1966
Third Antitanks
Commanding Officer: Maj. C. R. Stiffler
Executive Officer: Capt. D. C. Satcher
Operations Officer: 1st Lt. J. C. Debilio
Logistics Officer: Capt. D. C. Satcher
Location and Operations Summary: Da Nang TAOR

Antitank combat operations during the month of December 1966 were limited considerably because of the monsoon weather. Crosscountry mobility was impossible in most areas with trafficability limited to road networks. The Ontos were utilized in high-ground-type firing positions to provide support by fire for continuing infantry operations. Additionally, the Ontos conducted H&I firing, both day and night.

The 3d AT's CC for December '66 is uncharacteristically devoid of several pieces of documentation of its action during the month, limited exclusively to that of Company C.

COs H&S Company: 1st Lt. D. K. Caswell and 2d Lt. C. P. Wager

Location: Da Nang TAOR

CO Company A (-) (Rein.): Capt. A. A. Compton
Location: Phu Bai TAOR

CO Company B: Capt. S. L. Camby
Location: Phu Bai TAOR

🎖 Robert C. Boyd, PFC, age 20, Newark, California, an Ontos crewman serving in Company B, 3d Antitank Battalion, died on Thursday, 22 December 1966, by "friendly" fire.

CO Company C (-): Capt. S. T. Flynn
Location: Phu Bai TAOR

🎖 Jay Paul, corporal, age 23, Philadelphia, Pennsylvania, an Ontos crewman serving in the 3d Platoon, Company C, 3d Antitank Battalion, was killed by an enemy-planted mine on Tuesday, 20 December 1966.

December 1966
Third Tanks
Commanding Officer: Lt. Col. W. R. Corson
Executive Officer: Maj. E. R. Larson
Operations Officer: Maj. E. L. Tunget
Logistics Officers: 2d Lt. R. J. Bright and J. P. Schultz
Location and Operations Summary: Da Nang (AT 989708)

During the month of December 1966, the battalion remained in support of *both* the 1st and 3d Marine Divisions. In the Da Nang TAOR, the Battalion H&S Company (-) and Company E (Rein.) were under the operational control of the commanding general, 1st Marine Division. In the Dong Ha TAOR, Company A (Rein.), Company C (Rein.), and the Forward Operating Group (Det., H&S Company) were under the operational control of the commanding general, 3d Marine Division.

The Forward Operating Group was established at Dong Ha on 7 December 1966 in order to relieve the operating companies of the logistical burdens associated with being separated from the Battalion Headquarters. AdCon of the entire battalion remained with 3d Marine Division.

On 5 December, a platoon from Company A was transferred to BLT 1/4 for rotation to Okinawa.

On 12 December, the tank platoon attached to BLT 3/26 was joined and assigned to Company B.

Tank combat operations during the month of December 1966 were limited considerably because of the monsoon weather. Crosscountry mobility was impossible in most areas with trafficability limited to road networks. The tanks were utilized in high-ground-type firing positions to provide support by fire for continuing infantry operations. Additionally, the tanks conducted H&I firing, both day and night.

The following support assignments were effective during the month:

    Company A—DS 3d Marines (Dong Ha)
    Company B—DS 9th Marines (Da Nang)
    Company C—DS 4th Marines (Dong Ha)

Companies A and C were committed in the Dong Ha TAOR in support of Operation PRAIRIE, which is continuing.

On 7 December, 3d Tank Battalion established a Forward Operating Group consisting of logistics, communications, maintenance, and supply personnel and equipment in the Dong Ha area to assist Company A and C operating in the Dong Ha TAOR.

H&S Company COs: 1st Lt. R. D. McDaniel and 2d Lt. A. W. Hauser Location: Da Nang (AT 989708)

CO Company A: Capt. A. W. Facklam Jr.

Location and Operations Summary: Dong Ha (YD 061545)

From 041645H to 041915H, Company A tanks in support of 3/3 at (XD 975567) received 75 mm recoilless rifle fire and heavy automatic small-arms fire from enemy positions inside of caves at (XD 966573). One tank took a complete armor penetration, which jammed the turret and the 90 mm gun. Tanks returned a heavy volume of 90 mm fire with excellent coverage of target. Results of fire were inconclusive as the area was not searched.

CO Company B: 1st Lt. D. B. Garner
Location and Operations Summary: Da Nang (AT 962611)

1 December: At 011345H, while in support of 3/7 located at (AT 877576), Company B tanks observed one boat containing four VC and cargo on a river at (AT 832548) and (AT 845557). Tanks fired 90 mm rounds into the target, resulting in four VC (KBGF) confirmed and one boat sunk.

At 022100H, Company B tanks in support of 3/7 at (AT 876574) fired 90 mm rounds into an enemy position believed to contain a platoon of VC who had a squad of infantry pinned down. Results of fire were two VC (KBGF) confirmed and the following items captured: one submachine gun .45 caliber, with two magazines; two Chicom grenades; two M-26 grenades; two ponchos; one raincoat; and one pack.

3 December: At 031445H, Company B tanks in support of 3/7 at (AT 877575) sighted one boat containing three VC at (AT 849551) fired 90 mm rounds, resulting in three VC (KBGF) confirmed, one secondary explosion, and one boat sunk.

4 December: At 040815H, Company B tanks in support of 1/26 at (AT 968604), while on mine sweep, received small-arms fire from (AT 973604). Tanks returned fire with 90 mm rounds. Results were inconclusive.

5 December: At 050950H, Company B tanks in support of 1/26 at (AT 933578) detonated an antitank mine while on a road mine sweep.

Results of the mine detonation were moderate suspension system damage, one tank crewman WIA, nonmedevac.

At 051200H, Company B tanks in support of 1/26 at (AT 927527) and (AT 934525) received heavy small-arms fire from enemy positions at (AT 941526), (AT 941520), and (AT 934528). Tanks returned 90 mm rounds into enemy positions. Results of fire were inconclusive.

6 December: At 060715H, Company B tanks in support of 3/7 at (AT 877576) observed a boat at (AT 848554) containing three VC and cargo. Tanks fired 90 mm rounds at the boat, resulting in three VC (KBGF) confirmed, one large secondary explosion, and one boat sunk.

At 071815H, Company B tanks in support of 3/7 at (AT 876575) observed a large concentration of VC on a riverbank at (AT 535553). Tanks fired 90 mm rounds into the area, resulting in three VC (KBGF) confirmed, two VC (KBGF) probable, and two secondary explosions.

9 December: At 092320H, Company C tanks in support of 3/4 at (YD 112705) received fifteen rounds of 81 mm mortars. Tanks did not return fire because enemy positions could not be determined.

10 December: At 101030H, Company B tanks at (AT 919539) were returning on Liberty Road from Thu Bon Bridge. One tank detonated a mine, causing moderate suspension damage. While initiating repairs, one tank crewman stepped on a booby-trapped 105 mm round. Results were one tank crewman KIA and four WIA.

Douglas J. Miller, sergeant, age 20, East Lansing, Michigan, a Tanker, died instantly as a result of an enemy-planted explosive device.

15 December: At 151900H, Company B tanks in support of 1/26 at (AT 968594) heard firing at (AT 967594) and (AT 969594). Tanks moved to position where two Ontos, two 6×6 trucks, and one jeep had been caught in an ambush. Tanks returned fire with 90 mm rounds

and .30- and .50-caliber machine gun fire. Area was searched with inconclusive results.

At 171150H, Company B tank in support of 1/26 at (AT 955584) detonated an antitank mine, causing moderate damage to the tank's suspension system.

19 December: At 190930H, Company B tanks in support of 3/7 at (AT 877575) observed a boat on the river at (AT 862563). Tanks fired 90 mm rounds, sinking the boat.

At 191140H, Company B tanks in support of 3/7 at (AT 877575) fired 90 mm rounds at a VC boat at (AT 832549). Results were one boat sunk and one VC (KBGF) confirmed.

At 191440H, Company B tank in support of 2/5 at (AT 928528) observed a number of enemy troops crossing the river at (AT 907529). Tanks fired 90 mm rounds with good target coverage. Results were inconclusive as the area was not searched. At 211120H, Company B tanks in support of 3/7 at (AT 829557) received sniper fire from a tree line. Tanks returned fire with 90 mm rounds, resulting in one VC (KBGF) probable.

At 211700H, Company B tanks in support of 3/7 at (AT 829557) observed two VC at (AT 814575). Tanks fired 90 mm rounds, resulting in two VC (KBGF) probable.

22 December: At 220745H, a Company B tank in grid square (AT 9763) was traversing a bridge culvert when a mine was detonated electrically under the culvert. There was no damage to the tank. A man was observed running away from the location. The tank fired .30-caliber machine gun; results were inconclusive.

26 December: At 260750H, Company B tanks in support of 3/7 at (AT 876574) observed three boats containing VC troops crossing the

river at (AT 852557). Tanks fired 90 mm rounds, resulting in eight VC (KBGF) confirmed, two boats sunk, and the third boat capsized.

COs Company C: Capt. P. F. Lessard and 1st Lt. R. C. Kinkead
Location and Operations Summary: Dong Ha (YD 234582)

18 December: At 181115H, Company C tank in support of 3/4 at (YD 146689) detonated an antitank mine. Results were moderate damage to the tank suspension system.

At 181800H, Company C tank in support of 3/4 at (YD 136674) received a hit by an antitank weapon believed to be an RPG-2. At the same time, small-arms fire was received. The round penetrated the fuel cell, but the tank remained operational. The tank returned 90 mm and .30-caliber fire, with inconclusive results.

26 December: From 282245H to 282300H, Company C tanks in support of 3/4 at (YD 146613) received approximately 150 rounds of 82 mm and 60 mm mortar fire. Results were two tank crewmen WIA. Direction and location of enemy fire could not be determined.

As noted above, Lieutenant Colonel Bill Corson was a staunch advocate of the Civic Action Program. He relinquished his command of the third tank battalion to join the III MAF staff to ramrod the CAP. He was so disenchanted the way the war was being run out of Saigon by COMUSMACV and General Westmoreland's staff that he was compelled to write *The Betrayal*, which caused a tsunami among the top brass from the Pentagon to Vietnam. Here is an explanation that bears reading from one of the Foundation's most loyal supporters.

The Betrayal—The True Story

by Lt. Col. Ev Tunget, USMC (Ret.)

I met (then lieutenant colonel) Bill Corson in September of 1966 in the RVN when he reported for duty as the commanding officer of the 3d Tank Battalion. At that time I was commanding Bravo Company. In early October 1966, I was transferred to the staff of the battalion to be his operations officer. A friendship of mutual respect was developed during this time, which was maintained through personal contact and correspondence over the years until his death. It was due to this friendship that I was made aware by him of the ordeal he went through to have *The Betrayal* finally published.

"Freedom of the Press/Speech," as part of an American's treasured Bill of Rights guaranteed by the Constitution of the United States, does not obtain to a person to say or write scurrilous, slanderous, or libelous things about another person or organization acting within duly constituted constraints. Certain caveats of law and custom serve to protect the innocent from unrestrained and unwarranted attacks. However, these same caveats can be, and often are, used to "muzzle" dissent and constructive criticism when such pronouncements run counter to an "official line," particularly in high government or military echelons.

Certainly, Bill Corson knew of the Department of Defense Directive, applicable to both military and civilian personnel of the federal government, which required that all such personnel refrain from making public statements or submitting written matter for publication if they pertained to governmental or military policies. All such matters are required to be forwarded through "channels" to be blessed with the "holy water" of official sanction before any action is taken. Bill knew that his book would not be approved for publication had he followed the norm laid down for him as an active duty military officer.

The plan to avoid the almost certain shelving of his work was simple and straightforward. In the spring of 1968, the book was in the final stages of editing, proofing, etc., in preparation for going to print. *While he was still on active duty*, the publishing date was to have been in early July, some days after his planned retirement from active duty on 30 June. Thus, the "plan of attack" was made to protect the book and Bill Corson, who faced certain censure plus the loss of months of dedicated thought and writing, if the book was to enter the labyrinth of official channels.

There were several copies of the rough manuscript of *The Betrayal* in existence in the spring of 1968, as a number of people involved in the publication of the book needed a copy to complete their final tasks. Although discretion was emphasized by the publishing company, somehow a copy of the manuscript "leaked" out and came into the hands of the very officials in the "channels" whom it was important to avoid. (To my knowledge, the culprit in this piece of "literary espionage" was never discovered.) "Hell hath no fury like a woman scorned" is a quote apropos to the flurry of activity touched off in the Department of Defense immediately following the "acquisition" of the manuscript. The rapidity with which a special literary investigative task force was formed and set to work hints at some pretty high level interest in this effort.

The literary investigative task force was composed of a large number of civilian and military personnel who were broken up into teams to read and analyze each chapter of the book. The specific mission of each team was to search for classified information which, if found, would justify the silencing of this work as a threat to national security if it were allowed to be published. In the final report of this investigative body, one team believed it had found a relatively minor breach of security, which could fall under the "Confidential" classification. This report was forwarded to a high-ranking Navy admiral who headed a directorate in the Department of the Navy concerned with such matters. After a realistic review of the report, the admiral determined that there was nothing of a classified nature in *The Betrayal* and therefore the work could not be given any type of security classification. With this pronouncement, the book was saved from the doom intended for it.

Meanwhile, back at the Department of Defense, there were those who still sought to discredit the author and who sorely wished to get their "pound of flesh." Formal charges were referred to the commandant of the Marine Corps, General Leonard S. Chapman, for action. General Chapman had no alternative but to convene a Pretrial Formal Board of Inquiry to determine if the charges warranted trial by general courts-martial. If convicted in such a military trial, Bill Corson could have faced confinement in a federal prison, loss of all pay and allowances for the term of the confinement, and dismissal from the service with a dishonorable discharge. Bill retained a civilian attorney to represent him, and the battle was on.

With the "hot potato" sitting squarely in his lap, General Chapman's decision was a hallmark one in terms of integrity, wisdom, and courage. Despite continued pressure from above for Corson's "hide," General Chapman refused to waver. After he reviewed the report of the formal inquiry, he dismissed the charges against Bill Corson. The punishment he handed down for stirring up this hornet's nest was an official "Letter of Reprimand." This type of letter constitutes a censure of the highest order and is the "kiss of death" against further promotions for a military officer. Given Corson's intention to retire in the first place, the reprimand lost a bit of its sting. It did, however, spell the end of a comic opera of events which failed to "muzzle" a man determined to have his contribution to history survive unadulterated.

Later, Bill presented me with an autographed and inscribed copy of the book. He pointed out that in the foreword of *The Betrayal*, he mentioned my name as one of many persons to whom he was indebted for their help and encouragement when he stated, "To Major Everett L. Tunget, USMC, who as my operations officer in Vietnam sharpened and honed the rather blunt instrument of a Marine tank battalion so that it could be effective in the entire spectrum of the Vietnam conflict and who was my most devastating critic in the best meaning of the term."

Operation PRAIRIE transitioned from a specific operation to an operations area. And while the operation itself was extended into 1967 and did prevent the NVA from establishing a base in Quang Tri Province, the cost was great: two hundred Marines were killed and just over a thousand wounded with but one thousand enemy killed. Further, the constant, perpetual shifting of units adversely affected III MAF's pacification program and reduced the combat effectiveness of units, arguably resulting in a higher than acceptable casualty rate.

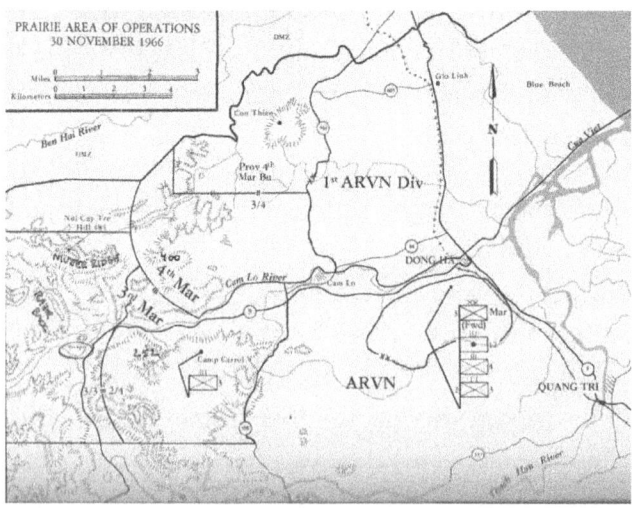

The NVA push did not materialize, and in fact, Marine forces by the end of 1966 III MAF reduced its forces in Quang Tri Province to just the 3d Marines operating with four infantry battalions. The 4th Marines relocated south to Hue in preparation for Operation CHINOOK.

The Da Nang TAOR became the responsibility of the 1st Marine Division.

In summing up the second year, General Walt felt that there was some success in drawing the enemy away from populated areas and into the rugged interior mountains where, with superior weapons and logistics support, he could win the war of attrition prescribed by General Westmoreland. General Walt commanded the largest U.S. Marine force deployed overseas since World War II. Observed was that the Corps was now fighting essentially two different wars: the 1st Marine Division in the Da Nang (and Chu Lai) TAOR(s) was prosecuting a guerilla war and continued in combination with large unit operations, while the 3d Marine Division in Northern I Corps was fighting a toe-to-toe, large unit operation, conventional war, operating largely in a "free-fire zone" environment.

Index

A

Adcock, Robert, 495
Allen, Art, 38, 130
Alvarado, Jose J., 496, 513
An Bong, 294
An Cuong, 161, 179, 181, 183, 192–94
Anderson, A. J., 329
Anderson, Donald F., 576
Anderson Trail, 386
Andrews, Wilbert I., 383
An Hoa, 292–94, 297, 428, 462, 526, 559–60, 563, 566–67, 569, 573, 597
An Khe, 142, 446
An My, 229
Arc Light, 296–97
Arizona Territory, 294, 560
Army of the Republic of Vietnam (ARVN), v, 3–4, 77, 85, 155, 157, 208–9, 215, 280–81, 322, 342, 358, 386, 414, 428, 475
Avalos, Alberto A., 407
A World Lit Only by Fire (Manchester), 275
Axis Blue, 436
Axis Brown, 436
Axis Red, 436
Axis Yellow, 436

B

Baccus, Jimmy D., 455
Backfire: A History of How American Culture Led Us into Vietnam and Made Us Fight the Way We Did (Baritz), 2
Bain, Herbert J., 249
Bain, H. J., 76
Banana Wars, 11
Bannister, John M., 252
Baritz, Loren, 2
Batangan Peninsula, 200, 206–9, 213, 258, 450
Battalion Flame Platoon, 479, 537
Battalion Landing Team (BLT), 11, 59, 74, 208, 245
Battalion Reaction Platoon, 335, 451
Bayne, James T., 538
Bell, Van "Ding Dong," Jr., 429
Benton, T., 195
Bertrand, H. A., Jr., 320, 334, 354
Betrayal, The (Corson), 281, 634–38
Binh Son, 198, 330, 450
Bodley, Charles H., 103, 118, 129–30, 159, 207, 254
Boyd, Robert C., 629
bracket method, 569, 571

Bright, Richard, 462
Brittain, Dan, 393
Brown, Joseph C., 463
Bumgarner, Charles, 218

C

Cam Ne, 114, 150–52, 255, 361
Camp Hansen, 36, 39–40, 52, 125, 131–34, 204, 216, 343–45
Camp J. J. Carroll, 595–96, 614
Camp Pendleton, 17, 22–23, 26–27, 30–31, 49–50, 57, 59, 67, 129, 132–34, 136, 159, 192, 197, 229, 234, 244, 309, 344, 346–47, 392, 464, 477, 534, 589
Carey, Dick, 148, 444
Carl, 82, 90, 200
Carl, Marion E., 82, 90, 252–53
Cereghino (colonel), 512, 579, 599
Chapelle, Dickie, 260
Chapman, Leonard S., 637
Chu Lai Airfield, 20–21, 45, 58, 143, 242, 320
Chu Lai Combat Base, 343, 354, 356–58, 407–8, 449, 478, 535–36
Chu Lai Defense Command (CLDC), 375–76, 378, 402, 405, 407–8, 444, 449, 478–79, 534–37, 590, 592–93, 610–11, 622
Civic Action Program, 85, 91, 93, 252, 301, 380, 569, 573, 634
Clement, David A., 88, 250
Coates, F. W., 292, 331, 349, 370, 388, 410
Cochran, Robert Fishel, Jr., 195
Cochrane, Bobby, 197
Colby, William, 14
Coleman, M., 351
Collins, William R., 252–53
Combined Action Platoon, 353

Combined Action Program (CAP), 244, 279, 281
COMUSMACV (Commander U.S. Military Assistance Command Vietnam). *See* Westmoreland, William
Connolly, H., 104
Conrad, Randy, 315
Con Thien, 579, 588, 599
Cook, Bertram E., Jr., 248
Coomes, W. A., 298, 314, 333, 353
Corsi, Bobby G., 480
Corson, William, 281, 634–37
Court (lance corporal), 179, 182, 187
Cox, Frank, 69
Cronkite, Walter, 213

D

Dan, Huynh Thi, 446
Da Nang Air Base, vi, 19, 69, 73, 75–76, 127, 144, 249, 252, 254, 273, 368, 390, 427, 560
Dance, Alan, 536
Dao, Thuy, 65
Dao, Tran Hung, 3, 6
Davis, Ray, 61
Decota, Walter J., 487
Demartino, Pasquale "Pat," 237
Denny, Rex C., Jr., 23
DePuy, William E., 282
Devers, P. A., 152
Diem, Ngo Dinh, 5
Dien Bien Phu, 7–8, 158
Dien Ngoc Village, 445–47
Dodgens, Jimmy M., 93
Dog Patch, 127, 368
domino theory, 4, 25
Don't Bunch Up: One Marine's Story (Van Zanten), 117

Doss, James G., Jr., 292, 331, 349, 388, 485, 600
"double hammer and anvil" plan, 159
Doublet, Alvin, 135–41
Downey, John, 60, 66, 559
Duoc, Hunh Thi, 445
Duoc, Nguyen Huu, 446–47
Dupras, Edward P., Jr., 252

E

Eagan, A. J., 343, 354, 374–75, 402, 406, 443, 477, 534
Earl, Q. V., 52
Easter Offensive, 10
Edmondson, O. R., 320, 334–35, 347
Erickson, E. L., 319, 333, 354, 374, 399, 410
Ewers, Norman G., 248, 254

F

Fairbourn, W. T., 57
Field Force Vietnam, 61, 137–38, 140–41
Fields, L. W., 343
Fierro, Robert, 132
Firing, F., 329, 338, 349, 364, 384, 409, 455
First Viet Cong Regiment, 156
Fisher, Bull, 159
Fleet Marine Force, Pacific (FMFPac), 55, 195, 257, 475
Flynn, John J., 524
Flynn, Kevin, 51
Flynn, S. T., 455, 481, 525–34, 540, 597, 616, 629
fog of war, 2
Force Service Regiment (FSR), 222
Fortunate Son: The Healing of a Vietnam Vet (Puller), 86
Foster, Gary J., 406
Frano, Peter J., 27–28, 48, 118, 130

free-fire zone, 12, 639
French Communist Party, 7
French Indochina, 3, 560

G

Gage, Robert Hugh, 444–45
Gagnon, Don, 75
Gao Lai, 439, 441–42, 597
Garretson, Frank E., 254
Gary, John H., 439
Giap, Vo Nguyen, 6–7
Gibson, Garry, 142
Gilbert, Oscar "Ed," vi, 282, 290, 331
Giovinazzo, Michael, 287–88, 290, 477
Greene, Wallace, 475
guerilla warfare, 11, 17, 55, 145
Guthrie, E. J, 524–33

H

Hall, William D., 253
Haller, Robert, 374, 576
Hanifin, R. T., Jr., 342
Harkins, Paul, 9
Harris, P. J., 82, 90
Harris, Robert E., 610
Hayes, Harold A., Jr., 428
Heflin, B. A., 93, 320, 334, 347, 360, 379, 408, 451
Henderson, Rod, 392, 398
Hika, Gene, 126, 128
Hildenbrand, L. I., 152
Hinojosa, Juan N., 162–63
Ho Chi Minh, 6–7, 10, 497, 504
Ho Chi Minh's Nightmare, 497
ho Chi Minh Trail, 5, 12–14, 245, 280
horseshoe, 309–10
Howard, Jimmie L., 401
Hunter, John, 38, 48–49, 130, 242
Hurst, E. H., 56
Hyde, Wayne, 406

643

I

I Corps, v, 8, 17–18, 66, 80, 88, 129, 176, 216, 249, 252, 255, 258–59, 261, 273–74, 276, 282, 385–86, 410, 414, 430, 473, 476, 505, 525
II Corps, 129, 136, 253, 255, 260, 284
III Marine Amphibious Force (III MAF), 8, 61, 85, 91, 122, 141, 157, 201, 238, 244, 253, 261, 264, 273, 277, 284, 294, 343, 573, 639
III Marine Expeditionary Force (III MEF), 6, 80, 89, 250, 252
Isley, Charles L., III, 610

J

Jarnot, Fidelas W., 149, 157, 229, 298, 313, 333
J. Donahue, R., 368
Johnson, Harold K., 474
Johnson, Lee G., 462
Johnson, Lyndon B., 8–9
Jones, Clarence W., 487
Jones, Donald R., 79, 88, 250
Jones, States Rights, Jr., 52, 60, 62, 124, 216

K

Karch, Frederick J., 64–66, 80, 89, 155, 249–50, 253, 255
Kelly, James P., 104
Kennedy, John Fitzgerald, 15
Kile, Leroy, 220
King, John H., Jr., 249
Koler, Joseph, Jr., 248
Kooney, Jim, 195
Kraus, R. C., 152
Krulak, Victor H., 11, 22–23, 55–58, 83, 141, 144, 285, 475–76
Kulick (sergeant), 420, 422, 424

L

La Hoa, 430
Laidlaw, William C., 160–61, 179, 184
Lamb, 149, 160, 174, 177, 198
Lamb, Allan, 27, 39, 122, 133, 346
Lamb, Allan W., 27, 31, 39, 122, 133, 149, 157, 159–60, 174–75, 177, 184, 198–200, 346, 370
Lancelot, 55–57
Lang Ke Ga, 262
Langley, Ric, 463–64, 470, 473, 505
Lanphier, R. F., 320, 335, 337, 348, 363
Larsen, Stanley, 137
Larson, E. R., 137, 140, 142, 360, 451, 480, 482, 544, 600
Leadfoot. *See* Hunter, John, 38, 40, 49
Leatherneck Square, 508
Lee, Arthur E., 72, 149, 237, 298–99, 333, 353, 371, 390, 431
Lemon, Carl, 45, 104, 198, 212, 215
Le My, 252, 336–37, 362, 371, 381, 452, 538, 595
Leprosy Colony, 97
Lessard, Paul F., 473, 483, 548, 579, 586, 607, 619, 634
Liberty Bridge, 420, 560
Liberty Road, 493, 546, 569, 575, 617, 632
Lochridge, Willard F., IV, 309, 313, 372, 374, 557–58, 568–69, 573
Lodge, Henry Cabot, 17
Ludecke, Carl, 30
Ludwig, Verle E., 144, 237–38, 253
Lullabies for Lieutenants (Cox), 69
Luong, Nguyen Thi, 445
Lyons, James, Jr., 406

M

Mackenzie, Mac, 46, 242
Maddox, Gerald W., 613
Manchester, William, 275

Marble Mountain, 72, 86, 94, 97–98, 114, 151, 153, 201, 228, 237, 243, 260, 292, 309, 322, 353, 372–74, 429, 560
Marine aircraft group (MAG), 6
Marine Air Ground Task Force (MAGTF), 74
Marine Corps Supply Depot (MCSD), 30, 51–52
Marine Task Unit 79.3.5, *4*
Massie, B. R. "Bucky," 82, 90
Mathews, J. T., 321, 361
Matthews, Earl, Jr., 580
Mattingly, Robert E., 281, 484
Maxwell, 21, 231–32, 237
Maxwell, H. L., 292
McCormick, Jerry, 425
McNamara, Robert Strange, 2, 15, 280
McPartlin, Charles E., Jr., 249
McQueary, Dan, 179, 181
Merlin, 55–56
Military Assistance Advisory Group (MAAG), 3, 5
Miller, Douglas J., 632
Miller's Ridge, 99
Mitchell, Bryan B., 428
Mixmaster Program, 235
Moore, W., 343, 354, 375
Mounted Combat in Vietnam (Starry), 15, 21
Muir, Joseph E., 159
My Hoa, 296

N

Nghiep, Nguyen Thi, 446
Nhuận, Lê Văn, 10
Nickerson, Herman, 589
9th Marine Expeditionary Brigade (MEB), v, 6, 22, 54, 65–66, 76, 78–79, 85, 89, 91, 155, 249, 251–52, 275
Noble, John D., 252
North Vietnamese Army (NVA), v, 1, 9, 13, 51, 55–56, 66, 119, 137, 209, 214–15, 245, 273, 279–80, 282, 284–85, 290, 293, 296–97, 342, 401, 508–9, 547, 559–60, 586–89

O

Odette, Allen, 219
O'Malley, Robert, 181
Operations
 BALTIMORE, 611
 BLACK FERRET, 199, 205, 260
 BLUE MARLIN, 205, 260–61
 BUILD-UP, 607
 CHEROKEE, 383–84, 399
 CHINOOK, 639
 COLORADO, 478–79, 537
 COUNTY FAIR, 238, 427, 461, 589, 623
 DAGGER THRUST, 123, 258–59, 262–63
 DEAD END, 337–38
 DOUBLE EAGLE, 282, 284, 288–91, 329, 334
 DRUM HEAD, 259
 EAGLE FLIGHT 49er, 315, 317
 FLORIDA, 438
 FRANKLIN, 448, 450
 FRESNO, 535
 GEORGIA, 371
 GLENN, 620, 623
 GOLDEN FLEECE, 237–38, 259, 366, 535, 589
 HARVEST MOON, 136, 205, 237–38, 263
 HASTINGS, 453–54, 481, 504–5, 508
 HOT SPRINGS, 357–58
 HUNTER, 340

IOWA, 354, 359
JACKSON, 480, 537
JUNGLE DRUM III, 78, 216, 225
KANSAS, 401–4
LAM SON 328, 614
LEE, 590–92, 610–11
LIBERTY, 410–11, 419–20, 425, 427, 429–33, 443, 560
LONG LANCE, 294
MACON, 462, 498, 547, 574, 606, 619
MALLARD, 292, 294, 296–97
MASHER/WHITE WING, 285
MIXMASTER, 117
MOBILE, 377
MONTEREY, 534
MONTGOMERY, 375–77
MORGAN, 377
NAPA, 535
NEVADA, 355–57
NEW YORK, 342
OAKLAND, 405
PAWNEE, 540
PAWNEE II, 540
  PIRANHA, 104–5, 200–203, 205, 207, 209–12, 215, 258, 286, 290
  PRAIRIE, 481–82, 522, 544, 547, 579, 599, 601, 607, 619, 630, 638
ROLLING THUNDER, 18
SHASTA, 617
SHUFLY, 4, 18, 61
SIERRA, 620
SILVER LANCE, 22–23, 55–57, 59
STOMP, 135–36, 138, 140–41
TRAIL BLAZER, 259
TRINIDAD, 620
TRIPLE PLAY, 259
UTAH, 342
VIRGINIA, 370
WAR BONNET, 298, 300, 314
WAR BONNET II, 299, 330
WAYNE, 383
WYOMING, 355

P

Paul, Jay, 629
Peatross, Oscar F., 47, 157–59, 207, 256, 342
Peavey, A. B, 76
Peavey, Robert E., vi, 86, 119
People's Army of Vietnam (PAVN), 1, 254
Perillo, John, 480
Phase Line Amber, 436
Phase Line Brown, 427
Phase Line Green, 427–28, 430, 436
Phong Bac, 93, 114, 152–53, 244, 281–82, 333, 353, 391, 483–84, 569, 611
Pierpan, Herb, 24
Pike, Douglas, 1
Plank, Milo W., Jr., 178, 180, 183–88, 219, 312
Platt, Jonas M., 284
Popular Forces (PFs), 280, 361, 380, 391
Powell, Colin, 2
Progress Offensive, 10
Provisional Rifle Platoon, 291, 449, 479, 535–37
Psychological Warfare (PsyOps) Team, 139
Puller, Lewis B., Jr., 86
Purnell, Richard M., 192, 195

Q

Quyen, Ngo, 3

R

Raphael, M. L., 292, 331, 349, 370, 388, 410, 461
Reckewell, Carl A., 429
Red Beach, v, 53–54, 60, 63, 65–66, 68–69, 72–73, 76, 79, 82–83, 90–91, 126, 148, 155, 249, 559

Reed (sergeant), 41, 71, 106–9, 111–14, 130–31
Revolutionary League for the Independence of Vietnam, 7
Revolutionary Youth League of Vietnam, 7
Reynolds, Pappy, 148
riot control CS gas, 135–36
Roalson, Larry, 318
Robinson, Robbie "Harvey," 315
Rockpile, 512, 540, 596, 599, 614
Rohleder, Donald W., 397, 601
Roseman, Michael D., 534

S

Sabo, Roy T., 592–93
Saikley, John, 71, 106–7, 111
Salinas, Jesse, 39, 46, 48–49
Sanders, Joe, 83, 158–59, 184, 216
Sanders, Joe P., 82–83, 90, 124, 149, 157–59, 180, 184, 216, 218
Scharnberg, George R., 254
Schmitt, Harvey, 104
2d ROKMC Brigade, 590–91, 610–11
Shaffer, James, 220
Sharff, K. E., 335–36, 347–48, 360, 379, 408, 451, 480
Sihanouk, Norodom, 13
Silver Shield, 27
Sipel, Ed, 183
Siron, Donald, 220
Siva, T. J., 315, 318
Small Wars (Krulak), 11
Snell, Albert W., 344, 358, 377, 407
South Vietnamese Army, 66, 86, 91
South Vietnamese Marine Corps, 4
South Vietnamese Regional Forces, 280, 297
Sparks, J. D., 319, 334, 346, 354, 359, 378, 407
Sparrow Hawk, 391, 394, 396, 414

Special Landing Force (SLF), 36, 74, 121–22, 124–25, 129, 244–45, 407
Starry, Donn A., 15, 21
Stewart, Ray, i–ii, xii, 2, 4, 6, 8, 10, 12, 14, 16, 18, 20, 22, 26, 31–32, 34, 36, 38–40, 44, 50, 120–22, 128–30, 154–56, 196–97, 304–6
Stolz, Frank V., 233–35, 237
Struggle Force, 385
Sullivan, Dan, 220
Suthers, Mark, 141

T

Tam Ky, 260–61, 401, 477–78
Task Force Alpha, 61, 79, 88, 137, 250
Task Force DELTA, 263, 284, 454–55, 599
Task Force X-Ray, 592, 611, 622
Task Group 76.5, *120*
Task Group Romeo, 381, 389–90
Taylor, Maxwell, 17, 21
Teske, Bernard A., III, 385
Tet Offensive, 10
Tews, Timothy, 585
Thi, Nguyen Chanh, 17–18, 65, 385–86, 445–47
Thieu, Nguyen Van, 18
Third Herd, 28, 35, 42, 45, 122, 398
Thomas, Turby, 416, 420
Thompson, Ky, 161, 183
324B NVA Division, 370, 481
Tilden, Richard, 242
Torres, Juan, 615
Tracked Vehicle Officer School (TVOS), 197, 229, 392
Tru, Le Huu, 158
Trung, Huynh Thi, 446
Trung Sisters, 3
Truong An, 296
Tuck, Tom, 204, 206

Tunget, Everett L., 371–72, 398, 432, 490, 556, 562, 600, 603, 617, 629, 635, 638
Tyson, Joe, 68, 72, 106–14

U

United States Military Assistance Command, Vietnam (USMACV), 4
U.S. Military Assistance Advisory Group (MAAG), 3
USS *Alamo*, 27–34, 36, 39, 131, 133, 155
USS *Cabildo*, 179
USS *Carter Hall*, 204
USS *Catamount*, 289
USS *Cavalier*, 345
USS *Colonial*, 345
USS *Frank Knox*, 36, 41, 103, 121
USS *Galveston*, 122
USS *General William Mitchell*, 204
USS *Henrico*, 63
USS *Iwo Jima*, 103, 117, 119–22
USS *Litchfield*, 592
USS *Marton*, 430
USS *Mount McKinley*, 63
USS *Paul Revere*, 260
USS *Point Defiance*, 29–30, 36–37, 40–41, 104, 118–22, 130–31, 159, 204
USS *Skagit*, 348
USS *St. Clair County*, 408, 410
USS *Talladega*, 120
USS *Thomaston*, 83–84
USS *Vancouver*, 63
USS *Vernon County*, 344–45
USS *Washtenaw County*, 125
USS *Whetstone*, 344–45
USS *Windham County*, 260
USS *Winston*, 344–45
Utter, Leon, 104, 122, 133, 135

V

Van Tuong Peninsula, 104, 156, 160
Van Zanten, William, 117
vertical envelopment, 119, 159
Viet Cong Regional Forces, 238, 280, 297
Vietnamese Communist Party, 7
Vining, Francis E., 399

W

Waggle, Charley, 44
Walt, Lewis W., 8, 157–58, 244, 253, 279, 284, 370, 385, 475, 599, 639
Warner, Bruce B., 291
Weaver, Greg, 386
Webb, Bruce D., 193
Westmoreland Plan, 280
Whaley, H. L., 351
Wheeler, Edwin B., 79, 88, 250
Where We Were in Vietnam (Kelley), 20
White, Jerry, 496–97
White Beach, 35–36, 92, 103–4, 131, 345
Whitehead, Gene, 413, 418, 420
Whitehead, Kenneth, 419–20, 430
Widdecke, C. F., 374
Williamson, Robert M., Jr., 486
Willy Peter (white phosphorous), 78, 318, 570
Wood, N. M. "Manny," 103
Wright, William, 194
Wyckoff, Don P., 158, 176

X

xenon searchlights, 304, 306–7, 561, 565–66

Y

Yen Bac, 93, 114, 152, 281–82, 361, 380, 451, 538

Z

Zebal, Ken, 84, 179, 436
Zitz, 84
Zitz, Ken W., 83–84
Zych, Joseph, 218

Lightning Source UK Ltd.
Milton Keynes UK
UKHW011835270519
343402UK00001B/38/P